THE SOVEREIGNTY OF LAW

Freedom, Constitution, and Common Law

The Sovereignty of Law

Freedom, Constitution, and Common Law

T. R. S. ALLAN

OXFORD

UNIVERSITY PRESS

OXFORD
UNIVERSITY PRESS

Great Clarendon Street, Oxford, OX2 6DP,
United Kingdom

Oxford University Press is a department of the University of Oxford.
It furthers the University's objective of excellence in research, scholarship,
and education by publishing worldwide. Oxford is a registered trade mark of
Oxford University Press in the UK and in certain other countries

© T Allan 2013

The moral rights of the author have been asserted

First Edition published in 2013

Impression: 1

Crown copyright material is reproduced under Class Licence
Number C01P0000148 with the permission of OPSI
and the Queen's Printer for Scotland

British Library Cataloguing in Publication Data
Data available

Library of Congress Control Number: 2013937735

ISBN 978-0-19-968506-6

Printed and bound in Great Britain by
CPI Group (UK) Ltd, Croydon, CR0 4YY

Preface

This book has been written during my tenure of a Leverhulme Major Research Fellowship, 2010–2012, and I am very grateful for the opportunity for uninterrupted research and reflection that the Fellowship provided. I am indebted to many friends and colleagues for their help and advice during this period, but most especially to John Allison, Peter Cane, David Dyzenhaus, David Feldman, Andrew Hillam, Jeff King, Stuart Lakin, Nick McBride, Alistair Mills, Nigel Simmonds, and Mark Walters for kindly reading and commenting on particular chapters. Andrew Hillam has generously read many chapters and given me invaluable advice on making my text more readily accessible to undergraduates as well as more experienced scholars. I am also grateful to Alex Flach and Natasha Flemming at Oxford University Press for their efficient and friendly assistance.

I have learnt much from the critical literature provoked by my previous writings on constitutional theory and public law. My critics have prompted me to think harder about my own conception of common law constitutionalism (as it is usually called); and I have taken the present opportunity to respond to their objections when it has seemed helpful to do so in order to advance or clarify my argument. My principal aim has been to explore some basic questions of method in the analysis of public law, attempting to lay bare the theoretical grounds of some of the major debates and controversies within the subject. I hope at least to clarify the jurisprudential roots of my own position, in respect of many of these controversies, even if I fail to bring all readers round to my own conclusions.

I have been very fortunate to enjoy the discussion of legal and constitutional theory with my friends John Allison, David Dyzenhaus, and Nigel Simmonds over many years; I have benefited greatly (if not greatly enough) from their scholarly wisdom. A great sadness during the writing of this book, however, has been the loss of my friend Amanda Perreau-Saussine de Ezcurra, after serious illness. A very fine common lawyer and legal theorist, Amanda was always both a generously appreciative reader and my most perceptive critic. The book would no doubt have been much improved if she had been able to scrutinize my draft chapters; I can only hope she would not have been too disappointed by the final text. I dedicate the book to her memory.

T. R. S. A.
Cambridge
January 2013

Contents

Introduction   1

1. Constitution and Constitutionalism   17

2. Constitutional Convention: Practice and Principle   55

3. The Rule of Law: Freedom, Law, and Justice   88

4. Parliamentary Sovereignty: Authority and Autonomy   133

5. Legislative Supremacy and the Rule of Law   168

6. Constitutional Foundations of Judicial Review   208

7. Judicial Review and Judicial Restraint   241

8. Democracy, Fundamental Rights, and Common Law   286

Appendix: Public Law and Political Theory   333

Index   351

Introduction

I

A student of British constitutional law is confronted by an intimidating series of antinomies; and it is quickly apparent that there is great scope for argument about fundamental ideas and doctrines. A doctrine of absolute 'parliamentary sovereignty' appears to make the principle of the 'rule of law' subservient to a fluctuating legislative majority. Yet the rule of law is normally understood by its defenders to provide the foundations for government according to law—the bedrock of liberal democratic constitutionalism. The paradox is deepened by what is sometimes presented as an opposition between the rule of law and democracy. If the former is broadly represented, in practice, by judicial enforcement of established legal principle, the latter consists (on that view) in the right of the people's representatives to override such principles in the larger public interest. For example, basic rights of fair trial for certain types of criminal defendant—perhaps suspected rapists or terrorists—might have to give way to considerations of public safety, as determined by elected members of Government or Parliament.[1]

The sense of paradox or contradiction is further deepened by an overarching conflict between so-called legal constitutionalism and its political counterpart. Whereas the former emphasizes the role of the judiciary in defending basic liberties, the latter gives pride of place to the ordinary political process, giving maximum weight to the popular voice on any issue, as reflected by opinions expressed and votes cast. A legal constitutionalist typically concentrates on the legal framework of the constitution, treating the judiciary as the ultimate guardians of a system of law designed to regulate the exercise of power and protect individual liberty. The political constitutionalist usually treats the legal framework as a transient and temporary arrangement of rights, duties, and powers, vulnerable to change at the will of a current political majority acting in the name of the people at large. If the content of fundamental rights is sometimes controversial, making it hard to disentangle lawyerly disagreement from political dispute, it is not clear (on that view) why judges should be entrusted with resolving the controversy rather than elected politicians.[2]

---

[1] The capital G of 'Government' indicates the executive (ministers and civil servants) by contrast with 'government', which I use as to encompass all main branches of the state (including Parliament, Government, and the judiciary).

[2] For a particularly robust defence of political constitutionalism and critique of its legal counterpart, see Adam Tomkins, *Our Republican Constitution* (Oxford: Hart Publishing, 2005). See also Richard Bellamy, *Political Constitutionalism: A Republican Defence of the Constitutionality of Democracy* (Cambridge: Cambridge University Press, 2007).

A further antinomy or opposition may now come forward, purporting to resolve an apparent conflict of basic principles. A purely formal conception of the rule of law, affirming a merely formal equality before the law, may be defended on the ground of its compatibility with parliamentary absolutism. On that view, the judicial role is simply to enforce whatever rules have been duly enacted by the legislature, without fear or favour: all are subject to the law, whatever its content, according to its enacted terms and without special exemptions (not expressly enacted) for powerful officials or their friends and allies. Any connection with substantive justice, such as rights to the enjoyment of free speech and other civil and political liberties, is merely incidental or contingent—the happy consequence of wise legislation by benevolent rulers. All rights and freedoms subsist at the will and pleasure of a parliamentary majority, which must be trusted to keep faith with our traditions of liberty even as it grapples with novel and pressing problems of governance. If Parliament is too easily manipulated by the executive Government, deploying the strength of its party domination of the House of Commons, the answer (according to the political constitutionalist) is political reform. A newly invigorated republicanism must nurture a greater independence for elected representatives, who may appreciate the virtues of liberty and defend it against governmental encroachment.[3]

By contrast with that merely formal account of the rule of law, a legal constitutionalist will insist on a broader and deeper conception. We see the point of formal equality before the law only when we understand it as being required by a deeper principle of equality or equal citizenship. The law is a shield against arbitrary power, whether wielded by influential private persons or organizations, bent on pursuit of their private interests, or by public officials, committed to conceptions of the public good that may be highly contentious or involve incidental costs that are hard to justify. By confining our conception of law to the regular enforcement of publicly promulgated rules, even when they have very damaging (and perhaps unforeseen) consequences for vulnerable persons or unpopular minorities, we deprive the principle of the rule of law of much of its power as a shield against oppression.[4] If the rule of law is a constitutional principle of real importance, capable of moderating the influence of majoritarian politics, especially in times of emergency or stress, it must be more than merely formal: it must embrace a range of familiar liberal rights and freedoms intended to guarantee each person's autonomy or independence. On this view, judges do not merely apply a law for whose content they take no responsibility; they rather apply a regime of legal principle whose integrity, as a systematic guarantee of basic liberties, it is their primary function to sustain.[5]

A thousand smaller controversies nestle amidst the clash of these contrasting versions of British constitutionalism. At numerous points, legal doctrine is torn

---

[3] See for example Tomkins, *Our Republican Constitution*, ch 4.

[4] There is here a further puzzling distinction: our concept of law is often treated as quite distinct from our ideal of the rule of law. See further Chapter 3, below.

[5] That has been a principal theme of my earlier books, *Law, Liberty, and Justice: The Legal Foundations of British Constitutionalism* (Oxford: Clarendon Press, 1993) and *Constitutional Justice: A Liberal Theory of the Rule of Law* (Oxford: Oxford University Press, 2001).

between rival visions of the constitution: it forms the anvil on which a larger resolution is hammered out in the course of legal and political evolution. The whole doctrinal basis of judicial review of administrative (or executive) action is contested by writers with varying understandings of the relationship between parliamentary sovereignty, on the one hand, and the rule of law, on the other. In its emphasis on the central place of legislative intention, the ultra vires doctrine seems a natural fit with absolutist conceptions of sovereignty; but its detractors give pride of place to common law doctrine, reflecting ideas of justice and fairness drawn from considerations of morality rather than authoritative political decision or instruction.[6] A formal doctrine, readily compatible with a formal account of the rule of law, confronts a more substantive engagement with political morality, which finds its natural expression in the articulation and development of the common law. And a lawyer who criticizes the thin formality of ultra vires, emphasizing instead the central role of the substantive common law, must equally acknowledge the thin formality of parliamentary absolutism. The nature and limits of parliamentary sovereignty are themselves (or so I shall argue) the products of common law—features of a common law constitution built on an elaborate mix of legal tradition and continuing popular and political allegiance.

Conflicting attitudes to the idea of separation of powers are closely related to these divergent theoretical viewpoints. A self-styled political constitutionalist is likely to look askance at the doctrine of separation of powers, fearful that too rigid a division of competence between different branches of government will frustrate political change or impede the implementation of policy.[7] For a legal constitutionalist, favouring legal guarantees of liberty, the separation of powers is an implication of the rule of law: only a strict division between legislator, executive government, and independent judiciary, marking the boundaries of separate jurisdictions, can preserve a sphere of individual autonomy in the face of state power. The subjection of public authorities to independent judicial scrutiny, bolstered by standards of procedural fairness that ensure an equality of arms between private citizen and public official, gives the rule of law a cutting edge: it promotes an accommodation between public policy and legal principle that might not otherwise be sought, let alone achieved. Questions about the justiciability of administrative action, or about appropriate styles of judicial deference to Parliament and Government, are closely bound up with contrasting attitudes to the separation of powers and the rival theories those attitudes invoke.[8]

A defender of the legal constitution as guarantor of individual liberty is likely to favour the proportionality standard of review: government action should not intrude on basic rights to any greater extent than is warranted, having regard to the gravity or urgency of the public interest in view. And a similar standard of

---

[6] See generally Christopher Forsyth (ed), *Judicial Review and the Constitution* (Oxford: Hart Publishing, 2000).

[7] See for example J A G Griffith, 'The Political Constitution' (1979) 42 MLR 1–21.

[8] See for example Jeffrey Jowell, 'Judicial Deference and Human Rights: A Question of Competence', in Paul Craig and Richard Rawlings, *Law and Administration in Europe: Essays in Honour of Carol Harlow* (Oxford: Oxford University Press, 2003), 67–81.

review should apply whether such basic rights are identified as part of the ordinary common law or, instead, find their formal source within the European Convention on Human Rights.[9] The Human Rights Act 1998, making the Convention rights directly applicable in domestic law, may be understood to further and consolidate an indigenous rights culture—a culture reflected in a developing common law tradition of respect for individual freedom or autonomy. But those who locate the constitution in the ordinary flux of political debate and decision, wary of legal frameworks policed by unelected judges, will typically have their doubts about proportionality. Surely, they protest, a balancing of rights and interests lacks objective grounding, independent of a judge's own moral and political opinions: a more relaxed standard of reasonableness, or rationality, leaves greater scope for governmental decision and action, which may be quite legitimate (in any particular case) even if a judge thinks it gives inadequate weight to individual rights or freedoms.

The Human Rights Act, although widely praised for achieving a masterly equilibrium between competing theories of constitutionalism, actually enshrines the ambivalence that such contrasting accounts engender.[10] While on the one hand purporting to preserve Parliament's unfettered sovereignty—giving Parliament the 'last word', as it is often put—on the other, it mandates a mode of interpretation of laws that strengthens the hand of the judiciary in resisting unwarranted encroachments on fundamental rights. While a legal constitutionalist is likely to emphasize section 3, which commands an interpretation of statute compatible with European Convention rights, as far as this is possible, his political counterpart will point to section 4, which by enabling the court to declare a provision incompatible with the Convention, but not to quash it, leaves it to Parliament—if it sees fit—to change the law. The critical point, however, is that the interaction of these provisions—the limits of the 'possible' as regards benign interpretation, promoting harmony between statute and Convention—itself depends on underlying theories of law and adjudication. Whether or not a judge can apply a statute consistently with Convention rights, or must instead make a declaration of incompatibility, rarely depends on the dictionary meanings of words beyond his control. It hinges rather on his interpretative ingenuity, stimulated by the strength of his commitment to fundamental rights. Or, at any rate, so I shall argue.

II

The student of constitutional law, however, confronts a further question—one of crucial importance to a satisfactory understanding. Alongside these striking divisions of opinion and attitude is a further complexity concerning their pertinence to the administration of justice, as opposed to academic debate and criticism. Textbooks on constitutional and administrative law typically strive to present the law 'as it

---

[9] Convention for the Protection of Human Rights and Fundamental Freedoms (Rome, 1950).
[10] Compare Jowell, 'Judicial Deference and Human Rights', at 69–70 (challenging the idea of a 'subtle compromise between two models of democracy').

is'—accurately reflecting the settled understanding—implicitly pushing debate and division to the periphery, where (it is often implied) the higher courts must make new law, when necessary, to resolve disagreement. If, then, lawyers disagree about whether a fair trial can take place in the absence of relevant evidence, kept secret by a government agency in the public interest, there is no law on the matter until a superior court has ruled one way or the other, or until such a ruling has been affirmed or denied by the Supreme Court. If lawyers disagree about whether there are any limits to parliamentary sovereignty, there are none (on this view) unless and until they are confirmed or imposed by a court sufficiently senior and influential to do so. If there is disagreement over the true nature and content of the rule of law, or the separation of powers, there is no real answer as a matter of 'strict law': there is only an academic discourse *external* to law as it actually exists in judicial practice.

It is the main burden of this book to challenge that familiar, 'common-sense' viewpoint: there is no law or legal practice (I shall argue) separate from, or independent of, the larger debates in constitutional theory and jurisprudence over basic doctrines and their moral and political justification. We cannot identify the content of law with a merely descriptive account of judicial practice, viewed as a matter of empirical fact: it is a product of normative *judgement*, in which we attempt to make good moral sense of an array of such familiar legal 'sources' as Acts of Parliament, judicial precedent and influential dicta. An account of English law on any specific subject is always a *theory* of how best to read the relevant legal materials, guided by notions of justice and coherence: we assume that the law, correctly interpreted, should as far as possible serve the interests of justice, rather than injustice, and be broadly coherent rather than confused and contradictory. And this is true even when we disagree about what justice requires, or about what would make the law more coherent overall. Lawyers characteristically impugn their opponents' interpretations by pointing to their unjust or inconvenient or untidy consequences for particular cases, whether actual or imagined.

The law on any issue is always a matter of informed opinion, not the incontrovertible product of authoritative decree. Even the explicit terms of an Act of Parliament must be construed or interpreted before they can be applied to particular cases. A general rule must be *held* applicable—or otherwise—on a reasoned basis, having regard to its enacted terms, its supposed rationale, and an identification of the concrete case as an instance falling appropriately within its compass. Does a general prohibition on the publication of offensive material necessarily preclude the transmission of a party political broadcast, at the time of a general election, if some viewers are likely to be offended by claims or images they deplore?[11] Does the imposition of an automatic life sentence on anyone convicted of a second 'serious offence', subject only to the existence of 'exceptional circumstances', apply to someone who poses no real threat to public safety?[12] If opinions differ, it is because

---

[11] *R (ProLife Alliance) v British Broadcasting Corporation* [2003] UKHL 23, considered in Chapter 1, below.
[12] *R v Offen* [2001] 1 WLR 253, considered in Chapter 1, below.

the statutory rule cannot be applied without interpretation; and interpretation involves moral or political judgement and not merely linguistic competence or expertise. We cannot ask what Parliament intended because cases arise that the legislators neither foresaw nor considered; we can only ask what decision would make their work, in retrospect, a better scheme of regulation—achieving its main objectives without unnecessary incidental harm to the broader public interest or to people's freedom and dignity.[13]

What is true of statutes is all the more plainly true of the common law. An analysis of precedent draws not merely on any general principles specifically mentioned in judicial opinions, but also on those further principles that enable us to find order and coherence in numerous previous decisions on particular sets of facts in related, but differing, circumstances. An account of common law rules and principles, in any field of law, is necessarily a theory about how best to understand why courts have reached certain decisions—not in the sense of explaining social or psychological phenomena, but rather of presenting reasons of justice or political morality for reading them in one way rather than another. If we are trying to make sense (for example) of the stronger control exercised by courts over public agencies in some cases than in others, we need a theory about the special demands of human rights and the implications for the scope of administrative discretion. We must try to construct an account which not only records judicial opinions and actions, but articulates a *justification* for such opinions and actions. We cannot, for instance, simply *describe* a doctrine of proportionality, by reference to a course of judicial decisions in human rights cases. A trend in judicial behaviour becomes a *doctrine*, worthy of analysis and criticism, only when we can discover reasons that might plausibly inform and explain it—even if it remains controversial whether, on due reflection, those reasons really do justify the practice in question.

If legal analysis is always an *interpretation* of statute and precedent, it cannot be a neutral description of what judges characteristically do or decide. Legal advice (to a client) may sometimes amount to the prediction of a court's decision; but the lawyer may quite coherently add that, in his considered view, the court would be making a mistake by giving inadequate weight to an important legal principle. An opinion about what the law permits or requires—what standard of review the High Court must adopt in an administrative law case, for example, or what restrictions on freedom of speech can be imposed by broadcasting companies—is an interpretative conclusion, based on a judgement of the balance of argument between divergent accounts. Lawyers disagree in 'hard' cases, when there are good arguments for competing conclusions, because they appraise the strength of the relevant considerations differently: their legal conclusions reflect contrasting moral judgements which might be resolved, eventually, by a larger and deeper exploration of moral or political theory than current circumstances (or expertise) permit.[14]

---

[13] The argument is presented in detail in Chapter 5, below.

[14] I draw inspiration here from the work of Ronald Dworkin: see especially Dworkin, *A Matter of Principle* (Oxford University Press, 1985) and Dworkin, *Law's Empire* (London: Fontana Press, 1986).

Cases reach the courts when lawyers are unable to resolve such interpretative disputes without judicial deliberation and decision. And since courts rightly confine their attention to the specific questions immediately arising, many larger questions will inevitably remain unsettled and controversial. Whether or not Parliament has power to curtail free speech by express provision, even at election time, is a matter of opinion; but an opinion can be more or less persuasive—more or less accurate—independently of judicial pronouncement. The answer depends on our larger theory of constitutional law—a theory every public lawyer must try to articulate, step by step, as she deepens her understanding of the relevant legal principles. And a thoughtful lawyer will not simply abandon her theoretical moorings as soon as the Supreme Court hands down a decision inconsistent with them. If she does not find the Court's reasoning persuasive, she will reject its conclusions, hoping to foster a debate that may lead, in due course, to a reappraisal and perhaps reversal of (what she considers) an erroneous precedent. A proper humility in the face of contrary opinion should not be confused with craven submission to reasoning found—after all due reflection—to be seriously flawed.[15]

We cannot, then, distinguish (as is often supposed) between an account of the present law, as it simply is for the time being, and our opinions about what, ideally, it ought to be, if the statutes and precedents were better understood. I do not mean, of course, that the law on any issue is what it would be in an ideal world of my (or your) own making: it must, on the contrary, be informed and guided by any relevant statutory text and any pertinent judicial decisions and opinions. But a *theory* of the law relating to the basis and grounds of judicial review of administrative action, or the nature and scope of the proportionality doctrine, or the requirements of procedural fairness (in some particular field) cannot be detached from the theorist's views about what would make constitutional law better rather than worse. Even a theory about the best way to read the Broadcasting Act 1991 must engage the relevant political values.[16] The plain words of the statute cannot relieve us from the responsibility to weigh, in any specific context, the respective demands of free speech, on the one hand, and broadcasting standards, on the other. Of course, the theory must be about how to read the Act, not one about what should replace it. But that is, inevitably, a rather subtle distinction in practice and one which only detailed, contextual argument can elucidate. I cannot defeat your own theory by pointing to your obvious political or moral convictions: I must try to show that they have misled you into adopting a construction which, for connected reasons of language, consistency, and democracy, is ultimately unsound.

The law student cannot, then, stand aloof from the arguments that rage over rival versions of British constitutionalism. There is no simple fact-of-the-matter about any questions of public law, however comparatively local or trivial: any statement

---

[15] Compare A W B Simpson, 'The Common Law and Legal Theory', in Simpson (ed), *Oxford Essays in Jurisprudence*, 2nd series (Oxford: Clarendon Press, 1973), 77–99, at 90: 'Nor does the common law system admit the possibility of a court, however elevated, reaching a final, authoritative statement of what the law is in a general abstract sense. It is as if the system placed particular value upon dissension, obscurity, and the tentative character of judicial utterances.'

[16] See *R (ProLife Alliance) v British Broadcasting Corporation* [2003] UKHL 23.

of law is always the conclusion of an interpretative *argument* over how best to read the relevant legal materials. The United Kingdom has a common law constitution not merely in the sense that it is the product of history and tradition, but also in the sense that its content is a complex mixture of shared understandings and theoretical argument. Every doctrine, no matter how well established or exalted, is embraced as a rough approximation to the applicable balance of reasons—adequate for most purposes, perhaps, but subject to reappraisal and refinement when tested in novel circumstances or in the light of changing moral attitudes. The theoretical arguments often presented as an introduction to public law cannot, then, be set on one side in order to study the law as it currently stands: they are intrinsic to any competent statement of the law, which has no separate existence or meaning outside a morally engaged, interpretative account.[17]

It was once a settled doctrine of common law that action taken under the royal prerogative—the powers traditionally enjoyed by the monarch without the need of parliamentary assent—could not be challenged in the courts. If the pertinent action fell within the prerogative domain, its manner of exercise lay within the unfettered discretion of Government ministers (acting nominally on behalf of the Queen). When, however, the Judicial Committee of the House of Lords agreed that, in certain contexts, the legality or fairness of prerogative action could legitimately be brought into question in the courts, it conceded that the previous understanding had been erroneous, or at least inaccurate.[18] It 'changed' the law only in the sense of acknowledging that earlier assumptions were not consistent with legal principle, more deeply and reflectively considered. While in many cases Government action under prerogative powers would not be justiciable—involving matters unsuited to judicial scrutiny—in other instances it was harder to justify the distinction, as regards judicial review, between statutory and prerogative power. Why, for example, should it make any difference that the conditions of employment of civil servants were amended by an order made under prerogative Order in Council, rather than a power delegated by Act of Parliament? Surely similar considerations of fairness, as regards notice and consultation, should apply in either case? Even the notion that many prerogative powers are in their very nature non-justiciable can be challenged as inimical to the rule of law; and more recent case law has chipped away at a suggested list of such powers, showing that judicial review can encompass a much broader range of governmental decision-making than formerly assumed.[19]

The point is that public law doctrine adapts to meet fresh challenges, political and moral. Any statement of the current position is necessarily tentative and provisional, dependent in detail on study of the implications of our shared commitment to legality—a moral ideal connected to related ideals of freedom, justice, and equality. We move between general principle and more concrete application, refining and

---

[17] Compare David Feldman, 'None, One or Several? Perspectives on the UK's Constitution(s)' [2005] CLJ 329–51, at 350: 'There can be no one source of authority for constitutional rules: authority and legitimacy stem from the process of argument about and justification for the rules.'

[18] See *Council of Civil Service Unions v Minister for the Civil Service* [1985] AC 374.

[19] Compare *R (Bancoult) v Secretary of State for Foreign and Commonwealth Affairs (No 2)* [2007] EWCA Civ 498, para 46 (Sedley LJ); *Bancoult* is considered in Chapter 8, below.

developing legal doctrine as we proceed. And while we can describe the outcome in terms of legal change or reform—initiated by a kind of judicial 'legislation'—it is for the lawyer or judge involved much more a process of exploration and discovery. We examine the consequences of our fundamental ideas as circumstances or social attitudes change and new interpretations of doctrine, which would once have seemed plainly misguided, now seem more plausible—presenting a serious challenge to our aspirations for justice and coherence. So a lawyer or legal theorist cannot simply describe events from the outside, as a historian might seek to chart the various stages of constitutional change. A statement of law is only as accurate as its theoretical grasp of the pertinent standards of legality: to be a lawyer is to be, at least in part, a legal philosopher, even if the philosophy is steeped in local tradition and shared experience.[20]

III

This book denies that there is any neutral, detached, descriptive ground on which a lawyer may stand in drawing conclusions about the requirements of English (or Scottish or European) law, in general, or the content of the British constitution, in particular. It insists that any statement of law is always a matter of interpretation, and that interpretation is (in the present context) necessarily normative: it draws on moral and political ideas and values to support one reading rather than another. I proceed to defend an interpretation of principles of parliamentary sovereignty, the rule of law, and separation of powers that, in my view, permits the constitution to be viewed as a bastion of liberty and justice. It may fall far short of the constitution I would design for a newly created republic of free and equal citizens, each of whom had assented to my acting as their founding father. But if we treat its principal doctrines of parliamentary sovereignty and the rule of law as affirmations of fundamental ideals of democracy and legality—each linked in complex ways to related ideals of equality and freedom—our existing tradition is plainly open to a benign or congenial interpretation, capable in principle of inspiring loyalty and allegiance.

Many readers will disagree with the details of my analysis, even if they accept my general interpretative stance; other readers will oppose my views with sharply contrasting interpretations of their own. If, however, we draw on familiar ideas and ideals, citing similar examples and precedents, we are engaged in genuine interpretative debate. We are seeking to understand (and thereby improve) our constitutional practice; we are not conducting a debate over politics or justice or morality that has only marginal relevance to questions of public law. It is important to emphasize the nature of this debate—its character as an internal argument over what, when correctly understood, our legal order already permits or requires. Many of the matters that are vigorously contested in public law and legal theory are obscured, in

---

[20] Compare Dworkin, *Law's Empire*, 90: 'So any judge's opinion is itself a piece of legal philosophy...Jurisprudence is the general part of adjudication, silent prologue to any decision at law.'

practice, by ambiguity over the kind of debate involved. Moves in an interpretative argument are often construed, erroneously, as pleas for radical change or reform—calls for the kind of new constitutional settlement that only a special Convention of leading statesmen or some revolutionary upheaval could bring about. Criticism of prevailing orthodoxy, on any question, is not illegitimate because it is unorthodox: it is encouraged by the method of the common law, whose health depends on its continuing ability to meet fresh challenges and absorb new ideas.[21]

It will not do, therefore, for supporters of absolute parliamentary sovereignty, who deny all constitutional limits on the scope of legislative supremacy, to say that their opponents are inciting revolution. The doctrine cannot be defended on the basis that it is what a majority of senior judges or other senior officials happen to think correct: it must be defended by arguments of principle, if indeed such a defence could be devised, consistently with our commitment to constitutionalism. There is no current fact-of-the-matter to which absolutists can appeal.[22] Nor can the justiciability of certain sorts of prerogative governmental action be settled by reference to judicial dicta in prominent cases: such dicta must be subjected to critical inquiry on the basis of legal principle, informed by a developed account of the central ideal of legality or the rule of law. And whether or not courts should defer to the views of other public authorities, as regards the compatibility of their actions with human rights standards, and in what circumstances they should do so, are again matters of constitutional theory. Differences of opinion on such matters are internal to an exploration of our present public law practice: they evince divergent understandings of that practice as a contribution to democratic governance, respectful of human rights and equal citizenship.[23]

The nature of A. V. Dicey's well-known exposition of constitutional first principles continues to be hotly contested.[24] For some public lawyers, Dicey's text is essentially descriptive and morally detached. He presents the law as it simply is, in the sense of a systematic account of settled judicial practice, viewed from the outside: his numerous appeals to the value of liberty and the merits of English tradition must be taken as rhetorical flourishes, decorating an otherwise austere descriptivism. This is Dicey as legal positivist: the content of law is determined by its authoritative sources, whether respectful or otherwise of rights or liberty; any overlap with morality or justice (or any lawyer's understanding of those values) is mainly contingent, depending on the goodwill or wisdom of those exercising political authority.[25] It is possible, however, to defend a different Dicey, more congenial to my own interpretative project. Now the references to liberty and

---

[21] Compare Simpson, 'The Common Law and Legal Theory', 90: 'As a system of legal thought the common law...is inherently vague; it is a feature of the system that uniquely authentic statements of the rules which, so positivists tell us, comprise the common law, cannot be made.'

[22] See further Chapter 4, below.

[23] See especially Chapter 7, below.

[24] A V Dicey, *Introduction to the Study of the Law of the Constitution*, 10th edn (London: Macmillan, 1964; first published in 1885).

[25] H L A Hart took 'Legal Positivism to mean the simple contention that it is in no sense a necessary truth that laws reproduce or satisfy certain demands of morality, though in fact they have often done

tradition—the contrasts with oppressive Continental regimes and the scepticism concerning enacted bills of rights—come centre-stage. Dicey, read in this way, attempts to provide a theory of the constitution intended to show that British democracy serves the interests of good governance, enhancing and protecting individual liberty. His 'rule of law', on this account, is as much the gift of historical tradition and respect for liberty as a merely formal doctrine, making everyone equally subject to whatever Parliament decreed as the law of the land. Here Dicey is himself an interpretivist, as much natural lawyer as legal positivist: the content of law is dependent on the 'spirit of legality' that animates his doctrine of the rule of law.[26]

The actual Dicey seems to have blended contrasting styles of analysis in a somewhat contradictory manner; perhaps that is part of his enduring influence, appealing to readers of different persuasions. In understanding his work as part of the tradition we are trying to explain and defend, however, we must identify the inconsistencies and expose the contrast between divergent understandings. If public lawyers read Dicey in contrasting ways, drawing rather different conclusions, it is largely because they begin with competing conceptions of the subject or of the nature of legal analysis. In that respect, continuing debate over Dicey's endeavour is a feature of the larger terrain of theoretical controversy that, to a significant degree, constitutes our public law.

My account of interpretation is developed more fully in Chapter 2, where I consider the familiar distinction between constitutional law and constitutional convention. That distinction, I argue, reflects a mainly descriptive stance, external to legal reasoning and adjudication. From the political scientist's perspective, legal rules enacted by Parliament or announced by judges can be readily distinguished from practices that politicians treat as morally binding: we can identify a category of rules that are mainly or wholly dependent, in practice, on political cooperation and consent. Dicey famously defined conventions as those rules observed by ministers of the Crown that were not enforced by the courts.[27] From an interpretative stance, internal to legal reasoning, however, such distinctions may prove unhelpful and misleading. The law consists of constitutional principles that may be illuminated as much by settled political practice as by enacted rules or judicial rulings: such principles try to make sense of the *whole* constitution, as an integrated legal and political order. Any feature of governmental practice may, in principle, become relevant to adjudication: settled convention, informed by ideas about good governance, is part of the normative background to any specific question of public law. And a judge cannot remain aloof, observing a practice whose content or significance he

---

so': Hart, *The Concept of Law* (first published in 1961), 2nd edn (Oxford: Clarendon Press, 1994), 185–6. John Austin observed (in 1832): 'The existence of law is one thing; its merit or demerit is another. Whether it be or be not is one enquiry; whether it be or be not conformable to an assumed standard, is a different enquiry.' (Austin, *The Province of Jurisprudence Determined*, ed Wilfrid E Rumble (Cambridge: Cambridge University Press, 1995), 157).

26 See further Chapter 1, below.
27 Dicey, *Law of the Constitution*, ch 14.

can simply take for granted.[28] I draw here on Ronald Dworkin's helpful account of legal interpretation, revealing the crucial linkage between practice and principle— matters of fact and attitude illuminated by reasons ascribed, in the last analysis, by the interpreter himself.[29]

In Chapter 3, I offer an account of the rule of law that invokes the idea of liberty as independence. Drawing on the work of F. A. Hayek as well as Dicey, I try to show the links between law and liberty that not only characterize republican political thought, but help to make sense of constitutional doctrine. Administrative discretion, though a necessary tool of modern governance, presents a threat to an ideal of individual autonomy or independence: judicial review of executive state action provides a necessary safeguard. The various connections between liberty, legality, and justice enable us to develop a much stronger conception of the rule of law than Dicey's well-known account initially suggests: it is ultimately a principle of equal citizenship, precluding arbitrary distinctions between persons, irrelevant to any legitimate public purpose. Our statements of law, as regards the content of individual rights or the scope of public powers, are informed by an implicit ideal of legality: they express an understanding of the manner in which, in the specific context in point, our legal practice serves our guiding political ideals.

The discussion of parliamentary sovereignty in Chapter 4 matches the logic of my account of legality. From an appropriately internal legal stance, rooted in the basic political values, Parliament's authority is confined by the limits of our ability (in any concrete context) to interpret its enactments as contributions to the public good. Our obedience is necessarily reasoned and reflective, attempting always to reconcile statutory instructions with constitutional principle, according to the circumstances in view. The responsibility to uphold legality—to keep faith with the rule of law—cannot be discharged by mere submission to literal meaning, divorced from its broader moral and political context. And it is ultimately a personal moral responsibility, linked to citizenship or membership of the political community. From an external vantage point, congenial to legal positivism, we might seek to identify a 'rule of recognition', summarizing the opinions of senior officials (including senior judges); there might be a broad consensus on the unqualified authority of Parliament.[30] But that would tell us nothing useful, as legal interpreters, responsible for making sense of Parliament's instructions in the infinitely varied contexts and circumstances we confront in practice. Our efforts to honour the demands of both democracy and legality, in any practical instance, must be morally engaged, not neutral and detached.

---

[28] Compare Feldman, 'None, One or Several?', 343: 'In theory, the convention [of collective cabinet responsibility] is established by consensus among actors in the political arena, and the courts merely take some form of judicial notice, for their own limited purposes, of that consensus. In reality, there may be no consensus, yet the courts have to assume or pretend that some consensus is to be found. In those circumstances, the judiciary creates a vision of the constitutional convention that is effective, at least for the court's own purposes.'

[29] Dworkin, *Law's Empire*. See also Dworkin, *Justice for Hedgehogs* (Cambridge, Mass: Harvard University Press, 2011), Part 2.

[30] For the rule of recognition, see Hart, *The Concept of Law*, ch 6; see also Jeffrey Goldsworthy, *The Sovereignty of Parliament: History and Philosophy* (Oxford: Clarendon Press, 1999), ch 10.

The implications of seeking harmony between parliamentary sovereignty and the rule of law are further explored in Chapter 5, where I defend a style of statutory interpretation that affirms both legislative supremacy and constitutional rights. The application of statutes to particular cases calls for deliberation and judgement: there is always a balance to be struck, according to the circumstances, between legislative aim or purpose (as revealed by the text) and conflicting individual rights and interests. The new interpretative regime under the Human Rights Act 1998 is, I argue, largely a reaffirmation of common law orthodoxy: a correct construction, compliant with the rule of law, gives as much protection to basic rights as possible, having regard to the legitimate public purposes a statute can be understood to further. I shall challenge the view that the Act prescribes a mode of construction that would not otherwise apply, at least in cases where European Convention rights run in parallel with constitutional rights at common law. Our discussion will broaden out into a study of the jurisprudential debate over statutory meaning and interpretation; we will examine the idea of 'legislative intention', a notion closely linked to certain conceptions of parliamentary sovereignty. I shall emphasize, in keeping with the main theme of the book, the contrasting perspectives of detached observer and committed interpreter. Our theoretical vision must match the demands of legal practice if constitutional theory is to play its proper role.

Chapter 6 considers the lively debate about the constitutional foundations of judicial review in the light of the principal themes of the book. Insofar as the ultra vires doctrine is anything more than a merely formal rationalization—squaring judicial enforcement of principles of legality with the empowerment of executive officials by a sovereign Parliament, free to impose such constraints and conditions as it pleases—it must draw sustenance from a *justification* of that sovereignty. And insofar as a rival common law theory, displacing ultra vires, locates the basis of judicial review in fundamental moral principle, it must repudiate any absolutist conception of sovereignty, inconsistent with the rule of law. It cannot (I shall argue) be neutral between competing conceptions of the legal and constitutional order, or take for granted any received ideas about the content of the 'rule of recognition'. It must, like any persuasive constitutional theory, be normative all the way down—rooted in a theory of legality that provides a context for parliamentary sovereignty, defining its reach and marking its boundaries.

In Chapter 7, I explore a range of issues concerning judicial review of administrative action, emphasizing the way in which legality depends on judgements about legitimacy: legal doctrine, although an important guide, must be adaptable to subtle variations of legal and political context. From an internal, interpretative viewpoint we can sometimes acknowledge the legitimacy of decisions or developments which from an external, detached perspective may look more doubtful. In some accounts, for example, the articulation of common law constitutional rights, in the decades before the Human Rights Act was passed, was a species of judicial activism that had no firm foundation in existing law: certain prominent judges manipulated the law for their own radical political ends (however noble such ends might be considered in themselves).[31] If, as I contend, we must appraise the legitimacy of such developments from the inside—from within the distinctive normative sphere that common law reasoning creates and maintains—we may reasonably reach quite different conclusions.

From an internal perspective, consistent with our commitment to legality as a moral ideal, a number of familiar doctrinal distinctions that serve mainly descriptive purposes look more questionable—procedure and substance, review and appeal, standards of legality and standards of review, European Convention rights and their common law equivalents, reasonableness (or rationality) and proportionality, judicial review of administrative action and the judicial enforcement of Convention rights. It is, I suggest, largely a failure to appreciate the fragility of such distinctions—the manner in which their application is sensitive to all the circumstances of any affront, or threatened affront, to legality—that underlies the calls for a specific doctrine of judicial deference, curbing the reach of judicial protection of fundamental human rights. Such a doctrine may duplicate what is already inherent in legal process, correctly understood, adding complexity rather than sophistication. From the perspective of adjudication, wisely conducted, deference to Parliament or Government means enforcing rights according to their true extent—if no further—having regard to the legitimate demands of the common good or public interest.

A number of prominent themes re-emerge in Chapter 8 by way of a concluding discussion. Questions about the rule of law and separation of powers, including the critical role of judicial independence, resurface in the context of fundamental rights. Whereas an external critique of 'legal constitutionalism' may attribute certain basic rights, such as freedom of speech or unimpeded access to the courts, to judicial 'invention' or dubious activism, an internal, more lawyerly, perspective may readily locate their legitimate interpretative foundations. Indeed, when the external critic dons the lawyer's robe, acknowledging the inherent role of the judiciary as guarantor of liberty, his scepticism may quickly disappear. A 'political constitutionalist', who recognizes only a very limited and subservient role for courts, risks an illuminating collapse into legal constitutionalism when he tries to confront questions of legality in the adjudicative context.[32]

A further distinction now appears which, though plausible from a primarily descriptive vantage point, proves brittle in more nuanced, interpretative hands. The Human Rights Act is presented (from the outside) as an example of 'weak' as opposed to 'strong' review: courts cannot quash or modify a statute that infringes constitutional rights but must obey it notwithstanding their declared objections.[33]

---

[31] See Tom Hickman, *Public Law after the Human Rights Act* (Oxford: Hart Publishing, 2010), 99–111. And compare Tomkins, *Our Republican Constitution*, ch 1, considered in Chapter 2, below.

[32] See my discussion of the work of Adam Tomkins and Richard Bellamy in (mainly) Chapter 8. Bellamy has been misled (I shall suggest) by Cass Sunstein's critique of Ronald Dworkin's account of adjudication: Sunstein's strictures about competing levels of theoretical sophistication (or 'conceptual ascent') make little sense from an internal, interpretative perspective (as Dworkin observes).

[33] See Jeremy Waldron, 'The Core of the Case Against Judicial Review' (2006) 115 Yale LJ 1346–406.

If, as I contend, however, statutory interpretation is at the same time constitutional interpretation—the content of law being always informed by the ideal of the rule of law—such distinctions between strong and weak review are in practice hard to sustain. The interpretative process is too subtle and discriminating for such labels to stick. The lawyer or judge strives to reconcile statutory purpose and individual right—or, more grandly, democracy and the rule of law. Judicial review is thereby rendered as strong as it needs to be to preserve legality. There is rarely any need to quash—or any sense in quashing—a provision whose full meaning and effect the court itself has helped to fashion.

Insofar as the standard debate over judicial or constitutional review assumes a rigid polarity—legislative versus judicial supremacy—I am challenging its practical utility. Common law constitutionalism, as I understand and defend it, resists that polarity. It denies that we have to choose between democracy and fundamental rights, or between parliamentary sovereignty and the rule of law, or between judicial deference and judicial activism. Our legal doctrine is only an attempt to summarize and systematize a tradition that has its own deeper momentum, rooted in conceptions of liberty and human dignity that may be hard to articulate in any comprehensive fashion. We resolve doctrinal conflicts by interrogating our tradition, confident that it has the resources to guide our deliberations. Even when doctrinal conflicts and inconsistencies suggest deeper divisions of moral or political opinion, our participation in a shared tradition holds out the promise of a larger, more complex vision, capable of resolving such conflicts and inconsistencies, at least for present purposes. There is rarely any genuine experience of *choice* available in ordinary legal practice, and hence in legal theory. There is, in practice, only the obligation to identify, by reference to the pertinent political values, what the law dictates in the circumstances we confront or suppose. Our differences are cognitive or intellectual, not (or not primarily) volitional or existential.

In an Appendix, at the end of the book, I consider a debate within public law about the relationship between the law and political theory, which is relevant to questions of method and interpretation. While the virtues and vices of my own approach will be apparent from my discussion of specific legal issues, it seemed appropriate briefly to reflect on that approach in the context of the wider debate. I also consider some further questions raised by Ronald Dworkin's interpretative approach to law and legal theory, developing themes explored in the earlier discussion of British constitutionalism.

IV

I have tried to make the earlier sections of each chapter accessible to students coming to the subject afresh, while developing my argument more fully in later sections. I envisage that the reader will move between chapters in the order he or she pleases, trusting that the introductory sections of each chapter will give sufficient guidance for the construction of an individual route-map. Later sections can be postponed, if the reader wishes, until a grasp of the larger argument across the book as a whole has been obtained. I have avoided separate subject headings within each chapter for the obvious reason that the material is closely interrelated, later sections pursuing, in more detail or in a different manner, themes already established in previous ones. I hope, nevertheless, that the index will enable the reader readily to locate discussion of specific cases or issues or writers. I have tried to be as systematic as my subject matter permits; but it is a general theme of the book that there are few straightforward divisions and distinctions: an interpretation must be an interpretation of everything—everything, at least, relevant to public law.

1

Constitution and Constitutionalism

I

What is the British Constitution and where can we find it? Being an 'unwritten'—more strictly, non-codified—constitution, we know it is vain to search for any special document that expresses the terms of an original contract, defining rights and distributing powers. The sources of constitutional law are multifarious; and they include ideas and ideals of liberty and justice, informing and inspiring our practice, both legal and political. The British Constitution today is the product of both history and morality: we have become accustomed to certain institutional arrangements, which are sustained by our commitments to democracy and the rule of law. We know that such arrangements are not perfect—in certain respects they may be very deficient—but they afford at least a basic structure for legitimate democratic government; they support a constitutional tradition (most of us think) worth maintaining and improving. In any case, we always start from where we are: change or reform must be brought about by agreement between people who are already united, for better or worse, by existing political arrangements.

We must interpret our constitution in the light of the demands of constitutionalism, as we conceive that noble ideal. The legislative supremacy of Parliament can be defended on democratic grounds: the people's representatives, fairly elected, ought to possess the power of changing the law when justice or the public good requires reform. And the principle of legality, that no public official (any more than a private citizen) should be able to exercise coercion without proper constitutional authority, is as much a basic precept of the British Constitution as an expression of the central idea of constitutionalism. To understand the constitution is therefore to grasp the principles that underpin and justify our practice. We must make sense of an evolving historical legal and political order, insofar as we can, by reference to the moral or political values that inform and explain our continuing adherence to it.

It is sometimes supposed that we can *describe* the constitution without reference to values or ideals, which may of course elicit debate and disagreement. No doubt we can identify the major institutions and catalogue their various powers and procedures, though even our selection of institutions and powers (among other possible objects of description) will reflect our value-judgements. Institutions and powers are *important* only from some perspective that informs our judgements of importance. Any coherent account of the constitution, viewed as a whole, however, must amount to a *theory* of it. The law of the constitution is something about which good lawyers often disagree. They may disagree, for example, about the limits of legislative supremacy (or parliamentary sovereignty) because they are divided about when, if ever, the assertion of such supremacy may contravene the rule of law. And they may well disagree about the nature and content of the rule of law, offering competing interpretations of the relevant precedents (or examples of conduct condemned by the courts). We can, of course, simply *report* these disagreements, observing that the constitution is, on many points, unsettled or indeterminate; but even fully to *understand* the phenomena we behold we must be more critical, forming our own view. We could not otherwise offer an account of the constitution— only an account of other people's conflicting opinions, none of which we might share in its entirety.

Public law textbooks sometimes suppress this crucial evaluative dimension. The law is presented, or summarized, as if it could be simply *learned*, as one might learn the rules of a game or the arrangement of the planets. The implication is usually that though there may be disagreement or uncertainty about rather minor, more technical points, there is no real doubt or debate over matters of fundamental importance. The ultimate 'sovereignty' of Parliament, for example, is often described as if it were a matter of *empirical fact*—something that no one who has looked at the legal precedents or has any knowledge of history could reasonably deny. If such an absolutist doctrine, denying all legal limits to legislative power, might seem to allow the gravest violations of justice to go unchallenged, we are assured that any such (unlikely) abuses would provoke resistance. A statute requiring the execution of blue-eyed babies might be legally *valid*, but no sane person would obey it.[1] So a statement of fact (everyone obeys whatever Parliament enacts) is supported by assurances that different facts (or anticipated facts) would occur to qualify it when necessary. But of course such assurances undermine the whole approach.

If Parliament is 'sovereign' it must be so in virtue of some theory that provides an *interpretation* of the relevant facts; and that theory, if it is to be persuasive, must account for the limits on legislative supremacy that any sane and decent citizen or official would insist on as a matter of practice. A different version of the empirical fact thesis says that Parliament has absolute power, at least as a matter of law, because members of Parliament and government ministers and other senior officials believe that this is so. If they all agree that an Act of Parliament is valid law, whatever its content may be, then there is a rule of practice to that effect, which an account of constitutional law must faithfully report. But how do we know that they would all agree? When confronted by an outrageous statute, apparently violating fundamental rights usually taken for granted, many judges or other officials might refuse to accept its validity even if a majority of members of Parliament thought differently. And even if the courts disclaimed any power to quash or disregard such an Act, they would be likely to interpret its provisions consistently with basic rights as far

[1] A V Dicey, *Introduction to the Study of the Law of the Constitution*, 10th edn (London: Macmillan, 1964), 81 (quoting Leslie Stephen, *Science of Ethics* (1882), 143).

as the language allowed (whatever the intentions or expectations of those promoting the Bill in Parliament might have been).

So we must reject any attempt to describe the law of the constitution as if its content were largely uncontroversial, or as if we were merely reporting the opinions of powerful officials, however distasteful we might find them. We are instead reporting our *own* opinion, based on a view of constitutional practice that we find defensible—an account of our practice that shows how legal doctrine furthers the moral and political values that a good constitution ought to serve. Since legislative supremacy is clearly related to the idea of democracy, its legal or constitutional limits will reflect our theory of democracy, which must explain how far a political majority may legitimately impose its will on a dissenting minority. Or at least considerations of democratic legitimacy must be a significant element of any plausible account of our own practice—one which we could defend as a reasonable basis for political cooperation. If no legislature, anywhere, even if popularly elected, could in our opinion legitimately pass a bill of attainder—singling out a named individual for special punishment—we have good grounds for denying Parliament such a power.[2] We are trying to elucidate the features of what (in common with most of our fellow citizens) we take to be a *legitimate* scheme of government, worthy of our attention and loyalty.[3]

This book is an exploration of the consequences for constitutional thought of emphasizing that normative or evaluative dimension of legal reasoning. I offer an interpretation of constitutional law that gives good reason, if it is persuasive, for maintaining and improving our practice rather than discarding it. In this first chapter, I will set the scene for what follows, giving a broad overview of my project. A short analysis of the *ProLife Alliance* case, on freedom of expression, is offered to illustrate our need to choose between rival conceptions of the British legal or constitutional order. We will look briefly at A. V. Dicey's famous work on the constitution, challenging the conventional reading. Dicey's apparently conflicting principles of parliamentary sovereignty and the rule of law can, I argue, be reconciled when correctly understood. The argument will be developed in subsequent chapters. I shall also introduce the jurisprudential debate over law, politics, and sovereignty by a preliminary review of Jeffrey Goldsworthy's critique of legal constitutionalism, as I defend it. He supports an absolutist version of parliamentary sovereignty that I reject.

We will also consider, later in the chapter, questions about the nature of law (and hence constitutional law) raised by the famous debate between H. L. A. Hart and Lon L. Fuller. Fuller's insistence that a theory of law should be a morally engaged account, revealing law as a form of governance respectful of the demands of human dignity, is highly instructive. Whereas Hart was content to distinguish

---

[2] Bills or Acts of Attainder, declaring someone guilty of an offence and inflicting a punishment, were sometimes enacted during the sixteenth and seventeenth centuries and treated as valid law. But such precedents are not, we must suppose, reliable guides to our present practice. See further Chapter 3, below.

[3] Compare Paul Craig, 'Public Law, Political Theory and Legal Theory' [2000] PL 211–39 (emphasizing the central normative dimension of constitutional theory and the common law tradition).

between internal and external perspectives on law, pointing to the way in which rules are treated as valid by citizens and officials, Fuller takes up the internal viewpoint itself. Legal philosophy becomes an implicit element of adjudication and legal reasoning.[4]

II

I am defending an interpretative approach to law that seeks to show, not merely what the law requires or permits, on correct analysis, but why that reading of the law is morally justified—consistent with basic political values that we can affirm as proper guides to the practice of liberal democracy. I am arguing that it is only within that general approach that we can find the resources—moral and intellectual—to make sense of our law, locating answers to legal and constitutional questions that would otherwise elude us. I am inviting you to take sides with me in favour of certain conclusions about legal rights and powers and duties (in the circumstances of particular cases) and against contrary conclusions; I need to appeal, therefore, to your moral and political judgement, not merely your knowledge of relevant statutes and precedents. You will need to be persuaded, if possible, that an attractive account of British constitutionalism, worthy of allegiance, can indeed be found—that the law, if not perfectly just, is at least legitimate.

Someone may, admittedly, be so repelled by the failure, as he sees it, of the legal order to uphold democracy or protect individual liberty (or some other important political value) that he does indeed deny its legitimacy. And in those circumstances he cannot do more than report its various failings, recording that there are differences of view over many important questions of legal authority. He can certainly call for radical reform or revolution; but he can scarcely engage in the minutiae of constitutional interpretation, defending one view as superior to another for reasons of justice, internal to legal reasoning, because he has already rejected the whole system as irredeemably bad. He cannot appeal to constitutional history and practice in support of political values he affirms: he condemns such history and practice as abhorrent.

On closer inspection, however, we might decide that this wholesale condemnation is only rhetorical. If our critic could embrace an account of the main principles and practices of British government, at least broadly consistent with notions of freedom and justice he endorses, he would not truly deny its legitimacy. He takes issue only with someone else's opinion of how best to understand constitutional law and practice; and it makes no difference, in principle, whether his adversary is an influential judge or politician or, alternatively, a minor official or private citizen. Our critic is entitled to stand his ground. Even Supreme Court judges can make

---

[4] This interdependence of theory and practice is also a feature of the work of Ronald Dworkin, introduced in Chapter 2, below. In an Appendix, at the end of the book, I look briefly at a debate, within public law itself, about the nature of public law and the proper tasks and approach of the public law scholar.

serious mistakes about the law, and they often disagree among themselves about major questions of constitutional interpretation.[5]

In *ex parte Zadig*, Lord Shaw dissented from the view of the House of Lords majority that Zadig was lawfully detained as a threat to national security.[6] Zadig was detained, without trial for any offence, under a regulation empowering the Secretary of State to order the internment of anyone of 'hostile origin or associations' when it was thought 'expedient for securing the public safety or the defence of the realm'. In denouncing the exercise of arbitrary executive power as 'poison to the commonwealth', Lord Shaw denied that the Government had been entitled to make such a regulation under the Defence of the Realm Consolidation Act 1914, whose general authority to issue regulations for 'the public safety and the defence of the realm' had, he considered, been exceeded. Although Shaw's conclusions were based on careful analysis of the statutory scheme, they also reflected his strong commitment to the liberty of the individual. They drew on an account of the rule of law, strongly resistant to discriminatory executive measures impinging on basic liberty, which underpinned the constitution as Shaw understood it. The speech amounted to a demand for adherence to legality in the face of what he conceived to be grave judicial error.

Lord Atkin's famous dissent in *Liversidge*, during the Second World War, made a similar appeal to an ideal of freedom that he took the constitution to serve.[7] The Emergency Powers (Defence) Act 1939 explicitly empowered the Crown to make regulations for the internment of those whose detention the Secretary of State considered to be 'expedient in the interests of the . . . defence of the realm'; so legal argument focused on the correct interpretation of Regulation 18B of the Defence Regulations, made thereunder. The Regulation permitted the minister to act where he had 'reasonable cause to believe any person to be of hostile origin or associations'; but though Lord Atkin held that the existence of such 'reasonable cause' should be determined by the courts, the House of Lords majority denied that the minister was subject to any such legal control. In the absence of proof of bad faith, executive discretion was unfettered. In reproving his colleagues as 'more executive minded than the executive', Atkin appealed beyond the prevailing judicial consensus to a vision of the constitution that afforded better protection of liberty.[8] What may appear on a superficial reading to be a somewhat technical debate about language—Atkin laid great emphasis on the ordinary legal implications of 'reasonable cause'—was in truth a more fundamental debate over the proper role of the judiciary. Viscount Maugham denied the relevance of any general principle that legislation dealing with the liberty of the subject should, if possible, be construed in favour of the subject and against the Crown: that principle had 'no relevance in dealing with an executive measure by way of preventing a public danger'.[9] Rival

---

[5] For elaboration of the argument in this paragraph, see Chapter 4, below.
[6] *R v Halliday, ex parte Zadig* [1917] AC 260.
[7] *Liversidge v Anderson* [1942] AC 206.
[8] Ibid, 244.
[9] Ibid, 218.

interpretations of law reflected deep-seated differences of constitutional vision: they exposed the gulf between underlying conceptions of the rule of law.

In more recent times, Lord Hoffmann has challenged the Government's power to derogate from Article 5 of the European Convention on Human Rights in order to detain without trial foreign suspected terrorists, who could not be lawfully deported (in view of the risk of torture in the receiving countries, contrary to Article 3).[10] Derogation from the right to personal liberty was permitted (under Article 15) only 'in time of war or other public emergency threatening the life of the nation' and only 'to the extent strictly required by the exigencies of the situation'. While a majority of the House of Lords was willing, admittedly with some reluctance, to accept the Government's view that the conditions for derogation were met, Lord Hoffmann denied that the threat of terrorism amounted to a threat to the 'life of the nation'. It was a duty of Government to protect people's lives and property, but one that it 'must discharge without destroying our constitutional freedoms'.[11] Significantly, Hoffmann denied that the case turned on 'some special doctrine of European law'. Freedom from arbitrary arrest and detention was a 'quintessentially British liberty', long enjoyed under the common law; and so there were fundamental values at stake: the question was 'whether the United Kingdom should be a country' in which a person who had fallen under suspicion could be seized and indefinitely detained.[12]

These cases are all striking examples of judicial disagreement over the most important questions of individual freedom, where the debate was concerned not with whether the law should be changed or reformed, but rather with how it should be correctly understood. Beneath the surface of the argument over the meaning or application of specific statutory (or Treaty) provisions lies a debate about basic principles; and we can only identify such principles, and determine their proper scope and application to particular cases, by reflecting on the moral qualities of our system of government. To *understand* a principle is to grasp its value within a larger system of ideas and values—to accord it weight as part of a grander scheme aimed at securing justice and the common good. So legal analysis cannot be detached from the fundamental questions of constitutional theory. We cannot decide, in each case, whether the majority or the dissenting judgment is the more compelling without first grappling with those fundamental questions. The content of law is at least partly a matter of what it *ought* to be in the light of the implicit ideals and principles that confer on the constitution whatever legitimacy we take it to have.

Legal analysis involves putting any specific issue in its broader constitutional context; we have to interpret the tradition we have inherited on the assumption (which we trust is widely shared) that it offers a reliable guide to the demands of liberty and justice. We draw on legal precedents as evidence of our adherence to tradition—to refute any suspicion that we are merely promoting a private political agenda, better pursued by political action and legislative reform than legal

---

[10] *A v Secretary of State for the Home Dept* [2004] UKHL 56, paras 86–97.
[11] Ibid, para 95.   [12] Ibid, paras 87–8.

argument. Lord Atkin cited copiously from the case law for exactly this reason: he was keen to establish that the statutory meaning he favoured had been 'accepted in innumerable legal decisions for many generations'.[13] Not only was he entitled, indeed morally bound, to oppose a majority opinion he considered erroneous, but his conclusions are today widely endorsed by good common lawyers. His 'classic dissent' is now accepted as correct not only on the construction of a specific regulation, but 'in its declaration of English legal principle'.[14] Indeed, Lord Hoffmann's assertion (in the course of his judgment) that during both World Wars habeas corpus was suspended by Parliament, and 'powers to detain on suspicion conferred on the Government', might well be contested. Habeas corpus—the basic right to have the legality of one's detention properly investigated by a court of law—was suspended only by effect of the majority decisions in *Halliday* and *Liversidge*.[15] These are matters of legal interpretation rather than observable empirical fact.

Nor should we accept uncritically Hoffmann's assumption that there are no legal limits on Parliament's power to authorize any and every breach of human rights. If, as he suggests, the 'real threat to the life of the nation, in the sense of a people living in accordance with its traditional laws and political values, comes not from terrorism but from laws such as these'—the provisions for detention under the Anti-terrorism, Crime and Security Act 2001—we should expect the courts to defend those traditions and values against unconstitutional encroachment.[16] Why should we accept, as Hoffmann supposes, that a law can be both valid and unconstitutional? If our conceptions of law and legal validity are linked (as I am arguing) to the values that inform and inspire our constitutional tradition, there must be internal limits to any legislative power that courts can enforce. *Legality* is always connected to *legitimacy*, even if the connection is sometimes complex. 'Parliament' is no more a mere matter of empirical fact, for purposes of legal reasoning, than any other legal or constitutional concept: it acquires its meaning (along with the scope and limits of the relevant powers) from the general theory we construct to make sense, as best we can, of our legal and constitutional practice.

I am assuming that any plausible theory of British constitutionalism must apply to the *whole* of our practice. It must be capable of showing how the various legal doctrines and political practices fit together into a coherent scheme of governance. It would be no good embracing conflicting principles of parliamentary sovereignty and the rule of law, for example, and leaving the conflict unresolved. Any decent theory must show how principles of legislative supremacy and legality are properly reconciled and brought into harmony. It would otherwise be a theory of two competing constitutions, leaving us without any guidance about how to choose between them. Dicey's account of the constitution has often been criticized on these grounds.

---

[13] [1942] AC 206, 228.
[14] *Khawaja v Secretary of State for the Home Dept* [1984] AC 74, 110 (Lord Scarman).
[15] See David Dyzenhaus, *The Constitution of Law: Legality in a Time of Emergency* (Cambridge: Cambridge University Press, 2006), 183. For helpful discussion of *Halliday* and *Liversidge*, see ibid, 149–60.
[16] *A v Secretary of State for the Home Dept* [2004] UKHL 56, para 97.

His strong assertion of absolute parliamentary sovereignty, giving Parliament the 'right to make or unmake any law whatever', seemed to conflict with 'the rule or supremacy of law', which forbade the exercise of 'arbitrariness, or prerogative, or even of wide discretionary authority'.[17] What if Parliament were to attempt to confer such arbitrary or discretionary power on officials, attempting perhaps to limit recourse to the courts by anyone affected?

As we shall see, Dicey's work contained helpful pointers towards a satisfactory reconciliation of principles of legislative supremacy and legality, or the rule of law; but they are easily missed on a superficial reading. Much of the problem lay in his failure to acknowledge the evaluative or prescriptive dimension of any competent legal analysis; he adopted (like so many of his successors) an apparently descriptive stance, as if legal principles were matters of empirical fact. Dicey wrote that his aim was to 'explain the nature of Parliamentary sovereignty and to show that its existence is a legal fact, fully recognized by the law of England', as if the content of law were a direct reflection of nature—presumably, the unalterable behaviour and attitudes of officials.[18] Even if it were true that a 'modern judge would never listen to a barrister who argued that an Act of Parliament was invalid because it was immoral, or because it went beyond the limits of Parliamentary authority', such a judge might sometimes be turning a deaf ear to a perfectly legitimate argument, if only in unusual circumstances.[19] The 'plain truth', that 'our tribunals uniformly act on the principle that a law alleged to be a bad law is *ex hypothesi* a law, and therefore entitled to obedience', is at best a sociological truth about standard judicial behaviour.[20] It does not establish whether such tribunals are *right* to assume, without argument, that respect for the rule of law (as a basic precept of British governance) does not sometimes demand a different conclusion.[21]

The rule of law also possessed an uncertain status, poised between political principle and traditional attitude or assumption. It was a 'peculiarity of English institutions', which had very beneficial consequences for the protection of liberty.[22] No doubt Dicey was right to believe that liberty and legality ultimately depended on their special place in the legal and political culture. Constitutional tradition is ultimately more important than formal declarations of liberty. Dicey had good reason to fear that a declaration or bill of rights, of the sort found in other constitutions, could be swept away in a political climate hostile to individual freedom. Where, as in England, 'the right to individual freedom is part of the constitution because it is inherent in the ordinary law of the land, the right is one which can hardly be destroyed without a thorough revolution in the institutions and manners of the nation'.[23] Nonetheless, those 'institutions and manners' assume the truth of

---

[17] Dicey, *Law of the Constitution*, 40, 184, 202.
[18] Ibid, 39.   [19] Ibid, 63.   [20] Ibid.
[21] Distinguishing between legal and 'political sovereignty', Dicey acknowledged that since Parliament was a representative body, the 'will of the electorate' would ultimately prevail; but that was 'a political, not a legal fact': ibid, 73.
[22] Ibid, 188.   [23] Ibid, 201.

certain principles or values. We need a *theory* of the rule of law that can illuminate the various elements Dicey described, capable of showing how politicians, officials and judges *ought* to act in defence of legality (not merely how they have often or usually done so).

To understand our legal and constitutional practice is to interpret it in the light of shared ideals of liberty and justice—ideals that give us reason to sustain that practice as a good tradition, worthy of continuing, if cautious and critical, allegiance. We want to be able to see how the past provides a solid foundation on which to construct the future—the precedents affirming the principles of an attractive liberal and democratic legal order. It is quite wrong to think that there is any 'fact of the matter' about constitutional law that must be grasped and digested, as a prelude to understanding and critique. Any statement about the current law is a conclusion based on analysis of relevant statutory provisions and case law, and since such analysis is always evaluative—accepting some readings and rejecting others on the basis of general principles—competent lawyers will disagree (at least in detail) over how best to combine or reconcile such principles in particular cases. It does not follow that they are all correct, or that one view is as good as another.[24] It does mean, however, that legal reasoning cannot eschew moral and philosophical argument, which must inform and enrich our analysis of public law.

III

Radically contrasting visions of the British Constitution are reflected by the decisions of the Court of Appeal and House of Lords, respectively, in *ProLife Alliance*.[25] Whereas the lower court offered an explicit defence of the judiciary as guardians of liberty, the higher court was far more reticent, treating itself as merely the servant of an unfettered parliamentary sovereignty. The Alliance, which was a political party registered under the Political Parties, Elections and Referendums Act 2000, put forward enough candidates in Wales at the time of the 2001 general election to entitle it to present a party election broadcast. The BBC and other broadcasters declined to transmit the intended broadcast, however, on the ground that its images of aborted foetuses would be offensive to viewers. Although the importance of the images to the Alliance's campaign against abortion was acknowledged, changes were demanded to ensure compliance with relevant guidelines on taste and decency. Subsequent versions were also rejected, however, until the final version was transmitted without any visual images at all.

The broadcasters' decisions were made with reference to regulations agreed between the BBC and the Secretary of State for National Heritage, which

---

[24] If we supposed that one view was as good as another, there would be no disagreement about the present law, which a court would be free to settle as it chose; and the litigants would have no rights, being at the mercy of unfettered judicial discretion.
[25] *R (ProLife Alliance) v British Broadcasting Corporation* [2002] EWCA Civ 297, [2003] UKHL 23.

reflected the terms (applicable to the other companies) of the Broadcasting Act 1990, section 6(1)(a), prohibiting anything 'which offends against good taste or decency or is likely to encourage or incite to crime or to lead to disorder or to be offensive to public feeling'. ProLife's application for permission to apply for judicial review was refused by Scott Baker J, who observed that the broadcasters had to perform a difficult balancing exercise between allowing freedom of speech, on the one hand, and upholding standards of taste and decency, on the other. In allowing ProLife's appeal, the Court of Appeal emphasized the constitutional context in which the court's supervisory jurisdiction is undertaken. Laws LJ explained that 'as a matter of domestic law the courts owe a special responsibility to the public as the constitutional guardian of the freedom of political debate', a responsibility which was 'most acute at the time and in the context of a public election, especially a general election'.[26] In other contexts, such as entertainment programmes or even 'day-to-day news reporting', the court should be readier to accept the broadcasters' judgement: 'But in this context the court's constitutional responsibility to protect political speech is over-arching. It amounts to a duty which lies on the court's shoulders to decide for itself whether this censorship was justified.'[27]

In striking contrast, the House of Lords denied that the court could enforce its own assessment of the demands of free speech: Parliament had already struck the balance of respective interests by imposing its restrictions on broadcasts that offended good taste. In censoring the Alliance's election broadcast, the BBC and other companies were only performing their statutory duty. According to Lord Hoffmann, the thrust of the Alliance's complaint (despite the absence of any challenge to the Broadcasting Act under Article 10 of the European Convention) was that 'the statute should be disregarded or not taken seriously'.[28] Lord Nicholls of Birkenhead also drew a sharp distinction between the initial decision by Parliament to subject party broadcasts to the general restriction on offensive material, on the one hand, and the broadcasters' performance of their duties in the particular case, on the other. The approach of the Court of Appeal amounted to 're-writing, in the context of party broadcasts, the content of the offensive material restriction imposed by Parliament'.[29] It was not appropriate for the lower court to carry out its own balancing of interests: 'That was not a legitimate exercise for the courts in this case. Parliament has decided where the balance shall be held.'

It is plain that Laws LJ regarded the common law as the primary source of the fundamental right to freedom of speech, attributing to the courts a special role in support of democratic constitutionalism: 'the courts are ultimately the trustees of our democracy's framework'.[30] Freedom of expression was one of a number of fundamental or constitutional rights that provoked close judicial scrutiny of executive decisions, and 'its enjoyment by an accredited political party in an

[26] [2002] EWCA Civ 297, para 36.
[27] Ibid, para 37.　　　[28] [2003] UKHL 23, para 52.
[29] Ibid, para 15.　　　[30] [2002] EWCA Civ 297, para 36.

election contest must call, if anything, for especially heightened protection'. The requirements of Article 10 of the European Convention on Human Rights and Fundamental Freedoms, as interpreted by the European Court of Human Rights at Strasbourg, formed only a 'convenient gateway' to consideration of the proper judicial response.[31] The English court was not a 'Strasbourg surrogate', its duty being 'to develop, by the common law's incremental method, a coherent and principled domestic law of human rights'; and in any case the core rights enshrined in the Convention 'by and large reflect the principles which the common law itself espouses'.[32] The focus on domestic constitutional law reflects the challenge contained in curtailments of free speech to the integrity of the British legal order.

The House of Lords, by contrast, effectively reduces the legal or constitutional order to the content of the discrete instructions contained in specific legislation, interpreted with minimal attention to the broader political context. Its assumption that the general provisions of the Broadcasting Act could be automatically applied to election broadcasts, with little or no reflection on the consequences for freedom of speech, betrays a narrow and somewhat authoritarian conception of the legal order. If freedom of speech is a genuine value, generating a constitutional right to free expression of political opinion, it must colour and inform an interpretative reconstruction of what, in the particular circumstances, a statutory text should be understood to mean. Whether or not material infringes standards of good taste or decency, or should be regarded as 'offensive to public feeling', depends on the specific context; such standards or judgements reflect a perception of the balance of interests, everything taken into account. Simon Brown LJ, in the Court of Appeal, rightly stressed that the relevant concepts were not 'absolute':

They cannot be detached from their surrounding circumstances. The context in which they fall to be applied is all-important. Images or other material which if broadcast in one context would quite clearly be distasteful and offensive would be quite differently regarded in another.[33]

What is acceptable in an election broadcast would not necessarily be acceptable in a quiz programme or a game show. The question was whether there was a 'pressing social need' to ban this particular broadcast:

Disturbing, perhaps shocking, though the images on this video undoubtedly are, they represent the reality, the actuality, of what is involved in the abortion process. To campaign for the prohibition of abortion is a legitimate political programme. The pictures are in a real sense the message. Words alone cannot convey...the essentially human character of the foetus and the nature of its destruction by abortion.[34]

---

[31] Article 10 provides that everyone has the right to freedom of expression, which includes 'freedom to hold opinions and to receive and impart information and ideas without interference by public authority'; but the exercise of these freedoms 'may be subject to such formalities, conditions, restrictions or penalties as are prescribed by law and are necessary in a democratic society, in the interests of national security, territorial integrity or public safety, for the prevention of disorder or crime' or for other specified public interests.

[32] [2002] EWCA Civ 297, paras 33–5.

[33] Ibid, para 56.   [34] Ibid, para 57.

In his dissenting speech in the House of Lords, Lord Scott of Foscote also pointed out the context-dependent nature of the relevant tests, observing that 'material that might be required to be rejected in one type of programme might be unexceptionable in another'.[35] He denied that a party broadcast, if factually accurate, not sensationalized, and relevant to a lawful policy on which candidates were standing for election, could properly be rejected as offensive to public feeling:

> Voters in a mature democracy may strongly disagree with a policy being promoted by a televised party political broadcast but ought not to be offended by the fact that the policy is being promoted nor, if the promotion is factually accurate and not sensationalized, by the content of the programme. Indeed…the public in a mature democracy are not entitled to be offended by the broadcasting of such a programme.[36]

The attitude of the House of Lords majority towards statutory interpretation is inconsistent not only with the defence of constitutional rights at common law, but also with the requirements of the Human Rights Act, section 3.[37] Just as there is a strong presumption against unjustified infringements of free speech at common law, so section 3 demands an interpretation of statute compatible with Article 10 of the European Convention, unless no such interpretation is possible. The notion that the Alliance's claims sought an impermissible rewriting of the Broadcasting Act is plainly at odds with established approaches to the construction of provisions that, when read literally, threaten fundamental rights. Instead, the courts were invited merely to comply with their obligation under the Human Rights Act to interpret the legislation consistently with the Convention right to freedom of expression.[38]

The *ProLife Alliance* case illustrates the way in which conceptions of language, authority, and law fit together as interlocking elements of rival theories of public law. Commitments to unqualified parliamentary supremacy, making even the most basic precepts of law subject to fluctuating expressions of majority will, invoke rather crude distinctions between 'interpretation' and 'amendment'. Even the smallest departures from literal meaning will undermine judicial subservience to Parliament by acknowledging the scope for creative adaptation. Courts that attempt a reconciliation of public interests in the context of a particular case display a constitutional independence that denies such subservience: taken seriously, the idea of fundamental rights must qualify the nature and scope of legislative supremacy. When it is understood that judges are primarily servants of the constitution or legal order, rather than mere agents of the legislature—or a legislative majority—their treatment of legislation will be reasoned and reflective, attuned to all the circumstances in which public power is employed or individual rights curtailed. There is a tension throughout constitutional law between competing visions of the legal order. It divides the judges in cases where legislation, literally construed, poses a challenge to common law principle; and that division is only deepened by attempts to comply

---

[35] [2003] UKHL 23, para 95.

[36] Ibid, para 98.

[37] Section 3(1) provides: 'So far as it is possible to do so, primary legislation…must be read and given effect in a way which is compatible with the [European] Convention rights.'

[38] Compare Eric Barendt, 'Free Speech and Abortion' [2003] PL 580–91, at 589.

with the Human Rights Act, section 3, while affecting to bow to the orthodoxy of absolute sovereignty.[39]

The House of Lords' attachment to the more authoritarian vision of the legal order is manifested by the judges' reliance on an overly rigid conception of the separation of powers. That conception is made explicit in Lord Hoffmann's speech, in the course of remarks that deprecate use of the term 'deference' to describe the relationship between the judiciary and other branches of government:

The principles upon which decision-making powers are allocated are principles of law. The courts are the independent branch of government and the legislature and executive are...the elected branches of government. Independence makes the courts more suited to deciding some kinds of questions and being elected makes the legislature or executive more suited to deciding others. The allocation of these decision-making responsibilities is based upon recognized principles. The principle that the independence of the courts is necessary for a proper decision of disputed legal rights or claims of violation of human rights is a legal principle.... On the other hand, the principle that majority approval is necessary for a proper decision on policy or allocation of resources is also a legal principle. Likewise, when a court decides that a decision is within the proper competence of the legislature or executive, it is not showing deference. It is deciding the law.[40]

In questioning the aptness of the term 'deference' for the proper acceptance of decisions falling within the jurisdiction of another branch of government, Hoffmann rightly links the separation of powers to the requirements of legality: respect for the proper division of powers is entailed by adherence to the rule of law. Insofar, however, as Hoffmann suggests that different sorts of decision must be allocated *exclusively* to particular branches, regardless of the particular circumstances in which the issue of separation of powers arises, the dictum carries a threat to the rule of law. In practice, governmental decisions will typically engage both matters of principle, including the demands of individual rights, and matters of policy or allocation of resources, including the reasonable limits to particular rights that broader public interests legitimately require. Adherence to an inflexible doctrine of separation of powers would preclude the far-reaching judicial inquiry that the appropriate balance between private and public interests demands.[41] And that was precisely what happened here: for Hoffmann, the only question was whether election broadcasts had been made subject to the same 'taste and decency' requirements as other sorts of broadcast, which in general terms they had; and in his view that was 'an entirely proper decision for Parliament as representative of the people to make'.[42]

Lord Hoffmann considered the compatibility of the Broadcasting Act, section 6, with Article 10 of the Convention, protecting freedom of expression, on the erroneous basis that the Alliance was, in effect, challenging the statute. His conclusions

---

[39] See the discussion of *Ghaidan v Godin-Mendoza* [2004] UKHL 30 and other cases in Chapter 5, below.

[40] [2003] UKHL 23, para 76.

[41] See the discussion of *Secretary of State for the Home Dept v Rehman* [2001] UKHL 47 in Chapter 7, below.

[42] [2003] UKHL 23, para 77.

rested, however, on a somewhat narrow view of the requirements of the Article, maintaining that the 'primary right' to receive and impart information and ideas without interference by public authority was not engaged: there was no interference because the Alliance was not prevented from using other avenues to impart its message. In the present context, there was only a right to 'fair consideration for being afforded the opportunity' of expressing opinions—a right 'not to have one's access to public media denied on discriminatory, arbitrary or unreasonable grounds'.[43] The choice of the manner and style of expression is, however, an important part of the right to freedom of speech, as Simon Brown LJ recognized; and the Alliance was unable to express its message in the way it thought likely to be most effective. In rejecting any allegation of unfair discrimination, Hoffmann asserted that the broadcast had little to do with the general election, in which abortion was not a major issue: 'The election merely gave it an opportunity to publicize its views in a way which would have been no more or less effective at any other time.'[44] In the result, a very narrow conception of the free speech rights at stake combined with a rigid view of the separation of powers to emasculate those rights: 'The Alliance had no human right to be invited to the party and it is not unreasonable for Parliament to provide that those invited should behave themselves.'[45]

Whereas under the House of Lords' approach the right to free speech is only a residue left by specific legislation, which may impose stringent limitations, for the Court of Appeal a more expansive conception underpins the structure and fabric of liberal democracy. Laws LJ was prepared not only to take a more flexible view of the statutory restrictions, adapting them to the specific context, but to extend the court's scrutiny of the broadcasters' decisions as far as the protection of freedom of speech required. The distinction between appeal and review—between the merits of the decision impugned and its legality—was reduced to vanishing point in all the circumstances. By contrast, the higher court was much more restrained. Lord Walker of Gestingthorpe, holding that the court's task is 'not to substitute its own view for that of the broadcasters, but to review their decision with an intensity appropriate to all the circumstances of the case', denied that the broadcasters had erred.[46] The Court of Appeal had engaged in 'something close' to a merits review, giving exaggerated weight to 'the disturbing images which the Alliance wished to transmit for their shock effect'. The fact that the Alliance's video, transmitted into people's homes, would 'indeed have extraordinary power to stir emotions and to influence opinions' was itself (on Walker's view) the justification for excluding offensive material: 'It cannot be a free-standing reason for disregarding the prohibition as discriminatory against those who (for whatever well-intentioned reasons) wish to shock television viewers.'[47]

[43] Ibid, para 58.
[44] Ibid, para 68.
[45] Ibid, para 73. For a trenchant critique, see Barendt, 'Free Speech and Abortion', at 582–4. Barendt also calls attention to the gravity of a prior restraint, confirming the correctness of the Court of Appeal's identification of impermissible censorship: ibid, 587–8.
[46] [2003] UKHL 23, paras 139–41.
[47] Ibid, para 140.

The *ProLife Alliance* case forces us to confront a fundamental division of approach and opinion. The more authoritarian approach favoured by the House of Lords combines a subservience to the literal meaning of statutes, and the weaker defence of basic rights consonant with that subservience, with a greater deference to executive judgements, balancing the respective interests. In the approach of the Court of Appeal, by contrast, a strong presumption in favour of free speech colours not only the meaning and effect of the statute—making its application highly sensitive to context and circumstance—but limits the scope of executive power: the court's review jurisdiction is adapted to the nature and scale of the threat to freedom of expression. The competing approaches reflect rival interpretations of British constitutionalism, which in turn embody rival conceptions of law. While the rule of law is, in the former approach, a constitutional safeguard that surrenders to the plainly expressed will of the legislature, in the latter it embodies the limits on public power inherent in a free and democratic society. If we think that law and liberty are necessarily connected values, regulating the permissible boundaries of governmental power, we will prefer the judgments of the Court of Appeal.[48]

IV

Treating law as an interpretative discipline, entailing argument rooted in basic political values, enables us more clearly to understand the nature of judicial disagreement in important constitutional cases. I have suggested that differences of opinion in particular cases reflects deeper disagreement at the level of fundamental principle: there are divergent conceptions of the constitution, which only theoretical analysis can clarify. And the attempt at clarification obliges us to enter the fray: we must engage our own moral and political judgements in the process of interpretation, enabling us to show why one view is more persuasive than another. We are required to take sides in debates about the legal foundations of the constitution, not merely about their implications in certain instances. A look at the continuing controversy over Dicey's theoretical structure will provide a useful beginning.

Recognizing the potential for conflict between Dicey's twin pillars of parliamentary sovereignty and the rule of law, many lawyers are tempted to accord the latter a very narrow meaning. They interpret the rule of law to mean only the very weak requirement of legality, in the sense that everyone, including government officials, must obey the law. Actions or decisions that exceed any power conferred on the relevant public official, whether by statute or the royal prerogative, have no validity and may be quashed or declared unlawful by the courts. An unbounded parliamentary supremacy, equivalent to the powers of an absolute dictator, is quite consistent with that merely formal account of the rule of law. An action or decision

---

[48] According to Adam Tomkins, the House of Lords' decision in *ProLife* reveals problems intrinsic to the 'model of legal constitutionalism': Tomkins, *Our Republican Constitution* (Oxford: Hart Publishing, 2005), 27–8. Tomkins' critique is considered (in the context of his desire to restrict the scope of judicial review) in Chapter 2, below.

may be morally abhorrent and grossly unjust while nonetheless within legal and constitutional limits: Parliament could, if it wished, confer the necessary power on the officials concerned. But though Dicey's attempted definition of the rule of law is superficially consistent with that formal account, I shall argue that he is better understood as writing in defence of a larger, more complex ideal of law as a safeguard of freedom and justice. Properly interpreted, Dicey's rule of law is closely connected to the substance of the common law, which is a framework of legal principles and values amounting to an enduring constitution—a common law constitution that provides the source of parliamentary supremacy and the context in which Acts of Parliament are construed and applied.

Dicey's well-known emphasis on the equal subjection of public official and private citizen to the 'ordinary law', administered by the ordinary courts, reflects the constitutional priority of private law—a vision of the state as, first and foremost, upholder of rules intended to secure the equal freedom and independence of every citizen.[49] The rule of law can be understood, consistently with the republican tradition of political thought, as a safeguard of liberty in the sense of *independence*: no one is to be at the mercy of arbitrary power, whether wielded by a public official or another private citizen (or group of citizens). Liberty (or freedom) is secured by the reliable enforcement of rules that, prohibiting harmful conduct and enabling people to acquire and transfer property, permit everyone to pursue his own interests or projects in a manner compatible with the similar freedom of others. When special powers are exercised by public authorities they must, when challenged, be shown to serve the public interest; any authorized departures from the 'ordinary' private law must meet the special standards of public law, which seeks to limit governmental restrictions of individual autonomy. The rule of law, as opposed to the rule of the powerful, official or otherwise, is ultimately the preservation of conditions under which each person's freedom is reconciled with a like freedom for others—where equal citizenship is an ideal that informs and illuminates all public discussion, deliberation, and decision.[50]

When we adopt the internal approach appropriate to an interpretation of law—an interpretation of the British constitution respectful of the value of individual freedom—we can perceive the right way to reconcile Dicey's superficially conflicting principles. From the internal viewpoint of lawyer or legal reasoner, parliamentary sovereignty is a *general principle of law* rather than a matter of empirical fact. It expresses a commitment to honour the reasonable decisions of elected representatives, in accordance with the proper demands of democratic equality. In a society marked by a wide divergence of moral and political viewpoints, the category of the 'reasonable' may have to be very broad; but we need the qualification, nonetheless, because no one could accept an obligation to obey any decision at all, however seriously it contradicted his most basic ideas of justice or fairness. He must be able to sustain his loyalty to a reasonably just political order, so that Parliament speaks or decides for him as well as other citizens even when he disagrees with its particular

---

[49] Dicey, *Law of the Constitution*, 193–6.   [50] See further Chapter 3, below.

decisions; he is otherwise an outsider, lacking allegiance to a constitution that is not, in any real sense, his own. As a principle of law, parliamentary sovereignty is one important strand within a larger constitutional tapestry; and it takes its full meaning (and limits) from the moral commitments that inform that larger picture.

As a settled principle of law, parliamentary sovereignty dictates obedience to duly enacted statutes: the courts and other public authorities must, like private citizens, obey an Act of Parliament. It is understood that Parliament is responsible for furthering justice and promoting the common good, whether by enacting legislation to correct abuses, deterring harmful conduct, or by calling the executive Government to account for its stewardship of the public finances and general conduct of policy. Within all reasonable bounds—within the limits of reasonable disagreement— Acts of Parliament should elicit the cooperation of both public official and private citizen. In a liberal democracy that enshrines the idea of equal citizenship—that everyone is of equal intrinsic worth, regardless of racial or ethnic origin or colour or class or wealth or talent or religion—there are likely to be few wholly unreasonable statutes (or, more strictly, purported statutes) that violate that fundamental precept. So parliamentary sovereignty, conceived as a fact about judicial obedience to statutes, largely coincides with parliamentary sovereignty understood as a general principle of law, *obliging* courts to defer to statute in all ordinary cases. Only in *extraordinary* cases would divergence become clear: a provision that (for example) drew distinctions of race or religion, wholly irrelevant to any legitimate public purpose, would have to be resisted rather than obeyed (if sovereignty is understood as a principle of law).

The superficial conflict between Dicey's main principles now disappears. When parliamentary supremacy is understood to mirror an underlying principle of democratic equality, requiring obedience to rules that represent the outcome of a fair and equal democratic process, the sovereignty of Parliament is only a manifestation of the *sovereignty of law*. Our ordinary democratic procedures (including fair elections for members of Parliament and decision by majority vote in the Houses of Parliament) are the appropriate means for settling the content of law: they enable us to reach agreement on what to do, at least in the short term, when unanimity on what would be wisest or fairest or otherwise most desirable remains elusive. Even when people are agreed on relevant principles and goals—they usually agree, for example, that it is wrong to convict anyone of a criminal offence without a fair trial before an impartial and independent judge, and that government has a duty to mitigate poverty and guarantee the provision of basic educational and healthcare needs for all—they invariably differ at the level of detail. We can argue about the requirements of a fair trial or about the proper standards of public provision; an Act of Parliament, adopted after full inquiry and debate, can often provide a reasonable solution, worthy of general support.

There is more to the rule of law, however, than strict observance of duly enacted statutes: such statutes must be properly *recognizable* as Acts of Parliament, made in the proper form and consistent in content with some reasonable account of the public good, compatible with the basic ideal of equal citizenship. An Act must not only be enacted according to accepted procedures (usually requiring the assent of

Commons, Lords, and Crown) but be composed of *general rules*. A bill of attainder, commanding the punishment of a named individual, would violate the rule of law and so (whatever the historical precedents) lie beyond the boundaries of any notion of legislative supremacy acceptable today. Without a separation of powers between Parliament and judiciary, ensuring that criminal charges are tried by independent courts, applying general rules to particular cases according to the evidence properly established, there is no rule of law—only the arbitrary power of the legislator.[51] But a statute that purports to make arbitrary distinctions between persons or groups—distinctions that have no defensible connection with any legitimate public purpose—fall into the same class as bills of attainder. Expressing only irrational hostility or prejudice, such purported laws contradict the assumptions of equal citizenship on which parliamentary sovereignty is based: flouting the democratic ideal that gives the doctrine of sovereignty its justification, they acquire no validity in virtue of that doctrine.

That reconciliation of legislative supremacy with the rule of law, capable of resolving questions raised by iniquitous laws, underlies a more general account of British constitutionalism. The same considerations that deny the validity of purported statutes, in quite extraordinary cases, apply to help determine the meaning of statutes in ordinary cases. We interpret an Act of Parliament on the assumption that it represents the outcome of deliberations conducted in good faith about the requirements of justice and the public good. Provisions that, on one reading, might do great damage to individual rights or legitimate interests without any countervailing public benefit, must be accorded a different construction. If necessary, the literal or prima facie meaning—the message the enacted words would most naturally convey—gives way to a more nuanced reading, compatible with the statute's apparent general purposes but less injurious to conflicting rights or interests. If there are no *explicit* exceptions for cases where adherence to the literal reading would result in manifest injustice, such exceptions may be treated as implied—the court seeking always an accommodation between general rule, on the one hand, and the special considerations arising in the particular case, on the other.

It is no objection that the breadth of the general rule is thereby curtailed: Parliament can only legislate for the standard case, and must rely on the court, when necessary, to determine the marginal or exceptional case. Parliament legislates against a complex background of existing law; and such existing law includes general common law principles whose integrity must be preserved as far as possible. Such principles affirm the rights and expectations that constitutional governance secures: their integrity, even in the face of pressure to achieve more immediate political aims, is the main point and purpose of the rule of law. The correct solution of the doubtful or marginal case, therefore, depends on an appraisal of the law in its entirety—not merely the statutory words, but the surrounding corpus of legal rules and

---

[51] A bill of attainder, though treated as valid law in earlier centuries, violates the principle that a statute must not be 'a special rule for a particular person or a particular case': *Hurtado v California* 110 US 516 (1884), 535–6. The United States Constitution (art 1, s 9, cl 3) provides that 'No Bill of Attainder or *ex post facto* Law shall be passed'.

principles. We ascertain the meaning of Parliament's enactments by examining the implications of alternative readings, preferring those that better conform to legal and constitutional tradition—so long, at least, as we do not frustrate any legitimate legislative purpose or intent, insofar as we can ascertain it.

On the House of Lords' approach in *ProLife Alliance*, a conflict between the rule of law and parliamentary sovereignty is simply resolved in favour of the latter.[52] A basic liberty of political speech, central to any plausible account of liberal democracy, is sharply curtailed by reference to Parliament's plain words: every broadcast, whatever the context, must conform to similar standards of 'good taste'. The Court of Appeal, by contrast, sought to reconcile Dicey's basic principles in just the manner that the Human Rights Act suggests: it interpreted the statutory commands in the light of constitutional principle, imposing a flexible standard capable of adaptation to context. And even if the Broadcasting Act had stipulated, even more firmly, that broadcasts of all kinds should be vetted for good taste and decency—'their subject-matter notwithstanding'—it would still have been open to the court to conclude that material which would be offensive in some contexts was not so (or not unreasonably so) in the case of a party election broadcast on a matter of great public interest and importance. The popular notion that parliamentary sovereignty ultimately overrides the rule of law is erroneous. Parliament's authority is constrained by its dependence on language; and words take their colour from the broader context in which they are used. We determine the content of Parliament's instructions in the light of those fundamental principles of law that give the British constitution its continuing authority and conceptual structure.

When, in *Anisiminic*, the House of Lords intervened to correct an erroneous construction of regulations by the Foreign Compensation Commission, notwithstanding a statutory bar on any 'determination' of the Commission being 'called into question in any court of law', it interpreted rather than defied the instructions of Parliament.[53] In holding that a seriously flawed decision was no true 'determination' at all, and so beyond the protection of the ouster clause, the court acted to preserve the rule of law in a manner that any parliamentarian ought to accept. If there were no recourse to law against a tribunal's decisions, no matter how far they exceeded any jurisdiction conferred by statute, the rule of law (including Parliament's law) would have surrendered to arbitrary power. Such limits on Parliament's ability to delegate unfettered powers to executive agencies or administrative tribunals flow from its own supremacy: its instructions must be obeyed by those who exercise the relevant powers. In affirming the *sovereignty of law*—the subjection of powerful bodies to legal principles, enforced by independent courts—the House of Lords bolstered the sovereignty of Parliament. These basic principles are mutually supporting rather than conflicting.[54]

---

[52] *R (ProLife Alliance) v British Broadcasting Corporation* [2002] EWCA Civ 297, [2003] UKHL 23 (considered above).

[53] *Anisminic Ltd v Foreign Compensation Commission* [1969] 2 AC 147; Foreign Compensation Act 1950, s 4(4).

[54] See also Laws LJ's judgment in *R (Cart & Ors) v The Upper Tribunal* [2009] EWHC 3052 (Admin), considered in Chapter 6, below.

In spite of the initial contradiction suggested by Dicey's notions of the rule of law and absolute parliamentary sovereignty, the route to reconciliation is indicated by Dicey himself. In contending that the sovereignty of Parliament 'favours the supremacy of the law of the land', Dicey was drawing attention to the manner in which authority attached only to formal *enactments*, which it was the courts' responsibility to interpret in the spirit of the rule of law.[55] Even 'extraordinary' powers, conferred on ministers or public agencies, were never truly unfettered or unlimited: they were 'confined by the words of the Act itself', as interpreted by the judges.[56] When we abandon Dicey's reliance on mere matters of fact—rejecting the external view of the sociologist or political analyst—and insist on an internal, normative engagement with legal principle, we can give the common law constitution a more coherent shape. We can show, not only that there is no intrinsic conflict between the rule of law and democracy—each resting on the same basic ideas of freedom and equality—but that there is no such conflict between the rule of law and parliamentary sovereignty.

Sovereignty or supremacy is a political idea and legal construct: it asserts a duty of obedience or allegiance whose validity is always a matter of moral judgement, albeit one made within the context of an established constitutional tradition. Once we abandon the notion that the content of English law is a matter of empirical fact, acknowledging its dependence on our *interpretation* of any relevant facts, we must concede the role of each person's moral judgement in resolving disputed questions of law. And if anyone's grasp of the law is better than another's, it can only be in virtue of the superior argument by which her conclusions are explained and justified. Just as we need a parliament to settle our differences over numerous aspects of our social and political life, so we must rely on courts to enforce the law as they understand it, even when we doubt the correctness of their interpretation. But the true content of law, dependent as it is on the considerations of justice that guide and inform any serious interpretation, remains a matter of argument—legal and moral—which is, in principle, open to everyone. Final responsibility for acting in accordance with the law, understood by reference to fundamental principles of liberty and justice, remains with each individual, whether judge, public official, or private citizen.[57]

V

According to Jeffrey Goldsworthy, the common law world has until recently known only two alternative constitutional models. The British model of parliamentary sovereignty can be contrasted with the American model of judicial review, which reposes responsibility for the protection of individual rights in courts of law.[58]

---

[55] Dicey, *Law of the Constitution*, 406.
[56] Ibid, 413–14.
[57] See further Chapter 4, below.
[58] Jeffrey Goldsworthy, *Parliamentary Sovereignty: Contemporary Debates* (Cambridge: Cambridge University Press, 2010), 79–81.

However, Canada, New Zealand, and Britain have recently adopted 'hybrid' models, which give enlarged responsibilities to courts for protecting rights but 'without altogether abandoning the principle of parliamentary sovereignty'. Such hybrid models (containing bills or charters of rights) offer the possibility of an attractive compromise between the traditional models, 'conferring on courts constitutional responsibility to review the consistency of legislation with protected rights, while preserving the authority of legislatures to have the last word'.[59] To defend a judicial power to override legislation that violates fundamental rights of equality or due process—implicit in my account of the rule of law as an ideal of just and democratic government—is, according to Goldsworthy, to support the American model against the alternatives. And while a power of judicial review may enable judges to resist grave injustice, it may also frustrate legitimate political decision-making:

The price that must be paid for giving judges authority to invalidate a few laws that are clearly unjust or undemocratic is that they must also be given authority to overrule the democratic process in a much larger number of cases where the requirements of justice or democracy are debatable. The danger of excessive judicial interference with democratic decision-making might be worse than that of parliamentary tyranny, given the relative probabilities of their actually occurring.[60]

Now if the content of law were merely a matter of whatever instructions a statute provides, according to some uncontroversial plain meaning, or according to the intentions of the legislators (capable of being straightforwardly ascertained), Goldsworthy's case would be more persuasive. We would have to decide which institution should, quite literally, have the 'last word'; and we would face a choice between competing constitutional models of the kind suggested. But since the content of law is, instead, a complex matter of *interpretation*, in which statutory provisions must be integrated within an existing web of legal regulation, based on both common law and statute, we do not in practice face the clear-cut choices that Goldsworthy indicates.

What may appear from the external perspective of the political scientist to be a radical difference of constitutional models may, from the internal viewpoint of the judge or public lawyer, be a more subtle variation. We are presented, instead, with contrasting, yet closely related, contexts in which to address very similar questions about legality or the rule of law. Reflection on the demands of legality, in all the circumstances of any particular case, may take a competent lawyer into territory only dimly illuminated by neat distinctions between governmental models. The appropriate accommodation between deep-rooted legal principle and current public policy will depend largely on the strength of the alleged justification for an encroachment on rights—rights which seek to preserve a strong measure of individual autonomy, whether elaborated at common law or enshrined within a formal bill or charter.[61]

---

[59] Ibid, 80.

[60] Ibid, 93–4, quoting his own previous work: see Jeffrey Goldsworthy, *The Sovereignty of Parliament: History and Philosophy* (Oxford: Clarendon Press, 1999), 269.

[61] Stephen Gardbaum adopts the external stance of the political scientist in order to clarify the difference between the various constitutional models, but he does so at the risk of oversimplification or

Although the Human Rights Act 1998 undoubtedly broadens the range of judicial rights protection, encompassing all the principal rights of the European Convention, there is a very substantial overlap with rights recognized at common law; and that same overlap enriches the common law, influencing its articulation and development.[62] And though the Act withholds any power to strike down primary legislation for breach of Convention rights, its requirement that legislation should, when possible, be read consistently with those rights confirms the constitutional role of the judiciary in preserving legality. Arguably, moreover, the interpretative function in respect of Convention rights is an analogue of a similar judicial role in relation to common law rights. In the result, while formally 'acknowledging the sovereignty of Parliament', in substance United Kingdom courts 'apply principles of constitutionality little different from those which exist in countries where the power of the legislature is expressly limited by a constitutional document'.[63]

There are, for Goldsworthy, no fundamental questions about the rule of law directly pertinent to adjudication. He thinks that law is ultimately a matter of fact (whatever Parliament has chosen to enact); and legal obligations, even when government aspires to do justice, are only 'the government's posited declarations of what its citizens morally ought to do', binding on them however implausible such declarations may be.[64] As a legal positivist, then, Goldsworthy acknowledges no intrinsic connection between the content of law, in any particular case, and the ideal of the rule of law (or legality). As a 'morally laden principle or ideal' the rule of law is allegedly quite distinct from the morally neutral concept of law in professional legal usage. Legal positivists 'insist that "the rule of law" is a distinctive concept, which includes criteria that are inapplicable to the concept of "law" *per se*'.[65] These theorists resist the notion that the basic values of human dignity and individual autonomy are necessary features of law—guiding ideals that inform the deliberations of legislators and lawyers in their efforts to construct and interpret a body of law fit for the democratic self-government of independent citizens. If, then, judges can strike down (or limit the effect of) unjust legislation, it is only because (on the positivist account) such a power has been formally conferred on them, and might, if the political context alters, at any time be withdrawn.

The legal positivist, however, occupies an external position, detached from the social and political practice he purports to describe. The moral neutrality of his

---

even caricature: his account of the Westminster parliamentary sovereignty model downgrades the significance of (what he terms) 'residual common law liberties'. His appraisal (for example) of the operation of the Human Rights Act 1998, being expressed in terms of a shifting balance of power between legislature and judiciary, is quite detached (as he appears to acknowledge) from lawyers' primary concerns with the content (in context) of the pertinent constitutional rights: see Gardbaum, 'The New Commonwealth Model of Constitutionalism' 49 Am J Comp L 707 (2001), and Gardbaum, 'Reassessing the New Commonwealth Model of Constitutionalism' (2010) 8 I·CON 167.

[62] The influence extends to private as well as public law, albeit in cautious, incremental fashion: see Gavin Phillipson and Alexander Williams, 'Horizontal Effect and the Constitutional Constraint' (2011) 74(6) MLR 878–910.

[63] *R v Secretary of State for the Home Dept, ex p Simms* [2000] 2 AC 115, 131 (Lord Hoffmann).

[64] Goldsworthy, *Parliamentary Sovereignty*, 89.

[65] Ibid, 88.

concept of law is designed to ensure the objectivity of his descriptive reports, which encompass not only the practice of liberal and social democracies, but any system of governance in which state officials exercise an ultimate monopoly of force. From that detached perspective there is perhaps something to be said for moral neutrality, though it will severely limit the power of any such theory to illuminate the operation of any particular system.[66] A positivist theory can only describe and predict the activities of state officials; and any legal conclusions or *judgements*, applicable to decision-making within that system, must be founded on the identification of some official *consensus* which, in many cases, will be hard to discern. The lawyer or constitutional theorist, by contrast, must cast aside such detachment, probing the correctness of any official consensus, which may be a poor reflection of legal principle, properly explained and understood; and she must come to her own judgement in cases where no consensus can be found, the question of law being a matter of interpretative dispute. So a constitutional theorist who wishes to participate in debate over the true nature of English (or Commonwealth) law cannot, like Goldsworthy, take shelter in the moral neutrality of a bland sociological notion of law.

When we recognize the interdependence of our fundamental concepts of law, liberty, and justice—each understood and developed in the light of the others—we can also appreciate the interconnection of legal and moral obligation. The law imposes a *moral* obligation of obedience: it is critical to the maintenance of the rule of law, and hence of individual liberty, that people honour their legal obligations, even when they doubt the wisdom or the justice of the laws (as inevitably they often will). It is the principal function of Parliament to give greater precision to the moral duties of cooperation that citizens owe each other; and legislation enacted in good faith for the furtherance of the public good should be treated respectfully, at least when any limitations of individual right are capable of reasonable justification. And it is normally right to accept judicial decisions as finally determining the legality and correct meaning of statutory provisions, when these matters are subject to dispute. There are important considerations of fairness and legal certainty in favour of deference to judicial decision, even when people entertain doubts about judicial wisdom or competence. The law imposes a general obligation of obedience that reflects the citizen's duty to cooperate in maintaining a viable and flourishing legal order, capable of securing liberty for all on a fair and equal basis.

That association of legal and moral obligation depends, however, on the *plausibility* of the claims of legislation (or other governmental action) to further the public good, within the general constraints of justice. While no one can properly expect the law to match in all respects his own opinions about the demands of justice or public policy, he must be able to *understand* it, at least, as a genuine contribution to the satisfaction of those demands, made in good faith. If legal obligation is a species of moral obligation, which the good citizen will recognize and honour, its limits are ultimately a matter of his own responsibility and judgement.

---

[66] It will also frustrate any attempt to grasp the critical role of the general idea of *legality* as a concept intimately linked with, if distinct from, concepts of justice and liberty. See especially Nigel Simmonds, *Law as a Moral Idea* (Oxford: Oxford University Press, 2007).

We all bear final responsibility for our own moral judgements, and the conduct they engender; and we cannot escape the obligation to decide, in any case where the state threatens very grave injustice, whether we should maintain our cooperation or, on the contrary, engage in civil disobedience. If our concept of law is linked to fundamental principles of liberty and justice, the law cannot have simply *any* content—even rules quite inimical to the defence of those principles. If either citizens or judges 'should disobey egregiously immoral legislation', as Goldsworthy accepts, such disobedience is not 'an exercise of moral authority' that (in the latter case) 'overrides the judges' legal duty'.[67] It is simply the result of taking seriously their moral obligation of support for good governance—within a broad but genuine conception of that ideal.[68]

For Goldsworthy, the distinction between legal and moral authority (and legal and moral obligation) is a 'conceptual device that helps prevent the extra-ordinary response of disobedience being resorted to excessively, thereby eroding the normal judicial stance of obedience, and undermining democracy'.[69] If judicial resistance to unjust legislation should be an extraordinary reaction, reserved only for cases of extreme injustice, it is better (he supposes) to regard judges' legal authority as a simple matter of obedience to Parliament. In the same way, since there are powerful reasons why individual citizens should obey legislation they regard as morally wrong, it is safer to treat disobedience as a matter of moral resistance to legally *valid* law: there is then less danger that they will disregard legislation with which they strongly disagree. But that luxury of conceptual refinement is only available if the law's content can be determined quite independently of one's moral judgement about the matters in view. If what the law requires is merely a question of fact—whatever Parliament has decreed—the legal obligation can be identified, if we wish, with the content of that decree. But if, on the contrary, the law must be painstakingly *constructed*—by reference to fundamental principles of the common law as well as the specific wording of statutory provisions—that neat distinction between legal and moral duty is unavailable. Whatever the statute provides, if it is not rejected altogether as irredeemably wicked, is itself in part *a product of our moral judgement*. We exercise our moral faculties in its *interpretation*, seeking to make sense of it as the kind of law a responsible parliament, attempting to further the public good, could reasonably enact.

It is a mistake to think that the law is merely a matter of fact, consisting in statutory instructions that no competent reader of English could fail to understand. Even when we can identify a general rule, by reference to an enactment's words read in the light of some plausible legislative purpose, we have yet to decide its application to what may appear doubtful or marginal particular cases. In resolving such questions of application we also settle the rule's boundaries, thereby making our initial construction more determinate. There is an interaction between general rule and particular case, reflection on the latter helping us to see the proper nature

---

[67] Goldsworthy, *Parliamentary Sovereignty*, 93.
[68] The argument is more fully developed in Chapter 4, below.
[69] Goldsworthy, *Parliamentary Sovereignty*, 93.

and reach of the former. If we treat law as an instrument of justice, rather than a tool in the hands of officials for whatever purposes they choose, our reflections amount to moral deliberations. Just as a common law rule is the product of applying general principles to different categories of case, distinguished on moral as well as purely historical grounds, a statutory rule is partly *constituted* by our efforts to apply it to a range of different circumstances, unfolding after its enactment.

The distinction between an interpretation of statute that avoids the infliction of serious harm on individuals, out of all proportion to any advancement of the public good, on the one hand, and the non-application (or invalidation) of a wicked statute, on the other, is only a distinction of degree. Since, moreover, it is a distinction identifiable only in relation to particular sets of facts, whether real or imagined, it cannot be the subject of any realistic practical theory of law or adjudication. A statutory provision amending criminal procedure, which is treated as being subject to an implicit exception in order to safeguard the fairness of a criminal trial, is not necessarily rendered futile.[70] It may well be applied in many cases without endangering the defendant's (common law) right to present his defence and challenge the prosecution case. If, however, there were very few instances, in practice, where its application would be consistent with fairness we should be forced to conclude that the statute was largely redundant—formally valid but substantively void. There would be no breach of legislative supremacy, correctly understood: we are entitled, and obliged, to resist (or narrowly restrict) a measure that Parliament could not legitimately impose. The right to a fair trial is an aspect of the basic idea of due process inherent in the rule of law.

According to Goldsworthy, we must choose between two quite different accounts of the role of the British courts in reading statutes, as far as possible, consistently with rights and liberties recognized by the common law. An interpretation of an Act that limits adverse consequences for individuals, when these are incidental to the general legislative purpose, can be fully squared with parliamentary sovereignty: we read the statute on the reasonable assumption that Parliament intended to show respect for basic rights, recognizing the limits they place on the legitimate exercise of governmental power. By contrast, the idea that Parliament is ultimately constrained by transcendent constitutional values, rooted in the requirements of the rule of law, is inconsistent with its sovereignty; it is even alleged that this idea 'renders the first justification otiose and disingenuous'.[71] Either courts obey their political masters, seeking to ascertain their will, or they oppose them to prevent injustice.

These are only different types of justification, however, if legislative intention is a matter of plain historical fact, so that any common law presumption must surrender to any plausible evidence of a contrary intention. But there is no single human mind that any such contrary intention can be attributed to: there is only

---

[70] Compare *R v A (No 2)* [2001] UKHL 25, considered in Chapter 5, below.

[71] Goldsworthy, *Parliamentary Sovereignty*, 99. If I am 'reluctant to choose' between these accounts of common law practice, as Goldsworthy observes, it is because I deny that they are, in the end, really different.

the institution of *Parliament*, whose expressions of will are confined to whatever the words of its enactments express, when correctly interpreted. The very same assumptions that justify the restrictive interpretation of an Act that, taken literally, would jeopardize basic rights, operate to exclude unconstitutional meanings—constructions that would violate fundamental rights in defiance of the rule of law. The extent to which a presumption in favour of constitutional rights must be displaced or qualified, if at all, is a conclusion of the interpretative process itself. Such rights may be limited only when *necessary* for the success of the statutory scheme, construed as a reasonable plan for advancement of the public good within the constraints of basic justice. And that is an interpretative *judgement*, reflecting the balance of competing considerations, not a capitulation to the legislative will viewed as the conscious intention of any individual lawgiver. We honour Parliament's instructions, consistently with democratic principle, when we strive to read and apply them appropriately—advancing their proper purposes in a manner that demonstrates the kind of concern for the welfare of individuals that any responsible legislator, respectful of people's rights, would certainly endorse.[72]

Admittedly, the Human Rights Act appears to envisage that Parliament should have the 'last word' about the enforcement of European Convention rights. While section 4 empowers the courts to declare an Act incompatible with the Convention, it does not authorize its invalidation. There may, however, be scope for judicial deference to parliamentary views about matters of social policy, affecting Convention rights, which would not necessarily exist (or exist to the same degree) in the context of constitutional rights at common law. Notwithstanding the substantial overlap between common law and Convention rights, the latter are arguably broader and more demanding—capable as interpreted by the European Court of Human Rights of very significantly curbing legislative discretion. A declaration of incompatibility may sometimes be the appropriate remedy when a court holds legislation to be in breach of the Convention, even though on a proper construction it meets basic common law standards of constitutional right. That remedy will be especially apt when a statutory scheme of regulation falls well short of what is needed to provide the administrative machinery necessary, in practice, to safeguard certain Convention rights.[73]

Such cases are likely, however, to be exceptional. In most cases an Act will be susceptible to benign construction, reconciling statutory purposes and Convention rights according to context. When such rights coincide with fundamental common law rights, such as the right to a fair trial, or to freedom of speech, the court's interpretation can be as robust as is necessary to safeguard the constitution against grave injury. Any potential breach of the fairness of a criminal trial, for example, must be met by stern resistance; but it is resistance only to an unconstitutional

---

[72] The argument is elaborated in Chapter 5, below.
[73] See for example *In re S (Minors) (Care Order: Implementation of Care Plan)* [2002] UKHL 10; for discussion see Aileen Kavanagh, *Constitutional Review under the UK Human Rights Act* (Cambridge: Cambridge University Press, 2009), 37–9.

construction, not to anyone's intentions about how defendants should be treated in particular cases, regardless of the risk of wrongful conviction. There is only judicial *disobedience*—marking the limits of legislative supremacy—if, when fairly construed, excluding possibilities of grave injustice, the statute has no practical application at all, making no appreciable difference to existing law. Such an outcome is likely to be a rare occurrence in a constitutional democracy built on respect for human dignity and freedom.

The Crime (Sentences) Act 1997, section 2, imposed an automatic life sentence on anyone convicted of a second 'serious offence', subject only to the existence of 'exceptional circumstances', which would preserve judicial discretion. In *Offen*, the Court of Appeal held that the youth of the offender at the time of the first offence, the lapse of time between offences, and the different nature of the offences involved could all be considered factors amounting to exceptional circumstances.[74] It did not matter that such factors were not uncommon in themselves: they helped to distinguish a case from the kind envisaged by the statutory purpose, which was plainly to protect the public from dangerous offenders. Earlier cases, which had adopted a more literal definition of exceptional circumstances, had lost sight of the statutory purpose and context. On the reasonable assumption that the section did not apply to someone who presented no future threat to public safety, the judges held it inapplicable to the case at hand: the case was not 'in the statutory context' a normal one, as envisaged by Parliament, and 'in consequence, for the purposes of the section, the position was exceptional'.[75] An offender who did not constitute a significant risk to the public need not be sentenced to life imprisonment.

Admittedly, the court relied expressly on the Human Rights Act, section 3, to reach that conclusion; but it is hard to see that the common law did not dictate precisely the same answer. If the court's construction were a legitimate one, reconciling the statutory purpose with fundamental rights of liberty and equality—an accused who poses no danger to the public should not be incarcerated indefinitely along with those who do—it was also the most appropriate reading. The Human Rights Act merely affirmed what constitutional theory already endorsed, as a matter of ordinary common law reasoning. Conor Gearty observes that 'however it is dressed up or explained away, the *Offen* case has effectively disembowelled a particularly savage legislative intervention, passed at the height of a panic about crime and...designed to inflict exactly the kind of punishment that was originally imposed on Offen'.[76] But the legislation was only a 'savage' intervention if we privilege the literal meaning, forcing an unnecessary wedge between the words enacted and their underlying purpose. When interpreted correctly, in its constitutional context, there is no conflict between the legislative will and common law reason: only the 'savage' reading is 'disembowelled', the statute being honoured in the manner that the rule of law requires.[77]

---

[74] *R v Offen* [2001] 1 WLR 253, approved in *R v Drew* [2003] UKHL 25, para 20.

[75] [2001] 1 WLR 253, 272.

[76] Conor Gearty, *Principles of Human Rights Adjudication* (Oxford: Oxford University Press, 2004), 77.

[77] See further Allan, 'Parliament's Will and the Justice of the Common Law: The Human Rights Act in Constitutional Perspective (2006) 59 CLP 27–50.

VI

Central to my account of the nature of public law is the distinction between the internal point of view of the lawyer or judge (or of anyone engaged in legal reasoning) and the external viewpoint occupied by a mere observer, detached from the relevant debates over meaning and interpretation. The detached observer can give a description of the legal phenomena that is at least relatively free from moral or political judgement: he might report, for example, that lawyers disagree about certain questions of law and predict (on the basis of a survey of previous decisions) how a court is likely resolve them. Like the radical critic I mentioned earlier, he will refrain from drawing any conclusions of his own about contested matters of law, denying any obligation to take sides between contending positions (and the moral judgements they entail). By contrast, the lawyer who offers an argument or conclusion about the content of the law—what it requires in particular cases—cannot enjoy a similar detachment. Her legal opinions are necessarily entwined with the moral judgements that accompany her efforts to distinguish better from worse interpretations of law, reflecting her own sense of which of the possible readings of the relevant legal materials would best help to sustain the legal tradition she accepts and supports.

  H. L. A. Hart drew a similar distinction between contrasting perspectives in his analysis of law and legal systems.[78] He identified legal rules as a category of social rules, imposing certain standards of behaviour. Hart distinguished the 'internal aspect' of rules, reflecting their *use* as criteria for action and judgement, from their external aspect, which consists merely in the 'regular uniform behaviour' they elicit or explain. A rule is distinguished from a mere social habit by making *normative* demands, which are generally accepted:

> What is necessary is that there should be a critical reflective attitude to certain patterns of behaviour as a common standard, and that this should display itself in criticism (including self-criticism), demands for conformity, and in acknowledgments that such criticism and demands are justified...[79]

Hart made the analysis of rules central to his account of law; but he denied that the 'ought' that accompanies the internal aspect of rules was necessarily a moral 'ought': the demand for compliance or conformity might, he considered, reflect a purely self-serving or similarly ignoble attitude.

  If, however, our concept of law is closely linked to our ideas about justice and freedom—we regard the 'rule of law' as itself a fundamental political ideal or value—Hart's legal positivism is hard to sustain. While a system of rules designed only to serve the selfish and perhaps nefarious purposes of a ruling clique might, for some purposes, be designated a legal system, it would arguably be a defective or

---

[78] H L A Hart, *The Concept of Law* (first published in 1961), 2nd edn (Oxford: Clarendon Press, 1994).
[79] Ibid, 57.

deviant instance—as judged by standards internal to the idea of law itself. Particular laws are invariably *presented* as serving the general public good, rather than some private end of the legislator, because any overt contrary admission would appear absurd and contradictory: an 'Administration of *Injustice*' Act would mock the very requirements it purported to impose.[80] Hart's distinction between internal and external aspects may therefore be harder to square with a strict separability of law from morality than he supposed. The idea of law we invoke in our effort to understand the British constitution—the idea of law implicit in the ideal of the rule of law—draws on basic moral and political values.

John Finnis (following Aristotle) proposes that we should attempt to delineate the 'central case' of the idea or phenomenon of law, enabling us to identify other more marginal instances as cases that fall short of the ideal to which the phenomenon corresponds.[81] Having distinguished the internal from the external point of view, Hart has no good reason for refusing to differentiate 'the central from the peripheral cases *of the internal or legal point of view itself'*. The central case of the 'legal viewpoint' must be the perspective in which 'legal obligation is treated as at least presumptively a moral obligation', and in which the establishment and maintenance of the legal order is 'regarded as a moral ideal if not a compelling demand of justice'.[82] When a legal order fails to meet the basic demands of justice and people fail to acknowledge any moral obligation of compliance with law, we are confronted on this view with a defective instance of law—one which falls well short of the ideal to which it inherently aspires. Law, we may fairly suppose, is intended to serve human well-being, securing justice and the common good.

Now, there is of course no inconsistency in recognizing the moral aspirations internal to the concept of law, on the one hand, and condemning the injustices and inefficiencies of any particular legal regime, on the other. If we thought that the British constitution denied important human rights we would condemn it as a defective and deviant version of the legal entity it (dimly) echoed. From *within* the practice of British constitutionalism, however, we cannot sustain that divergence between the ideal and the actual. Just as the legal theorist should give priority to the central case of the internal point of view, the legal interpreter must adopt the perspective it indicates: he offers an account of the law, applicable to particular cases, that takes the commitments to justice and the common good for granted. His interpretation of (constitutional) law embodies his efforts to understand its various prescriptions as parts of a larger whole—aspects of a coherent scheme of regulation for the attainment of justice.[83] The scheme's faults and failings cannot be ignored; but they can at least be minimized by giving priority, in making good

---

[80] See Neil MacCormick, 'Natural Law and the Separation of Law and Morals', in Robert P George (ed), *Natural Law Theory: Contemporary Essays* (Oxford: Clarendon Press, 1992), 110–18; see also Robert Alexy, *The Argument from Injustice: A Reply to Legal Positivism*, translated by Stanley L Paulson and Bonnie L Paulson (Oxford: Oxford University Press, 2002).

[81] John Finnis, *Natural Law and Natural Rights* (Oxford: Clarendon Press, 1980), ch 1.

[82] Ibid, 13–15.

[83] Compare Jeremy Waldron, 'The Concept and the Rule of Law' (2008) 43 Ga L Rev 1–61, at 32–6.

sense of it, to those general principles of liberty and justice that underpin its more attractive features. If an interpretation that builds on such general principles is possible—recognizable to other people as a viable and appealing account—then it is unlikely that any residual defects will be too severe. If fundamental human rights were really denied, for example, no such interpretation would be available; if it is indeed available, such rights are not—on a proper view of the matter—denied.[84]

It is natural to encounter the objection that a focus on the ideal may blind us to imperfections in the actual: if we view the constitution through rose-tinted spectacles (as the objection is often put) we will overlook its many deficiencies as a framework for justice and liberty. Could we not adopt a mid-way position between the radical critic, on one hand, and the Supreme Court justice on the other? Perhaps our legal tradition is in some respects admirable and in others shameful or dishonourable? Nick Barber objects that while Finnis's approach is helpful when we value the phenomenon studied, it falls down when we are confronted with a harmful practice we deplore.[85] So we should not, in his view, seek an idealized version of the practice in question: 'Our ethically informed test of importance can pick out bad features of a practice as well as the good; it can show a practice to be potentially harmful as well as potentially valuable.'[86] What from the outside may be viewed as potentially harmful, however, is from the inside a basis for good. The participant in a practice—such as the legal interpreter—can (and plainly should) choose the potential for good, suppressing as far as possible any potential for harm. If a statute is capable of being construed consistently with basic human rights, perhaps by giving it a narrower application than its literal terms would initially suggest, it is the lawyer's duty to adopt that construction. If the law should be an instrument of justice rather than injustice, it is irrelevant that an alternative construction, endangering basic rights, would be available instead.

Lon Fuller, a staunch opponent of Hart's legal positivism, suggested that the Nazis had taken advantage of the legal philosophy dominant in Germany in the 1930s, exploiting its insistence that a morally iniquitous law was nonetheless a law, demanding obedience.[87] Barber thinks Fuller's case against positivism was mainly strategic, complaining that he was wrong to suppose that the success of an interpretation should be judged by the beneficial consequences of adopting it: 'The point of an interpretation of a contemporary social practice is to explain and illuminate the important features of the practice as it currently exists.'[88] We should not allow our pursuit of the ideal to obscure the actuality of what we behold. It

---

[84] Compare Ronald Dworkin's interpretative theory of law as 'integrity', which seeks consistency of principle across the whole corpus of state law, insisting that 'the law—the rights and duties that flow from past collective decisions and for that reason licence or require coercion—contains not only the narrow explicit content of these decisions but also, more broadly, the scheme of principles necessary to justify them': Ronald Dworkin, *Law's Empire* (London: Fontana, 1986), 227. For discussion and critique, see Chapter 4, below.

[85] N W Barber, *The Constitutional State* (Oxford: Oxford University Press, 2010), 13.

[86] Ibid, 14.

[87] Lon L Fuller, 'Positivism and Fidelity to Law—A Reply to Professor Hart' (1958) 71 Harv L Rev 630–72, at 657–61.

[88] Barber, *The Constitutional State*, 15.

was the whole point of Fuller's philosophy of law, however, to show that the search for a morally neutral account of law was confused. From his perspective, *internal* to the practice of law, Nazi law was necessarily a gross distortion of law, properly conceived. Our concept of law is built on assumptions about the importance of respecting human dignity. To govern through law is, at a minimum, to respect human agency, allowing everyone to take responsibility for their own efforts to conform to published and practicable standards.[89] In breaching the ordinary precepts of the rule of law—by resorting to violence against opponents, retrospective laws to validate it, and intimidation of judges—the Nazis preserved only a parody of law. Rule by terror is not rule by law.[90]

What is true of the concept of law, in general, is also true of interpretations of the content of particular laws. Since it is only from the internal perspective of the judge or lawyer, applying reasoned *judgement*, that there is any answer to a question of law, we cannot sever that answer from the moral outlook on which it is ultimately based. An Act of Parliament means what the best interpretation indicates; and the best interpretation is one that will commend itself as a useful contribution to justice and the public good. That judgement will normally leave considerable discretion to the legislature, which may choose among the many possible forms of remedy for some perceived social evil or injustice. It is only in the light of our grasp of the problem being addressed, however, that we could understand the chosen solution; if our conceptions of justice and the public good diverged too far from those of Government or Parliament (or a parliamentary majority) we could make little sense of the rules enacted. Law, as Fuller emphasized, is the product of cooperation and collaboration—by legislators, officials, judges, and citizens—in search of a public good that can elicit the necessary support.

Fuller made this point in the context of Nazi decrees, exploring the difficulties of interpreting such measures in the context of the trial of spies and informers in the aftermath of the regime. If the legal positivist insists that Nazi decrees and statutes were undoubtedly *law*, even if wicked law, we should ask about their proper meaning. Should we interpret them by reference to our own standards of morality and justice, or by reference to Nazi standards (disregarding limitations helpful to an accused)? And would the post-war German courts 'really have been showing respect for Nazi law if they had construed the Nazi statutes by their own, quite different, standards of interpretation?'[91] We cannot, then, glibly assume that whatever purports to be law must be so merely because it is accompanied by state coercion:

We have instead to inquire how much of a legal system survived the general debasement and perversion of all forms of social order that occurred under the Nazi rule, and what moral implications this mutilated system had for the conscientious citizen forced to live under it.[92]

[89] Lon L Fuller, *The Morality of Law*, revised edn (New Haven: Yale University Press, 1969), 162. It was, moreover, the 'very essence of the Rule of Law' that in its coercive actions 'a government will faithfully apply rules previously declared as those to be followed by the citizen and as being determinative of his rights and duties' (ibid, 209–10).
[90] Compare Waldron, 'The Concept and the Rule of Law', 18.
[91] Fuller, 'Positivism and Fidelity to Law', 655.
[92] Ibid, 646.

A constitutional theorist is in the same boat as the constitutional lawyer. It is only by taking up the internal point of view, acknowledging the law's inherent aspiration to justice, that we can engage in serious discussion of the requirements of public law. To draw legal conclusions about facts or events is to engage, in some specific context, in reflection on the demands of legality or the rule of law—an ideal of governance premised on commitments to the values of human dignity and individual autonomy. There is no external space to occupy, advancing a 'bad interpretation' of some elements of legal practice and a more sympathetic view of other parts.[93] There is only a choice between external description of the facts about official conduct or attitudes (or predictions of future official conduct) and internal analysis of the nature and content of public law.[94] Moral condemnation is an appropriate response to systems of law we despise and whose purported duties or obligations we reject or deplore. If, however, we grant the legitimacy of our own constitution—embrace its capacity to generate morally binding rights and duties—we can only condemn erroneous *interpretations*, which misconceive those rights and duties when correctly understood. Our moral debates over law are closely tied to accounts of our practice: we invoke our ideals of liberty and justice to help make that practice more consistent—closer to the ideal of legality it already struggles to embody.

The common, but mistaken, view that the law can be identified by reference to facts alone—without engaging moral judgement—gains plausibility from a conception of law as statute. Surely, it may be said, the enacted words of a statute have a certain independence of the moral judgements we may need to make in applying them in quite unusual circumstances? It is very doubtful, however, whether they really do. Even instances of central application, when events appear to fall plainly within the scope of a provision, are only cases that exemplify the policy we take the legislation to serve. The distinction between 'core' and 'penumbra', or between central and peripheral cases of application, does not rest on semantic considerations alone.[95] We recognize a marginal case by seeing that, though it might fall within the statute on one construction, the unwelcome consequences (whether for legislative policy or constitutional principle) suggest that another reading may well be preferable. Fuller observed that lawyers are accustomed to posing hypothetical borderline cases, in seeking to elucidate meaning, 'in order to know where the penumbra begins'.[96] Such cases help in understanding the 'fabric of thought' that informs the statute:

This fabric is something we seek to discern, so that we may know truly what it is, but it is also something that we inevitably help to create as we strive (in accordance with our obligation of fidelity to law) to make the statute a coherent, workable whole.[97]

---

[93] Barber, *The Constitutional State*, 15.

[94] Compare Ronald Dworkin, 'Hart's Postscript and the Point of Political Philosophy' in his collection *Justice in Robes* (Cambridge, Mass: Harvard University Press, 2006) denying the availability of 'Archimedean' positions, external to the legal and moral discourse they purport to analyse.

[95] For the distinction between core and penumbra, see H L A Hart, 'Positivism and the Separation of Law and Morals' in his collection *Essays in Jurisprudence and Philosophy* (Oxford: Clarendon Press, 1983).

[96] Fuller, 'Positivism and Fidelity to Law', 666.

[97] Ibid, 667.

Even if statute law may be thought congenial to sharp divisions between clear and doubtful cases, however, the common law is not. Common law rules are only provisional formulations of underlying principles, whose implications can be discerned only by exploration, case by case, of the relevant 'fabric of thought'. Our conclusions of law reflect our moral judgements: we interpret a precedent in the light of the reasons that best justify the court's decision; and we need not accept the court's own proffered reasons if, in the light of moral reflection, we come to think that they were misleading or inadequate (or contrary to better reasoning in other cases). As Fuller observed, there is a sense in which common law is tantamount to 'unwritten law': the judges look 'behind the words of a precedent to what the previous court was trying to say, or to what it would have said if it could have foreseen the nature of the cases that were later to arise, or if its perception of the relevant factors in the case before it had been more acute'.[98] The law is always a work in progress, steered and inspired by the vision of justice it already embodies, at least in outline—a collaboration between earlier and current generations, as tradition is adapted and reinterpreted to meet fresh challenges to settled ways of thought.

What is true of law in general, and of common law in particular, is especially true of constitutional conventions, where the notion that a rule might operate with little or no reference to its underpinning reasons (even in core or central cases) is highly implausible. Many important matters are regulated by constitutional convention, such as the requirement that a Government that has lost the support of the House of Commons (after losing a general election or being defeated on a motion of no confidence) should resign from office. These conventions are the product of established practice, informed by political principle (such as the principle of democracy, requiring a Government to retain parliamentary approval). Since in most cases, however, there is scope for argument over the demands of principle, in light of all the circumstances, there is space for controversy as regards the requirements of convention. The precedents rarely speak for themselves, but rather call for interpretation—and sometimes *repudiation*—by appeal to the general virtues of the political order as they are understood by the statesmen or politicians involved.

Dicey wrote that such 'customs, practices, maxims, or precepts' were not, despite their normative character, to be regarded as law: they were neither enforced nor recognized by courts.[99] Later writers have generally accepted Dicey's strict dichotomy, denying that conventions, being created or adopted by politicians to govern their own conduct, could be a source of law. As I shall argue, however, it is only the adoption of an external viewpoint, detached from any practical concerns about just and lawful governance, that could explain that approach. The related idea that the law is wholly derived from certain authoritative 'sources'—to the exclusion of the moral and political principles and assumptions that lend such sources whatever authority they are taken to possess—is simply dogmatic and, ultimately, misleading. Important constitutional cases derive their significance from the *questions arising about such sources*—the nature and scope of their authority in all the relevant circumstances.

---

[98] Lon L Fuller, *Anatomy of the Law* (Harmondsworth: Penguin Books, 1971), 130.
[99] Dicey, *Law of the Constitution*, 417.

In relying on the facts of the matter, as he perceived them, Dicey made no attempt to *justify* the distinction between law and convention by reference to the ideal of legality or any other basic political value. Like parliamentary sovereignty, the dichotomy purported to be (or be dependent on) empirical fact. But the facts alone establish very little. Even if it were true that courts have generally paid little attention to constitutional conventions, treating them as rules to be enforced, if at all, by political pressure alone, it would not follow that such a course was necessarily justified—or justified in all circumstances. There may well be occasions on which the rule of law requires judicial recognition and enforcement of conventions; and a proper account of law and legality should identify those occasions. We cannot elevate our observations of past judicial practice into legal *doctrine* without an account of the relevant principles that we find persuasive. Why should the judges ignore established rules or conventions, adopted by politicians in the public interest, if these are relevant to matters of legality arising in the courts? And if conventions are based on political principles, reflecting genuine constitutional values, why should anyone think they might not sometimes be relevant to—sometimes even conclusive of—questions of constitutional law?

These are questions of real practical importance, and not merely academic interest, because they are closely related to contrasting visions of the legal order. The British Constitution is sometimes portrayed as a purely 'political' arrangement, in the sense that the most fundamental questions about power and liberty and justice are to be determined largely through the political process, marginalizing the role of the courts. The requirements of legality, on this view, are ultimately determined by politics; legal theory and political morality must alike give way, if necessary, to majority vote in Parliament. It is consistent with that view that constitutional convention, like many other strictly 'political' matters, should be placed beyond judicial scrutiny. The separation of powers between the main organs of government may be thought a feature of the political constitution that, like other settled practices, courts must simply accept as part of the constitutional landscape that they cannot question. A contrasting view, however, denies that the constitution can be divided in that way between the legal and the political; it insists that all questions in public law are both legal *and* political, in the sense that the requirements of legality depend on the specific context. The separation of powers is not merely an institutional feature to be *described*, or (depending on one's favoured definition) *denied*. It is an implicit requirement of legality that demands judicial recognition, exposition, and protection.[100]

VII

Dicey's remarkable appeal and influence, making his work an almost indispensable reference point for all succeeding writers on the constitution, owe a great deal to

---

[100] See further Chapters 2 and 3, below.

what is implicit rather than explicit in his argument. Despite his dubious assertions of 'legal fact', suggesting a purely external, descriptive stance, Dicey's constant appeal to general principles and political ideals points to a different approach. Beneath the apparently neutral and descriptive style of discourse lies something closer to the interpretative viewpoint, seeking to integrate legal custom or practice with the political values capable of conferring legitimacy. Judicial practice, however firmly fixed by professional attitude and assumption, we might infer, is ultimately justifiable (in its main lines) by a moral tradition of respect for liberty and justice.

Admittedly, Dicey explained his task as being 'neither to criticize, nor to venerate, but to understand': a professor of constitutional law should 'perform the part neither of a critic nor of an apologist, nor of an eulogist, but simply of an expounder; his duty is neither to attack nor to defend the constitution, but simply to explain its laws'.[101] In seeking to distinguish his role as constitutional expounder from that of the legal historian or political theorist, however, Dicey plainly exaggerated the necessary analytical detachment. As with the sharp contrast he draws between laws, in the 'strictest sense' of the term, and mere conventions or practices, which are 'not enforced by the courts', Dicey's main purpose here is to delineate a legal territory distinct from both legal history, reserved for historians, and political theory or political science.[102] The objective is to 'know and be able to state what are the principles of law which actually and at the present day exist in England'.[103] Dicey wants to confront and refute the possibility that 'so-called "constitutional law" is in reality a cross between history and custom which does not properly deserve the name of law at all'.[104] Once he embarks on his (necessarily interpretative) endeavour, seeking 'the guidance of first principles', the studied neutrality of the detached observer must give way to the commitment of the engaged participant: criticism and veneration, in appropriate degrees, must be invoked in aid of understanding.[105]

Insofar as Dicey's method was 'that of observation and objective description through the composition of sets or categories and the division or subdivision of their components' (such as the contrast between law and conventions), it suffered from the various deficiencies John Allison identifies.[106] In particular, a 'formal scheme of sets and distinctions' leaves the constitution's appeal or 'sources of fidelity' obscure. If, however, the *Law of the Constitution* is not 'as methodologically consistent or coherent as his own exposition of his analytical method would seem to have required', there being copious references to historical works as well as continental European comparisons, it may be because the analytical structure obscures a deeper, interpretative substructure.[107] While in one sense, as Allison observes,

---

[101] Dicey, *Law of the Constitution*, 3–4.
[102] Ibid, 23–4.
[103] Ibid, 14–15 (Dicey's first edition was published in 1885).
[104] Ibid, 22.
[105] Ibid, 34–5.
[106] J W F Allison, *The English Historical Constitution: Continuity, Change and European Effects* (Cambridge: Cambridge University Press, 2007), 8–9. According to Allison, Dicey's analytical method was 'confounded by three problems—fidelity, ossification and insularity'.
[107] Ibid, 13.

the references to 'legal triumphs in the constitutional struggles of the seventeenth century' were 'strictly extraneous to his legal analysis', they nevertheless helped to explain the constitution's capacity to inspire loyalty as a source of protection for important political values.[108] If, as Allison affirms, Dicey's approach 'was intended to benefit the student, the lawyer and the judge', he needed an internal, interpretative response to his source materials.[109] His analysis of contemporary constitutional law had to appeal to the ideals and values that inspired his readers' allegiance to the British governmental scheme.[110] Far from being merely rhetorical, and though highly selective and even questionable, Dicey's historical and comparative references (as Allison notes) were in 'the English legal and political community…a source of unity, appeal and historic legitimacy'.[111]

Examining the *Law of the Constitution* in the light of Dicey's other published works and unpublished manuscripts, Mark Walters has challenged the 'orthodox view of Diceyan constitutional theory as analytical, formalist, scientific, descriptive and positivist': if Dicey did not reject such approaches to legal method, he nevertheless 'consciously integrated them within an overarching legal theory that also embraced comparative, historical and normative approaches'.[112] A study of Dicey's views about legal writing and legal literature suggests to Walters 'a legal scholar who, on balance, favoured an interpretive approach to law that does not fit easily into the broad intellectual tradition associated with legal positivism'.[113] Analytical method had to be supplemented, in Dicey's view, by 'a comparative method that included philosophical accounts of "ideal" constitutionalism as well as the "spirit" animating the "letter or form" of particular constitutional laws'.[114]

If John Austin's jurisprudence was representative of legal positivism, defining law as the commands of the sovereign—the will of the person or persons habitually obeyed by the law's subjects—Dicey distanced himself from that view, defining law as the rules that the courts enforce.[115] Rejecting Austin's conception of the 'political' sovereign (referring to the ultimate source of power) Dicey favoured a 'legal' sovereignty, located in the Crown-in-Parliament. In that way, as Walters observes, law precedes sovereignty, rather than being the product of it: 'sovereignty

---

[108] Ibid, 14.　　　[109] Ibid, 8.

[110] It follows that there may not, on a sympathetic reading of Dicey, be such a great distance between his analytical approach 'in pursuit of a logically coherent formal scheme of constitutional legal rules and principles' and the 'liberal normativist' approach, 'preoccupied with liberal principles of legal and political morality in constitutional interpretation' (ibid, 29).

[111] Ibid, 185. 'Dicey's account of the rule of law, supposedly but only partly analytical, was attractive and enormously influential because of the normative comparative history with which he eloquently demonstrated the superior development and operation of the English historical constitution that his account repeatedly evoked' (ibid).

[112] Mark D Walters, 'Dicey on Writing the *Law of the Constitution*' (2012) 32 OJLS 21–49, at 47. '*Law of the Constitution* is really a book about general principles, not rules, and these principles gain their meaning through Dicey's narrative; any attempt to peel away literary form from legal substance is thus bound to fail' (ibid, 33).

[113] Ibid, 48.　　　[114] Ibid, 42.

[115] See John Austin, *The Province of Jurisprudence Determined* (1832), ed Wilfred E Rumble (Cambridge: Cambridge University Press, 1995), Lectures V and VI.

flowed from law'. Dicey's definition of law can itself be understood as a 'normative proposition of law', based on a view of the British constitution, rather than an empirical statement of fact, and 'it flowed directly from a larger theory of normative constitutionalism in which principles of parliamentary sovereignty and the rule of law are reconciled'.[116] Even if Parliament were 'sovereign' and could legislate as it pleased, independent courts enjoyed the final say on matters of interpretation.[117]

My discussion of Dicey's account of the rule of law, in Chapter 3, will emphasize the central place of the common law, viewed as an evolving scheme of legal principle focused on the protection of individual liberty. Allison objects that 'to read into Dicey's analytical exposition of the rule of law the entire organic functioning of the common law—its principled reasoning and systematic exegesis by reference to precedent—is contrary to Dicey's expository analytical method'.[118] But the objection overlooks the interpretative dimension to Dicey's analytical endeavour: legal exposition cannot proceed in disregard of general moral and political ideas and commitments, as Dicey's text so clearly demonstrates. Allison points to Dicey's disparaging reference to precedent as 'merely a useful fiction by which judicial decision conceals its transformation into judicial legislation'.[119] But this is made in the context of Dicey's dismissal of the notion of an original pure constitution that subsequent legal practice has obscured:

The fictions of the courts have in the hands of lawyers such as Coke served the cause both of justice and freedom, and served it when it could have been defended by no other weapons. For there are social conditions under which legal fictions or subtleties afford the sole means of establishing that rule of equal and settled law which is the true basis of English civilization.[120]

It is a familiar feature of common law reasoning that the strength or weight of precedent varies with its degree of approximation to general constitutional principle: the mistakes of the past are repudiated while we build on what are now understood to be its achievements.[121] Elsewhere, Dicey defends the rational, interpretative method of the common law that gives rise to 'judicial legislation':

New combinations of circumstances—that is, new cases—constantly call for the application, which means in truth the extension of old principles; or, it may be, even for the thinking out of some new principle, in harmony with the general spirit of the law, fitted to meet the novel requirements of the time.... The main employment of a Court is the application of well-known legal principles to the solution of given cases, and the deduction from these

---

[116] Walters, 'Dicey on Writing the *Law of the Constitution*', 40.
[117] See Chapter 5, below.
[118] Allison, *The English Historical Constitution*, 210.
[119] Dicey, *Law of the Constitution*, 19.
[120] Ibid, 18.
[121] Dicey's critique of Coke CJ's judgment in *Prohibitions del Roy* (disallowing James I to sit in person as a judge) as pedantic, artificial, and unhistorical (which Allison cites at 166–7) is the prelude to the celebration of the principle of separation of powers, central to the idea of the rule of law: Coke's efforts established a rule 'essential to the very existence of the constitution', ie to its existence as a constitution of law, consistent with fundamental principle.

principles of their fair logical result.... The duty of a Court, in short, is not to remedy a particular grievance, but to determine whether an alleged grievance is one for which the law supplies a remedy.[122]

And if, as Allison further contends, there is something of a leap from Dicey's 'jurisdictional equality' (equality before the law administered by the ordinary courts) to an overarching ideal of equal citizenship—an equality of fundamental rights and liberties—it is a movement promised by judicial decision-making attuned to the ideal of liberty or independence that illuminates the value of legality itself.[123]

I am arguing only that the enduring appeal of Dicey's principle of the rule of law, as a basic precept of British constitutionalism, cannot be explained if we take too literal a view of his formal exposition. If we acknowledge that Dicey's expository method entailed resort to moral or political principles, which could *justify* the selection of one version of constitutional sources and consequences rather than another, we have reason to set the formal analysis within its broader context. We can fend off misguided attacks, which may even inspire hostility to the very idea of the rule of law, by emphasizing the interdependence of fact and value: the internal perspective, characteristic of lawyer, judge, or jurist, makes issues of justification and legitimacy directly pertinent to an analysis of current law. If Dicey did not know he was engaged in an interpretative endeavour along these lines—not appreciating the methodological problems with his odd mix of analysis, national pride, reverence for legality and freedom, and selective comparative and historical references—we are entitled to distinguish the text from its author's self-understanding. We must read the *Law of the Constitution* in light of the political values that could justify its continued authority. If Dicey's work is best understood by reference to a moral ideal of law or legality, which informs and illuminates the text, we can fairly claim it as part of the tradition we want to explain and defend.

---

[122] A V Dicey, *Lectures on the Relation between Law and Public Opinion in England During the Nineteenth Century*, 2nd edn (London: Macmillan & Co, 1962), 363–5. See also Dicey's Appendix, Note IV, 492–3: 'The notion that judges pretended to expound the laws which they really made is based upon ignorance of the fact that fiction is not fraud, and that legal fictions are the natural product of certain social and intellectual conditions.'

[123] Allison, *The English Historical Constitution*, 211–12. See further Chapter 3, below.

2

Constitutional Convention: Practice and Principle

I

I have argued in Chapter 1 that public law cannot be reduced to facts about legal practice, even if we have in mind the regular practice of courts and judges. The facts must be interpreted in the light of the ideals—most notably, the ideal of legality—that we take our legal practice to serve and exemplify. Even settled legal rules do not apply themselves to particular cases; moral judgement is required in determining their proper application whenever reasonable doubts arise about their meaning and scope. Common law rules do not even possess the definitive textual form of enacted rules, but serve only to indicate the balance of reasons in the standard or typical case they chiefly envisage. Constitutional conventions are similar. These rules, making obligatory certain sorts of behaviour by government ministers, must be understood in the light of their underpinning reasons: what they require depends on all the circumstances, having regard to relevant considerations of political principle. If it is an important convention that ministers should be accountable to Parliament for the conduct and policy of the government departments over which they preside, the form of that accountability—what it requires in particular instances—must depend, in the last analysis, on the principles of responsibility and democracy that lend the convention sense or meaning.

We must distinguish, it follows, between the external perspective of someone who seeks only to describe what others do—recounting examples of politicians' behaviour that reveals what those politicians believe about the pertinent rules—and the internal perspective of the interpreter, who seeks to establish what, if anything, the rules actually require in all the circumstances. Since interpretation involves *judgement*, discriminating between true and false, or better and worse, accounts of the conduct required, it must take sides between the competing theories or viewpoints. It cannot rest content with simply recording politicians' conduct in the past and noting the terms of any controversy over that conduct and its propriety or impropriety. A statement about the content of constitutional convention—about what good practice actually requires—asserts or assumes a theory about how the rules help to sustain democracy or good governance, or at least must do so if intended to make any serious contribution to discussion of constitutional affairs.

It is customary for public lawyers to distinguish between constitutional law, on one hand, and convention, on the other; but that distinction largely reflects the external or descriptive perspective, appropriate for the detached political scientist, perhaps, but not for the lawyer or legal theorist. Certain rules can be classified as conventions on the ground that, though they are normally treated by politicians as binding, they are rarely, if ever, enforced by means of legal sanctions, applied by courts. A.V. Dicey famously distinguished English constitutional law from the 'customs, practices, maxims, or precepts' that were not to be regarded as law because they were neither enforced nor recognized by courts.[1] No doubt conventions are rarely 'enforced' by courts in any literal sense: unconstitutional conduct by ministers is more likely to elicit political criticism than give rise to a specific legal cause of action. Conventions receive judicial 'recognition', however, whenever the general principles they reflect or embody are relevant to legal proceedings. From the internal perspective appropriate to constitutional interpretation, principle and practice are interdependent: legal principles reflect the moral standards that underpin and protect our democratic practice.

Although Dicey distinguished formally between 'constitutional morality' and constitutional law, he emphasized their critical interdependence. Convention regulated the exercise of discretionary governmental power in the interests of democracy. The principal conventions were rules for the proper exercise of the royal prerogative, or non-statutory governmental power, and were intended to ensure that ministers retained the support of Parliament:

The conventions of the constitution now consist of customs which...are at the present day maintained for the sake of ensuring the supremacy of the House of Commons, and ultimately, through the elective House of Commons, of the nation. Our modern code of constitutional morality secures, though in a roundabout way, what is called abroad the 'sovereignty of the people'.[2]

While unable to envisage the enforcement of convention in the course of ordinary legal proceedings, Dicey argued that the continuing breach of convention (such as a failure to convene Parliament) would ultimately lead to breach of the law (the Government lacking the necessary legal authority to collect tax and spend money). Accordingly, the law of the constitution was the 'true foundation' of the English polity, giving 'even to the conventional element of constitutional law' such force as it possessed.[3]

In this chapter I shall challenge the arguments of several defenders of a strict dichotomy of legal rule and political practice. When we take up the internal, normative perspective of legal reasoner, as opposed to the external, descriptive stance more suited to political science, we will find that no clear distinction between law and convention can be sustained. Public law concerns the conduct of government; and legal interpretation cannot be divorced from political practice, whose principles and assumptions are necessarily pertinent to competent legal analysis.

---

[1] A V Dicey, *Introduction to the Study of the Law of the Constitution*, 10th edn (London: Macmillan, 1964), 417.

[2] Ibid, 430–1.

[3] Ibid, 470.

We will see that those who insist on trying to draw sharp boundaries between legal and political practice adopt a view of law shaped by the philosophy of legal positivism.[4] If law consists of rules enacted by the legislature or laid down by judges, in exercise of a quasi-legislative discretion, it can be distinguished from convention by its sources: conventional rules are adopted by statesmen or politicians to regulate their own behaviour. If, instead, law embraces general moral principles, whose requirements are rather the commands of reason than those of authorized officials, it cannot so easily be described and identified by reference to specific sources. Our study of conventional rules may therefore help to illuminate also the character of statutory and common law rules: in all cases, I am contending, we cannot obtain a clear grasp of a rule's requirements, in concrete instances, without reflection on the values or purposes the rule should be understood to serve.

The positivist assumptions that inspire the drawing of sharp boundary lines between law and convention are related, in the work of some theorists, to a distrust or disparagement of judicial review and its enforcement of general legal principle. Fearing that the application and development of general principles may draw judges too deeply into the governmental process, threatening the decision-making power of officials more directly accountable to Parliament or the electorate, these writers proclaim the superiority of the 'political' over the 'legal constitution'.[5] Seeking to limit the judicial role in the constitution, they question the 'justiciability' of disputes over rights, powers or duties that ought, in their view, to be resolved by politicians alone. Such writers would exclude from the ambit of judicial review substantial areas of governmental activity, much as those who insist on the radical difference between law and convention deny the relevance of the latter to questions of administrative legality. I shall challenge the coherence of any such distinction between legal and political constitutions, however, insisting that our legal and political practice is too intertwined and interdependent to sustain it.

For many years it was assumed that the royal prerogative, which places extensive non-statutory powers in the hands of the executive Government, could be deployed entirely without judicial supervision: no one could bring a legal challenge to the fairness or reasonableness of its mode of exercise, even when individual interests (such as those of an applicant for a passport or a pardon) were directly affected. Even when, in an important case, the House of Lords acknowledged that assertions of prerogative power were reviewable in principle, the judges considered that many such powers (including the power to pardon a convicted offender) were not in their nature amenable to judicial scrutiny.[6] Those restrictions have, however, largely crumbled away as particular cases have arisen to challenge their compatibility with

---

[4] It is notoriously hard to find an agreed definition of legal positivism; I refer to the assumption that matters of legal content and legal validity have no necessary connection with moral value, being ultimately determined by the facts of official practice (as opposed to any interpreter's appraisal of the moral implications of that practice). See generally Hart, *The Concept of Law*, 2nd edn (Oxford: Clarendon Press, 1994).

[5] See for example Adam Tomkins, *Our Republican Constitution* (Oxford: Hart Publishing, 2005), especially ch 1.

[6] *Council of Civil Service Unions v Minister for the Civil Service* [1985] AC 374.

central precepts of the rule of law.[7] Treated as a description of the general nature of the prerogative power, or the sphere of governmental activity in view, 'justiciability' is a concept better suited to the external viewpoint: it suggests that judicial review will rarely be an appropriate or effective remedy for administrative error or impropriety. From the internal perspective of the public lawyer, justiciability—or susceptibility to review—is, instead, a function of the specific legal challenge to an exercise of power in all the circumstances. It is, I shall argue, properly the *outcome* of legal analysis rather than a straitjacket confining its course from the start.

The topics of convention, prerogative, and justiciability are, then, closely linked. If, as Adam Tomkins maintains, ministerial responsibility to Parliament is a constitutional convention informed by an important principle of political responsibility—not merely, as J. A. G. Griffith seemed to suggest, a statement of current practice—it must be as much a part of the legal as the political constitution.[8] When we shift from descriptive to normative ground, we must be prepared to reappraise our expository categories and classifications. We are in the realm of first principles and the moral and political judgement they elicit in our efforts to apply them.

II

In an interesting case, the Supreme Court of Canada concluded not only that conventions were different from statutory rules, which the courts must obey and enforce, but also from common law: 'They are not based on judicial precedents but on precedents established by the institutions of government themselves.'[9] Enforcement of such institutional precedents, indicating proper governmental practice, depended on the assertion of political pressure against those tempted to disobey. When law and convention are thus conceived, it is possible to identify conflicts arising between them. Convention may impose constraints on the exercise of legal powers, which would otherwise be unfettered, even if those constraints are not enforced by courts. The legal rule that allows the Queen or Governor-General of Canada to withhold assent from a bill passed by both Houses of Parliament creates a discretion which settled convention 'completely neutralizes'.[10]

That external, descriptive perspective, however, places stringent limits on any coherent discussion of the interplay of the various sources of obligation, or of the subtleties and complexities of either legal doctrine or political practice. For one can only offer an argument about the requirements of law or convention (or their combined operation or overlap in any particular case) from an *internal* perspective—the perspective of politician or official or citizen, whose view of the relevant distinctions will reflect the *context* in which (and *purposes* for which) they are made. A judge

---

[7] See for example *Lewis v Attorney-General of Jamaica* [2000] 2 AC 50, considered below.

[8] Tomkins, *Our Republican Constitution*, 36–8, discussing J A G Griffith, 'The Political Constitution' (1979) 42 MLR 1–21; see further below.

[9] *Reference re Amendment of the Constitution of Canada (Nos 1, 2 & 3)* (1982) 125 DLR (3d) 1, 84–5.

[10] Ibid.

may be unwilling to acknowledge the validity of a bill which lacks any mark of royal assent; but no competent adviser would inform the monarch that she may, if so desired, apply a veto. Nor can a constitutional court, confronted by a fundamental question of legitimacy, properly take the distinction between law and convention for granted, at the outset, in the manner of the Canadian Supreme Court. That distinction may be called into question by the very nature of the legal issues arising; its survival, for the purposes in hand, will then be the *outcome* of the court's deliberations (if indeed it does survive) rather than an unchallengeable conceptual assumption.

The Canadian Supreme Court elevated Dicey's descriptive categorization of rules into legal *doctrine*, thereby confusing descriptive and normative (external and internal) viewpoints.[11] Whether or not established convention—in that case a convention serving to protect Canadian federalism—deserves judicial recognition or 'enforcement' must depend on all the circumstances. The appropriate judicial response depends on considerations of constitutional principle that transcend any merely descriptive categorization of rules. Because both legal rules and constitutional conventions form parts of a larger system of governance, in which subtle distinctions between law and politics depend so much on the specific context, it makes little sense to turn Dicey's distinction into legal doctrine, independent of the circumstances of the particular case. The content of any rule, however classified, is always partly dependent on its underlying general principles.

Since even settled and time-honoured customs and practices will nonetheless be vague or *unsettled* in relation to certain, perhaps novel, circumstances, they call for interpretation. But to interpret a practice or convention is to offer *reasons*, related to its apparent point or purpose, why it should (or should not) be extended to the case in view. And such reasons cannot merely describe what others think or characteristically do: there is, *ex hypothesi*, no such uniform attitude or conduct to appeal to. So any interpretation must appeal to the *role* of the pertinent custom or convention within the polity, providing an account of how it contributes to good government or some aspect of political morality. When government is conducted within the limits of the rule of law, as in a well-ordered liberal or social democracy, the relevant considerations of good governance will naturally reflect the requirements and objectives of legality: good political practice will support the maintenance of the rule of law, just as preservation of the rule of law will protect and enhance the working of democracy. To be a student of constitutional convention, therefore, is necessarily to be a constitutional theorist, not merely a historian or sociologist or descriptive political scientist. And the theorist's perspective is ultimately the same as the participant's: one can draw useful and interesting conclusions about the requirements of convention, and their relevance to public law, only from within the legal and political order one wishes to describe. Description and prescription then go hand-in-hand; the former, if not mainly superficial, entails the latter.

---

[11] The case is considered more fully below.

Geoffrey Marshall expresses this difference between external and internal per-spectives in terms of a distinction between 'positive morality' and 'critical morality'.[12] Whereas the former describes the beliefs and attitudes of the relevant 'political actors', from a strictly detached perspective, the latter reflects the theorist's own understanding of the value or point of conventions: they are conceived as 'the rules that the political actors *ought* to feel obliged by, if they have considered the precedents and reasons correctly'. Marshall thinks the 'critical' approach superior because it allows someone to say that 'although a rule may appear to be widely or even universally accepted as a convention, the conclusions generally drawn from earlier precedents, or the reasons advanced in justification, are mistaken'.[13] He prefers the view of Sir Ivor Jennings, who insisted on the role of reasons in judg-ing whether the precedents established a constitutional rule, to that of O. Hood Phillips, who defined conventions as 'rules of political practice which are *regarded as binding* by those to whom they apply'.[14]

If we could not criticize the views of statesmen or politicians on the require-ments of convention, we would be unable to resolve any doubts or ambiguities, or even to offer useful suggestions: we could merely report the existence of doubt and disagreement, mentioning only the reasons for any suggested rule that may have figured in political debate, in whatever terms those reasons were couched. Nor could we appraise the merits or demerits of any conventional rule as a contribu-tion to good governance. Any coherent appraisal would depend on first having a clear grasp of the *content* of the rule; and whenever that was uncertain or disputed (which in some contexts, at least, it almost inevitably would be) we could not reach any clear conclusions. We would need first to join the practice as participants, engaging with them on their own ground—offering, endorsing, and rejecting reasons for and against any particular interpretation of the historical precedents.

A participant interpreting a social practice, as Ronald Dworkin explains, 'proposes value for the practice by describing some scheme of interests or goals or principles the practice can be taken to serve or express or exemplify'.[15] That does not mean, of course, that he can impose on the practice whatever goals or principles he favours, regardless of whether these ends or values are shared by others; and he must respect the history and structure of the practice, which will rule out a great many interpre-tative possibilities.[16] An honest (and plausible) interpreter must be able and willing to distinguish between his substantive social or political views, on the one side, and his convictions, on the other, about how far the justification he offers 'must

---

[12] Geoffrey Marshall, *Constitutional Conventions: The Rules and Forms of Political Accountability* (Oxford: Clarendon Press, 1984), 10–12.

[13] Ibid, 12.

[14] Sir Ivor Jennings, *The Law and the Constitution*, 5th edn (London: University of London Press, 1959), ch 3; O Hood Phillips, *Constitutional and Administrative Law*, 7th edn (London: Sweet & Maxwell, 1987), 113 (emphasis added).

[15] Ronald Dworkin, *Law's Empire* (London: Fontana, 1986), 52.

[16] For the collective and interactive nature of interpretation of a common practice, which Dworkin may be thought to under-estimate, see Gerald J Postema, '"Protestant" Interpretation and Social Practices' (1987) 6 Law & Phil 283–319. (I consider the complex nature of interpretation further in the Appendix, below.)

fit the standing features of the practice' in order 'to count as an interpretation of it rather than the invention of something new'.[17] But though respectful of other people's attitudes and assumptions, he is forced to take sides when they disagree. It is not enough merely to report the different opinions within the community about what is required: he must distinguish between people's divergent conceptions of the practice, on the one hand, and the real demands of the practice itself, on the other. The theorist must, then, 'join the practice he proposes to understand'; his conclusions are not 'neutral reports' about what others think but rather claims about practice '*competitive* with theirs'.[18]

We could not, for example, criticize a convention allowing the Prime Minister to advise a dissolution of Parliament (hence choosing the date of a general election) before deciding whether, on due consideration, any such convention really existed, despite its rather dubious historical and democratic credentials. We need not call for radical constitutional upheaval: we should rather reject extravagant claims of prime ministerial power, which reflect a misapprehension of the conventions as we believe they are correctly understood. If 'no adequate constitutional foundation' existed for the prevailing view, that view would have to be rejected.[19] Even a 'common or widespread conviction' may rest on 'misconstruction of earlier precedents or on unconvincing assertions of principle'. Constitutional conventions are 'established through the medium of belief and conviction'; and, as Marshall rightly observes, even in politics convictions 'are sometimes changed by argument'.[20]

N. W. Barber complains that 'if a rule is widely accepted and followed by political actors, it would be odd for a constitutional commentator, or even for one of those political actors, to deny that it was a convention'.[21] It would be odd, in Barber's view, because he thinks that conventions, like other rules, must stand apart from the reasons that animate them: they must 'pre-empt...consideration of the reasons on which they depend'.[22] So statesmen and politicians may follow a rule whose purpose or value they have long forgotten or even deny altogether. Barber concedes that it is often useful to inquire about the reasons behind the rule. A 'historical' reason may be given for the rule's adoption; a 'psychological' reason may be offered to show why people adhere to the rule; and a 'justificatory' reason may be supplied to indicate the rule's value. But though every constitutional convention must have a reason in the first two senses, it need not (according to this account) be justifiable: 'some conventions may just be pointless, or wrong'.[23] If, however, conventions do not on correct understanding pre-empt, but rather *demand*, consideration of the reasons on which they depend, Barber's analysis is quite confused. From a fully internal stance, alongside the political actors themselves, the commentator cannot

---

[17] Dworkin, *Law's Empire*, 67.

[18] Ibid, 64.

[19] Marshall, *Constitutional Conventions*, 51. Marshall denies the existence of any genuine convention giving the Prime Minister sole power to choose the date of a general election.

[20] Ibid, 51–53.

[21] N W Barber, *The Constitutional State* (Oxford: Oxford University Press, 2010), 83.

[22] Ibid, citing Joseph Raz, *The Morality of Freedom* (Oxford: Oxford University Press, 1986), 57–62.

[23] Barber, *The Constitutional State*, 84.

repudiate a convention as being 'pointless or wrong': a pointless convention is simply no convention at all.

Barber concedes that a scholar's interpretative role has an evaluative dimension, if only because scholarly work may help to shape the practice it describes:

Within the elastic confines of the interpretations of the convention provided by political actors and other writers, she must try to identify the (justificatory) reason for the convention, and then clarify the rule in the context of that reason. She has a responsibility to her community to seek to show the convention in its best light or—if this cannot be done—to advocate that it be discarded or changed.[24]

A convention is shown in its best light, however, by explaining its role within the legal and political order, revealing the links between the various aspects of political practice and constitutional principle. When a convention is interpreted in that broader context, its value is revealed by reference to the reasons that sustain it; and those reasons will support one view of what it truly requires of the political actors, repudiating inconsistent opinions. Perhaps, on correct analysis, a conventional rule will have a much more limited sphere of application than has sometimes been supposed; but there will be nothing left to *discard or change*, except for the mistakes or misconceptions that fuel competing (erroneous) conceptions of the relevant constitutional duties.

If the scholar's account of convention necessarily combines description and evaluation, presenting its requirements in the light of their point or purpose, as she conceives it, so must any politician's account—whether, for example, he is accusing his opponents of flouting good constitutional practice or defending himself against similar criticism. Unless such a politician is insincere, acting only for short-term party advantage, his appeal to constitutional propriety must exhibit the same responsibility as the scholar, 'a responsibility to . . . show the convention in its best light'. For no one, acting in good faith, can condemn another for contravening 'pointless' requirements he himself rejects; and he can quite properly defend himself against accusations of impropriety by challenging the authenticity of the rule he is alleged to have broken— either because it does not, when properly interpreted, apply in all the circumstances or because it would be inimical to good practice, at odds with constitutional principle. Rule and reasons are interdependent: the rule is only a rough approximation of the reasons applicable to judgement, and quickly surrenders to those reasons when there is any doubt about its meaning or scope or validity in the particular case.

Since constitutional conventions generally owe their existence to a mix of precedent and principle, and do not normally depend on authoritative pronouncement, let alone formal *enactment*, they can be fairly characterized as 'non-systematic social rules' (where the rules induce a regularity of conduct, but do not constitute the formally arranged scheme found in a modern legal order).[25] As Barber concedes, such rules are generally treated as morally justified:

Whilst it is plausible to imagine that there are some within the community who obey through fear or hope of advantage, for a non-systematic social rule to exist a significant

---

[24] Ibid, 85.   [25] Ibid, 61–2.

portion of the community must believe that the rule is justified…If this is lacking, the apparent rule is not a rule at all: it is a threat or bribe.'[26]

So a 'significant portion' of the political community, at least, must believe a convention to be justified. If, then, a convention may nonetheless be 'pointless' or 'wrong', it must at least be the case that many statesmen and politicians believe otherwise— that they think the rule is justified and could give reasons for that view if pressed to do so. If treated as a purely external descriptive observation, Barber's assertion that a convention need not be justifiable is therefore mistaken. But if treated as an *internal* claim, of the kind any participant could make about its point or value, it amounts to the denial that any such rule or convention (in the terms commonly asserted) actually exists. Moreover, Barber's suggested distinctions between historical, psychological, and normative reasons for convention are highly artificial. From the internal, participant's perspective, it is implausible to suppose that anyone would try to defend a rule, if challenged, for reasons that bore no relation to constitutional history, or would adhere to the rule for reasons unrelated to their normative justification.[27] All such reasons are reflexive and intertwined, any valid interpretation appealing to both history and morality.

Joseph Jaconelli is more sympathetic than Barber to the idea of conventions as a form of critical morality, in Marshall's sense. He observes that conventions determined merely by patterns of behaviour, lacking any significant underlying reason, are 'not typically to be found in matters constitutional'.[28] Instead, many constitutional conventions are 'permeated by values—democracy, the separation of powers, responsible government—which are generally regarded as possessing independent and permanent worth'. It does not follow, he explains, that conventions can survive repeated breaches of their demands. Unlike 'critical morality' of the kind that is wholly independent of currently accepted attitudes or established norms of social conduct, conventions are contingent on their continued acceptance: they are, in that sense, 'matters of positive morality'.[29] There are *elements* of critical morality because such values as democratic accountability are independent of their observance or non-observance by particular legal systems; but since those values are given expression in diverse ways in different constitutions, the relevant conventions are better characterized as examples of *conventional* morality: the existence of a social rule or practice is a necessary basis for the obligations that ensue.[30] There must be

[26] Barber, *The Constitutional State*, 62. Barber cites John Finnis's characterization of the *central* case of the participant's internal point of view as one treating a rule as morally justified: see John Finnis, *Natural Law and Natural Rights* (Oxford: Clarendon Press, 1980), 9–18.

[27] The reasons for the Queen's adherence to the convention that she should assent to parliamentary bills (Barber's own example) would encompass both history and morality—matters of political power, 'tradition', and democracy (see Barber, *The Constitutional State*, 84).

[28] Joseph Jaconelli, 'The Nature of Constitutional Convention' (1999) 19 LS 24–46, at 44.

[29] Ibid, 43. Here Jaconelli follows H L A Hart's distinction between 'critical' and 'positive' morality, the former being the 'general moral principles' invoked in the critique of 'actual social institutions' and prevailing attitudes: H L A Hart, *Law, Liberty and Morality* (Oxford: Oxford University Press, 1963), 20.

[30] Jaconelli, 'The Nature of Constitutional Convention', 44, quoting Dworkin's distinction between 'concurrent' and 'conventional' morality (the latter depending on the existence of a social practice for its general acceptance): Ronald Dworkin, *Taking Rights Seriously* (London: Duckworth, 1977), 53.

precedents as well as reasons, though the importance of the latter means that the requirements of convention will in practice be marked by interpretative dispute.

Now that interaction of reason and precedent marks a striking analogy with the common law; and the analogy exposes the implausibility of any sharp conceptual division between law and convention. By contrast with formally enacted legislation, which alters future legal relations between affected persons, a judicial decision at common law draws on principles embedded in, or illustrated by, precedent: it seeks a solution to the present dispute that is, if possible, both morally defensible and consistent with established practice. As in the case of convention, *legitimacy* is a function of both morality and history: the court defers not merely to justice, in its universal character, but to its local manifestation, as reflected in the customs, practices, and understandings of society and polity. That does not mean, of course, that we cannot, as descriptive political scientists, distinguish between law and convention: not all social rules are suitable for legal enforcement or typically maintained by recourse to law. It does mean, however, that a *common lawyer* could only determine the consequences of a breach of social norms by consideration of all the circumstances: in some contexts, settled expectations and shared understandings will provide the appropriate content of legal obligations.[31]

We cannot properly classify the common law as either critical (universal) or positive morality. It is a complex admixture of both; and the same must be true of constitutional conventions. Jaconelli cautions that 'though animated by some of the most basic values of political theory, their content is not to be derived simply from abstract considerations of correct governmental conduct'.[32] But we can say much the same about the principal rules of constitutional law. Insofar, moreover, as convention does reflect fundamental political values, independent of their immediate context, it is wrong to dismiss the suggestion that 'there exists a uniquely correct constitutional morality applicable to all governmental systems'.[33] And hence it is wrong to suppose—as Jaconelli supposes—that the binding quality of convention can only be explained on the basis of pragmatic adjustment between opposing political parties for mutual advantage, so that the majority party desists from abusing its power in the expectation that its opponents will be as merciful when they in turn attain office.[34]

Jaconelli too quickly dismisses the intrinsic appeal of conformity to ethical values one recognizes, reflecting perhaps a sense of loyalty to the community whose well-being is served by compliance. He concedes that his analysis could not apply to such important conventions as those requiring the monarch to assent to bills duly passed by both Houses of Parliament, and the House of Lords to pass

---

[31] Jaconelli denies that enforcing a legal rule can be equated with a court's 'choosing to create a rule the contents of which are drawn from convention' ('The Nature of Constitutional Conventions', 26, n 10); but his assumption that courts may exercise discretion or *choice* in this manner is controversial, and almost certainly false. See Dworkin, *Taking Rights Seriously*, 31–9.

[32] Jaconelli, 'The Nature of Constitutional Convention', 46.

[33] Joseph Jaconelli, 'Do Constitutional Conventions Bind?' [2005] CLJ 149–76, at 171.

[34] Ibid, 170–5, quoting Hume's discussion of the foundations of justice and property: David Hume, *A Treatise of Human Nature*, 2nd edn by Selby-Bigge (Oxford: Clarendon Press, 1978), 490.

bills from the lower House that are based on the government's election manifesto: 'There will clearly be strong reasons of a prudential nature for the observance of these conventions, but that would appear to be all that could be said of them.'[35] Treating convention as a discrete corpus of rules, independent of both law and morality, Jaconelli reaches somewhat lame conclusions; his descriptive analytical method ultimately leads him astray.

III

I am arguing that the distinction between law and convention is the product of a purely external stance, appropriate perhaps for the political scientist, operating at a high level of descriptive generality, but quite inappropriate for the constitutional lawyer or theorist, whose perspective must be much closer to the view of the political actors themselves. From a suitably internal perspective, there are both questions of good governmental practice and questions of public law; but since such questions are in practice very closely related, it makes little sense to try to divide all the pertinent rules and principles between two separate categories. This is not to deny that some rules may be better enforced, if at all, by politicians than by judges. If, for example, a government minister's credibility depends on his retaining the confidence of the House of Commons, any alleged lack of integrity or competence is essentially a matter for parliamentary judgement; the relevant requirements of convention will be settled outside the courts. Since, however, matters of convention may sometimes be relevant to legal proceedings, they are a legitimate source of *normative judgement* that a court cannot properly ignore.

If the Attorney-General seeks an injunction to prevent the publication of a former minister's diaries, on the ground that their disclosure of Cabinet discussions would constitute a breach of confidentiality, the court may be obliged to determine the content and scope of the convention of collective ministerial responsibility. When that convention imposes the relevant duties of confidentiality, its correct interpretation will be critical to the court's finding of any breach of the minister's legal duty of confidence. He cannot be in breach of a duty of confidence that the convention, on correct understanding, does not impose in the circumstances arising. And since interpretation, as we have seen, involves an *evaluation* of the precedents, by reference to constitutional principle or good practice, a judge must make up his own mind about which view of the requirements of convention, if they are disputed, is actually correct. His study of political practice must be informed by a grasp of constitutional principle. His decision whether or not to grant an injunction should reflect his view of what would best protect the proper functioning of Cabinet government—subject to any reservations prompted by his broader conception of representative democracy, which will limit restrictions on free expression in the interests of well-informed debate and accountability. If there is an interval of some

---

[35] Jaconelli, 'Do Constitutional Conventions Bind?', 174.

years between Cabinet discussion and publication, sufficient to ensure that current deliberations would not be compromised by the risk of an early disclosure of divergent opinions, the demands of collective responsibility may be outweighed by those of free speech.[36]

N. W. Barber wants to distinguish between *direct* judicial enforcement of convention and *indirect* enforcement, the latter applicable where there is a separate and established rule of law such as the one prohibiting breaches of confidence. But that distinction simply assumes the dichotomy between law and convention in issue: it supposes that a court may only have regard to convention as a source of background information, independent of the primary questions of law. It may, of course, be necessary to invoke a specific *cause of action*, if seeking an injunction to prevent a publication by civil suit; but there may also be judicial review of governmental action on the basis of illegality or irrationality or procedural unfairness—anything that amounts, in the light of constitutional propriety, to an abuse of power. Unless we suppose that such judgements of propriety need take no account of the general principles that guide the conduct of statesmen and politicians, as servants of a liberal democracy grounded on the rule of law, we cannot relegate those principles to a special category, lacking legal status. How could we distinguish between legal and political principles? It could hardly depend on whether, or how often, a particular principle happens to have been mentioned in the course of a legal judgment, or on whether the relevant principle has been invoked in any particular (semantic) form.

We can accept a clear distinction between law and convention only if we treat them as composed of separate bodies of rules, sufficiently clear and self-contained to be applicable without recourse to any underlying reasons; for as soon as we turn to consider such underlying reasons, when a rule's requirements are doubtful or contested, law and convention merge in a broader reflection on constitutional principle. A principle is simply a general reason for a more specific conclusion, based on particular facts; and its strength or weight depends on its interaction with other principles, which may also have a bearing on the correct resolution of the case at hand.[37] We can distinguish, if we wish, between moral reasons and purely prudential or self-regarding reasons, like those of a corrupt politician who hopes to evade detection. But we cannot divide moral reasons into 'political' and 'legal' categories: expressing the perceived demands of justice and good government, they are as relevant in the legislative assembly or at the Cabinet table as in the courtroom. It is the whole purpose of democracy, through its various institutions, to determine their content, whether framed as general principles or as resolutions of particular cases.

---

[36] See *Attorney-General v Jonathan Cape* [1976] QB 752; Allan, *Law, Liberty, and Justice: The Legal Foundations of British Constitutionalism* (Oxford: Clarendon Press, 1993), 245. Lord Widgery expressly affirmed (at 771) that, in his view, the 'maintenance of the doctrine of joint responsibility within the cabinet is in the public interest, and the application of that doctrine might be prejudiced by premature disclosure of the views of individual ministers'.

[37] Compare Ronald Dworkin, *Taking Rights Seriously*, 22–8.

Since long-standing social norms do not automatically give rise to legal rights and duties, corresponding to the relevant practices, Jaconelli proclaims the existence of a 'clear conceptual divide between laws and conventions'.[38] But the division he discerns is only the reflection of his external, descriptive stance; and even if we grant his claim that the precise definition of constitutional conventions is not merely 'an arid exercise in classification', the conceptual division has little or no relevance either to legal or political practice.[39] He objects to the suggestion that, in the context of the Crossman Diaries case, the court's 'recognition' of collective ministerial responsibility amounted to 'enforcement'.[40] A typical example of a social rule is the requirement that men should remove their hats in church, one which might well meet with judicial approval: 'It does not follow that judges would be right to express their approval in the shape of inflicting a *legal* sanction on the occasional man who has refused to bare his head in church.'[41] Of course it does not *necessarily* follow; but it is not hard to imagine circumstances in which similar discourtesy might have consequences for judicial reasoning, perhaps because it offends legitimate expectations entitled to recognition in the resolution of a civil dispute or the determination of a criminal complaint. It all depends on the circumstances and the legal context in which they arise. Civil and criminal law both make frequent recourse to standards of reasonableness, which depend for their concrete content on the social norms that regulate the behaviour in question. (Think of the implications for a negligence claim of an accident caused by driving on the left-hand side of the road when, by convention if not by virtue of legal requirement, the custom is to drive on the right.) Distinctions appropriate to descriptive analysis or categorization may have little relevance to practical reasoning of the kind necessary for lawyers, judges, and statesmen.

The Attorney-General must, by convention, maintain a scrupulous independence from his ministerial colleagues when deciding whether or not to authorize a prosecution, or to stop a prosecution by entering a *nolle prosequi*. Although he may seek their advice when a case may have important public policy implications, he remains responsible for making his own decision in exercise of an independent quasi-judicial function: 'It must be taken on the merits of the case, which may include political considerations in a wide sense but no consideration of party advantage.'[42] The courts are usually disinclined to interfere with the decision to commence a prosecution, wishing to maintain a clear separation of functions between judges and prosecutors; and in *Barton*, the High Court of Australia declined to review the Attorney-General's decision to file an information ('*ex officio* indictment'), refusing to consider a claim that the Attorney had acted on the instructions of the State Premier.[43] It was accepted, however, that the court could grant a *stay of proceedings*, once commenced, in

---

[38] Jaconelli, 'Do Constitutional Conventions Bind?', 153.

[39] Jaconelli, 'The Nature of Constitutional Convention', 26. Although Jaconelli's discussion is undeniably of great interest, his arguments for its practical significance seem somewhat contrived.

[40] See discussion above of *Attorney-General v Jonathan Cape* [1976] QB 752; Allan, *Law, Liberty, and Justice*, 244–5.

[41] Jaconelli, 'Do Constitutional Conventions Bind?', 160–1.

[42] Marshall, *Constitutional Conventions*, 113.

[43] *Barton v R* (1980) 32 ALR 449.

order to prevent an abuse of process and ensure a fair trial. And it is very doubtful whether a decision to prosecute someone, taken by the Attorney at the dictation of the Prime Minister or Cabinet, would be compatible with a fair trial.

Fairness is not simply a matter of impartial trial procedure based only on relevant and admissible evidence: earlier breaches of constitutional propriety, affecting the defendant's presence within the jurisdiction or the manner in which evidence against him has been obtained, may taint the subsequent trial. It is not only improper conduct that impinges directly on the conduct of the trial that may give rise to an abuse of process: any serious official malpractice undermines the moral authority of any verdict against the defendant.[44] In a case, for example, in which the defendant had been forcibly abducted abroad, in breach of proper extradition procedures, the House of Lords decided that the prosecution should be stayed as an abuse of process: by undermining the moral foundation for the state's pursuit of justice, the executive actions had tainted the intended trial.[45] There would therefore be good grounds for ordering a stay of proceedings which had been initiated in clear breach of convention; a defendant should not be treated as an enemy of the party in government, nor the process of criminal justice abused to punish a political opponent. The breach of convention, if established, would point to a violation of the rule of law, requiring appropriate judicial remedy.

The relationship between convention and law is complex, reflecting the context in point. The courts will usually protect a person's legitimate expectation, as regards the exercise of an official discretion, if in all the circumstances it would be unfair for a public authority to depart from an earlier promise or settled practice or established policy: only an overriding public interest will normally suffice to justify the failure to satisfy such an expectation, reasonably entertained. In the *GCHQ* case, for example, the House of Lords accepted that a settled practice or convention, which required consultation with civil servants before changes were made to their conditions of service, could limit the prerogative power to amend such conditions.[46] It would be unfair to remove trade union membership rights from a group of civil servants without previous consultation, in accordance with established practice; or at least that would be so unless an overriding public interest (such as that of national security) could be shown to justify the government's action. The wider constitutional canvas, however, is critical to the scope and application of legal doctrine. The quasi-judicial nature of the duties of the Government law officers, in particular, is bound to qualify the operation of the doctrine of legitimate expectations; and law and convention are again conceptually interdependent, equally informed by underlying principle.

Statements by government ministers, concerning their intentions or the future conduct of their officials, cannot constitute the basis of any legitimate expectation about future decisions of the Attorney-General or the Director of Public

---

[44] See Allan, *Constitutional Justice: A Liberal Theory of the Rule of Law* (Oxford: Oxford University Press, 2001), 81–4.

[45] *R v Horseferry Road Magistrates' Court, ex p Bennett* [1994] 1 AC 42.

[46] *Council of Civil Service Unions v Minister for the Civil Service* [1985] AC 374 (see Allan, *Law, Liberty and Justice*, 241–2).

Prosecutions, as regards the prosecution of offences. Precisely because the Attorney (or the Director) must exercise independent judgement, he cannot be bound by any statement made on behalf of the executive, and 'no reasonable person alert to his constitutional role could expect him to be so bound'.[47] If, however, the Attorney or Director has established a policy in respect of some special category of case, determining the appropriateness of prosecution in the public interest, it would be arbitrary and unfair to override that policy in any particular instance unless unusual circumstances obtained. That policy would be analogous, at least, to a constitutional convention, operating in substance to limit the scope of the relevant offence on (for example) general grounds of compassion or respect for personal autonomy. The House of Lords acknowledged the legitimacy of such constraints on the Director's discretion in *Purdy*, when it ordered him to publish the guidelines he followed in cases of assisted suicide.[48] Notwithstanding the unqualified sweep of the ban on assisting suicide in the Suicide Act 1961, section 2(1), convention or practice had, in effect, generated a closely circumscribed exception for cases that merited special treatment. Any departure from that convention, when the facts made it applicable, would plainly raise important questions of fairness and legality.[49]

The assimilation and interaction of law and convention is especially well illustrated, however, in another context. It would be hard to imagine a clearer example of a general principle being dependent on judicial support, when political pressure for conformity proves unavailing, than the principle of Canadian federalism. In seeking judicial affirmation of the relevant conventions, the governments of Manitoba, Newfoundland, and Quebec sought to establish that it would be an unconstitutional attack on federalism for the Canadian Constitution to be amended (at the behest of the federal government) in the teeth of provincial opposition.[50] It was intended that a joint resolution of the two Houses of the Canadian Parliament would, by means of an address to the Queen, request enactment of new legislation by the United Kingdom Parliament. As well as terminating residual British legal authority in Canada, the legislation would enact a charter of rights binding on both federal and provincial governments. On appeal from advisory opinions of the respective provincial Courts of Appeal, obtained under statutory provisions, a majority of the Canadian Supreme Court held that such a procedure would indeed be unconstitutional: convention required the federal authorities to obtain a 'substantial degree' of provincial consent to any scheme for constitutional amendment. Canadian federalism would plainly be undermined if the legislative powers of the provinces could be altered by unilateral action on the part of the federal authorities.

---

[47] *R v Director of Public Prosecutions, ex p Kebilene* [2000] 2 AC 326, 339 (Lord Bingham of Cornhill CJ).

[48] *R (Purdy) v Director of Public Prosecutions* [2009] UKHL 45.

[49] The Suicide Act 1961, s 2(4) requires the consent of the Director for the institution of proceedings. For further discussion, see Chapter 5, below. The Director's *Policy for Prosecutors in Respect of Cases of Encouraging or Assisting Suicide* was published (on the official Crown Prosecution Service website) in February 2010.

[50] *Reference re Amendment of the Constitution of Canada (Nos 1, 2 & 3)* (1982) 125 DLR (3d) 1.

Although that decision effectively compelled the federal government to secure provincial cooperation, the Supreme Court clung to the strict law-convention dichotomy, as a matter of legal form, denying that there was any legal impediment to what was proposed: 'What is desirable as a political limitation does not translate into a legal limitation, without expression in imperative constitutional text or statute.'[51] Although the federal principle might be relevant to the interpretation or application of the British North America Act 1867, which established the constitutional scheme, the court was unwilling to grant it independent legal standing as a constraint on governmental action. It followed that there was no legal barrier, in the court's opinion, to the procurement by resolution of what the constitution forbade the federal Parliament to attain by legislation. The federal division of powers could be undermined in breach of the scheme and spirit of both the 1867 Act and the Statute of Westminster 1931, which while conferring the power to repeal or amend United Kingdom statutes, in general, excluded any power of constitutional amendment.

As the joint dissenting judgment observed, the resolution procedure was an attempt by the federal Parliament to accomplish indirectly what it was legally precluded from doing directly, 'by perverting the recognized resolution method of obtaining constitutional amendments by the Imperial Parliament for an improper purpose'.[52] The view that such an abuse was unlawful seems the natural conclusion; and only an inability to grasp the interdependence of law and convention, in the context of a threat to a fundamental constitutional principle, could explain the majority's contrary view. How could the principle of Canadian federalism be a proper source of guidance in the interpretation of the 1867 Act if it did not enjoy legal status as a basic constitutional norm? Somewhat ironically, a majority of the court endorsed the assertion of Colin Munro that 'the validity of conventions cannot be the subject of proceedings in a court of law', quoting his view that 'the idea of a court enforcing a mere convention is so strange that the question hardly arises'.[53] These proceedings arguably refuted both propositions.[54]

Defending Dicey's claim that laws, but not conventions, were judicially enforced, Munro invokes H. L. A. Hart's conception of *law* as a system of primary and secondary rules.[55] Secondary rules of recognition, change, and adjudication provide for the authoritative identification and amendment of primary (duty-imposing) rules, and empower officials to determine whether such rules have been infringed. Whereas a legal label attaches to a rule as a result of its 'mode of creation', conventions are less easily identified:

There is no authoritative mark of their existence, so that uncertainty abounds.... The existence of a legal rule is shown by reference to a formal sign that it is of a *system*, but conventions have no system. The existence of a convention is tested, so far as it can be, by its individual

---

[51] Ibid, 29.

[52] Ibid, 77 (Martland J and Ritchie J).

[53] Colin R Munro, 'Laws and Conventions Distinguished' (1975) 91 LQR 218–35, at 228.

[54] The question of *justiciability* is considered below. For further analysis of this case, see Allan, *Law, Liberty, and Justice*, 246–53, and *Constitutional Justice*, 179–84.

[55] See H L A Hart, *The Concept of Law*, chs 5 and 6.

content—an inference has to be made according to the strength and purpose of the particular political practice involved.[56]

While Hart's theory might appear to confirm Munro's position in the case of *statute*, however, it gives very doubtful support as regards the distinction between convention and the *common law*. Even if formally enacted statutes carry the authoritative mark of their creation, as Munro supposes, the principles of common law are identified, instead, in much the same way as convention: an inference has to be made according to the strength and purpose of accepted practice, interpreted in the light of the requirements of justice or the public good. Common law rules do not possess an 'authoritative mark' of their 'creation': they are inferred or constructed from judicial precedent, which exemplifies the application of general principles to particular cases, tempering independent moral judgement with respect for settled understanding and established practice.

The Supreme Court rejected the suggestion of analogy between conventions and common law, insisting that the former were not 'judge-made rules'; but the idea that there are two distinct sets of rules, made by politicians and judges respectively, simply ignores the inevitable overlap and interdependence that results from the operation of general principle, which resists any rigid dichotomy between political morality and political practice. If the 'main purpose' of conventions is 'to ensure that the legal framework of the Constitution will be operated in accordance with the prevailing constitutional values or principles of the period', such as the 'democratic principle', there could not be any strict division between law and convention unless such values or principles were irrelevant to the content of law.[57] Even the idea that a convention might 'crystallize' into law, which the court considered and rejected, suggests that it must undergo a transformation; whereas a convention may remain largely a matter of political practice yet give shape, in appropriate circumstances, to the enforcement of legal principle. There is only a 'leap from convention to law' if we assume that one rule, detached from the reasons that justify it, is displaced by another, equally independent of any underlying reasons for compliance.[58]

The idea, moreover, that law and convention typically *conflict*, the latter limiting the exercise of broadly defined rights and powers, also assumes a clash of inconsistent *rules*. When the rules give way to an examination of principle, invoking the reasons behind the rules, an apparent conflict may often be satisfactorily resolved.[59] It is a

---

[56] Munro, 'Laws and Conventions Distinguished', 232–3.

[57] *Reference re Amendment of the Constitution of Canada (Nos 1, 2 & 3)* (1982) 125 DLR (3d) 1, 84.

[58] Ibid, 29. The 'paradoxical' nature of the Court's decision was noted by Kuldip Singh J in the Supreme Court of India, which held that conventions could in appropriate circumstances be judicially enforced: *Supreme Court Advocates-on-Record Association v Union of India* (1993) 2 SCC 441, 654. The President of India had no power to appoint senior judges without the approval of the Chief Justice: the convention underpinned judicial independence, which was itself a mainstay of liberty and democracy (see especially 646–9, 662–4).

[59] According to the Canadian Supreme Court, conventions were generally in conflict with legal rules that the courts were bound to enforce. For example, the Queen is legally entitled to refuse her assent to legislation, but convention obliges her to act otherwise. If, however, convention is here an expression of democratic principle the conflict dissolves: a bill that sought to dismantle democracy itself might properly elicit a veto reserved, in the modern constitution, for the gravest abuses of legislative power.

familiar feature of public law that powers, even if generously framed, must be exercised within the constraints of legality, which will in practice sharply curtail a public authority's discretion. Administrative practice may in some circumstances generate legitimate expectations, for example, obliging an authority to treat someone in its customary manner unless it has given due notice of a change of policy, or unless meeting such expectations would involve disproportionate damage to the public interest. An unrestricted prerogative power to amend the terms of employment of civil servants may, for instance, be modified by a settled tradition of prior negotiation, which can be legally enforced in the absence of cogent reasons for a departure from custom in the particular case.[60] Formally conflicting rules are brought into harmony through an elaboration of general principle, applied to the competing claims of the litigants as justice or fairness requires.

IV

Mark Elliott acknowledges the difficulty of maintaining a clear separation between law and convention when both embody constitutional principles, which may play an important role, in particular, in the interpretation of statutes.[61] He notes that the development of conventions is likely to underpin the success of arrangements for the devolution of power from Westminster, and may in practice curtail Parliament's ability to override the European Convention rights given domestic legal status by the Human Rights Act 1998. For example, the Sewel Convention, affirmed by a Memorandum of Understanding, expresses the principle that the United Kingdom Parliament should not normally legislate for Scotland, within the area of devolved powers, without the consent of the Scottish Parliament; such understandings may evolve into firm conventions affecting not only legislative practice but, ultimately, the limits of legislative power.[62] We may further anticipate that Parliament will seek to avoid any action in breach of the European Convention, loyally amending statutes which the courts have declared incompatible with it. A theory of absolute parliamentary sovereignty that, without a heavy overlay of convention, bears little relationship to practical affairs, is due for reappraisal: the gap between constitutional theory and 'political reality' becomes too wide.

N.W. Barber interprets Elliott's argument as 'a call to the courts to render some conventions legally binding' even though they have no legal power to do so: 'it is a call for juridification through bare-faced judicial *fiat*'.[63] He observes that judges 'often have more power to change the law than the legal system accords them', especially in times of crisis (such as when a court may have to adjudicate

---

[60] *GCHQ* case, above.

[61] Mark Elliott, 'Parliamentary Sovereignty and the New Constitutional Order: Legislative Freedom, Political Reality and Convention' (2002) 22 LS 340–76.

[62] The Scotland Act 1998, s 28(7) formally preserves the power of the United Kingdom Parliament to make laws for Scotland even within the sphere of devolved powers (which extends to all matters except those over which competence is explicitly withheld).

[63] Barber, *The Constitutional State*, 93.

on the 'legality' of a revolution). Barber even suggests that *Factortame*, in which a convention governing the relationship between English and European Community (Union) law was given legal effect, was an instance of extra-legal— yet legitimate—judicial power.[64] Sir William Wade had described that decision, in which the House of Lords held that an Act of Parliament could not be applied in breach of Community law, as 'revolutionary', allowing us to conclude that the court acted beyond its strict legal powers while remaining, nonetheless, 'within its constitutional powers in limiting Parliament's law-making capacity'.[65]

Now we can be quite confident that Elliott would disavow that interpretation of his argument. He specifically rejects Wade's conception of sovereignty as simply 'a matter of political fact', unchanging unless by revolution, as 'normatively barren'; and he denies that recognition of directly effective European Community law, limiting Parliament's competence, was a judicial *imposition* rather than a response to the changing constitutional landscape.[66] Elliott has nevertheless invited Barber's interpretation by his resolutely external perspective, pointing to a gulf between theory and practice which he anticipates may prove unsustainable. His critique is detached from his own judgements of legal and political principle, just as Barber's account of law is detached from any normative theory of law or constitutionalism: it identifies what is wrong with the prevailing orthodoxy but leaves it to others to lead the heralded rebellion (Laws LJ being in the vanguard).[67] Although critical of the notion of sovereignty as 'political fact', Elliott's position is only marginally and subtly different: the judicial consensus on which Wade's theory depends is displaced by a broader consensus among all senior officials.[68] He is right, of course, to emphasize the significance of shared practice; but the legal interpreter cannot merely predict or record it: he must defend a specific account of that practice that is likely, at least at the level of detail, to provoke debate and controversy.

Since judges are obliged to respect the rule of law they must justify their decisions by reference to existing legal principles, identified and illuminated by common law precedent. To act beyond the bounds of the constitution is to renounce the judicial office; it means repudiating one constitution in favour of another, usually at a time of major political upheaval. If there is an eligible interpretation of legislative supremacy that accommodates the primacy of European law, as *Factortame* affirms, it is because that doctrine is sensitive to constitutional principle: it is not simply a matter of official consensus, detached from any inquiry into the reasons that might *justify* such a qualification of domestic legislative authority. Constitutional

---

[64] *R v Secretary of State for Transport, ex p Factortame (No 2)* [1991] 1 AC 603.

[65] Barber, *The Constitutional State*, 94–5; Sir William Wade, 'Sovereignty—Revolution or Evolution?' (1996) 112 LQR 568–75.

[66] Elliott, 'Parliamentary Sovereignty and the New Constitutional Order', 367, 371 (n 142). See also Mark Elliott, 'Embracing "Constitutional" Legislation: Towards Fundamental Law?' (2003) 54 NILQ 25–42, especially 35–40.

[67] Ibid, 368–70 (reviewing Laws LJ's judgment in *Thoburn v Sunderland City Council* [2002] EWHC 195, considered in Chapter 4, below).

[68] Elliott cites Jeffrey Goldsworthy's account of the 'secondary rules' of the legal system, dependent on consensus among senior officials: see Goldsworthy, *The Sovereignty of Parliament: History and Philosophy* (Oxford: Clarendon Press, 1999), 240–1.

theory must be an *account* of 'political reality', in the sense that it should explain the legal consequences of political change: it must exhibit the moral basis on which political change has been accepted as legitimate. In a common law legal order, legislative authority is the product of an arrangement of rights, powers, and duties that embodies a theory of legitimate government; and the constitutional scheme develops in tune with an evolving political morality—one which today embraces features of liberal democracy too deeply entrenched to permit abrogation by a temporary legislative majority. The gulf between the legal and political constitutions—between Elliott's legal theory and 'political reality'—is the disjunction between two descriptive accounts, *external* to the ordinary process of legal interpretation. From an appropriately internal perspective, faithful to both the rule of law and democratic principle, the gulf disappears: the content of public law depends as much on political morality, correctly understood, as on the commands or opinions of those best placed to wield political power.

Elliott draws our attention to the way in which principles of construction, protecting fundamental rights against inadvertent or unnecessary interference, have been justified by reference to reasonable expectations about legislative and governmental intentions: the courts presume that Parliament would not enact, nor the executive promote, legislation contrary to basic constitutional values.[69] Constitutional convention affords an appropriate basis for the identification of limits on legislative supremacy for similar reasons: the relevant limits can be understood as deriving from the constitutional order itself, as opposed to any 'unilateral imposition, by the judiciary, of its own moral preferences'.[70] But he does not draw the natural conclusion, which is that legislative supremacy is already qualified by a style of judicial interpretation inimical to any infringement of fundamental rights—an approach demanded by adherence to the rule of law, reflecting basic values of liberty and equality. Geoffrey Marshall observes that the rule of law gives rise to what he terms the 'most obvious and undisputed convention' of British government, that 'Parliament does not use its unlimited sovereign power in an oppressive or tyrannical way'.[71] When that convention is given legal force through appropriate presumptions of legislative intent, the *formal* principle of absolute power has been displaced, for all practical purposes, by a far more subtle and discriminating constitutional *substance*.

Barber denies that judicially recognized conventions need to be equated with legal principles, protesting that judges 'recognize and indicate approval of lots of rules which are not, ordinarily, considered laws'.[72] He instances the 'hand-written rules taped to a municipal lawn-mover'. He cannot see the distinction between constitutional principles, manifested in accepted political practice, and rules for lawn-mowers because he stands outside the practice he surveys: stripped of any connection with the basic legal values of liberty and equality, all kinds of rules possess much the same character. For Barber, conventions can become laws only

---

[69] Elliott, 'Parliamentary Sovereignty and the New Constitutional Order', 365.
[70] Ibid, 375.
[71] Marshall, *Constitutional Conventions*, 8.
[72] Barber, *The Constitutional State*, 92.

through a sort of quasi-constitutional usurpation by the judiciary, or else by a process of formalization, illustrated by the incorporation of aspects of ministerial responsibility into the published Ministerial Code.[73] From an internal perspective, however, of the kind appropriate for the judge or lawyer or conscientious politician, convention has force only when it has a justifiable basis in political morality; and that force does not disappear when convention has some relevance to a legal question calling for judicial resolution.

The interaction of law and convention is illuminated by a recent case arising out of current arrangements for devolved government. In *Robinson*, a question arose about the legality of an election of the First Minister and deputy First Minister of the Northern Ireland Assembly, which had taken place after the expiry of the six week period specified by the Northern Ireland Act 1998, section 16.[74] Although a dissenting minority of judges in the House of Lords held that there was no power of election outside the strict terms of the Act, emphasizing the limited status of the Assembly as a creature of statute, the majority took a more nuanced view, placing the statutory instructions within their broader constitutional context. There was plainly a real danger that tentative steps towards devolved government, based on the Belfast Agreement between representatives of rival unionist and nationalist communities, might be frustrated by an overly rigid interpretation; there was good reason to encourage an election of ministers once the necessary cross-party agreement had been obtained, notwithstanding the Secretary of State's duty to propose a date for dissolution once the statutory six-week period had expired. Slavish adherence to the literal terms of the statute was eschewed in favour of an approach that evoked the flexibility enjoyed by the executive under ordinary British constitutional practice. The matter of whether and when to seek a dissolution was left to the judgement of political leaders: 'Where constitutional arrangements retain scope for the exercise of political judgement they permit a flexible response to differing and unpredictable events in a way which the application of strict rules would preclude.'[75]

By treating the Act as assuming, by way of political background, a general power of election of ministers—whether within or outside the six-week period—it was possible to allow the Secretary of State a discretion to delay his proposal for a dissolution date when discussions or negotiations seemed likely to produce a successful outcome.[76] Pursuing the analogy with Westminster, Lord Hoffmann observed that, while the Secretary of State must propose a date for a poll for the election of a new Assembly (under section 32), he could not be compelled to advise the Queen to make an Order in Council dissolving the Assembly, which is traditionally treated as a matter of royal prerogative, governed by convention:

It is for the Secretary of State to advise Her Majesty to make the Order in Council and there is nothing in the Act which obliges the Secretary of State... to give such advice. Such

---

[73] Ibid, 98–103.

[74] *Robinson v Secretary of State for Northern Ireland* [2002] UKHL 32.

[75] Ibid, para 12 (Lord Bingham of Cornhill).

[76] Lord Millett thought it 'would subvert the purpose of the Act if the Secretary of State were obliged to take steps to dissolve an Assembly which had succeeded in electing a First Minister and deputy First Minister in order to obtain a new Assembly which might not be able to do so' (ibid, para 91).

a discretion is inconsistent with a scheme under which an immediate election becomes mandatory after the six weeks has expired.... There would be deadlock under which the Secretary of State could not be compelled to hold an election but the Assembly, even if able to do so, could not validly elect a First and Deputy First Minister.[77]

In invoking the analogy with British constitutional practice governing dissolution, Lord Hoffmann rightly treats convention as a legitimate source of guidance to the correct meaning of the Act: the literal statutory instructions are adapted to the scheme that best satisfies the requirements of political morality, as the court understands them. Legislative supremacy is honoured by constructive interpretation, making constitutional practice part of the context, and hence content, of specific statutory provisions.[78]

Jaconelli quickly dismisses Elliott's suggestion that convention might spawn limits to parliamentary sovereignty. Why, he asks, should the idea that convention might crystallize into law apply only to limits on sovereignty? And if it were to apply more generally, 'it would raise the problem of identifying those conventions which are genuinely constitutional and those which are not'.[79] Nor could Jaconelli 'envisage a constitutional convention which would be apt for judicial enforcement'. All these pseudo-problems arise, however, on the back of an assumption that, since law and convention are like chalk and cheese, some strange alchemy must operate to amalgamate them. When we acknowledge that law and convention reflect both principle and practice, according to the circumstances, we can recognize that a legal principle may be affirmed as such, and given concrete specification, by reference to well-established practice. As Elliott indicates, judges thereby discern the implications of their own jurisdictional arrangements rather than (as it might otherwise appear) imposing their own political preferences. Whether or not it is appropriate to draw on conventional practice in this way must depend on the nature of the legal claim, and the context in which it arises; it will not depend on questions of general classification of the sort that interest Jaconelli.

The analogy that Jaconelli draws here between convention and prerogative is also instructive. He suggests that Elliott's argument proceeds by analogy with recent judicial treatment of the royal prerogative:

From a situation where all prerogative powers were placed beyond judicial control the courts have moved to a position in which only those touching on matters of high policy will continue to be treated in this way. Those, by contrast, which involve matters of little political moment will now be subject to judicial review. By the same token, many constitutional conventions admittedly involve matters which would be regarded as not justiciable. The remainder, by implication, could in time become ripe for judicial enforcement.[80]

For purposes of descriptive analysis, at a suitably abstract level of description, the distinction between matters of 'high policy' and those of small 'political moment'

---

[77] Ibid, para 31.
[78] *Robinson* is further considered in Chapter 5, below.
[79] Jaconelli, 'Do Constitutional Conventions Bind?', 162.
[80] Ibid.

is perhaps acceptable; but if transplanted to the sphere of practical legal reasoning it would badly distort our grasp of the common law. The notion that prerogative powers could be neatly divided into two separate categories ignores the fact that justiciability is always a function of context and circumstance. Even the Home Secretary's grant or denial of a pardon, or the Foreign Secretary's grant or denial of a passport, can give rise to political controversy in particular cases. And questions relating to the making or execution of international treaties, or regulation of the armed forces, if not the permissibility of engaging in military conflict, may become justiciable in certain circumstances.[81] When the scope of legal rights, duties, or powers is called into question, in particular instances, questions of broad doctrinal or descriptive classification are as likely to obscure, as to illuminate, the questions of moral and constitutional principle on which sound legal judgement ultimately rests.[82]

V

Insofar as they have any practical significance, attempts to separate law from convention should be understood as efforts to limit the judicial role—excluding 'political questions' from the scope of constitutional adjudication. The underlying idea is to forge a division between the (so-called) legal and political constitutions, inhibiting judicial interference in a sphere of policy-making better reserved for politicians. It is reminiscent of the stance of the dissenting judges in the *Fire Brigades Union* case, who considered that any breach of a minister's duty to bring statutory provisions into force within a reasonable period lay beyond judicial concern.[83] The Criminal Justice Act 1988 authorized the minister to appoint a day, 'by order made by statutory instrument', for the commencement of new statutory arrangements for compensating the victims of violent crime. The minister, however, had chosen instead to substitute a modified (and less generous) version of an

---

[81] See *Laker Airways Ltd v Dept of Trade* [1977] QB 643; *R v Ministry of Defence, ex p Smith* [1996] QB 517. See also *R (Bancoult) v Secretary of State for Foreign and Commonwealth Affairs (No 2)* [2007] EWCA Civ 498, para 46 (Sedley LJ).

[82] The sphere of administrative 'quasi-legislation' or 'soft law' created by the concordats between the United Kingdom Government and the devolved administrations in Scotland, Wales, and Northern Ireland may give rise to legal disputes, in which constitutional principle would reflect (be partly constituted by) administrative practice and understanding. There is plainly an analogy with constitutional convention. Richard Rawlings notes that a breach of the provisions of a concordat may lead to challenge via ordinary principles of judicial review; the doctrine of legitimate expectation would be particularly relevant: see Richard Rawlings, 'Concordats of the Constitution' (2000) 116 LQR 257–86, at 282–4. The (formally non-legal) concordat provisions would have to be interpreted in their proper political and administrative context: the law and political practice would be intertwined and interdependent. As Rawlings remarks of the principal agreement, setting out general principles of cooperation, or comity, 'Locked in the Memorandum of Understanding, and waiting to escape, is a fundamental constitutional principle' (ibid, 267).

[83] An analogy with the American 'political questions' doctrine is drawn in Eric Barendt, 'Constitutional Law and the Criminal Injuries Compensation Scheme' [1995] PL 357–66, at 365.

existing *ex gratia* governmental scheme.[84] While a majority of the House of Lords held that this amounted to unconstitutional conduct, overriding the statute, Lord Mustill thought that such 'essentially political and administrative judgements' were not properly justiciable.[85] Lord Keith of Kinkel also condemned what he considered to be 'an unwarrantable intrusion by the court into the political field and a usurpation of the function of Parliament', whose task it was to hold the minister to account for his actions.[86]

It may well be that the balance of argument on all the facts of the case lay with the dissenting minority.[87] Parliament had not stipulated that the relevant provisions should be brought into force on any particular day (or within any specified period), and even though the minister had expressed an intention to leave them dormant, he (or a successor) could always change his mind: his conduct might generously have been interpreted as a *postponement*, awaiting improved economic conditions. (The court agreed that financial or economic circumstances could justify the minister's continuing delay in bringing the statutory provisions into force.) Nevertheless, the majority was right to resist the notion that the sort of executive action involved was inherently non-justiciable. There is no such thing as an 'essentially political and administrative judgement', conceived independently of all the circumstances: whether or not there are legal limits, curtailing the scope of discretionary governmental power, is a matter dependent on close analysis, focused on the actual use (or disuse) of the power under scrutiny and its consequences for those affected. The victims of violent crime had rights in public law, if not in private law, arising from the existing scheme for *ex gratia* compensation; and there were clearly pertinent questions about the effect on those rights of the minister's actions.[88] Treating the whole matter as non-justiciable, in the manner of the dissenting judges, simply disregards such rights without the detailed analysis they deserve.

Blunt-edged justiciability doctrines, which remove areas of executive power from judicial scrutiny regardless of the consequences for those affected, are inimical to the rule of law. Considerations of legality are suppressed in favour of political accountability, which depends on whether sufficient interest can be aroused to make suitable space in a crowded parliamentary timetable. Certain sorts of complainant, in the relevant fields, are deprived of access to the courts for the vindication of their rights—or the correction of wrongs—without any inquiry into whether, in all the circumstances, an exclusive reliance on political or administrative remedies is consonant with justice. Earlier restrictions on judicial review of the exercise of prerogative powers were removed for precisely this reason; it was acknowledged that the royal prerogative, like powers delegated by statute, could be abused in circumstances

---

[84] The non-statutory compensation scheme was regarded as having been established under the royal prerogative, though it was arguably only a governmental version of the kind of charitable scheme that did not depend on the exercise of the special powers of the Crown.

[85] *R v Secretary of State for the Home Dept, ex p Fire Brigades Union* [1995] 2 AC 513, 563.

[86] Ibid, 546.

[87] For further discussion, see Allan, *Constitutional Justice*, 167–73.

[88] The legislation, when implemented, gave statutory force to the original *ex gratia* scheme: see Lord Browne-Wilkinson, [1995] 2 AC 513, 552–3.

where the courts could and should afford a remedy.[89] Admittedly, the House of Lords sought to divide the prerogative between justiciable and non-justiciable powers, on the basis that certain powers were inherently unsuited to judicial oversight; but the case-by-case development of the common law has gradually whittled away such artificial barriers to scrutiny.

Until recently, a ministerial exercise of the prerogative of mercy, in deciding whether or not to pardon a convicted offender, was treated as non-justiciable: it was supposedly the assertion of a wholly unregulated personal discretion, beyond the limits of judicial scrutiny.[90] In *Lewis v Attorney-General of Jamaica*, however, the Judicial Committee of the Privy Council upheld the right of a convicted murderer to natural justice in relation to his plea for mercy.[91] The Governor-General of Jamaica, who could set aside the sentence of execution, was advised by a committee (the 'Jamaican Privy Council') required by the Constitution to consider the trial judge's report and such other information as the Governor-General might require to be provided. It was held that the offender was entitled to see the material placed before the advisory committee and to make any representations he wished; a dismissal of the plea for mercy would otherwise be invalid. It was rightly—if belatedly—recognized, that non-justiciable, arbitrary powers are inconsistent with the rule of law: a power to pardon an offender, or commute a death sentence, must be exercised fairly and impartially, according to criteria consistently applied to all those who may appeal for clemency. The English High Court, also resisting earlier Privy Council authority, had recognized that the court could intervene to correct an abuse of discretion: a refusal to pardon an offender on an irrational and discriminatory basis—on grounds, for example, of 'sex, race or religion'—would be unlawful.[92]

A power that had once been subject only to very weak political accountability, if any, was now fully governed by legal and constitutional principle.[93] And insofar as there are constitutional conventions governing exercise of the prerogative of mercy, justiciability may be a necessary consequence of judicial efforts to defend legality. The relevant conventions, developed by statesmen to ensure fairness and

---

[89] See *Council of Civil Service Unions v Minister for the Civil Service* [1985] AC 374.

[90] *de Freitas v Benny* [1976] AC 239; the Privy Council (on an appeal from Trinidad and Tobago) held that in tendering his advice to the Queen, the Home Secretary (in Britain) performed 'the exemplar of a purely administrative act', by contrast with the exercise of a quasi-judicial function (ibid, 247).

[91] *Lewis v Attorney-General of Jamaica* [2000] 2 AC 50.

[92] *R v Secretary of State for the Home Dept, ex p Bentley* [1994] QB 349, 363; Allan, *Constitutional Justice*, 175–6.

[93] B V Harris, while welcoming *Lewis*, rejects the concept of 'primary' in favour of 'secondary' justiciability, requiring determination of the justiciability of particular executive decisions on the basis of the relevant circumstances and the pertinent grounds of review: B V Harris, 'Judicial Review, Justiciability and the Prerogative of Mercy' [2003] CLJ 631–60. It is not clear, however, why the various indicia of justiciability suggested do not, when applied to a particular decision, simply duplicate the ordinary process of determining legality; the suspicion must be that such various 'considerations' describe from an external viewpoint what, from an internal judicial perspective, would be factors relevant to the precise nature and scope of review in all the circumstances (see further Chapter 7, below).

impartiality, have therefore acquired a truly legal significance: they enable the demands of the rule of law to be applied to the specific administrative context. The convention that the prerogative of mercy is exercised on behalf of the Queen by the Home Secretary alone, rather than by the Cabinet on behalf of the government as a whole, reflects its special nature as an element of the administration of criminal justice. The Home Secretary must exercise an independent, quasi-judicial judgement, free from political pressure or influence; it would normally be thought improper for him even to consult his ministerial colleagues, let alone accept their instructions. A disappointed applicant for clemency who could show that there had been such a departure from accepted practice would have a strong case for judicial review; he is entitled to the same standards of administrative fairness as are enjoyed by other convicted offenders, under similar circumstances. Constitutional convention is of direct, not merely indirect, importance: law and convention are inextricably linked. Justice or fairness is, at least in part, defined by adherence to good practice, which should be followed consistently. In enforcing compliance with convention, by quashing a decision contaminated by improper influence, the court would be preserving an equality of procedural justice—maintaining the rule of law as the context requires it to be observed.

The Canadian Supreme Court's firm response to a plea of non-justiciability, in the *Amendment* reference, confirmed the implausibility of its own dogmatic distinction between law and convention.[94] In repudiating a claim by the federal authorities that the existence or otherwise of the relevant convention was a political matter, unsuited to judicial determination, the Court acknowledged its responsibility to decide an important matter of constitutional propriety. It could not evade determination of a 'fundamental issue of constitutionality and legitimacy', even if it were not one of 'pure legality'.[95] By pronouncing on convention the Court made it impossible (as a matter of realistic politics, at least) for the federal authorities to proceed with constitutional change in opposition to the will of most of the Canadian provinces. The Court's claim, therefore, that it was not asked to enforce a convention, but merely to recognize its existence was, in context, somewhat fanciful. It was sufficient, for any practical purpose, to condemn the proposed procedure as an unconstitutional breach of convention. Questions of constitutionality and legitimacy plainly transcend any formal distinction between law and convention. Whether or not convention demands judicial protection (whether 'recognition' or 'enforcement') is itself a question of legality, whose answer depends on all the circumstances.

VI

I have argued that the distinction between law and convention, though a familiar feature of standard accounts of the British constitution, has very limited relevance

---

[94] *Reference re Amendment of the Constitution of Canada (Nos 1, 2 & 3)* (1982) 125 DLR (3d) 1 (considered above).

[95] Ibid, 88.

to adjudication or appraisal of the legality of governmental action. The distinction reflects an external, descriptive stance, being made for reasons of convenient exposition: while the law consists of statutes and judicially created rules, the conduct of politics is governed by weaker customs and practices fashioned by politicians, dependent on political pressure as a means of enforcement. From an internal viewpoint, characteristic of judge or lawyer asked to determine the legality of a specific action or decision, that distinction is quite unhelpful. Convention and practice may form an important part of the context in which a question of law must be addressed: it may help identify applicable general principles, showing how abstract ideas of good governance are given sharper definition and precise understanding in particular, concrete circumstances. Questions of legality and constitutionality are normative questions: they are determined by reflection on principles of justice or fairness or propriety that call for sophisticated moral judgement, not the classification or categorization of empirical phenomena.

If lawyers are nonetheless drawn to the law-convention dichotomy, employing it in their legal reasoning, it must be chiefly because they treat the law as simply the product of specific sources in the manner characteristic of legal positivism. If the law is to be found in the rules prescribed by statute or laid down by judges in exercise of a discretion to make law in the gaps between existing rules, it need have no systematic connection with convention. Conventions are made by politicians or statesmen, by contrast with the common law, which is made by judges; and so, it seems to follow, courts must take a convention as they find it. Convention consists in whatever a majority of statesmen, or perhaps only a majority of the wisest and most experienced statesmen, take it to require. I have been trying to show why that approach is quite unsound. Neither common law nor convention is made, whether by judges or politicians, as an act of will: each is a *construction of reason*, based on argument about the requirements of justice and good governance in particular instances. Just as a court finds the common law by exploring the principles that best explain and justify the most important precedents, seeking to extend the implications of those principles to novel circumstances, so an actor on the political scene behaves likewise: she attempts to comply with convention according to the reasons, as she perceives them, which identify correct behaviour in the circumstances arising. She is obliged to interpret an unfolding practice, whose character her own conduct may help to mould. Practice and principle march hand-in-hand.

And when matters of convention are raised in court, the judge becomes a political actor for the limited purposes of that case. Like Lord Widgery in the Crossman Diaries case, he must form his own view about the existence and demands of the alleged convention as a necessary step to legal judgement.[96] He cannot determine what, if anything, a convention requires until he obtains a grasp of its rationale, which must then be placed in the broader context of legal and political principle. If the convention is relevant to legal questions arising, it is relevant only insofar as it really does require or justify what the litigant who invokes it claims; and the judge must therefore make up his own mind. He defers not to politicians' assumptions

---

[96] *Attorney-General v Jonathan Cape* [1976] QB 752, considered above.

or assertions about the demands of convention, but to the reasons they can offer to support those demands—reasons the judge can weigh against any contrary reasons that may apply in all the circumstances. He cannot apply a normative standard without normative *judgement*. Determining its relevance and weight, on the facts in view, entails the characteristic internal attitude: it requires endorsement of that standard as *appropriate*, having regard to the balance of reasons in play.

As we have seen, from an external, detached perspective, law and convention can conflict: the law may authorize conduct that constitutional convention pro-scribes (as the Canadian Supreme Court observed).[97] And this observation may encourage a positivist approach, separating out competing sources of legal and moral or political judgement. Admittedly, a legal positivist may be willing to countenance judicial resort to general moral principles, provided that the nec-essary conditions are met—those specified by a 'rule of recognition' of sources of law accepted by officials.[98] But if it is controversial whether conventions are a source of law—whether the principles they embody or assume have any legal relevance—there is not the official consensus that the rule of recognition requires. So a positivist judge or lawyer may be forced to accept the distinction between law and convention that the textbooks affirm. She must struggle to separate legal rules and principles from their conventional counterparts, even if that means drawing legal conclusions that make little sense in terms of general constitutional theory (as the Canadian Supreme Court's judgment made little sense in the context of Canadian federalism).

A similar misguided philosophy underlies a good deal of the efforts of many legal and political theorists to limit the judicial domain, whether by endorsing restrictive theories of justiciability or by defending narrow, largely formal conceptions of the rule of law. Boundaries and distinctions that serve primarily descriptive purposes are pressed into the service of constitutional theory, where they obscure more than they reveal. At its most extreme, the opponent of judicial review in defence of legal and constitutional rights denies that the constitution has any normative content at all, being 'no more and no less than what happens'.[99] On that view, the constitution is simply a matter of empirical fact and the detached description of events is all that is available: 'Everything that happens is constitutional. And if nothing happened that would be constitutional also.' J. A. G. Griffith's adherence to legal positivism entailed the denial that 'the concept of law is a moral concept' and the belief that 'laws are merely statements of a power relationship and nothing more'. From that perspective, the judicial defence of individual rights or constitutional principle could only amount to an illegitimate intrusion into a political struggle for power:

I am arguing then for a highly positivist view of the constitution; of recognizing that Ministers and others in high positions of authority are men and women who happen to exercise political power but without any such right to that power which could give them a

---

[97] *Reference re Amendment of the Constitution of Canada (Nos 1, 2 & 3)* (1982) 125 DLR (3d) 1, considered above.

[98] See H L A Hart, *The Concept of Law*, 100–10.

[99] J A G Griffith, 'The Political Constitution' (1979) 42 MLR 1–21, at 19.

superior moral position; that laws made by those in authority derive validity from no other fact or principle, and so impose no moral obligation of obedience on others; that so-called individual or human rights are no more and no less than political claims made by individuals on those in authority; that a society is endemically in a state of conflict between warring interest groups, having no consensus or unifying principles sufficiently precise to be the basis of a theory of legislation.[100]

Understood as merely a detached description of British politics, external to the concerns of judges or statesmen committed to the cause of justice or the common good, Griffith's assertions can be ignored as irrelevant to normative constitutional theory. Reading between the lines, however, we can see that a moral and political stance is masquerading as a statement of empirical fact: naked political struggle is being celebrated as superior to a form of governance based on fundamental moral principles, enforced by courts. The fear is that adoption (for example) of a bill of rights must inevitably 'pass political decisions out of the hands of politicians and into the hands of judges'; to require 'a supreme court to make certain kinds of political decisions does not make those decisions any less political'. So Griffith advocates a 'political constitution' in preference to one that would leave important decisions of principle to courts: he doubts either the objective standing of such principles or the courts' ability to discern their content.[101]

Adam Tomkins is also suspicious of judicial review, apparently regarding a strong judicial role in defence of the constitution as inimical to the British tradition of democratic decision-making. He identifies a 'shift from the political to the legal constitution', which reflects a widespread view that the former has 'broken down'.[102] A Parliament dominated by the political parties has lost the independence from the Government necessary to hold ministers to account, obliging the courts to intervene instead to remedy abuses of power. Tomkins would prefer a reinvigorated Parliament, better able to monitor and criticize Government decisions; and he applauds Lord Mustill's dissenting speech in the *Fire Brigades Union* case, questioning the need for judicial interference in a matter concerning the relationship between Parliament and the executive.[103] Tomkins seeks to bolster his defence of the political constitution by explicit reference to the republican values furthered by government according to the wishes of elected representatives: he is anxious to plug the normative gap left by Griffith's superficially descriptive method.[104]

It is very doubtful, however, whether such attempts to limit the judicial role are either desirable or feasible, or even whether the notion of a competition between the legal and political constitutions makes much sense. Insofar as the legal constitution acknowledges the legislative supremacy of Parliament, and

---

[100] Ibid.

[101] See also J A G Griffith, 'The Common Law and the Political Constitution' (2001) 117 LQR 42–67. For similar doubts about Griffith's alleged 'descriptivism', see Graham Gee and Gregoire C N Webber, 'What Is a Political Constitution?' (2010) 30 OJLS 273–99, at 276–81.

[102] Adam Tomkins, *Public Law* (Oxford: Oxford University Press, 2003), 24.

[103] *R v Secretary of State for the Home Dept, ex p Fire Brigades Union* [1995] 2 AC 513, considered above.

[104] Adam Tomkins, *Our Republican Constitution* (Oxford: Hart Publishing, 2005), 37: 'When it came to discussing constitutional questions, Griffith only ever described—he never prescribed.'

enforces (by judicial review) a strict separation of powers between Parliament and Government, it assumes and affirms the 'political constitution'.[105] Its conception of equal citizenship underpins both parliamentary democracy and the rule of law.[106]

Moreover, we should challenge Tomkins's complaint that the majority judges in *Fire Brigades Union* disguised the constitutional significance of the case by framing their speeches as if it 'were merely a straightforward and uncontroversial case of statutory interpretation (a traditional judicial task)'.[107] Lord Browne-Wilkinson considered the case to raise the question of whether 'at the present day, prerogative powers could be validly exercised by the executive so as to frustrate the will of Parliament expressed in a statute'; and Lord Lloyd of Berwick thought it would come as a 'surprise to the man on the Clapham omnibus that legislative provisions in an Act of Parliament...can be set aside...by a member of the executive'.[108] And in resisting the suggestion that Parliament did not intend to confer on the courts any power to judge the legality of the minister's conduct, Lloyd rightly rejected the artificiality of any such speculations about 'intention': if a minister had acted unlawfully, in excess of his statutory powers, it was the court's 'ordinary function' to grant an appropriate remedy. It was that ordinary function that sustained the constitutional balance of powers.

Once again, distinctions or categories that might play a largely descriptive role serve only to generate confusion in the context of analysis. It is simply fallacious to suppose that there is any important distinction between ordinary cases of statutory interpretation, on one hand, and cases of constitutional dimension, on the other. All cases of interpretation involve complex judgements of constitutional propriety; these provide the basis and context for resolving disputed questions of meaning. Parliament 'intends' whatever the best interpretation, most faithful to the relevant constitutional values, indicates.[109] The proper division of authority between the courts and other branches of government is ascertained by study of the legal questions arising on the facts in issue: it is not a matter that can be determined a priori on the basis of a general preference for political rather than legal resolution (or vice versa). There are no helpful distinctions between constitutional law and administrative law, or between cases about common law principle and cases about statutory meaning—any more than between constitutional law and constitutional convention.[110] All these matters are, from an interpretative perspective, integral

---

[105] Compare Tom R Hickman, 'In Defence of the Legal Constitution' (2005) 55 UTLJ 981–1022, at 1017–19, noting that the effect of the *Fire Brigades Union* case was 'to *supplement*, not supplant, the political constitution', making it necessary for the Secretary of State to return to Parliament to enact his preferred scheme.

[106] The role of the court in defence of the 'political' constitution and in defence of traditional civil liberties is, however, recognized and affirmed in Adam Tomkins, 'The Role of the Courts in the Political Constitution' (2010) 60 UTLJ 1–22.

[107] Tomkins, *Public Law*, 28.

[108] [1995] 2 AC 513, 552 (Browne-Wilkinson), 568 (Lloyd).

[109] See Chapter 5, below, for fuller argument.

[110] Eric Barendt also drew a questionable distinction between constitutional and administrative law in his discussion of the case: see Barendt, 'Constitutional Law and the Criminal Injuries Compensation Scheme' [1995] PL 357–66.

features of a seamless garment. Justiciability is itself a function of legal principle: a matter is justiciable insofar as questions arise about the legality of governmental action; and if we think the courts should loyally accept an executive decision, it is because it falls, on correct analysis, within the scope of a lawfully bounded discretion.[111]

Tomkins draws a similar distinction between minor administrative law and major constitutional law questions in his critique of *Simms*, a case in which the House of Lords held that the Prison Act gave no authority for the making of prison rules that would prohibit all interviews of prisoners by journalists, or allow them only on unreasonable terms.[112] Since such interviews were sometimes necessary to assist a journalist's investigation into the reliability of a prisoner's conviction, they should not be routinely banned. If a prisoner was alleged to be the victim of a miscarriage of justice, there would need to be a strong case, based on the needs of prison discipline and management, to justify such an interference with the interests of free speech and criminal justice. According to Tomkins, a 'big question' about prisoners' freedom of expression was reduced by lawyers to a 'far narrower' one about the legality of the restrictions placed by a prison governor on interviews with journalists.[113] But this is plainly a false antithesis. Since every question about constitutional rights arises within the context of an existing legal order, composed of interrelated requirements of statute and common law, it cannot be assigned exclusively to either courts or legislature. Particular cases can only be determined by courts, drawing on constitutional principle to clarify and supplement existing rules. And the more narrowly the court adheres to the facts of the case, giving due weight to the competing considerations directly in view, the weaker the objection that, in exercising jurisdiction, it is somehow usurping a political judgement better left to elected officials.[114]

The breadth or depth of the court's inquiry into general principle must be dictated by the nature of the specific issue arising. In *ProLife Alliance*, considered in Chapter 1, the House of Lords neglected the broader constitutional implications of a challenge to the legality of a ban on the transmission of a party election broadcast.[115] Tomkins objects that in the result 'a potentially enormous case concerned with a right that many legal constitutionalists consider to be the most important of all—the right to freedom of political expression—became transformed into a perfectly ordinary administrative law case about the proper construction and

---

[111] In *R (Bancoult) v Secretary of State for Foreign and Commonwealth Affairs (No 2)* [2007] EWCA Civ 498, 787, Sedley LJ noted that many of the prerogative powers described by Lord Roskill as non-justiciable in *GCHQ* no longer enjoyed such special immunity: 'the grant of honours for reward, the waging of a war of manifest aggression, or a refusal to dissolve Parliament at all, might well call into question an immunity based purely on subject matter'; see *Council of Civil Service Unions* case [1985] AC 374, 418 (Lord Roskill). *Bancoult* is considered fully in Chapter 8, below.

[112] *R v Secretary of State for the Home Dept, ex p Simms* [2000] 2 AC 115. *Simms* is further considered in Chapter 7, below.

[113] Tomkins, *Our Republican Constitution*, 29.

[114] Tom Hickman argues that *Simms* represented a 'delicate, highly contextual balance' between the legal and political constitutions: Hickman, 'In Defence of the Legal Constitution', 1019.

[115] *R (ProLife Alliance) v British Broadcasting Corporation* [2003] UKHL 23 (see Chapter 1, above).

application of a particular set of statutory obligations'.[116] This is, once again, a false dichotomy: the proper application of the regulations depended on correct analysis of the relevant constitutional principles. And the failure to give free speech the protection it deserved was not the consequence of any shortcomings in 'legal constitutionalism', as Tomkins asserts. It was, instead, the result of dubious reasoning by the House of Lords, undermining the robust defence of free speech provided by the Court of Appeal, whose decision is a far better illustration of the demands of the common law constitution.[117]

Underlying Tomkins's distrust of the judicial process—his hostility to legal constitutionalism—is a legal positivist orientation similar to Griffith's. His argument seems to be that it is better to determine questions about prisoners' rights or freedom of political speech in the round, rather than allow courts to legislate (on a blank slate) about such matters in a haphazard manner, according to the facts of particular cases that happen to arise. Such questions should be removed from the legal to the political forum for more widely informed, democratic decision. Tomkins overlooks the possibility that general principles can be deduced from analysis of judicial practice and legal tradition, enabling courts to resolve particular cases by recourse to law which they find rather than make. It does not follow that because competent lawyers can argue both sides of a question with some degree of plausibility that one answer is as good as another; a claim of right may well deserve recognition, as an implicit element of settled law, even if its opponents are adept at proposing public policy grounds by way of resistance. Tomkins considers, for example, that the basic constitutional right of access to the courts was 'invented' in *Leech*, when the Court of Appeal denied the legality of an interference with a prisoner's correspondence with his solicitor about intended litigation.[118] But others will acknowledge the foundation of such a right in the principle of judicial protection against abuse of executive power.

According to Tomkins, the principles of legality that courts apply in reviewing the conduct of governmental action displace executive discretion with 'untrammelled judicial discretion', allowing judges to interfere as they please.[119] In the absence of a detailed statutory code, he supposes that general principles of legality must be the 'creations' of the courts, as if requirements (enforced against public authorities) to be guided by relevant considerations and disregard irrelevant ones, or to act fairly and reasonably, were not intrinsic to the very idea of government according to law. Law cannot be reduced to the instructions of authorized officials, identified by recourse to a rule of recognition: it extends to those principles that animate the ideal of the rule of law, insulating individuals from the exercise of arbitrary power. Far from being judicial 'creations', with all the arbitrary voluntarism that such language implies, the various principles of judicial review can be defended

---

[116] Tomkins, *Our Republican Constitution*, 28.
[117] See further Chapter 1, above.
[118] *R v Secretary of State for the Home Dept, ex p Leech* [1994] QB 198, considered in Chapter 7, below.
[119] Tomkins, *Our Republican Constitution*, 22.

as articulations of a universal ideal of fair administration, both respectful of the public purposes for which a specific power is conferred and sensitive to the settled rights and reasonable expectations of the citizen affected by its exercise.[120]

Many of the divisions and categories constructed by public lawyers to limit the scope of judicial review—narrowly circumscribing the sphere of the justiciable—reflect or assume a narrow conception of law as a body of discrete rules, imposed by official authority. When we take a larger view of law, encompassing the general principles developed by the common law tradition to protect both individual freedom and orderly, rational administration, these divisions may well look suspect. From the internal perspective of the legal reasoner, confronted by the complexities of particular cases, distinctions and categories designed chiefly to facilitate descriptive exposition usually prove unhelpful. The judge or lawyer cannot exclude constitutional conventions or constitutional rights or general principles of legality from her deliberations on the basis of any sweeping doctrine of justiciability. She must examine all those aspects of legal and political practice relevant, or arguably relevant, to the specific question of legality arising on the facts; the full significance of those facts, in their wider context, will sometimes become apparent only in the light of prominent features of political practice or convention. Questions of legality are intimately linked with considerations of legitimacy, undermining neat divisions between public law and political principle. Distinctions drawn between legal and political questions should reflect the analysis made of specific constitutional claims: they should be part of the conclusions of that analysis rather than its premises.[121]

---

[120] See further Chapter 6, below.
[121] The argument is more fully developed in Chapter 7, below.

3

The Rule of Law: Freedom, Law, and Justice

I

When we point to the rule of law as a basic principle of British government, we identify our constitutional foundations with the value of law itself—law or legality understood as a moral or political value, closely connected with such other fundamental values as freedom and justice. The precise nature of these connections is complex and controversial, but their exploration is a necessary part of constitutional theory; and it is only by theoretical reflection on the primary elements of constitutional law and practice that we can hope to advance our understanding. As a doctrine of English or Scottish law, the rule of law asserts the law's compliance with the standards of governance implicit in that basic political value: it imposes those requirements of procedural fairness and substantive justice that follow from a persuasive account of what it means to enjoy government according to law. The rule of law—as distinct from the rule of particular men and women whose integrity or impartiality we may distrust—is a noble ideal that our legal practice aspires to match. The British Constitution is, no doubt, an imperfect representation of what a liberal, democratic regime ought ideally to be. If that ideal is nevertheless reflected in our legal and constitutional arrangements, giving them a coherence and unity, it will serve as a guide of fundamental importance.

According to the interpretative account of law and legal practice I am defending in this book, the rule of law is not merely an ideal or aspiration *external* to the law—a yardstick by which the law can be measured for its compliance with an important political value, and against which it may fall short. It is a value internal to law itself, informing and guiding our efforts to ascertain the legal rights, powers, and duties created by statutory enactment, judicial precedent, and constitutional custom or practice. We cannot know the extent of the broadcasters' powers of censorship, in relation to party election broadcasts, or the scope of judicial discretion in relation to the punishment of serious offences, or the justiciability of an exercise of the prerogative of mercy, without confronting the relevant implications for the rule of law.[1] We must read the pertinent statutes and precedents in the light of our commitment to constitutionalism, which inspires the theoretical framework in which we work. The answer to any legal question—whether it involves the meaning of a statute, the implications of a common law doctrine, or the legality of

---

[1] See the discussion of *ProLife Alliance*, *Offen*, and *Lewis* cases in Chapters 1 and 2, above.

any specific action or decision—will ultimately draw on the guidance furnished by the rule of law. Our more immediate judgements, focused on concrete instances, will reflect our deeper theoretical grasp of the underlying value of legality.

The idea of the rule of law (or legality) is best understood, I argue in this chapter, as compliance with those conditions under which each person's freedom (or liberty) is secured, consistently with the enjoyment of a similar freedom for everyone. The kind of freedom I have in mind is autonomy or independence, understood as a guarantee against arbitrary interference—interference at the will or pleasure of other persons, whether private citizens or public officials, unregulated by legal rules enforced by independent courts. The rule of law is an ideal that informs and characterizes our concept of law: we see the nature and point of law, as a form of systematic state regulation of persons and property, when we grasp the underlying idea of legality as a basic moral and political value. Law and liberty are closely connected values: our liberty, understood as an immunity from arbitrary interference, depends on the regular and reliable enforcement of those legal rules that define the scope of official powers and frame the content of the civil and criminal law. When the law is reliably enforced and fairly and consistently applied, our liberty is secure: each person is guaranteed, so far as possible, a private sphere of thought, deliberation, and action consonant with his dignity as a free and independent citizen.

A. V. Dicey's well-known account of the rule of law can be regarded as an effort to express these important connections between law and liberty; and his work is illuminated by reflection on the writings of F. A. Hayek, who in a similar manner seeks to elucidate a conception of liberty under law.[2] Hayek invokes the republican tradition of political thought in which liberty as independence takes pride of place. Liberty is the freedom secured by a legal regime that disallows ad hoc, arbitrary interference in the lives of citizens. It is the liberty defended by John Locke in his theoretical justification of the Glorious Revolution of 1688.[3] This chapter explores the strong antipathy of both Dicey and Hayek to the exercise of administrative discretion when it involves interference with individual liberty; it can be understood as a natural response to the threat such discretion poses to an ideal of liberty under law. Instead, however, of rejecting the ideal of the rule of law as incompatible with the modern welfare-regulatory state, in which governmental discretion is inescapable, we should recognize the need for safeguards against abuse of such discretion. We should acknowledge, in particular, the critical role of judicial review by impartial and independent courts of law.

Law displaces arbitrary power when, first and foremost, it consists in the application to particular cases of published general rules, indicating in advance of people's actions the relevant legal consequences. The rule of law obtains only when state officials must act within the constraints of such general rules, prohibited from

---

[2] A V Dicey, *Introduction to the Study of the Law of the Constitution*, 10th edn (London: Macmillan, 1964); F A Hayek, *The Constitution of Liberty* (London: Routledge & Kegan Paul, 1960).

[3] John Locke, *Two Treatises of Government* (originally published 1690; London: Dent, Everyman, 1924).

interfering in people's enjoyment of their liberty beyond any powers granted by those rules. The precept *nulla poena sine lege*, condemning punishment for acts that were not forbidden when performed, forms a central plank in the structure of the rule of law. But it is also important that officials should respect the limits of the ordinary civil law when they act in furtherance of public policy: advancing the public interest (as a public authority conceives it) is not an automatic justification for an interference in personal liberty. The exercise of special powers, permitting conduct that would otherwise amount to trespass or assault or some other legal wrong, requires specific authorization. There can be no presumption in favour of the power of state officials to act in disregard of ordinary legal constraints, however pressing they consider their governmental objectives: 'with respect to the argument of state necessity, or a distinction... between state offences and others, the common law does not understand that kind of reasoning, nor do our books take notice of any such distinctions'.[4]

The rule of law consists, at a minimum, in the impartial enforcement of legal rules against both private citizens and public officials: arbitrary conduct by powerful persons or groups, unconstrained by rules, represents the antithesis of law.[5] In identifying a legal order—a legal or constitutional regime by contrast with an oppressive tyranny—we would treat compliance with the rule of law in this minimal sense as the critical mark of distinction. From the internal viewpoint of legal interpreter, however, we treat this minimal concept of law as the basis for a more elaborate account. Our own democratic legal order embodies the assumption that citizens have an equal status: we assume that legal rules must serve the general interest or the common good, in the sense, at least, that there is no systematic discrimination against despised minorities or political opponents. We do not suppose that the rule of law is maintained by the enforcement of rules that serve the interests only of a small clique of government officials, or a privileged social elite, even if the regularity and predictability of such enforcement curtails the scope for ad hoc intrusions into liberty. Beyond the formal equality—equality before the law—secured by the even-handed administration of justice, we embrace a deeper, more substantive equality: the rule of law entails an equality of citizenship, conferring the equal protection of the law.[6]

Our liberty as independence rests not only on the absence of unpredictable official coercion, but also on our assurance that extravagant governmental powers will not be conferred by Parliament, jeopardizing our most basic rights and interests. We make our plans and pursue our personal projects on the assumption that the fundamental

---

[4] *Entick v Carrington* (1765) 19 St Tr 1029, 1073 (where Lord Camden CJ, in the Court of Common Pleas, held that there was no valid lawful excuse for the trespass to the plaintiff's house and goods committed by officials, who had arrested him for publishing seditious writings).

[5] Compare Tom Bingham, *The Rule of Law* (London: Penguin, 2011), 8: 'The core of the existing principle is... that all persons and authorities within the state, whether public or private, should be bound by and entitled to the benefit of laws publicly made, taking effect (generally) in the future and publicly administered in the courts.' (Bingham cites both Dicey and Locke.)

[6] Bingham proposes as part of the rule of law the principle that 'the laws of the land should apply equally to all, save to the extent that objective differences justify differentiation' (ibid, 55).

freedoms on which they depend will not be swept away by a 'sovereign' legislature, temporarily deaf to pleas on behalf of individual liberty. We do not want freedom from arbitrary arrest and detention, for example, merely to escape the immediate misery entailed: we take for granted such immunity in constructing and executing our plans; and we agree that only very exceptional circumstances could justify new legislation that seriously curbed our personal freedom. We also assume that when discretionary powers are granted to officials they must be deployed with proper restraint. Coercive powers must be invoked only for legitimate public purposes and do no further damage to private rights and interests than are really necessary; and we do not think that public officials should be the final judge in their own cause on the question of necessity. The rule of law is more than regularity or predictability: it imposes a requirement of *justification*, connecting restrictions on liberty to a public or common good, open to fearless public debate and challenge.

When we adopt the internal perspective appropriate to legal interpretation—the viewpoint of citizen, judge, or official who seeks to ascertain the law on any issue—we are guided by a vision of the rule of law as a scheme of justice, implicit in our existing constitutional arrangements, at least when these are favourably regarded. Even if the law on many questions falls some way short of the ideal of legality, preserving a genuine equality of freedom, we try to bring it as close as we can. We interpret statutes and precedents in the manner that best secures freedom as independence for everyone, insofar as all the circumstances allow. Common law presumptions against retroactive criminal legislation, or in favour of the requirement of *mens rea*, or in support of evidential rather than probative burdens being imposed on defendants, are important means of preserving central elements of the rule of law.[7] But such presumptions are only instances of a style of statutory interpretation designed to maintain the rule of law's integrity in the face of legislation with the potential to undermine it. Similar presumptions in favour of such fundamental common law rights as freedom of speech, conscience, and association, or rights to personal liberty or fair trial, also serve to sustain a defensible legal regime—one in which liberty as independence is, as far as possible, secured.

In this chapter, then, I shall defend an account of the rule of law that embraces much more than a narrow conception of legality—legality in the sense of mere formal equality before the law (however oppressive or discriminatory that law may be in substance). As the basic principle of the British constitution, underpinning its character as a liberal democratic polity, the rule of law means the sovereignty of the principle of liberty: it upholds the freedom and dignity of those independent citizens who comprise the political community.[8] While, however, the rule of law

---

[7] See discussion of *R v Lambert* [2001] UKHL 37, as regards the imposition of burdens of proof on the accused, in Chapter 5, below.

[8] I treat liberty (or independence) as a requirement of respect for human dignity. For a helpful account of the idea of human dignity, see Ronald Dworkin, *Is Democracy Possible Here? Principles for a New Political Debate* (Princeton: Princeton University Press, 2006), 9–21. Dworkin identifies two principles as defining the basis and conditions of human dignity: every human life is of intrinsic potential value; and everyone has a responsibility for realizing that value in his own life. It follows, as Dworkin observes, that the state must honour everyone's human rights, including those of non-citizens (ibid, ch 2). See also Dworkin, *Justice for Hedgehogs* (Cambridge, Mass: Harvard University Press, 2011), ch 9.

prohibits the violation of citizens' basic rights—allowing only (modest) limitations and restrictions when really necessary for the public good—it does not prescribe the detailed content of the laws. Because there are many different arrangements compatible with liberty and equality, Parliament enjoys the right to settle the numerous questions of justice and public policy that constitutional theory leaves unanswered. But parliamentary sovereignty must be employed in the service of the sovereignty of law and liberty: it is not a power to dispense with the fundamental building blocks of a just regime, respectful of the independence and dignity of equal citizens.[9]

In its guise as a comprehensive system of private law, regulating the relationships between private citizens, the common law seeks solutions for doubtful cases from within a fabric of thought constructed from existing practice: the law is larger than a summary of explicitly stated rules, extending to the general principles of justice that infuse and sustain its detailed requirements. In public law, the common law must generate an equivalent structure of constitutional and administrative justice; but here we confront a distinct and often difficult interpretative task. Our general principles apply in a myriad of contexts involving complex questions of governance and public interest, requiring great subtlety and sensitivity of judgement. The more extensive the coercive powers invoked by public officials, however, the more urgent the need for independent judicial oversight. I shall suggest that common law adjudication, focused on ascertaining existing rights and duties, presents an ideal toward which administrative decision-making should itself aspire, according to the seriousness of the consequences for particular (identifiable) individuals. The rule of law requires a proper balance between public and private interests: the standards of fairness and due process enforced by judicial review seek to bring administrative decision-making as close to an ideal of impartial adjudication as the relevant public objectives permit in all the circumstances.

Our discussion will include a brief review of some pertinent jurisprudential discussions of the rule of law. I shall consider, and reject, Joseph Raz's suggestion that the rule of law is a defence against the dangers of arbitrary power presented by the law itself: it is, instead, a defence against the assertion of power unconstrained by law.[10] It will be helpful to refer to Ronald Dworkin's theory of law as 'integrity' in considering the connection between the rule of law and justice: integrity enforces the scheme of justice implicit in legal practice; it does not deny that legal practice may fall short of anyone's view of justice, abstractly conceived.[11] And, in a final section, I shall suggest that Kant's Doctrine of Right may be understood as an

---

[9] Endorsing a conception of the rule of law that embraces the protection of basic human rights, but unwilling to countenance any legal limits to parliamentary sovereignty, Bingham is forced to concede the existence of a 'serious problem': our 'constitutional settlement has become unbalanced' (see Bingham, *The Rule of Law*, 168–9). However, an interpretative approach, characteristic of adjudication, can normally redress the balance (I shall argue) in the process of resolving concrete cases in the manner legality demands.

[10] Joseph Raz, *The Authority of Law: Essays on Law and Morality* (Oxford: Clarendon Press, 1979), ch 11.

[11] Ronald Dworkin, *Law's Empire* (London: Fontana, 1986).

affirmation of my account of the rule of law, reconciling the state's authority with individual autonomy.[12]

<h1 style="text-align:center">II</h1>

The rule of law is a bulwark against any assertion of arbitrary power. When we are governed by law we are free to act as we wish, subject only to the known (or knowable) constraints of the civil and criminal law and the similar freedom of action of others. No one may force us to act or refrain from acting as we wish, otherwise than by simply taking advantage of opportunities or facilities available to all. Or at least, no one may so interfere except insofar as he is *authorized* to do so by legal powers or duties previously conferred; and the nature and scope of such powers must be publicly ascertainable and sufficiently precise to give warning in advance of their use and enable an independent court to determine, in retrospect, any complaint of excess or abuse. A public official no less than a private citizen is constrained by rules, enforceable by a court of law: he must pursue only authorized public ends and use only authorized means. Our liberty depends, at a minimum, on formal equality before the law: citizen and official are alike answerable for wrongful coercive action, beyond the limits of any legally sanctioned power.

Freedom or liberty inheres, however, in each individual's status as citizen: the rule of law in a just state secures an equal liberty, consonant with a basic equality of citizenship. Accordingly, the scheme of rights, duties and powers established by legal rules must itself be non-arbitrary, in the sense that it is justified in terms of a *public or common good*—one that we can fairly suppose favours a similar freedom for all. The impartiality and circumspection we demand of public officials, furthered by strict legal limits to their discretion, would be mocked by rules that themselves made arbitrary distinctions between persons or groups, irrelevant to any legitimate public purpose capable of eliciting broad assent. The rule of law requires not merely that legal rules should be strictly enforced, according to their true meaning, but that their requirements should, so far as possible, be ones that all citizens can affirm without loss of self-respect. If the rules draw distinctions between persons, as all rules must, they must be relevant to defensible public purposes—purposes consistent with a vision of equal, independent citizens who cooperate to secure the enjoyment of their civil and political freedoms.[13]

We can clarify our conception of the rule of law by identifying its most flagrant violation. A 'bill of attainder' purports to authorize the punishment of a specified individual or group of individuals, who are thereby deprived of the ordinary

[12] Immanuel Kant, *The Doctrine of Right (The Metaphysics of Morals*, Part I), in Mary J Gregor (ed), *Practical Philosophy* (Cambridge: Cambridge University Press, 1996), 363–506.
[13] Since we assume that lawfully resident non-citizens are entitled to the same protections as citizens demand for themselves—especially respect for their human rights, fundamental to human dignity—discrimination between the two groups needs justification consonant with its scale or severity: see discussion of *A v Secretary of State for the Home Department* [2004] UKHL 56, below.

safeguards of a fair trial on charges of having breached the criminal law. Liberty is infringed by state action beyond anything contemplated by previously promulgated general rules; independence (or autonomy) is undermined by the mere threat of such interference, which renders a person subject to the direct and immediate will of the legislators. The equal protection of the law is plainly denied. In abandoning even the pretence of even-handedness or impartiality, such a bill is an Act of Parliament only in the most technical sense of satisfying the formal conditions for enactment. It would not qualify as 'law' in the sense entailed by the principle of the rule of law, and accordingly generates no genuine legal powers or duties. It flouts the division of powers that the rule of law both assumes and requires: Parliament acts as prosecutor, judge, and jury, breaching the fundamental constitutional separation between legislature and judiciary—between the making of rules and their application to particular cases.

The rule of law is preserved in, and illustrated by, judicial enforcement of the ordinary private law, regulating relations between citizens. The enjoyment of our personal property and protection from various kinds of interference depends on other people's respect for the law, which prohibits assault and trespass and other established legal wrongs. When the rule of law obtains, we each enjoy a sphere of independent private action in which we can pursue our own aims and ambitions; we have sufficient assurance that if we avoid breaches of legal rules that cause damage or injury to others, we will in turn avoid unwarranted interference by those who might disapprove of our plans and seek to frustrate them. This ideal of cooperation and mutual tolerance depends on the regular and reliable enforcement of legal rules: such enforcement acts as a deterrent, reducing the likelihood of breaches of the private or criminal law, and enabling people to recover compensation for unlawfully inflicted injury or damage. Not only must state officials enforce the law when necessary, but they must not themselves use coercion beyond the strict limits of their allotted powers. Such unauthorized coercion, exceeding limits strictly defined in advance of any exercise of governmental power, plainly violates the rule of law: it presents the same threat to the individual's sphere of independent action as the unlawful interference of other private citizens.

The equality of private citizen and public official, in this important respect, was a major theme of A. V. Dicey's well-known exposition of the rule of law as a principle of British government. No man is above the law, and 'every man, whatever be his rank or condition, is subject to the ordinary law of the realm and amenable to the jurisdiction of the ordinary tribunals'.[14] While officials may possess special powers to be deployed in the public interest, they are nonetheless liable to punishment, or to pay damages, for acts done in excess of their lawful authority: 'every official, from the Prime Minister down to a constable or a collector of taxes, is under the same responsibility for every act done without legal justification as any other citizen'. The 'legal equality' between citizen and official, emphasized by Dicey, is superficially at least only a *formal* equality: it does not preclude the grant of extensive powers to state officials for specific purposes, curtailing the private spheres of action of individuals.

---

[14] A V Dicey, *Law of the Constitution*, 193.

In the context, however, of Dicey's defence of a 'judge-made constitution', in which individual rights are the product of litigation determined by courts on the basis of general common law principle, it is reasonable to suppose that formal 'legal equality' is underpinned by a more fundamental notion of equal citizenship.[15] Equality before the law would not be satisfied, on that view, by allowing officials to make arbitrary distinctions between persons or groups—distinctions irrelevant to any genuine public purpose, compatible with at least a plausible (even if contestable) view of the public or common good.

When we identify the rule of law as a fundamental precept of British governance, we refer to an ideal of constitutionalism that includes, but goes well beyond, the notion that government—like everyone else—should obey the law. Certainly, state officials must be made to comply with the law that defines their duties and limits their powers; their actions and decisions must be challengeable before independent courts, which can review any complaints of illegality with appropriate detachment and impartiality. Judges must also, of course, obey the law: their judgments must be guided by the standards and requirements imposed by existing rules of law (whether statutory rules or rules or principles of common law). But the nature and content of those standards or requirements is crucial; it is not just a matter of their being loyally applied. The rule of law would not be satisfied if an official were free to exercise sweeping powers, in some area of governmental regulation, in any manner he thought fit. It would hardly be enough to point to an Act of Parliament that authorized him to do whatever he considered 'necessary or expedient in the public interest' (even if we construed that authorization as excluding actions reflecting bad faith or improper motive). The rule of law would not be satisfied because it would leave everyone too much at the mercy of the official's discretion, however eccentric or misguided his view of the public interest or the appropriate means of advancing it: there would be no defence against arbitrary or whimsical assertions of governmental power.

Central to this characterization of the rule of law, then, is an appeal to the idea of individual liberty—the freedom or liberty that consists in the enjoyment of a protected private sphere of decision and action, immune from interference either by fellow citizens or public officials. It is a private sphere constituted by the regular and reliable enforcement of the ordinary criminal and private law, together with the strict observance by officials of the limits of their powers, which must be as narrowly defined as their proper efforts to advance the public good reasonably permit. Although the law is often viewed as a system of *constraints* on liberty, the real truth is quite the opposite: our liberty depends on the law, which secures the boundaries of our freedom against encroachment, whether by other citizens or state officials. The connection between law and liberty is deep and fundamental, though we must take care to identify the relevant conception of liberty. Adherence by government, like other citizens, to the rule of law protects individual liberty chiefly in the sense of *independence*: we are free to live our own lives within ascertainable legal

---

[15] Ibid, 195–6; an interpretation of Dicey's work along these lines is developed below.

boundaries, confident that no official body can intervene at pleasure to obstruct our plans or punish us for conduct it chooses to condemn. It is an immunity to arbitrary interference—coercive intervention at the will or pleasure of public officials. Even if people's domains of freedom are closely circumscribed by the content of rules and regulations, the rule of law preserves a valuable sphere of independence, appropriate to the acknowledgement of human dignity: no one is subject to the will of another as to what he should say or do.

The value of liberty as independence may be grasped by comparison with the position of a slave, who is wholly subject to the will of his master. Such freedom as a slave is permitted to enjoy is always precarious, subject at any moment to his master's interference. Even if he is allowed an extensive freedom, encompassing a large range of optional conduct, it remains dependent on the master's will and pleasure. Even if, in practice, the slave suffers little interference in the conduct of his affairs, he is nonetheless subject to *domination*, or *vulnerability* to interference.[16] A free man, or citizen of a free state, by contrast, does not suffer from domination. In the republican political tradition, emphasizing freedom as independence or non-domination, citizenship and freedom are treated as equivalents, based on a suitable legal regime: 'As the laws create the authority that rulers enjoy, so the laws create the freedom that citizens share.'[17] The rule of law is in place when the laws protect people from domination by other private parties—the *dominium* of those would otherwise exercise arbitrary power—but do not thereby introduce any new domination that could result from governmental *imperium*: the law must be made by the people's representatives and reflect their common interests.[18]

The essential link between law and liberty lies at the heart of John Locke's account of legitimate government, published in 1690 as a defence and justification of the Glorious Revolution of 1688. In the second *Treatise of Government*, on 'The True Original, Extent and End of Civil Government', Locke contrasted the mislead-ing idea of liberty as freedom *from* laws with the true conception: 'freedom of men under government is to have a standing rule to live by, common to every one of that society, and made by the legislative power erected in it'.[19] Freedom, properly understood, is the 'liberty to follow my own will in all things where that rule prescribes not, not to be subject to the inconstant, uncertain, unknown, arbitrary will of another man'. The law constitutes a 'compact' whereby obedience is owed to a 'limited power', by contrast with the condition of slavery, characterized by subjection to an 'absolute, arbitrary, despotical power'.[20] The law serves the com-mon good by enabling everyone to enjoy his liberty in accordance with rules that

---

[16] Compare Philip Pettit, *Republicanism: A Theory of Freedom and Government* (Oxford: Clarendon Press, 1997), 21–7.

[17] Ibid, 36.

[18] Ibid, 36–7. See also Quentin Skinner, *Liberty Before Liberalism* (Cambridge: Cambridge University Press, 1998), especially ch 2. As Skinner summarizes the 'neo-roman' theory of liberty (at 70), 'if you live under any form of government that allows for the exercise of prerogative or discretionary powers outside the law, you will already be living as a slave'.

[19] John Locke, *Two Treatises of Government*, II, para 22.

[20] Ibid, paras 22–4.

guarantee a similar liberty for all; and even if the legislature is the 'supreme power' in every commonwealth 'it is not, nor can possibly be, absolutely arbitrary over the lives and fortunes of the people'.[21] The dangers of arbitrary power are greatly reduced by a separation of powers, whereby general rules, enacted by the legislature, are applied to particular cases by independent judges:

And so, whoever has the legislative or supreme power of any commonwealth is bound to govern by established standing laws promulgated and known to the people, and not by extemporary decrees; by indifferent and upright judges, who are to decide controversies by those laws; and to employ the force of the community at home only in the execution of such laws, or abroad to prevent or redress foreign injuries and secure the community from inroads and invasion. And all this to be directed to no other end but the peace, safety, and public good of the people.[22]

The fundamental distinction between free man and slave is also drawn by F. A. Hayek in explaining the essence of freedom or liberty.[23] It is not a matter of the range of choice available, which will depend on all the circumstances, but rather on whether it is possible for someone to 'shape his course of action in accordance with his present intentions'.[24] Freedom is the independence that the slave is denied. It means 'the possibility of a person's acting according to his own decisions and plans, in contrast to the position of one who was irrevocably subject to the will of another, who by arbitrary decision could coerce him to act or not to act in specific ways'.[25] No degree of material comfort or even power over others can alter a slave's basic dependence on the arbitrary (unfettered) will of his master: 'But if he is subject only to the same laws as all his fellow citizens, if he is immune from arbitrary confinement and free to choose his work, and if he is able to own and acquire property, no other men or group of men can coerce him to do their bidding.'[26] Here Hayek equates freedom as independence with the impartial administration of the ordinary civil and criminal law, which protects each person's 'private sphere' against illegitimate coercion exerted by other persons. In a free society the state enjoys a monopoly of force, exercised only when it is necessary to prevent coercion by private persons. Such necessary state coercion is constrained by the operation of published general rules, so that arbitrary private coercion is not replaced by arbitrary state action:

Being made impersonal and dependent upon general, abstract rules, whose effect on particular individuals cannot be foreseen at the time they are laid down, even the coercive acts of government become data on which the individual can base his own plans. Coercion according

---

[21] Ibid, para 135.
[22] Ibid, para 131. Compare William Blackstone, *Commentaries on the Laws of England* (1765–9; 9th edn, London, 1783), vol 1, 126: 'laws, when prudently framed, are by no means subversive but rather introductive of liberty; for (as Mr Locke has well observed) where there is no law there is no freedom'.
[23] F A Hayek, *The Constitution of Liberty*, 12–20.
[24] Ibid, 13.
[25] Ibid, 12.
[26] Ibid, 20.

to known rules...then becomes an instrument assisting the individuals in the pursuit of their own ends and not a means to be used for the ends of others.[27]

Hayek places his own work in the republican tradition, in which law and liberty are interdependent rather than opposed, citing Harrington's reference to an 'empire of laws', and invoking Cicero as showing that 'during the classical period of Roman law it was fully understood that there is no conflict between law and freedom and that freedom is dependent upon certain attributes of the law, its generality and certainty, and the restrictions it places on the discretion of authority'.[28] Hayek also calls attention to Locke's *Second Treatise* as an important part of a tradition of the rule of law and separation of powers, which is given the 'fullest statement' in the work of William Paley, who emphasized the value of the separation of legislative and judicial powers: 'Parliament knows not the individuals upon whom its acts will operate; it has no case or parties before it; no private designs to serve: consequently, its resolutions will be suggested by the considerations of universal effects and tendencies, which always produce impartial, and commonly advantageous regulations.'[29]

The rule of law is distinguished from rule by men or women in the critical sense that the law preserves a zone of independent decision and action, wherein each person is insulated from the coercive interference of others so long as her conduct conforms to the known or readily accessible requirements of the general law: 'What distinguishes a free from an unfree society is that in the former each individual has a recognized private sphere clearly distinct from the public sphere, and the private individual cannot be ordered about but is expected to obey only the rules which are equally applicable to all.'[30] The general rules, of course, require interpretation; and it is a crucial feature of the separation of powers that a court should determine doubtful cases by reference to general principles, implicit in the existing constitutional scheme. Many rules will not, in practice, be given explicit written form but will be 'recognizable only because they lead to consistent and predictable decisions', expressing a 'sense of justice' capable of acting as a guide to conduct: 'Many of the general principles on which the conclusions depend will be only implicit in the body of formulated law and will have to be discovered by the courts.'[31] It is plainly critical to individual freedom that a judge has no discretion in the sense of 'authority to follow his own will to pursue particular concrete aims',

---

[27] Ibid, 21.

[28] Ibid, 166–7. See James Harrington, *The Commonwealth of Oceana and A System of Politics* (1656), ed J G A Pocock (Cambridge: Cambridge University Press, 1992), 8: 'an empire of laws, and not of men'.

[29] William Paley, *The Principles of Moral and Political Philosophy* (London, 1824), 348 ff, cited by Hayek, *The Constitution of Liberty*, 173–4.

[30] Hayek, *The Constitution of Liberty*, 207–8. Compare Hayek, *Rules and Order*, in *Law, Legislation and Liberty* (London: Routledge & Kegan Paul, 1982), 85–6: 'The law will consist of purpose-independent rules which govern the conduct of individuals towards each other, are intended to apply to an unknown number of further instances, and by defining a protected domain of each, enable an order of actions to form itself wherein the individuals can make feasible plans.'

[31] Hayek, *The Constitution of Liberty*, 209.

but only a duty 'to discover the implications contained in the spirit of the whole system of valid rules of law or to express as a general rule, when necessary, what was not explicitly stated previously in a court of law or by the legislator'.[32]

There is plainly a tension here between the certainty and predictability obtained by the consistent application of published and prospective rules, at least when these are clearly framed, and the desirability of the law's conforming to a more diffuse sense of justice, dependent on conformity to general principles whose application will depend on judgements of value that cannot be precisely delineated in advance. The court must tread a delicate line between adherence to the 'letter of the law', when such strict adherence is essential to the law's stability and predictability, and a more fluid and flexible invocation of deeper principles or underlying standards, when such principles or standards reflect widely shared expectations or assumptions about the requirements of justice. In practice, the acknowledged rules may be applied with sensitivity to context, permitting interpretations that enable the rules to be applied to novel and unforeseen instances in a way that does not violate settled principles and expectations. The tension between rule and principle, or between narrower and broader styles of reasoning, may be resolved, ideally, according to context—a commercial or criminal context, for example, requiring a strictness of approach appropriate to the needs of business confidence or the protection of liberty.

There is a parallel tension between formal and substantive equality—equality before the law, whatever its content may be, and the equal protection of the law in the sense that all are governed by the same general principles and standards, even if their application is necessarily sensitive to differences in people's needs, entitlements, or circumstances. The closer the law corresponds to the sense of justice that gives coherence and unity to the legal order as a whole—the principles and ideals that underpin its more concrete and particular rules—the more confident we can be that people are treated equally, in the sense that they are regarded as of equal worth and importance. When the law aspires to substantive rather than merely formal equality, the distinctions between persons drawn by legal rules must be justified by reference to fundamental ideas of justice. Discrimination on such grounds as race, gender, or sexual orientation is particularly suspect, requiring strong justification compatible with the assumption of citizens' fundamental equality. In other cases, it may be much harder to decide whether the criteria for distinguishing between persons, or between groups, are justifiable; but they must be closely related to purposes or policies that can be shown to advance a genuine public good, capable in principle of being endorsed by all groups or classes of citizens.[33]

The ideals of liberty and equality are accordingly closely aligned, and each is dependent for its realization on the rule of law or respect for legality. Liberty as independence—the preservation of a personal sphere of action and decision,

---

[32] Ibid, 212. Compare Hayek, *Rules and Order*, ch 5.

[33] Hayek observes that such distinctions 'will not be arbitrary, will not subject one group to the will of others, if they are equally recognized as justified by those inside and those outside the group'; when 'only those inside the group favour the distinction, it is clearly a privilege; while if only those outside favour it, it is discrimination' (*The Constitution of Liberty*, 154).

immune from interference—is most securely achieved when legal rules are treated as integral parts of a larger scheme of governance, expressing as a whole a consistent vision of justice. We are then not only protected from ad hoc interference, whether by officials or other private citizens, but also from the imposition of *new rules* (or even the reinterpretation of existing rules) contrary to our legitimate expectations—expectations generated by the faithful administration of an existing order of justice, recognizing certain basic individual rights. When government adheres to human rights standards, whether enshrined in a bill of rights or charter (such as the Human Rights Act 1998) or implicit in the development of the common law, it affirms the rule of law by strengthening the individual's sphere of independence. A guarantee of immunity from new legislation restricting that sphere is added to the ordinary protection secured by the operation of general rules, limiting official or private coercion; or, at least, there is a guarantee against new restrictions that cannot be convincingly justified by reference to the public good, recognizable by an independent court.

It is important to see that we must not be forced to choose—as legal theorists often require us to choose—between formal and substantive equality. It is wrong to identify the rule of law exclusively with either conception. The rule of law imposes a formal equality insofar as it insists on the regular enforcement of existing rules, disallowing arbitrary exemptions or dispensations—special privileges for favoured citizens or officials who are permitted to disregard the law. But insofar as those rules require *interpretation* in doubtful cases, or *supplementation* by new rules to meet changing events or altered perceptions of justice, the rule of law demands a high level of theoretical coherence. Only by striving to understand the law as a consistent scheme of justice, compatible with certain fundamental human rights and moral values, can we avoid making arbitrary (indefensible) distinctions between persons or groups. Whenever a court adopts an interpretation of existing rules informed by consideration of general principles, it serves the ideal of substantive, not merely formal, equality. When it develops the common law, by extrapolating general principles from previous decisions as a guide to decisions in novel circumstances, it brings the common law closer to an ideal of substantive justice, treating all alike according to those principles.

Although Dicey presented his account of the rule of law in apparently formal terms, he plainly thought it an important foundation for individual liberty. He regarded the strict adherence to law, by public officials as much as private individuals, as symptomatic of an underlying respect for human freedom and dignity. Adherence to law, when public policy might more readily be advanced by departures from law, signalled a recognition of the value of individual autonomy or independence; a formal legal equality furthered the more basic ideal of equal citizenship. When principles of law are 'mere generalizations drawn either from the decisions or dicta of judges, or from statutes which, being passed to meet special grievances, bear a close resemblance to judicial decisions', they forge a vital link between political ideals and legal practice.[34] Abstract ideals of freedom and justice

---

[34] Dicey, *Law of the Constitution*, 197.

are given a concrete legal form in which individual right is aligned with practical legal remedy: 'In England the right to individual liberty is part of the constitution, because it is secured by the decisions of the courts, extended or confirmed as they are by the Habeas Corpus Acts.'[35] Effective legal protection against arbitrary arrest or detention is plainly an important element of any system of law that reflects the value of freedom as independence. Independence depends on people's assurance that the right to personal liberty will be enforced as a matter of ordinary legal practice: 'The Habeas Corpus Acts declare no principle and define no rights, but they are for practical purposes worth a hundred constitutional articles guaranteeing individual liberty.'[36] Individual freedom can survive only when it is affirmed by a strong legal tradition; and the rule of law requires not merely the regular enforcement of the law against everyone, including public officials, but the participation of all branches of government—especially courts and Parliament—in maintaining that tradition.[37]

III

On the surface, at least, Dicey's account of the rule of law amounts to little more than the barest idea of *legality*—the principle that public officials are bound by the law and cannot exercise any power over the ordinary citizen that is not conferred by law. His initial definition of 'the supremacy or the rule of law' makes an explicit contrast with 'the exercise by persons in authority of wide, arbitrary, or discretionary powers of constraint': 'no man is punishable or can be lawfully made to suffer in body or goods except for a distinct breach of the law established in the ordinary legal manner before the ordinary courts of the land'.[38] His mention of the 'ordinary courts' indicates the implicit dependence of the rule of law on a separation of powers: only judges who are independent of the executive Government can be trusted impartially to enforce the law against officials who overstep the limits of their powers.

The second meaning ascribed to the rule of law—formal equality before the law—is largely a restatement of the first meaning: in England not only is no one above the law but, further, 'every man, whatever be his rank or condition, is subject to the ordinary law of the realm and amenable to the jurisdiction of the ordinary tribunals'.[39] If everyone is subject to the general civil and criminal law, administered by the ordinary courts, there is a burden cast on every official to show special authority for any prima facie legal wrong that causes another injury or loss: 'The

---

[35] Ibid.

[36] Ibid, 199.

[37] The British tradition of respect for liberty was invoked by the dissentients in *R v Halliday, ex p Zadig* [1917] AC 260 and *Liversidge v Anderson* [1942] AC 206, as well as by Lord Hoffmann in *A v Secretary of State for the Home Dept* [2004] UKHL 56: see Chapter 1, above. The efforts of Parliament and Government to enhance national security in response to the threat of terrorism has obliged the courts to seek to defend a tradition thereby placed under considerable strain (see further below).

[38] Dicey, *Law of the Constitution*, 188.

[39] Ibid, 193.

Reports abound with cases in which officials have been brought before the courts, and made, in their personal capacity, liable to punishment, or to the payment of damages, for acts done in their official character but in excess of their lawful authority.'[40] And superficially, the third meaning does little more than echo the second. English constitutional rights and principles are 'inductions or generalizations' based on particular judicial decisions about the legality of official actions:

> We may say that the constitution is pervaded by the rule of law on the ground that the general principles of the constitution (as for example the right to personal liberty, or the right of public meeting) are with us the result of judicial decisions determining the rights of private persons in particular cases brought before the courts; whereas under many foreign constitutions the security (such as it is) given to the rights of individuals results ... from the general principles of the constitution.[41]

Lacking an explicitly public law dimension, on Dicey's view, the rule of law is simply the vulnerability of officials to the rules of private and criminal law applicable to ordinary persons: 'the principles of private law have with us been by the action of the courts and Parliament so extended as to determine the position of the Crown and of its servants; thus the constitution is the result of the ordinary law of the land'.[42]

While it is tempting, and fashionable, to dismiss Dicey's exposition as both out-dated and parochial—overtaken by more recent developments and inexcusably hostile to foreign, especially Continental European, legal systems—it is more profitable to identify the deeper theory at which the surface rhetoric only gestures. Implicit in the emphasis on ordinary law and ordinary courts is the idea that the exercise of official powers of coercion, however necessary to just and effective governance, should be narrowly circumscribed—limited by close and jealous judicial scrutiny of the *source* of such powers, interpreted in the light of the legitimate public purposes in view. Legality, in the pertinent sense, is plainly *not* satisfied merely by the grant to officials of whatever powers they deem necessary to accomplish general state objectives, deployed in whatever manner they see fit. The exercise of 'wide, arbitrary, or discretionary powers of constraint' is contrary to the rule of law even if such powers are formally conferred by statute or royal prerogative on government ministers or officials. All Dicey's emphasis on the proud tradition of English liberty would be absurd if he had supposed that a dictator, exercising unfettered power bestowed on him by a formal written constitution, was in any real sense subject to the rule of law. The 'singularity of England' in the eighteenth century may have been 'not so much the goodness or the leniency as the legality of the English system of government'; but the distinction between rule by law and rule by official whim or 'caprice' depends on the existence of ascertainable limits to the scope of governmental powers.[43]

---

[40] Ibid.

[41] Ibid, 195–6.

[42] Ibid, 203.

[43] Ibid, 189–90 (Dicey here contrasts English law with Voltaire's experience of the arbitrariness of French law in the early years of the eighteenth century; in England, Voltaire found a land where 'men were ruled by law and not by caprice').

Dicey celebrates the writ of habeas corpus, whereby anyone imprisoned can be brought before the High Court and released if, on inquiry, he is found to be unlawfully detained:

The authority to enforce obedience to the writ is nothing less than the power to release from imprisonment any person who in the opinion of the court is unlawfully deprived of his liberty, and hence in effect to put an end to or to prevent any punishment which the Crown or its servants may attempt to inflict in opposition to the rules of law as interpreted by the judges.[44]

It would make little sense to portray the judiciary as an effective guarantor of personal liberty if someone could be lawfully imprisoned on general grounds of 'public interest', or in pursuit of broadly defined discretionary powers granted to officials. Habeas corpus can be an effective remedy, exemplifying the rule of law in practice, only if powers of detention are narrowly defined by law, and their exercise rigorously scrutinized by judges who embrace an ideal of individual liberty.

Nor should we suppose that Dicey's disparaging reference to 'those declarations or definitions of rights so dear to foreign constitutionalists'—however quaint it may appear in the present-day light of the European Convention on Human Rights—signalled any antipathy to or lack of reverence for the liberties such declarations proclaim.[45] His point was that if they are to be truly effective in protecting citizens from the abuse of state power, such rights and liberties must be ingrained in the constitutional culture—part of the taken-for-granted background of any issue of legality and reflected in the daily practice of the 'ordinary' courts. If constitutional rights are regarded as 'something extraneous to and independent of the ordinary course of the law', they can be suspended by a governmental regime keen to stifle political opposition.[46] When, by contrast, a right is considered part of the ordinary law, expressing a principle inherent in the justification of judicial precedent, it can 'hardly be destroyed without a thorough revolution in the institutions and manners of the nation'.[47]

If the liberty of the press is a 'special feature of English institutions', according to Dicey, it is simply because 'the relation between the government and the press' has been characterized by the rule or 'supremacy' of law: press freedom is a 'mere application of the general principle, that no man is punishable except for a distinct breach of the law'.[48] Accordingly, no scheme of licensing or censorship prevents publication of material that might be critical of government or officials; and 'press offences' are merely breaches of the ordinary law of libel (whether 'defamatory, seditious, or blasphemous') and tried and punished by the ordinary courts.[49] It is true, of course, that freedom of speech might be very limited, in practice, if the law of libel or sedition or blasphemy were very onerous; but Dicey's point again seems to be that respect for ordinary legal processes goes hand-in-glove with a sense of

---

[44] Ibid, 222.   [45] Ibid, 197.
[46] Ibid, 200–1.   [47] Ibid, 201.
[48] Ibid, 247–8.   [49] Ibid, 247–52.

the value of liberty in general, and the special value of free speech in particular. By contrast with state control of printing and publication in France before the revolution, in England 'the doctrine has since 1700 in substance prevailed that the government has nothing to do with the guidance of opinion, and that the sole duty of the state is to punish libels of all kinds, whether they are expressed in writing or in print'.[50] If press freedom prevailed in England and not in France, the explanation lay 'deep in the difference of the spirit which has governed the customs and laws of the two countries'.[51]

What, then, seems superficially an identification of the rule of law with mere legality, in the sense that everyone (including every official) is subject to law, is actually an attempt to defend a richer and deeper account—to identify and endorse the 'spirit of legality', rooted in a conception of the state as servant of a free people, permitting no special rights or privileges for officials that could not be defended as necessary to the preservation of that freedom.[52] Dicey's notorious opposition to French *droit administratif*—a distinct body of public law applied by special tribunals to disputes between citizen and government—reflected his anxiety that an independent regime of official law, separate from the ordinary law applied by the regular civil courts, would give systematic precedence to state interests at the expense of the citizen's liberty. He identified the existence of an 'elaborate administrative system', beyond the 'control of the ordinary tribunals', with a strong central state responsible in France for press censorship and the exercise of discretionary powers, hostile to individual liberty.[53]

If, then, 'the constitution is pervaded by the rule of law' because its general principles are exemplified by judicial decision in particular cases, Dicey can be understood as pointing out the law's dependence on a structure of moral or political ideas, rooted in evolving common law tradition. A preference for common law reasoning over continental declarations of rights does not in itself invest the rule of law with any particular content, as Paul Craig observes.[54] But when judges represent a constitutional tradition of respect for individual liberty, sceptical of official claims that would erode such liberty, the rule of law acquires a substantive content. Legality means the consistent and fearless defence of general principles of law, preserving an important sphere of individual autonomy, in the face of actions or measures that would flout them from whatever quarter (public or private) they may appear. The third limb of Dicey's account of the rule of law indicates the link between the merely formal idea of bare legality and the deeper conception, whereby strict adherence

---

[50] Ibid, 253.

[51] Ibid, 265.

[52] Dicey stresses 'the predominance of the spirit of legality which distinguishes the law of the constitution': ibid, 264.

[53] Ibid, 265–7. Note Lord Bingham's observation that 'it is for us, in our own tradition, a source of strength that claims, whether against the government, or a minister or an official, or against a private citizen or a corporation, come before the same judges in the ordinary courts of the land': Lord Bingham of Cornhill, 'Dicey Revisited' [2002] PL 39–51, at 51.

[54] Paul Craig, 'Formal and Substantive Conceptions of the Rule of Law: An Analytical Framework' [1997] PL 467–87, at 473–4.

to legal form involves the subjection of government to standards of respect for individual freedom and dignity.[55]

Dicey's claim that the concept of 'administrative law' was 'utterly unknown to the law of England', and 'fundamentally inconsistent with our traditions and customs', undeniably overrated the protection of freedom afforded by the 'principles of private law'.[56] Only the application of public law principles, whether by special tribunals or ordinary courts, can give protection against the abuse of administrative discretion; and the exercise of official discretion is plainly essential to the performance of many basic state functions. Nevertheless, just as it is fundamental to the rule of law that the state should enforce the rules of private law impartially between citizens, so it is equally important that state officials should themselves conform to the ordinary private law in the absence of explicit and justified exemption. If an official is liable for trespass or assault or false imprisonment, in the same manner as a private citizen, he carries the burden of showing special justification for actions otherwise contrary to law; and while the necessary powers may be granted by statute, such statutes are subject to the interpretation of independent judges—guided or influenced by the 'general spirit of the common law'.[57]

It is simply a misunderstanding of Dicey's project to object that, as a matter of fact, public authorities in Britain do exercise broad discretionary powers (and did so even when Dicey wrote in 1885).[58] The fact that the naturalization of an alien may fall within the discretion of the Home Secretary, or that a public health authority can take land compulsorily in order to build a reservoir, hardly serves to refute Dicey's theory; nor does Parliament's exercise of extensive law-making discretion show that legality is not, when properly explained, a precious ideal of constitutionalism. To complain that the idea of the rule of law 'is apt to express the political views of the theorist and not to be an analysis of the practice of government' is to suppose that we confront a stark choice between descriptive analysis, on one hand, and normative political argument, on the other.[59] Dicey's interpretative approach, if correctly understood, combines description and evaluation in the only way such an approach can proceed. It seeks to deepen our understanding of our own legal and constitutional heritage by reflection on the principles and ideals that make it worthy of notice and respect. The assertion that the 'only fundamental law is that Parliament is supreme' is a theory challenging the ideal of legality, presented as if it were a statement of undeniable empirical fact.[60]

We can further our grasp of Dicey's conception of the rule of law by attending to the distinction emphasized by F. A. Hayek between law, in its primary sense

---

[55] For further argument, see Allan, *Constitutional Justice: A Liberal Theory of the Rule of Law* (Oxford: Oxford University Press, 2001), 13–21.

[56] Dicey, *Law of the Constitution*, 203.

[57] Ibid, 413.

[58] Sir Ivor Jennings, *The Law and the Constitution*, 5th edn (London: University of London Press, 1959), 55–8.

[59] Ibid, 60.

[60] Ibid, 65.

of general rules governing relations between citizens or between citizen and state, and 'so-called laws' that are rather 'instructions issued by the state to its servants concerning the manner in which they are to direct the apparatus of government and the means which are at their disposal'.[61] Hayek observed that, while discretion is a necessary part of managing its own resources, under the rule of law 'the private citizen and his property are not an object of administration by the government', or a means to be used for its purposes.[62] Accordingly, an administrative decision, affecting the citizen's private sphere, should ideally 'be deducible from the rules of law and from those circumstances to which the law refers and which can be known to the parties concerned'.[63] The decision should not be affected 'by any special knowledge possessed by the government or by its momentary purposes and the particular values it attaches to different concrete aims, including the preferences it may have concerning the effects on different people'.

Hayek and Dicey draw the same fundamental distinction between law and discretion: discretionary power is, in principle, 'arbitrary' in the sense that it leaves people vulnerable to official determinations of public policy or public interest, made in full view of all the circumstances of the particular case. When an official can use coercion against the citizen to further a general policy objective, rather than enforcing a previously established rule, the citizen becomes an object of state administration: his plans and interests are liable to unpredictable disruption at governmental pleasure. The law cannot serve as a bulwark against such interference with a person's private sphere unless it consists of rules that prescribe clear limits to state action, enforceable by independent courts that do not share the specific policy objectives of the executive Government. Legal rules, whether common law or statutory, not only define the legitimate boundaries of governmental action, but provide a basic guarantee of impartiality, defining the permissible grounds for distinguishing between cases or persons:

The [pertinent] conception of freedom under the law...rests on the contention that when we obey laws, in the sense of general abstract rules laid down irrespective of their application to us, we are not subject to another man's will and are therefore free. It is because the lawgiver does not know the particular cases to which his rules will apply, and it is because the judge who applies them has no choice in drawing the conclusions that follow from the existing body of rules and the particular facts of the case, that it can be said that laws and not men rule.[64]

It is reasonably clear that Dicey shares Hayek's ideal of the rule of law, whereby the law serves to insulate the individual from all arbitrary interference—interference that has no justification in terms of general rules or standards that serve the public interest, treating all fairly as entitled to equal respect.[65] It is an ideal to be attained

---

[61] F A Hayek, *The Constitution of Liberty*, 207.
[62] Ibid, 213.
[63] Ibid, 213–14.
[64] Ibid, 153.
[65] J W F Allison distinguishes between Diceyan and Hayekian conceptions of the rule of law largely by attributing an exaggerated formality to the former; and even if 'Dicey's rule of law was directed at individuals—officials and private persons', while 'Hayek's was directed at the state administration', the

as fully as circumstances permit—the ideal that informs Dicey's 'spirit of legality'—rather than a rigid barrier to governmental action that may encroach, when truly necessary, on an individual's private sphere. Hayek concedes that it will be fully effective only insofar as the legislature (not merely the court) strives to honour it: 'In a democracy this means that it will not prevail unless it forms part of the moral tradition of the community, a common ideal shared and unquestioningly accepted by the majority.'[66] Hayek concedes that the rule of law is an ideal that, in some circumstances, 'we can hope to approach very closely but can never fully realize'. At the same time, if people reject it as an impracticable or undesirable ideal and cease to strive for its realization, a 'society will quickly relapse into a state of arbitrary tyranny'.

When we grasp the manner in which Dicey's general principles express an implicit ideal toward which the administration of law should strive, we can see how merely formal equality (equality before the law) is linked to a deeper, more substantive equality. Not only must there be rules that constrain the scope of official discretion, so that the formal equality between private citizen and public official amounts to a genuine safeguard against the abuse of power, but the *exercise* of such discretion must itself be justified—if necessary, by reference to general policies and public aims that an independent court can verify as legitimate reasons for official coercion. If administrative discretion that affects a person's property or trade or occupation, for example, cannot be wholly confined by rules laid down in advance, it should at least be closely regulated by such rules; and even if an agency cannot take its decisions in complete disregard of its 'momentary purposes' or current 'concrete aims' (as Hayek would prefer) it should be held nonetheless to high standards of *due process*: it must act fairly on the basis of an accurate view of the facts and in accordance with a plausible view of the public interest, avoiding irrational discrimination between persons.

At the centre of the ideal of legality is the concept of adjudication according to known rules and settled principles. The judge has no discretion, in the sense of scope for exercising will or choice: his task is to discern the requirements that reflect 'the spirit of the whole system of valid rules of law', expressing as a general rule what was previously only implicit within the corpus of common law and statute.[67] That he has no discretion, in the sense that an administrator has discretion, is shown by the fact that his decision is subject to review by a higher court which needs to know only the existing rules and the facts of the case.[68] From the perspective of the ideal of the rule of law, we can insist that an official or agency, though permitted to have direct regard to matters of public policy when exercising coercive powers, should

outcome is much the same: state officials should not exercise coercive powers on the basis of their ideas about the public good, beyond the specific remit of established general rules: see Allison, *The English Historical Constitution: Continuity, Change and European Effects* (Cambridge: Cambridge University Press, 2007), 202–4; see also discussion of Allison's views in Chapter 1, above.

[66] Hayek, *The Constitution of Liberty*, 206.
[67] Ibid, 212.
[68] Ibid.

nevertheless adhere as closely as possible to judicial standards of impartiality or objectivity: its decision must be not only *authorized*, falling within the scope of its jurisdiction, but *fair and reasonable*. Hayek argues that when individual rights must be curtailed in the public interest, there should be respect for people's legitimate expectations. The payment of compensation for the compulsory acquisition of land (for example) is 'our chief assurance that those necessary infringements of the private sphere will be allowed only in instances where the public gain is clearly greater than the harm done by the disappointment of normal individual expectations'.[69] The public benefit must, in other words, be *proportionate* to the private injury, any other result being unreasonable in all the circumstances.

Instead, therefore, of reading either Dicey or Hayek as wholly at odds with the modern regulatory state, in which the boundaries of the individual's private sphere are necessarily indistinct, we can read them, more profitably, as highlighting an ideal of legality implicit in our general political and constitutional arrangements.[70] It is an ideal that imposes on government officials high standards of due process, in their dealings with private citizens—as close to the paradigm of adjudication at 'ordinary law' as is practicable in the light of their functions. The closer an administrative function comes to the formulation of policy, based on general considerations of the public interest, the weaker the analogy with judicial reasoning and legal procedure, and the narrower the scope for judicial review of official decision-making. As an administrative function approaches the judicial, by contrast, in the sense that it entails the application of existing rules or policy to particular cases—where a correct decision depends to a significant extent on factors specific to those cases—the greater the need for rigorous standards of due process; and judicial review to enforce such standards is required. If, at the extreme, a government minister is obliged to exercise a quasi-judicial discretion, akin to a court's infliction of punishment on a convicted offender, he should be guided by judicially determined principles.[71]

When an executive or administrative agency is granted broad discretionary powers in the public interest, it ought to exercise them consistently, according to self-made rules or policies that limit the scope for arbitrary decisions in particular cases—decisions that curtail people's rights or damage their interests on inadequate grounds. Adherence to such rules or policies, which specify the criteria for decision in individual cases, serves both the value of certainty and the goal of fairness or substantive equality. Such rules enable people to predict the consequences of the authority's intervention in their affairs, improving their ability to make plans and pursue their own objectives; and the consistent application of the rules ensures that

---

[69] Ibid, 217–18.

[70] Compare Walters, 'Dicey on Writing the *Law of the Constitution*' (2012) 32 OJLS 21–49, at 35: 'Dicey's three propositions on the rule of law are, as strict rules, descriptively false and normatively problematic, but as general principles they may be, even today, both factually true and morally compelling.' It is important to note that Hayek recognizes a wide range of legitimate government action for public purposes; his conception of the rule of law is by no means equivalent to any principle of laissez-faire or non-intervention (see Hayek, *The Constitution of Liberty*, ch 15.)

[71] See the discussion of *ex p Venables* [1998] AC 407, *ex p Pierson* [1998] AC 539, and *Anderson* [2002] UKHL 46 in Chapter 5, below.

all are treated alike, according to relevant and ascertainable criteria. The common law doctrine of legitimate expectation serves both these aspects of the rule of law, obliging a public authority to justify its departure, in any particular case, from its usual practice or from any explicit statement of its intentions. When a person has acted in reasonable reliance on the continuation of that practice (or adherence to stated intentions) it is unfair to dash those expectations unless it is really necessary in the public interest; and the authority should not be the final judge in its own cause on the issue of necessity. The more a decision depends on the particular facts of the case in hand, and the smaller the consequences for public policy in general, the tighter the court's control should be: the gulf between law and policy is here at its narrowest, the court rightly imposing standards of due process that come close to the quasi-judicial.[72]

While an authority's failure to adhere to its own rules or statements of intention may cause injustice, it is equally a source of injustice for rules or policies to be applied inflexibly, with insufficient attention to the circumstances of the particular case. Even when strict adherence to rules or policies promotes certainty, enabling people to predict an agency's decisions, it may nevertheless entail unfairness by treating different cases as if they were all alike: there is no merit in sticking to rules of practice when, in the particular case, their application would do little or nothing to advance the public interest. Common law doctrine disallows the fettering of administrative discretion by rigid adherence to self-imposed rules or policies. It is not simply that the attainment of public purposes may be jeopardized by such rigidity, destroying the benefits of flexibility that attend the exercise of discretion, but also that any interference with people's rights and interests may be unjustified, causing injury or damage in cases where there is minimal public benefit. There is here an implicit principle of proportionality: the advantages of administrative convenience or efficiency, obtained by adoption of rules and policies to regulate the exercise of discretion, should not be bought at the price of an inflexibility that results in unnecessary damage to private interests.[73]

These rule-of-law standards of fairness or due process, applied to administrative agencies, reflect the essential method of common law adjudication. Common law rules are generalizations drawn from judgments in particular cases, lending an important element of certainty or stability to what might otherwise be a highly abstract jurisprudence, critically dependent on all the circumstances of individual cases. Adherence to settled rules makes the judicial resolution of disputes quite predictable across a broad range of social interaction. Since, however, the rules are ultimately only summary generalizations of underlying principles, there is always scope for adaptation of the rules when justice requires it. Previous cases can be distinguished, when necessary, by reference to general principles; exceptions to

---

[72] See *R v Secretary of State for Education and Employment, ex p Begbie* [2000] 1 WLR 1115, 1129–31 (Laws LJ), considered in Chapter 7, below.

[73] See further Allan, *Constitutional Justice*, 125–33. A policy requiring a convicted murderer to serve a minimum 'tariff' sentence before consideration for parole could not be straightforwardly applied to a child indefinitely detained; the child's progress and development were important distinguishing considerations: *R v Secretary of State for the Home Dept, ex p Venables* [1998] AC 407.

existing rules, consistent with those principles, can be made (or discerned) in acknowledgement of legitimate differences between cases or categories. There is no *direct* analogy between administrative and judicial decision-making because the former is guided by the needs of specific policy goals or objectives, permitting a type of discrimination between persons that would not be tolerable if made by judges, bound by general principles of law. But the imposition on administrative bodies of similar constraints of rationality or fairness, consistent with their duties to further the public interest, is demanded by fidelity to the ideal of the rule of law.

IV

Legal theorists often identify the rule of law with a species of formal or procedural legality, applicable to lawmaking or legislation. Lon Fuller identified a number of conditions, which taken together constituted an 'internal morality of law'; while lawmakers can only strive to fulfil such conditions to the best of their abilities, a complete lack of success in doing so must result in their failure to make effective law at all.[74] There must be published general rules, by contrast with ad hoc commands, and such rules should be sufficiently clear to provide effective guidance; the rules should be normally prospective (since no one can comply with rules made retrospectively), reasonably stable rather than constantly changing, and the rules must not be self-contradictory or require the impossible. Moreover, coercive official action must be congruent with the written law, the administration of the law reflecting its published content. When these various conditions are met, not only are people able to orientate their behaviour by reference to the rules, but the degree of certainty and security they engender marks official recognition of respect for human dignity and individual autonomy:

> Every departure from the principles of the law's inner morality is an affront to man's dignity as a responsible agent. To judge his actions by unpublished or retrospective rules, or to order him to do an act that is impossible, is to convey to him your indifference to his powers of self-determination.[75]

If Fuller's canons of formal legality are, on the one hand, necessary conditions of lawmaking (or governance by rule) and, on the other, moral requirements of respect for human dignity, he has established a necessary or intrinsic connection between law and morality, or law and justice. Insofar as our concept of law assumes the regulation of conduct by general rules, the applicable requirements of formal legality amount to an ideal of governance respectful of human dignity. Joseph Raz observes that 'the extent to which generality, clarity, prospectivity, etc., are essential to the law is minimal and is consistent with gross violations of the rule of law'; it is only a total failure of any of the canons of formal legality that would be incompatible with the existence of law.[76] Yet our concept of law is itself arguably

---

[74] Lon L Fuller, *The Morality of Law*, revised edn (New Haven: Yale University Press, 1969), ch 2.
[75] Ibid, 162.
[76] Joseph Raz, *The Authority of Law*, 223–4.

oriented to an implicit ideal of legality: violations of the precepts of formal legality result in instances of *defective* law, which fall short of standards internal to the concept of law. Fuller may be understood to argue that the concept of law is best understood by reference to an archetype, consisting in full compliance with each of his canons; and such full compliance embodies a moral aspiration of respect for human dignity: 'The necessary connection between law and morals that Fuller sought to delineate is grounded in the fact that instances of law count as such by their approximation to an archetype that constitutes a moral ideal.'[77]

The pertinent moral aspiration is the same ideal that we have discerned at the heart of the accounts of the rule of law given by Dicey and Hayek: rule by law is an essential condition of liberty as independence, marking out personal spheres of freedom of action, resistant to interference by other citizens or public officials. A citizen's legal duties will have definite limits, and those limits will not be dependent on the will or whim of any other person:

> Law represents the only possible set of conditions within which one can live in community with others while enjoying some domain of entitlement that is secure from the power of others. When a government pursues its objectives through the rule of law, it governs consistently with those conditions.[78]

According to Raz, the rule of law is a merely 'negative value': it is intended to minimize the 'great danger of arbitrary power' created by the existence of law.[79] There is less danger to people's freedom and dignity when the law satisfies the conditions of formal legality. Here, however, Raz introduces a questionable dualism, separating the idea of law from the ideal of the rule of law. Whereas for the lawyer 'anything is the law if it meets the conditions of validity laid down in the system's rules of recognition', to the layman 'the law is essentially a set of open, general, and relatively stable laws'.[80] The rule of law is a doctrine that constrains the making and application of law: '*the making of particular laws should be guided by open and relatively stable general rules*'. As Nigel Simmonds observes, however, the lawyer can only invoke a rule of recognition to identify the law if it is the rule of recognition of a system of *law*; and a regime in radical breach of Fuller's canons of legality (such as one where all the laws are kept secret) would hardly deserve that description. So the lawyerly and lay senses of 'law' are indeed closely related.[81] Our concept of law itself depends on our grasp of the ideal of the rule of law, whereby law is constituted a necessary safeguard of liberty as independence.[82]

Rather than a safeguard against the abuse of law, the rule of law is an ideal that helps to define what we mean by law itself: governance through law is the means

---

[77] Nigel Simmonds, *Law as a Moral Idea* (Oxford: Oxford University Press, 2007), 81.
[78] Ibid, 143.
[79] Raz, *The Authority of Law*, 224.
[80] Ibid, 213.
[81] Simmonds, *Law as a Moral Idea*, 50.
[82] Elsewhere Raz recognizes that a 'common image' of the rule of law views it as 'an ideal rooted in the very essence of law', so that in conforming to it 'the law does nothing more than be faithful to its own nature': see Joseph Raz, 'Formalism and the Rule of Law' in Robert P George (ed), *Natural Law Theory: Contemporary Essays* (Oxford: Clarendon Press, 1992), 309–40, at 309.

by which we protect ourselves from the abuse of political power. Law is itself the remedy, not the problem that an independent ideal—the rule of law—seeks to remedy.[83] These reflections serve to confirm the basic idea of the rule of law that I have attributed to Dicey, by analogy with the approach of Hayek. Their repudiation of administrative discretion was not, as it is usually portrayed, an idiosyncratic or ideologically suspect stance, which a superior notion of the rule of law might displace. Such discretion is conceptually antithetical to law, threatening the coherence of our commitment to constitutionalism; its control by independent courts is as important as legislative efforts to comply with Fuller's canons of legality (or the application of presumptions of legislative intent, such as the presumption against retroactive effect). We can explore the content of the British constitutional doctrine of the rule of law by reflection on the concept of law itself; we are seeking to understand the moral and political values implicit in any and every considered judgement about the legality—or constitutionality—of governmental actions or decisions.

Once we accept that respect for the rule of law demands more than bare legality, in the sense of some formal source of authorization (such as derivation from a rule of recognition), we discover that there is no clear division between form and substance. When a penal statute satisfies the (allegedly) formal requirement that it should have no application to past events, there are substantive implications: no one is subject to punishment for acting in a manner that had not then been forbidden. No one doubts that it is a requirement of the rule of law that legal rules should be fairly and accurately applied to the facts of particular cases; and it follows that the principles of natural justice, which require a fair hearing before an impartial judge or arbitrator, may be accounted part of the meaning of the rule of law. It is as important to the correct application of the law, however, that a judge or official should understand the law correctly as that she has an accurate grasp of the facts; if there are competing considerations to be accommodated, requiring judgement in all the circumstances, the rule of law demands that they be fairly weighed and balanced. Certain outcomes would fall outside the boundaries of proper and reasonable judgement, demanding (if available) correction on appeal.

Similar conclusions are warranted in the case of administrative discretion. Even if there is scope for policy choice, where an official may choose which public ends to pursue and to what extent, that choice must be constrained by all the factors that define and limit his 'jurisdiction'. A public official acts *ultra vires*—in excess of jurisdiction—if he flouts the ordinary demands of procedural fairness, refusing to listen to representations made on behalf of persons affected, or acts for extraneous purposes, irrelevant to the public function entrusted to him, or overlooks relevant considerations, or otherwise acts unreasonably. All the ordinary standards of administrative legality, imposed on officials and agencies by the common law and enforced by judicial review, must be considered integral features of the rule of law; they serve, like Fuller's precepts of legality, to secure the citizen's freedom in the

---

[83] Compare Jeremy Waldron, 'The Concept and the Rule of Law' (2008) 43 Ga L Rev 1–61, at 11.

sense of independence from arbitrary power. The safeguards of natural justice or procedural fairness are broadened to include the protections of *due process*, which constitute a powerful bulwark against improper, uncontrolled coercion.

The familiar distinction between review for legality, regarded as an inherent jurisdiction of the High Court, and appeal on the substantive merits, available only when conferred on a court by statute, acknowledges the legitimacy of administrative discretion: the court should secure the boundaries of lawful executive power but must not usurp the decision-making function entrusted to the public official or agency. Lord Greene's articulation of the various grounds of review in *Wednesbury* can be understood as a summary restatement of that distinction between appeal and review.[84] As well as having due regard to relevant matters, and paying no attention to irrelevant ones, an administrative decision must not be so 'absurd' as to constitute an excess or abuse of power. The dismissal of a teacher for having red hair would amount to the consideration of extraneous matters: 'It is so unreasonable that it might almost be described as being done in bad faith; and, in fact, all these things run into one another.'[85] The rule of law is satisfied when a public authority remains within the 'four corners' of its jurisdiction, delimited by these requirements of due process or administrative justice.

If the quashing of a decision for absurdity or unreasonableness seems at first sight inconsistent with the primary judicial focus on the manner of exercise of discretion, rather than its substantive merits, it is only because we have drawn too sharp a distinction between procedure and substance. It is in fact only a distinction of degree; the concept of due process contains elements of both procedure and substance. In most cases, a proper attention to all the relevant criteria, undeflected by irrelevant issues, will point to a rather limited range of acceptable (lawful) conclusions, ruling out a great many impermissible ones. An unreasonable decision, outside the acceptable range, is simply one in which the relevant considerations, if they were properly taken into account at all, were apparently accorded a wholly indefensible weight in all the circumstances. In some instances, when the potential consequences for a person's rights or interests are very serious, a suitably rigorous procedure, administered by fair-minded officials, will generate only one tenable outcome; the distinction between review and appeal has disappeared because the rule of law excludes any effective discretion in the circumstances of the particular case. *Wednesbury* unreasonableness, in other words, expresses the *conclusion* of legal analysis, which encompasses all the relevant rule-of-law criteria as they apply to the facts or circumstances in view.

It is ultimately the sensitivity of the scope of official discretion to all the circumstances that establishes the link between formal and substantive equality. We insist on judicial review by an independent court because we assume that the boundaries of executive discretion are not determined by policy considerations alone; the relevant considerations are not confined to matters of efficacy or efficiency, for example,

---

[84] *Associated Provincial Picture Houses Ltd v Wednesbury Corporation* [1948] 1 KB 223.
[85] Ibid, 229; the example was suggested by Warrington LJ in *Short v Poole Corporation* [1926] Ch 66, 90–1.

but extend to the consequences of different courses of action for the rights and interests of affected groups or individuals. The public benefits of any course of action must be appraised in the light of the related disadvantages for identifiable persons; we would otherwise compromise the objectivity or impersonality of law, underpinning the idea of governance by general rules and critical to preserving liberty as independence. If rule must be displaced by discretion, in the interests of greater flexibility, that discretion must be fairly exercised: the public benefit must be proportionate to any incidental damage or injury to individuals. In ascertaining the degree of harm to individuals, moreover, the court must give great weight to those rights and interests that enjoy a special place in common law tradition: such rights and interests partly constitute the private sphere of independent judgement and action protected by the rule of law. Equality of citizenship includes the equal enjoyment of all the familiar civil and political rights that supplement, in public law, the ordinary rights of protection for person and property in private law.[86]

The ideal of equality, expressed by the principle of rationality, lay at the heart of the issues arising from the scheme of preventative detention under the Anti-terrorism, Crime and Security Act 2001. Enacted in the wake of the terrorist attacks in the United States on 11 September 2001, the statute provided for the detention without trial of an alien (or foreign national) whom the Home Secretary suspected of being a terrorist, but whose deportation (under immigration rules) would expose him to the risk of torture or inhuman treatment abroad, contrary to Article 3 of the European Convention on Human Rights. The European Court of Human Rights had ruled that such an expulsion was prohibited even when the suspect posed a danger to his present country of residence.[87] The Government's Human Rights Act (Designated Derogation) Order 2001 was made in order to circumvent any breach of Article 5 of the Convention, which guarantees 'the right to liberty and security of the person' for everyone within the state's jurisdiction. Derogation from Article 5 is permitted by Article 15 'in time of war or other public emergency threatening the life of the nation', but only 'to the extent strictly required by the exigencies of the situation'. Several foreign nationals, detained under these provisions, challenged the legality of their treatment before the Special Immigration Appeals Commission, which upheld the challenge. The Court of Appeal subsequently allowed the Home Secretary's appeal, but that decision was in turn reversed by the House of Lords.[88]

Although the House of Lords accepted the claim that there was a public emergency sufficiently grave, in principle, to justify derogation from Article 5, the court was not persuaded that such measures were 'strictly required'. The threat of terrorism came not only from foreign nationals but also from British citizens, some of whom were known to support Al-Qaeda but were not subject to any similar regime of preventative detention. If the danger posed to national security by these

---

[86] In Chapter 7, below, I challenge the conventional assumption that there is a choice to be made between contrasting standards of review, arguing that rationality (or reasonableness) *entails* a proportionality judgement in many circumstances.

[87] *Chahal v United Kingdom* (1996) 23 EHRR 413.

[88] *A v Secretary of State for the Home Department* [2004] UKHL 56.

British nationals could be dealt with without infringing their rights to liberty, it was hard to see why similar measures could not be employed to answer the threat from aliens. The choice of an immigration measure to address a problem of national security had resulted in irrational discrimination between citizen and non-citizen. The legislation permitted the detention of people who, even if suspected of having links with Al-Qaeda, did not necessarily harbour hostile intentions towards Britain; and while leaving British suspected terrorists at large, it allowed foreign suspects to leave the United Kingdom to pursue their activities elsewhere if they could find another state willing to receive them.

For similar reasons, the court upheld a legal challenge based on unjustified discrimination on grounds of nationality or immigration status, under Article 14. Lord Bingham drew attention to the fundamental importance of the principle of equality, quoting Lord Hoffmann's remark that 'treating like cases alike and unlike cases differently is a general axiom of rational behaviour'.[89] Of course, a judgement of rationality depends on the criteria of likeness we adopt; and those criteria must be ascertained by close inspection of the specific context: there must be a sufficient connection between the relevant criteria and the avowed object of the legislation. We determine likeness or otherwise by reference to the aims and objectives officially proclaimed, looking with appropriate scepticism at how they are supposedly served by the distinctions made between persons. In the present case, the distinction between national and foreigner was not rationally connected to the supposed legislative objective.

Lord Bingham quoted Justice Jackson's celebrated statement of the 'salutary doctrine' that American local and federal governments 'must exercise their powers so as not to discriminate between their inhabitants except upon some reasonable differentiation fairly related to the object of regulation'.[90] Such equality was not merely an abstraction:

The framers of the Constitution knew... that there is no more effective practical guaranty against arbitrary and unreasonable government than to require that the principles of law which officials would impose upon a minority must be imposed generally. Conversely, nothing opens the door to arbitrary action so effectively as to allow those officials to pick and choose only a few to whom they will apply legislation and thus to escape the political retribution that might be visited upon them if larger numbers were affected. Courts can take no better measure to assure that laws will be just than to require that laws be equal in operation.

Although Lord Woolf CJ, in his judgment in the Court of Appeal, also quoted Jackson's remarks, his conclusions appeared to ignore their warning. He observed that, in order to avoid discrimination between nationals and aliens, the minister would have to exercise more extensive powers of detention than he apparently thought necessary: 'By limiting the number of those who are subject to the special measures, the Secretary of State is ensuring that his actions are proportionate to

---

[89] *Matadeen v Pointu* [1999] 1 AC 98, 109.
[90] *Railway Express Agency Inc v New York* (1949) 336 US 106, 112–13.

what is necessary.'[91] The 'rational connection' that Lord Woolf discerned between the detention of foreign suspects and the minister's purpose took the suitability of (what was in substance) an immigration measure for granted. This approach exemplifies a common conception of *Wednesbury* review, permitting judicial intervention only when a measure seems contrary to 'common sense' or otherwise absurd, in the sense of flouting accepted attitudes or unexamined assumptions. If we are really concerned to safeguard the members of unpopular and vulnerable minorities, in line with Jackson's ideal of equality, we must insist instead that rationality depends on whether the complainant has been fairly treated, not primarily as a member of a limited group or class, but as a separate individual, entitled to the same basic rights and liberties as other persons.

Once we have established the link between equality and rationality, however, we can see that it applies as much to primary legislation as to any other acts of public authorities. A statute that draws indefensible distinctions between persons, or specified groups of persons, has no validity; it is analogous to a bill of attainder, singling out individual enemies for special treatment. Legislative authority is conferred or acknowledged for reasons of the public good: it enables *general* rules to be enacted for the benefit of the whole political community, distinguishing between persons for proper reasons, related to legitimate public purposes. It may be only rarely that legislation is wholly resistant to a benign interpretation, capable of justifying the distinctions made between persons; but the Anti-terrorism, Crime and Security Act 2001, construed as read by the courts in *A*, seems to provide an example. If, as the House of Lords maintained, there were no rational basis for a power to detain foreign nationals suspected of being terrorists, when British nationals considered to be equally dangerous remained at large, the statute was plainly an abuse of legislative power: it deserved no recognition from judges committed to the basic principles of the rule of law. Not being *law*, in the proper sense of the term, the relevant provisions should have been struck down, or at least ignored; and the detainees' release should have been ordered as a necessary consequence. Their liberty had been unlawfully curtailed.

Consider Baroness Hale's rhetorical inquiry about the limits of legitimate legislative authority. She asked whether it would be justifiable to detain 'black', 'disabled', 'female', or 'gay' suspected terrorists by contrast with 'white', 'able-bodied', 'male', or 'straight' ones.[92] Since such arbitrary distinctions would violate the rule of law, they cannot be incorporated *into* the law without reducing it to incoherence. We can make sense of a general rule, identifying its scope and limitations, only by recourse to some account of its *purpose* as a contribution to justice or the public good; but a measure that consists of wholly arbitrary categories or distinctions has no intelligible purpose, or at least none consistent with any legitimate public

---

[91] *A v Secretary of State for the Home Dept* [2002] EWCA Civ 1502, para 53. Lord Walker of Gestingthorpe, in his dissenting speech in the House of Lords, took a similar view: he thought that 'in the context of national security' the limited number of persons actually detained (then 'significantly fewer than 17') was 'relevant to the issue of proportionality': [2004] UKHL 56, para 218.

[92] *A v Secretary of State for the Home Department* [2004] UKHL 56, para 238.

ends. Yet the judicial remedies actually awarded scarcely served to restore legality. Although the Derogation Order was quashed, the relevant statutory provision was simply declared incompatible with the Convention (under the power to make such declarations conferred by the Human Rights Act, section 4), leaving the complainants unlawfully—unconstitutionally—detained.

It is arguable, however, that the 2001 Act was open to an interpretation which, while not ensuring the detainees' immediate release, nonetheless extended a more rigorous form of protection, requiring release if there were no realistic prospect of deportation within the foreseeable future. Although the statute purported to author-ize *indefinite* detention, if deportation proved impossible, which would inevitably amount to a breach of Article 5, it did not preclude more modest measures that might not have flouted Convention rights. Quite apart from the obligation arising under the Human Rights Act, section 3, to try to maintain compatibility with the Convention, common law principles of interpretation would direct a similar effort to safeguard existing rights to liberty. Arguably, on the best interpretation, the statute permitted a contravention of Article 5 only if that were a necessary consequence of detention in any particular case; but in many cases indefinite deten-tion would be unnecessary. If it could be shown that a complainant's detention was genuinely a step towards deportation, as soon as circumstances allowed, the distinction between nationals and non-nationals would no longer look irrational. Foreign nationals do not possess the right of abode enjoyed by British citizens; they may in principle be deported if they pose a threat to national security.

The statute authorized (by reference to the Immigration Act 1971) detention pending removal: it permitted continued detention for as long as 'bona fide and duly diligent efforts were being made to remove the alien terrorist-suspect detainee (and provided he remained a reasonably certified threat)'.[93] Since ministers were attempting to obtain reliable undertakings from other states in relation to the proper treatment of detainees, if deported to those states, it might have been a fair conclu-sion that the requisite bona fide and diligent efforts were being made. The Home Secretary should have been required to satisfy the Special Immigration Appeals Commission that he was taking active and diligent steps to secure deportation; there should otherwise have been an order for the suspects' release.[94] Merely declar-ing a statute illegitimate, in the manner of a declaration of incompatibility with Convention rights, challenges the legality of the public policy impugned while failing to secure for those affected the genuine protection of the law.

The reader may wonder whether it would be compatible with democratic prin-ciple for judges to ignore, let alone strike down, a duly enacted statute, even if its irrationality is clear and irremediable. The doctrine of legislative supremacy cannot, however, be allowed to trump the principle of the rule of law: otherwise Parliament is free to substitute arbitrariness and tyranny for equality and freedom. In denying that the courts were precluded by 'any doctrine of deference' from investigating

---

[93] John Finnis, 'Nationality, Alienage and Constitutional Principle' (2007) 123 LQR 417–45, at 430.
[94] Ibid, 435.

the legality of the statutory provisions, Lord Bingham rightly rejected the Attorney General's distinction between 'democratic institutions' and the courts.[95] The judges were neither elected nor answerable to Parliament; but Parliament, the executive, and the courts had different constitutional roles: 'the function of independent judges charged to interpret and apply the law is universally recognized as a cardinal feature of the modern democratic state, a cornerstone of the rule of law itself'. The division of responsibilities was determined by a proper 'demarcation of functions' and considerations of 'relative institutional competence':

> The more purely political...a question is, the more appropriate it will be for political resolution and the less likely it is to be an appropriate matter for judicial decision....It is the function of political and not judicial bodies to resolve political questions. Conversely, the greater the legal content of any issue, the greater the potential role of the court, because under our constitution and subject to the sovereign power of Parliament it is the function of the courts and not of political bodies to resolve legal questions.[96]

The precise division between law and politics, however, must depend on the nature of the question in point and the kind of evidence needed to answer it. Lord Bingham was willing to defer to 'the judgement of the Home Secretary, his colleagues and Parliament' on the question of whether there was a 'public emergency' within the meaning of Article 15. He held that this was a 'pre-eminently political judgement', which depended on factual predictions about the future behaviour of various people around the world and its likely consequences. It may be doubted whether the court should so readily have accepted the existence of a public emergency, especially when the parliamentary Joint Committee on Human Rights (in a series of reports) had expressed serious doubts. Such acquiescence endangers the freedom the Convention rights are meant to secure.[97] Nor could the 'sovereign power of Parliament' be permitted to alter the basic division of functions, which is intrinsic to the rule of law.

Once we perceive, however, that the distinction between law and politics is highly contextual, reflecting the different components of any question about the limits of public authority in particular cases, we can answer the 'democratic' objection to judicial review.[98] Equality is both a democratic and a legal virtue. It demands an equal voice for all in the free public discussion on which democracy depends, and (at least rough) equality of representation in the legislature. It also commands the equal protection of the laws, in the sense that legal rules and principles are evenly and fairly applied, according to all relevant circumstances. No 'sovereign' Parliament can command an unequal protection, reflecting irrational distinctions, or authorize arbitrary executive action. Its supreme legislative power is limited to

---

[95] *A v Secretary of State for the Home Department* [2004] UKHL 56, para 42.

[96] Ibid, para 29.

[97] See David Dyzenhaus, *The Constitution of Law: Legality in a Time of Emergency* (Cambridge: Cambridge University Press, 2006), 178–81. See also Tom Hickman, *Public Law after the Human Rights Act* (Oxford: Hart Publishing, 2010), 338–43.

[98] See also David Feldman, 'Human Rights, Terrorism and Risk: The Roles of Politicians and Judges' [2006] PL 364–84, at 372–77.

the enactment of *law*, which has its own intrinsic moral form and nature. The formal equality summarized by Fuller's canons of legality is only part of a broader substantive equality of justice—the justice that obtains when the rights and freedoms acknowledged as general principles of British law are extended to all those to whom they rationally apply.[99]

V

The rule of law is an ideal of fair and just governance which embraces both form and substance. It imposes standards of equality and due process. It subjects every assertion of public power to rigorous constraints of procedural fairness and impartial judgement, attuned or adapted to the judicial or administrative context. No one should be at the mercy of any other person's whim, dependent on an official's good nature or present disposition to act fairly towards him; a public official must disregard any personal antipathy or political attitude irrelevant to the governmental function in question. We are subject to law, as opposed to the arbitrary will of officials, when public powers are exercised only in the public interest—when a decision adverse to our interests can be justified by reference to an intelligible account of the public good, allowing us to acknowledge its legitimacy even if, doing our best to be impartial, we continue to doubt its wisdom or justice.

When correctly understood, the rule of law amounts to a theory of legitimate government. Political authority is justified as essential to the provision and enforcement of legal arrangements under which freedom as independence is secured; and although there are many such possible arrangements, compatible in principle with individual freedom, the rule of law requires that the benefits of cooperation and mutual tolerance be extended to everyone. Adherence to the rule of law converts what would otherwise be an assertion of governmental will or power into an exercise of legitimate *authority*, showing respect for the governed as equal, independent citizens. If the British constitution is rightly understood as a free and democratic legal order, its division of powers and inherent common law rights must be interpreted in the light of that basic ideal of equal freedom. Dicey's account of the rule of law only scratches the surface of what is a much deeper and more robust conception of legality, linked to the related values of liberty and justice; and his insistence on the unfettered sovereignty of Parliament (echoed by Lord Bingham's dictum above) must be treated with reserve.[100]

---

[99] The serious challenge to the rule of law presented by the control order regime, substituted for detention of suspected terrorists (whether foreign or British) by the Prevention of Terrorism Act 2005, is emphasized by K D Ewing and Joo-Cheong Tham, 'The Continuing Futility of the Human Rights Act' [2008] PL 668–93. But the authors' appraisal of the courts' role in tempering the worst features of that regime might be thought rather too harsh: see Aileen Kavanagh, 'Judging the Judges under the Human Rights Act: Deference, Disillusionment and the "War on Terror"' [2009] PL 287–304, stressing the acute difficulties faced by courts in assessing the justification of measures taken in defence of national security.

[100] See Chapter 4, below.

Legal authority is sometimes treated simply as an *empirical* matter concerning the exercise of power: if people are in the habit of obeying a 'sovereign' ruler or lawmaker, who himself acknowledges no such duties of obedience to anyone else, then he is the ultimate source of law.[101] If, accordingly, Parliament is widely treated as the sovereign lawmaker for the United Kingdom, Acts of Parliament are binding on everyone whatever their content and however much they may flout our ideas about freedom or justice.[102] Not only may a statute (on this view) ride roughshod over the basic rights of individuals, but it may authorize officials to exercise unfettered discretion in the attainment of their objectives. If authority is understood in this way, as a matter of purely descriptive or empirical analysis, there is an apparent conflict between sources of law: parliamentary supremacy may be asserted in breach of rights or freedoms intrinsic to the rule of law. Since, however, we are concerned with *legitimate* authority—the exercise of power consistent with respect for individual freedom and dignity—our analysis must be normative, rooted in a theory of the rule of law as a moral and political ideal. Whether or not Parliament is sovereign, in the sense that its power is unlimited by any moral constraints, cannot be merely a question of what officials may think or may have thought in the past, even if they were unanimous in their opinion. If the scope of legitimate authority is defined by an accurate conception of the rule of law—an ideal that underpins our very concept of law—a valid Act of Parliament must be informed by at least a plausible conception of the public good, held in good faith and capable of coherent public explanation and defence.[103]

Parliament derives its constitutional authority from its democratic credentials, as the body representing the people as a whole and charged with the advancement of their collective interests. If its enactments cannot be viewed, even by those of goodwill, as a real contribution to the common good, but only as instruments of oppression of political enemies or despised minorities, they could assert no authority: such measures, furthering only private interests, would not *count* as legitimate Acts. Dicey was wrong to suppose that a statute ordering the killing of blue-eyed babies would be *law*, even if people would be mad to obey it.[104] Being *unintelligible* as a contribution to the public good, its invalidity would be fully apparent. It could not be obeyed as laws are meant to be obeyed—by reference to some conception of the public good sufficient to give anyone (citizen or official) a sense of purpose and direction in the circumstances of a particular case. A statute

---

[101] See John Austin, *The Province of Jurisprudence Determined*, ed Wilfrid E Rumble (Cambridge: Cambridge University Press, 1995), Lecture VI. Although Austin identified Parliament as the British seat of sovereignty, he also considered elected members to be trustees acting on behalf of their constituents: 'consequently, the sovereignty always resides in the king and the peers, with the electoral body of the commons' (ibid, 194).

[102] See Dicey, *Law of the Constitution*, 39, where Dicey asserts the 'existence' of parliamentary sovereignty as 'a legal fact', being also 'the dominant characteristic of our political institutions'.

[103] Dicey sets off against the sovereignty of Parliament the interpretative powers of the judiciary, informed by the 'general spirit of the common law', so that 'the supremacy of the law of the land both calls forth the exertion of Parliamentary sovereignty, and leads to its being exercised in a spirit of legality': *Law of the Constitution*, 413–14.

[104] Ibid, 81 (adopting an example provided by Leslie Stephen).

is a text awaiting *interpretation*: we cannot obey it until we have determined its meaning; and statutory meaning (as I shall argue more fully in due course) is as much a function of the public responsibilities we attribute to the legislature as of the literal meanings of words.[105]

The ideal of the rule of law is most fully realized in the common law, which is the ultimate foundation for the authority of court decisions, even those that apply statutory provisions. For the scope and limits of parliamentary authority, and the content of the principles of statutory interpretation, are themselves elements of the *legal order*, whose nature and implications are worked out, case by case, in the evolution and development of the common law. A judge who decides a case at common law, whether in private or public law, normally has no discretion: the parties are entitled to an adjudication of *rights*, in which the answer is, in principle, fully determinable by law. The judge is therefore an exemplar of the ideal of public office, seeking the correct solution to a dispute even when he might *prefer* a different answer—whether for reasons of public policy or even considerations of justice, excluded by the most persuasive interpretation of the applicable law. Since it ought to make no difference which lawyer occupies the judge's seat, if the law is truly the determinant of the pertinent rights and duties, the court must seek to discern the true content of the common law, offering reasons that (so far as possible) demonstrate the correctness of its conclusion on the facts of the case. The fact that lawyers inevitably disagree in practice, or that judgments are often overturned on appeal, does not threaten our ideal of legality. Such disagreement takes place within the structure of a system whose implications for large swathes of social and economic life are relatively certain and uncontentious.[106]

The distinction between formal and substantive equality evaporates in the practice of the common law. Many common law rules are initially identifiable by reference to authoritative judicial statements in the superior courts; summaries of the law made by senior judges in the course of giving their reasons for judgment may provide convenient points of departure for legal argument in subsequent cases. Such pronouncements have no real authority, however, unless they are ultimately *persuasive*: whether or not they provide the true justification for a decision, or only an explanation that finally proves unsatisfactory, is a question for lawyers to resolve as they argue over their implications for legal practice as a whole.[107] Any doctrinal statement of the common law, even when contained in the judgment of a superior court, is only as sound as the reasons that underpin and justify it; there is a continual process of adaptation and refinement, as formal equality, comprising

---

[105] See Chapter 5, below. As David Dyzenhaus points out, Dicey's imaginary statute would also be a bill of attainder, flouting the 'fundamental moral values of legality': see Dyzenhaus, *The Constitution of Law*, 215.

[106] Compare Hayek, *The Constitution of Liberty*, 208: 'the degree of the certainty of the law must be judged by the disputes which do not lead to litigation because the outcome is practically certain as soon as the legal position is examined'.

[107] Compare Fuller's description of precedents as a 'common language', preserving 'those systematic elements of the law without which communication between generations of lawyers, and among lawyers of the same generation, would be impossible': Lon L Fuller, *Anatomy of the Law* (Harmondsworth: Penguin Books, 1971), 136.

the consistent application of legal rules to all alike, regardless of rank or wealth or power, is supplemented by a deeper substantive equality—an equality of justice, whereby general principles of law, tested and refined through legal practice, are applied without fear or favour, according to their true tenor and weight.

If legality is related to the idea of freedom as independence, we must suppose that the content of common law rules is, in principle, knowable in advance of action that might infringe them: we should not have to await retrospective judicial pronouncement. Precedents may be distinguished or refined or even reconsidered in the light of changed circumstances or novel events, not contemplated when the original decisions were made; but such developments in the law should not normally take good lawyers by surprise. Especial care must be taken in the criminal law not to violate the precept *nulla poena sine lege*: no one should be punished for conduct that had not been declared unlawful at the time. But even here there is some scope for judicial adaptation or refinement to acknowledge social change which has made some feature of the law anomalous, provided that such adaptation is well signalled in advance. The courts' removal of a husband's previous immunity to a charge of raping his wife, when intercourse has taken place without her consent, is often cited as an example of common law development at odds with the principle of legality.[108] It is doubtful, however, whether such an objection can be sustained. The defendants' claims to have suffered a breach of their rights under Article 7 of the European Convention on Human Rights, enshrining the principle against retroactive criminal law, were rejected by the European Court: the decisions of the English courts had merely continued a line of case-law development dismantling the husband's immunity. The evolution of the criminal law in this context was a legitimate process, consistent with the rule of law: 'judicial recognition of the absence of immunity had become a reasonably foreseeable development of the law'.[109]

Our concepts of law, liberty, and justice are closely related; and any determination of the content of law, in any specific context, must reflect the moral or political values implicit in the presiding ideal of the rule of law. While a judgement of law is necessarily directed to the particular events or circumstances in view, it is informed by the ideal of legality (or rule of law) to which English law—like any system of law, properly so called—inherently aspires. If the law in practice falls short of our ideal it is because the circumstances of application are invariably challenging: legal interpretation is complex precisely because we have to give due weight to many competing considerations, giving scope for judgement and disagreement. If the efficient prosecution of public policy requires the delegation of substantial discretion to officials, there is a concomitant risk of abuse of power; and while judicial review is a valuable safeguard, it also carries the danger of unwarranted interference, damaging to legitimate public objectives. While reasonable stability is a necessary feature of a system of law capable of being obeyed, social and technological change makes regular legal reform or reinterpretation essential. And although retrospective legal

---

[108] *R v R* [1992] 1 AC 599.
[109] *SW v United Kingdom* [1995] 21 EHRR 363, para 43.

change is generally inimical to the rule of law, it is sometimes necessary to repair injustices or to acknowledge significant changes in social attitudes, threatening fidelity to the law as a bastion of justice.[110]

The fact that adherence to the rule of law entails good judgement and conscientious struggle, however, does not mean that the value of legality can be traded off against other benefits; for the legitimacy of state coercion depends on compliance with the rule of law. Joseph Raz can suppose that we should not sacrifice 'too many social goals on the altar of the rule of law' only because he treats the rule of law as 'essentially a negative value', minimizing the harm caused by law in the pursuit of its goals.[111] As I have argued, the rule of law is, on the contrary, an essential safeguard against abuse of power from any source; and the pursuit of public ends through law is the means of ensuring that protection. Raz is right to reject the notion that the rule of law should be identified with anything so nebulous as a right to 'the establishment of the social, economic, educational and cultural conditions' essential to the 'full development' of personality; and in that limited sense there is force in his objection that if the rule of law 'is the rule of the good law then to explain its nature is to propound a complete social philosophy'.[112] The ideal of legality is compatible with a great diversity of opinion about the social, economic, and cultural conditions that best uphold human dignity. But Raz carries his scepticism about the demands of the rule of law to implausible lengths:

It is not to be confused with democracy, justice, equality (before the law or otherwise), human rights of any kind or respect for persons or for the dignity of man. A non-democratic legal system, based on the denial of human rights, on extensive poverty, on racial segregation, sexual inequalities, and religious persecution may, in principle, conform to the requirements of the rule of law better than any of the legal systems of the more enlightened Western democracies.[113]

If, of course, the rule of law were merely an effective instrument for achieving political goals (as a sharp knife is good for cutting), the law could make any distinctions between persons or groups that served its authors' purposes.[114] And individual autonomy, or liberty as independence, would be served by officials' rigorous observance of such distinctions, enforcing the law according to its express terms; everyone would know what to expect by way of state coercion or protection (or lack of such protection). But in a more fundamental sense liberty as independence would be denied: members of racial or religious minorities, for example, would not enjoy the same autonomy as others, their personal spheres of independent action curtailed for reasons that would not be thought to justify general restrictions on liberty. Freedom from the danger of arbitrary interference should extend to

---

[110] See Fuller's discussion of the complexities entailed by adherence to the various precepts of formal legality in *The Morality of Law*, ch 2.
[111] Raz, *The Authority of Law*, 228–9.
[112] Ibid, 211.
[113] Ibid.
[114] Ibid, 225–6.

the threat of enacted laws that, by treating certain persons or groups as inferior to others, use those persons as means to the lawmakers' ends. Measures that draw distinctions between persons, or groups of persons, that cannot be justified on grounds that all could recognize—grounds consistent with equal citizenship—are no different from bills of attainder, singling out individuals for special punishment or inferior treatment. Renouncing the idea of legal equality, in the fundamental sense of equal citizenship, they flout the ideal of the rule of law; and in flouting that ideal they cease to be *law* in any sense relevant to legal interpretation or judicial responsibility.[115]

Hayek argues that, when a constitution enshrines the principle that people can be subject to coercion 'only in accordance with the recognized rules of just conduct designed to define and protect the individual domain of each', and when the Legislative Assembly is limited to the enactment of 'universal rules intended to be applied in an unknown number of future instances', a bill of rights is unnecessary.[116] The traditional civil and political liberties are not absolute rights but instead subject to limitations imposed 'in accordance with law'; and that proviso subverts the protection given by a bill of rights unless by 'law' is meant 'only such rules as can be described as laws in the narrow sense' of general rules of just conduct, applicable to all. Nor did the traditional liberties exhaust the scope of personal freedom: 'What the fundamental rights are intended to protect is simply individual liberty in the sense of the absence of arbitrary coercion.'[117] This is a valuable reminder that liberty and equality are demands of human dignity that generate, but are not confined to, the civil and political rights that our tradition has taught us to treat with especial reverence.

The idea of equal citizenship is central to the legal philosophy of Ronald Dworkin, whose emphasis on the role of legal principle reflects the importance of including everyone within the general protection of the law. Dworkin rejects a merely formal conception of the rule of law in favour of a more substantive account, closely related to the imperatives of justice. The 'rule book' conception 'insists that, so far as possible, the power of the state should never be exercised against individual citizens except in accordance with rules explicitly set out in a public rule book available to all'.[118] The 'rights conception', by contrast, insists that citizens' moral and political rights should be recognized in positive law, enforceable through the courts: 'It does not distinguish, as the rule-book conception does, between the rule of law and substantive justice: on the contrary it requires, as part of the ideal of law, that the rules

---

[115] Fuller noted the descent of law and adjudication into arbitrariness when courts are forced to draw racial distinctions that, expressing only prejudice, have no scientific basis or legitimate purpose, undermining any view of the apartheid regime in South Africa as having combined 'a strict observance of legality with the enactment of a body of law' that was 'brutal and inhuman': *The Morality of Law*, 160. For a helpful critique of Raz's argument, see Dyzenhaus, *The Constitution of Law*, 220–7; see also David Dyzenhaus, *Hard Cases in Wicked Legal Systems: Pathologies of Legality*, 2nd edn (Oxford: Oxford University Press, 2010), ch 9.

[116] Hayek, *The Political Order of a Free People*, in *Law, Legislation and Liberty*, 109–10.

[117] Ibid, 111.

[118] Ronald Dworkin, *A Matter of Principle* (Oxford: Clarendon Press, 1986), 11.

in the rule book capture and enforce moral rights.'[119] Naturally, Dworkin concedes that the 'rule book' is relevant to adjudication, even on the rights conception: 'people have at least a strong *prima facie* moral right that courts enforce the rights that a representative legislature has enacted'. Moreover, the 'rule book' continues to exert an influence, even when the rules do not dictate a determinate answer on their own; for a judge cannot apply a general moral principle, defining the parties' respective moral rights, unless it is consistent with the wider body of law: 'The principle must not conflict with other principles that must be presupposed in order to justify the rule he is enforcing, or any other considerable part of the other rules.'[120]

The language and context of Dworkin's discussion—his examples are mainly cases involving statutory interpretation—initially suggests a striking gulf between enacted rules, on the one hand, and judges' moral theorizing, on the other: judicial theories of natural right must be curtailed, or constrained, by the need to respect Parliament's decisions. But such an image would oblige a court to choose between enforcing the law and doing justice to the parties.[121] No doubt, we should understand the 'rule book', more broadly, as including the rules of common law; but then the gap between source-based law and moral or political principle quickly recedes. For the common law is more than a body of discrete rules, applicable to diverse, specific issues: its elaborate texture of rules and principles invites the kind of moral theorizing that Dworkin recommends, though always informed and guided by legal and constitutional tradition.

Dworkin argues that in 'hard' cases, where good lawyers disagree, the disagreement arises from contrasting views about citizens' moral rights; but it is doubtful how far we should view such divergence as a clash of beliefs about justice in the abstract—a conflict of political theories conceived independently of lawyers' understanding of the conception of justice implicit in (or assumed by) existing law. Rival interpretations of legal rules, whether statutory or common law, may reflect different accounts of the weight that is properly attributed to familiar and widely shared principles in particular circumstances. The relevant conceptions of justice are themselves *interpretations of law*; and while any judge's legal philosophy is in the end dependent on features of her broader moral and ethical outlook, her opinions about legal rights and duties will be heavily dependent (if she is a good judge) on her grasp of the implications of a shared tradition.

In Dworkin's later work the distinction between justice and legality is given sharper definition. His conception of law as 'integrity' requires the law to be interpreted as a consistent and coherent body of principle, informed by legal history and tradition. Legal or moral principles must provide a persuasive justification of judicial decisions and statutory rules without collapsing into the interpreter's favoured theory of justice, which might not be acceptable to others. Integrity is

---

[119] Ibid, 12.
[120] Ibid, 17.
[121] Paul Craig is led to suppose that Dworkin's connection between law and justice leaves 'no place for a *separate* concept of the rule of law as such at all'. See Craig, 'Formal and Substantive Conceptions', 478: 'The very need to preserve a firm distinction between "legal" rules and a more complete political philosophy is rejected by the thesis itself.'

distinct from both *justice*, regarded as an ideal scheme of liberties or allocation of resources, and *fairness*, in the sense of an appropriate distribution of political power or influence. It is a principle of equality that 'requires government to speak with one voice, to act in a principled and coherent manner toward all its citizens, to extend to everyone the substantive standards of justice or fairness it uses for some'.[122] The effect is to substitute for formal equality before the law (secured by the formal conception of the rule of law) a deeper, more substantive equality. The equal protection clause of the Fourteenth Amendment to the United States Constitution is understood to prohibit 'internal compromises over important matters of principle':

The equal protection cases show how important formal equality becomes when it is understood to require integrity as well as bare logical consistency, when it demands fidelity not just to rules but to the theories of fairness and justice that these rules presuppose by way of justification.[123]

It would, of course, be mistaken to think that integrity or equality could be wholly independent of justice: it is rather a best *approximation* to justice in a society where there is lively disagreement about what, in detail, justice truly requires. It must be supposed that divisions over justice, even if deep-seated, are not so radical as to preclude common understanding and goodwill. Integrity displaces justice, for all practical purposes, whenever what Jeremy Waldron calls the 'circumstances of justice' obtain. There is sufficient agreement throughout the community to sustain adherence to a general scheme of justice, based on existing arrangements which, though admittedly imperfect, are considered worth defending: they are not regarded as pervasively and irremediably corrupt and unjust.[124]

Legality, then, is inherently linked to justice, though the connection is complex. Since the requirements of law are moral demands, dependent on appraisal of all the relevant moral or political values, they are ultimately a matter of individual moral judgement—even if for practical purposes we must accept the court's decision as binding on all affected, at least until it is overturned on appeal. Dworkinian integrity, reflecting the articulation of moral principle characteristic of the common law, places the individual conscience, whether that of public official or private citizen, at the heart of the deliberative endeavour. It elicits an interpretative, self-reflective attitude: 'It is a protestant attitude that makes each citizen responsible for imagining what his society's public commitments to principle are, and what these commitments require in new circumstances.'[125] The 'creative role of private decisions' is affirmed by the 'regulative assumption that though judges must have the last word, their word is not for that reason the best word'.

I shall argue in Chapter 4, below, that there are important implications here for the citizen's obligation to obey the law. It is a moral obligation that assumes

---

[122] Ronald Dworkin, *Law's Empire*, 165.
[123] Ibid, 185.
[124] Jeremy Waldron, *Law and Disagreement* (Oxford: Oxford University Press, 1999), ch 9. See further Chapter 4, below.
[125] Dworkin, *Law's Empire*, 413.

that the law as a whole—and therefore each and every part of it, when correctly understood—is capable of being interpreted as a broadly just scheme, worthy of the citizen's allegiance. Although Dworkin supposes that a prima facie obligation of obedience may be overridden in exceptional cases, where the law is gravely unjust, it is very doubtful whether any such obligation (to obey a wicked law) arises in the first place.[126] Even if a statute purports on its face to authorize some iniquity, its correct interpretation will depend on legal principles too deeply rooted to be simply overridden or displaced; its apparent meaning will be misleading. A great many such statutes, furthermore, would so change the constitutional context as to threaten the coherence that general principles provide; and the committed, interpretative attitude would then be inappropriate: the conscientious interpreter, whether private citizen or public official, should repudiate the whole system as irredeemably unjust, deserving resistance rather than loyalty.

While the protestant attitude to law facilitates internal moral debate—argument over the correct interpretation of statutes or precedent—its plausibility depends on a substantial measure of agreement about many features of legal practice. We must not overlook the *collaborative* dimension of legal practice in service of established tradition. Even settled rules or doctrines are subject to potential challenge as being inconsistent with legal principle, when viewed as features of a larger moral theory; that is why the highest courts can sometimes overturn established doctrine in pursuit of a grander vision, closer to the demands of justice implicit in the broader scheme. As Gerald Postema observes, however, the feasibility of such internal challenge to particular doctrines depends on the stability achieved by shared understandings across the broader spectrum of legal practice.[127] Dworkin presents the tension between competing elements of interpretation as a feature of the lawyer's private deliberations; but such deliberations cannot normally diverge too far from those of other participants in a collective practice.[128] In this way, legal judgements reflect widely held convictions about the demands of justice, pertinent to people's moral rights in the context of a flourishing and valued legal tradition.

In conforming to law, when it meets the essential conditions of the rule of law, we also serve the requirements of justice, having regard to the legal and constitutional tradition within which justice must be pursued in collaboration with others. There is, however, no question of a judge simply imposing his own moral judgements on the litigants whenever the content of law is open to reasonable doubt. His duty is to deepen and clarify a scheme of principle already implicit, if indistinct, in accepted rules and standards, even if he cannot avoid recourse to moral judgement (and hence his own convictions about justice) in performing that duty. In practice, a judge's beliefs about the requirements of law and justice are

---

[126] Dworkin distinguishes between the *grounds* and *force* of law—between the circumstances in which propositions of law are true and 'the relative power of any true proposition of law to justify coercion in different sorts of exceptional circumstance': ibid, 110. I argue in Chapter 4 that rejection of legal positivism undercuts the distinction, which invokes a conception of law rooted in empirical fact.

[127] Gerald J Postema, '"Protestant" Interpretation and Social Practices' (1987) 6 Law and Phil 283–319.

[128] Dworkin, *Law's Empire*, 65–8, 239.

likely to be interrelated; his convictions about people's moral rights will reflect his experience of seeking to make sense of, and find value within, his own historical legal order.[129]

VI

The rule of law is ultimately an ideal of legitimate governance that explains the citizen's moral obligation of obedience. It seeks to reconcile governmental authority with individual autonomy, revealing the conditions under which compliance with positive state law is consistent with the freedom and self-respect of the morally responsible citizen. The connection between law and liberty, emphasized above, suggests a Kantian understanding of the ideal of the rule of law. Individual sovereignty, or independence, follows from the Universal Principle of Right, which states that 'any action is *right* if it can coexist with everyone's freedom in accordance with a universal law, or if on its maxim the freedom of choice of each can coexist with everyone's freedom in accordance with a universal law'.[130] If we treat the relevant freedom as *negative* liberty, or the freedom to pursue one's ends unhindered by other people, it is hard to see how equal freedom could be secured without judging the worth or value of people's differing aims. When people pursue different purposes their exercise of negative liberty will generate conflict, each person's project interfering with another's. If, however, we substitute the idea of liberty as *independence* from the power or choices of another, so that everyone is free to pursue his own purposes with his own property, subject only to respect for the similar freedom of others, we can give a coherent account of the connections between human dignity, freedom, and the rule of law. When freedom is understood as independence there is a fundamental equality in the sense that everyone can decide what ends to pursue with the means he has available (or can legitimately acquire): 'a system of equal freedom is one in which each person is free to use his or her own powers, individually or cooperatively, to set his or her own purposes, and no one is allowed to compel others to use their powers in a way designed to advance or accommodate any other person's purposes'.[131]

Interpreted in this way, Kant's theory of law shows how political authority can be made consistent with individual autonomy: the state's legitimacy derives from its essential role in sustaining a system of equal freedom. The purpose of public law is to secure the rightful civil condition under which the system of private right, or private law, can operate: the state has an obligation to secure and maintain a rightful condition, whereby everyone can enjoy the independence conferred by the Principle of Right. As Arthur Ripstein explains, the constraint a system of

---

[129] For consideration of the common law ancestry of Dworkin's theory of law, see Mark D Walters, 'Legal Humanism and Law-as-Integrity' [2008] CLJ 352–75.
[130] Immanuel Kant, *The Doctrine of Right (The Metaphysics of Morals*, Part I), in Mary J Gregor (ed), *Practical Philosophy* (Cambridge: Cambridge University Press, 1996), 6:230.
[131] Arthur Ripstein, *Force and Freedom: Kant's Legal and Political Philosophy* (Cambridge, Mass: Harvard University Press, 2009), 33.

equal freedom imposes on conduct is unqualified and unconditional. The right to freedom is not a right intended to bring about a certain state of affairs, or to further a specific interest, such as an interest in leading a fully autonomous life; such a right would be conditional on the extent of its instrumental value in all the circumstances. It is simply 'the right to act independently of the choice of others, consistent with the entitlement of others to do the same'.[132]

If negative liberty were the ultimate value, there would be no room for such positive rights as those to state provision of education or welfare or health care— rights generally viewed as legitimate creations of democratic deliberation and decision. Even when the state can provide such benefits or services without restricting people's freedom of action, they must be funded by means of taxation. When our guiding value is liberty as independence, however, positive rights can be endorsed as necessary to complete the original contract; they do not threaten the rule of law.[133] Since no one could consent to laws that would consign them to a condition of dependence on others, there must be arrangements made to protect people from the poverty that would make them wholly dependent on others. Those who hold property are entitled to its exclusive enjoyment only insofar as the system of justice sustains a rightful condition, so that 'the system of private rights really is part of a system of equal independence of free persons'.[134] It is for elected officials to decide how a rightful condition is best attained, in the concrete circumstances of time and place, and hence on what concrete positive rights should be guaranteed: 'Democratic politics has an ineliminable place in determining such matters, because the purpose of public institutions is to make the requirements of right apply systematically, not to discover some detailed blueprint that exists apart from those institutions.'[135]

Kant's Doctrine of Right shows how the rule of law and democracy may be reconciled, exhibiting the relationship between natural and positive law. The constitutional rights of citizens are those natural rights implicit in the basic idea of freedom as independence. The innate right of humanity, or 'independence from being constrained by another's choice', contains such fundamental rights as freedom of expression, freedom of conscience, and freedom of association.[136] Such rights are necessary elements of the system of equal rights under which everyone is '*his own master (sui iuris)*'.[137] Innate right also dictates the presumption of innocence when someone is accused of wrongdoing: everyone is entitled to be treated as a 'human being *beyond reproach (iusti)*' on the ground that 'before he performs any act affecting rights he has done no wrong to anyone'.[138] There is a role for positive law in adapting these rights to current circumstances, ensuring their operation as integral

---

[132] Ibid, 35.
[133] The priority apparently given to negative rights by Sir John Laws appears to reflect his principle of 'minimal interference': see Laws, 'The Constitution: Morals and Rights' [1996] PL 622–35.
[134] Ripstein, *Force and Freedom*, 283.
[135] Ibid, 285.
[136] Kant, *The Doctrine of Right*, 6:237.
[137] Ibid, 6:238.
[138] Ibid.

parts of the whole: 'The task of judgment and justification requires specification of the incidents of innate right through positive law and the exercise of judgment in their application to particulars.'[139] Positive law cannot, however, revoke these fundamental rights or balance them out against competing interests. The state's enforcement of the scheme of rights is necessary to secure equal freedom; coercion and freedom are hence two sides of the same coin.[140] The use of force is permissible, however, only when it is consistent with innate right: 'positive legislation is only legitimate if it could be a law that free persons could impose on themselves, where the test of the possible imposition is their rightful capacity to bind themselves, that is, consistency with their rightful honour'.[141]

Kant wrote that every state contains three authorities, coordinate with one another and, having distinct functions, being unable to usurp each other's power. The 'sovereign authority', in the form of legislator, could not act as ruler, or executive authority, because 'the ruler is subject to the law and so is put under obligation through the law by *another*, namely the sovereign'.[142] Moreover, an executive government that was also a legislature would be despotic. And neither sovereign nor ruler could act as judge, but 'can only appoint judges as magistrates'. Under the terms of the original contract, by which a people forms itself into a state, all three 'civic dignities' exercise true sovereignty, in harness to each other. A state's well-being consists in their being united, where well-being means 'that condition in which its constitution conforms most fully to principles of right'.[143] Only when the basic separation of powers is preserved can the citizen's status be assured, consisting of 'lawful *freedom*' (or 'the attribute of obeying no other law than that to which he has given his consent'), 'civil equality', and 'civil independence', viz. 'owing his existence and preservation to his own rights and powers as a member of the commonwealth, not to the choice of another among the people'.[144]

The separation of powers is not primarily an instrument or scheme for the *dispersal* of power, as many writers suggest, but rather a necessary response to the defects of the state of nature in which equal freedom cannot be attained.[145] In the absence of a public authorization, representing a general or omnilateral will, there can be no private acquisition of anything that can bind other people, and so private rights cannot be established or enforced.[146] Moreover, no one can be required to desist from interference with other people's possessions unless he has assurance that others will accord him the same respect; and 'only a collective general (common) and powerful

---

[139] Ripstein, *Force and Freedom*, 214.
[140] Rather than administering a *sanction* for breach of the law, that state uses force (and the threat of force) to hinder hindrances to freedom, sustaining the victim's right to independence: ibid, 52–6.
[141] Ibid, 213.
[142] Kant, *The Doctrine of Right*, 6:317.
[143] Ibid, 6:318.
[144] Ibid, 6:314.
[145] See for example Philip Pettit, *Republicanism: A Theory of Freedom and Government* (Oxford: Oxford University Press, 1997), 177–80; Eric Barendt, 'The Separation of Powers and Constitutional Government' [1995] PL 599–619. Barendt's essay is nevertheless an effective critique of sceptical treatments of the separation of powers in the British context.
[146] See Ripstein, *Force and Freedom*, 148–59.

will' can give everyone such assurance.[147] And since the application of concepts to particulars is always potentially indeterminate, requiring judgment, there must be public institutions authorized to determine questions arising about the application of rules. Equal freedom requires an objective standard for the determination of rights; the judiciary must therefore have authority to apply the law to particular cases. Since both executive (or ruler) and judiciary must act in accordance with existing law, and since the legislature is composed of elected representatives, the original contract establishes a genuine republic in which the people govern themselves consistently with the demands of human dignity and independence. The rule of law requires that the laws should be consistent with each person's innate right to independence; democracy, in further enforcement of the rule of law, dictates that legislation be self-imposed in a manner that represents the general will, reflecting the principle of equal dignity.

Ripstein explains Kant's reliance on the critical distinction between person and office.[148] The actions of the state are legitimate when they are done by authorized officials, acting for solely public purposes within their proper remit: they are not then simply the unilateral acts of particular power-holders. The idea is that officials act for the citizens as a whole, as the means whereby the people can act collectively. According to Kant, public right is a '*system of laws for a people, that is, a multitude of human beings…which, because they affect one another, need a rightful condition under a will uniting them, a constitution (constitutio)*, so that they may enjoy what is laid down as right'.[149] By making, applying and enforcing the law officials unite the governed into a people; and if those officials create a rightful condition, they are entitled to be obeyed: 'A multitude of human beings is a people just because institutions act for them; the institutions are the principle of their unity, and the acts of those institutions are the acts of the people.'[150]

Government has authority over its citizens because 'when you cannot avoid living side by side with all others, you ought to leave the state of nature and proceed with them into a rightful condition'.[151] Moral authority attaches to positive law, then, because such law is both *necessary* to constitute and complete a rightful condition and *legitimate* when imposed or enforced by authorized officials acting within their powers; and 'the fact that different laws, or different official decisions, with different outcomes could *also* have been authorized by law does nothing to make the actual decisions lack authority, because the rule of law constitutes its authority by creating reciprocal limits on freedom through common institutions'.[152] That does not mean, of course, that *any* positive law enjoys authority, solely by virtue of its source. Officials must act only for public purposes within their respective jurisdictions; even the legislature must act within its powers, respectful of the demands of human dignity and freedom as independence.

---

[147] Kant, *The Doctrine of Right*, 6:256.
[149] Kant, *The Doctrine of Right*, 6:311.
[151] Kant, *The Doctrine of Right*, 6:307.
[148] Ripstein, *Force and Freedom*, 190–8.
[150] Ripstein, *Force and Freedom*, 195.
[152] Ripstein, *Force and Freedom*, 197–8.

Common law constitutionalism can be understood in a similar way. The jealous scrutiny it demands of the coercive actions of public officials does not signal any hostility to the exercise of public power in principle, whether in support of negative or positive rights. On the contrary, the common law confers extensive powers of legislation on Parliament in order that, through its agency, the people can give themselves the laws necessary to the maintenance of a rightful condition. It also enforces the duties imposed on executive officials to implement the laws in specific cases. Autonomy as independence depends on strict compliance with the law by both citizens and officials. And in making the courts the ultimate guardians of the system of law, the common law ensures that both the making and execution of law conforms to the basic Principle of Right. In a truly republican government, in which people rule through their chosen representatives, the legislature cannot impose laws that the people could not give themselves consistently with their entitlement to equal freedom. When obliged to resolve a question about the content or validity of any measure or official action, a court must necessarily determine a question of law; and the question of law is ultimately one about an action's compatibility with the Principle of Right, whereby limitations on freedom are squared with each person's 'innate right', attaching to everyone by virtue of his humanity.[153]

If we follow Kant in conceiving of positive law as making determinate a scheme of moral rights and duties that is otherwise partially indeterminate, we can see more clearly how the rule of law and legislative supremacy must be harmonized. The supposedly absolute sovereignty of Parliament consists in its unchallenged power to determine how a rightful condition should be established, maintained, and defended. Parliament's supremacy reflects its role as the collective voice of the people, given expression through their elected representatives. It is only when Parliament determines how state power shall be deployed to secure the general conditions of freedom that the law is truly binding, representing the general will. In giving concrete form to that ideal of freedom, of course, Parliament cannot violate the moral rights it is supposed to be affirming. While legislation, for example, may regulate the transmission of party election broadcasts or the time and place of public meetings, it cannot abrogate the freedom of political speech. It is only through the exchange of information and opinion that citizens can contribute to the maintenance of a rightful condition in which liberty as independence is secure. It follows, however, that the courts must not assume anything so preposterous to be intended; they must interpret a statute in whatever manner best advances whatever *legitimate* purposes can be discerned, integrating their duty of faithful application with their responsibility for the protection of fundamental rights.

---

[153] Kant, *The Doctrine of Right*, 6.237.

4

Parliamentary Sovereignty: Authority and Autonomy

I

In this chapter I want to explore the doctrine of parliamentary sovereignty, which is the rather infelicitous British name for legislative supremacy. It is infelicitous because it attributes to one institution an authority that should strictly attach to the constitution from which Parliament derives its very extensive powers. Admittedly, Dicey defended an apparently absolutist version of the doctrine, denying limits of any kind on Parliament's legislative authority; but on a closer look we can adopt a more subtle interpretation, giving space to a counterbalancing judicial role, moderating Dicey's absolutism.[1] We will need to examine recent judicial dicta pointing to a more qualified account of the doctrine than the absolutist version; and we must consider what we can learn from the doctrine's adaptation to the circumstances of British membership of the European Community and Union. Unless we detach Dicey's formal definition of the rule of law (emphasizing formal equality before the law) from the 'spirit of legality' he sought to explain and celebrate, his theory of the constitution seems, superficially, to leave the two principles of parliamentary supremacy and the rule of law in irresolvable, potential conflict; but a more subtle reading points the way towards reconciliation. If parliamentary sovereignty is only a grander name for the doctrine of legislative supremacy, it may operate within the constitutional framework of the rule of law.

It will be necessary, however, to examine the notion of sovereignty as a fundamental rule, or 'rule of recognition', binding on everyone within the jurisdiction; most contemporary discussions either assume or explicitly defend an account of the doctrine along those lines. There is a strong affinity, in particular, between H. L. A. Hart's idea of a 'rule of recognition' and Sir William Wade's notion of sovereignty as a political fact.[2] Each points towards the alleged existence of a social or political practice that the lawyer or legal theorist must simply take for granted, any moral qualifications or reservations being (from a strictly legal perspective) entirely beside the point. So entrenched has this approach become that all major constitutional

---

[1] A V Dicey, *Introduction to the Study of the Law of the Constitution*, 10th edn (London: Macmillan, 1964), Part I.
[2] H L A Hart, *The Concept of Law*, 2nd edn (Oxford: Clarendon Press, 1994), 100–10; H W R Wade, 'The Basis of Legal Sovereignty' [1955] CLJ 172–97, at 188.

developments are usually analysed in terms of the rule of recognition—whether or not it has changed and, if so, in what respects. I shall challenge that approach, arguing that there is no such thing as a rule of recognition, any more than there are political facts that simply have to be accepted. Or at least, I shall contend that any such general rule exists chiefly as a matter of external observation—as a primarily sociological phenomenon—and is largely irrelevant to the practical legal issues arising before the courts.

It is doubtful whether legal positivism of the sort Hart endorses—the denial of any necessary conceptual connection between law and morality—is ultimately compatible with our general idea of law, with its associated ideas of legality and legitimacy.[3] If we think the idea of law is closely related to the moral ideal of the rule of law, which regulates the way in which laws are made and enforced as a safeguard against arbitrary infringements of liberty, we will doubt whether the concept of law itself can ever be reduced to a matter of empirical fact (or official attitudes).[4] So a theory that identifies law by pointing to the existence of a rule of recognition observed by officials provides a dubious foundation for the doctrine of parliamentary sovereignty. Even if Hart could convince us of the truth of his account of law as a general idea—a persuasive sociological concept of law—we would still have good reason to reject it as a basis for British constitutional theory. Hart did not seek to defend parliamentary sovereignty as a legal doctrine; and in any event the constitutional theorist does not stand outside the legal system like a sociologist, detached from the contentious debates over questions of law and politics that rage within it. A legal theorist of the British constitution occupies the same ground as any other judge or lawyer. His account of legislative supremacy (and every other legal doctrine) must be informed by reasons capable of persuading other lawyers of its strength or cogency. It must, then, have a moral foundation, even if people often disagree about what morality (and hence law) requires in particular instances.[5]

A theory of the British constitution must grapple with an important question of legitimacy: Parliament's legislative powers must be *justified*; and even if settled practice is part of the justification, we still need reasons for supporting and sustaining it. We cannot, I shall argue, simply point to the facts of the matter, as Hart's legal theory might appear to suggest. Any settled practice of allegiance to statute will prove indeterminate in many cases, in the sense that disagreement will break out about what the practice requires in particular instances. When we are confronted by arguments in favour of a departure from the ordinary rule of obedience to statute in particular circumstances—such as a case involving an apparent conflict with European law or fundamental rights—we cannot respond by pointing to a supposed

---

[3] It is sometimes suggested that Hart is better understood as simply denying any necessary connection between the *validity* of a law and its substantive justice or injustice, though that view is hard to square with Hart's insistence that officials might accept the rule of recognition for any reasons at all, moral or non-moral (ie purely self-interested): see Nigel Simmonds, *Law as a Moral Idea* (Oxford: Oxford University Press, 2007), 69–76.

[4] See Simmonds, *Law as a Moral Idea*, especially chs 3 and 4. Simmonds argues that the *legality* of a rule is critical to any justification of its enforcement and that the idea of legality cannot be reduced to conformity with a rule of recognition accepted by officials: ibid, 123–43.

[5] Compare Ronald Dworkin, *Law's Empire* (London: Fontana, 1986), especially chs 2 and 3.

fundamental rule. If legal arguments pose a coherent challenge to that rule, denying that its application would be consistent with important constitutional values, they can be met only on their own moral ground. We must confront the challenge in order to decide what, in context, fidelity to our practice actually requires. Adherence to a general rule, when good reasons are offered to the contrary, cannot be justified merely by pointing to the rule; and when the nature and scope of the rule are raised as questions of law, in the course of legal proceedings, the relevant moral issues cannot be dismissed as extrinsic to the application of law.

At first sight, these jurisprudential issues may appear to lead us too far from the elements of legal doctrine on which a lawyer may prefer to concentrate; but to cling to received doctrine while eschewing legal theory is only to join one side of a jurisprudential debate without any understanding of it. The principal cases concerning legislative supremacy—which include all those cases that ponder the limits of interpretative possibility under section 3 of the Human Rights Act as well as those that deal with the supremacy claims of European Community law—raise difficult questions about the nature of law and the demands of legality. Since such cases test the nature and limits of parliamentary supremacy they must reach beyond it to the constitution itself; and in a common law legal order like that of the United Kingdom, the constitution is a multi-faceted creature of common law thought, rooted in fundamental moral values.

Moreover, as we shall see, the question of sovereignty, or ultimate source of law, is closely connected to questions about the moral basis of the citizen's obligation to obey the law. If we are willing to contemplate the possibility that what purports to be an Act of Parliament may, on the best theory, lack legal validity, we must ask whose judgement is final on the question of validity. If we are unwilling to allow Parliament to trample on fundamental rights, implicit in the moral ideal of respect for persons, why should we accept judicial rulings that uphold such enactments, contrary to our own best moral judgements? How can we square the authority of legal institutions with the sovereign moral authority of the independent private conscience? These are, of course, large questions that we should approach with humility and caution; but we should not pretend that they are irrelevant to constitutional law or its conception of legal sovereignty. I shall offer an account of the common law constitution that seeks to reconcile claims of authority and autonomy according to context, making individual moral judgement an intrinsic element of the ascertainment of law. Whatever the merits of my account, as a general theory of our constitutional practice, it repudiates any absolutist version of the doctrine of parliamentary supremacy; and my critics cannot plausibly retreat behind mere assertions of empirical fact or the statements of legal principle in their preferred judicial dicta.

From the internal perspective appropriate to legal reasoning or interpretation, I shall argue, we do not confront a choice between rival specifications of a rule of recognition; we need not choose between 'continuing' and 'self-embracing' (or 'old' and 'new') conceptions of sovereignty.[6] That is merely the choice suggested

[6] See Hart, *The Concept of Law*, 149–50. The 'new view', allowing Parliament to bind itself as to the 'manner and form' of future legislation, was defended (for example) by R F V Heuston:

by Hart's alternative characterizations of the rule of recognition. Recourse to such a rule, or to one version of it rather than another, involves stepping outside or beyond the ordinary process of legal reasoning, invoking some set of political facts or supposed political reality: it abdicates responsibility for *judgement*, as if the facts imposed their own solution. By its very nature, as a normative discourse, law involves judgement about appropriate action in the light of the facts: the element of judgement cannot be subsumed by the facts themselves. And since such judgement is dependent, in large part, on the moral values that underpin our constitutional arrangements—supporting certain implications of the principle of legislative supremacy and denying others—moral responsibility cannot be evaded.

Presented with an Act that seems, on its face, to require or authorize some grave injustice—so grave as to lie outside any reasonable legislative discretion—the lawyer must try to reconcile the statutory instructions with constitutional principle, even if that means defending an interpretation that draws on general ideas about liberty or justice, susceptible to moral and political disagreement. He cannot seek shelter behind a simple rule of parliamentary supremacy because it gives no answer to the question he confronts; it no more determines the particular case than it could settle a concrete case about the relative claims of British and European Community law, when a potential conflict of authority arises in particular circumstances. So the nature and limits of parliamentary sovereignty must be worked out, case by case, as we seek to honour democratic deliberation and decision while preserving the conditions that ensure their legitimacy. What from the outside may look like a consistent rule of practice, exhibiting very few exceptions, is from the inside a much more complex and subtle exploration of *doctrine*: a general principle of legislative supremacy exerts its force within a larger framework of constitutional thought.

Ronald Dworkin's proper insistence on the role of moral judgement in competent legal interpretation supports my account of parliamentary sovereignty; but his theory of integrity is, in certain respects, ambiguous. Dworkin is sometimes understood to mean that, in the British context, any plausible interpretation of law would have to reflect an absolutist conception of sovereignty—that conception being one of the standard features that an interpretation has to fit. In the final section of this chapter, I shall show why that understanding is mistaken. There is a closer connection between the 'integrity' of law, as Dworkin conceives it, and the personal integrity of its interpreter than is usually perceived. A 'protestant' approach to interpretation, emphasizing the central place of personal moral conscience and commitment, has important implications for the boundaries of parliamentary sovereignty. Such boundaries (if they exist) are the *conclusions* of a theory of constitutional law, rather than preconceived matters of official opinion that any theory has to fit. Official opinion, of the sort recorded by a rule of recognition, must submit to sceptical scrutiny; it has no more authority, legal or moral, than the power of the reasons that can be given to justify it.

see Heuston, *Essays in Constitutional Law*, 2nd edn (London: Stevens, 1964), ch 1. For an overview, see Colin Turpin and Adam Tomkins, *British Government and the Constitution: Text and Materials*, 7th edn (Cambridge: Cambridge University Press, 2011), 71–9.

II

In Chapter 1, I questioned Dicey's aim to demonstrate that parliamentary sovereignty was a 'legal fact', which any statement about the content of English law had to recognize.[7] If there is a general *rule* requiring obedience to statute, it must be linked in some manner to other rules and principles of constitutional law; and that background of common law principle is bound to confine and colour the meaning and scope of legislative supremacy. The *rule of law* is plainly a normative principle whose implications cannot be ascertained as a matter of empirical fact: it is not identical with what any particular judge or official thinks about it, nor with propositions on which a majority of them presently agree. So the interaction between the rule of law and legislative supremacy must likewise be a matter of normative *argument*, based on considerations of legal or political principle; it cannot be a matter of plain fact, based on official opinion, even in the unlikely event that such opinion turned out to be uniform and wholly uncontroversial. We could challenge that opinion (if we saw fit) by reference to the very principles of political morality that, at an abstract level, must underpin official support for the rule of law.

The law's requirements and authorizations are not matters of fact, capable of being ascertained in the manner that we might ascertain the rules of a game (by consulting an official guide) or of social etiquette (by reference to well-informed opinion). Law is a complex social practice in which questions of political morality are relevant to the correct *interpretation* of the pertinent facts. We cannot know what the law requires or forbids, in any particular case, without some grasp of the ideal of the rule of law—or general principle of legality—which can help to explain why we treat certain kinds of social decision (likes statutes and judicial precedent) as 'sources' of legal obligation. Having very serious consequences for the lives, liberty, and security of everyone within the jurisdiction, legal obligations must be *justified*—if only by reference, in some cases, to the urgent need for collective agreement on complex and contentious questions of social cooperation. The normative dimension is inescapable; and it is also a *moral* dimension. Even such a basic doctrine as that of legislative supremacy must be capable of rational defence—sufficient to convince our sceptical fellow citizens—if we are to treat it as an element of the British constitution, giving rise to specific legal rights and duties enforceable by the courts.

It is sometimes supposed that the content of law is a matter of fact in the sense that it represents the commands or instructions of a sovereign ruler, whether that sovereign be a person or an institution like Parliament: the law is whatever has been commanded, according to accepted methods of reading those instructions. John Austin argued that laws were commands issued by the sovereign to subjects who were in the habit of obeying such commands; the sovereign, by contrast, was not habitually obedient to any other person or body.[8] As H. L. A. Hart observed,

---

[7] Dicey, *Law of the Constitution*, 39.

[8] John Austin, *The Province of Jurisprudence Determined* (1832), ed Wilfred E Rumble (Cambridge: Cambridge University Press, 1995); see eg ibid, 118: 'every positive law, or every law strictly so called, is a direct or circuitous command of a monarch or sovereign number in the character of political superior'.

however, Austin's thesis overlooked the normative dimension of law: the lawmaker is regarded as having an *entitlement* to legislate, which is not the same as merely taking advantage of (or acquiescing in) a habit of obedience.[9] Nor could law be reduced to a series of coercive orders (like the gunman's order to a bank clerk to hand over money). A legislator exercises power pursuant to a pre-existing rule, which confers the necessary constitutional *authority* and provides for an orderly succession of legislators (for example, by popular elections), preserving the continuity of law-making power. For the misleading notion of a habit of obedience to a legally unlimited sovereign Hart substituted an 'ultimate rule of recognition', stipulating the conditions of validity of legal rules. A properly enacted British statute is valid by virtue of the rule that 'what the Queen in Parliament enacts is law'.[10]

Although Hart's theory of law contributes to our understanding of constitutions and the authority they confer on designated officials, it is not a *constitutional theory*, internal to the British (or any other) legal order. The rule of recognition, or ultimate legal rule, is a mere matter of fact, being constituted by the practice of senior officials in treating Parliament (or some other institution) as having the right to legislate. Ordinary statements about the validity of legal rules adopt the participant's internal point of view: they apply an unstated rule of recognition, *accepted* as the appropriate source of the criteria of validity. All rules, Hart explains, have both external and internal aspects: the regularity of behaviour they enjoin, as a matter of observable practice, must be accompanied by a general *acceptance* that such behaviour is indeed obligatory. But whereas the obligatory nature of an ordinary rule may derive simply from its enactment in accordance with the rule of recognition (or ultimate rule), there can be no such explanation of the binding character of the rule of recognition itself:

The assertion that it exists can only be an external statement of fact. For whereas a subordinate rule of a system may be valid and in that sense 'exist' even if it is generally disregarded, the rule of recognition exists only as a complex, but normally concordant, practice of the courts, officials, and private persons in identifying the law by reference to certain criteria. Its existence is a matter of fact.[11]

Now reference to a practice among senior officials to treat certain sources of law as binding may help to explain the efficient operation of a legal system, just in the way that the adherence of government ministers to certain constitutional conventions explains the relatively stable operation of democratic governance. But whether or not such a practice should be accorded *legal status*, requiring its recognition and enforcement by British judges in the course of litigation, is a normative question of constitutional principle. It is a question, more precisely, of whether the courts are justified in applying a legal *doctrine* of legislative supremacy; and questions of justification cannot be answered merely by reporting the facts of the matter, as regards official practice. There must be good *reasons* for treating that practice as a source of rights, duties, and powers in particular cases coming before the courts—reasons

[9] H L A Hart, *The Concept of Law*, 51–61.
[10] Ibid, 100–10.
[11] Ibid, 110.

that judges could give for joining or sustaining the practice rather than ignoring or overriding it.

Of course, the practice of senior officials—members of Parliament, civil servants, and judges—is important. It helps to identify principles of political morality on which we can converge as elements of our own flourishing legal order (not just an ideal constitution imagined by legal theorists). We can interpret the loyal acceptance of statute as a source of legal rights and obligations as an implication of democracy: judges normally defer to Parliament's decisions, as expressed in legislation, because they reflect the wishes or judgements of the people's representatives, who (unlike themselves) can be removed at a general election if they abuse their trust. That practice of obedience to statute, however, is dependent on a continuing ability to read legislation as a contribution to justice, or the general public good, of the kind that people elect a Parliament to make. Democracy is not a principle that operates in a vacuum: its power derives from our related commitments to equality and justice; and these values govern the *interpretation* of statutes. The courts enforce statutes consistently with settled constitutional principles, protecting basic liberties and human rights, because respect for such principles (we may fairly suppose) is a condition of the judges' willingness to recognize Parliament as a body *entitled* to loyal obedience. Legislative supremacy is accepted on the basis that the United Kingdom Parliament 'legislates for a European liberal democracy founded on the principles and traditions of the common law'.[12] However broadly that legislative discretion is conceived, it cannot logically violate those principles and traditions—imposing restrictions on liberty incapable of reasonable justification in all the circumstances—without destroying the moral foundations of the doctrine of supremacy.[13]

Hart was reluctant to acknowledge any necessary moral basis for the rule of recognition. He insisted that there could be a single unified legal system only if the ultimate legal rule was 'regarded from the internal point of view as a public, common standard of correct judicial decision, and not as something which each judge merely obeys for his part only'.[14] But though the officials must respect these common standards and 'appraise critically their own and each other's deviations as lapses', a legal system need not 'rest on a sense of moral obligation or on the conviction of the moral value of the system'. People's allegiance 'may be based on many different considerations: calculations of long-term interest; disinterested interest in others; an unreflecting inherited or traditional attitude; or the mere wish to do as others do'.[15] So senior officials might agree that parliamentarians could exercise

---

[12] *R v Secretary of State for the Home Dept, ex p Pierson* [1998] AC 539, 587 (Lord Steyn).

[13] It would, admittedly, be possible to construct a more austere Hobbesian account of moral foundations, emphasizing the security obtained by unquestioning obedience to Leviathan's commands; but my own account is offered as a more attractive and plausible interpretation of the contemporary constitution. See Thomas Hobbes, *Leviathan* (first published 1651; Harmondsworth: Penguin Books, 1968). For a pertinent reappraisal of Hobbes, see David Dyzenhaus, 'How Hobbes Met the "Hobbes Challenge"' (2009) 72(3) MLR 488.

[14] Hart, *The Concept of Law*, 116.

[15] Ibid, 203.

their power (it would seem to follow) for purely self-interested reasons having nothing to do with democracy or justice.

It is doubtful, however, whether Hart's theory of law can explain the important connection between legality and legitimacy. Having a legal obligation is quite different from being forced to obey a gunman because the reference to legality imports the notion of legitimacy: if we do indeed acknowledge the difference, it is because we accept that a genuine legal obligation has a moral basis in the constitution, which we endorse (from the internal point of view) as a legitimate foundation for government. In any case, however, we must distinguish our own internal perspective, as lawyer or legal theorist, from Hart's external descriptive stance: our own concept of law must be tied to ideas of legality and justification even if Hart's broader, sociological concept need not be.[16] From an internal perspective, the claim that a rule is legally valid makes implicit reference to the legitimacy of the constitution on which validity depends; an acceptance of validity carries an acknowledgement of moral and political justification.

A British judge or official who invokes legislative supremacy, to justify obedience to (or the enforcement of) an Act of Parliament, is doing more than pointing to a doctrine that others accept (for whatever reason they see fit): he is supposing that the legal doctrine is itself defensible on moral grounds. It serves democracy by ensuring that everyone obeys the laws enacted by a representative assembly; contentious matters of justice and public policy are better resolved, in most cases, by officials who are elected and are in that sense directly accountable to the people. By the same token, however, the doctrine cannot intelligibly be invoked to justify measures that would *destroy* democracy (such as the abolition of elections) or infringe such basic rights as the freedoms of speech and association, which can fairly be considered intrinsic to democracy. Admittedly, lawyers may disagree about the limits of legislative supremacy, their disagreement reflecting their differing definitions of fundamental democratic rights; but they are likely to agree (on reflection) that there must be some such limits. It would be plainly self-contradictory to invoke the principle of democracy to justify obedience to rules which, in one's considered opinion, violate the basic precepts of democracy.

Dicey's assertion that parliamentary sovereignty is a 'legal fact' must be understood as the claim that legislative supremacy is a well-established and widely accepted *doctrine* of English law; and legal doctrine rests not on mere facts about general practice, but rather on the reasons that inform and justify such practice (at least in the eyes of those who do accept it). Since those reasons are themselves part of the doctrine—giving it the shape and character it possesses—they indicate the limits or boundaries of legislative supremacy in the very course of supplying a justification. The reasons that justify judicial application of a statute authorizing the Government to raise revenue by imposing taxes, for example, would not apply to justify obedience to a bill of attainder, ordering the imprisonment of a Government critic for his denunciation of public policy. No one is likely to think that the latter

---

[16] For the distinction between sociological and doctrinal concepts of law, see Ronald Dworkin, *Justice in Robes* (Cambridge, Mass: Harvard University Press, 2006), Introduction and ch 8.

would impose any genuine legal obligation—whether on the victim or judges or officials—unless he thought that parliamentary sovereignty was a rule that was wholly independent of its underpinning reasons. But that could only be the *outsider's* viewpoint, observing official behaviour and attempting to predict official reaction to new developments.[17] From the internal point of view of anyone who embraces legislative supremacy as a legal principle, the validity of a bill of attainder depends on a study of the reasons that justify legislative supremacy in those circumstances when it does indeed apply.

A bill of attainder derives no support from the doctrine of legislative supremacy, correctly understood, because it lacks even the *form* of a valid statute. Instead of enacting a general rule, binding on people whose circumstances bring them within its ambit on a reasonable construction, it singles out an individual for special treatment: it is a *measure* intended to strip someone of the normal protection of legal process.[18] In substance, moreover, a bill of attainder falls outside any coherent doctrine of legislative supremacy because of its *irrationality*: a genuine law, enacted for defensible public purposes, is based on reasons applicable (at least in principle) to all those people who satisfy its stipulated conditions. If the only reason for a measure is the desire to victimize a specific individual, who has incurred official displeasure, it need not be taken seriously as a ground of legal obligation. Form and substance are intimately connected. A bill of attainder flouts on its face the idea of equality basic to a liberal-democratic polity: its enforcement severs all connection between the principle of formal equality before the law and the underlying idea of equal citizenship, or equal protection of the laws. A measure that is wholly unreasonable or irrational, in that sense, cannot qualify as a valid law.[19]

Exactly the same would be true of a statute that appeared to order the execution of blue-eyed babies.[20] Since its irrationality, thus construed, would be self-evident, it could make no claim to anyone's serious attention as a possible basis of legal rights or duties. Dicey's claim that the Act would make the preservation of blue-eyed babies illegal, even it were generally ignored, supposes that a statutory rule has an existence quite independently of any reasons that might explain and justify it. But what sort of existence could that be? The operation of an Act as part of the legal order, conferring rights and imposing duties, cannot be divorced from its *meaning*; yet a plainly irrational measure, lacking any plausible justification, has no meaning at all—or none that anyone seeking to make sense of its contribution to the legal order could discover. Since a legal doctrine such as parliamentary supremacy marshals and summarizes reasons of political morality endorsed by its adherents, its *application* cannot be independent of those same reasons. If Acts of Parliament are normally obeyed on the ground that there is good reason for deference to the will of an elected assembly, they must be interpreted as the outcome of that

---

[17] For a fine repudiation of attempts to explain legal obligation in terms of the chance or likelihood of the application of force, see Hart, *The Concept of Law*, especially 33–5, 83–4, 136–47.

[18] See further Chapter 3, above.

[19] For further discussion of the connection between the rule of law and equality, see Chapter 3, above.

[20] See Dicey, *Law of the Constitution*, 81.

assembly's deliberations about the demands of justice and the public good. If they cannot be so interpreted—because they appear to ignore or scorn such demands— they exert no legal force. Lacking any defensible meaning, consistent with the most basic elements of justice, a measure—even if formally valid—is in substance void (whether or not there are any formal powers of judicial invalidation).[21]

In practice, an abuse of legislative power is rarely so obvious. Even when a measure is fiercely contested as inimical to the public good, there is normally a challenge to the wisdom rather than the good faith or sanity of the parliamentary majority; and a bill's opponents will usually acknowledge Parliament's right to enact it into law, while pledging to try to secure its repeal at the first opportunity. When, however, an Act is condemned as a violation of fundamental rights, wholly inconsistent with basic justice, the denunciation implicitly challenges its legal status. A measure that exceeds the limits of legislative supremacy, however generously that doctrine is conceived, obtains no authority from its purported enactment; and this is true even if opinion is deeply divided about the relevant questions of justice and legality. For all practical purposes these questions must be settled, at least for the time being, by the courts—ultimately, if necessary, by the Supreme Court. Moreover, the courts may approve a construction of the measure which, though departing from any 'ordinary' or prima facie meaning, enables it to be applied without grave injury to fundamental rights. An Act that authorizes draconian restrictions on personal liberty may be capable of salvage, for example, by implying (or imposing) appropriately rigorous requirements of due process or procedural fairness.[22]

Nevertheless, even the Supreme Court cannot confer validity on a measure that is, on correct analysis, invalid; anyone who believes it to violate the constitution is both entitled and bound (after due reflection) to maintain his dissent. He may even practice civil disobedience, refusing to accede to statutory demands which (as interpreted by the courts) he repudiates as unlawful and unconstitutional. When legality is annexed to legitimacy, as it must be when we embrace the ideal of the rule of law, there is no escape from individual moral judgement. Neither judge nor official nor citizen can avoid her responsibility for obedience or disobedience to a measure whose legality is open to serious doubt; even the Supreme Court must offer reasons for its own conclusions, which must pass the test of scrutiny by the conscientious sceptic, who awaits to be convinced. To suppose that judges might validate an invalid statute, by declining to disobey or disapply it, is to treat the court as if it were itself an absolute legislature—able to override the most basic elements of justice, affirmed by a constitutional tradition of adherence to the rule of law.

We would be entitled, then, to deny the validity of the blue-eyed babies statute even if, absurdly, the Supreme Court affirmed it. Our resistance would not amount

---

[21] The blue-eyed babies statute would in any case constitute a bill of attainder: see David Dyzenhaus, *The Constitution of Law: Legality in a Time of Emergency* (Cambridge: Cambridge University Press, 2006), 215.

[22] See *Secretary of State for the Home Dept v MB* [2007] UKHL 46; *Secretary of State for the Home Dept v AF (No 3)* [2009] UKHL 28. Such questions of interpretation are explored in Chapter 5, below.

to a violation of law but rather an attempted defence of law against the assertion of arbitrary and illegal force. To deny this is to take up a purely *external* stance, noting the possibility that wicked officials might succeed in their murderous exploits. Such denial is reminiscent of Austin's insistence that a measure radically contrary to justice is nonetheless a 'law', capable of imposing legal obligations:

Suppose an act innocuous, or positively beneficial, be prohibited by the sovereign under the penalty of death; if I commit this act, I shall be tried and condemned, and if I object to the sentence, that is contrary to the law of God, who has commanded that human lawgivers shall not prohibit acts which have no evil consequences, the Court of Justice will demonstrate the inconclusiveness of my reasoning by hanging me up, in pursuance of the law of which I have impugned the validity.[23]

From the external point of view, perhaps, such reasoning is inconclusive if the court proves obdurate. From the internal viewpoint of the victim, however, who supposes that state law ought to conform to minimum standards of morality and justice, the reasoning is perfectly valid; and Austin's Court of Justice contravenes the law.

III

Despite the many judicial dicta purporting to affirm the unqualified nature of parliamentary sovereignty, all good lawyers know that absolute rules of any kind are repugnant to the common law. Common law rules, even those relating to the interpretation and validity of statutes, are grounded in reason, which ensures their susceptibility to adaptation and revision in the face of changing circumstances and novel challenges. A rule requiring obedience to an Act of Parliament, passed in the customary manner, may be perfectly adequate for almost all practical purposes; but a statute that threatened basic legal principles without any apparent justification would test the boundaries of such a rule. As Lord Steyn expressed the point, in *Jackson*, while 'the supremacy of Parliament is still the *general* principle of our constitution', as a 'construct of the common law' it may be subject to exceptions:

In exceptional circumstances involving an attempt to abolish judicial review or the ordinary role of the courts, the...Supreme Court may have to consider whether this is a constitutional fundamental which even a sovereign Parliament acting at the behest of a complaisant House of Commons cannot abolish.[24]

The context of Lord Steyn's anxiety was the court's decision that there were no limits on the powers of the House of Commons to legislate without the consent of the House of Lords, under the Parliament Acts 1911 and 1949, except for the explicit ban in the 1911 Act on its use to extend the life of a Parliament beyond five years, postponing a general election.[25] He was concerned by the prospect that

---

[23] Austin, *The Province of Jurisprudence Determined,* 158.
[24] *R (Jackson) v Attorney General* [2005] UKHL 56, para 102.
[25] Parliament Act 1911, s 2(1).

the 1949 Act, which reduced the period of delay before a bill could be enacted without the Lords' approval from two years to one, might allow a Government to introduce 'oppressive and wholly undemocratic legislation', perhaps including outright abolition of the upper House. Lord Steyn's concerns were shared by Baroness Hale of Richmond, who asserted that the courts 'will treat with particular suspicion (and might even reject) any attempt to subvert the rule of law by removing governmental action affecting the rights of the individual from all judicial scrutiny'.[26] While *in general* 'the constraints upon what Parliament can do are political and diplomatic rather than constitutional', various qualifications 'may emerge in due course'.

Rather than treat these remarks as a threat to overthrow the established legal order, with which the courts have become disenchanted, we should interpret them—much more plausibly—as a reminder of qualifications already latent within the supremacy doctrine, awaiting elaboration if and when circumstances dictate. The message is confusing because the judges tend to waver between internal and external points of view, often treating the doctrine as a 'rule of recognition' that simply exists (or has previously existed) as a matter of 'legal fact'. From that external stance, the only limits on the rule are those that judges, for any reason or none, choose to invent or impose. A good example is Lord Steyn's suggestion that, while 'strict legalism' seemed to support the Attorney-General's argument that the Government could invoke the 1949 Act to force major constitutional change, an 'exorbitant assertion of government power' would 'test the relative merits of strict legalism and constitutional legal principle in the courts at the most fundamental level'.[27] But there is no genuine distinction between 'strict legalism' and 'constitutional legal principle' unless one supposes that Parliament may lawfully abuse its legislative power in breach of the constitution; and that is simply to detach the supremacy rule from the reasons that support it—to sever the rule from the larger constitutional *doctrine* from which it is drawn.

Although Lord Hope of Craighead acknowledged that the 'rule of law enforced by the courts is the ultimate controlling factor on which our constitution is based', granting the courts a role 'to play in defining the limits of Parliament's legislative sovereignty', he appeared reluctant to pursue the logic of his insight.[28] Lord Hope observes that 'the principle of parliamentary sovereignty which, in the absence of higher authority, has been created by the common law is built upon the assumption that Parliament represents the people whom it exists to serve'.[29] But he fails to elaborate the circumstances in which that assumption would be called into question, as a matter of common law, apparently relying solely on political remedies to deal with unconstitutional action. The 'rule of recognition', underpinned by 'what others have referred to as political reality', depended 'upon the legislature maintaining the trust of the electorate'. But what about inherent common law limits and the courts' role in defining (and enforcing) them? Like Dicey, Lord Hope falls back

---

[26] [2005] UKHL 56, para 159.   [27] Ibid, para 101.
[28] Ibid, para 107.   [29] Ibid, para 126.

on mainly external limits to deter abuse of legislative supremacy: 'Parliamentary sovereignty is an empty principle if legislation is passed which is so absurd or so unacceptable that the populace at large refuses to recognize it as law.'[30]

Hart's notion of a rule of recognition, then, is unhelpful and misleading. It may indicate the relevance of uniform official practice to the existence of a working legal system, regarded from a purely external or sociological viewpoint; but from the internal perspective of anyone interested in the content of English law—seeking to interpret its scheme of legal rights and duties—the rule of recognition is irrelevant. The doctrine of legislative supremacy it indicates must be analysed by reference to the reasons that sustain it: its requirements and limits are matters of doctrinal *argument*, which must wrestle with interwoven questions of principle about legality and democracy—about individual freedom and legitimate public authority. Law and political morality are interconnected, and cannot be neatly severed by reference to any supposed 'legal fact'. An interpretation of the facts about official (including judicial) practice must seek the reasons that guide and justify it; and these are necessarily moral reasons about the proper limits on the powers of legislative majorities, even when popularly elected.[31]

No more helpful than Dicey's 'legal fact' is Sir William Wade's 'political fact', which is another version of the rule of recognition. According to Wade, the rule requiring judicial obedience to statute is 'in one sense a rule of common law, but in another sense—which applies to no other rule of common law—it is the ultimate *political* fact upon which the whole system of legislation hangs'.[32] Wade is right, as a matter of descriptive historical observation, that 'the relationship between the courts of law and Parliament is first and foremost a political reality'; but he overlooks the point that, from the internal, participant's perspective, that relationship depends on reasons rather than simply on facts. He has been misled by John Salmond's assertion that the source of legislative supremacy is 'historical only, not legal', and hence a merely historical fact: 'It is the law because it is the law, and for no other reason that it is possible for the law itself to take notice of.'[33] On that view, any departure from a rule of absolute obedience to statute, under any circumstances, would be a 'revolution' whereby the courts—for whatever reasons they think fit—abandon their former allegiance. And consistently with his own theory, Wade treats the courts' willingness to recognize the primacy of European Community law, even when it conflicts with British legislation, as revolutionary—a

---

[30] Ibid, para 120. In *AXA General Insurance Ltd v Lord Advocate* [2011] UKSC 46, Lord Hope held the powers of the Scottish Parliament (under the Scotland Act 1998) subject to judicial review at common law in defence of the rule of law, which prevented attempts to deny individuals access to the courts: 'The rule of law requires that the judges must retain the power to insist that legislation of that extreme kind is not law which the courts will recognize' (para 51). Compare Lord Reed at para 153: since the UK Parliament 'legislated for a liberal democracy founded on particular constitutional principles and traditions', it 'cannot be taken to have intended to establish a body which was free to abrogate fundamental rights or to violate the rule of law'.

[31] Compare Stuart Lakin, 'Debunking the Idea of Parliamentary Sovereignty: The Controlling Factor of Legality in the British Constitution' (2008) 28 OJLS 709–34.

[32] Wade, 'The Basis of Legal Sovereignty' [1955] CLJ 172–97, at 188.

[33] John Salmond, *Jurisprudence*, 10th edn (London: Sweet & Maxwell, 1947), 155.

dramatic change of allegiance to a new European legal order, binding on Parliament as long as British membership of the Community continues.[34]

What may look from the outside like a revolutionary break with tradition, however, may be merely an adaptation and renewal of existing tradition, as the interpreter perceives it—a legal tradition responsive to political developments that cannot be ignored. Whereas the external observer reports the facts of judicial behaviour, as far as the available evidence allows, the legal reasoner must weigh the considerations for and against obedience to a specific Act of Parliament in particular circumstances. The legal reasoner can discriminate carefully between different instances—distinguishing, for example, between express statutory departures from European law and arguably implicit, but perhaps inadvertent, ones—in a manner that an outside observer, detached from the issues of legal principle, cannot.[35] Only his external stance, dependent on identifying the current rule of recognition, could explain Wade's view that the court in *Factortame* had confirmed a 'new doctrine' that made 'sovereignty a freely adjustable commodity whenever Parliament chooses to accept some limitation'.[36] By contrast with such an inflexible rule, purporting to reflect 'political reality', a true legal *doctrine* is much more subtle, enabling the courts to determine, case by case, what judicial loyalty to statute—as an expression of the democratic will—actually requires in all the circumstances. It can allow the judicial response to statute to be tailored to the context in point:

Understanding a constitution is not understanding any single rule internal to it as fundamental; it is understanding how the rules interact and cross-refer, and how they make sense in the light of the principles of political association that they are properly understood to express. If there is a fundamental obligation here, it is an obligation toward the constitution as a whole. It is the obligation to respect a constitution's integrity as a constitution, an obligation that has significance both in moments of relative stasis and in more dynamic moments. These are moments when, in response to changing circumstances, legislators or the people in a referendum make amendments, or judges engage in interpretative adjustment of principles and doctrines in a way that may produce great constitutional change but that does not thereby amount to radical or revolutionary discontinuity.[37]

Encumbered by the notion of a fundamental legal rule or rule of recognition, constitutional lawyers have felt obliged to specify its content; and there has been a competition between rival specifications. Sir William Wade defended a version of the rule that made the entrenchment of special laws impossible. The courts were required to obey the most recent Act, passed in the ordinary manner, even if earlier

---

[34] Sir William Wade, 'Sovereignty—Revolution or Evolution?' (1996) 112 LQR 568–75, appraising *R v Secretary of State for Transport, ex p Factortame (No 2)* [1991] 1 AC 603.

[35] Compare *Macarthys v Smith* [1979] 3 All ER 325, 329; see Allan, *Law, Liberty, and Justice: The Legal Foundations of British Constitutionalism* (Oxford: Clarendon Press,1993), 275–77.

[36] Wade, 'Sovereignty—Revolution or Evolution?', 573.

[37] Neil MacCormick, *Questioning Sovereignty: Law, State, and Nation in the European Commonwealth* (Oxford: Oxford University Press, 1999), 93. MacCormick distinguishes between rules of 'recognition' and 'change', arguing that Wade has conflated them. See also Pavlos Eleftheriadis, 'Parliamentary Sovereignty and the Constitution' (2009) 22 CJLJ 267–90, especially 282–90, emphasizing the interdependence of relevant principles, provoking interpretative deliberation.

legislation had attempted to impose additional hurdles, such as a requirement to obtain a special majority in Parliament or the approval of the electors at a referendum (requirements themselves protected against repeal by similar safeguards). Later Acts always repealed earlier ones, whether expressly or merely by implication, insofar as they were inconsistent.[38] If, then, the European Communities Act 1972 had acquired a special status, requiring later as well as earlier Acts to give way to contrary European law, there must have been a radical alteration of the fundamental rule: the old law had surrendered to a new political reality, which the courts were in no position to challenge.

A competing version of the fundamental rule, however, does permit entrenchment: if Parliament alters the law regulating the 'manner and form' required for future legislation on specified matters, a later Parliament must comply with those new rules in order to make valid law on the matters in question.[39] On that view, a bill of rights or other legislation of special constitutional importance can be protected against later repeal by ordinary majority vote: the courts would be obliged to reject any later measure that failed to comply with the new requirements of manner and form. Special legislation may even be placed beyond practicable amendment: it may be impossible to muster the necessary special majority or satisfy other, perhaps onerous, conditions for valid change or repeal. These contrasting versions of the rule of recognition reflect what Hart called a 'choice between a *continuing* omnipotence in all matters not affecting the legislative competence of successive parliaments, and an unrestricted *self-embracing* omnipotence the exercise of which can only be enjoyed once'.[40]

We are being offered a false choice between two versions of a non-existent fundamental rule. From the internal viewpoint of the legal reasoner, confronted by the choice between obedience to a recent Act, passed in the ordinary manner, and obedience to an earlier Act, stipulating special conditions for amendment, the choice of fundamental rule is an irrelevant distraction. While in some circumstances there may be very strong reasons to insist on compliance by Parliament with such special conditions, in other cases it may be an affront to the democratic will of the current Parliament to ignore its instructions, enacted in the ordinary manner. The relevant questions of manner and form cannot be severed from questions of moral and political substance. An attempt to entrench a bill of rights (such as the Human Rights Act) against repeal by ordinary majority vote in the House of Commons would at least deserve judicial respect; the British Government is already bound by the European Convention on Human Rights in international law. An attempt to entrench large parts of Government social and economic policy, frustrating the ordinary political process of democratic change, would by contrast need to be resisted; yet the 'self-embracing' version of the fundamental rule would permit such entrenchment, enabling a Government (with the support of its backbenchers)

---

[38] See *Ellen Street Estates Ltd v Minister of Health* [1934] 1 KB 590.
[39] See R F V Heuston, *Essays in Constitutional Law*, 2nd edn (London: Stevens, 1964), ch 1; Sir Ivor Jennings, *The Law and the Constitution*, 5th edn (London: University of London Press, 1959), ch 4.
[40] Hart, *The Concept of Law*, 149.

to place formidable obstacles in the way of any future efforts to reverse its political programme.

The special entrenchment of European Community law, made by the European Communities Act as subsequently interpreted, reflects the urgent need to secure harmony between British and European law. Rather than making or acceding to a change of rule of recognition, suggestive of some extra-legal, non-judicial act, the House of Lords in *Factortame* merely adopted an interpretation of the relevant statutes capable of producing that essential harmony. The European Communities Act, section 2(4), provided that 'any enactment passed or to be passed...shall be construed and have effect subject to the foregoing provisions of this section', giving legal force to the rights, powers, and duties arising by or under the Community Treaties. Lord Bridge explained that the effect was the same 'as if a section were incorporated in...the 1988 [Merchant Shipping] Act which in terms enacted that the provisions with respect to registration of British fishing vessels were to be without prejudice to the directly enforceable Community rights of nationals of any member state' of the Union.[41] It was a reasonable assumption, after all, that members of Parliament did not intend, in enacting the later statute, deliberately to repudiate the requirements of European law; it would be an unreasonable *construction*, at least, that entailed that consequence. When questions of interpretation are squarely faced, giving proper weight to the relevant considerations of legal principle, the irrelevance of competing versions of a rule of recognition is made apparent.

Lord Justice Laws's masterly exposition of the constitutional relationship between the United Kingdom and the European Union, in *Thoburn*, reflects the primacy of European law, as regards its substantive provisions, and the legislative supremacy of Parliament as a matter of British constitutional law.[42] Since the common law does not allow Parliament to surrender its legislative supremacy, the European Communities Act cannot grant any power to European institutions to qualify that supremacy: 'The conditions of Parliament's legislative supremacy in the United Kingdom necessarily remain in the United Kingdom's hands.'[43] However, substantive Community rights currently prevail over the conflicting terms of any domestic statute, even if passed after 1972. As a 'constitutional statute', having special importance for the 'legal relationship between citizen and state', the European Communities Act is protected against all but express repeal: the ordinary doctrine of implied repeal does not apply.[44] The Act has thereby secured a qualified immunity similar to that enjoyed by common law fundamental rights; and it joins a class of special statutes, including Magna Carta, the Bill of Rights 1689, and the Acts of Union between England and Scotland 1706 and 1707:

A constitutional statute can only be repealed, or amended in a way which significantly affects its provisions touching fundamental rights or otherwise the relation between citizen and state, by unambiguous words on the face of the later statute.[45]

---

[41] *R v Secretary of State for Transport, ex p Factortame Ltd* [1990] 2 AC 85, 140.
[42] *Thoburn v Sunderland City Council* [2002] EWHC 195 (Admin).
[43] Ibid, para 59.
[44] Compare MacCormick, *Questioning Sovereignty*, 88–91.
[45] *Thoburn*, para 63.

Reflecting the balance of reasons for and against competing *interpretations* of statute, the common law has no need of revolutions to explain its continual process of assimilating change within the general, overarching fabric of constitutional principle. Even Sir John Laws's talk of 'constitutional statutes' imposes rather too much rigidity on an interpretative process capable of responding to all the relevant circumstances. It may be hard to know, in the abstract, whether or not a particular statute qualifies for such special status; and the question is likely to distract us from more nuanced matters of construction, tailored to the facts of the case in view. If the Merchant Shipping Act could be read compatibly with the European Communities Act, giving due weight to the pertinent considerations of legal principle, no genuine question about implied appeal actually arose.

While, moreover, the Human Rights Act may also be dignified by Laws as a 'constitutional statute', having special importance for the relationship between citizen and state, there could be no question of implied repeal: the Act protects European Convention rights against infringement only insofar as it is 'possible' to interpret subsequent legislation accordingly.[46] If a compatible interpretation of later statutes cannot be found, the Convention rights are simply overridden. Admittedly, we would expect the courts to strive very hard to achieve a compatible meaning, avoiding any unnecessary conflict between domestic and Convention law; and so, in practice, only an express repeal—or repeal pro tanto (for the purposes in hand)—may be sufficient to displace the Convention rights. It depends on how fiercely the courts defend them by interpretative means, invoking a strong presumption in their favour.[47] But the special status of Convention rights is then the consequence of a style of interpretation focused on the competing demands of policy and principle, according to the facts of particular cases. It does not reflect the requirements of any special rule about constitutional statutes, whose classification will be of greater interest to the detached observer than to the committed legal reasoner (such as judge or lawyer).[48]

Wade's opinion that a 'new doctrine' had made the rule of obedience to statutes 'a freely adjustable commodity', subject to Parliament's own legislative choices, is largely defended by recourse to *Factortame (No 2)*, in which Lord Bridge denied that there was any improper or novel 'invasion' of parliamentary supremacy:

If the supremacy within the European Community of Community law over the national law of member states was not always inherent in the EEC Treaty, it was certainly well established in the jurisprudence of the Court of Justice long before the United Kingdom joined the Community. Thus, whatever limitation of its sovereignty Parliament accepted when it enacted the European Communities Act 1972 was entirely voluntary.[49]

---

[46] Human Rights Act 1998, s 3(1).

[47] These matters are explored in Chapter 5, below.

[48] Alison Young reaches rather similar conclusions, defending a 'pragmatic' interpretation of Laws LJ's distinction between constitutional and other statutes: Alison L Young, *Parliamentary Sovereignty and the Human Rights Act* (Oxford: Hart Publishing, 2009), 40–5. Young's account of *Thoburn*, however, is part of her defence of an absolutist conception of sovereignty, based on Dicey's view of sovereignty as a 'legal fact'. For a perceptive critique, see Stuart Lakin, 'How to Make Sense of the HRA 1998: The Ises and Oughts of the British Constitution' (2010) 30 OJLS 399–417.

[49] *R v Secretary of State for Transport, ex p Factortame Ltd (No 2)* [1991] 1 AC 603, 658.

This observation, however, was a response to the hostile 'public comments' on the decision of the European Court of Justice, affirming the primacy of European law.[50] It was an explanation or reminder of the political events that had led to the current position, denying any impropriety on the part of the Court of Justice or the national courts. As is so often the case, the failure to distinguish between internal and external points of view—the perspectives of legal reasoner and detached observer—has caused confusion. If Lord Bridge's remarks in the first and second *Factortame* cases are apparently in conflict, as Wade supposed, attention to these contrasting perspectives is the key to their reconciliation. The apparent conflict is only superficial. In the first case Lord Bridge explains the court's interpretation of the applicable law; in the second, he describes the circumstances in which the pertinent questions of law had arisen and required to be addressed.[51]

IV

In *Jackson*, Lord Steyn appeared to endorse a version of the 'rule of recognition' that enabled Parliament to bind its successors, entrenching legislation against repeal by an ordinary majority. Citing a number of Commonwealth cases, in each of which a colonial legislature had been required to adhere to special manner and form requirements for certain purposes, he asserted that 'apart from the traditional method of law making, Parliament acting as ordinarily constituted may functionally redistribute legislative power in different ways', such as by requiring special majorities in each House: 'This would involve a redefinition of Parliament for a specific purpose. Such redefinition could not be disregarded.'[52] Baroness Hale of Richmond also suggested that 'there is no reason why Parliament should not decide to redesign itself, either in general or for a particular purpose'. Citing some of the same Commonwealth cases, she observed:

If the sovereign Parliament can redefine itself downwards, to remove or modify the requirement for the consent of the Upper House, it may very well be that it can also redefine itself upwards, to require a particular parliamentary majority or a popular referendum for particular types of measure.[53]

The court accepted the validity of the Parliament Act 1949, enhancing the powers of the Commons to legislate without the consent of the Lords, even though it was itself enacted under the provisions of the Parliament Act 1911, permitting enactment by the Commons alone subject to compliance with specified conditions. Rejecting suggestions that the House of Commons was acting under the

---

[50] In *R v Secretary of State for Transport, ex p Factortame Ltd*, Case C-213/89, [1990] ECR I-2433 the Court of Justice held that any rule of national law that inhibited the grant of interim relief, protecting Community law rights, must be set aside by the national court.

[51] Compare P P Craig, 'Sovereignty of the United Kingdom Parliament after *Factortame*' (1991) 11 YEL 221–55, at 249–50.

[52] *R (Jackson) v Attorney General* [2005] UKHL 56, para 81.

[53] Ibid, para 163.

Parliament Act 1911 as a 'delegate' of Parliament as ordinarily constituted (both Houses giving their consent), the court held that the Act merely provided 'for an alternative mode by which Parliament, as reconstituted for specific purposes, may make laws'.[54] So the objection that, as a 'delegate', the lower House could not lawfully enlarge its own delegated powers could not be sustained.

It was, however, quite unnecessary to choose any particular version of any fundamental rule; nor would such a choice, adopted wholesale, have made any sense. Even if the House of Commons were entitled under the Parliament Acts to legislate with the same authority as Parliament itself, subject to meeting the relevant conditions, it would hardly follow that either Commons or Parliament could entrench legislation against repeal by ordinary majority vote. Different questions of principle would arise and relevant distinctions would need to be drawn, according to the balance of argument. Moreover, though the court held that an Act passed under the Parliament Act procedure enjoys the same constitutional status as other primary legislation, such an Act's validity derives from the 1911 Act. The Hunting Act 2004, whose validity was under challenge, owed its legal force to compliance with the 1949 Act, which in turn rested on the first Parliament Act. However the court preferred to *describe* the status of these Acts, there was in substance a delegation of power from Parliament as ordinarily constituted.[55] In principle, the power of the Commons to legislate without approval of the Lords could always be revoked.

In emphasizing that the *intention* in 1911 was not to enlarge the powers of the House of Commons, but rather to restrict those of the House of Lords, the court assumes that Parliament was free to act as it chose; but that is to beg the question at issue, which concerns the validity (and limits) of any such attempt to redistribute legislative power. Could Parliament decide to transfer its power to the Cabinet or Prime Minister? Should the courts simply accept such a transfer, acceding to the validity of 'primary legislation' issued by the Government? A focus on the historical events of 1911 has blinded the judges to the critical questions of legality and legitimacy that necessarily arose.[56] If Parliament was entitled in 1911 to redistribute its power in the chosen manner, it must be because there were strong democratic considerations in support of that conclusion: it was intolerable that the Upper House (with its hereditary membership) should be able to frustrate the policy of an elected Government by maintaining a permanent block on its attempts at legislative reform. No doubt similar considerations supported the further changes made in 1949; and the established use of that Act in enacting subsequent statutes (besides the Hunting Act) contributed an element of legitimacy based on settled custom and expectation.[57] There was, in effect, a constitutional convention that

---

[54] Ibid, para 94 (Lord Steyn). Compare Lord Bingham of Cornhill at paras 22–6. The validity of the 1949 Act was challenged on the ground that 'delegates' of legislative power (the Queen and Commons) could not constitutionally invoke that power to enlarge or vary the powers delegated to them.

[55] Parliament Act 1911, s 4(1) requires that such an Act must state that it is made 'in accordance with the provisions of the Parliament Act, 1911, and by authority of the same'.

[56] See especially Lord Bingham's speech: [2005] UKHL 56, paras 9–25.

[57] See Lord Nicholls of Birkenhead: ibid, paras 67–9.

enabled the House of Commons to legislate under the 1911 Act as, apparently, amended in 1949; and *Jackson* affirmed the legal force and validity of that convention.[58] None of these considerations would apply, or apply in the same way, to any attempt to entrench legislation by limiting the available means of future amendment or repeal.

Nor were the Commonwealth cases necessarily in point. In the *Trethowan* case, for example, the New South Wales legislature was held unable to abolish the Legislative Council (or Upper House) without first obtaining the approval of the electors at a referendum, as required by an earlier statute.[59] As a colonial legislature, however, it was subject to the Colonial Laws Validity Act 1865 (enacted by Parliament at Westminster) which provided, in section 5, that constitutional amendments must be made in such manner and form as was currently required, whether by Act of Parliament, prerogative Order in Council, or colonial law. The referendum condition was therefore enforceable in the courts. Since the New South Wales legislature was subordinate to the British Parliament, the attempted constitutional change was ultra vires by virtue of the restrictions imposed by the 1865 Act. There was no direct analogy with the position of the United Kingdom Parliament itself.[60]

And similarly, though in *Ranasinghe*, Lord Pearce observed that 'a legislature has no power to ignore the conditions of law-making that are imposed by the instrument which...regulates its power to make law', even if it is otherwise a 'sovereign' Parliament, there is no such 'instrument' in the case of the Westminster Parliament.[61] The legislature of Ceylon (Sri Lanka) operated subject to Orders in Council, made in London, that imposed special conditions on purported constitutional amendment; in the absence of a special majority vote (certified by the Speaker) a bill conflicting with the terms of those Orders could not become a valid Act. There can be no plausible reliance on such cases to support a particular version of any British rule of recognition: determined by the principle of ultra vires, they have no bearing on the general principles of political morality that provide the limits of the powers of the United Kingdom Parliament.

To invoke a version of some fundamental rule, dictating the nature and limits of legislative supremacy for any and every purpose, is a means of evading responsibility for *judgement* in all the relevant circumstances. Any such rule could only be a very rough approximation of the requirements of legislative supremacy, apt to describe the likely outcome of certain kinds of political action. Different versions of the rule would describe the predictable consequences of various sorts of action.[62] But

---

[58] Lord Hope of Craighead held that a court could not ignore the 'political reality' of 'a general acceptance by all the main parties and by both Houses of the amended timetable which the 1949 Act introduced': ibid, para 124. The connection between law and convention is explored in Chapter 2, above.

[59] *Attorney General for New South Wales v Trethowan* (1931) 44 CLR 394 (High Court of Australia), [1932] AC 526 (Judicial Committee of the Privy Council).

[60] Compare Wade, 'The Basis of Legal Sovereignty' [1955] CLJ 172–97, at 182–3, 189–90.

[61] *Bribery Commissioner v Ranasinghe* [1965] AC 172, 197–8 (Judicial Committee of the Privy Council).

[62] Notably, Lord Hope of Craighead reasserted the traditional view that it 'is impossible for Parliament to enact something which a subsequent statute dealing with the same subject-matter cannot repeal', while adding that there was no doubt that 'in practice and as a matter of political reality, the 1911 Act did have that effect': *R (Jackson) v Attorney General* [2005] UKHL 56, para 113.

the requirements of law or legality must be discerned by analysis of constitutional principle, focused on the merits and demerits of contrasting judicial responses to political events. Questions about legality and democracy arise to demand our attention; and because the answers must be found by recourse to legal and political theory we cannot take refuge in mere assertions about official practice, as if bare uninterpreted precedent could spare us from any concern with political morality. In *Jackson*, the judges not only disagreed about the *extent* of the powers conferred by the 1911 Act; their reasoning betrays various differences of approach and emphasis, reflecting the complexity of the underlying theoretical issues. A focus on the specific moral and political context made the judges' tentative observations on the nature of any fundamental rule redundant—irrelevant to the questions of practical judgement at issue.[63]

If the proper construction of the Parliament Act 1911 enables the House of Commons to achieve any legislative purpose it desires, subject only to the express exception in section 2(1) for a 'Bill containing any provision to extend the maximum duration of Parliament beyond five years', there is no reason in logic why the House might not invoke the Act to repeal that constraint before using it again to extend its own life—postponing a general election, perhaps indefinitely. That view was defended by the Attorney-General and endorsed by Lord Bingham of Cornhill.[64] The logic of fundamental rules, based simply on historical fact and official opinion, can dictate very unpalatable conclusions. Significantly, the majority recoiled from such conclusions, holding that the 'express legislative intention' could not be defeated in this way.[65] Lord Brown of Eaton-under-Heywood acknowledged the 'strict logic' of the Attorney-General's position, but was unwilling to give any ruling that would 'sanction in advance' such use of the Act.[66] Lord Rodger of Earlsferry was reluctant to accept the removal of a safeguard of 'fundamental constitutional importance', which might 'undermine the democratic basis of the British system of government'.[67] These reservations indicate the limits of reliance on general rules of recognition, supposedly descriptive of 'political reality'. Questions of legitimacy ultimately arise to force appraisal of the nature and grounds of such rules, smudging any neat distinctions between public law and its underpinning constitutional morality.[68]

---

[63] Compare Lakin, 'Debunking the Idea of Parliamentary Sovereignty' (2008) 28 OJLS 709, 720–8. Alison Young suggests that there are only 'two possible explanations' of *Jackson*, forcing us to choose between a 'shift in the rule of recognition', representing the court's surrender to the political facts, and a 'change to a self-embracing theory of parliamentary sovereignty', obliging courts to accept the new regime: Young, *Parliamentary Sovereignty and the Human Rights Act*, 171–4. Her essentially descriptive stance, detached from the relevant issues of legality and legitimacy, leads her to overlook a third explanation: the validity of the Hunting Act was, all things considered, the better conclusion as a matter of legal and constitutional principle.

[64] *R (Jackson) v Attorney General* [2005] UKHL 56, para 32.

[65] Ibid, para 59 (Lord Nicholls of Birkenhead).

[66] Ibid, paras 189–94.

[67] Ibid, para 139. Lord Carswell indicated that there might be further limits on powers conferred by s 2(1), 'though the boundaries appear extremely difficult to define': ibid, para 178.

[68] R F V Heuston's defence of his 'new view' of sovereignty was rooted in a misguided quest for a constitutional logic that would insulate the common law from questions of political morality.

V

Since H. L. A. Hart's 'rule of recognition' was merely a reflection of accepted practice, its content depended on official agreement. Insofar as opinions differed about what custom and convention required, the fundamental rule was indeterminate. While current practice endorsed a rule that granted Parliament a 'continuing sovereignty', so that statutes could not normally be protected against repeal, the validity of attempts to impose manner and form requirements for particular purposes remained uncertain. There were no legal answers to the many questions that might arise about the extent of Parliament's powers to bind the hands of its successors. Answers could only be supplied by the courts as they saw fit, by analogy with their role in settling the meaning of an indeterminate statute:

> The truth may be that, when courts settle previously unenvisaged questions concerning the most fundamental constitutional rules, they *get* their authority to decide them accepted after the questions have arisen and the decision has been given. Here all that succeeds is success.[69]

Jeffrey Goldsworthy calls the dilemma that would confront a court, considering the validity of a statute that does not comply with any special manner and form requirements, previously enacted, a 'hard case': the judges would have to look 'behind' the doctrine of parliamentary supremacy to underlying principles of political morality.[70] This would 'exemplify Hart's thesis, that judges must sometimes exercise a law-making discretion', reaching 'beyond the law'. If the issue needs to be settled, no doubt other senior officials will accept the result. It would not follow, however, that in an 'easy case', in which the doctrine of parliamentary sovereignty was clear, 'other senior officials would accept that the judges had authority to overrule the doctrine, and invalidate a statute on the ground that it is inconsistent with deeper principles'.[71]

   In one sense, of course, Hart and Goldsworthy are right: we can often predict that, though opinion is divided about the correct answer to a question of law, including a question about the nature and limits of legislative supremacy, everyone will loyally accept whatever the Supreme Court finally decides. But though the observation is right, it is also irrelevant. We are interested not in what may be described or predicted from a purely detached, external point of view; adopting the internal perspective of judge or lawyer, having to make a *judgement* in all the circumstances, we are concerned with what legality actually requires. From our perspective as participant, rather than outside observer, our recourse to principles

---

See, by way of analogy, Heuston, *Essays in Constitutional Law*, 30: 'The common law has found it almost impossible to transmute into satisfactory judicial decisions the important but curiously evasive principles of natural justice.'

[69] Hart, *The Concept of Law*, 153.

[70] Jeffrey Goldsworthy, *The Sovereignty of Parliament: History and Philosophy* (Oxford: Clarendon Press, 1999), 259.

[71] Ibid.

of political or constitutional morality is an integral part of finding the law. If it is legitimate to have regard to such principles at all—as Goldsworthy plainly concedes—they guide our efforts to determine what the law requires: any lawyer who ignored them, on the basis that they lay 'beyond the law' and so could be disregarded at her pleasure, would be rightly thought incompetent.

This is true, moreover, whether we have in mind statutory ambiguities or the limits of legislative supremacy itself; indeed the distinction is itself a product of the legal positivism that Goldsworthy adopts from Hart. While it is usually a matter of general agreement that an Act of Parliament should be obeyed, there is often serious doubt about what a specific provision actually *means*; and the doubt cannot be resolved by reference to any legislative 'intention' (which on matters of detail is usually non-existent, if not altogether meaningless) but only by recourse to considerations of public policy and legal and moral principle.[72] The distinction between legal rules and principles, on the one hand, and moral or political principles, on the other, exists only in the mind of the detached observer, whose grasp of the law is confined to the visible activities of officials and the specific explanations of them that such officials (including judges) choose to offer. That is, of course, why any overlap between legal rules and moral principles is (from that perspective) necessarily contingent, depending on the character and commitments of officials. From the internal viewpoint, however, in which law is conceived as an instrument of liberty, justice, and democracy, there is no such distinction between legal and moral rules or principles: the content of law is an interpretation of legal practice informed by those ideals.

Nor is there any useful distinction between 'hard' and 'easy' cases: the latter are merely cases in which general principles indicate answers which, in all the circumstances, elicit broad agreement. There would, therefore, be no question of judges scandalizing other senior officials by 'overruling' any doctrine of absolute sovereignty in an 'easy' case, as Goldsworthy suggests. In practice, the critical question will concern the true *meaning* of a provision capable, on one construction, of doing grave injustice or flouting fundamental principles. There is no doctrine of supremacy that prohibits judicial efforts to interpret a statute consistently with justice; and no such doctrine would be acceptable to anyone working in the common law tradition. In applying a provision in a manner that avoids great injustice, therefore, the court *conforms* to the doctrine of legislative supremacy as that doctrine is correctly understood. Statutes are interpreted as the product of a deliberative process intended to further justice and the public good; legislative supremacy is acknowledged on that understanding.[73] If a statute ever proved wholly impervious to a reasonable interpretation, consistent with constitutional principle, it could not be applied; but judicial resistance would constitute not an *overruling* of parliamentary supremacy, but rather an enforcement of its limits.

---

[72] See further Chapter 5, below.
[73] Note Coke CJ in *Bonham's case* (1609) 8 Co Rep 107, 118: an Act of Parliament made 'against common right and reason' would be 'void' at common law; or, more diplomatically, 'some statutes are made against law and right, which those who made them perceiving, would not put them in execution'. Compare *R v A (No 2)* [2001] UKHL 25, para 45 (Lord Steyn), considered in Chapter 5, below.

It must be doubted whether Goldsworthy is really entitled to take Hart's theory of law as a basis for his own defence of parliamentary absolutism. He argues that, since 'the most senior legal officials, including judges, have for a very long time recognized as legally valid whatever statutes Parliament has enacted, and have often said that they are bound to do so', parliamentary sovereignty is a 'central component' of the British 'rule of recognition'.[74] Hart is not, however, purporting to offer either a theory of British constitutionalism or a theory of parliamentary supremacy, even if he invokes the latter as an example to illustrate his arguments. Hart's 'concept of law' is an account of the nature of legal systems in general, attempting to elucidate their most important features. His emphasis on the uniformity of official practice is intended to explain the basis of the complex system of rights, duties, and powers associated with a national or municipal legal order, having regard to the regularities and expectations characteristic of such an order. Even if it is true that official attitudes are an essential part of any explanation of law, as a general social phenomenon, it does not follow that Hart is *endorsing* any particular attitude as a matter of British constitutional law or theory. Even as he emphasizes the importance of the 'internal attitude' of officials to an understanding of law, Hart's own perspective is clearly *external*: he takes the stance of the puzzled observer, demanding a theory of law in general (as a sociological phenomenon) rather than a theory of British (or liberal democratic) constitutionalism.

It is a controversial question whether Hart's philosophical method is defensible, and even more doubtful whether his efforts to employ it are successful.[75] Even if Hart's theory could be accepted as a reliable guide to the general character of legal systems, however, it would provide no support for Goldsworthy's position. A lawyer who wants to defend an absolutist view of legislative supremacy, denying all possibility of constitutional limits, must offer an argument drawn from moral and political theory. He cannot refute his opponents by pointing to any uniform practice that simply *constitutes* the doctrine he defends. There is no such uniform practice because on matters of detail lawyers, judges, and senior officials clearly disagree; even if they accept (or say they accept) absolute parliamentary supremacy, as a working general rule, they differ over the nature and extent of the qualifications they should read into statutes to safeguard common law values.

Official practice may converge in many instances, where agreement can be sustained on the basis of arguments everyone, or nearly everyone, finds persuasive. It may be widely agreed that, on almost all matters of current concern, disagreement is best resolved by adherence to whatever Parliament decides after due deliberation. But the legal rule of legislative supremacy is embedded in a complex tapestry of legal *doctrine*, which reflects such constitutional values as the rule of law, the separation of powers, the protection of individual rights and the fairness of criminal trials. If legislative supremacy were employed radically to undermine those values, it would disrupt and destroy the fabric of doctrine that sustains it. Senior officials (especially

---

[74] Goldsworthy, *The Sovereignty of Parliament*, 238.
[75] See especially Dworkin, *Justice in Robes*, ch 6, and Simmonds, *Law as a Moral Idea*, chs 3 and 4.

senior judges) as well as ordinary citizens would challenge the legitimacy of such action, thereby raising doubts about the *legality* of any such 'exorbitant assertion of government power'.[76]

Anyone's interpretation of the law must reflect her own moral judgements about the grounds of its constitutional legitimacy. Her account of the law will be constructed from a variety of legal 'sources', widely recognized as relevant; but statutes, precedents, and customs or understandings must be fitted to some larger scheme that makes coherent sense of people's claims of right or duty. The interpreter cannot divorce her construction from her own moral opinions. She proceeds on the assumption that the purpose of law is to instantiate some scheme of *justice*, responsive to her fellow citizens' reasonable expectations about the protection of liberty and furtherance of the collective welfare. So any rule of obedience to statutes must be grounded in that larger vision: it must be much more than merely a *report* that senior officials (for whatever reasons they see fit) think that Parliament is legally omnipotent. No doubt their opinions are *relevant*: their loyalty to the results of democratic decision-making is part of the general practice to be explored and interpreted. But an interpretation must try to make *good sense* of the practice, including the attitudes of other participants; exploration of the nature and limits of legislative supremacy is itself a feature of the practice in which everyone is necessarily engaged. Every 'hard case' that raises real doubts about the propriety of legislative action, undertaken for questionable purposes or with dubious consequences, also tests the boundaries of Parliament's jurisdiction. It presents the interpreter with a moral challenge that she cannot evade by hiding behind the attitudes of senior officials—attitudes she might deplore on moral grounds directly relevant to her general interpretative understanding.

If it were true that the opinion of senior officials (or at least of a majority of them) settled the requirements of constitutional law—the law being merely a matter of empirical fact—we should have to join Goldsworthy in distinguishing between legal and moral obligation. We should say that a wicked statute, productive (despite our best interpretative endeavours) of very grave injustice, imposed valid legal duties of compliance but ought, nonetheless, to be disobeyed. Goldsworthy contends that though in an 'extraordinary case' judges 'might be morally bound to disobey a statute', just as any citizen or official might be so bound, they are precluded by the doctrine of parliamentary supremacy from holding statutes invalid on the 'ground that they are unjust or undemocratic'.[77] But since the scope of legislative supremacy is *not* simply a matter of majority official opinion, but rather a matter of legal *judgement* resting on an interpretation of legal practice—informed by the ideals and principles that inspire that practice—the distinction between legal and moral obligation is, in this context, only a device to prop up Goldsworthy's legal positivism. The limits of legal obligation track the boundaries of moral obligation. Judge, citizen, and official are alike required to obey any statute *legitimately* enacted

---

[76] *R (Jackson) v Attorney General* [2005] UKHL 56, para 101 (Lord Steyn).
[77] Goldsworthy, *The Sovereignty of Parliament*, 266.

(having due regard to reasonable differences of view about matters of justice and the public good); what is *not* legitimate is not law, and so binds no one.

Admittedly, people's judgements about legitimacy will vary: they will sometimes differ not only about the demands of justice or the public good, but also about the scope for reasonable disagreement (and hence the extent of governmental discretion). So must there not be an institution to determine finally and for all purposes any question of legal validity? And if so, as Goldsworthy argues, may not an elected Parliament be a better final authority than unelected judges? If it is useful to ask whether a *statute* requiring that blue-eyed babies be killed could possibly be valid, 'it is equally useful to ask whether a judicial decision that a blue-eyed baby be killed could possibly be valid'.[78] And could that really be a legitimate question for every legal interpreter—even an ordinary citizen, anxious to decide what his legal obligations really are, and so whether or not to accept the court's ruling as correct? According to Goldsworthy, anarchy can be avoided only 'if some officials have legal authority superior to that of others, and citizens, to decide what legally ought to be done'. Yet the *moral* duty to resist supposedly valid, but wicked, 'laws' or 'judgments' (which Goldsworthy grants) must give rise to precisely the same risk. Anarchy is no more likely to ensue from the assertion of a citizen's right to judge the *validity* of evil (or radically unjust) state demands than from his resistance to such demands on independent moral grounds. In substance, the citizen's moral dilemma is exactly the same—whether or not to accept a measure or ruling as a legitimate governmental act, demanding his obedience.[79]

It is true, of course, that officials should not desist from enforcing the law as they understand it to be. There would indeed be anarchy if no law or judgment were ever enforced against anyone who challenges its validity or correctness, even if the challenge is made in good faith. People are often mistaken about the requirements of law, even when they are right to question the wisdom or justice of particular statutes or judicial decisions; and officials must not allow such people to impede the ordinary processes of law and administration. Fairness to other citizens limits the scope for official tolerance of civil disobedience. No one can expect the law to match her own judgements about what justice or public policy requires; everyone must leave a considerable latitude to government to make reasonable, if contestable, decisions in the public interest. But no one assents to *whatever* her government may seek to impose, abandoning all responsibility for distinguishing between law, properly so called, and assertions of arbitrary will. If it is her duty to *interpret* statutes and judicial rulings as contributions to a scheme of justice—a scheme sufficiently just to elicit her allegiance, notwithstanding its many imperfections—she could make no sense of truly oppressive measures, radically contradicting that scheme.

---

[78] Ibid, 262.
[79] Goldsworthy supposes that an insistence on the validity of oppressive laws helps to ensure that disobedience is an extraordinary response to extreme injustice: Jeffrey Goldsworthy, *Parliamentary Sovereignty: Contemporary Debates* (Cambridge: Cambridge University Press, 2010), 92–4. Even if this were plausible, however, the argument simply assumes that the law can be determined quite independently of the relevant moral considerations; and that assumption is mistaken. (See also my response in Chapter 1, above.)

Unable to locate any rational basis for obedience, she would have to regard them as meaningless (or void).

Although civil disobedience is usually treated as a form of resistance to unjust *laws*, whose validity is taken for granted, it is often better understood as a repudiation of the *legality* of the measures impugned. If civil disobedience is, ideally at least, a 'public, non-violent, conscientious yet political act contrary to law', addressed to the sense of justice of those in power (or a majority of the electorate), it is 'contrary to law' only in the sense that resistance may be maintained even if the courts affirm the validity of the 'statute' concerned.[80] The appeal to the sense of justice of officials or the political majority, seeking a change of heart over their support for the measure, is primarily a call for those officials or that majority to adhere more faithfully to the constitutional principles they purport to recognize. They are called on to be more *consistent*, conceding the disparity between legal principles and their present actions: the dissentient 'invokes the commonly shared conception of justice that underlies the political order'.[81] A person who refuses to comply with an Act of Parliament, in the manner that its official interpretation requires, is best regarded as invoking the limits of legislative supremacy, as she understands them. She does not normally intend to flout the constitution, whose authority she accepts, but rather to deny that the constitution—its corpus of common law principle—permits enforcement of the measure she decries.[82]

An important element of Lon Fuller's critique of legal positivism was his complaint that its insistence on the separability of law and morality—its refusal to countenance any necessary conceptual linkage between law and justice—left the idea of a citizen's moral obligation to obey the law (or the 'moral obligation of fidelity to law') without a coherent basis.[83] How should the obligation of fidelity be understood in relation to other moral obligations, such as the duty to resist injustice and condemn governmental oppression? We usually suppose that the citizen has a moral obligation to obey the law of his community, when the constitution makes arrangements for government which are reasonably just. In the absence of agreement on perfect justice, it is right to support a constitution that treats people fairly and equally, enforcing a consistent scheme of private law and protecting their autonomy from excessive state interference in matters of conscience and private lifestyle.[84] A regime may be *legitimate* and so justify people's allegiance even when they remain divided in opinion on many matters of justice and public policy: such matters must be decided fairly by democratic means. Any moral obligation

---

[80] John Rawls, *A Theory of Justice* (Oxford: Oxford University Press, 1972), 364–5.

[81] Ibid, 365.

[82] See further Allan, *Constitutional Justice: A Liberal Theory of the Rule of Law* (Oxford: Oxford University Press, 2001), 95–106.

[83] Lon L Fuller, 'Positivism and Fidelity to Law—A Reply to Professor Hart' (1958) 71 Harv L Rev 630–72, at 656.

[84] It is the state's primary role in maintaining a system of private law (or private right) that provides the chief source of its legitimacy; only such a system can secure individual autonomy, or liberty as independence from the power of others (whether fellow citizens or officials): compare Immanuel Kant, *The Doctrine of Right (The Metaphysics of Morals, Part I)*, in Mary J Gregor (ed), *Practical Philosophy* (Cambridge: Cambridge University Press, 1996), 6.230–238.

of obedience must be dependent, however, on government's faithful adherence to the principles of justice and equality that underpin its legitimacy: it is cancelled or overridden when those fundamental principles are flouted; and the citizen himself must be the final judge of where, in all the circumstances, his moral (and hence legal) duties lie.

When Shabina Begum declined to accept her school's uniform policy, refusing to attend unless she could wear a jilbab rather than the shalwar kameeze that she had formerly worn, she challenged the *application* rather than the content of the general law.[85] She sought protection for her freedom of conscience in the right to manifest her religion and beliefs under Article 9(1) of the European Convention on Human Rights: she believed, contrary to the opinion of the school governors, who had taken their own advice, that the kameeze was not an appropriate form of dress for a Muslim girl who had reached puberty.[86] The House of Lords ultimately rejected Begum's complaint, holding that even if the school had interfered with her right under Article 9, which was doubtful in the light of her ability to attend another school with different uniform rules, the interference was justified in the interests of tolerance and harmony (minimizing tension between distinctive groups of pupils). Nevertheless, the girl's refusal to attend school was a form of civil disobedience grounded as much on her constitutional rights, as she understood them, as on her religious convictions. She appealed to an interpretation of the constitution that would allow her to maintain her school attendance in good conscience. It was an interpretation that a court could properly reject only with the greatest caution and reluctance.[87]

There is no difference, for present purposes, between conscientious resistance to an administrative decision and principled disobedience to a (purported) Act of Parliament. Whether a measure inflicts a grave injustice on the dissentient or on other people, disobedience marks the limits (for the dissentient) of Parliament's legitimate legislative power. If any legal interpreter believes that individuals have fundamental rights that even elected officials cannot properly override, she will not countenance an interpretation that entails the violation of those rights. Her ability to reconcile legislative supremacy with the protection of basic human rights, as she conceives them, is critical to her constitutional allegiance—to her acceptance of a moral obligation to obey the law. She cannot condone the breach of what she regards as essential requirements of respect for human dignity, even if her scruples are not widely shared; she must either defend a construction of the measure impugned that limits its potential for injury, or deny its legality on grounds of constitutional principle. The mere fact that senior officials agree on the measure's validity, if they do, is quite irrelevant to the objector—except insofar as they offer reasons capable of persuading her to alter her own legal judgement. For she cannot accede to their

---

[85] *R (Begum) v Head Teacher and Governors of Denbigh High School* [2006] UKHL 15.

[86] Article 9(1) affirms the 'right to freedom of thought, conscience and religion', which includes the freedom, either in public or in private, to manifest one's religion or belief 'in worship, teaching, practice and observance'.

[87] *Begum* is further considered in Chapter 7, below.

view, abandoning her own principled stance, without at the same time concluding that the legal order, which permits such iniquities, has no legitimacy. In bowing to the official verdict, against her own considered view of the question of legality, she denies any *moral* obligation of obedience: the law has become an instrument of force for any purpose that suits officials; and the dissentient is pushed outside the interpretative debate, reduced to the status of detached observer of a legal system she condemns.

VI

In its denial of the validity of a specific measure or administrative decision, consistently with fidelity to law, civil disobedience is analogous to the refusal of the dissenting judge in court to endorse the conclusion of the majority. In both cases the dissentient contests the official or majority interpretation, denying that it represents the law, correctly understood. Ronald Dworkin has emphasized the citizen's right to make his own appraisal when there are good reasons to doubt the official view: 'A citizen's allegiance is to the law, not to any particular person's view of what the law is, and he does not behave unfairly so long as he proceeds on his own considered and reasonable view of what the law requires.'[88] He does not act unfairly in following his own judgement when the law is uncertain, 'in the sense that a plausible case can be made on both sides'. But a plausible case can be made on both sides whenever a measure threatens rights or moral values whose integrity is critical to the legitimacy of the legal order, as the dissentient perceives it. And plausibility is only an *external* judgement for others to make in responding to his disobedience. The citizen (or judge or other official) must ultimately decide for himself, taking moral responsibility: every citizen is a guardian of the constitution he affirms, entitled—indeed bound—to consider whether his cooperation with dubious state demands is, in all the circumstances, really justified.

When Jehovah's Witnesses refused to accept a decision of the Supreme Court of the United States, upholding the validity of a state law requiring school children to salute the American flag, they invoked the freedoms of belief and conscience (we may fairly suppose) that they took the Constitution to honour. While acknowledging the flag as 'a symbol of fairness and justice', they refused to join a ceremony condemned by their religion. When the Supreme Court reversed its decision only three years later, in *Barnette*, the Witnesses' interpretation of law was vindicated.[89] Dworkin has rightly defended their right to disobey the first decision, which was indeed erroneous: 'The Court did not simply hold that after the second decision failing to salute the flag would not be a crime; it held... that it was no crime after the first decision either.'[90] Admittedly, Dworkin stresses

---

[88] Ronald Dworkin, *Taking Rights Seriously* (London: Duckworth, 1977), 214.

[89] *West Virginia Board of Education v Barnette* (1943) 319 US 624, reversing *Minersville School District v Gobitis* (1940) 310 US 586.

[90] Dworkin, *Taking Rights Seriously*, 213.

that an individual may not altogether *disregard* a court decision; and he must grant the courts the general power to alter the law by operation of the doctrine of precedent. But no one could concede an *unqualified* power to courts to change the law without abandoning his allegiance to the constitution. His allegiance depends on the preservation and protection of certain fundamental rights and values; their infringement ruptures the essential harmony between his moral obligations of civic loyalty, on the one hand, and respect for justice and the public good, on the other.

Ronald Dworkin's theory of law challenges a division of labour between legal and political theorists encouraged by legal positivism. It denies that the question of political obligation—whether or not there is any general moral obligation to obey the law—can be severed from questions about how the law's content can be determined. A 'full political theory of law' must address both the grounds of law—the means of determining the truth of legal propositions—and its force, or the 'relative power of any true proposition of law to justify coercion in different sorts of exceptional circumstance'.[91] The law's content—the correct interpretation of statutes and precedents—is determined, at least in part, by moral considerations which are also relevant to the existence of an obligation of obedience. Dworkin purports, nonetheless, like many other lawyers 'to recognize a difference between the question what the law is and the question whether judges or any other official or citizen should enforce or obey the law'.[92] So a prima facie obligation of obedience may in exceptional cases be overridden: the law, even when interpreted in the light of the moral and political principles that the constitution affirms, may be gravely unjust; and in those circumstances (Dworkin supposes) morality may counsel disobedience. The Fugitive Slave Act, which did grave injustice in the years before the American Civil War, may have been part of United States law even if morally repugnant:

If a judge's own sense of justice condemned that Act as deeply immoral because it required citizens to help send escaped slaves back to their masters, he would have to consider whether he should actually enforce it on the demand of a slave owner, or whether he should lie and say that this was not the law after all, or whether he should resign.[93]

It is very doubtful, however, whether these concessions to legal positivism are justified. The idea that a judge should either lie or resign to avoid enforcing a wicked measure makes sense only if the content of law is ultimately a matter of empirical fact, however much it may contravene the principles of political morality central to the legal order (as the interpreter understands it). But that view is scarcely consistent with Dworkin's proper insistence that interpretation involves an *evaluation* of the facts, in the effort to bring legal practice sufficiently close to an ideal of just governance (qualified by other dimensions of political morality) as to *justify* state coercion.

Although Dworkin's conception of law as 'integrity' departs from justice, which is treated as an independent ideal, it is nonetheless a system of good governance

---

[91] Dworkin, *Law's Empire*, 110.   [92] Ibid, 109.   [93] Ibid, 219.

in which the value of justice has pride of place.[94] Integrity demands adherence to the *scheme of justice* that represents the best interpretation of a country's political and legal record, regarded from a moral point of view: 'It requires that the various standards governing the state's use of coercion against its citizens be consistent in the sense that they express a single and comprehensive vision of justice.'[95] Not only will that single vision reflect legal and political history, but it must accommodate the demands of fairness, in the sense that political power must be distributed in a defensible manner (and the outcomes of democratic deliberation duly acknowledged).[96] There is little scope, however, for the kind of injustice involved in irrational discrimination between persons or groups that politics might otherwise engender. Even if the Dworkinian 'model of principle' falls short of the *correct* principles of justice and fairness, viewed from a utopian standpoint, its consistent application at least secures a fundamental equality: 'its command of integrity assumes that each person is as worthy as any other, that each must be treated with equal concern according to some coherent conception of what that means'.[97]

The critical point, however, is that the normative standards that equal concern secures for everyone must qualify as standards of *justice* (if not perfect justice) in the eyes of the legal interpreter, whose moral conscience is fully and centrally engaged:

Political obligation is…not just a matter of obeying the discrete political decisions of the community one by one, as political philosophers usually represent it. It becomes a more protestant idea: fidelity to a scheme of principle each citizen has a responsibility to identify, ultimately for himself, as his community's scheme.[98]

The legal reasoner must, then, be able to interpret the law of his jurisdiction as a broadly just scheme of rights and duties, capable of retaining his loyalty—sufficiently just to sustain the internal perspective of *participant* in a flourishing legal order, worthy of his continued allegiance. Any gross violation of that scheme, infringing rights fundamental to its overall integrity, would challenge that allegiance. He must either adopt an interpretation of law that denies any such violation—declaring the offending measure invalid or defending a meaning more consonant with basic legal principle—or else withdraw his support from a system he now condemns. In the latter event, he would have become a 'sceptic', abandoning the internal point of view in favour of a purely *external* perspective (from which there is neither valid law nor any obligation of fidelity, but only the forms of legal practice that legal positivism purports to describe).[99]

---

[94] Dworkin endorses the familiar notion of the common law 'working itself pure' over time: latent within 'inclusive integrity' (responsive to all the political values) is 'pure integrity', which 'consists in the principles of justice that offer the best justification of the present law seen from the perspective of no institution in particular and thus abstracting from all the constraints of fairness and process that inclusive integrity requires' (ibid, 407).

[95] Ibid, 134.

[96] Integrity requires that the state should act 'on a single, coherent set of principles even when its citizens are divided about what the right principles of justice and fairness really are': ibid, 166.

[97] Ibid, 213.

[98] Ibid, 190.

[99] Dworkin distinguishes between internal and external versions of scepticism itself. Internal scepticism denies all possibility of a valid interpretation; external scepticism is a metaphysical stance that denies the objective status of an interpretation, however attractive in its own terms: ibid, 78–85.

Judge Siegfried (Dworkin's imaginary judge in Nazi Germany) exemplifies the sceptic, who denies the justice and hence the legitimacy of his legal order. If he thinks that legal practice in his jurisdiction provides no justification for state coercion, interpretation grounded in moral judgement is impossible: 'Siegfried should simply ignore legislation and precedent altogether, if he can get away with it, or otherwise do the best he can to limit injustice through whatever means are available to him'. [100] There is, in the pertinent sense, no law at all from that perspective: 'nothing in the mere fact that his nation has law in the preinterpretive sense provides any litigant with any right to win what he seeks in its courts'.[101] In the absence of any possibility of appeal to an attractive interpretation of the legal record overall, there are no resources with which to tame or limit the particular iniquities that the interpreter deplores. Dworkin suggests that, in some circumstances, legal practices might justify certain claims of legal right 'even though we believe these practices as a whole to be so defective that no general supportive interpretation is possible'; but when lawyers disagree about how to treat apparently wicked statutes, the normal recourse to an attractive overall interpretation of law is unavailable (except to those who share its morally reprehensible attitudes).

Accordingly, a lawyer who condemned the Fugitive Slave Act would, if faithful to integrity, have denied its legal status: it was inconsistent with a constructive account of law as a whole, capable of sustaining any general moral obligation of obedience.[102] Alternatively, he would have denied that the Act, if valid, really required what it superficially appeared to require: a correct construction would be one that made the statute consistent with basic principles of justice, even if the result might have surprised the draftsmen and many members of the legislature. As Dworkin had himself previously observed, there were principles of justice of much greater importance to the law as a whole than the 'particular and transitory policies of the slavery compromise' that the courts in the Northern states reluctantly enforced:

The general structure of the American Constitution presupposed a conception of individual freedom antagonistic to slavery, a conception of procedural justice that condemned the procedures established by the Fugitive Slave Acts, and a conception of federalism inconsistent with the idea that the State of Massachusetts had no power to supervise the capture of men and women within its territory.[103]

---

[100] Ibid, 105.

[101] Ibid. Law in the 'preinterpretive' sense consists in the empirical sources (such as statutes and precedents) which are generally agreed to be relevant to any interpretation of law: ibid, 91–2.

[102] In more recent work, Dworkin acknowledges that an integrated account of law and morality, as a unified system of thought, 'all but erases the difference' between 'the questions of what the law is and whether judges should enforce that law': Ronald Dworkin, *Justice for Hedgehogs* (Cambridge, Mass: Harvard University Press, 2011), 410. The 'moral emergency' (ibid, 411) that trumped any political right of slaveholders to regain their slaves (under the Fugitive Slave Act), making an otherwise valid Act 'too unjust to enforce', must also have been, in an integrated account, a legal emergency, affecting legal validity.

[103] Ronald Dworkin, 'The Law of the Slave-Catchers', *Times Literary Supplement* (London: 5 December 1975), 1437, reviewing Robert M Cover, *Justice Accused: Antislavery and the Judicial Process* (New Haven: Yale University Press, 1975).

Only a sceptic, sickened by the pervasive injustice of the legal order and repudiating any moral obligation of fidelity, would have contemplated the possibilities of lying or resignation. Those are means of resistance or escape for a judge whose internal stance has been surrendered: he occupies the position of external critic, lamenting the displacement of law (correctly so called) by naked force, deployed as a means of oppression.

Although the interpreter can distinguish her legal from her other moral obligations, with which they might sometimes come into conflict, she cannot conclude that the law flouts the basic principles of justice, underpinning its legitimacy, without thereby impugning its authority. She cannot divorce her interpretation of law from the conditions that preserve her own allegiance to it; she would otherwise succumb to scepticism. In extreme cases, therefore, involving serious threats of grave injustice, a 'protestant' approach will leave little, if any, space between the content of law and independent moral conviction: in determining the true requirements of law, as part of a system worthy of allegiance, the interpreter must try to keep faith with her own commitment to sustaining the practice. An interpretation that permitted iniquitous rules to generate grave injustice in particular cases would undermine the law's authority: legal practice, thus interpreted, would forfeit its moral capacity to justify coercion. When the gulf widens too far between integrity, as applied to the practice of law, and justice, as determined by her convictions about political morality, the lawyer must choose between principled dissent (like that of the dissenting judge in court) and scepticism (contesting the existence of any general obligation of obedience to the demands of an illegitimate regime).[104]

Fundamental conflicts between law and justice are excluded by integrity, which enforces a standard of equal concern, recognizable as such by the legal reasoner whose constructive interpretation of legal materials constitutes the law.[105] Grave departures from justice, as the interpreter conceives it, would deny appeal to any *plausible* conception of equal concern, critical to the fraternal community that generates duties of obedience, according to Dworkin's account of political obligation.[106] Contrary, then, to Dworkin's view that a prima facie legal obligation might sometimes be outweighed by countervailing moral obligations, political obligation is *all or nothing*: radical departures from justice must be challenged as

---

[104] Compare Leslie Green, 'Associative Obligations and the State' in Justine Burley (ed), *Dworkin and his Critics* (Oxford: Blackwell Publishing, 2004), 276, observing that Dworkin's protestantism 'turns principled civil disobedience into obedience to true law, since the disobedient are merely trying to keep faith with their own intentions in maintaining the practice of law'.

[105] Like personal integrity, political integrity requires, in addition to coherence, that the relevant standards amount to a 'defensible moral view': see Scott Hershovitz, 'Integrity and *Stare Decisis*' in Herschovitz (ed), *Exploring Law's Empire: The Jurisprudence of Ronald Dworkin* (Oxford: Oxford University Press, 2006), 103–18, at 114. Equal concern is a standard that occupies a 'moral middle ground' between mere consistency and true justice: see Stephen Perry, 'Associative Obligations and the Obligation to Obey the Law', ibid, 183–205, at 199.

[106] Dworkin characterizes political obligation as a form of associative obligation, akin to those applicable to family relationships. A 'community of principle', showing all its members equal concern and respect, 'can claim the authority of a genuine associative community and can therefore claim moral legitimacy . . . in the name of fraternity': Dworkin, *Law's Empire*, 214.

merely unwarranted official claims that law as integrity denies.[107] Confronted by a gross violation of human rights, or the breach of moral standards he considers fundamental to decent government, respectful of the governed, the Dworkinian interpreter must denounce the state's actions as both illegitimate and unlawful.[108]

It is only when we acknowledge the legitimacy of law as a broadly (not perfectly) just scheme of governance, yet wish to disobey it, nonetheless, on wholly independent moral grounds, that there is any genuine conflict between legal and moral obligation. Perhaps, for example, it would be right to help a close friend, in great pain from a terminal illness, to die, even if we think, on balance, that the law should prohibit such conduct in all cases, as a safeguard against involuntary euthanasia—or at least that Parliament could properly make that judgement. In such cases, our personal and civic obligations compete; and in resolving our moral dilemma we must stand, temporarily, outside the legal order we otherwise support. In cases of governmental injustice or oppression, however, we remain inside the interpretative dialogue, trying to keep our political allegiance alive: we deny the validity of action that offends moral principles internal to the constitution we endorse.

It should be quite plain that, consistently expounded, Dworkinian integrity excludes any *absolutist* doctrine of parliamentary sovereignty. Legislative supremacy is an element of British legal practice qualified by those dimensions of political morality that secure, for each interpreter, the essentials of a minimally decent scheme of justice, capable of generating a moral obligation of obedience. The absence of formally entrenched constitutional rights is immaterial: their substance will be part of any lawyer's understanding of the limits of legitimate governmental action. Absolute sovereignty is a feature of 'conventionalism', which demands respect for such settled legal conventions as obedience to statute, except in special cases when the law can, exceptionally, be overridden by appeals to justice.[109] Integrity, by contrast, makes every legal doctrine sensitive in application to considerations of political morality, which means in the last resort the interpreter's best understanding of that morality.

Any proposed interpretation of British practice must, of course, satisfy the constraints of 'fit': it must navigate a delicate boundary between interpretation and invention.[110] And so any plausible theory would disqualify 'outright' any

---

[107] Dworkin suggests that 'even genuine associative obligations may conflict with, and must sometimes yield to, demands of justice' (ibid, 214). But if the conflict is very serious, such obligations are not genuine at all. The best interpretation will be a wholly sceptical one: 'that no competent account of the institution can fail to show it as thoroughly and pervasively unjust, and that it should therefore be abandoned' (ibid, 203).

[108] It is no objection that the content of basic rights may be controversial, so that lawyers' accounts of law will diverge. Integrity displaces justice only under favourable conditions. Redundant in a utopia, in which the requirements of justice are not contested, integrity is also impracticable in a *dystopia* where ideological opinion is too deeply divided: see Jeremy Waldron, *Law and Disagreement* (Oxford: Oxford University Press, 1999), 192–4.

[109] Dworkin, *Law's Empire*, 116. 'Conventionalism' is Dworkin's reconstruction of legal positivism as an interpretative theory of legal practice—in which, of course, the distinction between the grounds and the force of law is comfortably at home.

[110] But even 'debate over fundamental practices like legislation and precedent' may proceed in the interpretative spirit, 'contesting discrete paradigms one by one, like the reconstruction of Neurath's boat, one plank at a time at sea': ibid, 139.

interpretation that denied 'legislative competence or supremacy'.[111] But a lawyer who doubts the validity of a wicked statute, or insists on a benevolent interpretation not shared by officials, does not deny legislative supremacy: he repudiates only an *absolute* doctrine, capable of authorizing grave breaches of individual rights. His acceptance of a general doctrine, according Parliament wide discretionary powers, is quite sufficient to meet the 'rough threshold requirement' of fit that an eligible interpretation must satisfy. He acknowledges Parliament's right to legislate in ways that offend his own ideals of justice; but he draws the line at very grave injustice, which would outweigh any countervailing considerations of political fairness.

The various dimensions of interpretation, as Dworkin presents them, are finally responsive to the interpreter's own moral judgement. The 'constraint fit imposes on substance' is the constraint of 'one type of political conviction on another in the overall judgement which interpretation makes a political record the best it can be overall, everything taken into account'.[112] An oppressive statute, violating rights fundamental to decent government, properly respectful of the governed, could not therefore qualify as law. Flouting the essentials of justice and good governance, it would have no foothold in political morality, and hence none in law. Any requirement of *fairness* to defer to the wishes of the majority, or its elected representatives, is overridden when confronted by iniquity. Basic justice must prevail to sustain a legitimate legal order, which judge, official, or citizen can in good faith acknowledge as a source of genuine obligation.[113]

---

[111] Ibid, 255.

[112] Ibid, 257.

[113] The argument is more fully developed in Allan, 'Law, Justice and Integrity: The Paradox of Wicked Laws' (2009) 29 OJLS 705–28. See also the Appendix, below, for further discussion of the nature of legal interpretation. For an illuminating discussion of the applicability of Dworkin's theory to radically unjust regimes, see David Dyzenhaus, *Hard Cases in Wicked Legal Systems: Pathologies of Legality*, 2nd edn (Oxford: Oxford University Press, 2010), esp 180–9, 250–7, 285–92.

5

Legislative Supremacy and the Rule of Law

I

In this chapter I shall explore the relationship between legislative supremacy and the rule of law, revealing the interdependence of these fundamental constitutional principles. Embodying the basic political ideas of democracy and legality, these principles lie at the heart of British constitutionalism, giving a distinctively common law expression to the twin imperatives of liberal democracy. The common law constitution makes the resolution of any tension between democracy and legality—between the popular will, on any issue, and respect for individual dignity and autonomy, implicit in the ideal of the rule of law—highly sensitive to all the circumstances. It honours Parliament's pre-eminent legislative role by according its enacted rules their proper authority; but it also insists that such rules should be tailored or adjusted, in their application to particular cases, in such a manner as to shield individual rights and freedoms from unjustified injury, disproportionate to any genuine public advantage. Statutes have no meaning before they are interpreted; and interpretation is a process inspired by the basic values of freedom, justice, and legality, even if the concrete demands of those values are often controversial.

I shall argue that familiar notions of conflict (or potential conflict) between parliamentary supremacy and the rule of law are false. There is never, in practice, a *choice* between opposing constitutional demands, requiring recourse to extraneous, extra-legal moral or other considerations. There is only a *process* of deliberation which, properly carried through, enables a good lawyer to decide a case in accordance with all relevant considerations, reflecting the weight that his broader conception of the constitution dictates when duly elaborated. When good lawyers disagree, they disagree about what in all the circumstances legality requires; they would rightly treat a quarrel over whether legality should be preferred to democracy, or vice versa, as beside the point—a debate framed for a different milieu, *external* to the practical business of deciding cases on grounds of legal principles, whose inherent moral force they cannot dodge or deny. In that sense, legislative supremacy is both conferred and constrained by law: its assertion *invokes* rather than challenges the principle of the rule of law.

We shall need to examine a number of prominent cases in some detail; and our study may shed new light on section 3 of the Human Rights Act 1998, which I shall argue is largely an affirmation, or reinvigoration, of the ordinary common law.[1]

---

[1] Section 3(1) provides: 'So far as it is possible to do so, primary legislation...must be read and given effect in a way which is compatible with the [European] Convention rights.'

First, the section reiterates the common law presumption that Parliament does not intend to legislate in breach of international law: the European Convention on Human Rights is a treaty legally binding on the United Kingdom. Secondly, there is a substantial overlap between Convention rights and the fundamental rights, such as freedoms of conscience, speech, and association, recognized at common law; and here the interpretative obligation under section 3 matches an equivalent common law duty, inherent in the constitutional status of these rights.[2] All such rights are part of the context in which a legislative provision should be read and understood: there is no separate, non-interpretative (or literal) meaning that has any independent authority. The widely held assumption that section 3 can lend a provision a special alternative meaning, not otherwise available, supposes that the Convention rights are irrelevant to the ordinary legal meaning; but why should that be so if we assume a legislative intention to honour them? How could section 3 generate a meaning compatible with the Convention rights from a legislative provision otherwise incompatible with them? It could do so only if the provision is read, initially, with little or no regard for these rights. But once fundamental rights are fully recognized as part of domestic law, whether deriving from the Convention or ordinary common law, the literalism that gives statutes an 'ordinary' meaning in breach of such rights is indefensible. What is 'possible' as a matter of interpretation depends on the interaction between text and context; and adherence to a narrow context, ignoring fundamental rights, requires quite as much justification (if any were available) as adoption of the broader context.[3]

I shall, in later sections, also consider the contributions made by a number of legal theorists to the debate over statutory meaning and interpretation—a debate intimately linked to the argument over the nature and limits of parliamentary sovereignty. At the root of the familiar image of conflict between fundamental doctrines lies a rather crude conception of the 'legislative intention' that courts should follow in their application of statutes. If we liken a parliamentary intention to that of a single individual lawmaker, whose wishes and expectations are pertinent to the meaning of his decrees, the courts may be forced to choose between abject obedience, on the one hand, and the defence of legal and constitutional principle, on the other. But when we appreciate the weakness of the analogy, noting that parliamentary intention is necessarily a judicial construction of the reasons and purposes that animate the text—a text reflecting the contributions of many persons over many months or even years—the image of conflict is itself undermined. For statutory meaning is a product of judicial deliberation, embracing fresh instructions pertinent to the resolution of disputes while simultaneously integrating change within the existing body of general principles. Textual meaning is always dependent on

---

[2] Compare Lord Rodger of Earlsferry in *Ghaidan v Godin-Mendoza* [2004] UKHL 30, para 104: 'Section 3...enacts the principle of legality as a rule of construction'. See further Lord Hoffmann in *R v Secretary of State for the Home Dept, ex p Simms* [2000] 2 AC 15, 132.

[3] It is usually claimed that the common law presumption in favour of compliance with international law (as opposed to the interpretative rule under section 3) only applies in cases of legislative *ambiguity*; but ambiguity is itself as much a product of interpretative context as the language of the text: it arises from an assumption that the Convention rights are (or were) external to 'ordinary' meaning. Compare Ronald Dworkin, *Law's Empire* (London: Fontana, 1986), 350–3.

context, which includes, where appropriate, the fundamental rights established at common law or affirmed by the European Convention on Human Rights.

The theoretical discussion will confirm our analysis of specific cases. The aim is to demonstrate the connections between legal principle and jurisprudential inquiry—connections dependent on adoption of the internal, interpretative stance appropriate to the study of constitutional practice. Lon Fuller's discussion of statutory interpretation emphasizes its creative dimension, showing that the judge often has, in effect, to complete a legislative scheme which does not address in any detail the circumstances of a particular case.[4] In a similar manner, Ronald Dworkin points to the critical role of the interpreter's own moral and political judgement in giving life and sense to an enacted text.[5] And in the context of the Human Rights Act, Aileen Kavanagh, noting that judges must make value judgements in interpreting a statutory text, argues that courts thereby make law as well as applying it: 'If there has not been a case in point and the judge has to decide on the basis of legal provisions which may be indeterminate on the issue, then the judge cannot decide the case without making new law.'[6]

We must distinguish carefully, however, between the detached perspective of the general theorist and the viewpoint of lawyer or judge, confronted by concrete questions of English law arising in the course of actual or potential litigation. In the latter context, a creative solution is one that, while not fully determined by semantic or linguistic constraints, seeks nonetheless to apply a legislative provision to the facts in a manner that respects its rationale while, at the same time, honouring the general principles that any constitutionalist would naturally take for granted. Its novelty is the consequence of unforeseen or unusual circumstances, not the result of judicial law-making in a space left open by indeterminate legal standards. A court supposes, as Parliament does not, that it must find an answer by extrapolation from existing materials and acknowledged standards—an answer that all good lawyers, if they have properly identified and weighed the relevant considerations, should acknowledge as correct. From within the deliberative process of adjudication, we seek the solution that legality dictates, which may well be different from the one we might prefer to impose (in a different role) as fresh legislation.[7]

In practice, of course, lawyers will disagree; but they disagree about the correct answer to a question of law, not (or at least, not usually) about whether there is any right answer to find. Judicial creativity is as much technical expertise as philosophical

<hr />

[4] Lon L Fuller, *The Morality of Law*, revised edn (New Haven: Yale University Press, 1969), 82–91.

[5] Dworkin, *Law's Empire*, ch 9.

[6] Aileen Kavanagh, *Constitutional Review under the UK Human Rights Act* (Cambridge: Cambridge University Press, 2009), 32. As Kavanagh rightly observes, even under traditional doctrines of statutory interpretation (apart from the Human Rights Act) 'judges have exercised a creative role by elaborating, supplementing, modifying and developing statutory meaning'. Such 'development and modification' are 'part and parcel' of interpretation (ibid).

[7] Compare Dworkin, *Law's Empire*, especially chs 6 & 7. For more detailed defence of the 'right answer' thesis, see Dworkin, *A Matter of Principle* (Oxford: Oxford University Press, 1985), chs 5–7. For a general defence of objectivity in moral argument, underpinning the objectivity assumed by the ideal of legality, see Dworkin, *Justice for Hedgehogs* (Cambridge, Mass: Harvard University Press, 2011), especially Part 1.

insight: it seeks a solution to a legal problem from within the fabric of existing law, drawing on conceptions of principle that the leading cases exemplify, when properly explained and understood. Acknowledging, as an external, descriptive observation, that judges must be creative (and, in that rather loose sense, make law) does not mean, from an internal viewpoint, that they can *choose* between different answers on the basis of personal predilection or a moral or political outlook distinct from the principles their ordinary legal analysis necessarily invokes. We do not, in recognizing the space for imaginative reflection—forging close connections between legal, moral, and political values—thereby abandon the rule of law. We believe that judges are as bound by the law as the rest of us; and we expect, in the common law tradition at least, that their reasons should show in some detail how their conclusions follow from widely shared and defensible premises.

To suppose that statutory provisions are invariably indeterminate, in the sense that judges must act like legislators to fill in the gaps between otherwise unambiguous instructions, is to set up a quite misleading polarity: the commands of a 'sovereign' Parliament are supplemented, in doubtful cases, by the choices of a 'sovereign' judiciary, free to rule in the spaces left open to it.[8] The truth is more subtle and more interesting. The law is constructed, by painstaking argument, from the building blocks provided by both statute and precedent, interpreted in a mutually supportive way. Only reason itself is truly sovereign, making law dependent on deliberation and debate. New instructions are assimilated into an existing practice or tradition, requiring sensitive adjustment between new and old—between fresh political initiatives and tried and tested safeguards for individual liberty.

II

Dicey's authoritative account of the law of the constitution seemed to create a conflict between fundamental principles of parliamentary sovereignty and the rule of law, a conflict that he apparently left unresolved.[9] Dicey is usually understood to mean that the integrity of the rule of law chiefly depended on the existence of empirical limits to Parliament's 'sovereign power'.[10] Serious abuses of power would meet with popular resistance, curtailing the scope for 'reactionary legislation'. That 'external limit' to the 'theoretically boundless sovereignty of Parliament' was accompanied by an 'internal limit'. A representative legislature was unlikely to countenance anything clearly contrary to the popular will: it was the 'essential property' of representative government 'to produce coincidence between the wishes of the

---

[8] A similar misleading polarity infects much of the debate over the ultra vires doctrine in administrative law: see Chapter 6, below.

[9] But he lay the ground, at least, for an appropriate reconciliation, along the lines proposed in this chapter: see especially section VII below.

[10] A V Dicey, *Introduction to the Study of the Law of the Constitution*, 10th edn (London: Macmillan, 1964), 76–85.

sovereign and the wishes of the subjects; to make, in short, the two limitations on the exercise of sovereignty absolutely coincident'.[11]

Public lawyers have usually acceded to Dicey's view of the vulnerability of the rule of law to the potential abuse of legislative power, insofar at least as they acknowledge a more substantial 'rule of law' than merely formal legality (or formal equality before the law). The emphasis on empirical limitations to sovereignty is, however, a counsel of despair: an implausible theory of legislative authority is tolerated on the basis of its substantial irrelevance to any practical purpose. A doctrine based on empirical fact—that courts have generally accepted without question whatever Parliament enacts—is moderated by countervailing facts: statutes are rarely *intended* to violate fundamental rights or delegate unfettered executive powers, open to serious governmental abuse. The presumptions of intent applied by courts to ambiguous legislation, which safeguard important precepts of the rule of law, are therefore legitimate guides (it is supposed) to the likely intentions of members of Parliament (or of those members who endorsed the measure in question).

A more discerning critic of an absolutist conception of sovereignty, however, will not be satisfied with these appeals to contestable facts, predictions, and estimates of probable intentions. A doctrine or principle of legislative supremacy, fit for a *theory* of British constitutionalism, must be defensible as an *interpretation* of legal practice, informed by considerations of legitimacy. The doctrine must be much more closely related to popular sovereignty, or conceptions of democracy, than the merely contingent connection that Dicey was apparently willing to concede.[12] And if rooted in a theory of democracy, the nature and scope of legislative supremacy will not be determined by official consensus (whether among judges or across a broader range of senior officials).[13] The doctrine's limits will depend on theoretical *argument*, not merely empirical realities (or supposed realities). Although there must be sufficient consensus to sustain constitutional practice across a broad range of political and administrative activity, it must ultimately rest on principles of good government which are subject to critical scrutiny—a scrutiny necessarily provoked by any governmental action that appears to challenge such principles, threatening the rights or reasonable interests of individuals or vulnerable minorities.

Mark Elliott rightly objects to a conception of parliamentary sovereignty that would allow the valid enactment of legislation 'utterly repugnant to the most fundamental of values'.[14] He identifies a gap between theory and 'political reality' that undermines the utility of the sovereignty doctrine, which misstates the true scope of Parliament's authority. Elliott would prefer that theory reflect reality, so that 'the

---

[11] Ibid, 84.

[12] Dicey distinguished between Parliament's legal sovereignty and the political sovereignty of the electorate, rejecting John Austin's attribution of sovereignty to Queen, House of Lords, and House of Commons' electorate: ibid, 71–6. See Austin, *The Province of Jurisprudence Determined*, ed Wilfrid E Rumble (Cambridge: Cambridge University Press, 1995), 194.

[13] Jeffrey Goldsworthy attempts to locate the basis of legislative supremacy in such a consensus of senior officials: see Goldsworthy, *The Sovereignty of Parliament: History and Philosophy* (Oxford: Clarendon Press, 1999), 238–46.

[14] Mark Elliott, 'Parliamentary Sovereignty and the New Constitutional Order: Legislative Freedom, Political Reality and Convention' (2002) 22 LS 340–76, at 341.

moral and political imperatives which shape the scope of Parliament's competence are taken into account at a theoretical, not merely a pragmatic, level'.[15] He observes, however, that those who challenge the absolutist doctrine of unfettered competence nonetheless defend only very modest limits. Lord Woolf, for example, has contended that Parliament may not enact legislation that discriminates unfairly on religious or racial grounds, or abolishes judicial review, or vests 'the property of all red haired women in the State'.[16] Elliott wonders whether the emphasis on extreme examples of legislative impropriety suggests that the gulf between theory and practice is not, after all, so very large. Perhaps the absolutist theory 'fits every situation which could ever realistically arise', or would do so, at least, if it were not for the altered landscape created by the Human Rights Act 1998 and the devolution of power to Scotland, Wales, and Northern Ireland, together with the conventions which are developing to accompany those constitutional changes.[17]

By imagining examples of outrageous statutes, violating fundamental precepts of political morality, we can put absolutist notions of sovereignty in perspective: we can demonstrate the absurdity of doctrines that, treated literally, would endanger the rule of law and hence the legal order from which Parliament derives whatever powers it truly enjoys. However, such reliance on improbable hypothetical examples, with the tacit admission that they are of little or no immediate practical concern, can be quite misleading. Elliott's critique shares an assumption that underlies some of the accounts of legislative supremacy he mentions. It supposes that a statute, once enacted, has a content that can be gleaned in a manner somewhat akin to a soldier's grasp of his superior's commands. The content will be plain and undeniable when the language is appropriate to convey its author's intentions. Insofar as a provision needs to be *interpreted*, the process of interpretation is assumed to be a rather marginal affair, focusing on any ambiguous elements of what are in the main clear legislative instructions. On that assumption, common law presumptions of intent serve only a very humble role: they assist in clarifying the content of Parliament's instructions when, as a result of some semantic ambiguity or oversight, the legislators' intentions have not been transparently conveyed.

When we appreciate the implausibility of this assumption we can grasp the deficiencies of the standard accounts of legislative supremacy. The meaning of a statutory provision is as much a function of the context in which its language appears as the dictionary meaning or meanings of its component words and phrases. And the context includes the broader constitutional backcloth against which any amendments to the current law must be viewed and understood. There is no clear separation between, on the one hand, the egregiously offensive statute that (read literally) shows a plain contempt for long-cherished constitutional values, and on the other, the statute that attempts to secure a genuine public benefit at the price of wholly disproportionate damage to individual interests. If we condemn the first as a repudiation of the rule of law, we have reason to read the second in a manner

---

[15] Ibid, 343.

[16] Lord Woolf of Barnes, '*Droit Public*—English Style' [1995] PL 57–71, at 68–9.

[17] See further Chapter 2, above.

that, so far as possible, avoids oppressive interference with personal liberty. Every statute is, in part, a *construction* by those who must interpret its language in the context of what are understood to be legitimate public ends, and in the light of basic constitutional principles whose integrity is normally taken for granted as a *sine qua non* of legislative change. We can no more treat legislation as akin to a soldier's orders than we can regard its parliamentary source as if it were equivalent to a superior officer, enforcing his will.

Treated as a general principle of legislative supremacy, the doctrine of parliamentary sovereignty is perfectly consistent with the rule of law because it does not threaten the integrity of basic constitutional values. Every case involving the application and interpretation of statute calls for an accommodation of legislative purpose and legal principle, attuned to the facts or circumstances in view. Just as it would be an affront to representative democracy for a court to disregard a statute's general purposes or ignore its specific provisions, so it would infringe the rule of law if a court invoked either purpose or text to justify the infliction of unnecessary damage to the rights of individuals, out of all reasonable proportion to the public ends envisaged. The principle of proportionality, widely viewed as a novel dimension of rights protection, imposed on domestic law by the terms of the European Convention on Human Rights and their interpretation by the European Court of Human Rights, is better understood as an element intrinsic to the interpretation of statutes required by English common law, appropriately sensitive to the demands of legal and constitutional principle.

If, in a criminal prosecution for possession of illegal drugs, the defendant is required 'to prove that he neither knew of nor suspected nor had reason to suspect the existence' of material facts, a literal interpretation, careless of the special constitutional context, would undermine the presumption of innocence.[18] The accused could be convicted of the offence, even though there remained some doubt about his guilt, if the court were not convinced on a balance of probabilities that his defence was true. It is not unreasonable to require the defendant to provide evidence of matters that lie peculiarly within his knowledge, alleviating what might otherwise be an unrealistic burden of proof on the Crown. It is sufficient, however, to impose an *evidential* burden on the accused, requiring him only to adduce enough evidence to raise serious doubt about his knowledge of the substance found in his possession; it is then for the prosecution to prove guilt beyond reasonable doubt. Accordingly, the words 'to prove' mean, in context, 'to give sufficient evidence': the literal or 'ordinary' or prima facie meaning gives way to the true meaning, reflecting all relevant considerations and their respective weights or importance. As the House of Lords held in *Lambert*, a reversal of the legal burden of proof—requiring the defendant actually to establish his innocence—would be a quite disproportionate response to the problems faced by the prosecution.[19]

---

[18] Misuse of Drugs Act 1971, s 28(2).
[19] *R v Lambert* [2001] UKHL 37. The defendant was charged with the offence of possessing a controlled drug (class A) with intent to supply another person, contrary to the Misuse of Drugs Act 1971, s 5(3).

Admittedly, the judges purported to rely on the Human Rights Act, section 3, to justify their interpretation of the statute; but such reliance, allowing the court to read the provisions compatibly with the presumption of innocence guaranteed by Article 6(2) of the European Convention on Human Rights, was made necessary only by initially adopting a literal construction. Lord Steyn's conclusion that the 'transfer of the legal burden', made by the Misuse of Drugs Act, did not satisfy the proportionality test obliged him to resort to section 3; but that conclusion contradicted his own appraisal of the balance of argument. According to Steyn's analysis, it was wrong to ignore the possibility that a guilty verdict might be returned in respect of an offence punishable by life imprisonment even though the jury thought it possible that the accused had been duped. But then that possibility was surely relevant to the correct construction of the statute *as a matter of common law*. The dangers or disadvantages of any particular reading are reasons against its adoption; or at least that is so when there are plausible alternative readings available. Either it was 'possible' to read the words consistently with the presumption of innocence or it was not; and once we acknowledge the importance of context (including constitutional context) we have good reason to eschew the literal in favour of the true or superior meaning.[20]

These conclusions are confirmed by Lord Clyde's admission that in 'the ordinary case, where the presumption of innocence has been recognized at common law long before its embodiment in the Convention', he would be reluctant 'to construe a criminal provision so as to impose a persuasive burden' on the defendant: 'While the Act uses the word "prove" it is perfectly possible to construe that as implying an evidential burden rather than a persuasive one.'[21] Naturally, then, Lord Clyde had no difficulty in achieving the correct result by application of the Human Rights Act: it was 'well within the scope of what is "possible" for the purposes of section 3'.[22] The correct construction, whether at common law or by virtue of section 3, reflected the balance of relevant considerations. On one side, there were the most serious potential consequences for the accused; on the other, the preferred construction was unlikely to cause any serious practical problem for the Crown. It should not be possible, accordingly, 'for an accused person to be convicted where the jury believed he might well be innocent but have not been persuaded that he probably did not know the nature of what he possessed'.[23] Drug trafficking was a notorious social evil; 'but if error is to be made in the weighing of the scales of justice it should be to the effect that the guilty should go free rather than that an innocent person should be wrongly convicted'.

Much the same can be said about *Oakes*, a case in which the Supreme Court of Canada struck down a similar provision for breach of section 11(d) of the Canadian

---

[20] Geoffrey Marshall's scepticism about the 'supposed new interpretative obligation' was therefore justified, even if he preferred a narrower, more literal approach, less protective of common law principle or Convention rights: see Marshall, 'The Lynchpin of Parliamentary Intention: Lost, Stolen or Strained?' [2003] PL 236–48.

[21] *Lambert*, para 131.

[22] Ibid, para 157.

[23] Ibid, para 156.

Charter of Rights and Freedoms, which protects the right 'to be presumed innocent until proven guilty according to law in a fair and public hearing by an independent and impartial tribunal'.[24] In placing a burden of proof on the defendant 'to establish that he was not in possession ... for the purpose of trafficking', section 8 of the Narcotic Control Act 1970 was held be a disproportionate infringement of section 11(d). Section 1 of the Charter guarantees the rights it proclaims 'subject only to such reasonable limits prescribed by law as can be demonstrably justified in a free and democratic society'. Even if a measure makes only the minimum curtailment necessary to achieve a legitimate public objective, there must (as the court affirmed) be a proper balance between its effects and that objective: 'The more severe the deleterious effects of a measure, the more important the objective must be if the measure is to be reasonable and demonstrably justified in a free and democratic society.'[25] In the absence, however, of any rational connection between the mere fact of possession (of a very small quantity of drugs) and the presumed fact of possession for the purpose of dealing, section 8 was over-inclusive, capable of leading to decisions that 'would defy both rationality and fairness'.[26] The ultimate balancing stage between the statutory aim and its adverse consequences for the presumption of innocence did not arise.

However, Dickson CJ's assertion that the phrase 'to establish' meant 'to prove' overlooked the alternative sense of 'to show by adducing evidence', leaving the ultimate burden of proving guilt on the prosecution. It would be possible, on that construction, for the accused to establish that he was not in possession for purposes of dealing in the sense of adducing evidence adequate, in all the circumstances, to prevent the Crown meeting the requisite standard of proof on the basis of possession alone. That superior reading had previously been affirmed by courts in several Canadian jurisdictions, and the Ontario Court of Appeal had held a similar provision, thus interpreted, consistent with the presumption of innocence guaranteed (in similar terms) by the Canadian Bill of Rights 1960.[27]

A superficial study of these cases might suggest that only resort to a bill or charter of rights, formally enacting limits to the powers of the legislature, could resolve a serious conflict between legislative supremacy and the rule of law. A closer inspection, however, shows that the truth is quite different. Neither the Human Rights Act nor the Canadian Charter was needed in *Lambert* and *Oakes* to secure an appropriate reconciliation of the respective claims of legality and democracy. Precisely the same balancing of relevant considerations was necessary, whether conducted under the aegis of the bill or charter or performed in the course of statutory construction at common law. Indeed, the latter is the more natural and suitable course: it attributes to Parliament an understanding of, and respect for, basic constitutional values, consonant with its pre-eminent constitutional role. No doubt judges are sometimes keen to pass responsibility to others, disguising their own essential interpretative role. It may be tempting to suggest that the literal meaning of legislative instructions leaves little or no

---

[24] *R v Oakes* [1986] 1 SCR 103.   [25] Ibid, para 71.
[26] Ibid, para 78.   [27] *R v Sharpe* (1961) 131 CCC 75.

room for manoeuvre, obliging the court to resist such instructions, when necessary, by recourse to a bill of rights approved by Parliament for that purpose. But judicial responsibility cannot be convincingly evaded in that way. Since the same judgements of context and degree must be made in application of the bill of rights, which is only a restatement of fundamental legal principle, it would be more straightforward—more conducive to both judicial self-awareness and public understanding—to acknowledge the moral complexity of the ordinary process of interpretation.[28]

I do not mean that every case should be decided on the overall balance of reasons (or general principles) as if there were no scope for the application of more narrowly formulated rules, making certain criteria determinative (regardless of other relevant considerations).[29] An enacted general rule is by its very nature over-inclusive: it will sometimes apply to determine a case contrary to the overall balance of reasons, everything taken into account. Since Parliament can assert its authority only by enactment of general rules, the courts would plainly usurp that authority if they decided every case on the balance of (common law) reasons, as if any pertinent statute made no difference. There are good democratic reasons for accepting legislative supremacy and its concomitant system of general rules: within the broad constraints imposed by respect for human dignity and fundamental rights, Parliament's solution to a question of justice or public policy can usually claim a legitimacy that an unelected court's determination cannot. Parliament has authority to change the law in response to new social problems or perceived defects in the current rules; and courts must respect that authority when resolving doubts about the scope or character of legislative reform. There are, in addition, considerations of certainty and efficiency that, in some fields, support the application of published general rules at the expense of the more discriminating, but less predictable, case-by-case regulation (informed by general principle) characteristic of the common law. It does not follow, however, that the pertinent rule must be identified largely by reference to the literal or dictionary meaning of particular words, or that its scope should be settled in disregard of the basic constitutional rights or values intrinsic to democracy itself—or at least to liberal democracy, with its special concern for individual autonomy or independence.

My claim is simply that the reasons in favour of governance by general rule, enacted by Parliament or adopted in pursuance of statutory authority, must be set against the countervailing reasons for a more individualized approach, akin to common law method, according to all the circumstances. Only in that way can

---

[28] According to Conor Gearty, it is 'hard to characterize such activism as other than the "judicial legislation" that the judges unanimously say they deplore': Gearty, *Principles of Human Rights Adjudication* (Oxford: Oxford University Press, 2004), 159. But we should welcome an 'activism' that consists merely in a reasoned departure from the literal meaning, as indeed Gearty (somewhat reluctantly) appears to do. See also the discussion of Gearty's views on *Offen* [2001] 1 WLR 253 in Chapter 1, above.

[29] For one prominent account of the distinction between rules and principles, see Ronald Dworkin, *Taking Rights Seriously* (London: Duckworth, 1977), 22–8, 71–80.

democracy and legality be united as kindred ideals, jointly based on equal citizenship. The true meaning and scope of a rule are always matters of reason and judgement, preserving an equilibrium between public objective and constitutional process. The application of a statutory formula to particular cases is as much dependent on reflective deliberation—setting the relevant aims and objectives in their broader constitutional context—as is that of any common law rule; and a common law rule is always merely a summary approximation of the reasons applicable to a class or category of case, vulnerable to review and adjustment when circumstances so require. Lacking a canonical and authoritative text, a common law rule hardly aspires to be more than a convenient distillation of relevant considerations, open to modification and reappraisal in the light of changing events or altered perceptions of justice. The definitive text of a statute certainly imposes tighter constraints; but the difference should not be exaggerated.[30] The interpretation of a text can change (as the Human Rights Act, section 3, appears to envisage in respect of statutes that pre-date it); and even an enacted rule can have unstated exceptions, whether implied (on the basis of assumptions attributed to its parliamentary authors) or imposed, as being a just and reasonable construction in all the circumstances.

An appearance of conflict between legislative supremacy and the rule of law is engendered by the treatment of statutes as if they were self-evident demands or instructions, applicable to particular cases without deliberation and judgement. That appearance quickly dissipates when we appreciate the subtleties of interpretation, recognizing the complex interaction between general legislative purpose—the projected aims that make best sense of the text—and the special features (if any) of the particular case in view. We acknowledge the claims of parliamentary authority when we bow to the operation of a general rule even in cases that might be differently decided by direct resort to first principles; but we do not deny that authority if, in some limited class of cases, we find the statute inapplicable in the face of powerful contrary moral reasons. We discern the true meaning and scope of a statutory rule in the very process of assisting its integration into the larger, complex tapestry of the general or common law. Without such integration and adjustment there could be no genuine equality before the law: such equality means the consistent application of the *whole corpus of law*, viewed as a coherent scheme of regulation—not merely the accurate enforcement of numerous ad hoc directives, with arbitrary lines being drawn to resolve their conflicts and inconsistencies as official whim dictates from case to case.[31]

The proper degree of judicial deference to the deliberations of the elected legislature is maintained by adherence to that constitutional balance, or accommodation, between general rule and particular case. There is no affront to democracy if courts loyally enforce the general rule, elaborated by reference to both statutory text and underlying purpose, while locating its boundaries and necessary exceptions

---

[30] See further Allan, 'Text, Context, and Constitution: the Common Law as Public Reason' in Douglas E Edlin (ed), *Common Law Theory* (Cambridge: Cambridge University Press, 2007), 185–203.

[31] Compare Dworkin, *Law's Empire*, 176–90.

by reference to the general law—including those basic rights embedded, as fundamental values, within the common law. The proportionality principle is implicit in statutory construction thus conceived. When application of a general rule would be quite *disproportionate* to any legitimate purpose, having regard to the serious adverse consequences for those affected, it should surrender to contrary general principle: a literal reading gives way to a more nuanced one as a more accurate determination of legality, all things considered. But there will usually be many different possibilities for regulation that meets that test: the court must enforce whichever lawful and proportionate response to a social problem provides the most persuasive interpretation of the statutory scheme.

In the context of a challenge to the mandatory sentence of life imprisonment for murder, Lord Bingham acknowledged that 'a degree of deference is due to the judgement of a democratic assembly on how a particular social problem is best tackled'.[32] Although there are serious objections to an automatic penalty, whose application takes no account of the circumstances in which the offence was committed, it was right to recognize the countervailing force of legal tradition: 'It may be accepted that the mandatory penalty for murder has a denunciatory value, expressing society's view of a crime which has long been regarded with peculiar abhorrence.' Moreover, the formal sentence of life imprisonment did not, in practice, normally represent the actual period of detention. A prisoner could be released on expiry of his 'tariff'—the specifically punitive element of the sentence—provided that he posed no continuing danger to the public; and the length of the tariff matched the trial judge's view of the gravity of the individual offence in all the circumstances. Setting the statute in the context of its actual administration, the formal sentence could not be condemned as arbitrary and disproportionate: previous authority refuted the notion, once widely entertained, that 'the convicted murderer forfeited his liberty to the state for the rest of his days, to remain in custody until (if ever) the Home Secretary concluded that the public interest would be better served by his release than by his continued detention'.[33] Form must be distinguished from substance. Admittedly, the prisoner remained liable to recall, even after his release, if his liberty was thought to endanger public safety; but the propriety of any recall would be subject to independent review by the Parole Board.

III

While a statutory text must be read in the light of its broader context, safeguarding constitutional rights, it is also right to have regard to its practical administration when assessing any challenge to its compatibility with fundamental values. What may on first impression appear to be a threat to legality (such as the automatic life sentence for murder) may sometimes be viewed in a more favourable light when we broaden our gaze to encompass executive practice, as regards the statute's application or

---

[32] *R v Lichniak* [2002] UKHL 47, para 14; Murder (Abolition of Death Penalty) Act 1965, s 1(1).
[33] Ibid, para 8.

enforcement. In some contexts, only a rule framed in relatively inflexible terms will adequately serve a statute's general purposes; and the court must then tread warily in finding (or imposing) implicit exceptions or qualifications. The proper balance between legislative and judicial authority may depend on many relevant factors, including any conventions that govern a statute's enforcement in varying circumstances. Here, as elsewhere, we cannot determine the true content of law in isolation from the conventions that operate in support of constitutional principle.[34]

The law relating to assisted suicide may provide a good example. Allowing a person to call on the assistance of others in ending her own life may carry a serious risk that other people's lives will also be terminated prematurely, without their full cooperation and consent: an important barrier to involuntary euthanasia is arguably removed. A general rule prohibiting assisted suicide may therefore be quite legitimate: it is a rule that Parliament has authority to impose in an unqualified form. The sacrifice of autonomy, as regards the fully competent and consenting candidate for assisted suicide, may be justified by the greater threat perceived to the autonomy of potential victims, vulnerable to pressure from others or fearful of being a burden to them; or at any rate, it is a balance of interest that may reasonably be left to democratic deliberation and legislative resolution. It may be hard to devise practicable safeguards that would serve reliably to distinguish the different sorts of case, making it necessary to adopt a general rule extending to all of them.

In *R (Pretty) v Director of Public Prosecutions*, the blanket prohibition on assisted suicide, under the Suicide Act 1961, section 2(1), was challenged as a breach of the claimant's rights of personal autonomy or self-determination.[35] Being paralyzed with a progressive degenerative illness from which she had no prospect of recovery, and dependent on her husband's assistance in ending her life when she wished to do so, Dianne Pretty sought an undertaking from the Director of Public Prosecutions that he would not consent to her husband's prosecution for aiding and abetting her suicide. The Director declined to give such an undertaking, and the House of Lords held that her application for judicial review of that decision had been rightly rejected. No breaches of Pretty's right to life, or her right against inhuman or degrading treatment, or right to respect for her private and family life, or to freedom of thought, or her right against unfair discrimination, had been established.[36] The European Convention on Human Rights, made applicable by the Human Rights Act 1998, did not confer or protect a right to assisted suicide, and the Director had no power to give an undertaking of the kind requested.

Because none of the complainant's rights was infringed or even engaged, in the court's opinion, it was unnecessary to decide whether the Suicide Act was unfairly discriminatory (for purposes of Article 14) by, in effect, preventing the disabled

---

[34] See Chapter 2, above.
[35] *R (Pretty) v Director of Public Prosecutions* [2001] UKHL 61. Section 2(1) makes liable to imprisonment any person 'who aids, abets, counsels or procures the suicide of another, or an attempt by another to commit suicide'; but s 2(4) requires the consent of the Director of Public Prosecutions for the institution of proceedings.
[36] European Convention on Human Rights, Arts 2, 3, 8, 9, and 14.

but not the able-bodied from committing suicide. The court denied that any *right* to commit suicide existed, even as a matter of English law: suicide (and attempted suicide) had been decriminalized because the offence was not thought to be a useful deterrent and resulted in the prosecution of injured parties 'in effect, for their lack of success'.[37] The recognition of any right to take one's own life was inconsistent with the imposition of a potentially severe punishment for anyone who aided or abetted suicide: the 'policy of the law remained firmly adverse to suicide, as section 2(1) makes clear'.[38]

The court was understandably reluctant to take sides in the contentious political debate over the justifiability of allowing assisted suicide, stressing its role as a court of law rather than legislative body or 'moral or ethical arbiter'.[39] In a case that raises so profoundly the location of the proper boundary between individual autonomy and state authority, we may have some doubts about the ease with which a court can distinguish, in practice, between law and public morality or ethics. By framing the case as a matter of the requirements of the European Convention, however, rather than any general implications of English legal principle (to which the Convention rights might contribute by way of illustration) the complainant failed to provoke any fundamental analysis of the conceptions of human dignity and autonomy that underlie and inform the various features of existing law. The Suicide Act, taken alone, was treated as representing the 'policy of the law', ignoring in particular the practice of the Director of Public Prosecutions in exercising his discretion, in some circumstances, against the prosecution of those who acted unselfishly to assist a terminally ill friend or relative to die. If it was legitimate for the Director to recognize compassionate grounds for refraining from prosecution, in cases of competent patients whose actions were duly considered and wholly voluntary, the law—when fully explored—was more nuanced and complex than the court in *Pretty* acknowledged.

The European Court of Human Rights, by contrast, recognized that personal autonomy or self-determination was a value underlying the safeguards for private and family life under Article 8, observing that a person was entitled to pursue physically dangerous activities, if he chose, and to refuse consent to medical treatment that would prolong his life.[40] The court echoed the observation of Lord Hope, in the House of Lords, that the way Dianne Pretty chose to pass the last moments of her life was 'part of the act of living' and so entitled to respect:

The very essence of the Convention is respect for human dignity and human freedom. Without in any way negating the principle of sanctity of life protected under the Convention, the court considers that it is under Article 8 that notions of the quality of life take on significance. In an era of growing medical sophistication combined with longer life expectancies, many people are concerned that they should not be forced to linger on in old age or in states

---

[37] [2001] UKHL 61, para 35 (Lord Bingham of Cornhill).   [38] Ibid.
[39] Ibid, para 2.   [40] *Pretty v United Kingdom* 35 EHRR 1, paras 61–3.

of advanced physical or mental decrepitude which conflict with strongly held ideas of self and personal identity.[41]

The critical question was therefore whether or not the prohibition of assisted suicide was compatible with Dianne Pretty's right to self-determination in respect of the time and manner of her death. Was it a proportionate restriction having regard to the need to protect the vulnerable from pressure to bring their lives to an end prematurely? It was argued that, even if many people would need such protection, Pretty did not: she was a mentally competent adult who had made a fully informed and voluntary decision, free from any improper influence. And it was no answer to say that laws are 'not made for particular cases but for men in general'.[42] Nor, contrary to Lord Steyn's assertion, was it 'a sufficient answer that there is a broad class of persons presently protected by section 2 who are vulnerable'.[43] The question was whether or not the prohibition was over-broad, encompassing some like Pretty's husband who could reasonably have been excluded.[44]

If, then, a blanket prohibition on assisted suicide was justified, it must be because it was too difficult to frame a general rule that, while affording sufficient protection for the vulnerable, excluded cases in which considerations of personal autonomy or self-determination were paramount. It was on that basis that the majority of the Supreme Court of Canada upheld the legality of a similar prohibition of assisted suicide in *Rodriguez*, Sopinka J calling attention to the difficulty of creating appropriate safeguards against abuse:

Attempts to fine-tune this approach by creating exceptions have been unsatisfactory and have tended to support the theory of the 'slippery slope'. The formulation of safeguards to prevent excesses has been unsatisfactory and has failed to allay fears that a relaxation of the clear standard set by the law will undermine the protection of life and will lead to abuses of the exception.[45]

Accordingly, there was no breach of the right to 'life, liberty and security of the person' under section 7 of the Canadian Charter of Rights and Freedoms, which guarantees the further right 'not to be deprived thereof except in accordance with the principles of fundamental justice'.

The European Court's conclusion, in *Pretty*, that a blanket prohibition was legitimate was based on the Director's ability to exercise his discretion against prosecution, in an appropriate case, as well as the wide range of permissible sentences, allowing any punishment to reflect the circumstances of the particular case. By such means

---

[41] Ibid, para 65.

[42] [2001] UKHL 61, para 29 (Lord Bingham of Cornhill, quoting Boswell's *Life of Johnson*, 3rd edn (1970), 735).

[43] Ibid, para 62.

[44] The European Court of Human Rights held that it was 'primarily for States to assess the risk and the likely incidence of abuse if the general prohibition on assisted suicides were relaxed or if exceptions were to be created': 35 EHRR 1, para 74.

[45] *Rodriguez v Attorney General of Canada* [1994] 2 LRC 136, 192–3. Four of the nine judges dissented, however, denying that the need to protect the vulnerable justified a blanket ban that left a severely disabled person unable to enjoy the same autonomy as other people with respect to suicide: sufficient safeguards could be fashioned to ensure genuine consent.

matters of retribution and deterrence were offset by countervailing considerations of compassion and self-determination.[46] In that way, personal autonomy was protected to a significant degree by means of executive prosecutorial discretion, which in practice modified the strict terms of the statutory prohibition. The undoubted benefits of an unqualified rule, defining the scope of the criminal offence, could be enjoyed without the unfairness or injustice that would accompany its inflexible enforcement.

As no such protection could be fully effective, however, without public knowledge of the criteria applied by the Director, as well as consistency in their application, he was required by the House of Lords in *Purdy* to publish appropriate guidelines.[47] Debbie Purdy, who suffered from progressive multiple sclerosis, wished to be able to travel to another country where assisted suicide was lawful, so that her husband could give the help necessary for her to bring her life to an end. She sought judicial review of the Director's refusal to publish the details of his policy in such a case; and the court held that, in the absence of such published guidance, there would be a breach of the requirement that any interference with rights under Article 8 should be sufficiently foreseeable. The general Code for Crown Prosecutors would, in normal circumstances, ensure predictability and consistency of decision-taking, as regards whether a prosecution would be in the public interest:

But that cannot be said of cases where the offence in contemplation is aiding or abetting the suicide of a person who is terminally ill or severely and incurably disabled, who wishes to be helped to travel to a country where assisted suicide is lawful and who, having the capacity to take such a decision, does so freely and with a full understanding of the consequences. There is already an obvious gulf between what section 2(1) says and the way that the subsection is being applied in practice in compassionate cases of that kind.[48]

While such considerations of predictability or foreseeability are pertinent to the protection of the citizen's autonomy, however, they do not exhaust its relevance. Debbie Purdy's autonomy was chiefly secured by what amounted, in substance, to an acknowledged exception to the general offence, tailored to the special circumstances of cases like her own. Admittedly, there could be no formal guarantee against prosecution, given in advance of any particular action intended to bring someone's life to a close.[49] Nor could the court effect a formal *change* in the law, usurping Parliament's role. But its interpretation of existing law, extended to include current executive practice, gives effect to all the relevant political values. By obliging the Director to adhere to an explicit prosecution policy, sensitive to the fundamental value of self-determination or autonomy, the court secures a defensible harmony between legality and democracy: Parliament's law is fairly applied, consistently with constitutional equality.

---

[46] *Pretty v United Kingdom* 35 EHRR 1, para 76.
[47] *R (Purdy) v Director of Public Prosecutions* [2009] UKHL 45.
[48] Ibid, para 54 (Lord Hope of Craighead).
[49] In *Pretty*, Lord Bingham suggested that such an undertaking would be an attempt to dispense with laws or the execution of laws, contrary to the Bill of Rights 1688: [2001] UKHL 61, para 39.

Lord Neuberger of Abbotsbury was right to insist that, as judges, the court was 'concerned with applying the law, not with changing the law', which was 'a matter to be decided by Parliament'.[50] But the significance of the court's broad and legitimate interpretative role was underlined by Lord Brown of Eaton-under-Heywood, explaining that it was implicit in the European Court's reasoning 'that in certain cases, not merely will it be appropriate not to prosecute, but a prosecution under section 2(1) would actually be *inappropriate*'.[51] A ban that operated in practice as a blanket prohibition, subject only to the occasional grant of merciful sentences, would not give sufficient weight to rights under Article 8. The giving of assistance to a loved one 'in desperate and deteriorating circumstances', who was determined to die, was not necessarily to be deprecated: 'Are there not cases in which (although no actual defence of necessity could ever arise) many might regard such conduct as if anything to be commended rather than condemned?'[52]

A court is sometimes obliged to take a statutory rule at face value, declining invitations to read in exceptions or qualifications that might better accommodate marginal cases, beyond the main focus of the rule. It may be too hard to define the exceptional cases in a manner that does not jeopardize the integrity of the rule, subverting the legislative aim or purpose: a faithful interpretation must seek to further the pursuit of a legitimate public purpose or policy. These cases about assisted suicide show, however, that there may still be a role for the court to play in holding public officials to a consistent and defensible mode of enforcement. There should be stable and published criteria for determining the 'public interest', which will not only limit the scope for arbitrary discrimination between offenders, but can provoke public scrutiny and informed debate. Such a dialogue between court and executive officials can generate a wider public discussion, in which questions of fair enforcement may broaden into consideration of the proper scope of the criminal law. In the result, the notion that the court must choose between enforcing the law and acting as 'moral or ethical arbiter' exaggerates a dichotomy that is, in practice, much less stark. When legal interpretation embraces the statutory and constitutional context, the court necessarily contributes to the argument over fundamental values: the judges' own moral attitudes both reflect and inform the public morality, in which competing conceptions of human freedom and dignity struggle for recognition and allegiance.

IV

When judgements of proportionality are made intrinsic to the interpretative process, as respect for the fundamental equality of persons requires, democracy and legality are jointly and equally satisfied. A defensible moral balance is maintained between individual and collective interests: no one is sacrificed for the general

---

[50] [2009] UKHL 45, para 106. (Compare Lord Hope at para 26.)
[51] Ibid, para 74.   [52] Ibid, para 83.

good as if his or her own welfare were of no account. It is only if such interpretative endeavours altogether fail that there is any need for judicial resistance to unreasonable legislative instructions. And only when it is quite impossible to construe a provision in accordance with legality—when any plausible legislative purpose *entails* the abrogation of fundamental rights—does benevolent interpretation prove futile. If, however, a measure discriminates between groups of citizens on grounds that are quite irrelevant to its supposed rationale—or to any legitimate rationale, consistent with constitutional equality—it is hard to treat it as *law*, imposing genuine obligations. Such a measure is akin to a bill of attainder, which singles out individuals for special punishment—flouting on its face the requirements of separation of powers and independent judicial trial fundamental to our understanding of the concepts of law and legality.[53] The requirement of proportionality, preserving a reasonable accommodation between individual right and public interest, is also a demand of *rationality*, implicit in the idea of equal citizenship internal to our basic concept of law.

A rational measure is one that respects equality; and the maintenance of a fair balance between individual and collective interests is a dimension of rationality or reasonableness, sensitive to the constitutional context in point. An enactment providing for the detention without trial of foreign, but not British, suspected terrorists must therefore present a challenge to law and legality, unless the relevance of nationality or immigration status can be established to the court's satisfaction.[54] Such a measure otherwise exhibits a lack of proportion that amounts to irrationality: the means are so far removed from any defensible connection with the purported ends as to call the legitimacy or bona fides of such ends into question. When a measure violates constitutional equality by curtailing basic rights without any plausible justification, the threat to legality must be squarely confronted: such a measure simply forfeits the status of law. When the irrationality is plain on the face of the statute it is barely distinguishable from a measure that lacks even the *form* of a statute, as an enactment of general rules.[55]

Adherence to constitutionalism entails the application or enforcement of statutes in accordance with their most reasonable interpretation; and that interpretation, correctly identified, must reconcile democracy and legality, or legislative supremacy and the rule of law. A statute will not apply, accordingly, when in any particular class or category of cases its literal injunctions would do wholly disproportionate incidental harm. There is, of course, always a risk that judges will move too far from the enacted terms, emasculating a legitimate statutory scheme; but they must at least expound their reasons, which can be publicly criticized and challenged (often before more senior judges). Reliance on literal or dictionary meanings, by contrast, is usually a substitute for reason, providing no answer to

---

[53] See Chapter 3, section II, above.

[54] *A v Secretary of State for the Home Dept* [2004] UKHL 56. For full discussion, see Chapter 3, section IV, above.

[55] The declaration of invalidity made under the Human Rights Act, s 4, in *A* (preceding note) was therefore too weak, failing to acknowledge (on the court's own reasoning) the wholly irrational nature of the suspects' internment.

legitimate questions about true meaning and scope. And no one should blame a judge for standing firm against an interpretation of statute that flouts the fundamentals of justice, enshrined in the constitution as she understands and honours it: her commitment to legality forbids any other course.

A provision, for example, that restricts the rights of the defendant in a criminal trial to challenge the prosecution case must be construed compatibly with his basic right to a fair trial. Limitations on his right to defend himself against a charge of rape, restricting his ability to adduce evidence of the complainant's sexual history, should be upheld as far as necessary to achieve their proper objectives; such evidence is often more prejudicial than probative, especially if introduced merely to embarrass the complainant or impugn her credibility. But a 'rape-shield' provision cannot be read as excluding evidence essential to the defence case. No judge can be required to preside over what she regards as an unfair trial or countenance the conviction of a man whose defence has not been duly heard. Evidence of the complainant's sexual experience with other persons will rarely be relevant; but the nature of her relationship with the defendant will sometimes be pertinent to the question of consent (or belief in consent).

The narrowly drawn provisions of section 41 of the Youth Justice and Criminal Evidence Act 1999 presented a challenge to the ordinary requirements of due process. It appeared to exclude all evidence about the complainant's sexual behaviour, in relation to the issue of consent, except in very rare circumstances. The decision of the House of Lords in *R v A (No 2)* is a fine illustration of judicial deliberation which, while adhering as closely as possible to the legislative directions, is nonetheless staunch in its defence of the rule of law. Lord Steyn acknowledged that earlier legislation had not achieved its object of preventing the improper use of evidence of previous sexual experience: 'There was a serious mischief to be corrected.'[56] The 1999 Act had, however, gone too far in constraining judicial discretion; and 'ordinary methods of purposive construction' could not cure the provision's 'excessive breadth': it 'pursued desirable goals' by means that 'amounted to legislative overkill'.[57] In those circumstances, he considered that the court should 'subordinate the niceties of the [statutory] language... to broader considerations of relevance judged by logical and common sense criteria of time and circumstances'.[58] It was 'realistic to proceed', he considered, 'on the basis that the legislature would not, if alerted to the problem, have wished to deny the right to an accused to put forward a full and complete defence by advancing truly probative material'. Accordingly, the statute should be read as subject to 'the implied provision that evidence or questioning which is required to ensure a fair trial under Article 6 of the Convention should not be treated as inadmissible'.

It is easy to see why any democrat might initially have reservations. Steyn's departure from the 'niceties' of the statutory language makes the Act rather plainly subordinate, in some circumstances, to common law principle. Lord Hope of

---

[56] *R v A (No 2)* [2001] UKHL 25, para 28.
[57] Ibid, para 43.   [58] Ibid, para 45.

Craighead, moreover, considered the Act a proportionate response to the mischief in view. There was a need to restore public confidence in a system supposed to protect vulnerable witnesses; and there were important safeguards for the accused, who was not in all circumstances prevented from adducing evidence of the complainant's sexual behaviour. It was an area where Parliament was better equipped than the courts to decide where the balance of considerations lay.[59] Lord Hope also doubted whether it was permissible under the Human Rights Act, section 3, to read into section 41 of the 1999 Act a provision that would allow the admission of evidence necessary to ensure a fair trial: so to enlarge the judge's discretion would contradict 'the plain intention of Parliament'.[60] There was, however, a smaller distance between judicial approaches than at first appears. On closer inspection it seems that Hope's objection was only to an *unnecessary* interference with the literal meaning: he stressed that the defendant had not yet shown, if he could, that evidence of his previous sexual relations with the complainant was actually relevant to his defence of consent, so that a risk of unfairness did not necessarily arise. Hope resisted the adoption of a general rule, modifying the literal text; but he was willing, nonetheless, to leave to the trial judge the task of construction of section 41 in the light of more detailed information about the circumstances, along precisely the lines Steyn had indicated.

The more robust and the more cautious interpretative approaches therefore reach the same conclusion in any case where evidence of the complainant's sexual history is, on close analysis, truly relevant to guilt or innocence. Lord Clyde considered that it might be possible in practice to admit relevant evidence 'without any straining of the language' of the section; but if necessary, 'the language would have to be strained' to avoid an injustice to the accused.[61] Lord Hutton at least recognized 'an argument' that the statute permitted the reception of relevant evidence; but it could in any event be so construed by recourse to the Human Rights Act, section 3.[62] It is, however, very doubtful whether such recourse was truly necessary, or whether talk of linguistic niceties and strain was justified: semantic strain was mainly the product of a literal or a contextual reading, divorcing the text from the context that lent it meaning. If it is legitimate to qualify statutory language to safeguard the right to a fair trial, pursuant to the courts' inviolable duty to preserve legality, it is immaterial whether reliance is placed on a bill of rights or the ordinary common law. The 'excessive breadth' of the statutory prohibition to which Lord Steyn objected was the consequence of his own prima facie, literal reading: its true breadth was what was needed, on careful study, to remedy the 'serious mischief' he identified.

The right to a fair trial is a fundamental common law right, which courts must preserve against unjustified or excessive encroachment. Article 6 of the European Convention runs in tandem with the common law, reinforcing a basic precept of the rule of law. No one should be liable to conviction of a very serious offence,

---

[59] Ibid, paras 99–104.   [60] Ibid, para 109.
[61] Ibid, para 136.   [62] Ibid, paras 159, 163.

carrying a severe penalty, as a result of flawed proceedings, excluding plainly relevant evidence: if a fair trial, in that sense, is impossible, the state should desist from prosecution. No matter how important the countervailing interests, and how narrowly judicial discretion is drawn in consequence, the essentials of a fair trial must be preserved. The critical question is whether or not it would be open to any responsible legislature, recognizing its duties to serve the interests of justice and the public good, to deny an accused the right to defend himself against a serious criminal charge. If the answer is reasonably clear, so is the correct construction of the statute: the scope or extent of any legislative change is always, in large part, a question of judgement sensitive to legal and constitutional principle.[63]

We can draw similar conclusions about the demands of the separation of powers in relation to a statute that, on a superficial reading, allowed a government minister to determine the length of a prison sentence. The Crime (Sentences) Act 1997, section 29, provided for the release of a convicted murderer by the Home Secretary after consultation with the judiciary and on the recommendation of the Parole Board, which would examine the question of public safety. As applied in practice, the Secretary of State would consider the question of release only after expiry of the prisoner's 'tariff', which reflected the requirements of retribution and deterrence. The tariff was fixed by the minister himself on the basis of advice given by the trial judge and the Lord Chief Justice. In *Anderson*, the House of Lords held that the 1997 Act was incompatible with Article 6 of the European Convention, which required an offender to be sentenced by an impartial tribunal, independent of the executive government.[64] If, of course, the Home Secretary were obliged to accept judicial advice as regards the proper length of the tariff, having no power to exceed it, the separation of powers would be substantially preserved; but Lord Bingham asserted that such a reading of the Act would be 'judicial vandalism' rather than interpretation.[65] On closer inspection, however, we may wonder whether the court's reading (and condemnation) of the Act was itself an instance of constitutional

---

[63] In *Secretary of State for the Home Dept v AF (No 3)* [2009] UKHL 28, the House of Lords accepted (following the ruling of the European Court of Human Rights in *A v United Kingdom* (2009) 49 EHRR 29) that a suspected terrorist, subject to imposition of a 'control order' under the Prevention of Terrorism Act 2005, would not receive a fair judicial hearing, before confirmation of the order, if the case against him were based mainly on closed materials, withheld from him on grounds of national security. According to Lord Scott (para 96), 'the common law, without the aid of Strasbourg jurisprudence' led to the same conclusion; and Lord Hope observed that the rule of law required the court to 'stand by principle', insisting that the person affected be told what is alleged against him (para 84). The Act was 'read down' in the manner determined in *Secretary of State for the Home Dept v MB* [2007] UKHL 46: the prohibition on disclosure of sensitive material was read subject to an implicit proviso, allowing disclosure where necessary to ensure a fair trial (see especially Baroness Hale at [2007] UKHL 46, paras 69–73).

[64] *R (Anderson) v Secretary of State for the Home Dept* [2002] UKHL 46.

[65] Ibid, para 30. According to Lord Steyn, such a reading 'would not be interpretation but interpolation inconsistent with the plain legislative intent to entrust the decision to the Home Secretary, who was intended to be free to follow or reject judicial advice' (ibid, para 59).

vandalism—evading a responsibility for the defence of fundamental principle which the court was perfectly able to fulfil.[66]

The Crime (Sentences) Act made no mention of any tariff, which was a matter of executive practice; but it is hard to see why the minister's duty to respect the Convention rights, under the Human Rights Act, section 6, did not preclude any exercise of his discretion inconsistent with them. Lord Hutton asserts that, in deciding for himself when to release a prisoner, the Home Secretary was (for the purposes of section 6(2)(b)) 'acting so as to give effect to' the 1997 Act.[67] But section 29 plainly empowered the minister to follow judicial advice if he thought it right to do so: he would not contravene the 1997 Act by acting in accordance with Article 6. Furthermore, the Crime (Sentences) Act should itself have been construed, under the Human Rights Act, section 3, in the light of Article 6: an interpretation that required the minister to follow judicial advice was superior to the more literal reading, which did not. Lord Hutton observes that the Parole Board could not recommend a life prisoner's release unless the Home Secretary had referred the case to it, and that the Home Secretary was not obliged to accept such a recommendation, even if made.[68] But such literalism begs the important interpretative issue. A duty to refer a case to the Parole Board before the tariff's expiry could, if appropriate, readily have been implied. Lord Bingham doubted whether 'it could ever be lawful to continue to detain a convicted murderer who had served the punitive term judged necessary to meet the requirements of retribution and general deterrence and whose release was not judged by the Parole Board to present any significant risk of danger to the public'.[69] Could, then, such restrictions on the minister's powers be circumvented by refusing to refer the case to the Board at the appropriate time? Would that view be consistent with the demands of legality? It appears that the court read the 1997 Act in isolation from the constitutional context, thereby foreclosing the possibility of an interpretation consistent with the Convention.

We can reach precisely the same conclusions at common law, without the aid of the Human Rights Act. The principle of separation of powers that frowns on the executive undertaking a judicial function, such as sentencing, is an important element of the rule of law: it is part of the common law constitution under which both Parliament and Government exercise their respective powers. It was already well established that, in setting a tariff, the Home Secretary was performing a sentencing task: it settled the substantive content of what was, in form, a mandatory sentence of life imprisonment. It had been held in *Venables* that in setting a tariff for a juvenile murderer, who was formally detained 'during Her Majesty's pleasure',

---

[66] A declaration of incompatibility, under the Human Rights Act 1998, s 4, passes responsibility to Parliament to amend the law but confers no legal obligation on Parliament to do so. (The duty to fix the tariff for mandatory life sentence prisoners was transferred to the sentencing judge by the Criminal Justice Act 2003: see s 269 and Schs 21 and 22.)

[67] [2002] UKHL 46, para 82. The Human Rights Act, s 6 makes it unlawful for a public authority to contravene a Convention right unless either obliged to do so by primary legislation or 'acting so as to give effect to or enforce' primary legislation which is inconsistent with Convention rights.

[68] Ibid, para 80; and see Lord Bingham at ibid, para 30.

[69] [2002] UKHL 46, para 11.

the Secretary of State could not follow the dictates of public opinion.[70] In performing a judicial task, the minister must be no more influenced by 'public clamour' than a judge, whose detached impartiality from government and public opinion is a principal safeguard of the rule of law. Lord Steyn had observed that Parliament must be taken to have conferred the relevant powers on the minister 'on the supposition that, like a sentencing judge', he would not act 'contrary to fundamental principles governing the administration of justice'.[71] And in *Pierson*, the House of Lords had denied that the Home Secretary could lawfully increase a tariff once it had been announced.[72] In undertaking a judicial function he must conform to quasi-judicial constraints on the exercise of his discretion; and there must, accordingly, be no violation of a 'deep-rooted principle of not retrospectively increasing lawfully pronounced sentences'.[73]

It would have been only a very small step beyond *Venables* and *Pierson* to have required the Home Secretary to follow judicial advice concerning the length of the tariff. It was a requirement imposed by the rule of law. The application of a uniform judicial standard of sentencing precludes arbitrary discrimination between comparable offenders: no one should be subject to discretionary punishment imposed by a politician, unconstrained by law. Although at one time the mandatory life sentence was treated as involving the forfeiture of the murderer's liberty to the state, subject only to his release at the Home Secretary's unfettered discretion, that view had since been rejected as erroneous. In *Stafford v United Kingdom*, the European Court of Human Rights observed that the former distinctions between mandatory life prisoners, discretionary life prisoners, and juvenile murderers, as regards tariff-setting, had been abandoned: the minister performed a similar sentencing function in each case.[74] In *Anderson*, Lord Bingham acknowledged the force of this reasoning, noting that in *Lichniak* the Home Secretary had sought to defend the mandatory life sentence on precisely the ground that an 'individualized tariff' was set and that after its expiry the prisoner could expect to be released once it was safe to do so.[75] In exercise of his quasi-judicial function, then, the minister was in point of law, correctly conceived, no more free to reject judicial guidance than to alter a tariff retrospectively, or to bow to public clamour.

Admittedly, the distinction made by the Crime (Sentences) Act between mandatory and discretionary life sentence prisoners supported a broader ministerial discretion as regards the former. In the case of a person sentenced to life imprisonment in exercise of the judge's discretion for offences other than murder, section 28 provided for the judge, rather than the Home Secretary, to determine the minimum period of detention before release. But analysis of legal principle, developing the

---

[70] *R v Secretary of State for the Home Dept, ex p Venables* [1998] AC 407.
[71] Ibid, 526.
[72] *R v Secretary of State for the Home Dept, ex p Pierson* [1998] AC 539.
[73] Ibid, 590. See further Chapter 7, below; see also Allan, *Constitutional Justice: A Liberal Theory of the Rule of Law* (Oxford: Oxford University Press, 2001), 141–8.
[74] *Stafford v United Kingdom* 35 EHRR 1121, paras 78–80.
[75] [2002] UKHL 46, para 18. The reasoning in *Stafford* was also approved by Lord Steyn (ibid, para 54) and Lord Hutton (ibid, paras 74–8). (*Lichniak* [2002] UKHL 47 is considered above.)

doctrine of separation of powers, had obliterated the distinction as a matter of the statute's practical administration. The 'plain legislative intent' which allegedly permitted the Home Secretary to fix his own tariff for a convicted murderer, over-riding judicial advice, was the kind of intention invoked by the dissenting minority in *Pierson* and *Venables*: it authorized the minister to increase a tariff, previously announced, or to have regard to public opinion regarding the deserts of a notorious offender. In those cases, Lord Browne-Wilkinson objected to the imposition of judicial constraints on what Parliament had determined should be an executive function.[76] But that view had been rejected as inconsistent with the rule of law, which enforces a distinction between executive and judicial powers—a distinction inherent in, and sustained by, the principle of judicial independence.

If, contrary to Browne-Wilkinson's opinion, Steyn was indeed correct in uphold-ing the separation of powers in *Venables* and *Pierson*, he was guilty of betraying that principle in *Anderson*. Whose 'legislative intent' must we suppose is pertinent to the meaning of the statute? Should we have in mind the imaginary member of Parliament who is assumed to have taken a rather literal view of the meaning of the 1997 Act at the time of enactment? Or should we instead locate the relevant inten-tion in the more abstract opinion of the member who thinks that statutes should be applied in accordance with the basic principles of the rule of law? Can we give any sense at all to the idea of legislative intent as a purely empirical matter, in the absence of any evidence about what the great majority of members actually thought or expected? The likelihood is that if the pertinent legal questions had been raised at the time, conflicting opinions would have been expressed about the answers envisaged. References to legislative intention must be understood as oblique invocations of statutory purpose or policy; and such notions of purpose or policy, while critical to the Act's integrity, must be refined and elaborated in the broader context of constitutional principle. We must seek to reconcile public policy and legal principle, as best we can, in all the complexity of their interaction in concrete instances.

V

It is an important general principle that legislative supremacy consists in the legal authority of the canonical text. It is only the words formally enacted, according to established legislative procedure, that provide a legitimate constitutional basis for the derivation of statutory rights, powers, and duties. The supposed inten-tions or expectations or aspirations of officials—whether draftsmen, sponsors of the bill, or prominent members of the legislative majority voting in favour—are generally irrelevant. Such intentions and expectations may or may not have been more widely shared; but in any case they are extrinsic to the *text*, which represents what Parliament as a whole has approved and which alone, therefore, is entitled

---

[76] *ex p Venables* [1998] AC 407, 503; *ex p Pierson* [1998] AC 539, 575–6. Lord Lloyd of Berwick expressed a similar view.

to the respect that enactments may properly elicit. Legislative supremacy and the rule of law converge on the understanding that, in looking for 'the intention of Parliament', the courts are seeking 'not what Parliament meant but the true meaning of what they said'.[77]

No doubt an element of intentionality is inherent in the form of legislation as a speech-act. It may be impossible wholly to separate sentence-meaning from a notion of individual intention: words mean what they would be commonly understood to mean when used by a competent user of the language to convey a message to the audience addressed. It does not follow, however, that we are entitled to look for legislative intentions that lie *beyond* the meaning of the statutory text, when that text is subject to interpretative dispute. In the case of a legislative body composed of many members there are no such relevant intentions: there is only the meaning embodied by the text, when construed according to accepted conventions and in the light of the specific context. We can properly ask what message a competent speaker of the language might be understood as wishing to convey, in the relevant circumstances, by his use of the words in question; but we cannot search for any further meaning by reference to anyone's intention without investing such a person with the authority that only Parliament itself enjoys.

Jeremy Waldron makes this point in conjunction with an eloquent defence of the constitutional function of a multi-member legislative assembly, charged with forging a legitimate common solution to a matter on which there may be radical disagreement: 'The authority of a law is its emergence, under specified procedures, as a *"unum"* out of a plurality of ideas, concerns, and proposals, in circumstances where we recognize a need for one decision made together, not many decisions made by each of us alone.'[78] Since it is those procedures and their identification of something as the legislative text that constitute the *unum*, there can be no justification for 'privileging *the mental states of any faction* in the legislature as canonical with regard to the decision that has been made by the whole'. If courts adopt a supposedly common view or shared sense of purpose, as discerned in committee rooms or parliamentary corridors, they are taking sides, unfairly, in what may actually be a division of opinion among elected representatives about the implications of what has been formally and officially agreed. Waldron concludes that 'we should abandon all talk of legislative intentions apart from the intentionality that is part and parcel of the linguistic meaning...of the legislative text itself'.[79] Any extraneous expressions of view or intention are necessarily irrelevant: 'There is simply no fact of the matter concerning a legislature's intentions apart from the formal specification of the act it has performed.'

If, then, we do talk of legislative intention (despite Waldron's plea) we must mean the intentions or purposes we *attribute* to Parliament, according to reasons that apply independently of its members' opinions or preferences. We construe an enactment in the light of what we know, or can fairly infer from its text, about

---

[77] *Black-Clawson International v Papierwerke Waldhof-Aschaffenburg* [1975] AC 591, 613 (Lord Reid).
[78] Jeremy Waldron, *Law and Disagreement* (Oxford: Oxford University Press, 1999), 144.
[79] Ibid, 142.

the social problem or legal deficiency it was designed to address or correct. As the Barons of the Exchequer resolved in *Heydon's Case,* it is necessary to determine the 'mischief and defect' for which the common law (or, we may add, previous legislation) did not provide, 'what remedy the Parliament hath resolved and appointed to cure the disease of the commonwealth', and also the 'true reason of the remedy', so that the statute can be construed in a manner appropriate to 'suppress the mischief, and advance the remedy'.[80] English courts have traditionally distinguished between the reports of inquiries or committees (such as Law Commission reports), which may explain the background and context of legislation, and parliamentary debates, in which alternative proposals and remedies may be canvassed before the canonical text is agreed. The distinction is precisely the difference between evidence of context, which may illuminate the text, and evidence of the intentions or opinions or desires of individual parliamentarians, which do not.

In *Pepper v Hart,* the House of Lords agreed to admit evidence of statements made in Parliament by a minister or other promoter of the bill, if legislation was ambiguous or obscure or led to an apparent absurdity, provided that those statements were themselves clear.[81] If, however, the effect is to substitute the minister's opinion or expectation for the legislative intention, properly conceived, there is a conflict with constitutional principle.[82] As Lord Steyn objected, writing extra-judicially, a minister speaks for the Government, not for Parliament: 'The statements of a minister are no more than indications of what the Government would like the law to be.'[83] There is nothing wrong with reference to *Hansard* to help identify the 'mischief' in view; what is improper is 'to treat the intentions of the Government as revealed in debates as reflecting the will of Parliament'.[84] The decision to admit ministerial statements in *Pepper* itself could be justified, exceptionally, on the basis that it was wrong for the Revenue to enforce a tax in a manner that was contrary to categorical assurances given to Parliament when the relevant statute was passed. The taxpayer could plead the equivalent of an estoppel; such a justification did 'not involve a search for the phantom of a parliamentary intention'.[85]

Jeffrey Goldsworthy argues persuasively that the courts conceive of statutes as utterances, so that utterance meaning is the proper object of statutory interpretation.[86] Whereas *sentence meaning* is simply the product of semantics and syntax (dictionary meanings of words and relevant grammatical rules), *utterance meaning* is enriched by context: it is 'the meaning of an utterance of a sentence by a particular person at a particular time and place'.[87] It is only in the light of the pragmatic considerations

---

[80] *Heydon's Case* (1584) 3 Co Rep 7a, 7b (76 Eng. Rep. 637).

[81] *Pepper v Hart* [1993] AC 593.

[82] Principle, however, is sensitive to changing legal practice: the question of legislative history is further considered below.

[83] Johan Steyn, '*Pepper v Hart*; A Re-examination' (2001) 21 OJLS 59–72, at 65.

[84] Ibid, 68.

[85] Ibid, 67. Steyn's proper concerns are echoed by Lord Hoffmann in *Robinson v Secretary of State for Northern Ireland* [2002] UKHL 32, para 40. (*Robinson* is considered below.)

[86] Jeffrey Goldsworthy, 'Implications in Language, Law and the Constitution', in Geoffrey Lindell (ed), *Future Directions in Australian Constitutional Law: Essays in Honour of Professor Leslie Zines* (Sydney: Federation Press, 1994), 150–84.

[87] Ibid, 151.

on which utterance meaning depends, such as conventions governing communication and 'pre-existing beliefs and values bearing on the subject-matter', that we can distinguish between the multiple semantic possibilities normally available. Goldsworthy stresses, however, that utterance meaning is dependent on *speaker's meaning* (the meaning a speaker actually intends to convey): 'Utterance meaning is essentially sentence meaning modified or supplemented by persuasive evidence of the speaker's meaning which is available to the hearer.'[88]

Implied meanings, in particular, depend on speaker's meaning in the sense that they rest on conclusions about the speaker's probable intentions in the light of available evidence. One category of implied meanings consists of assumptions that supplement or qualify express meaning: such *implicit assumptions* are part of the taken-for-granted background to any attempt at communication. Since such assumptions may not be consciously adverted to either by speaker or hearer, it may be inapt to say that the speaker *intends* to communicate them; but it does not follow that speaker's meaning is irrelevant: 'When we say that something is implicit in an utterance in the sense that it is taken for granted, we are saying that the speaker has taken it for granted.'[89] Since it is impossible to make everything explicit, even in a carefully drafted written document, a great deal must be left to implication. In the case of statutes, established legal principles, which will affect the manner in which an Act is applied and interpreted, are necessarily implied; the operation of such principles must be attributed to legislative intent, the statutory equivalent of speaker's meaning.

It hardly follows, however, that 'legislative intent' must refer to the designs or intentions of identifiable individuals; there is no one who enjoys such a privileged status. In the absence of anything truly equivalent to an individual author or speaker, we must substitute a *notional* speaker—the author of the words enacted in a context that includes not only any admissible evidence of the social problem or legal deficiency the statute was intended to remedy, but also more enduring legal and constitutional principle. If we assume that a statute leaves general principles intact as the taken-for-granted background, qualifying and curtailing its operation accordingly, we do so on the legitimate and defensible ground that such an approach reflects the 'intention' of any suitably delineated author—an author whose responsibilities encompass not only the rectification of the deficiencies or injustices in view, but also the preservation of the rule of law and the general conditions of individual autonomy and dignity. We treat the precept *nulla poena sine lege*, for example, as an implicit assumption, denying any new statutory offence a retrospective operation: any relevant author, appropriately conceived, would (we insist) take such a basic principle of criminal law for granted.

The relevant author for purposes of any pertinent legislative intent is therefore an *ideal or representative* legislator, constructed by constitutional theory to provide the necessary reconciliation between immediate ends and more enduring values—between current public policy and overarching legal principle. The ideal legislator

---

[88] Ibid, 152.   [89] Ibid, 159.

is the author of a text that conveys Parliament's instructions in a manner that fairly and accurately reports the outcome of deliberation and decision; but he takes for granted, as the background of such deliberation, the fundamental rights of citizens as equal members of a just polity. We may even imagine a dialogue in which the ideal or representative legislator is the court's interlocutor whenever questions of interpretation arise. What inferences and implications would he confirm as author of the text, treated as a coherent set of instructions for the attainment of specific public objectives? And what constraints and qualifications on the pursuit of those objectives (and on the exercise of relevant statutory powers) would he acknowledge or affirm in the light of countervailing public interests and individual rights? Of course, any such imaginary dialogue is wholly dependent on the moral and intellectual resources of the interpreter; it is only a device to make vivid the appraisal of competing claims that efforts to apply a statute to particular cases will typically involve. But whether the interpreter is judge, official, or conscientious citizen, puzzling over the implications of a statutory provision, a similar argumentative process is unavoidable. It is entailed by the obligation to interpret the legislative scheme as the work of a reasonable lawgiver, who seeks to further justice and promote the common good.

Utterance meaning, which makes reference to speaker's meaning, is necessarily constrained by sentence meaning. The literal meaning of the words continues to exert a degree of independent force, even when pragmatic considerations of context, convention, and shared beliefs are brought to bear: the 'semantic autonomy' of language, reflecting general understandings within the wider linguistic community, limits our scope for interpretative ingenuity.[90] Any eligible interpretation of statutory language must take the associated 'semantic intention' fully into account: it must acknowledge the deliberate choice of the words actually employed. But utterance meaning—the meaning ascribed to those words in the light of relevant considerations of policy and principle—is the result of interpretative efforts that fuse questions of fact and value. It is not simply an inquiry into what particular statesmen must have 'intended', having regard to their use of language, but also into what the text's prescriptions should be understood to authorize or require or forbid in present circumstances—usually unforeseen and, in relevant detail, often unforeseeable at the time of enactment.

In his attack on speaker's meaning, as a plausible focus of interpretation, Ronald Dworkin shows that the identification of an author or authors, in the case of statutes, is a complex and contestable matter of political morality.[91] Do they include, for example, those representatives who, after a statute's enactment, decided not to amend or repeal it? And how may a group or collective intention be discerned or constructed? Even if a single representative legislator could be identified, there would be difficult choices to be made between competing mental states: the legislator's support for a measure might reflect his political ambitions or private interests

---

[90] See Frederick Schauer, *Playing by the Rules: A Philosophical Examination of Rule-Based Decision-Making in Law and in Life* (Oxford: Clarendon Press, 1991), 55–7.
[91] Dworkin, *Law's Empire*, 313–37.

rather than genuine political conviction. Any search for authorship in empirical fact will end in recourse to normative theory: our identification of author and our construction of his intent will provoke a primarily jurisprudential rather than historical or factual inquiry. Even if the idea of speaker's meaning cannot be eliminated from our explanation of utterance meaning, therefore, it offers no escape from the creative or constructive mode of interpretation that the application of statutes inevitably requires.

Challenging Dworkin's conclusions, Richard Ekins objects that we need not identify legislative intention with the mental states of any individual representative, or even with those of the majority of the assembly voting in favour of a bill: a group intention may be found in the shared adherence to a joint plan of action, designed to further a common end.[92] Legislators act jointly to make law to further the common good; a proposal to change the law is a plan of action for Parliament, acting as a group or institution. On this view, the pertinent legislative intent is simply the content of the proposal, and we must ask how the legislators themselves should understand that proposal: 'What is open to legislators is the set of propositions that a reasonable, rational legislature, of the kind the legislators jointly aspire to be, would be likely to intend to convey in uttering this statutory text in this context.'[93] They will take into account the available evidence from which their readers will try to infer the intended meaning: 'Hence interpreters infer what Parliament intends—the legal meaning of the statute—by reflecting on what it is likely that a rational language user, legislating reasonably, would be likely mean.'

While this is an effective response to any over-hasty dismissal of speaker's meaning, revealing the linkage between legislative intention and institutional author, it concedes the interaction of fact and value: meaning is constructed in the light of context, which includes Parliament's responsibility to legislate reasonably for the common good. It is true, of course, that we cannot say 'that what is meant is simply what it would be reasonable to mean'; the context may show that alternative and otherwise preferable meanings are excluded. But the interpreter's moral and political judgement is nonetheless fully engaged: she cannot determine what rules have been adopted, in the detail necessary to resolve particular cases, without reflection on what rules *ought* to have been agreed to complete a just and effective statutory scheme. And some meanings will be ruled out as simply quite unreasonable. The 'presumptively rational and reasonable legislature', to which Ekins alludes, is incapable of enacting measures wholly *contrary* to justice or the common good— hostile to the freedoms nurtured by legal tradition—even if it still enjoys a wide discretion to act within elastic constitutional boundaries.[94] We could not readily identify such measures as Parliament's work, reflecting its responsibilities to promote the public good.

---

[92] Richard Ekins, 'The Intention of Parliament' [2010] PL 709–26.
[93] Ibid, 719.   [94] Ibid, 726.

In the deliberations of Dworkin's exemplary judge, Hercules, the fusion of fact and value is complete; he must seek moral and political coherence, interpreting the statute in the light of all relevant considerations:

Integrity requires Hercules to construct, for each statute he is asked to enforce, some justification that fits and flows through the statute and is, if possible, consistent with other legislation in force. This means he must ask himself which combination of which principles and policies, with what assignments of relative importance when these compete, provides the best case for what the plain words of the statute plainly require.[95]

Hercules's pursuit of integrity, or systematic coherence, reflects the familiar style of common law adjudication, elaborating the meaning and effect of statute against the broader canvas of legal and constitutional principle. The various presumptions of legislative intent, which qualify literal meaning to safeguard basic rights, assist the integration of new provisions into an existing legal regime; such rights survive intact unless their qualification is a necessary consequence of legitimate legislative change. As Sir Rupert Cross explained, such general presumptions of intent are not merely supplementary to the enacted text: they operate also 'at a higher level as expressions of fundamental principles governing both civil liberties and the relations between Parliament, the executive and the courts'.[96]

In the result, it makes little sense to treat even the legislation of a 'sovereign' Parliament as discrete commands or instructions, which must serve as a *substitute* for practical reasoning by citizens or officials. On the contrary, its interpretation involves recourse to moral and constitutional considerations that will colour its meaning and control its application to concrete events. Since these conclusions appear to undermine anything but a purely formal (and somewhat empty) notion of absolute or unfettered parliamentary sovereignty, Goldsworthy defends a distinction between 'genuine interpretation', which *reveals* the meaning of a legal text, and 'creative interpretation', which 'involves *constructing* the meaning of a text, by modifying it or adding to it meaning which it did not previously possess'.[97] Although he concedes that it is often difficult to decide whether a court is revealing or constructing meaning, Goldsworthy insists nonetheless that the distinction exists; in particular, implications can be revealed only by 'genuine' interpretation, not added by 'creative' interpretation. Courts should not, in his view, 'conceal their creative activity behind talk about make-believe implications'.[98] These tendentious distinctions depend, however, on giving the kind of prominence to speaker's meaning which is untenable in the case of statutes. When there is no single human author, whose mind we can try to probe, we cannot distinguish (even in theory) between what a text necessarily contains and what we think, on reflection, it should be treated as containing: the interpreter is part author of the text to be construed. The meaning

---

[95] Dworkin, *Law's Empire*, 338.

[96] Sir Rupert Cross, *Statutory Interpretation*, 3rd edn by John Bell and Sir George Engel (London: Butterworths, 1995), 166.

[97] Goldsworthy, 'Implications in Language, Law and the Constitution', 162. Goldsworthy's defence of absolute sovereignty is considered in Chapter 4, section V, above.

[98] Ibid, 163.

is revealed as we attempt to *apply* the text to the multitude of particular instances that arise, in the course of unfolding events, to test our understanding. The creativity of imaginative reconstruction is summoned by the very duty of faithful obedience that legislative supremacy entails.[99]

VI

In the celebrated *Elmer's Case*, the New York Court of Appeals held that a man who had murdered his grandfather was disqualified from inheriting his victim's estate despite being named as beneficiary in the will.[100] Even if the murderer qualified as beneficiary within the literal meaning of the Statute of Wills, a majority of judges denied that a literal construction was appropriate: statutes could be 'controlled in their operation and effect by general, fundamental maxims of the common law', including the principle that no one should profit by his own wrong.[101] Dworkin explains that the court had to construct the 'real' statute—an account of the difference it made to legal rights—from the enacted text on the basis of a 'theory of legislation'.[102] There were cogent considerations of political morality both in support of a literal construction (favoured by the dissenting judge) and against it; and the true content of the law could only be determined by judging the weight of these competing considerations. We cannot explain the outcome by reference to speaker's meaning: there would be no relevant intentions either way. The uncertainty arising and its best resolution alike reflect the interpreter's proper concerns about the potential damage to the law's integrity—the coherence of its scheme of legal and constitutional values.[103]

In applauding the result as a reflection of general legal principle, if not of 'sheer common sense', Goldsworthy undermines his distinction between 'genuine' (or 'clarifying') and 'creative' interpretation; for he concedes, in effect, that any effort to uncover or clarify meaning is necessarily creative or constructive. Even when the court invokes a well-recognized general principle, reflected in other parts of the law, it must still determine its weight in all the circumstances, having regard to the consequences of its application for the broader statutory scheme. The process of integrating the statute with the general law is subtle and complex, requiring moral sensitivity and judgement. The decision in *Riggs* (or *Elmer*) was the result of an interpretation aiming to reveal the intentions of our ideal or representative legislator—the meaning that best reflects the statutory purposes that the general scheme suggests, qualified by the countervailing demands of legal principle.

The interpretative complexity inherent in applying statutes to particular cases is plainly inconsistent with the familiar view that there is radical conflict, or potential conflict, between the doctrines of parliamentary sovereignty and the rule of

---

[99] See further the discussion of Lon Fuller's work, below.
[100] *Riggs v Palmer* 22 NE 188 (1889). Compare *Re Sigsworth* [1935] 1 Ch 89.
[101] 22 NE 188, 189 (1889).
[102] Dworkin, *Law's Empire*, 17.
[103] Ibid, 351–2.

law. Legislative supremacy operates within a *milieu* in which the rule of law has pride of place; any responsible interpreter must treat legislation as a contribution to governance in accordance with legality, promoting a conception of the public good consistent with the basic rights of individuals. Judges who limit or qualify the application of literal meanings do so in obedience to Parliament's laws as they are correctly understood—bowing to the demands or instructions of our *ideal* legislator, seeking harmony between changing political aims and enduring constitutional values. We may, of course, disagree in any particular case about the wisdom of the court's reconciliation of competing imperatives; and judges will often disagree among themselves. But we cannot then accuse the court of wilfully flouting its legislative instructions: there are no such instructions, distinct from our best interpretative construction, capable of being flouted. Nor is there any human legislator (or group of such officials) whose personal desires and expectations have any bearing on the content of law.

Frederick Schauer has emphasized the importance of the canonical text in defining the content of a statutory rule; the literal terms possess a semantic autonomy that resists any collapse into underlying aims or purposes.[104] A rule diverges from its underlying justification by entrenching a generalization closely tied to a specific verbal formulation. In Schauer's view, the Statute of Wills dictated a morally unacceptable result in *Riggs*: the relevant facts 'fell rather plainly within the linguistic grasp' of the applicable rule.[105] Accordingly, the statute was *overridden* by reference to common law principle. In Schauer's analysis, statutory rules have only presumptive force, giving way in the face of strong countervailing reasons: considerations of certainty and predictability must sometimes surrender to the desirability of reaching the best answer from a moral point of view. That explains 'not only why Riggs's grandson did not inherit, but why a host of almost but not quite as unworthy beneficiaries *do* inherit'.[106] We can, however, with equal felicity say that the rule contained an implicit exception to its literal terms, ascertained by reflecting on the qualifications that anyone acquainted with the general law would reasonably expect or require.

Naturally, Goldsworthy objects to Schauer's account, observing that it is inconsistent with the court's own analysis, which offers an *interpretation* of the statute, not reasons for overriding it.[107] It also offends the principle of legislative supremacy which, according to Goldsworthy, means that statutes must override inconsistent common law principles, not vice versa: the principle is applicable in the United States, as in Britain, even if the authority of American legislatures is subject to their national and state constitutions. If judges have power to override or amend the New York Statute of Wills, to give effect to the common law principle

---

[104] Schauer, *Playing by the Rules,* ch 4.
[105] Ibid, 209.
[106] Ibid, 203.
[107] Jeffrey Goldsworthy, 'Legislative Intentions, Legislative Supremacy, and Legal Positivism', in Jeffrey Goldsworthy and Tom Campbell, eds, *Legal Interpretation in Democratic States* (Aldershot: Ashgate/Dartmouth 2002), ch 3, 55–8.

that no one should be permitted to profit from a wrong, 'they must have power to override or amend other statutes to give effect to other common law principles'. Judges would then be superior to statute law, being 'arbiters of the extent to which they should exercise their supremacy'.[108] But perhaps this is not so very far from the truth of the matter—no further, at any rate, than absolutist notions of parliamentary sovereignty. The fact that *Riggs* can be so easily reconciled with the doctrine of legislative supremacy, according to the characterization Goldsworthy prefers, suggests that his disagreement with Schauer is largely semantic. Schauer offers a provocative description of a process whose legitimacy is not fundamentally in question.[109]

There is no clear-cut distinction between elaboration of a statutory scheme to meet unforeseen events, on the one hand, and its curtailment or qualification to forestall unwanted consequences, on the other. It is always a matter of *judgement* how far from the literal sense of a provision the court may properly travel, better to reconcile the competing claims of public policy and legal principle. If that conclusion is hard to square with Goldsworthy's conception of legislative supremacy, which treats judges as servants of an empirically ascertainable legislative will, so much the worse for that conception. He readily acknowledges that literal meanings must often give way for the sake of 'other values, intentions or purposes':

If these are the actual or presumed values, intentions or purposes of the legislature, then legislative supremacy over statutes is preserved. The judicial role is that of an agent striving to interpret and apply statutes equitably, so as better to serve the legislature's values, intentions and purposes. If, instead, the judiciary can change or override the literal meanings of statutes to make them consistent with its own values, intentions or purposes, then it has effective supremacy over statutes.[110]

In the absence of any individual lawgiver, however, whose state of mind can generate a distinctively personal expression of values, intentions or purposes, the supposed division between legislative and judicial attitudes is wholly unrealistic. Whether or not, in any particular instance, an interpretation amounts to a faithful application of the statute, sensitive to context, or instead an impermissible 'amendment' will depend on all the circumstances. It is a conclusion—either way—that summarizes the balance of argument, all things considered, not one that can be stipulated independently on the basis of an abstract account of parliamentary sovereignty.[111]

---

[108] Ibid, 59.

[109] Note also the discussion of *R v A (No 2)*, above.

[110] Goldsworthy, 'Legislative Intentions, Legislative Supremacy, and Legal Positivism', 66.

[111] A similar response may be made to Richard Bellamy's attempt to define the limits of permissible interpretative creativity: Bellamy, 'Political Constitutionalism and the Human Rights Act' (2011) 9 I·CON 86–111, at 102–10. A 'political constitutionalist' makes common cause with a legal constitutionalist when he asks 'if it is possible to have a concept of law that conjoins Convention rights with parliamentary sovereignty in a coherent way that might constrain the sorts of legal reasons judges could offer for their decisions'; but he reverts to a very crude conception of adjudication in asking whether, in particular, there can be 'legal norms that prevent judges from simply interpreting the law so that it accords with an outcome they personally believe best realizes human rights in the case at hand' (ibid, 104). The best realization of human rights in any particular case is always, in large part, a reflection of the legislative and constitutional context in point. Bellamy's views are further considered in Chapter 8, below.

The House of Lords' interpretation of the Rent Act 1977, in *Ghaidan*, given under the aegis of the Human Rights Act, involved a clear departure from the literal meaning.[112] In adding homosexual partners to the categories of relationship which qualified the survivor to become the 'statutory tenant' on the death of the original tenant, the court contradicted the ordinary grammatical meaning. The Rent Act provided that a person who was living with the original tenant 'as his or her wife or husband' should be treated as 'the spouse of the original tenant'. As Lord Millett (in a dissenting speech) observed, the Act apparently contemplated a relationship between persons of the opposite sex. In overruling its previous decision that the Act did not extend to persons in a same-sex relationship, the court reinterpreted the statute so as to avoid the unwelcome conclusion that it offended rights to respect for a person's home, under Article 8 of the European Convention, guaranteed against discrimination by Article 14. Once Parliament had extended the statutory protection to include unmarried but cohabiting heterosexual couples, by the Housing Act 1988, there was no justifiable basis for excluding same-sex couples. Even if it were a policy objective of the 1988 Act to increase the number of properties available to rent, that objective provided no reason for the discrimination involved. In the absence of good reason to prefer the more obvious or literal reading, it made perfect sense to construe (or adapt) the legislation in a way that made it compliant with fundamental rights.[113]

The lesson we should draw is that statutory meaning depends critically on context, which includes the strength of any applicable reasons for deference to the specific prescriptions that the language most naturally provides. Questions of meaning, context, and legitimacy are interwoven, dependent on all the circumstances; we cannot, in practice, make neat distinctions between legislative and judicial values, intentions or purposes. Admittedly, the court laid great weight on the special effects of section 3 of the Human Rights Act, which was held 'apt to require a court to read in words which change the meaning of the enacted legislation, so as to make it Convention-compliant'; but without resort to context and circumstance there is no independent meaning to 'change'.[114] There is no way of determining the limits of the 'possible' by reference to the enacted words alone; and the futility of the court's efforts to give general guidelines ought to make this clear. Once it is conceded that the court cannot allow a focus on the literal wording to make interpretation a 'semantic lottery', there are no convenient markers that stand outside the pertinent matters of policy and principle.[115] To say that the meaning declared should

---

[112] *Ghaidan v Godin-Mendoza* [2004] UKHL 30, overruling *Fitzpatrick v Sterling Housing Association Ltd* [2001] 1 AC 27.

[113] See especially Lord Nicholls of Birkenhead at [2004] UKHL 30, paras 13–20; compare Lord Rodger of Earlsferry at para 128. Arguably, *Fitzpatrick* was wrongly decided, the discrimination being irrational with or without the Human Rights Act. The Act, as applied in *Ghaidan*, would otherwise have had a questionable retrospective effect on vested rights: see David Mead, 'Rights, Relationships and Retrospectivity: The Impact of Convention Rights on Pre-existing Private Relationships following *Wilson* and *Ghaidan*' [2005] PL 459–67.

[114] [2004] UKHL 30, para 32 (Lord Nicholls).

[115] Ibid, para 31. Compare Lord Rodger of Earlsferry at para 123: 'What matters is not so much the particular phraseology chosen by the draftsman as the substance of the measure which Parliament has enacted in those words.'

be consistent with the 'underlying thrust' of the statute, or 'go with the grain of the legislation', or be consistent with the 'fundamental features of the legislative scheme', is after all only to state the obvious.[116]

We must be able to say that, in the light of all relevant considerations, the meaning ascribed is genuinely an *interpretation* of the statute; but the distinction between interpretation and illegitimate amendment is implicit in our conclusions, not a boundary we can identify in advance of the analysis. Moreover, our reasoning must reflect the balance of competing arguments we now find convincing. The meaning of a statute depends not on what anyone supposed at the time of enactment (perhaps long ago) but rather on our own view of what its successful integration into the corpus of current law demands. In that respect, section 3 of the Human Rights Act affirms a common law tradition in which statutory meaning may change to reflect the evolution of the general law. An interpretation that once seemed unassailable, even if it entailed the infringement of rights we would today acknowledge as fundamental, can now be disowned in the light of changes to the moral environment.

We should, therefore, treat Lord Steyn's description of section 3 as a 'remedial measure' with caution, even while assenting to his view that section 4 is a 'measure of last resort'.[117] A declaration of incompatibility is an admission of interpretative failure: a provision is, on any plausible reading, in breach of the Convention rights. But section 3 is not, in the strict sense, a remedy for incompatibility: it is an *interpretative guide to the true meaning* of the statute. In the same manner as a presumption of intent at common law, the section affirms the correctness of a construction that respects, rather than flouts, the basic rights of the citizen. We should not, then, say with Kavanagh that 'in cases where the rights violation is substantial and a remedy is required, there will be strong reasons in favour of a "strained" interpretation under section 3'.[118] It is true that a declaration of incompatibility would be of no 'remedial use' to the complainant, and therefore distinctly second-best. But when correctly analysed, there is no rights violation at all, when section 3 applies, and so nothing requiring a 'remedy'. The accepted interpretation is 'strained' (as Kavanagh seems inclined to agree) only from a literalist perspective, ignoring the wider constitutional context.[119]

---

[116] See ibid, para 33 (Lord Nicholls), para 121 (Lord Rodger), para 67 (Lord Millett). How can a meaning be 'intellectually defensible' if it is also 'unnatural or unreasonable', as Lord Millett asserts? If the court can 'do considerable violence to the language and stretch it almost...to breaking point', in what sense is its interpretation possible or legitimate? Such contradictions exemplify the consequences of divorcing text from context: section 3 can help only by what (on Millett's account) must be deemed judicial amendment. For a pertinent critique, see Aileen Kavanagh, *Constitutional Review under the UK Human Rights Act*, 82–8, observing that Millett, unlike the other judges, identified the legislative purpose without any reference to the relevant Convention right.

[117] *Ghaidan v Godin-Mendoza* [2004] UKHL 30, para 46.

[118] Kavanagh, *Constitutional Review under the UK Human Rights Act*, 124.

[119] The point is important because Kavanagh is misled by Steyn's characterization into defending a judicial discretion that affords a *choice* between the competing 'remedies' of sections 3 and 4 (ibid, ch 5). There is no such choice, on correct analysis, and therefore no warrant for the kind of legislative remedial discretion Kavanagh attributes to the court, dependent on matters external to ordinary legal analysis (see Chapter 8, below).

VII

Lon Fuller's discussion, in *The Morality of Law*, is perceptive and pertinent. He repudiates any mistaken identification of fidelity to enacted law with a 'passive and purely receptive attitude on the part of the judge'.[120] As regards the conflict between those who celebrate judge-made law, and welcome creativity, and those who 'distrust judicial power', suspicious of a 'reaching for personal power', Fuller is rightly dismissive: 'When issue is joined in these terms the whole problem is misconceived.' He imagines an inventor leaving the sketch of an invention which, on his deathbed, he asks his son to bring to fruition. In carrying out his father's wish the son would have to determine (in the manner of the common law 'mischief' rule) 'what defect or insufficiency of existing devices' the invention was intended to remedy, and then to grasp its underlying principle (the 'true reason of the remedy').[121] The son is then faithful to his father's 'intention' in the sense of collaborating in the project: he seeks the 'intention of the design', akin to the useful metaphor, 'the intention of the statute'. It would make no sense to attribute either praise or blame for adopting such an approach: the son is simply meeting the demands of his assignment: 'The time for praise or blame would come when we could survey what he had accomplished in this inescapably creative role. So it is with judges.'[122]

Fuller's emphasis on the creative aspects of interpretation dovetails with his deprecation of theories of law that treat 'a hierarchic ordering of authority as the essential mark of a legal system'.[123] His scepticism about the notion of unqualified parliamentary supremacy reflects its 'intimate association' with such theories. The objection is to what amounts to an unrealistic focus on formal sources of authority at the expense of proper concern for the law's integrity as a just and effective scheme of social regulation—a 'fatal abstraction from the enterprise of creating and administering a system of rules for the control of human conduct'.[124] Dicey's suggestion that Parliament could 'extinguish itself by legally dissolving itself and leaving no means whereby a subsequent Parliament could be legally summoned' exemplified the departure of his doctrine from constitutional sense and experience.[125] A doctrine that made no allowance for the reasonable expectations and aspirations of the citizen, reflected in their interpretative responses to enacted laws, might permit Parliament to assign all its powers to a dictator, or 'decide that all future laws...shall be kept secret from those subject to them'.[126] An account of the judicial role as wholly subservient to an indomitable legislative will, akin to the irresistible commands of a military leader, entails the destruction of the rule of law, contradicting our

---

[120] Fuller, *The Morality of Law*, 87.
[121] Ibid, 85 (see *Heydon's Case*, considered above).
[122] Ibid, 87.
[123] Ibid, 113.
[124] Ibid, 115.
[125] See Dicey, *The Law of the Constitution*, 68–70 (extended note).
[126] Fuller, *The Morality of Law*, 117.

assumptions about constitutional government: 'At some point we take leave of
the gravitational field within which the distinction between law and not-law
makes sense.'

Absolutist theories of parliamentary sovereignty downgrade the interpretative
function of the courts by overlooking, or underestimating, the 'open texture' of
language, whereby any general rule will at some point prove indeterminate: 'Open
texture is the ineliminable possibility of vagueness, the ineradicable contingency
that even the most seemingly precise term might, when it confronts an instance
unanticipated when the term was defined, become vague with respect to that
instance.'[127] H. L. A. Hart observes that it is unrealistic even to cherish as an ideal
the conception of a rule so detailed that its application to any particular case is
always determined in advance, without further reflection:

It is a feature of the human predicament (and so of the legislative one) that we labour under
two connected handicaps whenever we seek to regulate, unambiguously and in advance,
some sphere of conduct by means of general standards to be used without further official
direction on particular occasions. The first handicap is our relative ignorance of fact: the
second is our relative indeterminacy of aim.[128]

When we confront the issues arising in a novel case, we render our initial aim more
determinate and thereby settle a question as to the meaning, for the purposes of
the rule, of the general words it employs. While in one sense a court must ascertain
what, in detail, its legislative instructions are, in another sense it must strive to
adapt those instructions (like the son of Fuller's deceased inventor) to meet the
circumstances arising; and we can make no clear distinction in practice between
these different responsibilities. As Fuller explained:

The interpretation of statutes is, then, not simply a process of drawing out of the statute
what its maker put into it but it is also in part, and in varying degrees, a process of adjusting
the statute to the implicit demands and values of the society to which it is to be applied.
In this sense it may be said that no enacted law ever comes from its legislator wholly and
fully 'made'.[129]

Dworkin elaborates this idea by rejecting the assumption, implicit in the 'speaker's
meaning' theory, that a statute's meaning is fixed at the point of enactment, leaving
courts with a choice between enforcing the original statute in changed circumstances
or 'amending it covertly to bring it up to date'.[130] Instead, Hercules 'interprets
not just the statute's text but its life, the process that begins before it becomes law
and extends far beyond that moment'. He must take account of subsequent legislation and common law development, which may properly affect his interpretation;
and admissible statements of legislative purpose, made at the time of enactment,
will gradually lose their force as a guide to the correct meaning in altered circumstances. As the statute is further absorbed into the general fabric of the law, we may

---

[127] Schauer, *Playing by the Rules*, 36.
[128] H L A Hart, *The Concept of Law*, 2nd edn (Oxford: Clarendon Press, 1994), 128.
[129] Lon L Fuller, *Anatomy of the Law* (Harmondsworth: Penguin Books, 1971), 85–6.
[130] Dworkin, *Law's Empire*, 348.

conclude, the more inapt and misguided is the idea of largely passive obedience to plain legislative instructions, literally construed.

The editors of the third edition of *Statutory Interpretation*, by Sir Rupert Cross, defend the principle that 'an Act is always speaking', in the sense that a provision should be treated as a norm of the current legal system, rather than merely the product of a particular historical Parliament: 'It has a legal existence independently of the historical contingencies of its promulgation, and accordingly should be interpreted in the light of its place within the system of legal norms currently in force.'[131] Lord Steyn considered that this principle was offended by judicial reference to *Hansard*, whereby 'the position is crystallized as explained by the minister at that time'.[132] As Dworkin explains, however, where aspects of legislative history are accorded a special role by legal practice, they enjoy a status intermediate between informal exchanges, made during debate, and the canonical text. There is a difference between the explicit terms of the statute and the explanatory facts of legislative history, akin to the distinction between a person's promise and his explanation or interpretation of it. The official statements about a statute's intended meaning or effect have a reporting rather than performative function:

Legislative history offers a contemporary interpretation of the statute it surrounds, an interpretation that may later be revised by courts or the legislature itself, even though any important revision would, in retrospect, make the legislative history a matter of regret.[133]

Legislation is better construed in a way that avoids any danger of people being misled by official statements of legislative purpose, but such statements are only 'reports of public purpose and conviction', not part of the statute itself, and so 'they are naturally vulnerable to reassessment'.[134]

The distinction between the statute, on one hand, and ministerial statements about its effect or design, on the other, was emphasized in a case which also provokes reflection on the value of interpretative flexibility or creativity.[135] In *Robinson*, the House of Lords affirmed the legality of an election of the senior ministers of the Northern Ireland Assembly outside the six-week period specified by the Northern Ireland Act 1998. Notwithstanding the requirement in section 16(1) that the Assembly 'shall, within a period of six weeks beginning with its first

[131] Sir Rupert Cross, *Statutory Interpretation*, 3rd edn by John Bell and Sir George Engel (London: Butterworths, 1995), 51–2.
[132] Steyn, '*Pepper v Hart*; A Re-examination', 68.
[133] Dworkin, *Law's Empire*, 346.
[134] Ibid, 350.
[135] *Robinson v Secretary of State for Northern Ireland* [2002] UKHL 32. Lord Hoffmann observed (para 40) that it was not 'sufficiently understood that it will be very rare indeed for an Act of Parliament to be construed by the courts as meaning something different from what it would be understood to mean by a member of the public who was aware of all the material forming the background to its enactment but who was not privy to what had been said by individual members (including ministers) during the debates in one or other House of Parliament'. Lord Hobhouse of Woodborough stated (para 65): 'It is fundamental to our constitution and the proper ascertainment of the law as enacted by Parliament that the law should be found in the text of the statute, not in the unenacted statements or answers of ministers or individual parliamentarians.'

meeting, elect from among its members the First Minister and the deputy First Minister', a majority of the court held that an election made after the period's expiry, on the successful conclusion of discussions to seek the necessary agreement, was perfectly valid. While the dissentients denied the existence of any power of election once the statutory period had elapsed, the majority placed greater weight on the larger constitutional context. Lord Bingham urged that the statute should be interpreted 'generously and purposively, bearing in mind the values which the constitutional provisions are intended to embody'.[136] The Act sought to implement the Belfast Agreement, intended to end decades of bloodshed and strife in Northern Ireland; flexibility was needed to enable the politicians to find a solution that would allow government to be sustained. Although the minority thought that any power to make an election must be a mere implication of the specific duty to do so, imposed by section 16, the majority inferred such a power, more broadly, from the statutory scheme as a whole: the statutory provisions were considered to 'assume as background the existence of a power to elect'.[137] Bingham's imaginative approach, attuned to the sensitive political context, contrasts sharply with Lord Hutton's opinion that there was nothing in the Act indicating any exception to the 'normal rule' that where a statutory body is empowered to perform an act within a specified period, it has no power to act outside that period.[138] In *Robinson*, if not in *Anderson*, Bingham was willing to reject a narrowly legalistic approach to questions of interpretation having major constitutional significance.[139]

Beyond any superficial contradiction between dual precepts of parliamentary sovereignty and the rule of law, Dicey's influential work pointed to their proper reconciliation, rightly emphasizing the centrality of the interpretative role of the judiciary. Far from conceding any necessary opposition, Dicey proclaimed that the 'sovereignty of Parliament favours the supremacy of the law of the land'.[140] The will of Parliament could be expressed only in the form of an Act, passed by due procedure, and the 'English Bench' would refuse to 'interpret an Act of Parliament otherwise than by reference to the words of the enactment', ignoring the opinions expressed in debate. Moreover, discretionary governmental powers, conferred by statute, were limited by judicial interpretation, which constituted a bulwark against arbitrariness:

Powers, however extraordinary, which are conferred or sanctioned by statute, are never really unlimited, for they are confined by the words of the Act itself, and, what is more, by the interpretation put upon the statute by the judges. Parliament is supreme legislator, but from the moment Parliament has uttered its will as lawgiver, that will becomes subject to the interpretation put upon it by the judges of the land, and the judges... are disposed to construe statutory exceptions to common law principles in a mode which would not commend

---

[136] Ibid, para 11.
[137] Ibid, para 24 (Lord Hoffmann). Compare Lord Millett at para 93.
[138] Ibid, para 54.
[139] *R (Anderson) v Secretary of State for the Home Dept* [2002] UKHL 46 is considered above.
[140] Dicey, *Law of the Constitution*, 406.

itself either to a body of officials, or to the Houses of Parliament, if the Houses were called upon to interpret their own enactments.[141]

Since it is accepted that the courts 'have no power to dispense with the laws enacted by Parliament', or (in normal circumstances) to override them, the principle that no one should be allowed to benefit from his own serious wrong operates, like other settled common law principles, as a rule of interpretation.[142] It applies even to cases where the performance of a serious crime might, on certain readings, be facilitated: 'Parliament must likewise be presumed not to have intended to promote serious crime in the future'.[143] Although treated as an implicit qualification of the statute's general terms, there is no requirement that the principle should have been authoritatively declared—and so formally drawn to Parliament's attention—before the statute was passed. Moreover, the various principles that operate to modify a statute's operation are those that the judges identify from time to time, as the infinitely varied circumstances of successive cases arise to complicate the statute's integration into the general law. Parliament is 'taken to have intended' that the statute should be adapted to such 'principles of public policy', as these are judicially developed and refined. Parliamentary sovereignty survives as an assertion of legislative supremacy; but its consequences are invariably controlled, or modified, by the overarching doctrine that 'the legislature must be presumed, unless the contrary intention appears, not to have intended to imperil the welfare of the state or its inhabitants'.[144]

Parliament cannot usurp the constitutional sovereignty that consists in adherence to the rule of law, conceived as an ideal of governance rooted in respect for the dignity of the individual person. Democracy consists in representative government, operating in tune with the basic interconnected values of liberty, equality, and justice, as these are explored and developed within a flourishing legal tradition. Law-making should be understood as part of a *dialogue* that seeks to persuade those affected of the need for change and cooperation; legislation is ultimately the voice of the people, whose status as both governors and governed rests on fundamental ideas of equal liberty and mutual respect. Authority is tamed by reason because the intelligibility and effectiveness of Parliament's injunctions alike depend on the mutual cooperation, understanding, and tolerance that, at the deepest level, underpin a republic composed of free and independent citizens. As Dicey shrewdly observed: 'If the sovereignty of Parliament gives the form, the supremacy of the law of the land determines the substance of our constitution.'[145]

---

[141] Ibid, 413–14. For the theoretical context and intellectual background to Dicey's work, supportive of this deeper, interpretative reading, see Mark D Walters, 'Dicey on Writing the *Law of the Constitution*' (2011) OJLS 1–29.

[142] *R v Registrar General, ex p Smith* [1991] 2 QB 393, 402.

[143] Ibid, 403–4.

[144] Ibid, 405 (McCowan LJ, accepting the submission of Mr John Laws).

[145] Dicey, *Law of the Constitution*, 471. See also Allan, 'Questions of Legality and Legitimacy: Form and Substance in British Constitutionalism' I·CON 9 (2011) 155–62.

6

Constitutional Foundations of Judicial Review

I

The constitutional basis of the High Court's powers of review of executive or administrative action is a matter that lies at the heart of any theory of British government, connecting and illustrating such important ideas as legislative supremacy, the rule of law and the separation of powers. It is a subject that has in recent years generated a good deal of disagreement and debate, which we shall need to examine.[1] The ultra vires doctrine confines a public authority within the jurisdiction conferred by Parliament, any transgression of the limits of that jurisdiction rendering an action or decision null and void. Jurisdictional boundaries are established, moreover, not merely by the explicit terms of the statutory grant of power, but in addition by an *implicit* obligation to satisfy such established common law standards of propriety as natural justice (or procedural fairness) and reasonableness.[2] A breach of any one of these general standards of administrative legality may justify judicial intervention, correcting an excess or abuse of power—power asserted inconsistently with (what is assumed to be) the will of Parliament. Parliament delegates power to public authorities, it is supposed, on the understanding that its exercise must comply at all times with the requirements of the rule of law.

The ultra vires doctrine has, however, been challenged by critics who locate the basis of judicial review in the general common law alone, contesting the need to invoke an express or implied 'legislative intent'. The court's powers of supervision of administrative agencies and executive public authorities may be understood to derive from its inherent jurisdiction to prevent the abuse of power, defending the rights of those affected. The pertinent standards of legality do not depend (on this view) on any special parliamentary sanction or instruction, implicit in any and every grant of power to an executive agency: they are, instead, entailments of the ordinary judicial duty to enforce the rule of law, according to the judges' own conception of what that ideal dictates in all the circumstances.

---

[1] For an overview of the debate, see the essays collected in Christopher Forsyth (ed), *Judicial Review and the Constitution* (Oxford: Hart Publishing, 2000).

[2] The nature of the *Wednesbury* doctrine of reasonableness or rationality is considered in Chapter 3, above (see *Associated Provincial Picture Houses Ltd v Wednesbury Corporation* [1948] 1 KB 223). The relationship between standards of reasonableness and proportionality (and between standards of review and standards of legality) is considered in Chapter 7, below.

A study of this debate will teach us much about the British constitution: it brings to light the interaction of fundamental legal principles in a particularly vivid and instructive context. I shall argue that rather than taking sides between the two main positions, we can learn something from the strengths and weaknesses of each. An emphasis on the common law, as a fundamental bedrock of constitutionalism, is to be commended; but the ultra vires doctrine can be understood, if we wish, as expressing a commitment to democracy: its invocation of 'legislative intent' can be construed as a reference to the statutory context in which the common law principles of legality take determinate shape. So ultra vires may be a merely formal label, asserting a legislative intention assumed for the sake of appearances (as its common law critics usually claim): then it conceals or disguises the underlying analysis, if any, rooted in common law values and reasoning. But it may instead, in the right hands, summarize the conclusion of a legal analysis that focuses on the specific administrative context, which will (if properly taken into account) inevitably inform and colour the application of the general grounds of review. Abstract principles of fairness and reasonableness must be applied with great sensitivity to the context in view: the rule of law and democracy operate in harness, each affirming and reinforcing the other.

We must, however, start with a warning: the match has been fixed. The terms of the debate have been set somewhat artificially by a rarely challenged assumption about its scope. It is generally supposed that we can discuss the basis of judicial review of administrative action without regard to any question about review of primary legislation. Almost everyone, it seems, takes absolute or unqualified parliamentary sovereignty for granted: Parliament may confer whatever powers it chooses on any public (or other) authority on whatever terms it sees fit; and the court's supervisory role is concerned only with the legality of the exercise by that authority of the powers conferred. When the debate is set up in those terms the ultra vires doctrine clearly has the advantage: any judicial intervention must, in principle, be consistent with whatever instructions or intention Parliament has given or revealed, whether expressly or impliedly. The various precepts or stand-ards of legality that inform the traditional grounds of review may be amended, curtailed, or abolished by express statutory provision, and their application in particular cases must not flout any special restrictions implicit in the form or content of a grant of executive power.[3]

The consensus on absolute, unfettered sovereignty threatens the coherence of the debate, making it very hard to see what, if anything, really separates the rival views. It must be challenged if we are to achieve a better understanding. I have rejected the notion of absolute sovereignty as an exaggerated and untenable form of the doctrine of legislative supremacy, which (unlike absolutist conceptions) is compatible with the rule of law.[4] It is in fact a controversial question whether it is possible in practice to draw a sharp line between review of governmental action, on

---

[3] The ultra vires doctrine cannot, however, apply to non-statutory powers, such as royal prerogative powers, and here the common law critics plainly have the advantage (see further below).

[4] See Chapters 4 and 5, above.

the one hand, and review of the grant of statutory powers, on the other; and the limits of the former cannot therefore be fairly considered without attention to the latter.[5] As we shall see, judicial review of the actions of public authorities rests on strong assumptions about the implicit or necessary limits on their powers—limits that Parliament may not, in practice, be allowed to override. We must not allow a purely *external* viewpoint, describing a general practice of obedience to statute, to obscure the far more complex and nuanced perspective of the judge or lawyer, who is obliged to find an appropriate accommodation between legislative supremacy and the rule of law, case by case, according to the specific context.

There is here a methodological question about the nature of the debate over ultra vires that we should confront at the outset. What sort of claim is being made by the doctrine's defenders or detractors? It might superficially appear that the debate is intended merely to clarify an existing state of affairs—to show, perhaps, what senior judges think about the matter when their various pronouncements are properly ordered and understood; or to show what courts are most likely to do under certain hypothetical conditions. But there are too many appeals to *legitimacy*—what it would be proper or improper for courts to do in specified circumstances—to make that view tenable. So the role of the ultra vires doctrine must be treated as a matter of constitutional theory, which attempts to connect legal practice with larger questions of general political principle. We should understand the debate, then, as an argument over the best *interpretation* of our legal practice: the competing views express divergent conceptions of how judicial review should be conceived and developed as supporting an ideal of administrative legality, attuned or adapted to British legal tradition and experience. There is no sharp distinction between matters of fact or official attitude, on the one hand, and questions of political morality, on the other. Judicial precedent and opinion is relevant as showing what specific form the safeguards of legality already take, pointing the way towards their rational elaboration and extension. But practice can be understood only in the light of the ideals or values it serves—those values that give us reason to pursue and sustain the practice and argue over its detailed implications. We cannot remain aloof, observing a practice of judicial review that simply exists; or at least we cannot do so if we want to understand and contribute to a debate over the place of that practice in a larger theory of British constitutionalism.[6]

There is a tendency, on both sides of the argument, to appeal to established facts or influential opinions as a way of foreclosing debate in favour of a certain outcome. Calling in aid the unqualified sovereignty of Parliament, which is conceived to give it the 'last word' on any matter of legality, is the most conspicuous example. An interpretative theory, rooted in considerations of legitimacy, cannot take such

---

[5] Paul Craig recognizes that various interpretative approaches to statute impose progressively tighter constraints on parliamentary supremacy: Craig, 'Constitutional Foundations, the Rule of Law and Supremacy' [2003] PL 92–111, especially 107–9. He insists, nonetheless, that 'Parliament can trump judicial doctrine' (by explicit direction), purporting to affirm both the 'sovereignty of Parliament' and a 'conception of shared sovereignty', shared between courts and Parliament: ibid, 93.

[6] See further Chapter 1, above. See also Allan, 'The Constitutional Foundations of Judicial Review: Conceptual Conundrum or Interpretative Inquiry?' [2002] CLJ 87–125.

supposed 'facts' for granted: the limits or conditions of legislative supremacy must themselves be part of the argument. And the same is true of legality or the rule of law. Paul Craig rejects the suggestion that 'those engaged in the *ultra vires* debate should spell out their views on the rule of law within this debate'.[7] But an interpretative theory of judicial review cannot be independent of the conception of law and legality that informs its account of legitimacy. Nor can we accept the contention that any connection between theory and judicial doctrine is merely contingent, depending on how the competing theories are applied in practice.[8] From the internal, critical perspective of an interpretative approach, there is no conceptual separation or division between general theory and judicial doctrine. The latter is fully dependent on the former; the shape and content of doctrine, and its manner of application to particular cases, will reflect the reasons that give judicial intervention in governmental decision-making its legitimacy, according to the theory in point. The notion that questions of sovereignty, legality, and doctrine are sufficiently independent of the debate over ultra vires to be set aside, for the purposes of that debate, indicates serious misunderstanding of the nature and point of an interpretative theory. Matters of empirical fact or official opinion obtain their relevance from a theory informed by moral and political values—a theory whose construction is foundational to any useful account of the practice of judicial review.

It is, moreover, only when we reconnect a rather narrow argument over the status of ultra vires with the larger debates over sovereignty, legality, and doctrine that we can further our understanding of constitutional theory. Unless our scrutiny of the doctrinal foundation of judicial review is informed by considerations of legitimacy—what could *justify* the varying kinds and degrees of judicial intervention in the operations of executive government—our conclusions will have no direct bearing on legal practice. Divorced from ordinary legal analysis of specific claims of illegality in concrete cases, on one side, and abstract ideals of democracy and legality, on the other, our theory of judicial review will be only an empty plaything for academic amusement. Since all participants in this vibrant debate plainly have loftier ambitions, seeking to improve our grasp of constitutional theory, we must try to make sense of their arguments in the light of those ambitions. If an interpretative theory of judicial review must set the pertinent institutions and procedures within a larger framework of political values, we should read the arguments over ultra vires as contributions to the construction of a coherent account of public law principles—principles that connect our most basic ideas about legality and democracy, via developing judicial doctrine, to the more mundane issues raised by specific complaints of abuse of power against a public official or agency.

Our appraisal of academic debate about the constitutional foundations of judicial review will therefore take us far beyond the conceptual puzzles that may initially appear so central. I shall try to show that beneath the more superficial argument over the merits of competing models or characterizations of judicial review lies a deeper level of agreement, at least among the main protagonists on

---

[7] Craig, 'Constitutional Foundations, the Rule of Law and Supremacy', 95.
[8] Ibid, 94–5.

either side. The value of judicial review as a means of protecting citizens from the abuse of official power is widely recognized. And there is also agreement about the threat that, if judges do not respect the boundary between legality and policy—marking out a sphere of legitimate administrative discretion—they will damage the democratic process, usurping powers properly conferred on other institutions. Doctrinal disagreement is the reflection of controversy about how best to draw that line between legality and policy in particular fields; and insofar as there is *agreement* about the content and application of public law, it reflects not the independence of doctrine from theory, but rather an instructive overlap between interpretative viewpoints. A meeting of minds, at both abstract and concrete levels, is what every interpreter hopes to forge. We seek agreement through debate, holding our interlocutors to the moral and political ideals they affirm—challenging conclusions on specific issues that we think betray those fundamental values.

II

If we agree with Sir William Wade that 'unfettered discretion cannot exist where the rule of law reigns', every grant of statutory power must be confined by its specific terms and general purposes in such a manner as to exclude unfettered discretion.[9] And the courts could not, consistently with the rule of law, acknowledge such discretion—giving a public authority the power to exercise coercion in any manner it chooses—even if Parliament has apparently imposed no limits (or even expressly excluded them). As Wade explains:

If merely because an Act says that a minister may 'make such order as he thinks fit', or may do something 'if he is satisfied' as to some fact, the courts were to allow him to act as he liked, a wide door would be opened to abuse of power and the rule of law would cease to operate.[10]

It should be clear already that Parliament's supremacy is being honoured here in a manner appropriate for a constitutional democracy; a largely formal principle of parliamentary sovereignty gives way, in practice, to the substance of the rule of law. Parliament is presumed to intend no violation of the rule of law, and grants of statutory power to public authorities are interpreted on that assumption.

According to Wade, the 'simple proposition that a public authority may not act outside its powers (*ultra vires*) might fitly be called the central principle of administrative law'; and since judicial review is designed to prevent the abuse of power by public officials, it is 'presumed that Parliament did not intend to authorize abuses, and that certain safeguards against abuse must be implied'.[11] Wade rightly emphasizes that these are 'matters of general principle, embodied in the rules of

---

[9] Sir William Wade, *Administrative Law*, 9th edn by Sir William Wade and Christopher Forsyth (Oxford: Oxford University Press, 2004), 35.
[10] Ibid.   [11] Ibid, 36.

law which govern the interpretation of statutes'. They need not be incorporated expressly: 'They may be taken for granted as part of the implied conditions to which every Act is subject and which the courts extract by reading between the lines.'[12] The principles of law that limit administrative discretion are found (or inserted) 'between the lines' because the court is unwilling to tolerate violation of the rule of law. And it is doubtful whether a court that did accede to such violation would continue to be a *court of law*, or whether instead it would be co-opted into a scheme for the *evasion* of law, surrendering all constitutional legitimacy.[13]

Any satisfactory reconciliation of legislative supremacy with the rule of law must leave an official agency with proper scope to fulfil its public functions: it must be free, within the bounds of legality, to exercise its statutory discretion according to its own (not the court's) view of the public interest. Wade is right, therefore, to stress the distinction between review and appeal: the High Court's role is to uphold the rule of law, or legality, rather than to substitute its own decision 'on the merits'. He acknowledges that limitations of purpose and requirements of reasonableness may sometimes severely restrict the scope of discretion, so that an action's 'merits determine its legality'.[14] He even observes that the 'further the courts are drawn into passing judgement on the merits of the actions of public authorities, the more they are exposed to the charge that they are exceeding their constitutional function'. But there he adopts a merely descriptive stance, external to the questions of legal principle involved in sustaining the rule of law: becoming exposed to a charge of impropriety is not the same as actually being guilty of it. Whether or not a court has improperly transgressed the limits of its own jurisdiction, intruding too far into the functions of the public agency, is a matter that depends on all the circumstances of the particular case. If, in context, the administrative discretion is rightly given a narrow definition, limiting the number of alternatives available for the agency to choose, there is no unconstitutional usurpation by the court: it merely enforces the rule of law as the circumstances require.

The ultra vires doctrine is plainly intended to reconcile legislative supremacy and the rule of law. The potential for conflict is removed by adopting a strong presumption that Parliament intends the rule of law to be observed, so that any abuse of power, in breach of the rule of law, is also a breach of the limits of the powers (or 'jurisdiction') conferred on the public agency. As inherent limits on any grant of powers made to a minister or other public authority, the various standards of legality enforced by judicial review—natural justice or fairness, reasonableness,

---

[12] Ibid. According to the 7th edition, the courts extract these implied conditions 'by reading between the lines or (it may be truer to say) insert by writing between the lines' (p 42).

[13] It is an unspoken assumption, underlying much of the debate over ultra vires, that the *rule of law* is an ideal quite distinct from *law*, which is ultimately a matter of empirical fact (derived from specific sources). But this is only a doubtful stipulation of legal positivism: see Nigel Simmonds, *Law as a Moral Idea* (Oxford: Oxford University Press, 2007), ch 2. The implicit challenge to legal positivism, which denies that law has any necessary, inherent moral value (related to the value of legality), is nevertheless identified by David Dyzenhaus: see Dyzenhaus, 'Reuniting the Brain: The Democratic Basis of Judicial Review' (1998) 9 PLR 98–110, and 'Form and Substance in the Rule of Law: A Democratic Justification for Judicial Review?', in Forsyth (ed), *Judicial Review and the Constitution*, 141–72.

[14] Wade, *Administrative Law*, 9th edn, 34.

proper purposes, and so forth—cannot be infringed without loss of jurisdiction: the authority automatically exceeds the scope of its powers, making any decision null and void. Not only may any such decision be quashed by the court, but it may be ignored by anyone affected as making no change to her legal position (unless she depends on the active cooperation of the authority, in which case she may have to rely instead on judicial review). There is no threat to parliamentary supremacy, of course: the court is simply policing the boundaries of the statutory powers conferred. As a merely formal rationalization, however, the ultra vires doctrine is consistent with whatever limits on administrative discretion the court decides that the rule of law requires.[15]

While a perfectly serviceable doctrine for practicable purposes, ultra vires depends on the court's adherence to the strong presumption in favour of the rule of law. It must be a non-rebuttable presumption, cast in that guise only to preserve the formally unlimited sovereignty of Parliament. While Parliament, being 'absolute', may in theory confer powers capable of being used unreasonably or unfairly or according to the unfettered discretion of a public agency, the courts will never acknowledge, in practice, that Parliament has actually done so (whatever the terms of the relevant Act). When Sir William Wade turns to examine the judicial treatment of ouster clauses, purporting to exclude the court's review jurisdiction altogether, he comes down clearly on the side of the rule of law. He is quite plainly defending only a formal doctrine of ultra vires, sustaining only a qualified form of parliamentary sovereignty, which cannot in practice be asserted, in defiance of the rule of law, to abrogate the citizen's right to judicial review of an executive decision of dubious legality.

In the *Anisminic* case, the House of Lords quashed a decision of the Foreign Compensation Commission on grounds of error of law, notwithstanding section 4(4) of the Foreign Compensation Act 1950, which provided that a determination of the Commission 'shall not be called in question in any court of law'.[16] In adopting a mistaken construction of an Order in Council relevant to their decision, the Commission had exceeded its jurisdiction; and the ouster clause could not protect an ultra vires decision. As a mere 'purported determination', falling outside the scope of the powers conferred, the decision was not saved by section 4(4), which merely excluded review of erroneous (but presumably less seriously erroneous) decisions made within jurisdiction. Whatever the merits of the distinction between jurisdictional and non-jurisdictional errors of law, and the plausibility of the court's application of that distinction on the facts of the case—matters about which public lawyers differ—*Anisminic* confirmed the court's ability to defend the rule of law, when necessary, by an appropriately nuanced interpretative approach to statutes. Wade goes so far as to assert that, in defence of the rule of law, 'the courts have been forced to rebel against Parliament', applying 'a presumption that

---

[15] The inability of such a formal doctrine, in itself, to provide substantive guidance or legitimacy is emphasized by Paul Craig: see Craig, 'Ultra Vires and the Foundations of Judicial Review', in Forsyth (ed), *Judicial Review and the Constitution*, 47–71.

[16] *Anisminic Ltd v Foreign Compensation Commission* [1969] 2 AC 147.

may override even their constitutional obedience, namely that jurisdictional limits must be legally effective':

> This is tantamount to saying that judicial review is a constitutional fundamental which even the sovereign Parliament cannot abolish and that any attempt to abolish it is an abuse of legislative power.... Parliament is mostly concerned with short-term considerations and is strangely indifferent to the paradox of enacting law and then preventing the courts from enforcing it. The judges, with their eye on the long term and the rule of law, have made it their business to preserve a deeper constitutional logic, based on their repugnance to allowing any subordinate authority to obtain uncontrollable power.[17]

Wade's recognition of judicial review as a 'constitutional fundamental', which Parliament cannot remove, is an admission that the absolutist version of parliamentary sovereignty is false: it is only a principle of legislative supremacy which cannot conflict with the rule of law, which defines its boundaries.

It is hardly surprising that, in these circumstances, Lord Woolf of Barnes should dismiss the ultra vires doctrine as a 'fairy tale', doubting whether the presumed intentions of Parliament can provide the basis of judicial review.[18] Insisting that 'our parliamentary democracy is based on the rule of law', Lord Woolf denies that Parliament could 'abolish the courts' entire power of judicial review in express terms': 'As both Parliament and the courts derive their authority from the rule of law so both are subject to it and cannot act in a manner which involves its repudiation.'[19] While some judges might invoke an 'unrebuttable presumption' against such statutory interference with the judicial role, there were advantages 'in making it clear that ultimately there are even limits on the supremacy of Parliament which it is the courts' inalienable responsibility to identify and uphold'.[20] Despite his doubts about ultra vires, however, Lord Woolf's position is substantially the same as Wade's, as indeed Wade acknowledges.[21]

The ultra vires doctrine is a fairly tale only if we cling to the notion of parliamentary omnipotence: it squares judicial practice with an implausible doctrine of absolutism. When we concede the necessary limitations on parliamentary supremacy, its role is more modest and plausible. The ultra vires doctrine preserves the link between judicial review and statutory interpretation, emphasizing the specific statutory context in which the general grounds of review must be applied: judgements of fairness or reasonableness or proper purposes are necessarily attuned to all the circumstances, which include the relevant statutory objectives or policies. And the doctrine need not be taken to deny the ultimate status of the rule of law, which imposes those constraints of procedure and substance that mark respect for human dignity and equal citizenship.[22] If Parliament cannot authorize administrative

---

[17] Wade, *Administrative Law*, 720–1; see also Sir William Wade, *Constitutional Fundamentals*, revised edn (London: Stevens & Sons, 1989), 87: 'In their self-defensive campaign the judges have almost given us a constitution ... They may be discovering a deeper constitutional logic than the crude absolute of statutory omnipotence.'

[18] Lord Woolf of Barnes, 'Droit Public—English Style' [1995] PL 57–71.

[19] Ibid, 67–8.

[20] Ibid, 69.

[21] Wade, *Administrative Law*, 721, citing Woolf's lecture with approval.

[22] See Chapter 3, above.

action that infringes the rule of law, any assertion of power made in violation of legality is necessarily ultra vires: the agency exceeds any jurisdiction that Parliament was competent to bestow.

Sir John Laws has joined the debate as a prominent sceptic, claiming that attribution of the various grounds of review to 'an intention of the legislature that statutory decision-makers should act reasonably and fairly' is fictitious:

They are, categorically, judicial creations. They owe neither their existence nor their acceptance to the will of the legislature. They have nothing to do with the intention of Parliament, save as a fig-leaf to cover their true origins. We do not need the fig-leaf any more.[23]

Although Laws might be understood as calling merely for a simplification of constitutional theory, dispensing with unnecessary fictions, he is more plausibly read as emphasizing the fundamental nature of the grounds of review, impervious to parliamentary interference. He affirms that the court's review jurisdiction 'vindicates the rule of law not only by confining statutory power within the four corners of the Act, but also by ensuring that the statute is not usurped by anyone—including the courts themselves'.[24] That reference to the rule of law is followed in the same article by an insistence on the 'imperative of higher-order law', protecting fundamental rights from legislative attack. Granting that Parliament enjoys a 'political sovereignty', Laws denies that it has a 'constitutional sovereignty':

Ultimate sovereignty rests, in every civilized constitution, not with those who wield governmental power, but in the conditions under which they are permitted to do so. The constitution, not the Parliament, is in this sense sovereign. In Britain these conditions should now be recognized as consisting in a framework of fundamental principles which include the imperative of democracy itself and those other rights, prime among them freedom of thought and expression, which cannot be denied save by a plea of guilty to totalitarianism.[25]

It is a reasonable inference, then, that the objection to the 'fig-leaf' of ultra vires is its ability to obscure not merely the judicial origins of, or inspiration for, the various grounds of review, but more importantly their status as constitutional fundamentals that Parliament cannot override.

The inference is confirmed by Laws's observation that the duty to obey Parliament is imposed by the common law, which is the 'higher premise' and represents the people's will in a different sense from the democratic voice that speaks through the legislature:

It represents a collection of fundamental civic aspirations which in one form or another are a necessary reflection of man's nature as a rational being, possessed of free will, living in community with others of his kind: justice, freedom, and order. The common law has to give effect to these aspirations because they are its *fons et origo*. . . . Wade's description of the *ultra vires* rule as the foundation of the court's constitutional function puts the cart before the horse; the common law is logically prior to statute, and its obedience to Parliament's law is not an axiom on which its jurisdiction proceeds, nor a defining limitation of it.[26]

---

[23] Sir John Laws, 'Law and Democracy' [1995] PL 72–93, at 79.
[24] Ibid, 77–8.
[25] Ibid, 92.
[26] Sir John Laws, 'Illegality: The Problem of Jurisdiction', in Michael Supperstone and James Goudie (eds), *Judicial Review*, 2nd edn (London: Butterworths, 1997), 4.12–13.

It ought to follow that those precepts of legality enforced by judicial review against public agencies are fundamental law; and though they must be adapted to the administrative context in view, they cannot be overridden. If, as Laws also argues, 'the developed doctrines of modern public law, including an increasing recognition of fundamental constitutional rights, are not in fact and logically cannot be a function of Parliament's law', they must be basic presuppositions or preconditions of that law.[27] These common law principles, which may operate formally as presumptions of legislative intent, are in truth impervious to any purported legislative abrogation. The relevant 'intent' presupposes compliance with legality because in conferring executive powers, Parliament invokes the idea of law: in making *law* it cannot logically repudiate the basic principle of legality. Legislative supremacy, correctly understood, is always asserted in compliance with the rule of law.[28]

III

Christopher Forsyth reaches similar conclusions about the pivotal role of parliamentary supremacy in the critique of ultra vires. He insists that a supposedly 'weak' critic, emphasizing the artificiality of reference to legislative intentions, is transmuted by force of logic into a 'strong' critic, who challenges absolute parliamentary sovereignty.[29] As he explains, a breach of administrative legality, as defined by common law, is either sanctioned by Parliament or not, at least in the sense that any judicial intervention inconsistent with a public agency's statutory mandate would deny Parliament's authority: 'what an all powerful Parliament does not prohibit, it must authorize either expressly or impliedly'.

Likewise if Parliament grants a power to a minister, that minister either acts within those powers or outside those powers. There is no grey area between authorization and prohibition or between empowerment and the denial of power. Thus, if the making of ... vague regulations is within the powers granted by a sovereign Parliament, on what basis may the courts challenge Parliament's will and hold that the regulations are invalid? If Parliament has authorized vague regulations, those regulations cannot be challenged without challenging Parliament's authority to authorize such regulations.[30]

The logic is unimpeachable even if we apply a strong presumption against any legislative intention to permit an authority to issue vague regulations, which threaten the

---

[27] Ibid, 4.18.

[28] As we will see below, Sir John Laws draws back from these conclusions. In insisting on a strict division, as regards the concept of law, between factual and normative questions, Laws fails to see how law is dependent on a vision of the rule of law; accordingly, he treats the 'mere idea of law itself' as morally neutral. His legal positivism misleads him: Laws, 'Judicial Review and the Meaning of Law', in Forsyth (ed), *Judicial Review and the Constitution*, 173–90, especially 178–80, 183–4. For reflection on the idea of public law and individual rights as themselves expressions of sovereignty, see Martin Loughlin, *The Idea of Public Law* (Oxford: Oxford University Press, 2003), ch 5.

[29] Christopher Forsyth, 'Of Fig Leaves and Fairy Tales: The Ultra Vires Doctrine, the Sovereignty of Parliament and Judicial Review', in Forsyth (ed), *Judicial Review and the Constitution*, 29–46.

[30] Ibid, 39–40.

citizen's liberty. Sir John Laws objects that merely because Parliament can authorize or prohibit anything it does not follow that 'all authorities and prohibitions must come from Parliament': there may be common law requirements that Parliament has neither authorized nor forbidden.[31] But the objection misses the point. All such common law rules or requirements remain (for the absolutist) vulnerable to legislative abrogation; so the jurisdiction of any public agency is in that sense always a function of the scope of its statutory grant, however broad or unfettered Parliament has chosen to make it.

Forsyth defends the ultra vires doctrine as a concomitant of the unqualified parliamentary sovereignty he endorses: he insists that 'the sovereignty of Parliament, for good or ill, remains a fundamental element of the constitutional order; and it is not for the judges acting on their own motion to try to change that'.[32] That assertion of absolutism is, however, undefended: a normative constitutional doctrine cannot be established, as I have argued at length, by reference to the supposed facts of the matter; and this is so even if (which is hardly the case) official opinion—the pertinent fact of the matter—were uniform and uncontroversial.[33] Laws's appeal to the 'constitutional sovereignty' from which Parliament's more limited 'political sovereignty' is derived must be met, if it can be, on its own terms. And the moral and political debate must be suitably nuanced. If democracy is itself an idea embracing such fundamental rights as freedom of speech, as Laws contends, Forsyth cannot simply invoke the value of democracy as a constraint on judicial review. If Britain is a parliamentary democracy (Laws may be understood to argue) Parliament is *already* subject to the constraints inherent in the best conception of democracy; and it is the judges' inescapable task to determine, when necessary, what that conception entails.

Unfortunately, misled by his reluctance to acknowledge Forsyth's logic, Sir John Laws denies any need to challenge parliamentary absolutism, rendering his attack on ultra vires incoherent. Observing that parliamentary sovereignty remains 'the plainest constitutional fundamental at the present time', he suggests that 'a departure from it will only happen, in the tranquil development of the common law, with a gradual re-ordering of our constitutional priorities to bring alive the nascent idea that a democratic legislature cannot be above the law'.[34] But this is to take up the external viewpoint of the observer, attempting to predict the future course of legal development. In view of his objections to absolutism it is clear that Laws has already grasped the 'nascent idea' of constitutional democracy, based on respect for certain fundamental rights of individuals. So his assumption of legislative absolutism is adopted merely for purposes of the present argument, perhaps to disarm his opponents—a concession that proves fatal to any serious objection to ultra vires and its implicit reference to legislative intent or instruction.

---

[31] Laws, 'Illegality', 4.17–18.   [32] Forsyth, 'Of Fig Leaves and Fairy Tales', 46.
[33] See Chapter 4, above.   [34] Laws, 'Illegality', 4.17.

Laws is anxious to protect both common law constitutional rights and settled standards of administrative legality from inadvertent or ill-advised interference; so he constructs a presumption of intention as strong as continued adherence to parliamentary absolutism will bear:

The judges' duty is to uphold constitutional rights: to secure order, certainly, but to temper the rule of the state by freedom and justice. In our unwritten legal system the substance of such rights is to be found in the public law principles which the courts have developed, and continue to develop. Parliament may (in the present stage of our constitutional evolution) override them, but can only do so by express, focussed provision.[35]

Laws maintains that 'prima facie the commitment of a final decision as to what the law is to any body other than the High Court is an infringement of the rule of law', though he accepts that an inferior court may be 'given the last word upon the law relating to matters within its remit'.[36] If government is to be held subject to a consistent and coherent body of law, extending similar safeguards against wrongful coercion to everyone, there is much to be said in favour of the High Court's unique responsibility. Since an ouster clause would remove that protection, the court must stand as a bulwark, seeking to vindicate the rule of law, such vindication being 'the constitutional right of every citizen':

So if it is to be breached by Parliament or Parliament's permission, the High Court will require express words to be used. Here is the true place of the idea of legislative intention. Parliament may override the rule of law, but only where it shown, on the face of the statute, that it *actually* intended to do so. In such a context, there is no room for "implied" intention....As the constitution presently stands the sovereign Parliament can override the rule of law, but only if it passes main legislation to say that that is what it is doing.[37]

But now the argument has gone badly awry; for it makes little sense to talk of an institution such as Parliament, composed of hundreds of members, actually intending anything. We can ascertain any relevant 'intention' only from a study of the words enacted; and then it is only a general plan or scheme constructed—whether by a judicial interpreter or an individual voting member of Parliament—to make the best sense possible of a collective action.[38] If we concluded that Parliament had chosen to breach the rule of law, contrary to the first principles of democratic constitutionalism, it would only be because we *attributed* such an intention to the legislature; and no one who truly values the rule of law, as a foundation of freedom and justice, would make such an attribution. We should not attribute to Parliament intentions that flout the very conditions on which the legitimacy of its enactments depends. The lesson of *Anisminic* is that the court's responsibility is always to interpret an Act in such a way as to advance its apparent general purposes while preserving the essentials of legality. While an ouster clause may serve to enlarge a public authority's discretion to develop and follow its own policy agenda,

[35] Ibid, 4.18–19. [36] Ibid, 4.23.
[37] Ibid, 4.23–4. [38] See further Chapter 5, above.

within certain broad limits, it cannot operate to exclude review of 'jurisdictional' error of the kind that causes serious injustice—injury to important rights or interests out of all proportion to any public advantage. An ouster provision is part of the text to be interpreted; but it cannot consistently with the rule of law exclude the interpretative process itself, attuned to the circumstances of the particular case.[39]

Such requirements of administrative legality as the duty to have regard to relevant considerations, while ignoring irrelevant ones, and to act only for the purposes envisaged (on correct construction) by the statutory grant of power, are implicit in the basic idea of government according to law. They are no less part of the rule of law than the precepts of legality that dictate the proper form of statutes, and whose infringement, if serious, threatens the idea of law itself. Just as an Act must mainly consist of reasonably clear, general, prospective, published rules, which do not contradict each other in such a manner as to render them meaningless, so must an administrative act comply with essential conditions of legality.[40] An action or decision that flouts the limits and purposes inherent in its empowering legislation is not a genuine exercise of a public jurisdiction, but rather a private action that constitutes unlawful coercion of other persons. As Wade clearly sees, the courts can permit such unlawful coercion only at the cost of undermining the legal framework of the state, threatening their own *raison d'etre* as guardians of the rule of law. If we are unwilling to take shelter in fictions and fairy tales we must come clean: there are limits to legislative supremacy that the courts must enforce in defence of legality.

Admittedly, Sir John Laws stresses the relatively recent origin of the grounds of review as a matter of English administrative law. Attributing the duty on administrative bodies to observe natural justice (or procedural fairness) to *Ridge v Baldwin*, and the proper purposes doctrine to *Padfield*, and noting that decision-makers have not in the past been required to honour legitimate expectations, Laws points to judicial creativity as the source of the modern law: the grounds of review are 'categorically, judicial creations'.[41] If we assume, however, that such innovations were legitimate, they were 'creations' only in the sense that they rectified deficiencies in the courts' previous enforcement of the rule of law. The landmark cases of the 1960s and 1970s restored or rediscovered an ideal of legality that had suffered indefensible neglect: the judges reasserted their constitutional function in the face of an expanding administrative state. In *Ridge v Baldwin*, Lord Reid observed that the principle *audi alteram partem* had been applied for centuries, its more recent eclipse being the result of the failure to appreciate its adaptability to the great variety of administrative contexts: 'What a minister ought to do in considering

---

[39] Compare *Pushpanathan v Canada (Minister of Citizenship and Immigration)* [1998] 1 SCR 982, 1003–12.

[40] For the canons of legality applicable to enacted laws, see Lon L Fuller, *The Morality of Law*, revised edn (New Haven: Yale University Press, 1969), ch 2.

[41] Laws, 'Law and Democracy', 78–9, citing *Ridge v Baldwin* [1960] AC 40 and *Padfield v Minister of Agriculture* [1968] AC 997.

objections to a scheme may be very different from what a watch committee ought to do in considering whether to dismiss a chief constable.'[42]

Insofar as the different principles of administrative legality are part of the common law, articulated and developed by the judges, they exemplify the common law's commitment to constitutionalism. As abstract ideals or general standards they embody an important dimension of the rule of law; their application to the particular circumstances of British government gives the ideal of legality a domestic and concrete content suitable to current needs and aspirations. The conditions of legality are discovered or worked out in the context of particular instances of apparent unfairness or alleged abuse of power: an abstract ideal acquires a more determinate shape in the course of judicial deliberation and doctrinal development. These principles are not dependent on any parliamentary sanction because they are inherent in the very concept of legality, applicable (in more general form) to any and every government subject to the rule of law. If the doctrine of ultra vires retains its place in the general scheme, it is only in the sense that a breach of legality is always, in a statutory context, in part a matter of statutory interpretation: the application of the grounds or heads of review must be sensitive to context, acknowledging (as Lord Reid's observations indicate) that what is unfair or unreasonable (or otherwise unlawful) inevitably depends on all the relevant circumstances.[43]

For all his denial of limits to parliamentary absolutism, one may wonder whether Christopher Forsyth really disagrees with these conclusions. After all, his defence of ultra vires is, in part, a warning about the potentially dire consequences for the rule of law of its demise. He observes that the courts' resistance to any literal application of ouster clauses depends on the doctrine of ultra vires: any action in breach of the various heads of review, by causing the public authority to exceed its jurisdiction, gains no protection from such a clause.[44] *Anisminic* is contrasted with a case in the Appellate Division of South Africa, in which vague regulations were held to be protected by an ouster clause, rejecting the ultra vires doctrine: the regulations were made 'under section 3' of the Public Safety Act 1953, and hence fell within the compass of the ouster clause, even if they were otherwise so vague as to offend the principles of Roman-Dutch common law.[45] Forsyth's anxiety about the 'evisceration of judicial review' that may follow the abandonment of ultra vires, whether justified or not, plainly reflects his strong adherence to legality: he does

---

[42] [1964] AC 40, 65. In respect of 'dismissal from an office where there must be something against a man to warrant his dismissal', Lord Reid found 'an unbroken line of authority to the effect that an officer cannot lawfully be dismissed without first telling him what is alleged against him and hearing his defence or explanation' (citing *Bagg's Case* (1615) 11 Co Rep 93b).

[43] 'If a minister is considering whether to make a scheme for, say, an important new road, his primary concern will not be with the damage which its construction will do to the rights of individual owners of land. He will have to consider all manner of questions of public interest and, it may be, a number of alternative schemes. He cannot be prevented from attaching more importance to the fulfilment of his policy than to the fate of individual objectors, and it would be quite wrong for the courts to say that the minister should or could act in the same kind of way as a board of works deciding whether a house should be pulled down': [1964] AC 40, 72.

[44] Forsyth, 'Of Fig Leaves and Fairy Tales', 35–9.

[45] *Staatspresident v United Democratic Front* 1988 (4) SA 830(A).

not wish the rule of law to be endangered by any too literal invocation of an apparently hostile legislative will.[46]

Although Sir John Laws rejects Forsyth's argument for the retention of ultra vires, relying (as we have seen) on a rule of construction that can only be expressly overridden, his own position is not substantially different. Once the misleading references to 'actual intention' are stripped away, we are left with a general principle of legality with which all delegations of power must comply. Any limitation of judicial review must be capable of justification by reference to the administrative context; and an ouster clause is only a tentative guide to the demands of that context, underlining the scope for (some measure of) genuine policy discretion. We have only to note the terms of Laws's prescription for an effective ouster of jurisdiction, in defiance of legality, to perceive how exaggerated are invocations of absolute sovereignty in the present context:

The statute would have to provide that the decision of the body in question could not be reviewed for any failure to comply with the principles of public law; it would be tantamount to a provision to the effect that the decision-maker was not obliged to be reasonable, or to be fair, or to act within the confines of the Act's purpose, or according to its correct construction.[47]

Any such provision would, of course, be a patent absurdity, analogous to the pragmatic self-contradiction entailed by an Act purporting to be for the implementation of unjust discrimination, or some similar injury to the public good.[48] It is the sort of nightmare conjured up by giving simplistic notions of absolute sovereignty free rein.[49]

The proper reconciliation between legislative supremacy and the rule of law is exemplified by Laws LJ's own judgment in *R (Cart & Ors) v The Upper Tribunal*, in which he held that neither the Upper Tribunal nor the Special Immigration Appeals Commission could be rendered immune from judicial review merely by being designated as, in each case, a 'superior court of record'.[50] While the Upper Tribunal, as an appeal court of wide jurisdiction, could be considered an alter ego of the High Court, the Commission was a court of limited jurisdiction subject to judicial review. The former, but not the latter, satisfied the pertinent principle of the rule of law that 'statute law has to be mediated by an authoritative judicial source, independent both of the legislature which made the statute, the executive

---

[46] Forsyth, 'Of Fig Leaves and Fairy Tales', 38.

[47] Laws, 'Illegality', 4.24.

[48] See Neil MacCormick, 'Natural Law and the Separation of Law and Morals', in Robert P George (ed), *Natural Law Theory: Contemporary Essays* (Oxford: Clarendon Press, 1992), 105–33, at 112.

[49] The fierce opposition provoked by the very elaborate ouster provision in the Asylum and Immigration (Treatment of Claimants, etc) Bill 2003 is recorded by Andrew Le Sueur, 'Three Strikes and It's Out? The UK Government's Strategy to Oust Judicial Review from Immigration and Asylum Decision-making' [2004] PL 225–33; see also Lord Woolf, 'The Rule of Law and a Change in the Constitution' [2004] CLJ 317–30, at 327–9.

[50] [2009] EWHC 3052 (Admin): see Tribunals, Courts and Enforcement Act 2007, s 3(5); Special Immigration Appeals Commission Act 1997, s 1(3), as amended by Anti-Terrorism, Crime and Security Act 2001, s 35.

government which (in the usual case) procured its making, and the public body by which the statute is administered'.[51]

The integration of legislative supremacy and legality is explicit in Laws's observation that the 'very effectiveness' of statute law depends on the existence of an impartial and independent judicial interpreter, charged with the function of making determinate what are otherwise 'only letters on a page'. If either legislature or executive were final interpreter it would be judge in its own cause, 'with the ills of arbitrary government which that would entail'. If the public authority itself were final interpreter, 'the decision-makers would write their own laws'. Judicial review is necessary to confine public bodies within their allotted powers; it is a constitutional fundamental:

Accordingly, ... the need for such an authoritative judicial source cannot be dispensed with by Parliament. This is not a denial of legislative sovereignty, but an affirmation of it: as is the old rule that Parliament cannot bind itself. The old rule means that successive Parliaments are always free to make what laws they choose; that is one condition of Parliament's sovereignty. The requirement of an authoritative judicial source for the interpretation of law means that Parliament's statutes are always effective; that is another.[52]

The reference to 'legislative sovereignty' can be read to mean legislative supremacy; and the respective conditions are equally demands of democracy. Parliament and courts cooperate to preserve the integrity of liberal democracy: the court permits a statutory tribunal to exercise the authority (including interpretative authority) appropriate to the constitutional function conferred by Parliament in exercise of its legitimate democratic role.[53]

In the view of the Court of Appeal, the Upper Tribunal was not an alter ego of the High Court but stood, instead, in the shoes of the various administrative tribunals it had replaced.[54] As part of a new tribunal structure intended to allow for the internal correction of errors, the Upper Tribunal would be subject to judicial review only in exceptional cases: 'outright excess of jurisdiction' (conducting an unauthorized adjudication) or a denial of 'fundamental justice' (such as a serious breach of natural justice) could be remedied even though less serious (non-jurisdictional) errors could not. It was necessary to reconcile two relevant principles: the 'relative autonomy' with which Parliament had invested the new tribunals must be squared with the 'constitutional role of the High Court as the guardian of standards of legality and due process'.[55] Legislative supremacy and the rule of law were thereby united: the appropriate form of judicial control, in all the circumstances, was one which secured the 'boundaries of the system' but did not 'invade it'.[56]

---

[51] Ibid, para 36.

[52] Ibid, para 38.

[53] Compare Lord Wilberforce in *Anisminic* [1969] 2 AC 147, 208: 'What would be the point of defining by statute the limit of a tribunal's powers if, by means of a clause inserted in the instrument of definition, those limits could safely be passed?'

[54] *R (Cart) v Upper Tribunal* [2010] EWCA Civ 859.

[55] Ibid, para 35.

[56] Ibid, para 42. The Supreme Court, however, denied that judicial review was confined to exceptional cases, embracing a more broadly defined oversight: *R (Cart) v Upper Tribunal* [2011] UKSC 28.

IV

When we acknowledge that a court must, in virtue of its constitutional function, adhere to the rule of law—upholding legality as it understands that complex requirement—the common law basis of the various grounds of judicial review can be understood. The common law is a corpus of general principles, refined and elaborated by judicial precedent, that embodies the ideal of legality as it applies in the context of the British administrative state. As elements of the rule of law, inherent in constitutional government properly respectful of the governed, the various principles of administrative legality cannot be displaced or abrogated by Parliament. Even a democratic assembly must comply with the rule of law: any delegation of power to a public authority must be applied to the furtherance of legitimate public purposes in a manner that satisfies general standards of fairness and reasonableness. No Parliament could be understood as authorizing an abuse of power; and since such 'abuse' is a function of all the circumstances, depending on the nature of the power and the consequences of its deployment against particular persons, its identification is necessarily a judicial function, bringing general principle to bear on the facts of the case in view.[57]

The appropriate integration of general legal principle and specific statutory purpose is a matter calling for reflection and judgement. From within the practice of law—by contrast with a merely external or descriptive viewpoint—there is neither an omnipotent Parliament nor any free-standing criterion of administrative legality, independent of context. There is only the subtle and nuanced process of interpretation, sensitive to social and political context, that the doctrine of ultra vires invokes when correctly understood. If proponents of ultra vires sometimes emphasize the legislative context at the expense of general principle, its opponents often seem to underestimate the pliability of the grounds of review, which in many cases serve mainly to summarize a finding of illegality closely dependent on all the circumstances. No one would doubt that a public agency should be required to have regard to relevant considerations and disregard irrelevant ones; nor would anyone think that the agency should normally have the last word about what, on correct construction of the statute, was relevant and what was not. The question of substance concerns the scope for discretionary administrative judgement on the

---

Lord Phillips observed (at para 89): 'The administration of justice and upholding of the rule of law involves a partnership between Parliament and the judges. . . . It should be for the judges to decide whether the statutory provisions for the administration of justice adequately protect the rule of law and, by judicial review, to supplement these should it be necessary. But, in exercising the power of judicial review, the judges must pay due regard to the fact that, even where the due administration of justice is at stake, resources are limited . . .'

[57] As David Dyzenhaus explains, the error made both by critics and defenders of ultra vires is to treat the principles of legality as only *contingently* relevant, in virtue of English legal tradition (which might have been, or become, more hostile). In that way they attempt to square their commitment to common law principle with adherence to parliamentary absolutism: Dyzenhaus, 'Formalism's Hollow Victory' [2002] NZLR 525–56, especially 529–40.

facts in view; and in maintaining legality the court, by keeping an agency to its statutory task, also upholds the legislative will.[58]

If Sir John Laws were right to claim that, by virtue of ultra vires, 'the decisions of the courts are only a function of Parliament's absolute power', we would have good reason to repudiate the doctrine.[59] But on correct analysis the doctrine makes (or need make) no such assumption. It is only the dubious assumption of unbounded sovereignty that induces that conclusion. If Parliament must honour the rule of law, ultra vires signals only the necessary interconnection between general legislative mandate, on the one hand, and specific determinations of legality or illegality, on the other. And whether or not it is objectionable that '*ultra vires* consigns everything to the intention of the legislature' depends on what is meant by the 'intention of the legislature'.[60] Since Parliament, being composed of hundreds of members, cannot literally have an intention in any ordinary sense, we can understand the expression only in a metaphorical sense. The relevant intention is the one we might attribute to a notional human legislator using the enacted words in the relevant context; it will depend as much on our understanding of the social problem being addressed, and our grasp of the character of the chosen remedy, as on any inference we can draw from the language alone.[61] Because our notional or representative legislator will acknowledge the demands of the rule of law—he represents a Parliament responsible for advancing the public good within the limits of legality—there is no question of his countermanding the application of administrative law. Our references to legislative intention, if coherent, signify only an attempt to read a provision consistently with its underlying general purpose—trying to make good sense of a scheme that promotes the public good within the constraints of respect for individual rights or legitimate countervailing interests.

We need, therefore, have no quarrel with Mark Elliott's 'modified ultra vires principle', which attributes not the detailed grounds of review to parliamentary intention but rather the general requirement that discretionary power should be exercised in accordance with the rule of law.[62] Elliott acknowledges the 'inherent normative value' of the principles of administrative legality. Insisting that Parliament's intention is consistent with respect for those principles 'simply recognizes that the constitutional order itself locates the legislature and the legislation which it passes within a framework which is founded on the rule of law, and which therefore

---

[58] Jeffrey Jowell rightly calls attention to the importance of context. See Jowell, 'Of Vires and Vacuums: The Constitutional Context of Judicial Review' [1999] PL 448–60, at 458: 'The judicial task is relatively circumscribed; it is not to impose its "creations" upon officials, but to articulate the foundations of a system in which both courts and the legislature are essential features with their own distinct institutional limits. Whether judges "make" or "find" the law, they do so within a relatively confined space in which a focused search for the concrete application of constitutional and institutional principle takes place.' Unfortunately, however, Jowell cannot throw off the usual allegiance to parliamentary absolutism, allowing Parliament 'to exclude a constitutional principle'—even, if the exclusion is sufficiently clear, to 'displace democracy's foundational features' (ibid).

[59] Laws, 'Illegality', 4.19.

[60] Ibid.

[61] See further Chapter 5, above.

[62] Mark Elliott, *The Constitutional Foundations of Judicial Review* (Oxford: Hart Publishing, 2001), especially ch 4.

attributes to the legislature an intention to act consistently with that principle'.[63] On that basis, 'judicial vindication of the rule of law through judicial review is seen to fulfil, rather than conflict with, the endeavours of the legislature'. We may wonder, however, whether Elliott's account truly differs from Sir William Wade's original version of the ultra vires doctrine.[64] When Wade observed that the judges 'have no constitutional right to interfere with action which is within the powers granted', he meant simply that the courts, being confined to matters of legality, must accept decisions made within jurisdiction.[65] The judge 'must in every case be able to demonstrate that he is carrying out the will of Parliament as expressed in the statute conferring the power' in the sense that he must point to some abuse of power, inconsistent with the statutory grant. And if, moreover, all such grants are necessarily curtailed by implicit standards of legality, the 'will of Parliament' coincides with the requirements of the rule of law.

Admittedly, Elliott declines to recognize more than very modest limits on parliamentary sovereignty. Even if certain theorists are right to contend that 'Parliament cannot abrogate the most basic tenets of the British democratic tradition', it does not follow (he supposes) that it cannot interfere with the principles of administrative legality:

> Completely abolishing all review in every context is an entirely different enterprise from statutory modification of the intensity, nature or availability of review in a particular area. While it may be possible to categorize the former as constitutionally anathema, the same is not true of the latter, which may well constitute a legitimate choice which is necessary, within a particular factual and policy environment, for effective government.[66]

But the distinction drawn here is suspect: it is not an 'entirely different enterprise' at all. No one doubts that the principles of legality must be sensitive to context. Their content and application must tread the delicate line between unwarranted interference with a public agency's functions, on the one hand, and failure to protect the victim of an abuse of power, on the other. And the explicit language of the statute may offer useful guidance about how to draw that line in ordinary cases, informing the court's interpretation of the scope of the discretion conferred. But an abuse of power is something *extraordinary*, entailing injustice or unfairness that no advancement of legitimate public purposes can justify; and no statute, properly interpreted, authorizes any such departure from legality. A court must, of course, be hesitant about finding an abuse of power, wary of frustrating the implementation of public policy; but it cannot decline to rectify what it concludes is indeed an abuse without, quite literally, giving up on *law*. An abdication of responsibility in

---

[63] Ibid, 113.

[64] Paul Craig argues that the 'modified ultra vires model' has conceded many of the objections made to the traditional model; but in view of the manifest deficiencies of the earlier model (as he describes it) one may fairly ask whether anyone could have seriously entertained it: see Craig, 'Competing Models of Judicial Review', in Forsyth (ed), *Judicial Review and the Constitution*, 373–92, especially 373–8.

[65] Wade, *Administrative Law*, 9th edn, 37.

[66] Elliott, *The Constitutional Foundations of Judicial Review*, 78–9.

respect of any specific departure from legality (falling under one or more heads of review) is no different from wholesale surrender; that is why ouster clauses are not taken at face value but permitted only, in appropriate cases, to enlarge the scope for 'error' (viz. policy choice or judgement) within jurisdiction.[67]

Elliott's stance is ultimately external and descriptive: he seeks to identify the 'prevailing conception of political morality' on which any limits to parliamentary sovereignty depend.[68] Even if it is conceded that there must be a normative grounding for any recognition of sovereignty, it must be sought (he supposes) in an empirically identifiable constitutional morality. We must turn chiefly to authoritative legal pronouncements, judicial and extra-judicial, and these do not support the view that sovereignty admits of any qualification. If, then, sovereignty requires a foundation in democratic theory, it must (in Elliott's view) be a very narrow conception of democracy. The empirical evidence supports only a 'relatively bare' conception, excluding any protection for human rights or principles of administrative legality.[69]

The legal interpreter cannot, however, remain detached from the political morality she seeks to articulate: her own moral judgements must play a critical role in supplying sense to and justification for the phenomena surveyed. If she concludes that the adherence of public authorities to certain elementary standards of legality is itself a democratic precept—part of any *legitimate* conception of democracy, operating within the constraints of the rule of law—she must defend that requirement against judicial assertions that betray or deny it. We cannot draw, as Elliott supposes, a sharp distinction between normative foundations and their purely empirical manifestation: judicial opinion and dicta are only contributions to a debate about constitutional theory that we must join, whether as legal commentators or equal citizens, on our own terms. A normative foundation that rests on a radically defective conception of democracy, inconsistent with the rule of law, could be accepted only at the price of wholesale scepticism: we would surrender our interpretative hat for the garb of anthropologist, excluded from a legal and constitutional argument we must observe from afar.[70]

From an internal, interpretative perspective, there is no clear distinction between modest and more flagrant violations of legality—between limited and substantial barriers to judicial review. It is a distinction of degree rather than kind: the more serious the abuse of power left without remedy, the graver the damage to the rule of law. In practice, however, interpretative disagreement will focus on how to discern the demands of legality in particular instances, in a specific constitutional context: the need for effective government will rightly affect our deliberations and

---

[67] See for example *South Asia Firebricks Sdn Bhd v Non-Metallic Mineral Products Manufacturing Employees Union* [1981] AC 363, affirming the dissenting judgment of Geoffrey Lane LJ in *Pearlman v Keepers and Governors of Harrow School* [1979] QB 56.

[68] Elliott, *The Constitutional Foundations of Judicial Review*, 66.

[69] Ibid, 71–3.

[70] The argument is more fully developed in Chapter 4, above. It is, of course, my own previous failure to make these points clear that now obliges me to quarrel with Elliott's interesting and careful critique of my earlier contributions to the debate.

appraisal. When we recall the proper sensitivity of judicial review to the context in point, the supposed antagonism between legislative supremacy and the rule of law dissolves. We need not recognize any power to suspend or curtail the principles of legality, even if we accept the propriety of their adaptation to the administrative context.

The principles of natural justice or procedural fairness provide a clear example of the way in which a basic precept of legality, critical to the impartial and accurate application of law or policy to particular cases, derives its detailed content from the context in view. When tailored to the circumstances in question, these principles both enforce legality and help give effect to the legislative scheme or purpose. In *Lloyd v McMahon*, which concerned the procedural rights of city councillors facing a possible finding of misconduct by the district auditor, Lord Bridge observed that the rules of natural justice were not 'engraved on tablets of stone':

> [W]hat the requirements of fairness demand when any body, domestic, administrative or judicial, has to make a decision which will affect the rights of individuals depends on the character of the decision-making body, the kind of decision it has to make and the statutory or other framework in which it operates.[71]

Whether or not the councillors were entitled to an oral hearing, in addition to the opportunity to make written representations, depended on what was necessary to ensure fairness in all the circumstances.

Christopher Forsyth and Mark Elliott invoke this judgment in support of their own defence of the role of the statute in guiding the application of the grounds of review.[72] They also stress the close analysis of the statutory context made by the House of Lords in *Padfield*, whose general principle is too abstract to be applied independently: 'It is the statutory background that will determine what are the relevant considerations and the proper purposes underlying the exercise of the discretion.'[73] But their proper acknowledgement of context is here carried to such extreme lengths as to endanger the principles of legality themselves. We cannot accept their suggestion that it is the 'statutory analysis rather than the common law' that determines the validity of the decision: this is plainly a false antithesis. If the general principle against unfettered discretion, unlimited by specific statutory purposes, 'emerges from the analysis of the statute', as Forsyth and Elliott argue, it does so because the court perceives the relevance of a fundamental precept of legality. We can no more dispense with general principles, endorsed by the common law, than with the statutory context in which they are given concrete effect.

Forsyth and Elliott are quite mistaken in contending that 'in many cases' there is 'no significant reliance upon the common law or any other extra-statutory source of law in determining the lawfulness of the decision'.[74] If that were true the whole subject of administrative law, as part of constitutional law, would be an illusion and Wade's efforts to give it structure and coherence would be futile. There would

---

[71] [1987] AC 625, 702–3.
[72] Christopher Forsyth and Mark Elliott, 'The Legitimacy of Judicial Review' [2003] PL 286–307.
[73] Ibid, 303.
[74] Ibid, 305.

merely be a large number of unconnected decisions about specific statutory powers; though quite how they could be decided without reference to general principles, guiding the *interpretation* of the various statutes, is not explained. Nor is there any important distinction, as Forsyth and Elliott propose, between ordinary cases of judicial review, on the one hand, and, on the other, a special 'class of important decisions in which principles drawn from the common law are used by judges in order to determine the lawfulness of the decision'. Here they have in mind such cases as *Witham*, in which the powers of the Lord Chancellor to set court fees, under the Supreme Court Act 1981, were interpreted in the light of the constitutional right of access to the courts—a common law right that could be abrogated, it was held, only by specific statutory provision to that effect.[75] The requisite interaction between common law principle and legislative context, which the authors rightly emphasize, is an integral feature of all the cases. The 'necessary reconciliation between the supremacy of Parliament and the creativity of the judiciary', or more accurately between parliamentary supremacy and the rule of law, is the aim of every appraisal of the legality of an administrative decision, not just a limited class of them.[76]

This attempt to segregate different classes of case is symptomatic of an error that figures on both sides of the debate over ultra vires. A misguided focus on competing *sources* of administrative law, characteristic of legal positivism, has deflected attention away from subtle practicalities of legal interpretation in particular instances.[77] Instead of trumpeting the superiority of common law over statute, or vice versa, we should recognize that the limits of an official's powers reflect an interpretation of statute made in the light of all the pertinent constitutional values. Neither the abstract precepts of administrative legality nor constitutional rights at common law take effect as external fetters on a statutory jurisdiction given independently. They are essential *presuppositions*, internal to the correct construction of the legislative powers conferred: they are as important to the discernment of 'legislative intent' as our assumptions about legislative purpose, and play a similar role in making sense of what Sir John Laws terms 'letters on a page'.[78] If the precepts of administrative legality truly 'take effect as interpretative constructs which, *ab initio*, operate so as to determine the reach' of delegated power, they inform the statute's meaning and govern its application.[79] The nature and scope of the powers conferred are a function of the interaction of legislation and common law, the statutory provisions acquiring the specific application to concrete events that fundamental principles dictate.

---

[75] *R v Lord Chancellor, ex p Witham* [1998] QB 575.

[76] Forsyth and Elliott, 'The Legitimacy of Judicial Review', 305.

[77] For discussion of the dubious notion that 'only deliberately made law is real law', divorcing law from an implicit aspiration towards justice or right, see F A Hayek, *Law, Legislation and Liberty* (London: Routledge & Kegan Paul, 1982), vol II, 44–8. Legal positivism makes the identification of official sources of positive law central to its conceptions of law and legality, marginalizing (or denying) the conceptual connections between law, liberty, and equality. (See further Chapter 3, above.)

[78] *R (Cart) v Upper Tribunal* [2009] EWHC 3052 (Admin), para 37 (see above).

[79] Forsyth and Elliott, 'The Legitimacy of Judicial Review', 305.

The exaggerated focus on contrasting sources of law is itself a feature of the external viewpoint, which by erecting a fence between theorist's description and practitioner's normative commitment, disables itself from effective legal analysis. When Forsyth and Elliott insist that 'the purpose of the ... *ultra vires* doctrine is to reconcile judicial review with the *existing* constitutional framework', and that 'the sovereignty of Parliament is still a key part of that framework', they treat questions of constitutional principle as matters of empirical fact.[80] They invoke (as we have seen) an official consensus, deduced from judicial dicta and other expressions of opinion.[81] While conceding that the common law framework within which legislative supremacy is exercised must be capable of adaptation to changing circumstances, Forsyth and Elliott dismiss such adaptation as 'a future possibility, not a present reality'. From their external perspective, the common law is regarded as mere custom or practice whose shape may be described and whose future evolution may be predicted. They overlook (or disregard) the nature of the common law as a continuing *argument* over fundamental questions of legality and legitimacy—an argument stimulated in practice by ever-present threats to constitutionalism and good governance. The law cannot be identified with whatever a majority of judges (or perhaps more senior judges) currently accept or assert, even if their views are elaborated in sufficient detail to give them definite shape in specific contexts. The law is rather the product of considered *judgement* in which general principle is brought to bear on the distinctive facts of particular cases, forging an accommodation between governmental aim, on the one hand, and the constraints of legality, on the other.

Nor does 'the absence of a written constitution' and, hence, 'the lack of any formal process' for constitutional amendment present a special problem, as Elliott and Forsyth mistakenly assert.[82] There is no formal process 'for amending or removing values which become entrenched through the organic development of the rule of law'. But how could moral values be 'removed' by formal declaration or enactment? Their importance, if they are genuine values, is either recognized or it is not. If, as Elliott and Forsyth happily concede, 'in most situations, any tension between legislative provisions and the rule of law may be resolved through judicial interpretation', the appropriate separation of powers between legislature and judiciary, in conformity to the rule of law, is already well established.[83] The judicial task of 'determining how constitutional values should be balanced against policies adopted by the legislature' is simply intrinsic to statutory interpretation; and so-called 'judicial disobedience to statute', when it is alleged, usually means adherence to an interpretation that other lawyers (or politicians) may question. *Anisminic* provides a good example.[84] Forsyth and Elliott are keen to classify

---

[80] Ibid, 299 (emphasis in original).
[81] Considerable reliance is placed on Laws LJ's judgment in *Thoburn v Sunderland City Council* [2002] EWHC 195 (Admin), considered in Chapter 4, above; but the heavily qualified endorsement of one eminent judge cannot put parliamentary absolutism beyond inspection and challenge.
[82] Forsyth and Elliott, 'The Legitimacy of Judicial Review', 295.
[83] Ibid, 294.
[84] *Anisminic Ltd v Foreign Compensation Commission* [1969] 2 AC 147, considered above.

the decision as 'an exercise in interpretation, rather than an example of judicial disobedience to Parliament', and so it is.[85] But 'judicial disobedience' is only an external description of what, from the internal perspective of legal reasoning, is a *conclusion* about the requirements of legality—all relevant factors properly taken into account.

If British judges 'are always extremely reluctant to conclude that Parliament has chosen to attenuate or exclude' the constitutional right of access to the courts, it is because they recognize the fundamental status of the rule of law.[86] Elliott and Forsyth demur at any suggestion that the *Anisminic* case presents a challenge to orthodox notions of sovereignty, and hence to the 'modified' ultra vires doctrine; Parliament can always abrogate constitutional rights 'if it expresses its intention with sufficient clarity'. Accordingly, *Anisminic*, and similar cases, '*must* be characterized as exercises in statutory construction', or else be 'regarded as constitutionally improper judicial usurpations'.[87] In practice, however, the distinction between construction, favourable to fundamental principle, and disobedience is quite artificial—no more than a rhetorical device to sustain an implausibly absolutist doctrine. Any 'disobedience' is to the literal meaning of the ouster only, ripped from its constitutional context, and any 'usurpation' only an insistence on respect for legality, on which legislative supremacy must itself (as a legal doctrine) ultimately depend.

How much clarity is necessary to overcome judicial adherence to basic principles of the rule of law? Suppose Parliament expressly authorized a departure from 'legality', or enacted that 'legality' should mean whatever a government agency determined in exercise of its unconstrained discretion. Could any self-respecting judge, sworn to uphold the law of the land, accord such absurdities their literal meaning? And would the citizen, acknowledging a duty to obey the law, be expected to treat such submission to arbitrariness as a genuine exercise of judicial power, deserving respectful compliance? If we foist on Parliament an 'intention' that statutory powers should be exercised in accordance with the rule of law, we do so on the basis that no contrary intention or assumption (whoever may actually be supposed to entertain it) would be consistent with our fundamental democratic ideal of governance in accordance with law.

V

It is plain that the ultra vires doctrine has no application to judicial review of the exercise of non-statutory power. As a conceptual rationalization of the imposition of common law limits on statutory power, consistent with parliamentary sovereignty, it is irrelevant to judicial scrutiny of assertions of prerogative power or the de facto monopoly power of quasi-governmental institutions (such as the Take-over Panel).[88]

---

[85] Forsyth and Elliott, 'The Legitimacy of Judicial Review', 298.
[86] Ibid.
[87] Ibid, 298–9 (emphasis in original).
[88] See *R v Panel on Take-overs and Mergers, ex p Datafin plc* [1987] QB 815. See generally Dawn Oliver, 'Is the Ultra Vires Rule the Basis of Judicial Review', in Forsyth (ed), *Judicial Review and the Constitution*, 3–27.

When extended to bodies that do not derive their power from statute, 'judicial review cannot be rationalized through the idea that the courts are delineating the boundaries of Parliament's intent'.[89] In holding, in the *GCHQ* case, that the availability of judicial review depended on the subject matter of the power rather than its source in the royal prerogative, the House of Lords removed artificial limits on the enforcement of the rule of law, at least when powers are deemed 'justiciable'.[90] The focus on subject matter rather than source underlines the largely formal nature of ultra vires, signalling (whether accurately or otherwise) that the court's intervention, in the case of a statutory body, is consistent with the legislative scheme and purpose concerned.

Paul Craig also draws attention to judicial development of the rules of civil liability in private law, which 'have substantive force because of the normative principles which comprise their content'; the application of such rules to public bodies does not depend on any special statutory authorization.[91] Even in the absence of explicit legislative instructions, however, the courts may qualify the application of private law 'where they decide that there is something in the nature of the statutory scheme which makes it necessary to exclude or modify these principles'.[92] In that formal sense, then, we may say if we wish that a breach of private law is ultra vires—beyond any jurisdiction conferred, and so contrary to the rule of law—though the statement only expresses the conclusions of our reasoning in the particular case. Subject to adjustment to the demands of the specific context, the principles of civil liability are applied to public bodies and private persons alike, according to their own internal force and logic.

The distinction between public and private law does, however, serve to illuminate an aspect of the ultra vires doctrine that ought not to be ignored. It relates to the wholly different functions that public and private law perform, and to the contrasting roles of the judiciary in respect of each branch of law. While enforcement of the rule of law consists, in private law, in the defence of the rights and duties that compose the established scheme of civil liability, in public law it means chiefly the prevention or correction of abuse of power by official state agencies. People are, of course, entitled to the benefit of whatever rights against the state are granted by statute; but the rights protected by judicial review are more abstract and inchoate—rights not to be the victim of an abuse of power, which can take any of the various forms of unreasonableness or illegality. Whereas the judicial role in private law is essentially to resolve uncertainties in the general scheme of regulation, in public law the court must intervene only to remedy excesses or abuses of jurisdiction by a public authority, which is normally entitled (and required) to pursue a policy agenda in furtherance of its own view of the public interest. Being fully dependent on the court's appraisal of the actions of a public agency in the circumstances—the boundary between legality and the merits reflecting all relevant considerations—public law rights lack the pre-emptive quality of their private law counterparts.

---

[89] Craig, 'Ultra Vires and the Foundations of Judicial Review', 53.
[90] *Council of Civil Service Unions v Minister for the Civil Service* [1985] AC 374.
[91] Craig, 'Competing Models of Judicial Review', 379.
[92] Ibid.

Private law rights, once established, may be asserted whether or not their enforcement (in the particular instance) would advance the public interest: they secure a sphere of individual autonomy immune from official calculations of collective benefit. But public law rights are mainly rights to *fair treatment*, having regard to the balance of public and private interests, and subject to reasonable deference to official estimations of public need: they allow private interests to be sacrificed when the public good reasonably demands it.[93]

A comparison between private law rights in contract or estoppel and public law rights to the protection of legitimate expectations may help to clarify the point. When a public authority has made a promise or representation that leads a person to expect the conferment of a benefit, it may be held legally bound to honour that expectation. If the promise has been made to relatively few people, so that the implications for the wider public interest are likely to be modest, the court may enforce the promise to prevent unfairness: there is an analogy with breach of contract or breach of a representation (giving rise to an estoppel) in private law.[94] It is only when the analogy is sufficiently strong in all the circumstances, however, that the court will intervene; and even then it will enforce the promise only if satisfied that to do so would not unduly impede the effective implementation of public policy, as determined by the public agency. The authority must adhere to its promise or representation unless there is an overriding public interest that justifies its failure to do so. The court itself may determine the balance of private and public interest rather than defer to the public authority, which, desiring to renege on the promise, would be judge in its own cause; but it must accept 'as part of the factual data' the authority's choice of general policy, including any decision to change the policy.[95] In the result, the complainant's right is a function of all the considerations that determine, in the court's judgement, the overall balance of fairness.

While invocation of ultra vires, with its implicit references to 'legislative intent', can sometimes deflect attention from the pertinent matters of substance, it may instead—if invoked more critically—focus our attention on the circumstances which, in the particular case, are alleged to constitute an excess or abuse of power. The doctrine may serve to remind us that the abstract grounds of judicial review, though valuable articulations of the rule of (public) law, are not self-executing: they summarize the nature of legal flaws or failings whose existence must be established by close appraisal of an agency's actions and their consequences for those affected. The statutory background—the enacted provisions and the policies and purposes that best appear to animate them—must form an integral part of any judicial appraisal: the unique contribution of the specific legislation involved is, as we have seen, part of the case of the defenders of ultra vires.[96]

---

[93] The central importance of ordinary civil and criminal law to the liberty preserved by adherence to the rule of law is a major theme of Chapter 3, above.

[94] See *Preston v Inland Revenue Commissioners* [1985] AC 835, 866–7 (Lord Templeman).

[95] See *R v North and East Devon Health Authority, ex p Coughlan* [2001] QB 213, para 82 (Lord Woolf MR).

[96] See Forsyth and Elliott, 'The Legitimacy of Judicial Review', considered above. In the context of legitimate expectation, the role of the statutory scheme (which envisaged only a limited ministerial

When we emphasize the constitutional importance of the common law grounds of review, as fundamental demands of legality, it is important also to stress the close dependence of their proper application on considerations specific to the administrative action under scrutiny. Steadfast adherence to the rule of law does not entail—nor does it permit—the abrogation of democracy or government by judges. The legitimacy of judicial review depends as much on its *manner of exercise*, sensitive to context, as on its basis in the rule of law, as an ideal of just governance. Like Sir John Laws, Paul Craig is inclined to resist charges of judicial supremacism by insisting on the ultimately unfettered sovereignty of Parliament, which may dispense with legality by explicit command.[97] But I have argued that we cannot interpret legislation as having such consequences without abandoning our allegiance to democratic constitutionalism. The search for a suitable integration of legislative aim and structure, on the one hand, and the constraints of legality, on the other, is the *raison dêtre* of public law adjudication: a court that reads a statute, however framed, as ordering a surrender of the rule of law ceases (in all but name) to be a court of law. Deference to Parliament, then, must occur at a micro rather than macro level: we have to meet charges of judicial overreaching, if we can, by analysis focused on the facts of the case in view. It is always a question not merely of what a statute explicitly provides (or fails to mention) but also of *interpretation*, sensitive to all the pertinent political values as the circumstances engage them.

Craig does not, of course, deny that judicial review is, in practice, dependent on interpretation of the statute; but he does say that the 'legislature will rarely provide any indications as to the content and limits of what constitutes judicial review'.[98] No doubt, Parliament would rarely attempt to specify the abstract requirements of legality; but that does not mean that considerations of statutory purpose and context will not have a critical influence on the way in which those requirements are applied. Insofar as the idea of legislative 'intent' has any coherent meaning, as a reference either to general purposes or their more specific application, it must be ascertained as much from statutory structure and context as from any express instructions. And referring to the 'paradigm' represented by the private law fields of 'contract, tort, restitution, and trusts', Craig observes that there is 'nothing odd or strange about a set of principles derived from the common law, which are then supplemented or complemented by specific legislative intent if and when this is to be found'.[99] But I have stressed the different dimensions of the rule of law enforced by public and private law. In public law, it is not so much that general principles are complemented by 'specific legislative intent', when it may be found, but rather that their application must be sensitive to a specific statutory context—determined in large part by the aims or purposes that the enacted terms reveal.

discretion for exceptional cases, precluding the acquisition of expectations that would enlarge it) is well illustrated by *R v Secretary of State for Education and Employment, ex p Begbie* [2000] 1 WLR 1115.

[97] See for example Craig, 'Competing Models of Judicial Review', 374: 'If the omnipotent Parliament does not like these [judicial] controls then it is open to it to make this unequivocally clear. If it does so the courts will then adhere to such dictates.'

[98] Ibid, 374.

[99] Ibid.

The ultra vires doctrine may serve as a useful reminder of the need to forge a defensible accommodation between legislative purpose, on the one hand, and the legal constraints of due process, on the other. We cannot take any statutory abridgments of due process at face value; but nor can we fall back on abstract grounds of review as a substitute for argument about their specific demands in all the circumstances. Neither legislative supremacy nor the rule of law operates independently: legality is ultimately a function of a complex adjustment of competing imperatives, according to the needs of time and place. In the course of such adjustment the distinction between statute and common law largely disappears: the demands of legality subsume our commitments to both democracy and constitutionalism. Too much emphasis on the independent operation of the common law, separately from statute, is a threat to democracy, just as incantations of parliamentary absolutism threaten the rule of law. The notion that the common law might operate quite independently (as a regime of private common law might so operate) until Parliament intervenes expressly (in any manner it pleases) imports both threats: democracy and legality alike are placed in danger.

Craig is right to observe that ultra vires provides no guidance on the right approach to the identification of jurisdictional error, being in itself compatible with any.[100] But it is also true that common law doctrine will rarely determine the outcome of individual cases, even if it indicates the correct approach. So much depends in practice on the balance of reasons for and against agency autonomy: the boundaries of an agency's jurisdiction will reflect all relevant considerations of subject matter, including official expertise and efficiency as well as any implications for individual liberty. Common law doctrine is a tool of analysis that embraces the full statutory and constitutional context. The collateral or precedent fact doctrine was invoked in *Khawaja*, for example, to prevent the detention and deportation of someone who was not, on the evidence, an 'illegal entrant' within the meaning of the Immigration Act 1971.[101] His immigration status was identified as a precedent fact, which the court could determine, because of the threat to the liberty of a person who enjoyed specific legal protection, akin to the position of a British citizen who possessed the ordinary right of abode. The court would naturally view 'with extreme jealousy' any 'claim by the executive to imprison a citizen without trial'.[102]

Nor is the doctrine of error of law a reliable guide to the limits of jurisdiction, despite its endorsement in *ex p Page*.[103] Dependent on making appropriate distinctions between law, fact, and policy, the doctrine is easily (and justifiably) manipulated to preserve a necessary degree of autonomy for the public agency to pursue its own policy agenda. Since there is no clear distinction between the *interpretation* of statute, as regards its correct meaning, and *application* to particular cases, in which matters of law, fact and policy may be closely interwoven, the court's intervention

---

[100] Craig, 'Ultra Vires and the Foundations of Judicial Review', 50.
[101] *Khawaja v Secretary of State for the Home Dept* [1984] AC 74.
[102] Ibid, 122 (Lord Bridge of Harwich).
[103] *R v Lord President of the Privy Council, ex p Page* [1993] 2 AC 682 (where the context led the court to make an 'exception' to the supposedly general doctrine).

for 'error of law' is only readily classifiable as such *ex post facto*. The distinction between review and appeal can only be maintained if on some questions, at least, a tribunal or agency is entitled to differ from the High Court; and if those questions cannot in practice be limited to matters of pure fact or pure policy, the distinction (acknowledged in principle in *Anisminic*) between jurisdictional error of law and error of law within jurisdiction must remain.[104] The distinction will be drawn, whether expressly or implicitly, by reference to the balance of argument for and against judicial intervention in all the circumstances. The doctrinal label 'error of law' signals that the separation of powers has been observed as befits the context, much as ultra vires may signal that proper account has been taken of the needs of the specific statutory scheme.[105]

Moreover, though an ultra vires action is in principle null and void, it is sometimes necessary for a complainant to seek judicial review: it is not always possible simply to ignore an invalid decision or challenge it collaterally, in the course of ordinary private law or criminal proceedings. It will generally be a good defence to a criminal prosecution to plead the invalidity of the bye-law under which the complaint arises.[106] But in some cases a challenge to the validity of a decision on which the prosecution is premised is not permitted within the criminal proceedings. Just as the concept of ultra vires cannot determine the outcome of particular cases, neither can a general doctrine of nullity: everything depends on analysis of context. In *Wicks*, the defendant was not permitted to challenge the validity of the planning enforcement notice that he was accused of breaching: for purposes of the criminal proceedings an 'enforcement notice' was held to mean a formally valid notice which, whatever its latent defects might be, had not been set aside on appeal or by judicial review.[107] There had been other opportunities to challenge the notice on public law grounds and reliance on similar objections at the criminal trial would endanger the effective enforcement of planning control. Lord Hoffmann observed that it was 'impossible to construct a general theory of the *ultra vires* defence which applies to every statutory power, whatever the terms and policy of the statute'.[108]

We do not, then, face a choice between a merely formal ultra vires doctrine, on the one hand, and common law doctrine, on the other: the application of doctrine must be sensitive to the administrative context, making the statutory background critical to the judgements of legality in any particular case. Any apparent or potential conflict between legislative supremacy and the rule of law is thereby dissolved: legislative aims are given concrete effect within a common law framework of fundamental values. The availability of collateral challenge—the chance to impugn a governmental decision in the course of ordinary private law or criminal proceedings— safeguards a person's rights or interests at the expense of administrative certainty

---

[104] See for example *South Asia Firebricks Sdn Bhd v Non-Metallic Mineral Products Manufacturing Employees Union* [1981] AC 363.
[105] Recognition of the distinction between jurisdictional and non-jurisdictional errors of law was explicit in *R (Cart) v Upper Tribunal* [2010] EWCA Civ 859 (above).
[106] See *Boddington v British Transport Police* [1999] 2 AC 143.
[107] *R v Wicks* [1998] AC 92.
[108] Ibid, 117.

and efficiency. Judicial review, by contrast, is a procedure better suited to enable a public authority to know the legality of its decisions and plan accordingly, even if it places the onus on the complainant to initiate proceedings. There is an unavoidable tension between the citizen's prima facie right to resist proceedings against him by a public authority, challenging the legal basis of its claim, and the authority's need, in some circumstances, to have confidence in the legality of its action in the absence of any direct proceedings against it for judicial review. It is a tension that we can only resolve or diffuse by seeking a balance of fairness attuned to the specific context.

A local authority may face serious administrative inconvenience and financial embarrassment if, long after its decision to increase council housing rents, a tenant (who did not promptly seek judicial review) is permitted to resist an action for unpaid rent, alleging that the rent increase had been unreasonable and therefore void.[109] Such inconvenience and embarrassment must, however, be 'set against the arguments for preserving the ordinary rights of private citizens to defend themselves against unfounded claims'.[110] As the beneficiary of private law contractual rights against his landlord, the tenant is entitled to resist the action on the basis that he is not liable for the money claimed; but as the tenant of a public authority it is arguable that his rights are only weaker public law entitlements, vulnerable to changes made by decisions that have not been set aside by the administrative court.[111] There is here a conflict between private and public law paradigms that only reflection on the various demands of legality can help to resolve. If we emphasize the landlord–tenant relationship, giving contractual rights priority over countervailing governmental considerations, we give preference to the private law paradigm and its strong protection of individual autonomy. A more collectivist orientation, focused on the needs of public administration, would give the tenant's autonomy and security less weight in the balance of argument over the demands of legality in its distinctively governmental (public law) character.[112] Our doctrinal solutions, even in a narrow class of cases, draw on deeper conclusions about the nature and implications of an underlying and complex ideal of the rule of law. [113]

The doctrinal heads and categories of public law are quintessentially markers for the role of constitutional principle in the appraisal of executive action. They indicate the nature of the argument necessary, in each case, to show that such action satisfies the demands of legality; and they obtain their concrete content from application to the circumstances of a specific complaint of illegality. Unlike rules of the kind that give content to private law, demarcating separate spheres of individual freedom or responsibility, they are only paths or gateways between basic political

---

[109] See *Wandsworth London Borough Council v Winder* [1985] AC 461.

[110] Ibid, 509 (Lord Fraser of Tullybelton).

[111] According to Ackner LJ (dissenting in the Court of Appeal) the tenant had no relevant private law right to enforce: he was instead challenging the decision of 'a public body, performing its public functions in a field of public law': ibid, 468.

[112] See Sir Harry Woolf, 'Public Law—Private Law: Why the Divide? A Personal View' [1986] PL 220–38, at 233–5.

[113] For further discussion of these issues, see Allan, 'Doctrine and Theory in Administrative Law: An Elusive Quest for the Limits of Jurisdiction' [2003] PL 429–54.

values, on the one hand, and allegations of unfairness or impropriety in individual instances, on the other. Moreover, the precedents *exemplify* the operation of these principles or values, but rarely dictate the resolution of subsequent cases: one cannot argue from case to case (in the manner characteristic of private law) without attention to the change of context, which may vary substantially from statute to statute, from one administrative regime to another.

Whether or not, for example, a person is entitled to legal representation before a prison Board of Visitors, hearing a disciplinary charge, has been held to depend on a wide range of factors, relevant to the exercise of the Board's discretion.[114] They included the seriousness of the charge and the nature of the potential penalty, the likelihood of points of law arising on which the prisoner would need assistance, the prisoner's capacity to present his own case, the possible need to interview potential witnesses in preparation for presentation of the case or for cross-examination, the desirability of conducting a timely adjudication, and the need for fairness as between prisoners and prison officers. Such considerations do not apply only to unusual cases lying at the perimeter of a settled rule: they determine what, in substance, natural justice actually *means* in all the circumstances of a particular case.

Judicial attempts to marshall cases on legitimate expectations, allowing different cases to be assigned to distinct categories according to their specific features, were met with appropriate disdain by Laws LJ in *ex parte Begbie*.[115] In some cases, a court will protect a legitimate expectation, founded on a public authority's previous conduct or promise or statement of intent, only when it would be quite unreasonable for the authority to override it. In other cases, the court will itself determine the balance of fairness between individual reliance and the wider public interest. But since the court must intrude as far as legality requires—*Wednesbury* review shading into proportionality review—there can be no hard-and-fast distinction between categories: 'The facts of the case, viewed always in their statutory context, will steer the court to a more or less intrusive quality of review.'[116] The court must prevent an abuse of power; but the identification of abuse depends on such matters as the number of those reliant on any promise or expectation as well as the nature and scale of the implications for the public interest:

The more the decision challenged lies in what may …be called the macro-political field, the less intrusive will be the court's supervision. More than this: in that field, true abuse of power is less likely to be found, since within it changes of policy, fuelled by broad conceptions of the public interest, may more readily be accepted as taking precedence over the interests of groups which enjoyed expectations generated by an earlier policy.[117]

---

[114] *R v Secretary of State for the Home Dept, ex p Tarrant* [1985] QB 251; see also *R v Board of Visitors of HM Prison, The Maze, ex p Hone* [1988] AC 379.
[115] *R v Secretary of State for Education and Employment, ex p Begbie* [2000] 1 WLR 1115. For the attempt to articulate separate categories of expectation, see *R v North and East Devon Health Authority, ex p Coughlan* [2001] QB 213, paras 56–60.
[116] *ex p Begbie* [2000] 1 WLR 1115, 1131 (Laws LJ).
[117] Ibid. Jeffrey Jowell purports to identify a 'fundamental shift' from ordinary judicial review to constitutional review in defence of individual rights, but his own analysis of *Coughlan* casts doubt on the distinction: the court's approach was 'part common (administrative) law …and part constitutional

Paul Craig is right to observe that the courts have developed 'more detailed principles within the heads of review', giving doctrinal coherence to the application of the precepts of legality to particular cases: 'The normative arguments that serve to justify these more detailed principles have force independently of the particular context in which they are applied.'[118] But we may question his claim that the fact that the courts have regard to the specific context—whether 'social welfare rather than licensing, tax rather than planning'—'tells one nothing as to whether there is any cognisable legislative intent as to how the principles of judicial review should play out' in the relevant context. He is right, of course, if 'legislative intent' invokes some conscious plan in the mind of a specific human legislator or draftsman; but he is wrong if such intent refers, more plausibly, to a reading or construction of the statute attuned to its underlying policy or purpose. The principles of review bring considerations of legality or rationality or fairness, very broadly conceived, to bear on a specific governmental context in which the nature, purpose, and scope of statutory powers are usually the critical questions at issue. Any pertinent 'intent' must be inferred from the statutory scheme, interpreted (or constructed) in the light of all the relevant constitutional values. There is no *gap* between the statutory instructions and the limits on administrative discretion, which the courts might fill by reference to the common law.[119] Those limits are ascertained by interpretation of the statute, informed and guided by common law principle—exemplified, but not exhausted, by precedent.

It is only the assumption of such a gap or gulf between (rather sparse) statutory instructions and the boundaries of administrative discretion, determined by the common law alone, that could justify the following assertion:

There will normally be nothing in the legislative text, or the legislative history, which sheds any light on matters such as the test for jurisdictional error, the criteria for substantive review, the intensity with which such review should be applied, what should occur in the event of invalidity, or the one hundred and one other such matters that arise before the courts.[120]

The truth is surely quite the opposite. When we read the text in the light of its history, or the general purposes such history supports, and against a larger background of common law principle, it illuminates all those questions. As mere 'letters on a page', the text is not enlightening; but interpreted as a contribution to the public good of a liberal democracy, framed by the common law constitution, it indicates the appropriate boundary between executive discretion and judicial oversight.

---

law (drawing on the Convention right of respect for one's home)': Jowell, 'Beyond the Rule of Law: Towards Constitutional Judicial Review' [2000] PL 671–83, at 678. His underlying mistake is to separate legality (or the rule of law) from the fundamental rights that make up a principal element of its (English law) content. See further Chapter 3, above.

[118] Paul Craig, 'The Common Law, Shared Power and Judicial Review' (2004) 24 OJLS 237–57, at 245.

[119] See Paul Craig and Nicholas Bamforth, 'Constitutional Analysis, Constitutional Principle and Judicial Review' [2001] PL 763–80, at 769: 'There is no necessity to manufacture legislative intent to fill the gap between legislative silence and the imposition of judicial controls.'

[120] Craig, 'The Common Law, Shared Power and Judicial Review', 239.

The statutory text changes the law, permitting or requiring governmental action that would otherwise be forbidden or unnecessary; the court's role is to determine whether such action (or lack of it) complies with the law, which now includes the Act in question. An excess or abuse of discretion is ultra vires the statute in precisely that complex, interpretative sense.

It is also the assumption of a gap between limited statutory instructions, standing alone, and the constraints on administrative discretion, deriving from the common law, that best makes sense of the claim, in relation to legislative supremacy, that 'present doctrine still leaves it to Parliament to have the last clear and unequivocal word'.[121] But there is no such gap, and hence no dead ground to fight over. When the statutory text is read as a whole, and the reading is informed by those common law principles that delineate the relevant demands of legality, questions of clarity or certainty are related, most suitably, to any statement of interpretative conclusions. If anyone has the 'last word', it is the court that determines legality in all the circumstances of the particular case; but of course legality is a function of statutory purpose and context as well as general constitutional principle. When adjudication achieves a proper integration of legislative aim and common law principle, the limits on administrative discretion are correctly discerned. Representing the *outcome* of the necessary interpretative inquiry, duly sensitive to context, the court's defence of the rule of law will fully and fairly accommodate the legislative will.[122]

---

[121] Craig, 'Constitutional Foundations, the Rule of Law and Supremacy', 109.

[122] See further Allan, 'Constitutional Dialogue and the Justification of Judicial Review' (2003) 23 OJLS 563–84; and Allan, 'Legislative Supremacy and Legislative Intent: A Reply to Professor Craig' (2004) 24 OJLS 563–83. See also Philip A Joseph, 'Parliament, the Courts, and the Collaborative Enterprise' (2004) 15 KCLJ 321–45, emphasizing the interdependence of legislative and judicial power. The nature and role of public law doctrine are further explored in Chapter 7, below.

7

Judicial Review and Judicial Restraint

I

This chapter explores a range of interconnected questions about the nature of judicial review and the desirability or otherwise of judicial restraint. Strictly speaking, we may distinguish between judicial 'restraint' and judicial 'deference': the former recognizes the legitimate discretion of a public authority in making its policy choices; and the latter acknowledges that courts must sometimes bow to superior expertise, on which judges may properly rely in gauging the consequences of alternative measures or actions.[1] Challenging demands for development of an independent *doctrine* of judicial restraint or deference, however, I shall argue that the relevant considerations of constitutional legitimacy and institutional expertise are already implicit constraints on judicial review—reflected in ordinary legal reasoning or met by an application of legal principle sensitive to the circumstances of the particular case. The argument develops the general theme of earlier chapters. I shall suggest that the demand for special rules to curtail judicial 'discretion', in response to doubts about the objectivity or reliability of judicial 'choices' with respect to constitutional rights, reflects an outsider's external viewpoint: it adopts an arm's length *detachment* that has no place within a fully internal, interpretative posture, appropriate to adjudication.[2]

A similar distinction between external and internal points of view—between the characteristic stances of social or political scientist and lawyer or jurist—generates equivalent tensions elsewhere. I shall challenge the familiar orthodoxy that draws clear lines between different 'standards of review', arguing that our concepts of reasonableness, rationality, and proportionality are interdependent—the distinctions reflecting our perceptions of the demands of legality in particular cases, in all the sophistication and complexity that our interpretative approach permits and requires. From an internal perspective we may also question the utility of the distinction between 'standards of review' and 'standards of legality': the former ought to be a direct reflection of the latter. Tom Hickman draws such a distinction, along with a related distinction between procedure and substance, in the course of a mainly descriptive account of judicial review; but within a normative account, directly pertinent to legal doctrine and adjudication, these distinctions may cast more shadow

---

[1] Compare Julian Rivers, 'Proportionality and Variable Intensity of Review' [2006] CLJ 174–207, at 199–200.

[2] See also the discussion of justiciability in Chapter 2, above.

than light.[3] Judicial review in defence of legal and constitutional rights enforces standards of *due process*, which resist any neat division between procedure and substance.

From Hickman's external viewpoint, common law constitutional rights are apparently the product of an ingenious judicial strategy that claims a spurious legal authority: substantive limitations on the power of public authorities were added to established procedural constraints by a dubious manipulation of doctrine.[4] The legal interpreter, however, may legitimately prefer a different story: the recognition of basic rights at common law merely renders explicit what was arguably implicit all along. An interpretation of legal doctrine governing judicial review is simultaneously an inquiry into the requirements of the rule of law. We must view the traditional distinctions between appeal and review, or substance and procedure, as helpful approximations only—aids to discerning a richer constitutional discourse attuned to the changing facts of political life. If an earlier reliance on largely intuitive judgements of reasonableness or fairness has been replaced today by more explicit analysis of legal rights and duties—treating the common law as a source of fundamental principle—the change is a welcome recognition of the need to articulate and develop an existing constitutional tradition.[5]

The common law constitutional tradition is strong enough to embrace the standards of good governance adumbrated in the European Convention on Human Rights and Fundamental Freedoms. These fundamental rights having been granted full domestic legal status by the Human Rights Act, common law and Convention jurisprudence can now develop in harmony: each source of law provokes a fuller appreciation and better articulation of the demands of legality. Contrary to current doctrine, moreover, we can no more countenance a sharp distinction between procedure and substance in respect of Convention rights than in the case of their common law counterparts. The Convention rights are necessarily 'relevant considerations' in the deliberations of public authorities, entitled to be accorded proper weight as part of a fair decision-making process. We should repudiate the notion that whereas common law rights are primarily matters of procedure, Convention rights are largely matters of substantive outcome.[6] All constitutional rights impose standards of due process: they demand that proper attention be given, whether by courts or public agencies, to the adverse consequences of decisions for the fundamental interests of those specially and directly affected. If courts must to some extent accept the judgements of such agencies, whether on grounds of democratic legitimacy or institutional competence, they should ensure that those judgements are made in full critical awareness of the rights they propose to qualify or curtail.[7]

---

[3] Tom Hickman, *Public Law after the Human Rights Act* (Oxford: Hart Publishing, 2010), 99–111 (for full discussion, see below).

[4] See for example Hickman's discussion of *Wheeler v Leicester City Council* [1985] AC 1054, considered below.

[5] Compare Jeffrey Jowell and Anthony Lester, 'Beyond *Wednesbury*: Substantive Principles of Administrative Law' [1987] PL 368–82.

[6] See *R (Begum) v Denbigh High School Governors* [2006] UKHL 15, considered below.

[7] When he resumes his internal, interpretative stance Hickman is a much more reliable guide, whether on the procedural dimension of Convention rights or on the subject of judicial deference (see further below).

My conception of constitutional rights at common law differs from standard accounts, which also invoke the 'principle of legality'; in standard accounts, legality gives way, under pressure, to political necessity or parliamentary override. I interpret that principle as a fundamental requirement of respect for the rule of law, whose precepts and implications define the judicial role: when we override legality, even for allegedly beneficial purposes, we cease to govern ourselves through the institution of law. It is commonly supposed that common law rights exert strong presumptive force against any interference, but that any such presumption may be displaced by clear, unambiguous legislative instructions.[8] I shall argue that the presumption is both more modest and more powerful: it excludes only *unjustified* or *disproportionate* interference, requiring close analysis of all the relevant circumstances; but that exclusion is nonetheless complete and conclusive. Only an analysis trained on the specific administrative context can reveal what constitutional rights require, when the imperatives of governmental purpose or policy are fully taken into account. In their nature, however, these rights amount to binding limits on public power. As implications of human freedom and dignity—more concrete specifications of what those ideals entail—constitutional rights enjoy a fundamental status; and their integrity is an implicit condition of the validity of both administrative action and parliamentary enactment.[9]

The various topics studied in this chapter are united by a focus on the role of public law doctrine. While conceding its critical function in promoting consistency and discipline in the exercise and development of judicial review, I shall nonetheless emphasize the fragility of doctrine as a bridge between constitutional theory and specific determinations of legality. However vital a link between territories, a bridge can only bear so much weight. In an interpretative approach, legal doctrine must be our guide rather than our master: it cannot eliminate the need for moral judgement focused on the special demands of the particular case. Just as we should not be misled by the doctrine of parliamentary sovereignty into supposing that we can evade moral judgement in resolving questions of statutory construction and application, so we should recognize the limits of the capacity of doctrinal tests and categories to resolve the hardest questions of legality and legitimacy.

II

In my discussion of the rule of law, I questioned familiar distinctions between procedure and substance and between formal and substantive equality: I argued that in the practice of judicial review such distinctions were mainly matters of degree.[10] Judicial review of administrative or executive action enforces principles of *due process*, which extend from basic requirements of natural justice (or procedural fairness) to the further demands of rationality or reasonableness. The distinction

---

[8] See discussion of *R v Secretary of State for the Home Dept, ex p Simms* [2000] 2 AC 115, below.
[9] See especially Chapters 3 and 4, above.
[10] Chapter 3, above.

between appeal and review, though critical to the court's role in preserving legality, is itself in practice a matter of degree: the scope of administrative discretion depends on all the circumstances, which will sometimes dictate a single correct answer, affirming a citizen's legal rights. When we appreciate that what is rational or reasonable usually depends on the *balance* of relevant considerations—any damage to people's rights or interests being duly offset by significant public benefits—we can see why formal equality before the law, in the context of executive discretion, demands an equality of substance: the adverse effects on individuals must be duly proportionate to the alleged advantages accruing to the wider community. And we judge those effects by reference, in particular, to the consequences for enjoyment of the basic civil and political rights that we treat as primary elements of equal citizenship.

A requirement of proportionality between governmental objective, on the one hand, and curtailment or qualification of individual right, on the other, is intrinsic to the demand for rationality or reasonableness. We cannot decide what is reasonable (or not unreasonable) without scrutiny of all the relevant circumstances, which must include the likelihood and seriousness of damage to affected rights and interests. Governmental action that simply *ignored* such rights would plainly violate the rule of law; but whether or not it takes proper or adequate account of them clearly depends on judgements of *weight*. A decision to limit the scope or enjoyment of a fundamental right for only marginal benefit to a competing public interest, particularly where the proposed limitation was severe, would signal an ignorance of, or contempt for, the right's legitimate demands. It is implicit in the recognition of rights that the associated personal interests enjoy a degree of resistance to competing public interests; they cannot be merely swept aside in a utilitarian balancing of interests that considers only the merits of the overall outcome, regardless of the scale of the sacrifice made by a few. Public law rights essentially consist in that resistance, demanding appropriate levels of official attention to, and respect for, the individual interests at stake.[11]

Any notion that courts must choose between rival standards of review, governing their appraisal of legislative or executive action, is therefore quite confused. There is no real choice to be made, for example, between standards of *Wednesbury* unreasonableness and proportionality because the recognition of individual rights *entails* the requisite standard of judicial protection: a public authority that imposes a disproportionate burden on the relevant individual interests has necessarily acted unreasonably, overlooking (or disregarding) the special status of those interests. A policy of discharging from the armed forces anyone identified as being homosexual, notwithstanding blameless conduct and an exemplary service record, showed a cavalier disregard of fundamental human rights of privacy and personhood; or at least it did so unless there was a cogent alternative case to be made on grounds of clear overriding public interest. In view of the relative weakness of the defence of government policy, whose emphasis on troop morale and effectiveness appeared

---

[11] It is important to note, however, that there will usually be individual interests on *both* sides of the balance: the public interest (or common good) is ultimately the well-being of individual persons, whose rights must be respected in the balance of judgement (see further below).

to pander to anti-gay prejudice, the English courts (unlike the European Court of Human Rights) appeared to condone an unreasonable interference with basic constitutional rights.[12]

In the Court of Appeal, Sir Thomas Bingham properly distinguished the court's role from that of the 'primary decision-maker'. It was 'not the constitutional role of the court to regulate the conditions of service in the armed forces of the Crown'; but it possessed, nevertheless, 'the constitutional role and duty of ensuring that the rights of citizens are not abused by the unlawful exercise of executive power'.[13] Accordingly, the test of 'irrationality' was required to fit the context:

The court may not interfere with the exercise of an administrative discretion on substantive grounds save where the court is satisfied that the decision is unreasonable in the sense that it is beyond the range of responses open to a reasonable decision-maker. But in judging whether the decision-maker has exceeded this margin of appreciation the human rights context is important. The more substantial the interference with human rights, the more the court will require by way of justification before it is satisfied that the decision is reasonable in the sense outlined above.[14]

More is required 'by way of justification' because only an interference with basic rights proportionate to a legitimate public objective can be entertained without, in effect, renouncing those rights altogether. It is doubtful, then, whether the court was entitled to rely, in dismissing the complaint, on the fact that current government policy enjoyed parliamentary support, or even the fact that its endorsement by a Select Committee of the House of Commons 'reflected the overwhelming consensus of service and official opinion'.[15] The court's own appraisal should be independent and impartial, bowing to official opinion only when it falls within a legitimate range of balanced judgement, focused on the rights in question. Although the Court of Appeal was unwilling to condemn the policy of excluding homosexuals on the basis of their rights under the European Convention, such rights having not yet acquired formal status in domestic law, its own adaptation of the *Wednesbury* doctrine demanded an appraisal of comparable rigour to that required by Convention jurisprudence. If, as Bingham suggested, there was 'room for argument' whether the interference in question answered a 'pressing social need' or was 'proportionate to the legitimate aim pursued', it was incumbent on the court to investigate those matters in order to confirm or refute the charge of irrationality.[16]

The critical point is that the proper division between governmental and judicial responsibilities depends on the context in view. Rationality and proportionality are only convenient labels for a form of review that must press as far, in each case, as is necessary to satisfy the court (and ideally also the complainant) that the action in question is truly justified. When a limitation of rights is defended by recourse to

---

[12] *R v Ministry of Defence, ex p Smith* [1996] QB 517.
[13] Ibid, 556.
[14] Ibid, 554 (endorsing counsel's formulation of the correct approach).
[15] Ibid, 553.
[16] Ibid, 558 (citing *Norris v Ireland* (1988) 13 EHRR 186, 198).

persuasive grounds of public policy, the court must normally accept the outcome: it should defer to the public agency as the appropriate body, whether on grounds of constitutional authority or technical expertise, to judge between permissible alternatives. There will usually be a number of policy choices open to Parliament or a public authority, which in meeting legitimate objectives in different ways and to varying degrees may each be consistent with respect for people's rights. In each case, however, what is reasonable (or not wholly unreasonable) must depend on whether the action taken is proportionate to any consequent curtailment of rights, or damage to the relevant personal interests.[17] A measure is normally proportionate whenever an alternative, less injurious to rights, would be significantly less effective. It is only *disproportionate*, and hence unlawful, if a less intrusive alternative would not be very much inferior as a means to the end in view. How could anyone suppose that the test of legality might be any less onerous?

Other scholars have rightly challenged the idea that the *Wednesbury* and proportionality principles dictate quite different sorts of review, noting how approaches such as that commended by Sir Thomas Bingham, in *ex parte Smith*, blur any strict division. Neither principle obliterates the distinction between appeal and review, even if proportionality review sharply reduces the discretion of the public authority: it is a distinction of degree rather than kind.[18] The related notion, however, that these principles represent different points on a spectrum may be questioned. It treats the question of 'intensity of review', or level of scrutiny, as a *separate* question from the pertinent questions of law or legality. It supposes that the court must determine the appropriate form of review, within the available spectrum, on criteria quite distinct from the substantive issue of *justification*, which inevitably depends on all the circumstances. But that view is scarcely plausible.

According to Mark Elliott, the 'precise level of judicial review which is applied in any given case reflects a judicial choice which is made in light of numerous factors, including the relative institutional competence of the judicial and executive branches and the constitutional significance of the values which are at stake'.[19] (Note the insistence on judicial *choice*, with its connotations of public policy formulation or change.) Each of the relevant factors, however, will *already* play a role in any defensible inquiry into whether or not a particular action or decision is justified, whatever label is attached to the style of review. Any clear disparity between the respective experience or expertise of court and agency must limit the scope of judicial inquiry, if only in the sense that, beyond a certain point of sceptical interrogation, the court should (if appropriate) acknowledge that the agency's defence of its actions has survived unscathed. In a similar manner, the 'constitutional

---

[17] Compare *R v Lord Saville of Newdigate, ex p A* [1999] 4 All ER 860, para 37: 'What is important to note is that when a fundamental right such as the right to life is engaged, the options available to the reasonable decision-maker are curtailed. They are curtailed because it is unreasonable to reach a decision which contravenes or could contravene human rights unless there are sufficiently significant countervailing considerations' (Lord Woolf MR).

[18] See Mark Elliott, 'The Human Rights Act 1998 and the Standard of Substantive Review' [2001] CLJ 301–36, at 311–15.

[19] Ibid, 315.

significance of the values' at stake will inform the inquiry into legality and proportionality directly: it does not need to be mediated through any separate inquiry about the appropriate level of scrutiny. A governmental policy that involves an intrusion into basic principles of privacy and personhood must elicit the closest scrutiny; and the respective, intersecting spheres of judicial and ministerial responsibility will depend on the nature and plausibility of the arguments offered in defence of the restrictions imposed.

Review for rationality or reasonableness ensures that freedom can be restricted only for proper purposes, consonant with legitimate public ends. It is not sufficient, however, for such purposes to be *asserted* by way of justification unless there is a genuine connection between ends and means. When the incidental consequences of a measure are out of all proportion to its alleged objective, we may fairly conclude that the purported justification is specious: the real purpose is an unacknowledged one of dubious legality. If an outright ban on homosexual servicemen and women seems an exaggerated response to a potential problem about inappropriate behaviour, it is likely that the real basis of the measure is an adherence to traditional attitudes or majority preferences or implicit moral disapproval. Yet such attitudes or preferences, if fully articulated, would provide very doubtful support: they are scarcely compatible with the ideas of equal respect and personal liberty that inspire the relevant constitutional rights.

Lord Steyn was therefore on shaky ground in concluding, in *Daly*, that 'differences in approach between the traditional grounds of review and the proportionality approach may...sometimes yield different results'.[20] When the court's demand for justification is properly attuned to the nature of the rights in question, and reflects the gravity of the threat to their integrity, its approach should be wholly indifferent to the matter of labels. Lord Steyn's suggested differences, as regards the 'intensity of review', have become accepted orthodoxy; but orthodoxy may be misleading. Each supposed difference reflects the mistaken idea that there are different standards of review, or varying levels of intensity, which are doctrinally independent of the pertinent questions of substance.

First, 'the doctrine of proportionality may require the reviewing court to assess the balance which the decision maker has struck, not merely whether it is within the range of rational or reasonable decisions'.[21] If, however, the range of reasonable decisions contracts to meet the requirements of fundamental rights, only those decisions that reflect a proper balance of relevant considerations will fall within it. Secondly, 'the proportionality test may go further than the traditional grounds of review inasmuch as it may require attention to be directed to the relative weight accorded to interests and considerations'.[22] But the coherence of the distinction between the *relevance* of particular considerations, on the one hand, and their proper *weight,* on the other, depends entirely on the context. Whether or not a

---

[20] *R (Daly) v Secretary of State for the Home Dept* [2001] UKHL 26, para 28.
[21] Ibid, para 27.   [22] Ibid.

public authority is free to attribute a lesser or greater weight to any matter than a court might have done, if charged with the same task, depends on its significance in relation to the rights or interests affected, as well as on any special agency expertise that the court may lack. How could we regard as rational a decision that, while acknowledging the relevance of a basic right, or the fundamental interests it protects, nonetheless accords it only minor or trivial weight in the overall balance of judgement?

Thirdly, 'even the heightened scrutiny test developed in *R v Ministry of Defence, ex p Smith*...is not necessarily appropriate to the protection of human rights'.[23] But we should not confuse the propriety of the test with the bungled application of it. According to the European Court of Human Rights, 'the threshold at which the High Court and the Court of Appeal could find the Ministry of Defence policy irrational was placed so high that it effectively excluded any consideration by the domestic courts of the question of whether the interference with the applicants' rights answered a pressing social need or was proportionate to the national security and public order aims pursued'.[24] A proper application of the 'heightened scrutiny' test, however, paying close attention to the balance of interests involved, would have addressed precisely the questions finally resolved by the European Court.

The fourfold structure of the proportionality doctrine adopted by the European Court of Human Rights, as well as a number of constitutional courts including the German *Bundesverfassungsgericht*, spells out what is plainly implicit in the notion that fundamental rights, once identified as such, deserve enhanced protection. The measure under scrutiny must serve a legitimate public purpose, capable in principle of qualifying the relevant constitutional right. It must be suitable, in the sense of being capable in practice of fulfilling the public purpose in view. It must also be *necessary*, in the sense that no less intrusive means would achieve a comparable degree of attainment of the end in view. And there must be a fair balance overall: a suitable and necessary encroachment on personal liberty, having regard to the public objective, must not impose an excessive burden.[25] An otherwise defensible interference may nonetheless go so deep as to challenge the original commitment to the protection of liberty, jeopardizing the integrity of the legal order. A ban on gay servicemen and women is a good example: a somewhat marginal and speculative enhancement of national security may not be purchased at such great cost to the dignity and self-respect of those excluded.

In *Smith and Grady*, the European Court of Human Rights acknowledged that a government policy intended to secure operational effectiveness was one that pursued the legitimate aim of maintaining national security. It also accepted that, in view of the strength of entrenched attitudes within the forces, it was reasonable to anticipate that revocation of the policy would cause some difficulties. However, the British government had failed to show that such difficulties could not be

---

[23] Ibid.

[24] *Smith and Grady v United Kingdom* (1999) 29 EHRR 493, 543.

[25] See Julian Rivers, 'Proportionality and Variable Intensity of Review', especially 177–82, comparing and contrasting common law and continental approaches. See further Robert Alexy, *A Theory of Constitutional Rights*, translated by Julian Rivers (Oxford: Oxford University Press, 2002), 44–69.

substantially mitigated by adoption of a strict code of conduct to prevent inappropriate behaviour. Only weighty reasons could justify such serious intrusion into a person's private life; and the threatened dangers to morale were largely based on antipathy and prejudice of the sort that any right of privacy must be intended to counteract. The government conceded that the policy was not based on any depreciation of the innate physical capability or courage or other relevant qualities of homosexuals. In view of the very dubious basis in homophobic sentiment of the policy's justification, it was plainly right to insist on a clear demonstration of public need. The availability of alternative arrangements, unlikely to be very much less effective in ensuring good discipline and morale, pointed to the violation of fundamental rights of personhood closely tied to the value of human dignity.

In judging the relative effectiveness of alternative measures, of course, the court will depend on evidence submitted by the public authority; it will rarely possess a similar expertise or experience. The appropriate *degree* of deference, however, should reflect the cogency (or apparent cogency) of the evidence adduced and its capacity to withstand critical scrutiny and challenge. In *Smith and Grady*, the Court was entitled to call attention to the use of disciplinary codes in ensuring the successful integration of women and members of racial minorities within the armed forces, as well as noting the satisfactory cooperation already achieved with allied foreign forces that included homosexuals. And it was entitled to doubt the government's view that nothing could be learned from the experience of those other European countries which now accepted gay servicemen and women. A proper hesitation before rejecting a defence based on past experience or expert risk assessment may be highly desirable; but the court bears the ultimate responsibility of protecting the complainant's rights against unjustified infringement. Judicial deference must be based on evidence and argument, in support of the decision or measure under review, that the complainant has not been able effectively to undermine. Any wider submission to official expertise would defeat the point of judicial review, threatening the court's impartiality and independence.

III

From an appropriately internal, interpretative stance, many of the distinctions and categories invented for purposes of analytical exposition lose their force—or at least serve only as very rough guides to the making of an evaluative legal judgement, dependent on all the circumstances. From an external vantage point, characteristic of the text-writer's detached perspective on institutional arrangements, Tom Hickman presents an interesting contrast between public law before and after the implementation of the Human Rights Act.[26] In charting the course of legal development he invokes a range of distinctions that, while helpful in illuminating his descriptive analysis, may serve only to confuse an interpretative account, offered as an integral part of legal reasoning. Distinctions between procedure and

---

[26] Tom Hickman, *Public Law after the Human Rights Act*, 99–111.

substance, standards of review and standards of legality, administrative law and constitutional law, legality and rationality, reasonableness and proportionality, may all be instructive at the level of detached analysis while nonetheless constituting only very tentative—sometimes even misleading—guides to correct judicial decision in particular instances. There is, of course, room for both sorts of analysis; but the difference between them should be kept firmly in mind.

I am contending that the style and scope of review adopted by the court must be appropriately matched to the relevant question of law: the smaller the discretion enjoyed by a public authority, in any given instance, the more intrusive judicial review must be if those affected are to enjoy the equal protection of the law. When we define with appropriate care the pertinent question of law, the separation of powers between court and public authority is preserved. It is simply a function of the court's duty of enforcing the law, which may or may not, on correct analysis, leave certain matters for purely legislative or executive decision. Hickman appears to challenge this view, however, by emphasizing the distinction between standards of *review* and standards of *legality*: he treats the scope or intensity of judicial review as a matter quite distinct (at least conceptually) from the principles of legality binding on a public authority. He concedes that the distinction is not always helpful and that 'some rules and principles resist classification as either standards of review or standards of legality', serving both functions simultaneously.[27] Noting, however, that Lord Greene's judgment in *Wednesbury* was directed to the question, 'What, then, is the power of the courts?', he classifies the case as one about the standard of review rather than the duties imposed on public authorities.[28]

The distinction is connected to a further distinction between procedure and substance. Administrative law traditionally limited common law standards of legality to matters of *procedure*, requiring compliance with the rules of natural justice; any substantive standards of legality were supplied by the terms of the empowering statute: 'The courts would require the statutory conditions to be observed.'[29] The substance of an administrative decision was otherwise controlled only by a restricted *Wednesbury* approach, focused on the appropriate standard of review:

The imposition of *substantive* principles that would condition the exercise of general powers was associated in the minds of lawyers with a written constitutional document or Bill of Rights, which the United Kingdom did not have.[30]

Reliance was placed on politicians' responsibility to the electorate, national and local, to ensure that cherished liberties were not curtailed, until constitutional orthodoxy was challenged by Browne-Wilkinson LJ in the *Wheeler* case.[31] Browne-Wilkinson LJ invoked standards of legality in support of judicial intervention

---

[27] Ibid, 100. Hickman stresses that the distinction 'is not one that is formally drawn in the law'; nor is it 'any part' of his thesis that it should be (ibid).
[28] *Associated Provincial Picture Houses Ltd v Wednesbury Corporation* [1948] 1 KB 223, 228.
[29] Hickman, *Public Law after the Human Rights Act*, 102.
[30] Ibid, 103.
[31] *Wheeler v Leicester City Council* [1985] AC 1054.

to protect common law liberties rather than resorting to the *Wednesbury* standard of review:

> In my judgement it is undoubtedly part of the constitution of this country that, in the absence of express legislative provisions to the contrary, each individual has the right to hold and express his own views.... In my judgement, general powers such as those conferred by the Open Spaces Act 1906 and the Public Health Acts cannot in general be lawfully exercised by discriminating against those who hold particular lawful views or refuse to express certain views.... If it were permissible in exercising such powers to take into account the views expressed or held by individuals, Parliament must be taken to have impliedly authorized the doing of an act by the local authority inconsistent with the fundamental freedoms of speech and conscience.[32]

Hickman observes that, even though Browne-Wilkinson LJ's view was 'scotched' in the House of Lords, which upheld his dissenting judgment on rather different grounds, that view was ultimately endorsed by a line of cases recognizing fundamental or constitutional common law rights. In *Simms*, Lord Hoffmann drew a direct analogy, as regards 'principles of constitutionality', with judicial review of legislation under a formal 'constitutional document': 'In the absence of express language or necessary implication to the contrary, the courts...presume that even the most general words were intended to be subject to the basic rights of the individual.'[33] According to Hickman, Lord Hoffmann thereby 'completed the exercise of joining the dots left unjoined by Browne-Wilkinson LJ's judgment in *Wheeler*'. It was now accepted that modern civil and political rights could be enforced 'as part of a common law constitution'; the House of Lords' judgment in *Wheeler* had been reversed *sub silentio*.[34]

The European Convention rights, given statutory force by the Human Rights Act, are not standards of review, Hickman observes: 'they are norms of general application and not principles directed to the courts'.[35] As Lord Hoffmann explains the position, the 'principle of legality', affirming fundamental rights, has been 'expressly enacted as a rule of construction', so that 'the principles of fundamental human rights which exist at common law' are 'supplemented by a specific text', namely the European Convention.[36] A danger of confusion arises, Hickman believes, from 'the tendency to approach the Human Rights Act from the perspective of administrative, rather than constitutional, law'.[37] While the distinction between standards of review and standards of legality has been readily understood in relation to such 'absolute' or unqualified rights as the right against torture and inhuman or degrading treatment or punishment, under Article 3, there has been confusion as regards such expressly qualified rights as those under Article 8 (right to respect for private and family life) or Article 10 (freedom of speech). In particular, it is not always appreciated that proportionality—the test

---

[32] Ibid, 1063–5.
[33] *R v Secretary of State for the Home Dept, ex p Simms* [2000] 2 AC 115, 131.
[34] Hickman, *Public Law after the Human Rights Act,* 108.
[35] Ibid.
[36] *ex p Simms* [2000] 2 AC 115, 131–2.
[37] Hickman, *Public Law after the Human Rights Act,* 109.

applied to determine whether an interference with 'qualified rights' is necessary and hence justified—is 'not a heightened standard of review but part of the definition of qualified rights'.[38] Such 'qualified rights', though permitting interference with freedom under certain conditions, are nonetheless standards of legality: 'if a public authority acts in a manner which represents an unnecessary interference with an individual's right to respect for his private life, the public authority has acted unlawfully'.[39]

While these interconnected distinctions may serve to dispel error or confusion, at the level of descriptive analysis, they should not necessarily play a commanding role in legal doctrine; in the latter context, where we take up the internal, interpretative viewpoint, such distinctions may prove misleading. If, as I have argued, *Wednesbury* unreasonableness is best regarded as a *consequence* of the sorts of errors of reasoning Lord Greene outlined—asserting an excess or abuse of jurisdiction that could, if we wished, be formulated in other (more instructive) ways—there is no clear-cut distinction between procedure and substance. Failures of *due process* are departures from legality and fairness that undermine the substantive outcome, rendering it an unlawful interference with private rights or interests. Admittedly, Lord Diplock distinguished between illegality and irrationality in *GCHQ*.[40] But that distinction ultimately holds, as an important doctrinal division, only if we suppose that all substantive duties derive directly from statute—the view Hickman attributes to common lawyers before *Wheeler* and its progeny. We should resist such an account, however, because it draws a sharp distinction between statute and common law that is not sustainable. No statute is ever directly addressed to the circumstances of a particular case; nor is it free-standing, independent of the surrounding context—a context replete with legal rules and principles that will inform and qualify the statute's application to specific events. We determine the conditions a statute imposes on public authorities by interpreting its express provisions in the light of such things as the general statutory purpose, the particular administrative context in point, and common law presumptions of legal and constitutional propriety. The substantive duties imposed by statute on a public agency are those that the best interpretation, all things considered, supports: they are the product of both statute and common law, interpreted in harmony, and not the statute taken alone.

The suggestion that the *Wheeler* case marked that start of a deliberate challenge to orthodoxy—coming, as Hickman puts it, 'out of the blue'—invites the objection that such judicial innovation was neither democratic nor legitimate.[41] Yet it is misleading to characterize the clarification of underlying ideas and commitments, already implicit in the law, as unorthodox or revolutionary. In lamenting the new 'polarization of political attitudes', and the failure of constitutional conventions to prevent the victimization of individuals who do not share the attitudes of the majority, Browne-Wilkinson LJ was merely explaining the need to enforce

---

[38] Ibid, 110–11.   [39] Ibid, 109.
[40] *Council of Civil Service Unions v Minister for the Civil Service* [1985] AC 374, 410.
[41] Hickman, *Public Law after the Human Rights Act,* 104.

principles that had formerly been observed as a matter of general expectation and understanding; such principles were as much *legal* in character as political, rooted in basic constitutional morality. The City Council had banned the Leicester Rugby Club from using a municipal recreation ground for practice because the Club had declined to denounce a proposed rugby tour of apartheid South Africa, which councillors opposed. Browne-Wilkinson LJ's recourse to the fundamental freedoms of speech and conscience, in explanation of the ban's illegality, made explicit what was already implicit in any finding of irrationality: people are entitled to express opinions at variance with those asserted by officials, even if such officials are elected representatives; they cannot be punished for lawful conduct that a public authority finds unhelpful. Browne-Wilkinson LJ correctly interpreted the Council's statutory powers by reference to the broader legal context, which included the common law. And even if he declined to denounce the Council's actions as unreasonable in the sense of 'perverse', he established the appropriate link with *Wednesbury*: if in exercising its discretion the Council had taken account of people's lawful views, or 'their willingness to express certain views', it had acted unlawfully by taking a 'legally irrelevant factor' into account.[42]

Admittedly, the Court of Appeal majority reached different conclusions, affirming the first instance decision in favour of the Council; and the House of Lords, while allowing the Club's appeal, did not specifically endorse Browne-Wilkinson LJ's reasoning. The much vaguer references to unreasonableness and 'procedural impropriety' in the House of Lords speeches nonetheless *required* an invocation of constitutional principle: they were in that respect conclusionary and unexplained. The fundamental rights of speech and conscience are, for example, the implicit foundations of Lord Templeman's insistence that a 'private individual . . . cannot be obliged to display zeal in the pursuit of an object sought by a public authority and cannot be obliged to publish views dictated by a public authority'.[43] Moreover, the emphasis given by the Court of Appeal majority to the Council's statutory duty (under the Race Relations Act 1976) to promote good race relations, to which the ban allegedly contributed, illustrates the deficiencies of an approach that divorces a statutory requirement from its broader common law constitutional context. As Browne-Wilkinson LJ observed, that section did not authorize discrimination against people who lawfully expressed their views on racial or other matters.[44]

For similar reasons, the claim that, in *ex parte Pierson*, Lord Browne-Wilkinson and Lord Steyn 'camouflaged their radical innovation in the trappings of uncontroversial and respected doctrine', smuggling new constitutional principles into public law, is—from an internal, interpretative stance, at least—very wide of the mark.[45] In objecting that the Home Secretary had increased the penal element of his life sentence retrospectively, Pierson was asserting rights to liberty and due process

---

[42] *Wheeler v Leicester City Council* [1985] AC 1054, 1065.

[43] Ibid, 1080.

[44] See also Allan, *Law, Liberty, and Justice: The Legal Foundations of British Constitutionalism* (Oxford: Clarendon Press, 1993), 137–8, 168–9.

[45] Hickman, *Public Law after the Human Rights Act*, 107; see *R v Secretary of State for the Home Dept, ex p Pierson* [1998] AC 539.

that lay at the heart of the rule of law. Since the tariff, or minimum period of detention, represented the minister's view of what the prisoner deserved by way of punishment, it was directly analogous to the sentence imposed by a judge in cases other than murder. Such a quasi-judicial power, even if conferred on a government minister, must be exercised in an appropriately judicial manner. A minister should no more be able to extend a sentence, once imposed, than a judge would be; and Parliament was rightly presumed not to legislate contrary to the rule of law, which imposed 'minimum standards of fairness, both substantive and procedural'.[46] Such minimum standards do not permit a person to be punished twice for the same offence; nor do they allow a person, already informed of his sentence, 'to be given in substitution for it a more severe punishment'.[47] The fair treatment of offenders—their punishments reflecting the gravity of their offences according to an impartial scale, administered by independent judges—is plainly a requirement of constitutional equality. No one should be at the mercy of an unfettered political discretion, responsive (it is reasonable to fear) to sustained media condemnation of the offender and resulting public clamour.[48] As basic requirements of the rule of law, these substantive elements of public law derive from common law principle, which frames and colours our interpretation of statute.

In observing that a general statutory power should not be taken to authorize actions 'which adversely affect the legal rights of the citizen or the basic principles on which the law of the United Kingdom is based', unless Parliament had clearly stated a contrary intention, Lord Browne-Wilkinson was simply affirming a basic precept of legality or the rule of law.[49] It was not, as alleged, a 'classic common law trick' for the judges to suggest that they were 'simply propounding the law as it had always been'.[50] It is central to the rule of law, as a principle of constitutionalism, that criminal justice should be administered fairly in accordance with the separation of powers between government and judiciary: it is these considerations of equality or fairness that ultimately distinguish the process of law from arbitrary power or political violence. Moreover, what to the detached observer might appear to be a species of judicial collaboration turns out, on closer inspection, to be an important interpretative disagreement. It makes little sense, then, to place Lord Steyn and Lord Browne-Wilkinson in the same constitutional camp: their conceptions of legality were, in substance, far apart. Lord Browne-Wilkinson's alleged creativity was not enough, in practice, even to secure an effective safeguard against abuse of executive power. He held, in a dissenting speech, that to require the Home Secretary to behave judicially would 'subvert' the legislative decision, made in the teeth of opposing constitutional opinion, to leave such a sentencing function in the hands of the executive. On that view, the rule of law can be overridden—the

---

[46] *ex p Pierson* [1998] AC 539, 591 (Lord Steyn).
[47] Ibid, 603 (Lord Hope of Craighead).
[48] Compare *R v Secretary of State for the Home Dept, ex p Venables and Thompson* [1998] AC 407.
[49] *ex p Pierson* [1998] AC 539, 573.
[50] Hickman, *Public Law after the Human Rights Act*, 107.

associated idea of legality denied—at the will of a hostile parliamentary majority, inferred from the statutory scheme.[51]

The *Wheeler* case shows not that the common law failed to impose substantive standards of legality, but rather that such standards long remained implicit and inarticulate. In their absence, judicial disapproval of 'unreasonable' governmental action would have been undisciplined and arbitrary—incapable of explicit justification. If, in subsequent cases, the courts 'set about modifying the *Wednesbury* standard of review, applying it with greater intensity and rigour', they did so in support of standards of legality, not (as Hickman claims) as an alternative.[52] It follows that the distinction between standards of review and standards of legality, while useful perhaps for limited purposes of exposition, is potentially misleading. The appropriate standard of review is dictated by the relevant standard of legality. Where the question before a public agency has a single correct answer, as a matter of law, the court must apply a 'correctness' standard of review. A rationality standard is appropriate for review of discretionary decisions that may fall anywhere within a limited range of lawful judgement. It implies that a public authority must give proper attention to all relevant considerations, giving them, moreover, what *in context* is a defensible weight, reflecting the pertinent constitutional values. If, in *ex parte Smith*, the English courts substituted a *Wednesbury* standard of review for the 'correctness' standard that was appropriate, as Hickman concludes, it was only in the sense that the court's appraisal—however classified or labelled—fell short of what was necessary to protect the basic rights in issue.[53]

An appreciation of the interdependence of the concepts of legality, rationality, and proportionality helps us to see the fragility of current doctrinal distinctions between standards of legality and reasonableness, as well as the doubtful utility of the distinction between standards of legality and standards of review. In playing a central role within the meaning or definition of most Convention rights, including certain rights expressed in unqualified terms, the proportionality doctrine operates to determine both the standard of legality and the standard of review. And the same is true of common law rights, even if they are usually regarded as imposing corresponding duties of substantive legality rather than merely enhancing the intensity of judicial review. In *Daly*, the House of Lords held unlawful a government policy that required prisoners to be excluded from their cells during searches for prohibited materials or equipment.[54] Such a blanket policy, applicable to disruptive and well-behaved prisoners alike, infringed the right to conduct confidential legal correspondence; there was too great a danger that such correspondence would be read by prison officers if the prisoner were absent. While Lord Bingham of Cornhill reached his conclusions 'on an orthodox application of common law principles...and an orthodox domestic approach to judicial review', he derived

---

[51] For further discussion, see Allan, *Constitutional Justice: A Liberal Theory of the Rule of Law* (Oxford: Oxford University Press, 2001), 141–8.

[52] Hickman, *Public Law after the Human Rights Act*, 104.

[53] *R v Ministry of Defence, ex p Smith* [1996] QB 517, considered above.

[54] *R (Daly) v Secretary of State for the Home Dept* [2001] UKHL 26.

the same result by reference to Article 8 of the European Convention.[55] The standard of review reflected the standard of legality, which required any interference with privileged correspondence to be strictly necessary—proportionate to the public ends in view.

Paul Craig has suggested that the protection of common law constitutional rights rests on the operation of a 'priority rule': such rights enjoy an automatic priority over conflicting legislative instructions or purposes unless Parliament has expressly stipulated to the contrary.[56] Such rules of construction might be thought to support a strong distinction between legality, circumscribing the boundaries of a public authority's jurisdiction, and rationality, concerning the exercise of that jurisdiction in particular instances. On closer inspection, however, we can see that there is danger here of form obscuring substance—descriptive analysis blinding us to interpretative subtlety. Rules of construction are only general guidelines, usually expressed as *presumptions* of legislative intent. And we cannot determine the meaning or effect of a statutory provision in isolation from the particular factual and normative context, within which common law rights obtain their specific *weight*. If, as Lord Hoffmann asserts in *Simms*, a common law right may be overridden by 'necessary implication', the best construction may be one that permits the right to be curtailed or qualified even though there are no *explicit* instructions to that effect: it surrenders, in part, to pressing contrary public needs. What is *necessarily* implied, moreover, depends on our judgements about the proper balance of rights or interests, sensitive to considerations of purpose and context: it cannot be gleaned from a scrutiny of the statutory words alone.

In *Simms*, the House of Lords held that the Home Secretary had unlawfully prohibited interviews of prisoners by journalists, or imposed unreasonable conditions. Simms wished to harness the resources of the media in aid of his campaign to overturn his conviction, which he alleged was mistaken: he hoped that a journalist, who had requested an interview, could uncover new information which would support a reference to the Court of Appeal. Any prison rule imposing an unreasonable impediment to access to the media, when such access served a legitimate purpose, advancing the public interest, would exceed the rule-making power conferred in general terms by the Prison Act 1952. Since, however, the prisoner's rights of communication were inevitably curtailed by his imprisonment, and since there were proper demands of prison security and discipline to be weighed in the balance, the illegality of the minister's ban reflected his failure to make an appropriate accommodation between the conflicting interests: the ban was, in effect, a *disproportionate* response to the legitimate needs of order and discipline.

The reasoning of the Court of Appeal in the earlier case of *Leech* brought out more clearly the dependence of judgements about legality on appraisal of all relevant circumstances—and hence on review of the *rationality* of administrative action, all things considered.[57] Prison rules, made by the Home Secretary, provided

---

[55] Ibid, para 23.
[56] Paul Craig, 'Constitutional and Non-constitutional Review' (2001) 54 CLP 147–78, at 166–7.
[57] *R v Secretary of State for the Home Dept, ex p Leech* [1994] QB 198.

for a prisoner's letters to be examined by the prison governor, who was empowered to prohibit any correspondence he thought objectionable. Leech's communications with his lawyer were intercepted under these rules, in contravention of the usual confidentiality bestowed by legal professional privilege. It was held that the general power under the Prison Act, to make rules for purposes of prison management and discipline, did not authorize such interference with a right that was ancillary to the fundamental right of access to the court. It was well established that a prisoner's 'unimpeded right of access to a solicitor for the purpose of receiving advice and assistance in connection with the possible institution of civil proceedings' formed 'an inseparable part of the right of access to the courts themselves'.[58] Although, in principle, a statute might authorize the curtailment of the right by ministerial rules, where the rule-making power was alleged to arise by necessary implication the executive bore a heavy burden of justification: 'the more fundamental the right interfered with, and the more drastic the interference, the more difficult becomes the implication'.[59]

Whether or not the statute permitted any encroachment on a basic constitutional right, and if so to what extent, were questions of substantive legality that depended on assessment of the need for such restrictions. What was formally a question of jurisdiction, based on statutory construction, was in substance a matter of the reasonable exercise of powers, consistent with limited qualification of a fundamental right if necessary in the public interest. Restricted powers of inspection and interception could be inferred from the need to ensure that mail was 'in truth bona fide correspondence' between prisoner and solicitor, where there was some reason to doubt that this was the case. The existence of any wider powers depended on whether a persuasive case could be made for them, having regard to the importance of protecting the prisoner's rights. The question was 'whether there is a *self-evident and pressing need* for an unrestricted power to read letters between a prisoner and a solicitor' and to stop them if considered objectionable.[60] Since no 'objective need' had been established, the relevant power did not exist.

Distinctions between procedure and substance, or between legality and rationality, or between standards of legality and standards of review, while sometimes useful for purposes of exposition—detached from the practical judgements involved in particular cases—must be employed with caution in an interpretative context. In practice, the separation of powers is more subtle and fluid than such distinctions allow. Common law constitutional rights, like their Convention counterparts, generate strong resistance to governmental measures inimical to the basic interests they protect: they impose substantial constraints of justification, exposing such measures to independent judicial scrutiny. But while certain sorts of government action are wholly forbidden, in all or almost all circumstances, for the most part these rights allow any measure capable of reasonable justification: they are rights to *fair treatment*, having regard to the respective public and private interests in play.

---

[58] Ibid, 210.   [59] Ibid, 209.   [60] Ibid, 212 (emphasis added).

The explicit terms of the enactment under which administrative powers are exercised are plainly relevant to the nature and scope of the jurisdiction conferred; but they are never decisive on their own. The statutory framework is a critical part of the constitutional context in which coercive state action must be justified, if challenged; but its true meaning and consequences for affected persons depend on appraisal of all the circumstances, an appraisal sensitive to the basic values that constitutional rights protect.

The interpretation of statute invokes considerations of constitutional propriety as well as those of legislative purpose and public needs. Lord Wilberforce explained that the process of statutory construction, whereby 'subjects are brought under the rule of law', as opposed to the rule of monarch or legislature, was not a matter of 'mechanical' semantic analysis but was focused on 'such matters as intelligibility to the citizen, constitutional propriety, considerations of history, comity of nations, reasonable and non-retroactive effect' as well as social needs.[61] It follows that the identification of constitutional rights at common law limits the scope of parliamentary supremacy by curtailing the boundaries of interpretative possibility. Operating as basic assumptions about the legitimate deployment of public power, such rights effectively restrict the legislature to measures than can be *justified* on intelligible grounds of justice or the public good. For we cannot both suppose that responsible legislators acknowledge the requirements of constitutional rights, as basic precepts of governance according to law, and think them willing to flout such rights for immediate political ends. If, as Dicey asserted (notwithstanding his supposed endorsement of absolutism) even 'extraordinary' powers, conferred or sanctioned by statute, are 'never really unlimited' because they are confined not merely by the words of the Act but 'by the interpretation put upon the statute by the judges', we should acknowledge the special nature of constitutional rights.[62] Their flexibility in the face of legitimate public ends, authorized by Parliament, is matched by their resistance to unjustified intrusion: they can be 'overridden' only in circumstances that justify curtailment, as determined by an independent judiciary, capable of resisting unreasonable assertions of public power in particular instances.[63]

Lord Hoffmann, admittedly, stated the opposite in the familiar judicial manner: 'Parliamentary sovereignty means that Parliament can, if it chooses, legislate contrary to fundamental principles of human rights.'[64] Any limitations on legislative power were 'ultimately political, not legal'. But we cannot draw such a sharp line between law and politics, or legal and political morality, unless we imagine that legislative instructions might be transmitted in a manner that treats judges and citizens as automata, having no responsibility for seeking a humane and defensible reconciliation between statutory purpose, on the one hand, and countervailing individual interests, on the other. If fundamental rights cannot be overridden by

---

[61] *Black-Clawson International Ltd v Papierwerke Waldhof-Aschaffenburg AG* [1975] AC 591, 629–30.

[62] A V Dicey, *Introduction to the Study of the Law of the Constitution*, 10th edn (London: Macmillan, 1964), 413–14.

[63] See further Chapter 5, above.

[64] *ex p Simms* [2000] 2 AC 115, 131.

'general or ambiguous words', it is not (as Lord Hoffmann asserts) because there is 'too great a risk that the full implications of their unqualified meaning may have passed unnoticed in the democratic process'. It is rather because the 'full implications' can rarely be known until events unfold to test the statutory scheme. Such implications are as much the product of judicial interpretation as of legislative fiat: they are discerned in the course of reconciling general aims with particular cases, in all their complex particularity.

And if judicial insistence on clear instructions means that 'Parliament must squarely confront what it is doing and accept the political cost', we should welcome the obligation on elected representatives to take responsibility for what may be unpopular political decisions.[65] But that does not relieve the judges and other legal interpreters of their *own* responsibilities for statutory construction faithful to the rule of law. There is no point at which legality simply surrenders to contrary political direction. The 'political cost' of interference with the rights of prisoners, or other minority or marginal groups, may sometimes be very small; the infringement of such rights may even pay significant political dividends.[66] Against their duty of respect for the deliberations of the legislature, as regards the general scheme of its provision for the public good, the courts must set an equal duty of loyalty to the basic precepts of the rule of law, including the protection of established fundamental rights.

IV

Our reflections on the relationship between the principles of legality and the standards of judicial review, together with the related questions of equality and rationality, may help to elucidate some further matters concerning procedure and process. The distinction between standards of legality and standards of review, like the associated distinction between jurisdictional conditions and requirements of rationality, can easily cloud our perception of more important matters of general principle. If compliance with constitutional rights is understood as a matter of *substantive legality*, quite independently of questions of reasonableness or rationality—and hence independently of any judicial appraisal of the *reasoning* of the public authority—it may well be supposed that the court should focus its attention solely on the legislative or administrative *outcome*. There would be no duty on a public agency to have regard to fundamental rights, provided that its decision turns out to be compatible with them. And even if the authority has given careful attention

---

[65] Ibid.

[66] Consider the generally hostile political reaction to the decision of the European Court of Human Rights in *Hirst v United Kingdom (No 2)* (2004) 38 EHRR 40, holding that the automatic loss of the right to vote accompanying a sentence of imprisonment in the United Kingdom, irrespective of the length of sentence or nature or gravity of the offence, was an indiscriminate restriction on the right to vote (Art 3 of Protocol No 1) falling outside any acceptable margin of appreciation. The failure of successive Governments to promote reform has clearly reflected the prevailing current of majority opinion, opposed to any modification of existing rules.

to the complainant's rights or interests, in the course of reaching its conclusions, its deliberations would be irrelevant to any judgement about whether those rights have indeed been infringed.

In the *Begum* case, the Court of Appeal was critical of the failure of the school authorities, when considering the demand of a Muslim pupil to wear the (full body-length) jilbab, to determine its response in the light of her right under Article 9 of the European Convention to manifest her religious belief.[67] Although the school's decision that the girl must comply with its uniform requirements (which did not permit the jilbab) might be legitimate, in principle, it was nonetheless held unlawful for failure to adopt the appropriate form of inquiry. Brooke LJ observed that the school might be able to justify its stance if it were to undertake an analysis of the kind performed by a court in assessing the justification for any interference with a Convention right. By contrast, the House of Lords insisted that the question was purely a matter of substance, endorsing an objection that the lower court's approach was a 'recipe for judicialization on an unprecedented scale'.[68] While in ordinary 'domestic judicial review' the court was usually concerned with 'whether the decision-maker reached his decision in the right way', in the present case what mattered was the 'result'.[69] A decision consistent with Article 9, as a matter of substance, should not be condemned on the ground that it was not the product of a quasi-judicial procedure.

Neither the approach of the Court of Appeal nor that of the House of Lords can be accepted as appropriate. We do not face a stark choice between the highly structured process of reasoning, required of public authorities by the former, and the exclusive focus on substantive outcome, endorsed by the latter. While compliance with constitutional rights (whether at common law or under the European Convention) is a requirement of *legality*, and hence a jurisdictional condition of validity, it is equally a demand of *rationality*: a proper exercise of discretion, within jurisdictional boundaries, must devote attention to the consequences of any possible decision for the enjoyment of those rights. Although individual rights may preclude certain governmental action as necessarily inconsistent with them, they will in many cases allow a range of reasonable and proportionate actions, any of which could be defended as a legitimate accommodation of personal and public interests. If, however, the court must defer to the public agency in its choice of legitimate actions, acknowledging the agency's entitlement to act on its own best view of the public good, there must be reassurance that officials have at least made a properly considered *judgement*, acting in full awareness of the importance to the complainant of the rights or interests concerned. In the ordinary language of administrative law, all relevant considerations should be fairly taken into account; and there are no more important considerations than the constitutional rights of those affected. A lawful and rational decision is not simply one that is *hypothetically*

---

[67] *R (Begum) v Denbigh High School Governors* [2005] EWCA Civ 199.

[68] See Thomas Poole, 'Of Headscarves and Heresies: the Denbigh High School case and Public Authority Decision-making under the Human Rights Act' [2005] PL 685–95.

[69] *R (Begum) v Denbigh High School Governors* [2006] UKHL 15, para 68 (Lord Hoffmann).

compatible with basic rights, in the sense that it can be defended, *ex post facto*, as serving an overriding public interest. It is a decision actually taken in the light of the harm inflicted on affected individuals, which is minimized by a serious attempt to reconcile the competing interests.

No doubt, head teachers and school governors cannot be expected to make decisions of the sort involved in *Begum* 'with textbooks on human rights law at their elbows', as Lord Hoffmann expressed it.[70] But it hardly follows that they cannot pay proper regard to the importance of a decision for their pupils' rights of conscience. In that case, indeed, the school authorities had demonstrated their appreciation of the interests at stake by the thoroughness of their inquiries. The school had not only consulted with parents, pupils, and local mosques when devising its uniform, but took further advice from appropriate religious authorities when the complainant expressed her objections. The shalwar kameeze, which met the uniform requirements, was understood to satisfy the obligation of modest dress for Muslim girls. The school was also concerned that an acceptance of the jilbab would lead to undesirable divisions between pupils, reflecting the strictness of their religious views; the uniform was intended to promote a sense of inclusion and social cohesion. It may well be thought that the school had adopted a rational and defensible decision-making process, consistent with its obligation of respect for human rights, even if its deliberations did not match the rigour appropriate for a court or tribunal.

In the absence of such reasonable deliberations, however, a complainant would have little protection.[71] Confined to review of the substantive outcome, even when informed of the parties' respective aims and assumptions, the court may be unable to challenge the conclusions of the public authority: it may lack the experience and expertise necessary to call into doubt the proportionality of the measures adopted. How much weight should be given to the *ex post facto* assurances of the authority that a different approach, more sensitive to the complainant's rights, would not have been a sufficiently effective means of achieving its objectives? No doubt the answer depends on the extent and cogency of the evidence and arguments the authority is able to muster; but there would normally be good reason for scepticism about the reliability of a self-serving case, presented in response to a complaint of unlawful action. How then should the court resolve the dilemma? It may be obliged to dismiss the complaint, despite its misgivings about the reliability of *ex post facto* assurances, because the complainant, lacking the expertise of the public authority, has not been able to challenge them effectively.

An emphasis on questions of legality, distinguished from rationality, and on substantive outcomes, as opposed to due process, has generated conceptual confusion. When constitutional rights are correctly analysed as rights to *fair treatment*, requiring no greater interference with the relevant interests than can be justified in all the circumstances, considerations of due process are fundamental: there is no pertinent distinction between fair treatment, as a matter of outcome, and fair

---

[70] Ibid.
[71] Compare Hickman, *Public Law after the Human Rights Act*, 239–42.

treatment in the sense having one's legitimate interests properly identified and considered. The citizen is entitled to a decision-making process that takes her interests fully into account, giving them a weight that reflects the importance they are ascribed by acknowledged constitutional standards. It is only in cases where the degree of interference was in all the circumstances inevitable—where a conscientious examination of competing imperatives would not have made any difference to the outcome—that the court's preoccupation with substance rather than process is justified. The complainant is otherwise deprived of the essence of her right, which consists in a decision-making process duly respectful of the important personal interests at stake. Since the true requirements of religious freedom were heavily dependent, in the circumstances of the *Begum* case, on a complex appraisal of relevant matters of fact and judgement, the court was inevitably reliant, in large part, on the quality of the deliberations of the school management; and it ought to have given the complainant more confidence in the justice of the outcome that those deliberations *preceded* the adverse decision, rather than being merely an after-thought.

The demands of due process are the quid pro quo of judicial deference. Lord Bingham observed that it would be 'irresponsible of any court, lacking the experience, background and detailed knowledge of the head teacher, staff and governors, to overrule their judgement' on so sensitive a matter.[72] The power of decision had been given to them 'for the compelling reason that they are best placed to exercise it'. It was proper to bow to the superior expertise and judgement of the school authorities, however, only if the court were confident that those responsible had exercised their discretion fairly, giving appropriate weight to the complainant's legitimate interests. If there were a variety of permissible uniform policies, each compatible with constitutional rights—*insofar as the court itself could judge*—it was important that the school should have made its own selection with the special interests of the complainant (or of those similarly placed) in mind. Otherwise *no one* has confronted the complexities involved in according fair treatment with the necessary reflection and insight. And if, as Lord Bingham suggested (notwithstanding the primary focus on substantive outcome) 'a challenger's task will be the harder' where it appears that the public body 'has conscientiously paid attention to all human rights considerations', it is because, in the absence of rather plain failings of judgement or understanding, the demands of due process (or fair treatment) will have been duly satisfied.[73]

What is necessary to meet the demands of due process must depend on all the circumstances. Whereas a court or tribunal must determine the rights of the parties to litigation, treating countervailing interests only as reasons to moderate their consequences, an executive public authority usually aims chiefly to serve some aspect of the public interest, treating any conflicting rights as necessary constraints on its course of action. It would be absurd to suppose that the reasoning with respect to constitutional rights should be identical in both situations. It should normally be

---

[72] *Begum*, para 34.   [73] Ibid, para 31.

enough for an administrative agency to attend to the rights of the citizen, or the interests those rights protect, as a significant part of its decision-making process: it need not perform a balancing of rights and interests in a formal, quasi-judicial manner. In *Begum*, the complainant's case amounted to a challenge to the general policy, not merely to her own obligation of compliance: the school could scarcely make an exception for her without substantially changing, or abandoning, the uniform requirement. Where the right and policy objective are closely bound up together in this way, as is usually the case in administrative decisions, the deliberations of the authority may legitimately reflect the nature of its executive function.

There is, then, an analogy with the ordinary principles of natural justice, or procedural fairness, which require a level of protection commensurate with the public function in question. An administrative agency would not normally be expected to offer the sort of elaborate formal hearing for interested parties that a court must provide for litigants; unlike a court, it is usually pursuing a policy objective in which the rights of individuals properly play only an incidental, if significant, role in its deliberations. The doctrine of legitimate expectations is similarly flexible, affording a barrier to unfairness defined by reference to the administrative context. While a public authority may sometimes act in defiance of a person's legitimate expectation, provoked by previous practice or even an explicit promise about future intentions, it may do so only when fairness allows. Not only must the authority give due consideration to any hardship likely to ensue from its change of policy; it may in some cases be forced to make an exception for the benefit of a complainant when to do so would not greatly damage the public interest. Any injury to the complainant must be proportionate to the wider public advantage.

When a legitimate expectation is shared by only a small number of identifiable persons, whose protection from disappointment would be unlikely to have significant implications for public policy, the court may properly make its satisfaction a condition of lawful administrative action: fairness dictates adherence to previous practice or promise unless there is an overriding public interest that should take priority. As Laws LJ has argued, the further a decision lies within the 'macro-political field', the 'less intrusive' should be the court's decision: 'in that field, true abuse of power is less likely to be found, since...changes of policy, fuelled by broad conceptions of the public interest, may more readily be accepted as taking precedence over the interests of groups which enjoyed expectations generated by an earlier policy'.[74] The court will defer to the authority more readily when there are 'wide-ranging issues of general policy', and it is harder to envisage the 'full consequences' of judicial intervention. That deference must, however, be offset—it is reasonable to suppose—by a duty on the public agency itself to take fairly into account the expectations it has engendered by its own previous conduct.

Accordingly, a local authority, empowered to grant a licence for premises to be used as a sex shop should have some regard for rights of free expression; it should not refuse a licence on policy grounds without weighing the legitimate interests

---

[74] *R v Secretary of State for Education and Employment, ex p Begbie* [2000] 1 WLR 1115, 1131.

that would be frustrated thereby.[75] Appropriate judicial deference, as regards substance, should be matched by a counterbalancing respect for due process. As Baroness Hale of Richmond observed, the court 'is bound to acknowledge that the local authority is much better placed than the court to decide whether the right of sex shop owners to sell pornographic literature and images should be restricted—for the prevention of disorder or crime, for the protection of health or morals, or for the protection of the rights of others'.[76] But then the authority should be obliged to demonstrate that it took all relevant considerations into account, including the complainant's interests. If, in such circumstances, the court 'would find it hard to upset the balance which the local authority had struck', it must be because the rights involved were duly satisfied.[77] And it may sometimes be safe to conclude that giving explicit attention to the rights at stake would have made no difference. Lord Rodger of Earlsferry considered that the Belfast City Council must have been well aware of the relevance of the right of freedom of expression, which had only 'modest value' in the circumstances. So due process requirements need not be unduly onerous or unsuited to the nature of the inquiry.

We cannot, then, accept Baroness Hale's view that the role of the court in 'human rights adjudication' is quite different from its role in 'an ordinary judicial review of administrative action'.[78] The idea that in its former role 'the court is concerned with whether the human rights of the claimant have in fact been infringed, not with whether the administrative decision-maker properly took them into account' is misconceived, presenting a false antithesis. The latter inquiry is a major part of the former, unless in all the circumstances a decision is 'obviously compliant with the right in question'.[79] Legality and rationality are closely linked, together marking the boundaries of the discretionary judgement reserved to the public agency. The greater the dependence of legal analysis on a sensitive judgement of complex and contested matters of empirical fact, especially where competing imperatives of constitutional right and public interest are finely balanced, the closer the court's intervention must move to a species of procedural review. The court's role must be to examine the quality of the administrative *process*, in which the public authority will enjoy a limited power to make its own appraisal of all the relevant circumstances, subject to the normal demands of rationality or reasonableness. The court has the final say on the appropriate reconciliation of public and personal, or general and particular, interests; but the judicial process should not be the *only* means of preserving the requisite balance between citizen and state. Or that is certainly the case unless there is reason to think the analogy between common law rights, which fit comfortably within the ordinary framework of judicial review, and European Convention rights is false.[80]

[75] See *Belfast City Council v Miss Behavin' Ltd* [2007] UKHL 19.
[76] Ibid, para 37.
[77] Ibid.
[78] Ibid, para 31.
[79] Ibid.
[80] See also *R (Nasseri) v Secretary of State for the Home Dept* [2009] UKHL 23, reiterating the procedure-substance dichotomy imposed in *Begum*; and see the effective critique in Hickman,

According to Lord Bingham, in *Begum*, the Human Rights Act 1998 was not intended to 'enlarge the rights or remedies' of the victims of breaches of Convention rights, but merely to enable those rights and remedies to be enforced by domestic courts; and the focus at Strasbourg was on whether rights had been infringed, not on whether a decision was the product of a defective decision-making process.[81] Even if Bingham were correct about the approach of the European Court of Human Rights, however, the Convention rights must be absorbed into an existing constitutional culture before they can make an effective contribution to administrative legality.[82] There is inevitably a large overlap between relevant standards, the Convention in many cases providing a more formal and elaborate basis for constitutional rights already implicit in the common law. Since, moreover, both Convention and common law constitute efforts to give more concrete and specific form to precepts inherent (if only in abstract conception) in the rule of law, it makes little sense to treat them as radically different creatures, bestowed by competing or contrasting political authorities. The 'sources' of these human or fundamental rights are ultimately located in our historical legal tradition, interpreted and reinterpreted in the light of the moral values that help us make sense of its new conditions.

The jurisprudence of the European Court of Human Rights, which British courts have accepted a general obligation to follow, may be understood as offering a challenge to the repeated failure of those courts, in numerous past cases, to fulfil the common law's promise of protecting liberty. Requirements of rationality, dependent on judgements about the scope and content of individual rights in specific cases, have often been too weakly applied—judges falling back on inadequately analysed assumptions about the public interest, or equating reasonableness with mere instrumental rationality (the serviceability of means to given ends). Decisions like those in *Wheeler*, *Leech*, *Pierson*, and *Simms* (considered above) signalled a welcome rejuvenation of the common law, less subservient to the political branches of state. If rights of conscience and freedom of expression underpinned coherent judgments of rationality in *Wheeler*, they were equally pertinent to the desire of the complainant in *Begum* to match her dress to her religious convictions. If it is only in rather plain cases of infringement of rights that the courts can quash executive decisions, confident that they do not wrongly trample on legitimate official discretion, we should expect it to be a condition of legality that, in more doubtful cases, the public authority has at least taken proper account of the significant individual interests at stake.

When the demands of Convention jurisprudence are fully integrated within domestic law, they must affect the constitutional context within which assessments

---

Public Law after the Human Rights Act, 234–5. And compare David Mead, 'Outcomes Aren't All: Defending Process-Based Review of Public Authority Decisions under the Human Rights Act' [2012] PL 61–84.

[81] *Begum* [2006] UKHL 15, para 29.

[82] For a different view of the Strasbourg approach, see Hickman, *Public Law after the Human Rights Act*, 242–4.

of legality and rationality are made: the Convention rights become relevant considerations which, at common law, should be accorded appropriate attention and weight.[83] At a deeper level these rights reinforce fundamental common law rights, which should themselves inform all coercive governmental action. The European Convention provided a legitimate source of reference, as regards the application and development of the common law, even before enactment of the Human Rights Act: its jurisprudence shed light on the meaning and scope of rights which had existing analogues in the common law, albeit that the common law equivalents were generally less clearly articulated. Sir John Laws had argued that the courts should treat Strasbourg jurisprudence in a similar manner to the decisions of other Commonwealth courts, as a source of enlightenment on relevant legal principles.[84] It was simply a natural development of the remedy of judicial review, recognizing that the *Wednesbury* doctrine could accommodate 'differential principles', including the principle of proportionality.[85] Lord Browne-Wilkinson had also argued that the common law could provide protection analogous to that afforded by the Convention, defending a strong presumption against legislative interference with fundamental human rights.[86] The rigid dichotomy of procedure and substance adopted by the House of Lords in *Begum* is therefore inconsistent with ordinary common law reasoning, which identifies the Convention rights—which run in many cases *in tandem* with similar rights at common law—as considerations relevant to the lawful exercise of governmental powers. The common law imposes standards of due process embracing both legality and rationality, insofar as these can be distinguished.[87]

Thomas Poole insists that competing responses to these questions about process reflect contrasting visions of public law.[88] Against his preferred view that a public authority need not consider the consequences of its actions for fundamental rights, he sets a 'hardline' alternative, imposing rigorous constraints of due process. He supposes that 'hardliners' would think that a rights-respecting culture would best develop if public authorities were required to articulate their decisions in the language of rights. A more relaxed view, focused on substance rather than procedure, would instead be more accommodating to the exigencies of public administration. The artificiality of this contrived opposition is apparent, however, from Poole's acceptance that, where an authority has in fact sought to balance the applicable

---

[83] For a similar argument, presenting the common law as a remedy for the deficiencies of Human Rights Act jurisprudence, see Hickman, *Public Law after the Human Rights Act*, 247–52.

[84] Sir John Laws, 'Is the High Court the Guardian of Fundamental Constitutional Rights?' [1993] PL 59–79.

[85] Ibid, 71.

[86] Lord Browne-Wilkinson, 'The Infiltration of a Bill of Rights' [1992] PL 397–410.

[87] Sir John Laws distinguished between *Wednesbury* review (adapted to include proportionality) and illegality (extending the *Padfield* doctrine to include a presumption against any interference with fundamental rights); but in practice the two approaches converged: there must be a presumption of intent to rebut any 'naked assertion of a power to interfere with fundamental rights without a demonstrated justification': Laws, 'Is the High Court the Guardian of Fundamental Constitutional Rights?' [1993] PL 59 at 78. A presumption of this kind is, indeed, *entailed* by the nature of these rights (when correctly understood) as barriers to unfair or disproportionate treatment.

[88] Thomas Poole, 'The Reformation of English Administrative Law' [2009] CLJ 142–68.

rights and interests, the court should intervene more reluctantly and cautiously. On pragmatic grounds, a public agency should be given an incentive to reflect on human rights requirements; such an approach 'represents the best route towards inculcating a plausible rights-respecting culture within the structures and pathways of administration'.[89] The space between the so-called hardline approach and Poole's alternative is evidently much smaller than his language would suggest; and this conclusion is confirmed by his own acknowledgement that in some circumstances, such as the discretion to deport someone from the United Kingdom, it is 'entirely appropriate' to require the decision-maker (even if a Government minister) to consider rights-related questions directly and specifically.[90]

In emphasizing pragmatic concerns, moreover, Poole loses sight of the point of upholding constitutional rights. As implications of the demands of human dignity and equal citizenship, these rights constitute limits to the legitimate exercise of governmental power: they cannot be traded off against other considerations as but 'one normative priority...amongst many'.[91] It is not a matter of devising administrative structures that will tend to enhance rights-protection over the long term, but rather a question of whether or not the complainant's fundamental rights have been infringed, contrary to the rule of law, in the particular case under review. Poole casts judges in the guise of superior administrative technicians, or managers, manipulating their responses to claims of illegality for strategic ends; and that view reduces the litigant's status to a tool for use in fashioning the grand design.

Poole's critique here, as elsewhere, is rooted in his conviction that we must choose between protecting rights, on the one hand, and attending to the administrative context, on the other; and this is, of course, a false antithesis. He purports to reject two 'related propositions': first, that administrative law is 'essentially a vehicle for protecting the rights of individuals' from the abuse of public power; secondly, that such rights 'are fundamental aspects of personhood that can only be properly protected by courts'.[92] Yet if the rights of individuals are implicit in their equal dignity as members of a genuine republic of independent citizens, it is right that the courts should defend them as central elements of the law that governs the relationship between citizen and state. Poole argues, nonetheless, that the two related propositions can be sustained only 'if administrative law is understood to operate as though it were a kind of hermetically sealed juridical order, removed from the concerns and realities of government'; such an approach is flawed 'because it is blind...to institutional context'.[93]

The notion that a resolute judicial defence of rights is necessarily insensitive to social or institutional context, however, is quite misguided. And the error is connected to the assumption that a stark choice must be made between a largely formal or procedural approach to rights protection, on the one hand, and a mainly

---

[89] Ibid, 164.
[90] Ibid, 150 (citing *R v Secretary of State for the Home Dept, ex p Razgar* [2004] UKHL 27).
[91] Ibid, 165.   [92] Ibid, 154.
[93] Ibid. Compare Thomas Poole, 'Questioning Common Law Constitutionalism' (2005) 25 LS 142–63.

substantive result-oriented stance, on the other. It is a product of the same mindset that wants to distinguish substantive *Wednesbury* unreasonableness from other familiar grounds of review as a problematic 'outlier to the conceptual system of which it was part'.[94] These false distinctions and dichotomies betray a failure to appreciate the intimate interdependence of doctrine and context, overlooking the manner in which broad conceptions of human dignity, independence, and due process must be adapted to the specific conditions in which they apply. A judgement about legality is always directed to the particular circumstances in view; and the fact that there should, in principle, be a direct chain of argument from abstract right to concrete judgement on the facts does not show that the relevant conceptions of right are sealed in a juridical order, unconnected to social and political context. It shows just the opposite: rights to fair treatment are necessarily dependent on judgements attuned to all the relevant circumstances, giving complainants the chance to show why, if at all, their individual cases merit specific attention. The Platonic 'Idea of the Rule of Law', as Poole conceives and condemns it, is a figment of his own imagination.[95]

V

If we are sceptical about the notion of varying standards of review, conceived independently of any particular context, we must be equally wary of the much vaunted 'doctrine of deference', alleged to be a requirement of proper democratic governance.[96] Courts must, of course, accept the legality of government action that lies within the jurisdiction of the public authority concerned; and in many cases the scope of that jurisdiction will encompass a variety of possible courses of action, giving the authority a discretion to choose whichever one best accords in its own judgement with the public interest. Furthermore, a court may be dependent, in some degree, on the authority's own expertise or experience when it determines the range of permissible state action: it may have to accept an official assessment of the practicalities of different courses of action in the absence of any effective challenge by other parties to the litigation. But these points are scarcely controversial; and they are implicit in any system of judicial review that preserves an appropriate separation of powers between the different branches of government.

There is no more need for a special *doctrine* of deference to limit the scope of judicial review than there is need for an independent scale of 'intensity'. The appropriate degree of deference is dictated, in each case, by analysis of the substantive legal issues arising. If properly conducted, the analysis will indicate the correct division of responsibilities between court and agency, making all due allowance for the exercise of administrative discretion and recourse to specialist expertise. That division

---

[94] Ibid, 143.

[95] Ibid, 164.

[96] See especially Murray Hunt, 'Sovereignty's Blight: Why Contemporary Public Law Needs the Concept of "Due Deference"', in Nicholas Bamforth and Peter Leyland (eds), *Public Law in a Multi-Layered Constitution* (Oxford: Hart Publishing, 2003), 337–70. For a sceptical response, see Allan, 'Human Rights and Judicial Review: a Critique of "Due Deference"' [2006] CLJ 671–95.

of responsibilities is itself the *outcome* of legal analysis attuned to the specific questions of legality arising: it cannot determine these questions, a priori, on the basis of general features of the separation of powers divorced from the specific constitutional context. The demand that courts should weigh up 'the relevant deference factors' in order properly 'to calibrate the intensity of review in the particular case' should therefore be resisted.[97] It seeks to erect a deference doctrine on the back of an artificial distinction between supposedly different standards of review.

When the court accepts a legislative or executive decision as a legitimate response to public needs, it does not 'defer' to Parliament or Government in any ordinary sense of that term: the court simply acknowledges that the decision falls within the proper scope of the relevant powers. As Lord Hoffmann observes in the *ProLife Alliance* case:

In a society based upon the rule of law and the separation of powers, it is necessary to decide which branch of government has in any particular instance the decision-making power and what the legal limits of that power are. That is a question of law and must therefore be decided by the courts.[98]

The courts' adherence to the separation of powers is not 'a matter of courtesy or deference', but is instead governed by legal principle: 'when a court decides that a decision is within the proper competence of the legislature or executive, it is not showing deference'. It is, instead, 'deciding the law'.[99] It follows from Hoffmann's analysis that showing deference, in the ordinary sense, would amount to an abdication of judicial responsibility for the defence of legal rights: the court would be ceding to officials powers of adjudication that belonged, on correct analysis, to the court itself.

The requirements of legality and the separation of powers are themselves, however, a reflection of the content of legal and constitutional rights in the circumstances of the particular case: these principles cannot function independently, allocating powers to the different branches a priori on the basis of some general classification of functions. Since, as we have seen, constitutional rights are fundamentally rights to fair treatment—constraining state power to accommodate the interests of affected individuals—they entail a reconciliation of competing imperatives. The scope of official discretion therefore depends on all the circumstances. Whether or not a limitation of rights is justified by an important countervailing public interest is ultimately a matter for the court to determine, even if it must give such weight to expertise as the plausibility of official explanations appears to require. Insofar as Lord Hoffmann purports to erect a rigid barrier between spheres of competence—suggesting that while their independence makes courts more suited to deciding certain questions, 'being elected makes the legislature or executive more suited to deciding others'—he threatens the coherence of judicial review. As Jeffrey Jowell

[97] Michael Taggart, 'Proportionality, Deference, *Wednesbury*' [2008] NZLR 423, 460.
[98] *R (ProLife Alliance) v British Broadcasting Corporation* [2003] UKHL 23, para 75.
[99] Ibid, para 76.

observes, conceding competence to another branch of government, when necessary, is not, in Lord Hoffmann's formalistic sense, a matter of law or legal principle:

> Lord Hoffmann is right that it is for the courts to decide the scope of rights, but there is no magic legal or other formula to identify the 'discretionary area of judgement' available to the reviewed body. In deciding whether matters such as national security, or public interest, or morals should be permitted to prevail... the courts must consider not only the rational exercise of discretion by the reviewed body but also the imperatives of a rights-based democracy.[100]

In the *Rehman* case, which concerned the deportation of an alien alleged to have links with terrorist groups operating abroad, Lord Hoffmann invoked the separation of powers in aid of a sharp distinction between executive and judicial concerns.[101] Whereas the meaning of 'national security' was a question of law for the court, the question of whether Rehman's deportation was 'in the interests of national security' (for purposes of the Immigration Act 1971, section 15) was a matter of 'judgement and policy', entrusted to the executive. Accordingly, the Special Immigration Appeals Commission had very limited power to overrule the Home Secretary on whether a person's support for terrorism abroad was a sufficient reason to deport him from the United Kingdom. Admittedly, Lord Hoffmann recognized that the Commission could intervene on the ground that there was no evidential basis for the minister's conclusions about the facts, or if the decision was wholly unreasonable; but there was little recognition that the distinction between law and policy should be sensitive to all the circumstances. The fairness of deportation must depend on a comparative appraisal of risk to national security, which might be very modest, and the humanitarian considerations likely to weigh heavily against it. Even if the Secretary of State is 'in the best position to judge what national security requires',[102] an independent and impartial appeal tribunal is better placed to decide whether, all things considered, the individual concerned has been fairly treated.[103]

A systematic doctrine of judicial deference, curtailing the scope of judicial review by reference to general considerations of institutional competence or legitimacy, would be tantamount to endorsing Lord Hoffmann's rigid conceptual approach. Instead of the separation of powers reflecting a careful analysis of claims of legal right in particular cases, permitting matters of law and policy to be disentangled in the light of all the facts, that principle would enjoy doctrinal priority—as if the preservation of clearly defined competences were of greater importance than vindicating constitutional rights. Such an approach betrays an anxiety that applying

---

[100] Jeffrey Jowell, 'Judicial Deference: Servility, Civility or Institutional Capacity?' [2003] PL 592–601, at 599 (quoting a term used by A Lester and D Pannick (eds), *Human Rights Law and Practice* (London: Butterworths, 1999), para 3.21). See also Jeffrey Jowell, 'Judicial Deference and Human Rights: A Question of Competence', in Paul Craig and Richard Rawlings (eds), *Law and Administration in Europe: Essays in Honour of Carol Harlow* (Oxford: Oxford University Press, 2003), 71–5.

[101] *Secretary of State for the Home Dept v Rehman* [2001] UKHL 47, paras 50–4.

[102] Ibid, para 26.

[103] Compare David Feldman, 'Human Rights, Terrorism and Risk: The Roles of Politicians and Judges' [2006] PL 364–84, especially 372–82.

a proportionality test to legislation or administrative action makes the court an arbiter of the public interest, forcing Parliament or Government to act as the court itself would act, if charged with similar functions. English judges were at one time fearful that a proportionality test would undermine the courts' detachment from politics or policy, involving 'a review of the merits of the decision' and risking 'an abuse of power by the judiciary'.[104] As I have argued, however, the proportionality test is already implicit in any proper judgement of the reasonableness or rationality of an interference with basic rights; and it does not obliterate the distinction between appeal and review. The appropriate safeguard against abuse of judicial power is an insistence on perspicacious and perspicuous legal reasoning, laying bare all the elements of the proportionality analysis for public inspection and criticism.

When the various stages of the proportionality test are identified, distinguishing clearly between questions of necessity (as regards the feasibility of alternative actions, less injurious to rights) and 'narrow' proportionality (comparing respective gains and losses), judicial reasoning can be more tightly structured: the plausibility of the relevant judgements of fact and value can be more readily appraised. In judging a governmental claim that no course of action less restrictive of the complainant's interests would have been as effective in securing the ends in view, the court must often defer to superior expertise. In principle, the question of necessity 'admits of only one correct answer (unless there are several ways of achieving the objective, all... equally, and minimally, restrictive of the right)'.[105] But judges are reliant on expert evidence as to what the correct answer is: 'To the extent that there is expertise, judges are correct to rely on the executive as part of "getting it right".'[106]

Questions of value-judgement, pertinent to concerns about democratic legitimacy, arise chiefly in relation to the narrow proportionality issue: does the attainment of the specific governmental objective justify the consequent damage to rights-protected interests, even if such damage is necessary? Once again, steadfast attention to the issue of legality, as it relates to the specific context, is sufficient to guide judicial decision-making. Any necessary deference here is the result of recognizing that, in some circumstances, there may be legitimate scope for disagreement: there will be no unlawful violation of rights within the limits of reasonable judgement. Unlike the case of deference to superior expertise, there may simply be no uniquely right answer to the correct accommodation of competing, and arguably incommensurable, interests—or none that the court can demonstrate to be correct.[107] We do not challenge the constitutional structure of rights, whose integrity must be the courts' primary concern, by granting that, in some circumstances,

---

[104] *R v Secretary of State for the Home Dept, ex p Brind* [1991] 1 AC 696, 758, 763 (Lord Ackner).
[105] Mark Elliott, 'Proportionality and Deference: The Importance of a Structured Approach', in Christopher Forsyth, Mark Elliott & others (eds), *Effective Judicial Review: A Cornerstone of Good Governance* (Oxford: Oxford University Press, 2010), 264–86, at 273.
[106] Julian Rivers, 'Proportionality and Variable Intensity of Review' [2006] CLJ 174–207, at 200.
[107] Elliott, 'Proportionality and Deference', 283.

there is scope for political judgement about their correct application, responsive to the complexity of social and economic affairs.[108]

Appropriately rigorous clarification of these separate questions removes any need for an independent doctrine of deference, which would either replicate them pointlessly or erect an artificial barrier to review, insensitive to the specific context. If the degree of deference required is whatever is indicated by the court's inability to match the expertise of the public authority, or whatever the legitimate scope of governmental discretion demands in all the circumstances, it is secured by proper application of the ordinary criteria of legality. The tests of rationality or proportionality subsume the issue of deference, leaving any special deference doctrine empty. If it is agreed that questions of 'relative expertise or authority' are irrelevant to the correct 'definition' of a constitutional right, which must be a matter of law for the court alone, but relevant instead to questions of concrete application, talk of a 'doctrine of deference' is mistaken.[109] We should not suppose that the application of rights to particular cases may be 'indeterminate', but rather that such rights may, on correct analysis, leave open more than one lawful course of action. That is merely to concede that there is, in such circumstances, no uniquely right answer to the complex problems of governance and administration arising; the correct answer, as a matter of law, is that any challenge to the legality of governmental action is misconceived.

If, as Laws LJ has suggested, there should be 'greater deference' paid to an Act of Parliament than to an executive decision or 'subordinate measure', it must be because in all the circumstances the statute reflects or embodies an expertise that the court cannot match.[110] Insofar as questions about public opinion or public confidence (for example, in the administration of justice) are relevant to a question of legality, Parliament's representative character plainly gives it an advantage. And its various facilities for investigation and debate can sometimes justify ascribing weight to legislative policy choices that have implications for constitutional rights. In *Huang*, Lord Bingham declined to give weight to the balance between individual and collective interests struck by the Immigration Rules, observing that they were 'not the product of active debate in Parliament, where non-nationals seeking leave to enter or remain are not in any event represented'.[111] He rejected any analogy

---

[108] In *R (Quila) v Secretary of State for the Home Dept* [2011] UKSC 45, Lord Brown (para 91) appeared to think that the attempt to prevent forced marriages by raising the age at which a British national could sponsor a fiancée or spouse seeking admission to the UK from 18 to 21 raised incommensurable issues: 'What value…is to be attached to preventing a single forced marriage? What cost should each disappointed couple be regarded as paying?' His conclusion that these were questions of policy for Government rather than courts, however, exhibited an exaggerated deference in all the circumstances: there was little evidence to suppose that the new restrictions, which were plainly a serious interference with Art 8 rights, would have any significant benefits (as the Supreme Court majority observed). Even if the respective interests were incommensurable in the abstract, they were susceptible to a balanced comparative judgement in the light of available evidence about the effects of the measure impugned.

[109] Alison L Young, 'In Defence of Due Deference' (2009) 72 MLR 554–80, at 575.

[110] See *International Transport Roth GmbH v Secretary of State for the Home Dept* [2002] EWCA Civ 158, paras 81–7. Laws LJ's various principles of deference exemplify the problematic nature of such doctrine, offering generalizations as a substitute for reasoning more finely tuned to the facts of individual cases: see further Allan, 'Human Rights and Judicial Review', at 674–6.

[111] *Huang v Secretary of State for the Home Dept* [2007] UKHL 11, para 17.

with the 'considered democratic compromise' embodied in legislation concerning the lease of property:

> Domestic housing policy has been a continuing subject of discussion and debate in Parliament over very many years, with the competing interests of landlords and tenants fully represented, as also the public interest in securing accommodation for the indigent, averting homelessness and making the best use of finite public resources.[112]

There is, however, no basis for any special deference to Parliament on the mere ground of its members' elected status: a representative body is as fully capable of infringing basic rights as any other; and the court's duty is to interpret its enactments (as far as possible) consistently with those rights, even if that interpretation departs significantly from 'ordinary' meaning.[113] In the Belmarsh internment case (discussed in Chapter 3, above) Lord Bingham explicitly repudiated the idea of deference based on the court's unelected membership, observing that 'the function of independent judges charged to interpret and apply the law is universally recognized as a cardinal feature of the modern democratic state, a cornerstone of the rule of law itself'.[114]

If it is true that a court should sometimes 'recognize that there is an area of judgement within which the judiciary will defer, on democratic grounds, to the considered opinion of the elected body or person whose act or decision' is impugned, as Lord Hope of Craighead has observed, it must be because, on correct analysis, fundamental rights *accord* such leeway in all the circumstances.[115] They are compatible with a range of decisions, each consistent with the fair treatment of those affected. The relevant 'area of judgement', however, depends on an appraisal of all the circumstances: the breadth of lawful judgement or discretion is discovered by analysis of the reasons for and against upholding the constitutional challenge presented. Whether or not, in the context of a mandatory sentence of life imprisonment for murder, for example, 'a degree of deference is due to the judgment of a democratic assembly on how a particular social problem is best tackled', depends on whether a plausible case can be made for singling out murder as a uniquely heinous crime, demanding a distinctive form of public denunciation.[116] Even then, the pertinent 'area of judgement' is limited by basic principles of liberty. As administered in practice, a mandatory life sentence does not prevent the release of the prisoner on the expiry of his 'tariff', which marks the true extent of the punishment deserved for the specific crime, unless he continues to pose a danger to the public welfare. If it were really the case, as sometimes contended, that a convicted

---

[112] Ibid (distinguishing *Lambeth LBC v Kay* [2006] UKHL 10).

[113] See Chapter 5, above.

[114] *A v Secretary of State for the Home Dept* [2004] UKHL 56, para 42, citing Jeffrey Jowell, 'Judicial Deference: Servility, Civility or Institutional Capacity?', at 597: 'The courts are charged by Parliament with delineating the boundaries of a rights-based democracy'. See also Hickman, *Public Law after the Human Rights Act*, 156–67.

[115] *R v Director of Public Prosecutions, ex p Kebilene* [2000] 2 AC 326, 380.

[116] *R v Lichniak* [2002] UKHL 47, para 14 (Lord Bingham, who accepted the view 'that the mandatory penalty for murder has a denunciatory value, expressing society's view of a crime which has long been regarded with peculiar abhorrence').

murderer simply forfeited his liberty to the state for the rest of his life—his release on licence being a matter of unfettered ministerial discretion—the legality of such a draconian regime would be very much more doubtful.

It is not, then, the subject matter of the pertinent governmental action, taken alone, that determines the nature or scope of judicial review, but rather the power of the legal challenge in all the circumstances. If the 'area of judgement' is treated literally, as a zone of political discretion immune from legal challenge (whether based on subject matter or special expertise or any other general criterion) it would amount to a principle of *non-justiciability*: the courts would be wholly excluded from an inviolable realm of pure political determination. It would be directly analogous to the idea of non-justiciable prerogative powers invoked in the *GCHQ* case, where the House of Lords suggested that certain kinds of prerogative power were inherently immune from judicial supervision.[117] And we cannot distinguish for these purposes between cases involving 'questions of social or economic policy' and those where the legal rights are 'of high constitutional importance or of a kind where courts are especially well placed to assess the need for protection'.[118] Any individual case may involve a complex mix of such different matters; and the development or implementation of social policy may, in particular circumstances, generate questions of legal and constitutional right that require judicial resolution.

Other writers have recognized the danger that a doctrine of deference will collapse in practice into a doctrine of non-justiciability, leaving regions of governmental decision-making invulnerable to legal challenge no matter what the circumstances giving rise to concern or complaint. Murray Hunt has rightly observed that 'much of the progress of modern public law has been in rolling back what were formerly considered to be zones of immunity from judicial review'.[119] The reasons for judicial restraint have instead been reintegrated into substantive public law as 'considerations which affect the particular, contextualized application of what have increasingly become accepted as universally applicable general principles'—a hard won victory for the rule of law, but 'constantly threatened by the failure to ground deference theory in anything other than crudely formalistic notions of the separation of powers and the supposed continued sovereignty of Parliament'.

In seeking to substitute a doctrine of 'due deference' for the defective 'spatial approach', however, Hunt ignores the logic of his own critique. Either the various considerations commending judicial deference are 'contextualized', wholly dependent on all the circumstances of the particular case, or they can be marshalled and applied independently, as a distinct and separate judicial process. On the former approach, the relevant considerations merely counsel judicial caution, reminding us of the limitations of legal process and judicial expertise. The latter approach, which amounts to a genuine doctrine of deference, raises a barrier to judicial review in certain sorts of case or in respect of certain kinds of challenge: when the

---

[117] *Council of Civil Service Unions v Minister for the Civil Service* [1985] AC 374; see Chapter 2, above, for discussion of justiciability in the context of judicial review.
[118] *Kebilene* [2000] 2 AC 326, 380 (Lord Hope).
[119] Hunt, 'Sovereignty's Blight', 347.

various criteria apply, governmental action becomes, in effect, non-justiciable. The distinction between legitimate deference, on the one hand, and a dubious doctrine of non-justiciability, on the other, is precisely the distinction between the ordinary process of review, sensitive to context, and separate doctrinal regimentation of general reasons for restraint, curtailing judicial review.[120]

On Hunt's model, a range of factors are deemed relevant to an inquiry into the appropriate degree of deference: they include, in addition to the nature of the right asserted and the particular constitutional context, the comparative expertise of decision-maker and court, as well as the 'relative institutional competence of the primary decision-maker', by comparison with the suitability of the court's adjudicative process to determine the matters in issue.[121] The 'deference inquiry' should also take notice of the 'degree of democratic accountability of the original decision-maker, and the extent to which other mechanisms of accountability may be available in the increasingly layered context in which power is exercised in contemporary conditions'.[122] While the fact that a decision has been made by a democratically accountable authority cannot be determinative, in a democratic society 'a reviewing court should give careful consideration to whether other avenues of accountability are available and more appropriate, and to how well democratic mechanisms are working in practice when deciding the degree of deference which is due to a decision-maker'.

The extent to which considerations of expertise and competence should constrain or circumscribe judicial deliberation, however, must depend on all the circumstances; and the proper limits of judicial inquiry cannot be determined as an independent matter, divorced from those circumstances. We cannot know *in advance* how far a judicial inquiry should press: everything depends on the nature of the complaint of illegality and the complexity and cogency of the reasons put forward by way of defence. Judges should bow to superior expertise only when they are satisfied that further inquiry would be futile, the proffered justification having proved resilient in the face of attack. These matters cannot be elevated into a doctrine of deference that operates independently of the relevant issues of substance; such a doctrine would have no content unless it amounted, in practice, to a principle of non-justiciability.[123] Nor are considerations of democratic accountability qualified to displace the ordinary rigour of judicial review in defence of legal and constitutional rights. A judge who accedes to a governmental decision of doubtful legality, on the grounds that the complainant has other potential avenues of redress, abdicates his responsibility to uphold the rule of law.

---

[120] See further Allan, 'Judicial Deference and Judicial Review: Legal Doctrine and Legal Theory' (2011) 127 LQR 96–117.

[121] Hunt, 'Sovereignty's Blight', 353.

[122] Ibid, 354.

[123] There is an analogy here with Cass Sunstein's attempt to block judicial resort to abstract theory by confining adjudication to narrow or 'low-level' principles, considered in Chapter 8, below: Cass R Sunstein, *Legal Reasoning and Political Conflict* (New York: Oxford University Press, 1996).

A doctrine of judicial deference would be necessary to preserve the separation of powers if the courts were otherwise entitled simply to substitute their own opinions for those of ministers or other public authorities, confusing the rule of law with government by the judiciary. Limited to a focus on questions of legality, however, courts apply the tests of rationality and proportionality that the rule of law identifies. Questions of expertise and competence are often relevant to the application of those tests. A court must hesitate to condemn as unlawful a course of action that may, when examined in the light of relevant expert knowledge, applied to the facts by an appropriately crafted procedure, be shown to be necessary and justified. The extent of the court's reliance on such expertise will vary, however, from case to case. Since, moreover, tests of rationality and proportionality do not permit judges to usurp governmental discretion, properly exercised within jurisdictional limits, they preserve the necessary constitutional boundaries. Requirements of deference are, then, already built into the doctrinal structure of judicial review, implicit in the ordinary tests of legality.[124]

In rejecting, as unnecessary mystification, arguments about 'due deference, discretionary areas of judgement, the margin of appreciation, democratic accountability, relative institutional competence', and such-like, Lord Bingham was simply resisting doctrinal regimentation of matters that present themselves—from an internal, interpretative standpoint—as implicit features of ordinary judicial deliberation.[125] In an immigration case, a wide range of considerations bearing on the fairness of a refusal of leave to enter or remain must be weighed. The minister's reasons may encompass both general considerations of effective immigration control and more specific reasons, applicable to the sort of case in view:

The giving of weight to factors such as these is not...aptly described as deference: it is performance of the ordinary judicial task of weighing up the competing considerations on each side and according appropriate weight to the judgement of a person with responsibility for a given subject matter and access to special sources of knowledge and advice.[126]

Since matters of weight are inherently dependent on all the circumstances, immune to predetermined doctrinal control, deference doctrine adds only complexity and mystification, duplicating elements of legal reasoning already engaged by conscientious resolution of a complaint of illegality.

We should not suppose, then, that judges have two quite distinct obligations in public law: first, to 'evaluate the legal issues on their merits', and secondly, to

---

[124] Tom Hickman also defends a 'non-doctrinal' approach to deference, noting the 'inherently fact-sensitive nature of this feature of decision-making': Hickman, *Public Law after the Human Rights Act*, 137. His critique of my own approach at 141–3 wrongly supposes that it allows 'deference factors' to 'influence the judicial interpretation of the right in question', altering the scope of the right. My argument, like his own, was intended merely to insist that such factors operate legitimately only in determining whether the right is infringed *in all the circumstances*; they should not operate independently, as second-order considerations that specify a distinct judicial approach or standard of review.

[125] *Huang*, para 14.

[126] Ibid, para 16 (Lord Bingham of Cornhill); see also Hickman, *Public Law after the Human Rights Act*, 130–45.

'consider questions of relative institutional competence, expertise and legitimacy'.[127] If these obligations were really separate, a court could properly decline to intervene in defence of legal rights, leaving the complainant without protection: 'institutional concerns' would 'sometimes outweigh the judge's view about the correct substantive outcome'.[128] The supposed doctrine of deference would indeed have collapsed into a non-justiciability doctrine: legal remedies would be withheld for extraneous reasons, irrelevant to the applicable legal principles. The notion that there might be a 'correct substantive outcome', identifiable by judges quite independently of considerations of expertise and legitimacy, is the result of overlooking the ordinary distinction between appeal and review. When courts are confined to review, judging governmental decisions on grounds of legality rather than political wisdom, their conclusions will perforce reflect constitutional constraints: answers to the questions of relative expertise and legitimacy are implicit within any findings of illegality. The correct substantive outcome is whatever conclusion follows from careful analysis of the legal issues arising, when the law is accurately applied to the evidence that the court accepts.

Any independent doctrine of deference must be built on a division between *first-order* considerations of substance or content and *second-order* considerations of institutional design, such as the goal of democratic accountability. While such distinctions may be illuminating as a matter of purely descriptive legal theory, they can easily lead us astray if we use them to draw normative conclusions, embodied in legal doctrine. Dimitrios Kyritsis has argued that a judge, as a conscientious state official, should often be willing to accept a legislative or governmental decision even when he thinks that the balance of first-order considerations supports a different outcome.[129] It is rational to trade a minor gain on the first-order side of the balance for a major second-order value, the enhancement of democracy. All this shows, however, is that judges should defer to other officials when those officials act *within their jurisdiction*; and an official body exceeds its jurisdiction, not only when it interferes in matters outside its remit, but also when it infringes constitutional rights or commits other serious legal errors. All relevant second-order considerations for deference are incorporated into the ordinary judicial process: they are made internal to adjudication by acknowledging the scope for legitimate, if limited, official discretion.

From the perspective of judicial analysis, there is no distinction between first-order and second-order considerations because the question of legality differs from appraisal of the merits. A judge's view of the *desirability* of a measure is irrelevant, except insofar as its necessity is pertinent to a question of proportionality. Nor could he usually form any *opinion* about its desirability without reliance on the evidence and arguments submitted by the parties to the litigation. Since the court

---

[127] Aileen Kavanagh, 'Defending Deference in Public Law and Constitutional Theory' (2010) 126 LQR 222–50, at 231.
[128] Ibid.
[129] Dimitrios Kyritsis, 'What is Good about Legal Conventionalism?' (2008) 14 *Legal Theory* 135–66, at 156–65.

has no independent basis for reaching any conclusions on the merits, being unable to conduct its own inquiries into the virtues of rival policies, it cannot juxtapose the argument of the public authority in defence of a measure with any separate judicial appraisal, comparing the extent of overlap or divergence. So the court cannot gauge an appropriate level of deference based on the 'severity of the rights violation', or the 'degree of confidence' it has in its own assessment, among other questions about 'the limits of judicial expertise and legitimacy'.[130] The severity of the rights violation, if any, and the court's confidence about its own conclusions are matters that depend on the judicial process itself, in which the court must assess the evidence and arguments presented by the parties to the best of its ability. Accordingly, all questions of expertise and legitimacy are wholly *internal* to ordinary legal analysis, based on the established tests of legality: there is no separate conceptual space for any doctrine of deference to occupy.[131]

VI

In a thoughtful and wide-ranging critique of both formalist and 'non-doctrinal' approaches to judicial review, Jeff King defends an 'institutional' approach to judicial restraint.[132] Formalism relies too heavily on such abstract categories as 'law', 'politics', and 'policy', treated as capable of defining the judicial role without further contextual analysis; sharp distinctions between law and politics, or principle and policy, lack the requisite subtlety to sustain a defensible judicial role. Non-doctrinal approaches, by contrast, rely too much on judicial discretion, leaving judges to determine the appropriate degree of restraint on a case-by-case basis. Such reliance on unregulated discretion, it is alleged, not only underestimates the possibility of judicial error, but is arbitrary and unpredictable: it offends 'our sense of being governed by the rule of law and legal principle, rather than the capacious discretion of some official'.[133]

If King were right about the dangers of non-doctrinal approaches, we would have good reason to reconsider our objections to the supposed doctrine of deference, and no doubt also our scepticism about different standards of review, expressing

---

[130] Kavanagh, 'Defending Deference', 226.
[131] A similar sort of second-order doctrine is proposed by B V Harris in relation to what he describes as 'the inherently discretionary determination of justiciability as a prerequisite to judicial review': B V Harris, 'Judicial Review, Justiciability and the Prerogative of Mercy' [2003] CLJ 631–60, at 635. His 'generic model' consists of various considerations, such as whether or not accountability is 'best facilitated by the courts' and whether the judicial process is suitable for the decision-making role envisaged (ibid, 637). What from an external, descriptive stance may be regarded as an exercise of discretion based on various criteria, detached from specific complaints of unlawful administrative action, may be understood quite differently by the judge, whose overriding commitment is (or should be) to do justice according to law. Harris's approach appears to reintroduce via 'secondary' justiciability what he accepts is illegitimate in the case of 'primary' justiciability—the exemption of certain types of decision from the constraints of the rule of law.
[132] Jeff A King, 'Institutional Approaches to Judicial Restraint' (2008) 28 OJLS 409–41.
[133] Ibid, 411.

divergent levels of 'intensity' or degrees of scrutiny. We do better, however, to challenge his premise. The judicial enforcement of rights may make great intellectual demands on judges, who are required to exercise *judgement* in what may often be finely balanced disputes, but it does not involve *discretion*, in the sense in which other state officials may enjoy a legitimate freedom of choice between competing alternatives.[134] Faced with a complaint that a public authority has violated a legal or constitutional right, the court must determine whether or not it is justified. The possibility that the court may have to appraise the quality of expert opinion (perhaps on the suitability of alternative courses of governmental action) does not alter its responsibility to decide, after careful review, whether the right in question has been unjustifiably curtailed. If the court gives weight to the experience and expertise of a public authority, it does so only insofar as its own relative ignorance appears to require it.

Nor is that responsibility diminished by the possibility that a proportionality test may confront the need to balance competing (even incommensurable) values. Insofar as there is scope for reasonable disagreement about whether an interference with rights is proportionate to the relevant aim—assuming that no less intrusive a measure is feasible—the court must affirm the legality of the measure impugned. The court can intervene only when a public authority has exceeded the limits of legitimate political choice, whether of ends or means: it cannot properly usurp the pertinent legislative or executive discretion. The fact that lawyers and judges, like other citizens and officials, will often *disagree* about whether or not a fundamental right has been unfairly qualified does not establish the existence of judicial discretion, in the sense of political choice. Their disagreement, if it makes any sense, is about whether a complaint of injustice (or infringement of rights) is true or false; and if it is not true, because the action impugned fell within the proper scope of official discretion, then it must be false.

King objects to 'the prominence given to right answers' as the basis of a non-doctrinal approach, observing that 'there is vast disagreement about the meaning of rights and justice', a problem compounded by that of judicial fallibility: 'Any theory putting such great emphasis on the objective nature of rights is bound to licence the imposition of judicial values to a greater than desirable or credible extent.'[135] Now, the problem of judicial fallibility is undeniable, and it certainly counsels caution and humility in the face of what may be highly complex and hotly contested legal disputes. But to reject the idea of right answers even in principle is misguided. If disagreement about the nature and content of rights, or the basic elements of constitutional justice, were too great to permit adjudication to proceed with any shred of moral authority—judicial decisions being widely rejected as nothing more than the expression of personal predilection or partisan affiliation—we should have to abandon judicial review and therewith much of the protection of the rule of law. It is important to remember that moral disagreement

---

[134] Ronald Dworkin distinguishes between 'strong' and 'weak' discretion, the latter alluding merely to the necessary exercise of judgement: *Taking Rights Seriously* (London: Duckworth, 1977), 31–9.
[135] King, 'Institutional Approaches', 413.

in the present context refers chiefly to disagreement about the application to particular cases of general principles which, when formulated at a more abstract level, usually command wide assent. In interpreting a flourishing constitutional tradition, respectful of individual liberty, the process of law affords a means of resolving moral disagreement in a piecemeal, evolutionary manner—constrained if not wholly constricted by precedent.

In its emphasis on 'incrementalism'—the principle that cases should be decided, where possible, on 'narrow rather than sweeping grounds'—King's own theory dovetails with common law constitutionalism: 'Reasoning by analogy, following precedent, and deciding cases on narrow grounds are all familiar tools of the common law judge.'[136] Furthermore, King defends 'contextual institutionalism' against a more 'restrictive institutionalism', which severely restrict the judicial role by 'bright line' rules about justiciability. Contextual institutionalists, having greater faith in the power of ideas and the value of human rights, believe that judges can be trusted to balance institutional factors in the course of adjudication.[137] An institutional approach offers various principles of judicial restraint relating to such matters as expertise and democratic legitimacy; but when these principles point in different directions, as they often will, the judge should try to 'balance and adjust' their application, employing an intuitive sense of justice.[138] A proper scepticism is reserved for Laws LJ's attempt to formulate general principles of deference in *Roth*.[139] And it is observed that a rather similar catalogue, aimed at gauging deference for the purposes of the proportionality inquiry under the Canadian Charter of Rights, section 1, has not 'caught on as a freestanding deference test'.[140]

In the result, it must be doubted whether, in rightly rejecting formalism, King has nevertheless 'travelled considerable distance' from the non-doctrinal approach, as he claims. Instead, he appears to offer a largely external, analytic description of an adjudicative process that, from an internal, interpretative viewpoint, is substantially 'non-doctrinal'. Significantly, Iacobucci J's judgment in the Canadian Supreme Court in *M v H* is cited as an effective rejoinder to Bastarache J's notion of free-standing principles of deference:

The question of deference... is intimately tied up with the nature of the particular claim or evidence at issue and not in the general application of the s. 1 test; it can only be discussed in relation to such specific claims or evidence and not at the outset of the analysis.[141]

The institutional approach differs from the non-doctrinal alternative, according to King, on the ground that non-doctrinal approaches are 'often set off against a background theory of right answers and a robust, anti-majoritarian conception of rights'; but judges adjudicating claims of right are inevitably concerned to find correct answers to questions about the limits, in context, of the powers of public officials, both elected and unelected.

---

[136] Ibid, 429.   [137] Ibid, 430.   [138] Ibid, 437.

[139] *International Transport Roth* [2002] EWCA Civ 158, paras 81–7.

[140] King, 'Institutional Approaches', 434–5; see Bastarache J's judgment in *M v H* [1999] 2 SCR 3.

[141] *M v H* [1999] 2 SCR 3, para 79; see King, 'Institutional Approaches', 439–40.

Insofar, moreover, as the familiar distinction between principle and policy is employed in support of arid conceptual formalism, we need have no quarrel with King's critique.[142] Ronald Dworkin distinguishes a standard that dictates a social or economic goal for the community in general (policy) from one that represents a 'requirement of justice or fairness or some other dimension of morality' (principle).[143] Whereas a court provides the 'forum of principle', matters of policy are remitted to the determination of the political branches of government, ensuring democratic accountability.[144] But since the consequences of a measure may be relevant to an argument about its consistency with justice or fairness, as Dworkin readily concedes, his distinction may be difficult to apply in practice; and King objects that the associated allocation of functions is too rigidly conceived: judges and legislators alike must often address both kinds of standard.

Dworkin is chiefly concerned to defend judicially enforced constraints on the pursuit of a broadly utilitarian approach to government: individual rights are 'trumps' over policies that seek to maximize the general happiness or welfare, conceived in a purely aggregative manner (harms to some being outweighed by the greater benefits for others). If, instead, we define the common good or the general welfare as the conditions that secure justice or freedom for all, there is no stark opposition between welfare and justice, or policy and principle. Legislation that limits the enjoyment of certain rights for the public good may be conceived as an attempt to reconcile competing rights: the liberty of suspected terrorists (for example) may be curtailed when necessary to preserve the lives and liberty of their potential victims. In deciding, moreover, whether restrictions on liberty are proportionate to legitimate ends the court must take account of estimates of risk: the relevant determinations of justice are dependent on complex factual assessments, which the court must appraise, if only at second hand.

The distinction between principle and policy may be reinterpreted, however, as marking the difference between the requirements of justice, encapsulated in the principles of public law, and the sphere of governmental discretion that remains when those requirements are met. In the realm of public law, the distinction replicates the familiar division between the legality of a measure and its substantive merits: the court's role is to determine the question of legality without intruding on what is properly a sphere of political judgement or choice. It is a distinction inherent in the idea of constitutional equality: the rule of law requires government to treat all alike in respect of the basic rights of citizenship, imposing constraints on officials' ability to discriminate between persons for public ends. It may, of course, be a legitimate complaint in any particular case that the distinction between principle and policy, or between legality and the merits, has been invoked as a substitute for analysis rather than as an aid to it. But the vice of conceptual formalism must be fought by insistence on better argument and analysis: our conceptual distinctions

---

[142] King, 'Institutional Approaches', 416–19.
[143] Ronald Dworkin, *Taking Rights Seriously*, 22.
[144] Ronald Dworkin, *A Matter of Principle* (Oxford: Oxford University Press, 1985), ch 2.

are only as valuable as their utility in explaining and supporting our normative judgements in particular cases.

It is a legitimate complaint against enacted bills of rights, by contrast with common law rights, that they can readily obscure these points by giving textual priority to certain rights, thereby depreciating (or appearing to depreciate) other rights and legitimate interests, which will sometimes be of equal or greater strength in particular circumstances. It is only a very abstract, if important, right to 'respect for...private and family life' that precludes interference by a public authority except where it is 'necessary in a democratic society in the interests of national security, public safety or the economic well-being of the country, for the prevention of disorder or crime, for the protection of health or morals' or, even more broadly, 'for the protection of the rights and freedoms of others'.[145] And there is only a breach of this right when an 'interference' is *not* justified as being 'necessary in a democratic society' for any of the general categories of reason listed. In view of the breadth of the permissible grounds for restriction of liberty it makes little sense to suppose that privacy (abstractly defined) could enjoy any automatic precedence. The proper balance between competing interests must be a function of all the circumstances, even if the burden of justification ultimately lies with the public authority.[146] When we recall that the various public or collective interests are readily equated with the rights or interests of individuals, which may clash with those seeking to defend their privacy, we can see that such an enactment adds very little, if anything, to the ordinary course of practical reasoning required (on correct understanding) by the common law.

It is easy to understand the objection that judicial enforcement of the Convention rights apparently passes to the judiciary a responsibility properly left to the legislature: the court must '*choose commitments*, backed by legal compulsion' in relation to numerous aspects of the common good.[147] Such judicial choosing, in exercise of a general discretion to determine the public interest, would of course be inconsistent with the rule of law: the courts are confined to discerning the demands of legal principle within a specific legislative or administrative context, when genuine questions arise about the fairness of the burdens imposed on particular persons or groups. But no general doctrine of deference or restraint can serve to secure the necessary division between principle and policy, or legality and the political merits. The only effective remedy against judicial overreaching into areas of policy, on the one hand, or judicial passivity in the face of unwarranted interference with rights, on the other, is an insistence on clearly articulated legal reasons, allowing for inspection and criticism of judicial decisions (and, when appropriate, appeal

---

[145] European Convention on Human Rights, Art 8.

[146] It is generally taken for granted, for example, that imprisonment for an offence (or even remand in custody) does not infringe Art 8, the proportionality of such detention being treated as axiomatic: see *Norris v United States (No 2)* [2010] UKSC 9, paras 52–4 (Lord Phillips). Not all interferences with privacy or family life amount to breaches of *respect* for those values, having regard to the context in point.

[147] J M Finnis, 'A Bill of Rights for Britain? The Moral of Contemporary Jurisprudence' (1985) 71 *Proceedings of the British Academy* 303–31, at 328.

and reversal). If adoption of a bill of rights inevitably led to usurpation of the role of the legislature, we should have to conclude, implausibly, that development and enforcement of the ordinary common law had the same effect.

An overly rigid application of the distinction between formal definition of a right, on the one hand, and grounds for legitimate qualification or restriction, on the other, can certainly generate confusion. As Bradley Miller argues, the distinction invites a crude principle–policy dichotomy, premised on the mistaken idea that all relevant qualifications reflect an aggregated collective interest rather than the countervailing rights and interests of individuals.[148] He offers the two-stage reasoning adopted by the Canadian Supreme Court, when applying the Canadian Charter of Rights and Freedoms, as an instructive example. According to the approach favoured in *Oakes*, once the complainant has established that state action affects his prima facie Charter rights, it is for the government to show that the 'infringement' or 'violation' is nevertheless justified under section 1, which guarantees the asserted rights and freedoms 'subject only to such reasonable limits prescribed by law as can be demonstrably justified in a free and democratic society'.[149] But since such reasonable and justified limits constitute part of the correct definition or scope of Charter rights, these rights cannot in any true sense be *violated* when such limits apply in any particular case:

The alternative reading—that reasonable limits are inherent in the rights themselves—would have avoided the conceptual muddle of asserting that something that is *justified* can be judged to be, all things considered, an infringement of someone's right. . . . Argument at this second stage of s. 1 analysis is best understood, not as a *justification* of a right *violation*, but as the *defeat* of the claim of right, having considered the competing claims and entitlements of others.[150]

The conceptual muddle is hardly conducive to sound adjudication, giving full weight to all relevant rights and interests. A constitutional right to the equal protection of the law is, moreover, particularly unsuited to such a rigid, formalistic approach because it amounts to nothing more than a reassertion of the rule of law. The prohibition of 'discrimination based on race, national or ethnic origin, colour, religion, sex, age or mental or physical disability' is already implicit in the ideal of fairness to which the principle of legality aspires.[151] All kinds of discrimination which cannot be justified, having regard to the legitimate ends in view and the equal status of persons, are necessarily abhorrent to democratic constitutionalism and violate the rule of law. So it makes little sense to have regard to questions of the common good under section 1 only *after* an initial finding of discrimination

---

[148] Bradley W Miller, 'Justification and Rights Limitations', in Grant Huscroft (ed), *Expounding the Constitution: Essays in Constitutional Theory* (Cambridge: Cambridge University Press, 2008), 93–115.

[149] *R v Oakes* [1986] 1 SCR 103, paras 62–71 (Dickson CJ).

[150] Miller, 'Justification and Rights Limitations', 96. Miller also calls attention to the remarkable suggestion by Bastarache J that 'the government's burden under s 1 is to justify a breach of human dignity', as if such a justification were conceivable, contrary to the whole idea of government under law (see *Lavoie v Canada* [2002] 1 SCR 769, para 48).

[151] Canadian Charter of Rights, s 15(1).

under section 15. The notion that the court should seek to differentiate between a legitimate 'distinction' and improper 'discrimination', independently of the broader inquiry, is quite misleading: it overlooks the necessarily value-laden and highly contextual analysis involved in any finding of impermissible discrimination.[152]

The closer judicial reasoning comes to common law reasoning, sensitive to all the relevant considerations that bear on the particular case, the safer the course a constitutional court is likely to steer between the numerous obstacles to good judgement. And that conclusion reinforces our earlier objections to an unduly formalist understanding of common law rights, dependent on rigid conceptual distinctions or categories. There is a delicate balance to be attained between democratic decision-making by an elected legislature, or its executive agents, on the one hand, and enforcement of the rule of law in defence of fundamental rights, on the other. But its attainment depends on the considered and conscientious responses of all officials, elected and non-elected, to the requirements of reason as they apply in particular cases and specific contexts; it cannot be achieved by adding new layers of legal doctrine, independent of those particularities and contexts, and hence disconnected from the substance of claims of right and the facts and judgements on which they rely.

Perhaps the reader will be disconcerted by reference to the 'requirements of reason', which implies a confidence in the objectivity of legal and moral argument that he or she may not share. It is easy to assume, without reflection, that there cannot be right answers to questions that give rise to disagreement between competent and well-informed lawyers and judges. It may be supposed that the apparent indeterminacy of legal reasoning reflects a deeper problem about the reliability of moral reasoning: disagreement about legal rights may be thought a product of the doubtful ontological status of conclusions about justice and morality. That kind of scepticism would not, however, be a good basis for the erection of institutional barriers to over-zealous or ill-considered judicial review; it would be a basis for rejecting the institution of judicial review altogether, along with our commitment to justice and the rule of law. We disagree in many instances about the requirements of justice and the rule of law, but we do not normally suppose that our disagreements are empty—competing assertions detached from any public discourse, grounded in shared experience and common standards of judgement.

As Ronald Dworkin has observed, the doubts of the *external* critic or sceptic, whatever his grounds for scepticism, are simply irrelevant to our arguments over the truth or soundness of legal propositions.[153] The external sceptic supposes he can check all interpretative judgements 'against some external reality whose content is not to be determined by arguments of the sort made familiar' by our legal practice but which 'is to be apprehended in some other way'.[154] But the correctness of a legal argument, in any particular case, can only be judged by application of ordinary

---

[152] Miller, 'Justification and Rights Limitations', 98–101.
[153] Ronald Dworkin, *A Matter of Principle*, 137–42, 171–7; and *Law's Empire* (London: Fontana, 1986), 76–86, 266–75. For a more recent discussion, see Ronald Dworkin, *Justice for Hedgehogs* (Cambridge, Mass: Harvard University Press, 2011), Part 1.
[154] Dworkin, *A Matter of Principle*, 176.

legal criteria: truth is a function of competent analysis *within* the established enterprise of legal and constitutional reasoning, reliant on the kinds of argument and evidence accepted by those who take up the internal role of participants. The fact that the right answer to a legal question may not be *demonstrable*, by reference to undisputed empirical fact, does not show that it may not be true in virtue of correct inferences from accepted legal authority or practice; and this is so even if legal practice makes systematic recourse to judgements of political morality, some of which will inevitably be controversial. The fact that people disagree strongly over moral questions does not show that their disagreement is absurd and pointless, as it would be if there were no criteria (acknowledged by all competent moral reasoners) for judging one argument better than another.

The external sceptic, who denies the sense or objectivity of moral reasoning, may be contrasted with his internal counterpart, whose scepticism concerns only the existence of a uniquely right answer to a specific question within the interpretative enterprise. Even a committed participant may sometimes think the arguments in favour of a proposition so well balanced by those against it that he refuses either to accept or deny its truth; he may think truth or falsity dependent on facts or circumstances not yet sufficiently well established (or specified in adequate detail). Such judgements do not challenge the coherence of legal or moral interpretation; they are not to be equated with the views of the external sceptic who, despite having his own views about particular questions of law or justice, somewhat inconsistently denies that such views have any real or objective or valid grounding. None of this of course denies that courts will often make mistakes in determining the content of legal rights. But other officials will also err, even when actually turning their minds, if they do, to questions of right and the limits of jurisdiction; and judicial review provides an independent safeguard that has the special virtues of detachment and impartiality—the impartiality inherent in elaborated reason, exposed to the glare of public scrutiny.[155]

---

[155] Questions about the nature and legitimacy of judicial review, as regards both primary legislation and executive action, are further explored in Chapter 8, below. The dependence of legal interpretation on moral deliberation and debate is further considered in the Appendix.

8

Democracy, Fundamental Rights, and Common Law

I

In this final chapter I shall draw together a number of threads of argument, seeking to show further connections between important questions of constitutional theory. Our study of the *Bancoult* cases, concerning the common law rights of the Chagossian islanders, will help to illustrate interconnected matters of fundamental rights, judicial review, justiciability, and deference.[1] It will provoke further consideration of the principle of separation of powers, assisted by reflection on some significant, related Commonwealth constitutional cases; these cases help us to see how the central doctrines of legislative supremacy, the rule of law, and separation of powers are interdependent parts of a larger theory of liberal democratic constitutionalism. I shall use the case law as a bridge to a wider discussion of the theoretical issues raised, in different ways, by previous chapters.

My defence of constitutional adjudication at common law will broaden to include a closer look at the work of recent critics of 'legal constitutionalism'. I shall challenge the coherence of the narrow 'political' constitutionalism of Adam Tomkins and Richard Bellamy, contending that their theories lack a convincing account of legal and constitutional interpretation: their implausible conceptions of law disfigure their accounts of the rule of law. Bellamy's critique of Ronald Dworkin's work in legal theory is inspired by the doubtful objections of Cass Sunstein, whose own approach to adjudication seems much closer to Dworkin's than he cares to admit. The radical distinction Tomkins and Bellamy want to draw between so-called legal and political constitutionalism disintegrates, or so I shall claim, when they turn their attention to interpretative questions of law.[2]

In a later section, we return to matters of interpretation under the Human Rights Act, examining some of the cases provoking lively debate about the nature and scope of the judicial role in defence of fundamental rights. I shall try to show why a proper understanding of the nature of adjudication is critical to any assessment of these controversial decisions, and why misunderstanding has fuelled exaggerated demands for judicial deference. I shall question the defence of the *Bellinger* decision

---

[1] For *Bancoult*, see Section II, below.   [2] See Sections IV and V, below.

offered by Richard Bellamy and Aileen Kavanagh, among other commentators, challenging the notion that sections 3 and 4 of the Human Rights Act provide alternative *remedies* for legislative violations of European Convention rights.[3]

And finally we will examine Jeremy Waldron's brand of political constitutionalism, probing his opposition to judicial review in defence of fundamental rights. We need not accept the underlying assumption that we must choose, at the level of constitutional design, between absolute parliamentary sovereignty, on one side, or judicial enforcement of a bill of rights, binding on the legislature, on the other. The common law constitution of the United Kingdom finds a middle course, tempering parliamentary sovereignty with those rule-of-law constraints inherent in liberal democracy, based on a fundamental equality of citizenship. Nor can 'strong' judicial review be clearly distinguished from its 'weaker' counterpart: as so often, what may seem useful descriptive categories, from an external perspective, lose their power when we adopt an internal viewpoint, characteristic of legal reasoning and constitutional adjudication. The Human Rights Act permits or mandates 'weak' review only in the sense that it confers no power to quash primary legislation; its strength, underpinned by common law reasoning and assumptions, lies in its affirmation of fundamental rights as inherent features of public law. In a similar manner to the common law constitutional framework in which it operates, the Act presents a challenge to any straightforward or rigid distinctions between familiar models of governance.

II

I have argued, in Chapter 7, that the distinctions customarily drawn between standards of review are misleading, indeed conceptually confused. A requirement of reasonableness excludes disproportionate interference with the enjoyment of constitutional rights: resistance to such improper interference is entailed by the special status of these rights. What matters in practice is not so much the labels affixed to varying standards of review, conceived in abstraction from concrete instances of dubious state action. Our focus should rather be on the nature and scope of the rights in question, and the circumstances giving rise to allegations of their infringement. In the *Bancoult* case, which involved the expulsion of the Chagossian islanders from their homeland by use of the royal prerogative, the judges all adopted a similar standard of review, treated as a matter of general constitutional doctrine; yet they were sharply divided over the principal questions of legality.[4]

The Chagos Islands in the Indian Ocean were separated from the British colony of Mauritius, and the office of Commissioner established as a legislature for the new colony, under the British Indian Ocean Territories Order 1965. The Commissioner made an Immigration Ordinance in 1971, which provided that no one could enter or remain in the territory without a permit, although by that time the British

---

[3] *Bellinger v Bellinger* [2003] UKHL 21; see Section VI, below.
[4] *R (Bancoult) v Secretary of State for Foreign and Commonwealth Affairs* [2008] UKHL 61.

government had already secured the removal of the population of Diego Garcia, the largest island, which was intended for use as a military base by the United States of America. In 2000, however, the High Court quashed the relevant provision, holding that the exclusion of the islands' population was not within the Commissioner's power to make laws for the 'peace, order and good government' of the territory.[5] Whether or not the *Wednesbury* reasonableness doctrine were applied (in preference to 'a more, or less, intrusive approach'), the removal of a people from their land could not, in the absence of some natural or other catastrophe making the land toxic and uninhabitable, be said to conduce to the territory's peace, order, and good government: the people were to be *'governed* not removed'.[6]

The British government initially accepted the ruling, removing the restrictions on the islanders' ability to return, and an inquiry was established into the feasibility of resettlement in the outer islands. However, restrictions were subsequently reimposed by Order in Council: section 9 of the British Indian Ocean Territory (Constitution) Order 2004 provided that no person had the right of abode in the territory or could enter it without authorization. A written ministerial statement referred to the conclusion of the feasibility study that, while short-term resettlement was possible on a subsistence basis, long-term resettlement would be 'precarious and costly'. The Court of Appeal upheld a finding by the High Court that the new restrictions were invalid; but a majority of the House of Lords finally took a different view.

The Law Lords were agreed that the legality of the Order in Council was open to judicial review. They rejected the argument that such an exercise of royal prerogative—being primary legislation made in exercise of the Crown's original legislative power, by contrast with the delegated power formerly exercised by the Commissioner—was immune to judicial control: the ordinary principles of legality, rationality, and procedural propriety applied.[7] Since it was held that the Human Rights Act 1998 (and hence the European Convention on Human Rights) did not apply to the territory, Lord Carswell thought that Sir Thomas Bingham's approach in *Smith* indicated the applicable standard of review.[8] Lord Hoffmann also accepted that an 'anxious' degree of scrutiny was appropriate, requiring demonstration of compelling justification for a measure affecting fundamental rights, or having 'profoundly intrusive effects'.[9] Both judges were, however, members of a majority that denied that the Order in Council could be deemed unreasonable, reversing the judgments of the lower courts. In view of doubts about the feasibility of resettlement, Lord Hoffmann considered the Chagossians' right of abode merely symbolic, and so of little practical value: the

---

[5] *R (Bancoult) v Secretary of State for Foreign and Commonwealth Affairs* [2001] QB 1067.

[6] Ibid, para 57 (Laws LJ).

[7] These principles had formerly been held applicable to the exercise of delegated prerogative powers: *Council of Civil Service Unions v Minister for the Civil Service* [1985] AC 374 (powers exercised under the authority of the Civil Service Order in Council 1982).

[8] [2008] UKHL 61, para 131 (see discussion of *R v Ministry of Defence, ex p Smith* [1996] QB 517 in Chapter 7, above).

[9] Ibid, paras 52–3.

islanders would be dependent on financial support which the British government was unwilling to provide. Lord Rodger also concluded that, given the terms of the expert report, the government's decision to legislate to prevent resettlement could not be held unreasonable.[10]

For the dissentients, by contrast, the irrationality of the measure followed from the relative weakness of the grounds put forward for removal of a fundamental right. The irrationality was implicit in the disproportionate curtailment, indeed abrogation, of what (following Sedley LJ in the Court of Appeal) Lord Mance called 'one of the most fundamental liberties known to human beings, the freedom to return to one's homeland, however poor and barren the conditions of life'.[11] It was wrong to conflate the legal freedom to return with the economic practicalities of resettlement; and if the right was likely to remain largely symbolic the alleged reasons for its removal lost their force. The professed wishes of the American government for the outer islands to remain uninhabited appeared to represent a belated attempt to strengthen the British government's hand in this litigation. For Lord Bingham, section 9 of the Order was irrational because there was no good reason for making it.

The general principles of legality and rationality, though important expressions or implications of the rule of law, have determinate content only in relation to the specific circumstances of the particular case. For Lord Bingham and Lord Mance, in *Bancoult*, these principles entailed appropriate scrutiny of a measure that purported to revoke a fundamental human and constitutional right. The irrationality of the measure was the consequence of its illegality as a wholly *disproportionate* interference. Such a measure could be justified, if at all, only in exceptional circumstances, such as the event of a natural disaster or real military emergency: 'the relationship between the citizen and the Crown is based on reciprocal duties of allegiance and protection and the duty of protection cannot ordinarily be discharged by removing and excluding the citizen from his homeland'.[12] Lord Mance explained that the people of a conquered or ceded territory acquired rights of abode against the Crown comparable to the immunity from exile that common law confers on a citizen of the United Kingdom. The Crown's power to provide a constitution for a ceded territory was, accordingly, a power 'intended to enable the proper governance of the territory, at least among other things for the benefit of the people inhabiting it'.[13] A constitution that exiled a territory's inhabitants was therefore 'a contradiction in terms'.

The failure of the majority to discern irrationality reflected their unwillingness to recognize a fundamental right of abode. In the case of a ceded colony, unlike the United Kingdom itself, the Crown enjoyed plenary legislative authority: according to Lord Hoffmann, the right of abode was a creature of the law, which both 'gives it and...may take it away'.[14] Nor would the majority accept that the legislative powers of the Crown were limited by any requirement that laws must be the 'peace,

---

[10] Ibid, para 113.   [11] Ibid, para 172.
[12] Ibid, para 70 (Lord Bingham of Cornhill).
[13] Ibid, para 157.   [14] Ibid, para 45.

order and good government' of the territory, which was merely 'the traditional formula by which legislative powers are conferred upon the legislature of a colony or a former colony upon the attainment of independence'.[15] Lord Hoffmann held that 'Her Majesty exercises her powers of prerogative legislation... on the advice of her ministers in the United Kingdom and will act in the interests of her undivided realm'; in the event of any conflict of interest, she was entitled to prefer the interests of the United Kingdom.

In the result, the challenged Order was, in effect, rendered impregnable. Rationality was reduced to whatever the Crown thought fit as regards the needs of defence or expediency: there was nothing to which any test of proportionality, and hence rationality, could be applied. Sedley LJ had suggested, in the Court of Appeal, that English courts would always have struck down an Order permitting torture to obtain evidence, or abolishing all recourse to law, or introducing forced labour. Lord Rodger was obliged, however, to deny the possibility of any legal, as opposed to political, remedy: he acknowledged no limits to the validity of an Order in Council based on repugnancy to any fundamental principles of justice.[16] When constitutional rights of abode and freedom from torture are denied, and recourse to law on the basis of fundamental principles rejected, it is hard to imagine what, in the present context, unreasonable government conduct would consist in. As regards those judges in the majority, invocation of the general principles of administrative legality was illusory: the content of such principles was empty.

An exaggerated deference to the executive had collapsed into non-justiciability. Even if it were conceded that the limits of the Crown's legislative powers were to be understood by reference to such general objects as 'peace, order and good government', those limits were not in practice legally binding: the sanction for inappropriate use of the Crown's legislative power was deemed to be 'political, not judicial'.[17] Even if a court might 'be strongly attracted to the view' that a measure that exiled the Chagossians could not be said to be for the 'peace, order and good government of the colony', the measure should not (according to the majority) be declared invalid on that ground: once the courts 'enter upon such territory they could very easily get into the area of challenging what is essentially a political judgement'.[18] Accordingly, 'the rule of abstinence should remain unqualified'. In the absence of any fundamental principles of substantive law, however, the application of tests of legality and rationality was hollow: any decision adverse to the British government was already precluded by the prior stance on justiciability.[19]

---

[15] Ibid, para 47.
[16] Lord Rodger (ibid, paras 101–2) cites *Liyanage v R* [1967] 1 AC 259 as authority for the rejection of the limit imposed by the 'fundamental principles' of common law invoked by Lord Mansfield in *Campbell v Hall* (1774) 1 Cowp 204, 209; 98 ER 1045, 1048. (*Liyanage* is considered below.)
[17] Ibid, paras 108–9 (Lord Rodger of Earlsferry).
[18] Ibid, para 130 (Lord Carswell).
[19] For a similar assessment, see Mark Elliott and Amanda Perreau-Saussine, 'Pyrrhic Public Law: *Bancoult* and the Sources, Status and Content of Common Law Limitations on Prerogative Power' [2009] PL 697, 720–1. For Lord Rodger and Lord Carswell, any challenge based on repugnancy to fundamental principles of law was also barred by the Colonial Laws Validity Act 1865, s 3, which enacted

It did not matter for any practical purpose, in *Bancoult*, whether the House of Lords majority concluded that the Crown's prerogative powers were unfettered by any requirement that they be exercised for the peace, order, and good government of the colony, or whether any such limits were not justiciable: in either case, the British government was accorded the status of absolute dictator (in substitution for the King or Queen as absolute monarch). In reaching this dismal conclusion, so plainly contrary to the rule of law, the judges drew a direct analogy with the sovereignty of Parliament, similarly unconstrained (in their view) by any requirements of rationality or legality. Lord Hoffmann held that, subject to the principle of territoriality, the formula 'peace, order and good government' had always been treated 'as apt to confer plenary law-making authority': 'The courts will not inquire into whether legislation within the territorial scope of the power was in fact for the "peace, order and good government" or otherwise for the benefit of the inhabitants of the territory'.[20]

Similarly, Lord Rodger held that even if 'Her Majesty's constituent power' could properly be described as a power to make 'laws for the peace, order and good government of the Territory', it was 'equal in scope to the legislative power of Parliament'.[21] He cited a unanimous judgment of the High Court of Australia, which reviewed the opinions of the Judicial Committee of the Privy Council in a number of earlier cases, concluding that 'a power to make laws for the peace, order and good government of a territory is as ample and plenary as the power possessed by the Imperial Parliament itself'.[22] The case concerned the scope of power conferred by section 5 of the Constitution Act 1902 to make laws 'for the peace, welfare, and good government of New South Wales'. The High Court denied that these words imposed any limitation: 'Just as the courts of the United Kingdom cannot invalidate laws made by the Parliament of the United Kingdom on the ground that they do not secure ... the public interest, so the exercise of its legislative power by the Parliament of New South Wales is not susceptible to judicial review on that score.'[23]

We are entitled to ask, however, whether these robust conclusions are not too broadly expressed—too sweeping a dismissal of the constraints of legality that ultimately underpin the state's legitimacy. Since the state is a creature of *law*, it cannot contain a sovereign legislature empowered to repudiate the substance of the rule of law; and we have rejected a narrow conception of the rule of law, limited to a purely formal equality before the demands (whatever their content) of an authoritarian regime. When, therefore, it is said that a power to make laws for the peace, order, and good government of a territory connotes 'the widest lawmaking power

---

that no 'colonial law' should be void or inoperative on the ground of repugnancy to the law of England (except an Act of Parliament or order or regulation made thereunder). Lord Hoffmann, by contrast, held that the Constitution Order was not a 'colonial law' for the purposes of the 1865 Act, which applied only to Orders in Council insofar as they formed part of the local system of laws administered by colonial courts; and Lord Mance agreed.

[20] [2008] UKHL 61, para 50.
[21] Ibid, para 109.
[22] *Union Steamship Company of Australia Pty Ltd v King* (1988) 166 CLR 1, 10.
[23] Ibid.

appropriate to a Sovereign',[24] it is necessary to ask whether there are inherent limits to 'sovereign' legislative power. Even if Lord Halsbury was right, in *Riel*, to deny that a statute was invalid merely because a court concluded that it was inapt 'as a matter of fact and policy' to secure the peace, order, and good government of a territory, it does not follow that *any* kind of measure can constitute a 'statute', whatever its terms or purposes.[25] Questions of 'fact and policy' may lie within the proper province of the legislature; but questions of law, which include the identification of genuine statutes, possessing legitimate authority, fall within the province of the judiciary.

Sedley LJ, in *Bancoult (No 2)*, drew the appropriate distinction between what, in the opinion of the British government (the relevant legislature in that case) was best for the well-being of a colony, and what, as a matter of law, fell within the constitutional boundaries of a legal order designed to further the interests of its citizen-members. It was not the court's function to criticize the Crown's judgement of what was conducive to peace, order, and good government, let alone 'to substitute their own view of what is best for a colony'. But it was nonetheless 'their constitutional function to decide whether what has been enacted, or what it is proposed to enact, is rationally and legally capable of providing for a colony's well-being'.[26] In holding that the traditional formula accorded 'a very wide discretion to the imperial state in deciding what is best for a colony', while affirming that 'like every discretion, it is limited by and to its own expressed objects', Sedley LJ echoed the judgment of Street CJ in an interesting case in the Court of Appeal of New South Wales: 'The words, by their very terms, confine the powers conferred to "peace, welfare, and good government" of the body politic in respect of which the legislature is being established.'[27]

The Chief Justice's reference to the 'body politic' contains a clue to the proper understanding of the conceptual boundaries of legislative power, and hence of the test of what is *legally and rationally capable* of being for the public good or the public welfare. Just as Laws LJ, in *Bancoult (No 1)*, insisted that the 'peace, order and good government' of a territory must have reference to its population, who were to be *governed* rather than removed, so in the *Builders' Labourers Federation* case, Street CJ held that both people and territory were united into a body politic, or 'political organism'.[28] For the purposes of section 5 of the Constitution Act 1902, which gave the state legislature 'power to make laws for the peace, welfare, and good government of New South Wales in all cases whatsoever', the term 'New South Wales' must be understood conceptually: 'That body politic or political organism is essentially a parliamentary democracy—an entity ruled by a democratically elected Parliament whose citizens enjoy the great inherited privileges of freedom and justice under the protection of an independent judiciary.'[29]

[24] *Ibralebbe v R* [1964] AC 900, 923 (Privy Council; cited in *Union Steamship*, above).

[25] *Riel v R* (1885) 10 App Cas 675, 678 (Privy Council).

[26] *Bancoult (No 2)* [2007] EWCA Civ 498, para 51.

[27] *Building Construction Employees and Builders' Labourers Federation of New South Wales v Minister for Industrial Relations* (1986) 7 NSWLR 372, 383.

[28] Compare *Amalgamated Society of Engineers v Adelaide Steamship Co Ltd* (1920) 28 CLR 129, 147.

[29] *Builders' Labourers Federation* case (1986) 7 NSWLR 372, 382.

Even a 'sovereign' legislature must acquire its sovereignty from a prior constitution, whether it be a codified one, like the New South Wales Constitution Act, or an unwritten one, like the United Kingdom constitution. It is necessarily implicit that such a legislature, even if sovereign in the sense that it is free to delegate legislative power to subordinate authorities, must act for the public good.[30] Its discretion is entrusted to it for the benefit of the citizens, united in a *rechtsstaat* (or polity governed in accordance with the rule of law). It is one thing to deny a broad judicial power to question the wisdom of legislative determinations of the public interest, made in good faith, especially when the legislature is properly representative of the people; it is quite another to suppose that a legislature (democratic or otherwise) might act for purposes entirely inimical to the well-being of all or some of its subjects, on any plausible view of their interests or welfare.

Street CJ's description of the 'body politic' encapsulates the essential elements of democratic constitutionalism: an elected and representative lawmaker is conjoined with an independent judiciary, charged to protect fundamental liberties. All state power exists only to guarantee the conditions of individual freedom, preserving and enhancing each person's autonomy compatibly with the equal autonomy of others. And since the ideal of the rule of law is fulfilled only in a democracy, whereby every citizen is empowered to participate in establishing those conditions of freedom, adapted to the needs of time and place, an elected legislature cannot lawfully repudiate its own democratic basis. The court's resistance to illegitimate measures, adopted in defiance or ignorance of the demands of the rule of law or democracy, is a necessary and proper consequence: 'Laws inimical to, or which do not serve, the peace, welfare, and good government of our parliamentary democracy...will be struck down by the courts as unconstitutional.'[31]

A measure intended to exile an entire population is as clear an illustration of action in breach of inherent conditions of peace, order, and good governance as one is likely to find. Sedley LJ's view, in *Bancoult*, that 'the permanent exclusion of an entire population from its homeland for reasons unconnected with their collective well-being' could not be a legitimate act of governance, reflected his opinion that the 'governance of each colonial territory is in constitutional principle a discrete function of the Crown', so that the interests of the colony will not necessarily coincide with those of the United Kingdom.[32] Since Lord Hoffmann, by contrast, considered that the United Kingdom and its dependent territories formed 'one realm having one undivided Crown', he denied that the Constitution Order was invalid because it was against the interests of the Chagossians.[33] Even if Lord Hoffmann's view were thought preferable, however, it may still be insisted that the injury inflicted on one part of Her Majesty's dominions should bear a reasonable

---

[30] Street CJ notes that references to 'plenary' or 'sovereign' power are usually found in cases where the court has rejected an argument that the legislature is a mere delegate of the English Parliament, and so unable to delegate further the law-making powers vested in it: ibid, 383.

[31] Ibid, 384.

[32] *Bancoult (No 2)* [2007] EWCA Civ 498, para 67.

[33] *Bancoult (No 2)* [2008] UKHL 61, paras 47–9 (citing 6 *Halsbury's Laws*, 4th edn (2003), para 716).

and defensible relationship to the benefits secured to the others. The dissenting speeches in the House of Lords attest to the grave illegality inherent in the inequitable balance between these conflicting interests: the exclusion of the Chagos islanders was wholly *disproportionate* to any supposed advantages that might have accrued from it.

The gross disparity between these respective burdens and benefits presents a challenge to those who would question the legitimacy of constitutional adjudication. It is often claimed that competing interests are typically incommensurable, there being no single value by reference to which the scale of respective benefits and burdens can be measured. Such a stance would appear to lend support to Lord Carswell's view that any legal challenge by reference to the criteria of peace, order, and good government would engage only 'political' considerations, justifying a judicial 'rule of abstinence'.[34] It would also appear to bolster Lord Rodger's opinion that, as regards the appropriate weight to be given to the 'economic, foreign affairs and defence interests of the United Kingdom', by comparison with the interest of the islanders, the government's conclusions were non-justiciable: 'In the absence of any relevant legal criteria, judges are not well placed to second guess the balance struck by ministers on such a matter.'[35] But many will wonder whether such wholesale judicial abstention is truly defensible.

The recognition of fundamental rights, implicit in the rule of law, imports a larger judicial responsibility, as the dissenting speeches of Lord Bingham and Lord Mance reveal. While the balance of interests may be solely a matter for ministerial judgement when they are relatively evenly matched, the islanders' rights of abode could not be rightly overridden except on grounds of overwhelming force, normally involving their own safety and security. In the context of a threat to 'one of the most fundamental liberties known to human beings', Mance's sceptical treatment of the purported justifications for the Constitution Order was fully justified.[36] The objection on grounds of incommensurability fails: incommensurability does not entail incomparability.[37] It is enough to show that a minor and somewhat speculative gain to defence or economic interests was outweighed by very substantial injury to the islanders' basic constitutional rights. It is true, of course, that each limb of the balance is measured in its own terms, there being no general value in play beyond such unhelpfully broad ones as liberty, justice, or security; but who could rationally deny that a minor gain on one side of the scales is outweighed by an associated injury on the other side of very grave proportions?[38]

---

[34] Ibid, para 130.

[35] Ibid, para 114.

[36] Ibid, para 172 (see discussion above).

[37] See Virgilio Afonso da Silva, 'Comparing the Incommensurable: Constitutional Principles, Balancing, and Rational Decision' (2011) 31 OJLS 273–302. See also Robert Alexy, *A Theory of Constitutional Rights* (translated by Julian Rivers; Oxford: Oxford University Press, 2002), 100–9, defending the rationality of balancing and emphasizing the role of value judgements in other dimensions of legal reasoning and interpretation.

[38] While insisting that Parliament or Her Majesty in Council enacted legislation for 'Her Majesty's possessions as a whole', Lord Rodger nonetheless observes that the 'underlying assumption' was naturally that 'the policies in question were for the ultimate benefit of all those possessions' (*Bancoult*

Incommensurability is largely a function of comparing very abstract accounts of relevant constitutional values: when we bring those values into focus in the context of specific threats to acknowledged fundamental rights, there is usually scope for making rationally justified comparisons.[39]

III

Chief Justice Street's identification of limits on legislative power, in the *Builders' Labourers Federation* case, was rightly based on the principle that the legislature, if it is to make valid *law*, must act in accordance with the rule of law: it must serve the 'body politic' constituted by parliamentary democracy and the protection of individual liberty. It is, however, an essential component of that conceptual polity, enshrining the rule of law, that judicial power must be exercised by independent judges, able to hold the other branches of government to account for unlawful action. The separation of the 'administration of common justice' by an independent judiciary from the exercise of legislative and executive power was celebrated by Blackstone as 'one main preservative of the public liberty': 'Were it joined with the legislative, the life, liberty, and property, of the subject would be in the hands of arbitrary judges, whose decisions would be then regulated only by their own opinions, and not by any fundamental principles of law; which, though legislators may depart from, yet judges are bound to observe.'[40]

The Builders' Labourers Federation (Special Provisions) Act 1986 was, accordingly, condemned by Street CJ as a 'legislative judgment', passed in breach of the principle of separation of powers: the New South Wales Parliament had 'directly intruded its power into the judicial process by directing the outcome of a specific case between particular litigants awaiting hearing' at the time of enactment.[41] The Industrial Arbitration (Special Provisions) Act 1984 had authorized the Government to cancel the Federation's registration under industrial relations legislation, depriving it of significant benefits (including the representation of members before industrial tribunals). The Federation challenged the legality of the cancellation, claiming a right to be heard under general principles of natural justice. The 1986 Act was passed between the dismissal of the Federation's claim at first instance and the hearing of its appeal to the Court of Appeal. Section 3 provided that the Federation's registration should 'be taken to have been cancelled' pursuant to the 1984 Act, and

---

(No 2) [2008] UKHL 61, para 114). Against any assumptions of incommensurability should be set Ronald Dworkin's persuasive case for the ultimate unity of value: Dworkin, *Justice for Hedgehogs* (Cambridge, Mass: Harvard University Press, 2011), chs 5 and 6.

[39] If we conclude that the pertinent values are, in all the circumstances, of equal importance—competing rights, for example, making equal moral claims—there is no justification for judicial interference; the solution lies within the legitimate discretion of Parliament or Government: see Afonso da Silva, 'Comparing the Incommensurable', above (discussing *Evans v United Kingdom* (2008) 46 EHRR 34).

[40] William Blackstone, *Commentaries on the Laws of England,* 1st edn (1765–9), vol 1, 259.

[41] *Builders' Labourers Federation* case (1986) 7 NSWLR 372, 378.

the necessary ministerial certificate as 'having been validly given'; such provisions were to take effect 'notwithstanding that any proceedings' had been instituted in relation to such a certificate.

By giving directions to the court about how to determine the legal questions in contention, the New South Wales legislature had trespassed into the province of judicial power. Street CJ drew attention to the serious implications for the rule of law and the impartial administration of justice: 'For Parliament, uncontrolled as it is by any of the safeguards that are enshrined in the concept of due process of law, to trespass into this field of judging between parties by interfering with the judicial process is an affront to a society that prides itself on the quality of its justice.'[42] The Federation was widely regarded as having done great harm to the trade union movement and to the conduct of industrial relations, but as the Chief Justice emphasized, 'the greater the hostility directed against a person or organization, the greater the temptation to distort the fundamental precepts' of the rule of law and democracy.[43] Yet though he considered the passing of the 1986 Act to be 'contrary both to modern constitutional convention, and to the public interest in the due administration of justice', he did not think it exceeded the constitutional limits inherent in the 'peace, welfare, and good government' formula.[44]

The danger is fairly obvious here that such a conclusion empties the concept of law, implicit in the Constitution's reference to the 'peace, welfare, and good government of New South Wales', of any substantial content. If the 'various protections of natural justice, absence of bias, appellate control, and the other concomitants that are the ordinary daily province of the courts' are 'fundamental safeguards of the democratic rights of individuals', as the Chief Justice asserts, their removal by legislative intrusion into the judicial process contravenes the rule of law—literally depriving the litigants affected of the protection of law.[45] Like Priestly JA, who also thought that a statute might, in principle, be struck down as 'manifestly not for the peace, order and government of the State', Street seems to reserve the court's power to resist oppressive legislation for extreme cases, involving the infringement of substantive rights.[46] Priestly alludes to the example of a statute requiring the murder of blue-eyed babies, famously treated by Dicey as legally valid (if politically unwise).[47] Yet the constitutional right to *due process*, allowing the alleged justification for an abrogation of substantive rights to be examined by impartial and independent judges, is a basic element of the rule of law—implicit in our concept of law.

The national counterpart of the Builders' Labourers Federation faced similar governmental action. The Building Industry Act 1985 empowered the Federal Minister for Industrial Relations to direct cancellation of the Federation's registration, provided that the Australian Conciliation and Arbitration Commission had

---

[42] Ibid, 376.   [43] Ibid, 379.
[44] Ibid, 381.   [45] Ibid, 376.
[46] See Priestly JA, at 421.
[47] A V Dicey, *Introduction to the Study of the Law of the Constitution*, 10th edn (London: Macmillan, 1964), 81.

first made a declaration that certain criteria were satisfied. However, the Builders' Labourers Federation (Cancellation of Registration) Act 1986 intervened by providing, in section 3, that the Federation's registration was 'by force of this section, cancelled'. The High Court of Australia rejected the complaint that the statute amounted to an improper exercise of judicial power, despite a well-established separation of powers doctrine applicable to the Federal Constitution: the statute simply deregistered the Federation, thereby making its proceedings against the Act—already begun in the High Court—redundant.[48] Parliament could legislate so as to alter rights in issue in pending litigation without improperly interfering with the exercise of judicial power; such legislation was to be distinguished from interference in the judicial process itself. It did not matter that 'the motive or purpose of the Minister, the Government and the Parliament in enacting the statute was to circumvent the proceedings and forestall any decision' that might result from them.[49]

The conclusions of the New South Wales Court of Appeal naturally reflect, in part, the ease with which the federal authorities attained similar ends by direct provision. It was assumed that the state Parliament 'could have achieved its object in the same way as did the Commonwealth Parliament, that is to say without interference with the judicial process'.[50] But that assumption meant that all the protections of judicial process depended on a technicality: they could be swept aside by more suitable statutory wording. If the motive or purpose of the legislation were truly irrelevant to the legal questions arising, it must be because the constitutionality of a statute should be ascertainable by inspecting its form and content. The true distinction between valid legislation, compliant with the rule of law, and invalid legislation, contrary to the rule of law, must consist in the difference between *general rules*, applicable to everyone who meets specified criteria, and ad hoc or ad hominem legislation, designed to alter the legal position of particular persons or groups, directly identified. No one's rights or liberties should be at the mercy of a hostile majority in parliament, however plainly the exercise of such rights may appear to have injured the public interest. Those rights, even if only statutory rights granted for limited purposes, should be curtailed by an independent authority in application of general criteria, publicly announced in advance.

Much attention was paid by the New South Wales Court of Appeal to the well-known decision of the Privy Council in *Liyanage*, which the judges were anxious to distinguish.[51] In that case a fundamental division of powers was inferred from the general nature of the constitutional arrangements made for Ceylon (Sri Lanka) by the Ceylon Independence Act 1947 and the Ceylon (Constitution) Order in Council 1946. At the time of introduction of the Order in Council, which made provision for the appointment and independence of the judges of the Supreme Court, the judicial system operated according to a Charter of Justice, similar to the charter establishing the judicial system in New South Wales. The Charter

---

[48] *Australian Building Construction Employees' and Builders' Labourers Federation v The Commonwealth* (1986) 60 ALJR 584.

[49] Ibid, 587.

[50] *Builders' Labourers Federation* case (1986) 7 NSWLR 372, 387 (Street CJ).

[51] *Liyanage v R* [1967] 1 AC 259.

directed that the administration of justice be vested exclusively in the courts it established. The Judicial Committee of the Privy Council invoked the separation of judicial power to strike down as invalid a statute designed to secure the conviction and punishment of the regime's political enemies. The decision remains an important example of unconstitutional ad hominem legislation, adopted in breach of the rule of law.

The Criminal Law (Special Provisions) Act 1962 was enacted in response to an attempted *coup détat*. It created a new criminal offence *ex post facto* and provided for a minimum sentence of ten years' imprisonment and mandatory forfeiture of property. As well as purporting to authorize breaches of criminal procedure which had already occurred, the statute sanctioned the receipt of evidence of confessions that were otherwise inadmissible. It empowered the Minister of Justice to direct that the accused be tried by three judges without a jury, and to nominate the judges, although a subsequent Act vested the power of nomination in the Chief Justice when executive nomination was ruled unconstitutional. It was provided that the new arrangements ceased to be operative after conclusion of the trial of the defendants. Upholding the contention that the statute constituted an interference with the functions of the judiciary, the Judicial Committee held it invalid as a 'legislative plan *ex post facto* to secure the conviction and enhance the punishment' of particular individuals.[52]

The principal ground on which *Liyanage* was distinguished in the *Builders' Labourers* case lay in the entrenchment of judicial power by virtue of the Ceylon (Constitution) Order in Council, section 29(4), which permitted amendment of the constitution only by a two-thirds majority vote in Parliament, certified by the Speaker. The Judicial Committee had held that in 'so far as any Act passed without recourse to section 29(4) of the Constitution purports to usurp or infringe the judicial power it is *ultra vires*'.[53] Since there was no similar entrenchment in the New South Wales constitution, restricting the possibilities of constitutional amendment, there was thought to be no true analogy with *Liyanage*: the state Parliament was free to 'abolish, alter or vary the constitution, organization and business of the Supreme Court'.[54] That distinction between the cases is only valid, however, on the assumption that, in the absence of any formal and *explicit* entrenchment of the separation of judicial power, there are no limits to legislative freedom to usurp such power. But that view is tantamount to the notion that the state Parliament may contravene the conditions of law-making implicit in our concepts of law and legality. So far from *legislating* for the peace, welfare, and good government of the polity, in a manner respectful of those objectives, the legislative majority would be enabled to act directly against its political opponents, or against anyone else who incurred its contempt or displeasure.

Despite its affirmation of the separation of judicial power, inferred from the general constitutional scheme, the Judicial Committee in *Liyanage* denied that

---

[52] Ibid, 290.   [53] Ibid, 289.
[54] *Builders' Labourers Federation* case (1986) 7 NSWLR 372, 401 (Kirby P).

the Ceylon Parliament was constrained by any 'fundamental principles' of justice: its legislative supremacy was not subject to a 'fetter of repugnancy to some vague unspecified law of natural justice'.[55] The court declined to accept that such limits might be based on Lord Mansfield's statement, in *Campbell v Hall*, that the King in exercise of his prerogative power in relation to colonies could not 'make any new change contrary to fundamental principles'.[56] Insofar as Lord Mansfield had intended any distinction between what was repugnant to English law, on the one hand, and fundamental principles of justice, on the other, no such limits survived to inhibit the legislative power conferred on the Parliament of Ceylon. In the *Builders' Labourers* case, the court similarly rejected an argument that certain common law rights were too deeply entrenched for even the 'plenary power' of a sovereign legislature to remove, including a right against legislative interference in existing legal proceedings. Kirby P regarded fundamental rights as 'extra-constitutional notions', unless 'anchored in a Bill of Rights duly enacted'.[57] Even Street CJ felt inhibited by the lack of modern authority from accepting any such doctrine of fundamental rights 'standing alone'.[58]

A doctrine of fundamental rights does not, however, stand alone; nor does it look outside the constitution except in the very narrow sense of 'constitution' that equates it with an entrenched or formally enacted text. Fundamental rights inhere in the very nature of a parliamentary democracy that embodies the rule of law: such arrangements are intended to enable every citizen to enjoy the maximum autonomy, for leading a life of his or her own choosing, compatible with the same freedom for others. The impartiality of public institutions is essential to such a scheme; and the independence of the courts from political interference is necessarily implicit in it. Street CJ's reluctance to acknowledge the existence of fundamental rights, resistant to measures that threaten the rule of law, is hard to square with his insistence on the judicial power to strike down laws inimical to the peace, welfare, and good government of the State. Nor is Priestly JA's reliance on *Liyanage* for the dismissal of the doctrine of fundamental rights consistent with his concession that a court could repudiate a statute as 'manifestly not for the peace, order and good government of the State', at least in extreme cases.[59] *Liyanage* itself was, after all, an illustration of the power of fundamental principles, safeguarding the constitutional right to due process dependent on the operation of independent and impartial courts of law.

The dissonance evident in the judgments of Street and Priestly betrays the characteristic tension in common law legal orders between respect for law, based on a grasp of the principles of the rule of law, and at least notional adherence to a doctrine of absolute legislative sovereignty, inconsistent with the rule of law. A similar tension was evident in *Bancoult*, where the judges were divided about whether the Crown's prerogative power in relation to colonies was subject to respect for

---

[55] *Liyanage* [1967] 1 AC 259, 284.
[56] (1774) 1 Cowp 204, 209; 98 ER 1045, 1048.
[57] *Builders' Labourers Federation* case (1986) 7 NSWLR 372, 405–6.
[58] Ibid, 387.
[59] More consistently, Mahoney JA rejected both lines of argument, treating them as one: ibid, 412–13.

the fundamental rights of their inhabitants.[60] Lord Rodger and Lord Carswell expressed a scepticism about fundamental principles analogous to the judicial attitudes in *Liyanage* and the *Builders' Labourers* case; Lord Bingham and Lord Mance, by contrast, understood the real significance of the right of abode as part of the social contract between government and governed. Sedley LJ, in the Court of Appeal, also struck a very different note from the House of Lords majority by observing that 'however vague the notion of fundamental principles had come to seem by the mid-twentieth century, they will have had a fairly solid meaning for Lord Mansfield and his contemporaries, starting with the inviolability, save by due process of law, of property and person'.[61]

Admittedly, none of the judges in *Bancoult* denied that Parliament itself could accomplish what was more doubtfully within the prerogative power of the executive. Rodger's observation that 'the sanction for inappropriate use of the legislative power is political, not judicial' carries an echo of Kirby's view that the 'chief protection' against oppression 'lies in the democratic nature of our parliamentary institutions'.[62] But there is too stark an opposition here between the legal and the political: democracy is not to be equated with majority rule alone but rather with the context in which such rule is effected. Parliamentary legislation is rarely an instrument for oppression because it is subject to judicial interpretation, which proceeds on the assumption that fundamental rights must be accorded due respect. In the *Builders' Labourers* case, Mahoney JA was quick to deny that the Constitution attributed 'to the acts of the bare, often temporary, majority a moral sanction', emphasizing the judicial interpretative role.[63] And Kirby's affirmation of the judicial power of benevolent construction comes close to refuting his own denial of boundaries to legislative supremacy: 'Often judges do surgery to legislation, in order to ensure its consistency with basic constitutional assumptions.'[64]

The notion of doing surgery to legislation, of course, invokes rather crude assumptions about legislative intention—pitting the personal intentions of legislators against the contrary intentions of judges. As I have argued in earlier chapters, such assumptions should be abandoned in favour of a more nuanced account of statutory interpretation, matching Street CJ's conception of the liberal-democratic body politic within which legislation acquires its meaning and effect. A view of legal rules as having a determinate meaning quite independently of their constitutional context, which operates only to mitigate the worst effects of free-standing statutory instructions, is rooted in an implausible conception of law. The various tensions and inconsistencies in the judgments in *Bancoult*, *Liyanage*, and the *Builders' Labourers* case reflect the assumption, characteristic of legal positivism, that the law can be reduced to specific rules, enacted or declared by authoritative institutions (whether

---

[60] *Bancoult (No 2)* [2008] UKHL 61, considered above.
[61] *Bancoult (No 2)* [2007] EWCA Civ 498, para 28.
[62] *Bancoult (No 2)* [2008] UKHL 61, para 109; *Builders' Labourers Federation* case (1986) 7 NSWLR 372, 405.
[63] (1986) 7 NSWLR 372, 413.
[64] Ibid, 405–6.

courts, Crown, or Parliament). These judgments betray a reluctance to embrace general principles of justice or good governance as equal sources of law—implicit in developed legal tradition—unless given specific textual definition in an enacted bill of rights.

Even when judges acknowledge a duty to protect the rule of law, or repudiate legislation contrary to 'peace, welfare and good government', they typically view it as a duty to resist extreme injustice of the sort that would threaten the character or stability of the legal order. We are reminded of Lord Steyn's distinction between 'strict legalism' and 'constitutional legal principle', in *Jackson*, pitting the law against the 'rule of law' in a manner that seems to deny the fundamental legal status of the constitution.[65] In the absence of respect for the common law as a source of fundamental rights—those rights that lend coherence to the complex legal edifice of constitutional government—the various grounds of judicial review lose their moorings. Judgements of legality or reasonableness appear as little more than conclusions about the nature or scope of statutory powers, interpreted by reference to a legislative 'intention' that focuses wholly on immediate ends or purposes. Divorced from the recognition of any fundamental rights, judicial review of prerogative legislation in *Bancoult* lacked significant content. It echoed the crude divorce between law, as a merely empirical phenomenon, and constitutional legality, as a moral ideal—a divorce inherent in notions of absolute, unfettered sovereignty.

There is a similar divorce between the ordinary grounds of review and basic legal principle in *AXA General Insurance Ltd v Lord Advocate*,[66] in which the Supreme Court affirmed the court's right to repudiate an Act of the Scottish Parliament (passed under powers conferred by the Scotland Act 1998) that flouted the rule of law, while denying the applicability of the common law grounds of review for irrationality or arbitrariness. Lord Reed rejected rationality review on the ground that, whereas administrative bodies were accorded limited powers for identifiable purposes, the Scottish Parliament enjoyed plenary powers: its exercise of law-making power needed 'no justification in law other than the will of the Parliament'.[67] Lord Mance, however, expressed a reservation which, in the light of his dissent in *Bancoult*, is of considerable interest. Recalling Lord Diplock's description of *Wednesbury* irrationality as something 'so outrageous in its defiance of logic or of accepted moral standards that no sensible person' could approve it, he observed that 'blatantly discriminatory' decisions were irrational 'irrespective of any limitation on the purposes for which the decision-maker might act':

If a devolved Parliament or Assembly were ever to enact such a measure, I would have thought it capable of challenge, if not under the Human Rights Convention, then as offending against fundamental rights or the rule of law, at the very core of which are principles of equality of treatment.[68]

---

[65] *R (Jackson) v Attorney General* [2005] UKHL 56, paras 101–2. See Chapter 4, above.
[66] [2011] UKSC 46.
[67] Ibid, para 147.
[68] Ibid, para 97 (see *Council of Civil Service Unions v Minister for the Civil Service* [1985] AC 374).

IV

Adam Tomkins's antipathy to 'legal constitutionalism' was briefly surveyed in Chapter 2, above. He objects both to the application by courts of general principles of legality, intended to prevent the abuse of executive discretion, and to judicial enforcement of constitutional rights, whose abstract nature—when treated as a matter of general political theory—leaves too much power in the hands of unelected judges. Tomkins defends a version of republicanism allied to a conception of 'political constitutionalism', which seeks to enlarge the role of decision-making by elected representatives and sharply reduce the role of the judiciary.[69] He deplores the transfer of 'political questions' to an unaccountable and unrepresentative body of judges; and he also challenges the effectiveness of legal constitutionalism as a safeguard of liberty.[70]

I suggested in Chapter 2 that Tomkins's critique was rooted in a doubtful philosophy of legal positivism, which draws too sharp a distinction between the law contained in enacted rules, on the one hand, and the (supposedly non-legal) moral and political principles beyond the rules, on the other. When, more plausibly, we treat legal rules as attempts to crystallize or clarify settled principles of good governance or individual right—principles already implicit in our institutions, practice and shared tradition—we can see that the distinction between 'legal' and 'political' questions is often elusive. From an external, largely descriptive viewpoint, we may discern a plain distinction between rule-governed decisions (typically, enforcing statutory provisions) and discretionary law-making (where rules give way to abstract principle or the general public interest). But from the internal perspective of the legal reasoner, that distinction largely disappears: the rules acquire their meaning and effect, in large part, from our efforts to apply them intelligently to particular instances. Neither judge nor arbitrator nor administrator, acting conscientiously, can divorce the letter of the law from her understanding of what, in any decent society of the kind she takes her own to be, such rules would mean for the particular cases (or categories of case) that make demands on her attention.

Political constitutionalism of the kind that sets itself up as a rival to legal constitutionalism is ultimately self-contradictory. On the one hand, judicial review of the exercise of executive power is condemned because it involves interference in political matters, which should be determined by people or agencies accountable to Parliament. On the other hand, the courts are expected to ensure that executive agencies actually perform the tasks entrusted to them, so that Parliament's instructions are not disregarded; and the courts must prohibit the performance of other tasks not so entrusted to the agency in question, or a performance that flouts the conditions contained, whether explicitly or implicitly, in the pertinent delegation of power. These are rather plainly inconsistent positions. If the court is to fulfil its

---

[69] Adam Tomkins, *Our Republican Constitution* (Oxford: Hart Publishing, 2005).
[70] Ibid, ch 1.

proper function of keeping a public body within the boundaries of its authorized remit, it must interpret the relevant legislation: it must ascertain those boundaries by analysis of the nature and scope of the powers conferred, according to the best construction of the statute. And while the explicit terms of the statute will provide important guidance, they will do so only through interpretation—resolving the uncertainties and ambiguities that their application to specific instances inevitably generates.

Such uncertainties arise, primarily, because (as I argued in Chapter 5) ambiguity springs from context: unforeseen events occur to challenge our rough-and-ready preconceptions, forcing us to think harder about how best to apply the statute (and so how to understand the limits of executive power) in all the circumstances. Since that context is, in part, composed of legal and constitutional values— the taken-for-granted assumptions about law and liberty that sustain our ideal of government according to law—the court cannot separate its view about what Parliament *actually* ordained from its view about what any reasonable Parliament, appreciative of the consequences of its instructions for justice and liberty, *ought* to have ordained. These ideas cannot be readily distinguished because they amount to substantially the same thing: Parliament has specified those limits to executive power which, while consistent with successful implementation of the means and goals that its language indicates, serve to preclude any unnecessary interference with individual freedom irrelevant (or even wholly disproportionate) to the statutory purposes. At least, that is the only way we can interpret parliamentary instructions in a manner that honours the important role elected representatives must play in a liberal democracy—a democracy that respects human rights and basic freedoms as integral parts of the common good we strive, collectively, to define and nurture.

J. A. G. Griffith's celebration of the 'political constitution' does not deter him from acknowledging the courts' role in preventing abuse of executive power, where it results in injury to individuals; but he fears that the further development of legal doctrine may have unacceptable consequences:

Hitherto, control by the courts has been directed to cases where Government has purported to exercise powers which it does not possess either under statute or the prerogative; or where its procedures are contrary to widely accepted principles concerning bias or irrelevance or bad faith; or, exceptionally, where the decision is manifestly absurd. Beyond these categories the argument becomes one about the desirable distribution of power.[71]

The suggestion here is that, beyond certain obvious delimitations of boundary and settled matters of procedure, legal constraints melt into political matters, distinct from or extraneous to considerations of the rule of law. The suggestion is scarcely tenable, however, because whether or not, in any particular case, a public authority has exceeded its powers is a complex matter of statutory interpretation. We cannot draw the jurisdictional lines in advance as neatly as Griffith would desire. Whether or not a government agency enjoys the power it has purported to exercise may depend on many relevant factors: adverse consequences for individual rights or

---

[71] J A G Griffith, 'The Common Law and the Political Constitution' (2001) 117 LQR 42–67, at 58.

interests may indicate limits that, on the most plausible view of the statutory grant, may not (in all the circumstances) be exceeded. We cannot know, for example, whether a prison governor's power to intercept a prisoner's correspondence extends to letters seeking legal advice (and so attracting legal professional privilege) until we have set the relevant statutory provisions in their broader constitutional context, and appraised the arguments either way.[72]

Nor are matters of procedure neatly severable from questions of substance, as I have argued in Chapter 7. Standards of due process encompass considerations of both procedure and substance. Questions of relevance are pertinent to conclusions about unreasonableness or irrationality: what may be a relevant matter in one context may be largely or wholly irrelevant in another; its weight may vary in a manner that a court, required to correct any abuse of power, cannot ignore. The same basic questions about the legal limits on power can be addressed from different angles, but their *substance* is substantially unaltered, distinct from the specific doctrinal tools that come most readily to hand. While a public agency may have wide discretion to formulate a policy in some sphere of regulation, it must apply that policy consistently, avoiding arbitrary exceptions and exemptions. If, moreover, its policy has generated legitimate expectations on the part of affected private citizens, such expectations should not be dashed unfairly or unreasonably—though questions of fairness and reasonableness inevitably involve the courts in delicate judgements of value and degree.

We cannot, then, fix the division between law and politics on the basis of abstractly formulated doctrinal categories, as Griffith seems to suppose. Enforcing the separation of powers between Parliament and the executive government, and so preserving legislative supremacy, involves robust judicial appraisal of the exercise of power in particular cases. It is an appraisal that, depending on the circumstances, may carry the court into deep constitutional waters where the distinction between the legal and the political is only a matter of labels—rhetorical flourishes that obscure rather than illuminate contrasting philosophical approaches. We can all agree, with Griffith, that 'the review of substantive policy decisions made by public authorities acting within the four corners of their statutory or prerogative powers should be out of bounds to the courts'; but the critical question, of course, is the extent of the territory enclosed by the 'four corners'.[73] The sphere of 'substantive policy' is precisely what judicial review of an exercise of administrative discretion must attempt to identify. If, as Griffith maintains, the decisions in *Anisminic, Padfield,* and *Pergau Dam* are examples of judicial overreaching, they are so only in the light of reasons that pertain to the cogency of the judgments given in all the relevant circumstances.[74]

---

[72] See *R v Secretary of State for the Home Dept, ex p Leech (No 2)* [1994] QB 198 (considered in Chapter 7, above).

[73] Griffith, 'The Common Law and the Political Constitution', 63.

[74] Ibid; see *Anisminic Ltd v Foreign Compensation Commission* [1969] 2 AC 147, *Padfield v Minister of Agriculture, Fisheries and Food* [1968] AC 997, *R v Secretary of State for Foreign and Commonwealth Affairs, ex p World Development Movement* [1995] 1 WLR 386.

Not only is a political constitutionalist precluded from taking shelter in imaginary distinctions between supposedly water-tight doctrinal categories, but he is equally unable to distinguish review for legality from the judicial protection of fundamental rights. Such rights are only manifestations of the legal and constitutional values which, through common law thought and development, form part of the necessary background of any competent construction of statutory powers. Whether or not a prison governor may intercept the legal correspondence of a prisoner depends, in large part, on whether a person's ability to obtain confidential legal advice is a necessary part of any realistic right of access to the courts. And whether or not a prisoner may be prevented from having any face-to-face contact with a journalist, seeking to expose a potential miscarriage of justice, depends largely on the significance of the role of the media in sustaining a reliable system of criminal justice.[75] Review of the legality of an exercise of powers cannot be detached from questions of constitutional right: such questions are necessarily pertinent to the scope of the powers actually conferred (on the most reasonable interpretation) on the public agency.[76]

When, therefore, Adam Tomkins contends that, where there is uncertainty about the scope of a public authority's lawful powers, 'the courts should rule in favour of the outcome that protects or best protects individual liberty', he declares himself as much a legal as a political constitutionalist.[77] He embraces the separation of powers between legislature, executive and judiciary internal to the rule of law, conceived as a bastion of individual liberty and shield against the assertion of arbitrary power. He concedes the necessity to grant judicial power over particular cases, even when judicial decisions may have important implications for the public interest, recognizing that only such an independent jurisdiction can contain what would otherwise be a grave risk of oppression. Tomkins assumes, however, that uncertainty or ambiguity is merely a matter of linguistic imprecision which a better draftsman might have corrected; yet a degree of uncertainty arises when we are confronted by the consequences of a literal reading for particular cases—instances never contemplated, in all their individual complexity, at the time of enactment. It is precisely our commitment to civil liberties that generates the ambiguity: could Parliament really be supposed to have authorized such measures in a case of the present kind? If, as Tomkins suggests, the appropriate rule is that the courts should 'hold that the government has the power to interfere with individual liberty only where it is unambiguous, clear, and certain that Parliament has conferred such a power', the power will exist only where, having regard to the legitimate needs of public policy, its conferral would be *justified* in a liberal democracy based on British legal traditions.[78]

---

[75] *R v Secretary of State for the Home Dept, ex p Simms* [2000] 2 AC 115, 131 (see Chapter 7, above).

[76] Compare Paul Craig, 'Political Constitutionalism and the Judicial Role: A Response' (2011) 9 *I·CON* 112–31, at 122–7.

[77] Adam Tomkins, 'The Role of the Courts in the Political Constitution' (2010) 60 UTLJ 1–22, at 9.

[78] Ibid.

These conclusions are confirmed by Tomkins's own highly critical appraisal of *Gillan*, where the House of Lords upheld the legality of sweeping and extraordinary powers of 'stop and search' under the Terrorism Act 2000.[79] Gillan was stopped and searched while cycling near the ExCel Centre in London's Docklands, intent on protesting peacefully against an arms fair. Section 44 of the Act permitted a constable in uniform to stop and search any person or vehicle in a place where such powers were authorized by a senior police officer (at least the rank of commander in the case of the Metropolitan Police); an authorization could be given only when it was considered 'expedient for the prevention of acts of terrorism'. Section 45 provided that though the power only extended to searching for 'articles of a kind which could be used in connection with terrorism', it could be exercised whether or not the constable had grounds for suspecting the presence of such articles. In light of the obvious scope for abuse, there were strong grounds against a literal interpretation of these provisions; it was argued that such powers were available only where there were reasonable grounds for considering that they were 'necessary and suitable, in all the circumstances, for the prevention of terrorism'.[80] Although an authorization could not be made for longer than a period of twenty-eight days, a series of such authorizations—for the entire Metropolitan Police District—had been made continuously for successive periods since section 44 had come into force (more than two years previously).

Although Lord Bingham of Cornhill acknowledged the desirability of giving the term 'expedient' a meaning 'no wider than the context requires', having regard to the ordinary principle that stop and search powers should be exercised only on the basis of reasonable suspicion, he pointed to the close regulation of the powers (imposing conditions on authorization and exercise) as 'leaving no room for the inference that Parliament did not mean what it said'.[81] Bingham reverted, then, to a literal meaning which, though bolstered by the accompanying text, disregards the broader constitutional context. He also acknowledged some merit in the objection that it was 'one thing to authorize the exercise of an exceptional power to counter a particular and specific threat, but quite another to authorize what was, in effect, a continuous ban throughout the London area'.[82] Nevertheless, since the necessary authorizations and confirmations 'complied with the letter of the statute', he was unwilling to find illegality. The principle of legality articulated in *ex parte Simms*, enforcing a presumption in favour of liberty, did not apply: even if the provisions infringed a fundamental right, which Bingham thought debatable, they did not do so 'by general words but by provisions of a detailed, specific and unambiguous character'.[83] The force of the principle of legality is thereby blunted, its implementation made dependent on a

---

[79] *R (Gillan) v Metropolitan Police Commissioner* [2006] UKHL 12; the terms 'extraordinary' and 'sweeping' were applied by the Divisional Court, as Tomkins notes: Tomkins, 'The Role of the Courts in the Political Constitution', 11.

[80] See *Gillan*, para 13 (Lord Bingham of Cornhill).

[81] Ibid, para 14.   [82] Ibid, para 18.   [83] Ibid, para 15.

doubtful distinction between clear and ambiguous legislation, drawn in isolation from the specific context in point.

Tomkins, by contrast, would give the principle of legality expressed in *Simms* a stronger role, more suited to the defence of liberty; but that stance undermines his critique of legal constitutionalism: it confirms his position as, in the last analysis, both legal and political constitutionalist. He rightly protests that it would be impossible, in practice, ever to make any effective challenge to the use of such very broadly conceived powers, observing that the various safeguards were plainly of little practical benefit.[84] It is odd, however, to mount so vigorous a defence of the right to freedom from the limited interference involved in being stopped and searched by a police officer in public while, at the same time, denying the value of judicial scrutiny of curtailments of such fundamental rights as those of free speech or conscience or privacy. The broader the scope of the right, having regard to its fundamental character, the more its specific requirements depend on analysis of all the factors relevant to the case in view—involving a delicate adjustment of the competing demands of individual right and public policy. Respect for rights therefore entails the sort of case-by-case oversight that only independent courts can provide.

Tomkins hopes to shift responsibility to Parliament, obliging it to give more specific authority for any intrusion into liberty; and in that respect his position is an echo of the legalist philosophy of *Simms* itself: when the authority is sufficiently clear, the judges must obey, setting their reservations to one side. But the truth is that the statutory words can never do all the work on their own: their interpretation will, if rational, reflect the context in point; and a commitment to liberty, if genuine, will not evaporate when confronted by the bare language of a potentially authoritarian measure or by its rigid enforcement, insensitive to the consequences for particular cases. And just as there is no real distinction between clear and unambiguous legislation—ambiguity being largely a reflection of context— there is no straightforward distinction between so-called 'absolute' rights, on the one hand, and 'qualified' rights, on the other.[85] Even such allegedly absolute rights as the guarantee against torture and inhuman or degrading treatment, under Article 3 of the European Convention on Human Rights, entail judgements of degree: a line must be drawn, according to the context, on what (for example) amounts either to torture or degrading treatment; and social convention and expectation will inevitably be relevant to the judgements made. Because it is only in respect of particular cases, which arise to challenge governmental aims or methods, that we can reach clear conclusions about the limits of acceptable state power, we cannot both affirm basic rights and make the application of law a simple, largely automatic process. A liberal democrat must temper his enthusiasm for representative decision-making with concern for the effects, often unforeseen, on those with legitimate interests that conflict with governmental policy or determinations of public good.

---

[84] Tomkins, 'The Role of the Courts in the Political Constitution', 12–14.
[85] Tomkins emphasizes the distinction at ibid, 4–7.

Tomkins's legitimate criticism of the courts' record in *Gillan* is hard to square with his antipathy to judicial enforcement of the fundamental rights guaranteed by the European Convention. If, as he claims, Griffith was right to contend that the Convention consisted merely of 'statements of political conflict pretending to be resolutions of it', its enforcement giving judges too much naked political power, it must follow that the House of Lords was justified in *Gillan* in sticking to the literal terms of the statute.[86] Whatever we may think of the judgments, they reflect the need to balance the respective demands of personal liberty and national security; and while there is no reason to suppose that a reasonable accommodation cannot be found, it cannot be derived from the words of the statute alone. Judgements about reasonableness and proportionality are (as I have argued in Chapter 5) necessary constituents of rational interpretation: they are implicit in any conclusion about the legality of an exercise of public power whatever the specific terms of the legislation involved. A judge who adopts the kind of nuanced construction of the powers conferred on police officers by the Terrorism Act 2000 that Tomkins defends should, in consistency, exhibit a similar scepticism in the face of extravagant jurisdictional claims under the Prisons Act 1952 (and prison rules made thereunder) or indeed any other assertions of statutory power that threaten traditional civil and political liberties.[87]

The distinction Tomkins draws between cases where the judicial defence of liberty is appropriate and cases where it is not—between the justiciable and non-justiciable, as he would identify the difference—is no more tenable than the distinction, considered in Chapter 2, between large constitutional cases and routine administrative cases. He objects to major political questions about the limits of free speech, of the kind raised by the *Simms* and *ProLife Alliance* cases, being determined in the course of deciding particular cases, where the answers inevitably reflect the specific context. But any question of legality, in almost any field, may involve major questions of constitutional principle: the relevant legislation will acquire its true meaning only in the light of general principles, which mediate between statutory purpose and common law tradition. It is, moreover, only in the light of specific cases, with their own rather special complexities, that we can fully work out the implications of the abstract principles that rights exemplify. Insofar as political constitutionalism depends on drawing such sharp lines between statutory language and context, or between constitutional and administrative law, or between absolute and qualified rights, it rests on very shaky foundations. It attempts to solve by arbitrary line-drawing problems of interpretation that can only be solved by detailed *argument*, duly sensitive to all the relevant legal or political values as they apply to the matter at hand.

In *ProLife Alliance*, the House of Lords overturned the finding of the Court of Appeal that the Alliance's party election broadcast, condemning the practice of abortion, had been unlawfully censored by the BBC and commercial broadcasters: the restrictions imposed were only a performance of the obligation, under the Broadcasting Act

---

[86] Ibid, 3–4; Griffith, 'The Political Constitution', 14.
[87] Compare Craig, 'Political Constitutionalism and the Judicial Role: A Response', 127–30.

1990, to avoid the transmission of anything contrary to 'good taste and decency' or 'offensive to public feeling'.[88] Richard Bellamy echoes Tomkins's complaint that the decision represents a failure to protect free speech—a failure of legal constitutionalism. According to Bellamy, plaintiffs 'may need to take certain of the broader considerations off the table in order to strengthen or present their case in law, even though these may involve the key constitutional issues'.[89] In the result, the court's duty to address the legal points selected by the litigants, rather than the wider issues of principle at stake, impairs its ability to consider the 'full moral implications of an issue'. But this is all quite confused. Insofar as the 'full moral implications' are side-stepped, the court properly avoids deciding matters better left to the political realm with its procedures for democratic participation and decision. And insofar as it is *necessary* to address broader issues of principle in order to grapple reliably with the specific issues raised by the litigation, the court is right to do so: judicial decision-making would otherwise be inconsistent, different cases failing to exhibit a coherent approach to legal and constitutional principle.

According to Bellamy, 'the general question of whether the prohibition on broadcasts "offensive to public feeling" complied with the principle of freedom of expression was conceded not to be at issue' in *ProLife*, 'leaving the Lords merely to consider the narrower legal point of whether or not the broadcasters had correctly applied this prohibition in this particular case'.[90] But the challenge was made, in effect, to the *applicability* of the prohibition to the sort of case in issue: the general principle of freedom of speech was fully engaged, even if the legality of the prohibition as regards other categories of case was not in question. The Court of Appeal was fully aware of the distinction—placing the case in the appropriate context of political speech at the time of a general election—even if the majority in the House of Lords failed to understand the nature of the challenge. The allegedly 'narrower' issue of application was precisely the pertinent question of principle: no one thinks that the principle of free speech is incompatible with any restrictions at all on broadcasting, whatever the circumstances. The question of principle concerned the *scope or extent* of the statutory prohibition, on correct construction—duly sensitive to the basic constitutional values at stake.[91]

Tomkins and Bellamy turn a proper criticism of the Lords' decision into a misguided critique of legal constitutionalism: the decision illustrates merely the undeniable deficiencies of weak, half-hearted judicial review. Their error is symptomatic of an underlying failure to understand the way in which political morality is sensitive to context. We are presented with a false dichotomy, placing judgements about rights either in the political sphere or the legal; whereas they necessarily transcend the division. Bellamy is right to protest against assertions that democratic decision-making is typically marked by self-interest or prejudice: it may instead

---

[88] *R (ProLife Alliance) v BBC* [2003] UKHL 23 (see Chapter 1, above).
[89] Richard Bellamy, *Political Constitutionalism: A Republican Defence of the Constitutionality of Democracy* (Cambridge: Cambridge University Press, 2007), 36.
[90] Ibid, 37.
[91] See the analysis of *ProLife* in Chapter 1, above.

reflect genuine commitments to justice.[92] But the consequence is that the judicial application of enacted laws must grapple with considerations of justice too: it could not otherwise begin to honour the product of democratic deliberation in the spirit of intelligent cooperation required. Bellamy is fully entitled to doubt whether an enacted bill of rights is necessary for a rights-culture to flourish, or even whether it is beneficial.[93] But he cannot sensibly suppose that such a culture could endure if courts failed to support it, enforcing constitutional rights when the facts of particular cases make it appropriate to do so.[94]

V

Richard Bellamy's rejection of legal constitutionalism presents a challenge to any theory of law grounded in a moral ideal of the rule of law.[95] Sceptical of theories that treat law as a counterweight to political power, he places his faith entirely in the beneficial operation of ordinary politics, allowing the competition between rival groups and interests to moderate the risk of domination or oppression. Too many versions of the rule of law, in Bellamy's view, embrace an implausible vision of law as the good law, capable of harmonizing individual and collective interests at a level above the cut-and-thrust of democratic politics: 'Enshrine good laws in the constitution and entrust a special caste of legal guardians to oversee them, and the rule of persons can be subordinated to the rule of law.'[96] Despite his affirmation of the republican ideal of government as an 'empire of laws' (in the neo-Roman conception of Cicero, Machiavelli, and Harrington) Bellamy resists reliance on any special form of law to eliminate the 'domination of arbitrary rule'. He takes literally the idea that the people, as citizens, should rule themselves: 'the rule of law simply is the democratic rule of persons'.[97]

F. A. Hayek and Ronald Dworkin are taken as exemplifying, in their different ways, a mistaken identification of the rule of law with an ideal of law above and beyond the ordinary practice of politics. Hayek's emphasis on general rules of just conduct, as opposed to particular rules concerned with specific policy objectives or identifiable persons, is condemned for impracticality: legislation is sometimes

---

[92] Bellamy, *Political Constitutionalism*, 35.

[93] Ibid, 48–51.

[94] There is a similar tension between the demand for a stronger judicial defence of the rule of law, on the one hand, and an asserted scepticism about the value of judicial review in defence of human rights, on the other, in K D Ewing and Joo-Cheong Tham, 'The Continuing Futility of the Human Rights Act' [2008] PL 668–93; for an effective response, see Aileen Kavanagh, 'Judging the Judges under the Human Rights Act: Deference, Disillusionment and the "War on Terror"' [2009] PL 287–305. Kavanagh complains (at 303) that 'democratic sceptics fervently oppose any expansion of the judicial power to protect rights on the basis that judges are unelected, unaccountable and lack sufficient legitimacy', while at the same time 'they heap scathing criticism on the courts when they fail to obstruct policies contained in primary legislation—even when the justification for that failure is a constitutionally appropriate judicial respect for the superior expertise, competence and legitimacy of the elected branches of government'.

[95] Bellamy, *Political Constitutionalism*, ch 2.

[96] Ibid, 54.   [97] Ibid, 80–3.

necessary to secure specific ends, and judicial discretion in the application of rules cannot be eliminated.[98] Dworkin's holistic approach to the law, whereby the content of law depends on an overarching general theory, grounded in moral principle, is also rejected: that approach is alleged (among other defects) to enhance rather than curtail judicial discretion.[99] Abandoning any aspiration to a society in which people could identify and endorse a genuine common good, underpinned by a moral ideal of the rule of law, Bellamy thinks we must fall back on a rough equality of bargaining power to prevent domination in a pluralistic society: 'justice emerges from a balance of power'.[100]

We may legitimately wonder whether Bellamy's view of the rule of law, insofar as its identification of law with representative democracy seems attractive, does not trade too heavily on its questionable characterization of legal constitutionalism. Neither Hayek nor Dworkin, when closely read, defend rule by 'philosopher kings'; nor does a strong judicial interpretive role depend on a codified constitution or the power of a Supreme Court to quash legislation considered to infringe it. It is a major theme of this book that statutory interpretation is by its very nature holistic: we can resolve uncertainties and conflicts rationally and fairly only by placing any specific dispute in its larger constitutional context, seeking the answer that best conforms to the principles of the legal order itself, treated as the charter of a free and equal society. Hayek and Dworkin both attempt to elucidate our sense, as lawyers, that disputes which appear irresolvable, when viewed in isolation, are usually susceptible of rational and impartial adjudication when we adopt a larger view, broadening the range of relevant considerations by reference to related or analogous areas of law. And, as I have stressed, once the correct interpretation of legislative provisions is attained, and their application made duly sensitive to the circumstances in view, the absence of any formal power to quash them is usually unimportant—irrelevant to the preservation of the rule of law.

Bellamy cites Cass Sunstein's defence of analogical, case-by-case reasoning, allowing decision by reference to agreed outcomes rather than deeper principles, about which there may be no agreement. There may be 'incompletely theorized agreements on particular outcomes, accompanied by agreements on the narrow or low-level principles that account for them'.[101] Low-level principles include 'most of the ordinary material of legal "doctrine"—the general class of principles and justifications that are not said to derive from any large theories of the right or the good, that have ambiguous relations to large theories, and that are compatible with more than one such theory'. There are various considerations that recommend judicial avoidance of high-level theory; but 'fundamentally, it is in the absence of a democratic pedigree that the system of precedent, analogy, and incompletely theorized agreement has such an important place'.[102] Sunstein contrasts his own

---

[98] Ibid, 67–74.   [99] Ibid, 74–9.   [100] Ibid, 81.

[101] Cass R Sunstein, *Legal Reasoning and Political Conflict* (New York: Oxford University Press, 1996), 37.

[102] Ibid, 46.

favoured approach with Dworkinian integrity: Dworkin's model judge, Hercules, guided by the ambition of a comprehensive theory of law, presents (it is alleged) a misleading image.[103]

Yet the gulf between Sunstein's apparently more legalistic stance and Dworkin's grander, holistic approach is, in practice, far narrower than it may at first appear. As usual, so much depends on the specific context within which we assess the most appropriate scale of theoretical ambition. Sunstein proceeds to explain the desirability of 'conceptual ascent' to higher-level theory in the face of doubts about the reliability or consistency of lower-level principles. He concedes, at least, that there is 'some truth' in the contention that low-level principles must be tested by reference to more ambitious forms of reasoning: 'In this way we might conclude that judges should think of incompletely theorized agreements as an early step toward something both wider and deeper.'[104] Sunstein also notes that analogies depend on reasons, so that analogical reasoning can lead to the study of abstract principle: 'concrete rulings may be synthesized', so that a more general principle emerges: 'Sometimes the process of low-level judging will yield greater abstraction or a highly refined and coherent set of principles—the conceptual ascent.'[105]

Dworkin is plainly entitled to doubt whether there is any real difference between Sunstein's approach and his own 'theory-embedded' account of adjudication.[106] Insofar as Sunstein commends a judicial approach focused primarily on the area of law directly concerned, structured by existing precedent, he echoes Dworkin's own principle of 'local priority', which helps to preserve stability and protect legitimate expectations. And Dworkin is equally entitled to object to the unhelpful nature of the distinction between low-level (or 'mid-level') and high-level principles, which inevitably depends, once again, so much on the context in which such labels are invoked. As Dworkin observes, 'the very idea of an *a priori* constraint on legal reflection, defined as a boundary of abstraction such reflection must not cross' is phenomenologically bizarre:

Lawyers (like other people) discover the scope of reflection they need to pursue in the course of inquiry, by finding where inquiry leads before a responsible resting place is reached. They do not—cannot—accept a methodology that stipulates in advance where they must stop no matter how inconclusive or unsatisfying their reflection to that point.[107]

The argument about adjudication is closely tied to the argument over political theory; and just as we can be blinded by a false antithesis in the case of the former—case-by-case reasoning versus examination of principle—so we can be equally misled

---

[103] See especially Ronald Dworkin, *Law's Empire* (London: Fontana Press, 1986).
[104] Sunstein, *Legal Reasoning and Political Conflict*, 51–2.
[105] Ibid, 55.
[106] Ronald Dworkin, *Justice in Robes* (Cambridge, Mass: Harvard University Press, 2006), 66–72. Dworkin is defending the claim that adjudication proceeds on the basis of principles 'embedded' in legal practice, i.e. that such principles 'offer the best justification of more general legal practice in the doctrinal area' concerned: ibid, 51–2.
[107] Ibid, 69.

by an exaggerated contrast between democratic deliberation and legal reasoning.[108] We cannot make any cast-iron distinctions between the political and judicial spheres based on appeal to democracy or the rule of law. As Dworkin says, in response to Sunstein's contention that 'the development of large-scale theories of the right and the good is a democratic task, not a judicial one', it is not clear how democratic deliberation could generate such theories 'unless judges accepted that it was part of their responsibility to identify which such theories were latent in legislation and other political events'. It is only through judicial 'interpretation of more concrete enactments that we can identify the principles which we have together embraced'.[109]

Bellamy complains that 'Dworkin's holistic approach to the law can often be arbitrary, encouraging the application of principles and considerations in settled parts of the law that are remote from, and inappropriate to, the case at hand'; but he plainly misunderstands that approach.[110] If the principles were 'inappropriate' it would be because they had no weight in the circumstances, or were clearly outweighed by countervailing principles. If, as Bellamy asserts, 'different parts of the law give different weights to different goods, values and types of moral claim', it is because the context is critical to any decent argument over legal or moral rights or claims. If civil and criminal cases 'tend to operate with different standards of evidence and notions of responsibility', it is because the relevant moral considerations differ. The difference between the civil and criminal standards of proof, for example, reflects the graver moral injury involved in mistaken conviction of a criminal offence than is typically involved in an erroneous finding of facts elsewhere. To reject coherence, at least at a relatively abstract level of principle, is to embrace irrationality and unjustified discrimination between persons or groups.

There would be a genuine dispute over the proper character of adjudication if Bellamy were understood to endorse a pluralism of the sort that attributed legitimacy to whatever emerged from an undiluted clash of competing interests: then the law would have to be treated as a series of unrelated compromises, reflecting the current balance of power across each of the numerous social and political issues that had generated specific legislation. Instead, however, Bellamy defends a version of republicanism that celebrates democratic deliberation through public reason, albeit a broader, more expansive form of public reason than John Rawls would allow.[111] Whereas Rawls's conception of public reason envisages a separation between people's full or 'comprehensive' moral outlooks and their commitment to certain principles underpinning their status as equal citizens, Bellamy prefers a more relaxed, less exclusive approach: individuals 'must be allowed to base their reasoning and arguments on their personal moral or religious views while accepting the need, as a matter of civility within a

---

[108] See also Allan, *Constitutional Justice: A Liberal Theory of the Rule of Law* (Oxford: Oxford University Press, 2001), ch 9.
[109] Dworkin, *Justice in Robes*, 70–1 (citing Sunstein, *Legal Reasoning and Political Conflict*, 53).
[110] Bellamy, *Political Constitutionalism*, 76.
[111] John Rawls, *Political Liberalism* (New York: Columbia University Press, 1993), especially Lecture VI.

democracy where all citizens are respected as autonomous reasoners, to couch them in terms others can be expected to recognize as reasons and argumentation'.[112] It is expected that such public discourse will filter out 'the most blatantly unjust and self-serving positions that fail to treat others with equal concern and respect'; and any resulting compromise will be the product of attempts to accommodate different perspectives within a coherent programme of government.[113]

There is no fundamental inconsistency between Bellamy's conception of deliberative democracy, based on the recognition of citizens' equal status, and a Dworkinian account of adjudication; insofar as Bellamy's reliance on Sunstein suggests the contrary, it evokes an exaggerated contrast between ordinary common law adjudication and the ideal of principled coherence latent within it. While dismissing Dworkin's example of 'chequer-board' compromises as a 'prime instance' of the legal constitutionalist's contempt for compromise, Bellamy observes that abortion statutes have not, in practice, made irrational distinctions between different groups of women (such as those born on odd numbered days of the month by contrast with those born on even-numbered days).[114] Bellamy and Dworkin would naturally agree that any acceptable solution must balance such different considerations as the right to life of the unborn child, at least in the later stages of pregnancy, and the potentially conflicting rights of the pregnant mother, especially where the mother's life is itself at risk. If we suppose that the resulting compromise represents a reasonable accommodation of rights or interests, any judicial interpretation in cases of doubt must probe the nature of that compromise—seeking to identify its implications for the resolution of conflict in doubtful or borderline cases.[115] If necessary, a judge would have to look to analogous areas of law, or even general constitutional principle, for further guidance. A rational compromise of the kind everyone might fairly be expected to accept must be rooted in values that, at a relatively abstract level, everyone (or almost everyone) can share.

Many readers will no doubt sympathize with Sunstein's view that 'there is no special magic in theories or abstractions', agreeing with him that 'theories are simply the (humanly constructed) means by which people make sense of the judgements that constitute their ethical and political worlds'.[116] On that view, the abstract 'deserves no priority over the particular; neither should be treated as foundational'. In common law thought, there is always an interaction of general and particular: principles are tested by reference to their power to justify settled and accepted precedents. As Sunstein says, 'any resulting theory will likely have been developed through generalization and clarifying incompletely theorized outcomes and doing

---

[112] Bellamy, *Political Constitutionalism*, 192. Dworkin also rejects Rawls's narrow conception of public reason: see Dworkin, *Justice in Robes*, 252–4.

[113] Bellamy, *Political Constitutionalism*, 192–3.

[114] Ibid, 193; see Dworkin, *Law's Empire*, 178–84.

[115] Compare Dworkin, *Law's Empire*, 179: 'If there must be compromise because people are divided about justice, then the compromise must be external, not internal; it must be compromise about which scheme of justice to adopt rather than a compromised scheme of justice.'

[116] Sunstein, *Legal Reasoning and Political Conflict*, 52.

so by constant reference to concrete cases, against which the theory is measured'.[117] Dworkin's theory of integrity can be understood as an attempt to encapsulate precisely that interaction of the abstract and the more concrete—the interdependence of precedent and principle. When Sunstein declares that judges 'should adopt a presumption rather than a taboo against high-level theorization', there is no reason for Dworkin to dissent.[118]

In his own defence of analogical reasoning and deference to precedent, Bellamy invokes a conception of law that scarcely differs from Dworkin's theory of integrity. His suggestion that precedent 'provides a common resource of diverse considerations' on which lawyers can draw, in their search for appropriate analogies, echoes the legal constitutionalist concern to connect legal tradition with current moral opinion, fusing legal and moral argument.[119] If the law 'becomes a means for expressing disagreements and differences within a common language', such disagreements and differences must be resolved by critical scrutiny of previous decisions: the law is developed and reformed in the very process of its application.[120] Significantly, Bellamy endorses the decision in *R v R*, in which the House of Lords declined to recognize a husband's immunity from prosecution for the rape of his wife, based on the implied consent to sexual relations formerly attributed to the marriage contract.[121] Resisting objections deriving from a 'positivist and democratic point of view', Bellamy observes that the judges were able to make 'incremental adjustments' that followed a general trend in earlier cases. If, however, as he contends, no reference were needed to 'any grand moral principles' beyond those implicit in the previous cases, it was because the court was building on the foundations laid by other lawyers, who had sought to interpret the law as a scheme of justice fit for a society that acknowledged the equal status of men and women.

Moreover, there is a smaller gulf between Bellamy and Hayek than might initially be obvious. Notwithstanding his emphasis on general rules as a safeguard against arbitrariness and oppression, Hayek acknowledged the need for rules to distinguish between different groups, according to their proper purposes. And his criterion for judging the legitimacy of such distinctions—whether they are equally recognized as justified by those inside and those outside the group concerned—is affirmed by Bellamy himself: the rule of law prevails when the law has the 'capacity to evince reciprocity and hence obtain mutual assent from citizens'.[122] Nor did Hayek believe that enacted rules could 'eliminate judicial discretion', as Bellamy

---

[117] Ibid, 56.

[118] Ibid, 57; Dworkin, *Justice in Robes,* 71–2.

[119] Bellamy, *Political Constitutionalism*, 85.

[120] Compare Lon L Fuller, *Anatomy of the Law* (Harmondsworth: Penguin Books, 1971), 136: 'The precedents become…like a common language; they preserve those systematic elements of the law without which communication between generations of lawyers, and among lawyers of the same generation, would be impossible. At the same time, while they may direct the course of change, they impose no unbreachable obstacle to it.'

[121] Bellamy, *Political Constitutionalism*, 86–7; *R v R* [1992] 1 AC 599 (see further Chapter 3, above).

[122] Ibid, 73; Hayek, *The Constitution of Liberty* (London: Routledge & Kegan Paul, 1960), 154 (see further Chapter 3, above).

contends: he rather maintained (in common with Dworkin) that judicial discretion, disciplined by legal principle, was a radically different notion from that of administrative discretion, whereby officials determine particular cases according to the demands of a governmental policy objective. Hayek had no illusions about gapless codes of law, but rather defended adherence to the *spirit* of the law when sticking to the letter wrought manifest injustice. His conclusion was not merely that the judge should fill in gaps in the written law 'by appeal to yet unarticulated principles', but further that, 'even when those rules which have been articulated seem to give an unambiguous answer, if they are in conflict with the general sense of justice he should be free to modify his conclusions when he can find some unwritten rule which justifies such modification and which, when articulated, is likely to receive general assent'.[123]

Hayek objected to the exercise of discretion in a sense that made individuals subject to the fluctuating and temporary judgements of officials about how best to achieve some policy goal or further the public interest, as they might define it from case to case. The judge's task was to 'discover the implications contained in the spirit of the whole system of valid rules of law or to express as a general rule, when necessary, what was not explicitly stated previously in a court of law or by the legislator'; he could not seek to secure specific results in the way that an administrator might wish to implement a current policy initiative.[124] The difference is that the law attempts to regulate relationships between citizens in the manner that best preserves individual autonomy, allowing each to pursue his own ends while respecting the similar independence of others. An administrative policy, by contrast, aims at a specific outcome (such as a cleaner environment or the advancement of a particular industry or economic region). Insofar as such a policy is pursued by exercise of administrative discretion, as opposed to the impartial application of general rules, private citizens are vulnerable to forms of interference that may be both unpredictable and insensitive to their own needs and interests: such needs or interests will usually be outweighed by the wider public interest, as judged by officials from time to time. In the result, benefits and burdens may be very unequally shared, and the shifting pattern of official judgements very hard to challenge.

While Hayek is, no doubt, overly fearful of administrative discretion, underestimating the value of judicial review as a defence against its oppressive exercise, Bellamy ignores it almost completely. There is little or no recognition of the dangers of domination presented by the delegation of administrative discretion to government officials and agencies, authorized to use coercion as a tool of public policy or to further contestable conceptions of the public interest. The administrative state is largely absent from Bellamy's account of political constitutionalism; but the omission gravely undermines the coherence of his assault on legal constitutionalism. The more freedom enjoyed by officials to discriminate between persons or groups, according to the needs of their own administrative programmes, the greater is the need for independent judicial protection. Only an impartial judiciary can provide

---

[123] F A Hayek, *Law, Legislation and Liberty* (London: Routledge & Kegan Paul, 1982), vol 1, 118.
[124] Hayek, *The Constitution of Liberty*, 212.

a remedy for disproportionate intrusions into personal liberty; and only by reference to a general scheme of constitutional justice can questions of proportionality be fairly and consistently determined. If the judicial record in curbing abuse of official power is as poor as Bellamy asserts, the solution must lie in more vigorous judicial scrutiny; political accountability is too diffuse, even when effective, to reach abuses of power in particular instances.[125]

More fundamentally, however, Bellamy appears to assume that review of executive action raises no questions about judicial appraisal of primary legislation—that one can concede the legitimacy of the former without any necessary implications for the nature and limits of legislative authority. As servants of a sovereign Parliament, the courts must ensure that ministers and executive agencies observe the terms and limits of their statutory mandates; and in thus enforcing the law (it is supposed) the judges may take the content of those statutory mandates largely for granted. It has been a major theme of this book that, to the contrary, the law's content is always a matter of interpretation, dependent on judgements of value that cannot be evaded by any responsible legal reasoner. What Parliament has authorized an official or agency to do in particular circumstances is always a matter of judgement, reflecting considered opinions about what, in such circumstances, it would be reasonable (or not unreasonable) to authorize. The meaning of legislative instructions cannot be divorced from the context in point: they derive their sense from the overarching tradition of governance to which they contribute. What it is lawful or reasonable for a public authority to do, in performance of its statutory tasks, cannot be answered in the abstract. It depends on the consequences for constitutional rights and settled expectations and equal citizenship—all those large dimensions of legality that opponents of legal constitutionalism appear, in theory if not in practice, to banish from public law.

VI

We may wonder whether, like Adam Tomkins, Richard Bellamy is a reluctant legal constitutionalist once he is forced to confront the complexities of governance according to law. His defence of both legislative supremacy and political constitutionalism leaves room for adjudication which is sensitive to legal principle. Admittedly, he identifies statutory interpretation with the mere resolution of ambiguities and inconsistencies; but the requisite judicial 'discretion' encompasses, in practice, the court's resistance to the blunt 'two-strikes-and-you-are-out rule' in *Offen*—the ruling that Conor Gearty thinks 'disembowelled a...savage legislative intervention' into criminal justice.[126] Bellamy's political constitutionalism is also flexible enough to accommodate *Ghaidan*, in which the House of Lords reinterpreted the Rent

---

[125] See Bellamy, *Political Constitutionalism*, 247–50.
[126] Richard Bellamy, 'Political Constitutionalism and the Human Rights Act' (2011) 9 I·CON 86–111, at 103–4; *Offen* [2001] 1 WLR 253, considered in Chapter 1, above (see Conor Gearty, *Principles of Human Rights Adjudication* (Oxford: Oxford University Press, 2004), 77).

Act 1977 as allowing same-sex couples the same rights, in respect of a secure tenancy on the death of a partner, as applied to those living as husband and wife (even if not actually married).[127] Bellamy considers that such non-literal interpretation, or reconstruction, was permissible on the ground that 'Parliament itself had amended the 1977 Act in 1998 to make provision for unmarried heterosexual couples, thereby implying a change of legislative focus from official marriage to cohabitation'.[128] It is, of course, a change of focus that has implications for legal principle. It is hard to resist the conclusion that, in the context of any specific attempt to reconcile statutory instructions with principles of justice and equality, the legal and political constitutionalist may find themselves on similar ground—ideological objections to all but formal conceptions of the rule of law implicitly laid aside. Admittedly, Bellamy would have preferred a declaration of incompatibility in *R v A*; but his discussion here too is nuanced, acknowledging the complexity of the interpretative task.[129]

In supposing, moreover, that there is an instructive contrast between *Ghaidan* and *Bellinger*, Bellamy echoes the view of other writers, including Aileen Kavanagh, who have also defended both decisions.[130] In *Bellinger*, the House of Lords had to decide whether a valid marriage subsisted between a couple who, though living together as husband and wife, had been through a marriage ceremony after the appellant, who was born male, had undergone gender reassignment treatment (including surgery).[131] The Matrimonial Causes Act 1973, section 11(c), provided that a marriage was void unless the parties were 'respectively male and female'; and the lower courts had held, following previous authority, that a person's sex at birth, as determined by chromosomal, gonadal, and genital tests, could not be changed for the purposes of that provision.[132] The House of Lords acknowledged that the failure to recognize gender reassignment for the purposes of marriage was not compatible with Articles 8 and 12 of the European Convention (protecting privacy and family life and guaranteeing the right to marry, respectively). In *Goodwin v United Kingdom*, the European Court of Human Rights had held that the failure to give legal recognition to gender reassignment, for various purposes besides marriage, had become unlawful, having regard to increasingly sophisticated types of surgery and hormonal treatment and changing perceptions of the balance between the relevant considerations in determining a person's sex.[133] The House of Lords declined, however, to read the Matrimonial Causes Act consistently with the applicable Convention rights, making instead a declaration of incompatibility under the Human Rights Act, section 4.

---

[127] *Ghaidan v Godin-Mendoza* [2004] UKHL 30, considered in Chapter 5, above.

[128] Bellamy, 'Political Constitutionalism and the Human Rights Act', 108.

[129] Ibid, 107–8; *R v A (No 2)* [2001] UKHL 25, considered in Chapter 5, above. Bellamy's conclusions about this case are prompted by his implausible attempt to mark off legislative 'scope' as a constraint on interpretation that would operate (it would appear) quite independently of constitutional context: ibid, 102–10.

[130] Aileen Kavanagh, *Constitutional Review under the UK Human Rights Act* (Cambridge: Cambridge University Press, 2009), ch 5.

[131] *Bellinger v Bellinger* [2003] UKHL 21.

[132] See *Corbett v Corbett (orse Ashley)* [1971] P 83.

[133] *Goodwin v United Kingdom* (2002) 35 EHRR 447.

Lord Nicholls of Birkenhead held that to ascribe a novel sense to the terms 'male' and 'female' in the 1973 Act would be a 'major change in the law', having far-reaching implications:

It raises issues whose solution calls for extensive inquiry and the widest public consultation and discussion. Questions of social policy and administrative feasibility arise at several points, and their interaction has to be evaluated and balanced. The issues are altogether ill-suited for determination by courts and court procedures. They are pre-eminently a matter for Parliament, the more especially when the government, in unequivocal terms, has already announced its intention to introduce comprehensive primary legislation on this difficult and sensitive subject.[134]

But this is to say merely that legislation should be made by Parliament rather than the courts. While it is true that it would be neither prudent nor legitimate for a court to try to resolve wide-ranging questions of social policy or administrative feasibility, it is perfectly possible for a court to declare a person's existing legal rights or status; and Mrs Bellinger (as the appellant was called throughout the proceedings) required only judicial recognition of her married status. If the Government proposed to bring forward new measures for Parliament's approval—measures that culminated in the Gender Recognition Act 2004—the court could proceed with greater confidence that a decision in favour of Mrs Bellinger would not create serious anomalies elsewhere. In any event, it is inherent in the judicial role that any decision will create a precedent that may force reconsideration of other parts of the law; but nothing is *prejudged* because in future cases, raising different issues, the court can distinguish the earlier decision of a specific question—in this case, Mrs Bellinger's marital status, having regard to the very substantial gender reassignment that she had undergone.

As Tom Hickman rightly observes, the court did not need to go beyond the circumstances of the case before it.[135] It did not need to look beyond the issue of marriage to other areas where the rights of transsexual persons to recognition of their acquired gender were not currently recognized: 'There was no substance to Lord Nicholls's fear that the court had to settle government policy on the legal entitlements of transsexuals across the board, or do nothing at all.'[136] As Thorpe LJ had noted, in his dissenting judgment in the Court of Appeal, the court was not required to resolve more general issues of policy but only a narrow question arising under the Matrimonial Causes Act, when correctly interpreted.[137] It is very doubtful whether information about government plans for legislative reform was relevant to the legal proceedings. Judicial speculation about such matters is clearly extraneous to the matter of a complainant's present legal rights, and may in any event prove unfounded. Hickman considers the possibility that *Bellinger* might have been followed by a change of Government with different legislative priorities.

---

[134] [2003] UKHL 21, para 37.
[135] Tom Hickman, *Public Law after the Human Rights Act* (Oxford: Hart Publishing, 2010), 91.
[136] Ibid.
[137] *Bellinger v Bellinger* [2001] EWCA Civ 1140, para 152.

If a new Government had abandoned proposals for reform, courts in future liti-gation would be 'helpless, discovering that the House of Lords had renounced the ability to assist transsexuals by denying the ability to embrace them within section 11(c)'.[138]

If the court's refusal to recognize the validity of Mrs Bellinger's marriage can be justified, it is on the basis that in *Goodwin* the European Court envisaged only a right to amendment of existing law: it did not question the Convention-compatibility of the Matrimonial Causes Act at the time of the purported marriage, which was not therefore valid. The Court had previously treated the United Kingdom's treat-ment of transsexual people as falling within the country's legitimate 'margin of appreciation'. Moreover, Lord Hope observed that the Human Rights Act itself had no retrospective effect, preventing reliance on section 3 to affirm the validity of a marriage ceremony conducted in 1981.[139] However, the court's preoccupation with the complexities of social policy and anticipated legislative reform betrayed, at root, a misguided view of section 3 as a *remedy* for the infringement of human rights. The question then becomes a matter of choosing the most appropriate rem-edy, having regard to alternative means of ensuring consistency between English and Convention law. When it is appreciated that section 3 is, instead, a guide to the *correct interpretation of existing law*, the nature of the judicial role in defence of legality can be more clearly understood.[140]

Aileen Kavanagh invokes *Bellinger* and the critical literature it has spawned 'to elucidate further the nature of the judicial choice between sections 3 and 4' of the Human Rights Act.[141] There is, however, no such *choice*: a declaration of incom-patibility is the measure of last resort when it is impossible to interpret existing law in line with Convention rights. Kavanagh argues that the courts 'have an important constitutional responsibility to ensure that they should only make those decisions which rest on an appropriate degree of expertise, law-making competence and legitimacy'.[142] But the pertinent expertise, in the present context, is legal expertise; there is no law-making involved, in the strict sense of the term; and legitimacy is a function of the ordinary judicial task of interpreting the law. There is no essential qualitative difference between statutory interpretation that draws on settled common law principle, on the one hand, and interpretation that takes full account of the European Convention rights, on the other. Section 3 simply extends or strengthens the court's jurisdiction to have regard to all relevant legal sources in determining the rights and duties of the parties before it. It does not confer a discretion to *change* the law if, in the judges' opinion, a change would be desirable, all things considered.[143]

---

[138] Hickman, *Public Law after the Human Rights Act*, 93.
[139] [2003] UKHL 21, para 65.
[140] See also the discussion in Chapter 5, above.
[141] Kavanagh, *Constitutional Review under the UK Human Rights Act*, 137.
[142] Ibid, 137–8.
[143] Elsewhere Kavanagh accepts that 'section 3(1) does not mark a radical departure from interpreta-tive methods and devices available to the courts prior to the HRA', changing only the 'constitutional context' in which the presumption in favour of protecting rights operates: *Constitutional Review*, 109.

It is a critical feature of the rule of law that a court, properly so termed, should decide cases according to the law that applies to the facts in issue: the parties are entitled to the court's best judgement of their rights or obligations. If judicial doubts about expertise or competence or legitimacy intervene to qualify that judgement, the parties are deprived of the protection of the law. Such considerations are sometimes relevant to the process of determining the law, counselling caution, for example, in reviewing the legality of decisions of expert officials or agencies; but they cannot justify the refusal to enforce what, after careful study, the court decides the law requires. Perhaps the subject of gender reassignment is a matter ideally regulated by systematic legislative reform, in preference to piecemeal case-by-case common law development; but it is an abdication of responsibility for judges to refuse to enforce the law in the particular case, even if that involves overruling a previous decision now understood to be erroneous—inconsistent with fundamental principles of law that the court affirms.

No doubt, it was hard to know precisely where to draw the line between transsexual persons who have undergone different degrees of treatment; but the common law method is always to proceed from case to case, demanding good reasons for drawing distinctions, pertinent to the specific issues arising. The possibility of a weaker claim by someone who had not undergone Mrs Bellinger's extensive treatment was no reason at all—despite Lord Nicholls's claim to the contrary—for a refusal to honour her own Convention rights.[144] If, as Hickman points out, any subsequent legislation were challenged for failure to comply with the Convention, or if a dispute arose over its interpretation, the court would inevitably have to determine the content of the applicable Convention rights. There would be no escape from the obligation to determine the justifiability of the relevant distinctions between male and female. The elements of social policy and administrative feasibility that concerned the House of Lords were mainly consequences of the breadth and novelty of the Convention rights in question: they could not be invoked as reasons for failing to enforce such rights without, in effect, denying the rights themselves.

Gavin Phillipson reaches similar conclusions, observing that 'the role of the courts is surely to do justice to the individual—in this case remedy a violation of her rights—and leave it to Government and legislature to sort out the overall legislative and administrative scheme'.[145] Kavanagh objects, in response, that merely because it is possible for judges to intervene does not mean that they should: 'judges must advance arguments to show that their conclusions are right, just or legitimate, not simply that they have taken an available option'. But the force of Phillipson's critique must be that it is *not* simply an available option: the rule of law means, in

---

Stephen Gardbaum's general preference for a greater use of section 4, which he regards as the distinctive mark of the new hybrid British constitutional model, also rests on a challengeable view regarding the permissible limits of interpretative construction of statutes (whether at common law or under section 3): see Gardbaum, 'Reassessing the New Commonwealth Model of Constitutionalism' (2010) 8 I·CON 167–206.

[144] [2003] UKHL 21, para 40.

[145] Gavin Phillipson, 'Deference, Discretion, and Democracy in the Human Rights Act Era' (2007) 60 CLP 40–78, at 66.

this context, the enforcement of legal rights by courts acting within their jurisdiction. As he rightly observes, there was no true question of alternative remedies, requiring *either* Parliament *or* the courts to act: 'the courts could have carried out their limited, but crucial judicial role of vindicating Mrs Bellinger's individual rights; Parliament could then have proceeded to do its job of bringing forward a comprehensive new legislative scheme for everyone'.

According to Kavanagh, Phillipson's mistake is to assume that 'the court's only duty is to do justice to the individual', whereas that duty must instead be balanced 'against values such as certainty and predictability in the law'. Moreover, the courts must acknowledge their institutional limitations: they cannot provide a remedy for every violation of rights. Underlying the disagreement, however, is the contrast between internal and external points of view that has been emphasized throughout this book. The treatment of sections 3 and 4 of the Human Rights Act as alternative remedies, offering a choice that invokes considerations of political strategy, is external to ordinary legal reasoning, when properly conducted. It turns judges into political operators who use the litigants as means to secure a different legal regime, contrary to their constitutional role as impartial arbiters, bound by principles they cannot set on one side for political convenience. From an interpretative viewpoint, rooted in legal and constitutional principle, speculation about governmental and parliamentary plans and their likely outcomes is irrelevant: they are matters of fact or prediction extraneous to legal judgement about existing rights and duties.

Phillipson and Fenwick have nevertheless suggested that resort to section 4 might have enabled the courts better to protect the rights of those made subject to control orders under the Prevention of Terrorism Act 2005.[146] Rather than acquiesce (in effect) in an attenuated version of Article 5 liberty rights, acceding to the legality of lengthy periods of house detention, the courts could have declared the whole scheme incompatible with the European Convention. And by reading into the scheme (under section 3) basic requirements of fair procedure, in *AF (No 3)*, the House of Lords overlooked the great 'rhetorical force' of a declaration of invalidity, capable of informing public debate.[147] While there is some truth in these points, it is very doubtful whether the political dimension of judicial review should deflect the court from its duty to enforce the law, correctly conceived, in the particular case. Constitutional debate and dialogue must be enriched to encompass the courts' critical interpretative role: that role should not be curtailed, at the expense of the individual suspect, stripped of an effective remedy, in order to stimulate or simplify debate. And as these writers concede, the various judgments have in any event provoked 'a lively political debate both within government and between government and Parliament'.[148]

---

[146] Helen Fenwick and Gavin Phillipson, 'Covert Derogations and Judicial Deference: Redefining Liberty and Due Process Rights in Counterterrorism Law and Beyond' (2011) 56 McGill LJ 863–918. For the nature of and background to control orders, which have imposed onerous restrictions on personal liberty, see ibid, 873–8.

[147] *Secretary of State for the Home Dept v AF (No 3)* [2009] UKHL 28 (see Chapter 5, above).

[148] Fenwick and Phillipson, 'Covert Derogations and Judicial Deference', 909.

Aileen Kavanagh's own account of adjudication is hard to square with our ordinary understanding of the rule of law and the role of the judiciary. It is central to the idea of legality that the law's prescriptions are binding on all, the judges included. It is the immutability of legal standards, applicable to the particular case, that constitutes an essential bulwark against arbitrariness: no one is subject to another's will, but only to enforcement of law; and in the present context that means that officials must honour the basic rights that the constitution affirms. There is no conflict of values of the kind that Kavanagh postulates: 'justice to the individual' means justice according to law; and though human rights law may be fraught with uncertainty, as we struggle to give concrete definition to abstract statements of value, it is the court's duty to resolve such uncertainty, insofar as the specific case requires, and enforce the law accordingly. Concerns about the limits of judicial expertise, as regards the social policy consequences of judicial decision, are legitimate grounds for caution in expounding legal doctrine: individual rights are sensitive to countervailing public interests, which affect their content and scope. Once such rights are ascertained, however, in accordance with ordinary legal procedure, they must be loyally enforced. The court otherwise surrenders its impartiality and independence, joining forces with the relevant public authorities against the victim of a breach of the law.[149]

VII

It is a mistake to suppose, as constitutional theorists generally do, that we face a choice between constitutional judicial review, American-style, and unfettered parliamentary sovereignty. There is an arrangement distinct from both judicial review of legislation (and governmental action) under a bill or charter of rights, on the one hand, and unqualified legislative supremacy, on the other. It is exemplified by the common law constitution of the United Kingdom, when the excesses and absurdities of absolutism (and literalism) are tamed or removed. Legislative supremacy is acknowledged subject to certain assumptions about the equal dignity of every citizen, which demands respect for basic common law rights, definitive of the British tradition of liberal democracy and the rule of law. For the most part, such rights are defended by judicial *interpretation*, reading statutes in the light of the constitutional framework of the rule of law. It is only in very unusual cases that judicial resistance to injustice must go beyond anything that (on any ordinary understanding) could readily be called interpretation—only when there is a threat to the very idea of law implicit in our basic commitment to the rule of law.

The common law constitution may be supplemented by a bill of rights, such as the Human Rights Act 1998, which gives the rights enunciated by the European Convention on Human Rights a firm foothold in United Kingdom law. Admittedly, the Human Rights Act does not authorize the judiciary to disapply or strike down statutes made in breach of the Convention, permitting only a declaration of

---

[149] See also the discussion of judicial deference in Chapter 7, above.

incompatibility with Convention rights, leaving the (domestic) legal rights of the parties before the court unaltered. The British bill of rights therefore permits only limited judicial review, by contrast with the stronger form adopted (inter alia) by the United States, Canada (subject to the possibility of legislative override of the Charter of Rights under section 33), and Germany. And because the Human Rights Act is not formally entrenched, it could be expressly repealed by ordinary majority vote in Parliament. But legal theory may support a deeper underlying unity between these variants of constitutional democracy, deriving from similar conceptions of liberty and equality.[150] And even if the Human Rights Act were repealed, the underlying common law constitution would remain untouched, including its implicit safeguards for the citizen's dignity and independence.

Common law rights include those fundamental rights that constitute the essential framework of a system of government respectful of individual freedom or autonomy. Being integral parts of a system of law that has legitimate authority, reconciling such authority with individual autonomy, they cannot be dispensed with or overridden without undermining the basis of legislative and executive power. Parliamentary supremacy is unqualified only within the (broad and generous) sphere of legitimate governmental authority: it represents the collective voice of the people, regarded as independent citizens who enjoy the rights associated with that fundamental moral status. Legislation is properly construed accordingly: statutes must be understood to sanction no further qualification of basic rights than the general public interest reasonably requires, consistently with the citizen's freedom and dignity.

There is no inconsistency in insisting that fundamental freedoms of speech, conscience, and association, together with the right to a fair trial and immunity from arbitrary arrest and detention, are integral parts of any legitimate regime, while at the same time recognizing that their precise specification depends on positive law and thereby conceding space for legislative initiative. There is scope for legitimate disagreement, for example, about how far the right of free speech should be qualified in the interests of public decency, or to protect members of racial minorities from expressions of racial hatred likely to undermine their self-respect as equal citizens. But there is no scope for legitimate dispute about the freedom to criticize the conduct of government or the justice of political and economic arrangements more generally. Nor could any government properly interfere with people's rights to belong to whatever groups or associations they choose for whatever purposes, short of the commission of criminal offences. Nor can a government stipulate what religious or other conscientious affiliations its subjects may acquire or express. Nor could it set itself up as an authority on matters of academic or literary or scientific knowledge or taste, or make adherence to some ideology a condition of the receipt of public benefits.[151]

---

[150] See further Allan, 'Constitutional Rights and the Rule of Law', in Matthias Klatt (ed), *Institutionalized Reason: The Jurisprudence of Robert Alexy* (Oxford: Oxford University Press, 2012), 132–51.

[151] Compare Alan Brudner, *Constitutional Goods* (Oxford: Oxford University Press, 2004), 213: 'Democracy is not defeated but protected if the court invalidates a law no free person could impose on

Jeremy Waldron's 'core argument' against constitutional judicial review—'strong' judicial review of legislation—is based on four assumptions which, if satisfied, suggest that it is more appropriate for matters of political disagreement, including contested issues of right, to be resolved by legislative assemblies than by judges:

'We are to imagine a society with (1) democratic institutions in reasonably good working order, including a representative legislature elected on the basis of universal adult suffrage; (2) a set of judicial institutions, again in reasonably good order, set up on a non-representative basis to hear individual lawsuits, settle disputes, and uphold the rule of law; (3) a commitment on the part of most members of the society and most of its officials to the idea of individual and minority rights; and (4) persisting, substantial, and good faith disagreement about rights (i.e., about what the commitment to rights actually amounts to and what its implications are) among the members of the society who are committed to the idea of rights.'[152]

Waldron argues that when members of society disagree about what rights require, they must possess a decision-procedure for resolving that disagreement that all can accept as legitimate. Distinguishing between outcome-related and process-related considerations, he maintains that the latter are predominantly in favour of decision by elected legislators rather than by the judiciary: our electoral and representative arrangements are designed to meet the requirements of political equality even if they do so imperfectly.

Waldron also offers reasons for doubting whether the judiciary is more likely to produce correct answers to such disagreements than the legislature. He assumes, for example, that the courts will be entrusted with enforcing a bill of rights, but observes that such an abstract text (adopted precisely to finesse disagreement) may be unhelpful: its 'platitudes may be exactly the wrong formulations to focus clear-headed, responsible, and good faith explorations of rights-disagreements'.[153] A rigid textual formalism may be encouraged: a legal right 'that finds protection in a bill of rights finds it under the auspices of some canonical form of words', and the words 'tend to take on a life of their own, becoming the obsessive catchphrase' to represent the right in question. Legislators, by contrast, can confront the moral questions involved more directly.

While there is undoubtedly force in Waldron's fears about textual formalism, the objection is inapplicable to judicial defence of common law rights, which do not depend for their meaning or application on any canonical formulas. The content of common law rights is dependent on general principles of moral and political theory, adapted to the specific context of the historical jurisdiction in question.

---

himself, for the majority has no more authority to pass such a law than an autocrat nor any jurisdiction to decide by fiat a question to which there is a correct legal answer.' Brudner grants that the common law constitution can be understood as the 'full constitution of the inclusive conception of public reason' (ie the full requirements of the rule of law) and may, furthermore, be entrenched without being codified. He contends, nonetheless, that there are reasons to prefer entrenchment through codification in place of reliance on judicial interpretation of statutes: see Allan, 'In Defence of the Common Law Constitution: Unwritten Rights as Fundamental Law' (2009) 22 CJLJ 187–203; Alan Brudner, 'A Reply to Critics of *Constitutional Goods*' (2009) 22 CJLJ 237–40.

[152] Jeremy Waldron, 'The Core of the Case Against Judicial Review' (2006) 115 Yale LJ 1346–406, at 1360.

[153] Ibid, 1381.

Moreover, the common law constitution escapes the opposition between legislative supremacy and judicial review that Waldron postulates: it envisages a division of functions between the enactment and the application of law, distributing responsibility between Parliament and judiciary according to context and circumstance. If there are circumstances in which a statute could not be applied, in accordance with its literal or ordinary meaning, without doing serious injury to fundamental rights, the necessary adjustments or modifications are legitimately made. A statute must be intelligently adapted to accommodate circumstances that could not have been foreseen or specifically addressed at the time of enactment; and it must be assumed that legislation was not intended (by any relevant draftsmen, sponsors, or assenting representatives) to violate fundamental rights, even if there might be some uncertainty or disagreement about the nature or scope of those rights in all the circumstances. It is the court's constitutional role to settle such doubts and disagreements as they arise on the facts of particular cases.

Waldron's objections to judicial review are, on reflection, of rather limited relevance to common law constitutionalism. Admittedly, his characterization of 'strong judicial review' includes not merely a judicial power to decline to apply a statute in a particular case (whether or not it is literally struck down or quashed) but also a power 'to modify the effect of a statute to make its application conform with individual rights (in ways that the statute itself does not envisage)'.[154] While the statute may not *expressly* authorize such modification or adaptation, however, it rather begs the question to suppose that the statute necessarily *precludes* it. Statutes acquire their full meaning, we may properly insist, only through reflection on the interaction of the text, underlying purposes or policy, and the specific context of application in view. The 'effect of a statute' always depends on questions of interpretation, requiring informed and considered judgement rather than mechanical responses to plain commands. So we can always ask, without offence to constitutional propriety, what changes to the previous law can most reasonably and legitimately be attributed to an enactment in the circumstances confronting us, thus reconciling legislative purpose and legal principle to the best of our ability.

When we take proper account of the interpretative role of the judiciary, the debate over the merits or demerits of strong judicial review begins to look somewhat crude. What is most important is not the formal characterization of judicial review, but rather the manner in which courts determine the content of fundamental rights, on the one hand, while showing proper deference to the legislative role of furthering the public good within the broad limits of those rights, on the other. An interpretative approach that gives due weight to fundamental rights will give them all the protection necessary in a generally benign regime of the kind Waldron has in mind. An adaptation or adjustment of the ordinary or prima facie meaning of the statute will serve, where necessary, to protect such rights—though the greater the potential threat to liberty or human dignity, the further the departure from ordinary meaning warranted to preserve the rule of law. In the result, a statute will properly be held inapplicable to a particular case (and hence cases relevantly similar) when

---

[154] Ibid, 1354.

there is no scope for any operation, in those circumstances, consistent with basic rights.

When Waldron's conditions are met, there are likely to be few instances of statutes being so narrowly construed that the relevant legislative aims or purposes are seriously prejudiced; such benign conditions will be conducive to cooperation between Parliament and judiciary, reinforcing the collaborative nature of just governance. If, as he supposes, the 'society-wide commitment to rights involves an awareness of the worldwide consensus on human rights and of the history of thinking about rights', legislation is unlikely to be seriously oppressive, at least in ordinary circumstances; this is all the more the case if we 'assume also that the society cherishes rights to an extent that has led to the adoption of an official written bill or declaration of rights of the familiar kind'.[155] But whether or not any particular judicial application (or even disapplication) of statute should provoke objection, as amounting to judicial usurpation of the legislative function, must depend on all the circumstances. Since it is plainly a question of degree and context, we should not exaggerate the contribution of abstract constitutional theory. The adoption of a charter of rights will not only elaborate and supplement common law rights, intrinsic to legitimate governance; it will rightly and inevitably affect what ordinary statutes are subsequently taken to permit or require. By proclaiming the importance of the specified rights, the charter will alter the *meaning* attributed (by anyone acquainted with constitutional law) to other statutes.

What these considerations show is that Waldron's distinction between strong and weak judicial review is unsustainable: to the extent that interpretation and application of statute is sensitive to the demands of basic rights, a court will always act to constrain legislative action capable of undermining them. Waldron offers the Human Rights Act as an example of weak review, permitting the courts to declare the incompatibility of a statute with the European Convention, while being nonetheless obliged to apply it as valid law. But he overlooks the importance of section 3, which requires the court to adopt an interpretation consistent with the Convention if it is 'possible' to do so. That section is arguably the key provision, enabling the courts to avoid the danger of incompatibility in the great majority of cases. The New Zealand Bill of Rights Act 1990, stipulating (in section 6) that the 'preferred' meaning of an enactment is that which is consistent with the enunciated rights and freedoms, may also be thought to provide all the protection necessary for practical purposes. If the courts 'may strain to find interpretations that avoid the violation' of human rights, they can match their interpretative efforts to the scale of the threat they perceive.[156]

Furthermore, there is a degree of tension between Waldron's third and fourth assumptions. How far is 'persistent, substantial, and good faith disagreement about rights' consistent with a general commitment 'to the idea of individual and minority rights'? If the disagreement is very deep, with little accord over even paradigm cases, we may wonder whether there is any shared commitment to the *same* idea.

---

[155] Ibid, 1365.   [156] Ibid, 1356.

Waldron assumes that 'the rights-disagreements are mostly not issues of interpretation in a narrow legalistic sense'; they are rather 'major issues of political philosophy with significant ramifications for the lives of many people'.[157] We should not infer that the general commitment 'covers the core of each right and that the right only becomes controversial at the outer reaches of its application'. Two people who disagree about whether restrictions on racist hate speech are acceptable 'may both accept that the right to free speech is key to thinking through the issue' and even agree that the problem of hate speech is 'a central rather than marginal issue relative to that right'. If they were unable to agree on any central issues at all, however, we would have to conclude not merely that they held 'different conceptions of the right', but were actually defending wholly different *concepts*.[158]

It is appropriate, then, for judges to defer to the considered conclusions of elected representatives within a certain broad range of judgement, normally satisfied in mature democracies. It is usually apparent that disagreement is reasonable, even if 'some positions are held and defended disingenuously or ignorantly by scoundrels (who care nothing for rights) or moral illiterates (who misunderstand their force and importance)'.[159] But reasonable disagreements must divide positions equally consistent with the root ideas of human dignity and independence that undergird a liberal democratic polity; and those ideas go well beyond any merely superficial rhetoric or empty gesturing. The freedom of political debate and criticism is already implicit in Waldron's assumptions; but there is much more to the idea of human dignity (on any plausible view) than freedom of political speech. We could not treat anyone who defended *torture*, even in exceptional cases, as being truly committed to the idea of human rights; nor, therefore, should courts acquiesce in its authorization. And while there may be reasonable disagreement over the rights of criminal suspects, and especially of terrorist suspects, the courts have an undeniable duty to preserve the integrity of their own procedures. They cannot properly accede to statutory demands that, taken literally, mandate the conduct of unfair trials or authorize the punishment of people whose actions infringed no law applicable at the pertinent time.[160]

Waldron might want to say that there may yet be reasonable disagreement over the correct understanding of such principles as natural justice, fair trial or *nulla poena sine lege*; courts should adhere as closely as possible to the outcome of parliamentary deliberations on such questions. But such adherence must take the deliberative form I have emphasized, seeking an interpretation that generates *appropriate* rules—rules appropriate not only to Parliament's role as representative legislator but also to the

---

[157] Ibid, 1367.
[158] Ibid. For the distinction between the concept of a right and competing conceptions of it, see Ronald Dworkin, *Taking Rights Seriously* (London: Duckworth, 1977), 134–6.
[159] Waldron, 'The Core of the Case Against Judicial Review', 1368.
[160] The House of Lords was right, therefore, in *Secretary of State for the Home Dept v AF (No 3)* [2009] UKHL 28, to accept the view of the European Court of Human Rights that a suspected terrorist, deprived of all knowledge of the evidence against him, could not have a fair trial; and it was equally right to 'read down' the Prevention of Terrorism Act 2005 accordingly (see further Chapter 5, above).

broader constitutional context in which that role is performed. There can be no question of submission to any plain 'legislative intent', whether based on the literal words of an enactment or on allegedly non-contentious expectations or assumptions: the pertinent legislative intention must be constructed in the course of a statute's application to unfolding events.[161] Judicial deference must take the form of a moral dialogue with a representative legislator, sensitive to considerations of basic justice as well as more diffuse or immediate political goals.[162] The constraints of legality leave no space for judicial discretion in the sense of political choice. A court must read a statutory provision in the manner that best protects the fundamental rights it considers intrinsic to the rule of law; those rights constitute the bedrock on which all state authority ultimately stands. After making all due allowance for contrary opinion, the court must adopt a construction that meets (what it takes to be) the requisite standards of constitutional propriety and legality. A judge's responsibility for his decision in the particular case cannot be evaded by reference to an unjust (or potentially unjust) enactment; he must show how his decision is consistent not only with a defensible account of legislative purpose and policy, but also with the constitutional safeguards for liberty that he regards as fundamental.[163]

Ronald Dworkin distinguishes constitutional from majoritarian democracy: the former denies the 'majoritarian premise', implicit in the usual objections to judicial review, which assumes that something of moral importance is lost whenever a political decision contradicts the preferences or judgements of the majority of citizens.[164] The constitutional conception of democracy supposes that certain conditions must be met before majoritarian decision-making has any special authority; majoritarianism can provide self-government only when all have full moral membership of the community: 'A political community cannot count anyone as a moral member unless it gives that person a *part* in any collective decision, a *stake* in it, and *independence* from it.'[165] His part in collective decision-making 'must not be structurally fixed or limited in ways that reflect assumptions about his worth or talent or ability, or the soundness of his convictions or tastes'. Further, moral membership involves reciprocity: 'a person is not a member unless he is treated

---

[161] As Waldron himself observes, there is 'simply no fact of the matter concerning a legislature's intentions apart from the formal specification of the act it has performed': Jeremy Waldron, *Law and Disagreement* (Oxford: Oxford University Press, 1999), 142.

[162] See Chapter 5, above.

[163] See also David Dyzenhaus, 'The Incoherence of Constitutional Positivism', in Grant Huscroft, *Expounding the Constitution: Essays in Constitutional Theory* (Cambridge: Cambridge University Press, 2008), 138, especially 140–54. The incoherence of 'constitutional positivism' arises from its implausible combination of resistance to 'strong' judicial review and acceptance of a human rights culture informing both 'weak' review (of primary legislation) and review of administrative action (on the basis of moral principles of legality). For a full-blown 'political positivist' (in the tradition of Jeremy Bentham, hostile to judicially enforced legal principles) what must be resisted is 'a change in political culture from one in which it is a sufficient condition for the legitimacy of a political decision that it has been voted into law by a majority in Parliament to a human rights culture, where a decision must also comply with human rights and other constitutional commitments' (ibid, 151).

[164] Ronald Dworkin, *Freedom's Law: The Moral Reading of the American Constitution* (Oxford: Oxford University Press, 1996), 15–35.

[165] Ibid, 24.

as a member by others, which means that they treat the consequences of any collective decision for his life as equally significant a reason for or against that decision as are comparable consequences for the life of anyone else'.[166] The requirement of independence sustains the self-respect of those who are encouraged to regard themselves as partners in a joint venture. A genuine political community must be composed of independent moral agents: 'It must not dictate what its citizens think about matters of political or moral or ethical judgment, but must, on the contrary, provide circumstances that encourage them to arrive at beliefs on these matters through their own reflective and finally individual conviction.'[167]

Under the constitutional conception of democracy, then, governments can have only qualified authority. In particular, respect for individual rights is a background condition of the legitimacy of representative majoritarian decision-making. It is only when people are treated fairly by their political institutions, as citizens entitled to equal concern and respect, that they have reason to accept the legitimacy of majority decisions on matters in dispute. Dworkin denies that there is any loss to democracy if a court strikes down a statute that infringes fundamental rights: if the court has made the correct decision, upholding rights against a genuine violation, democracy has been *improved* rather than defeated. Admittedly, democracy is impaired when a court rejects a statute on the basis of mistaken conclusions about what the conditions of moral membership require, but no more than when a statute that contravenes those conditions is allowed to stand: 'The possibility of error is symmetrical.'[168]

Waldron objects that Dworkin's claim may be read in two ways: '(1) democratic procedures are legitimate only among people who hold and act upon the correct view of one another's rights; or (2) democratic procedures are legitimate only among people who take one another's rights seriously and who in good faith try as hard as they can to figure what these rights are.'[169] Since the first reading is plainly too strong, we are left with the second; but 'then Dworkin's premise is satisfied for the sort of society' under consideration. So Dworkin has not, it is alleged, refuted the democratic case against judicial review. If the democratic case has been overstated, however, by postulating too stark a choice between strong review, on the one hand, and interpretative sensitivity, on the other, Dworkin's democratic conditions survive as accurate, if very abstract, guidance on the ultimate responsibilities of courts.

The first interpretation of Dworkin's conditions is not too strong if we are appropriately modest in our claims about the fundamental rights central to human dignity and independence. For it is not reasonable to suppose that *everything* is open to legitimate dispute; we are entitled, and bound, to hold the line against ignorant scoundrels and 'moral illiterates'. To take human rights seriously is, in part, to discountenance the sorts of treatment meted out, for example, to dissentients in wicked regimes, and to insist on the proper functioning of judicial procedures, detached from immediate political pressures, whether of governmental hostility or

[166] Ibid, 25.   [167] Ibid, 26.   [168] Ibid, 33.
[169] Waldron, 'The Core of the Case Against Judicial Review', 1400.

popular prejudice. If we then reiterate the point that judicial review is in reality a matter of degree—the court's interpretative stance being attuned to the scale of the potential injury to liberty—we can insist that judicial adherence to statute must always be informed, and qualified, by a vision of the genuine political community, composed of independent moral agents, whose government may act only on their behalf.

Since any argument for the legitimacy of law must show how state coercion can be reconciled with individual autonomy, giving reason for the compliance of independent-minded persons who will often doubt the law's justice or wisdom, it is not enough to invoke the will of the majority. It is necessary to establish the conditions under which that will should be treated as binding. And while a general acceptance of the importance of rights, in principle, is a good start, it cannot do all the necessary work: the moral concepts in play must be at least *recognizable* as interpretations of the basic ideal of individual autonomy or independence. And just as there is no way to avoid a degree of entanglement with the substance of rights, when reflecting on questions of legitimacy, so there is no means for a court to practice a similar abstinence when determining, in any concrete context, what a statutory provision should be understood to mean or require. Democracy must be understood to consist not merely in the deliberation of representative legislative assemblies, but in the accompanying moral discourse among free and equal citizens. That discourse encompasses both democratic deliberation and legal interpretation; and it is an argumentative process that can be understood only from the inside—by those who join it in the spirit of participant, moulding and reforming its content and conclusions in the very act of seeking to articulate an understanding.

APPENDIX

Public Law and Political Theory

I

My discussion in Chapter 1 of contrasting interpretations of Dicey's work raises more complex issues than could be conveniently considered there, so I add an appendix to explore them further. I also examine here certain aspects of Ronald Dworkin's theory of interpretation (on which I draw) in greater detail than the context of earlier discussion conveniently permits. Rival approaches to constitutional law reflect different conceptions of the relationship between public law, on the one hand, and legal and political theory, on the other; competing approaches embody contrasting conceptions of law. These are undeniably deep and rather daunting waters, but the additional plunge may be thought worthwhile in view of the interest and importance of the subject matter.

In a provocative challenge to recent academic emphasis on the theoretical dimension of public law, Peter Cane has suggested that debate over the relationship between law and theory 'has diverted attention away from legal values and on to styles of legal and theoretical scholarship'.[1] In Cane's view, the contribution of political theory to our understanding of public law is limited by the abstract nature of political values and disagreement about their practical implications. It is better to focus on the values immanent within the law itself; and so the common law must take centre stage: the courts' role is to maintain the integrity of society's legal culture 'by interpreting and applying legislation, and by making and applying the common law, in ways that respect and preserve traditional legal values'. The immanent or 'background' values of the law are to be found in the complex interaction between legislative and judicial activity:

Because courts are required to promote consistency and coherence not only in common-law rule-making but also in the interpretation and application of legislation, judge-made law provides a framework of values into which legislation is introduced and within which the forward-looking outcome-oriented values of legislation have to be accommodated.[2]

Cane distinguishes immanent or background values from 'foreground' values provided by political theories such as pluralism, liberalism, or republicanism, which are external to the law: such moral or political values have priority in practical reasoning (reasoning about what one ought to do) and so provide a basis for criticizing the law. Law is an authoritative institution that enables us to overcome the problems associated with the abstractness of political values and unresolvable disagreement:

Legislation and judicial rule-making concretize political (and moral) values by applying them to particular social problems and issues. Adjudication concretizes values even more by applying legislative and common-law rules to individual cases....Legitimate laws provide people with authority-based reasons for action that are independent of the normative content of the laws.[3]

---

[1] Peter Cane, 'Theory and Values in Public Law', in Paul Craig and Richard Rawlings (eds), *Law and Administration in Europe: Essays in Honour of Carol Harlow* (Oxford: Oxford University Press, 2003), 3–21, at 14.

[2] Ibid, 6 (footnote omitted).

[3] Ibid, 18.

Cane's distinction between immanent and critical values helpfully captures our sense that public law has a certain degree of autonomy from abstract political theory.[4] We expect the higher judiciary to seek consistency and coherence of legal principle—preserving the integrity of our legal culture—without direct resort to abstract political theory of a kind that would be deeply contentious, taking a judge well beyond his role as interpreter of existing law. Lawyers' invocation of general theory must be carefully tailored to the needs of a flourishing legal order; legal practice has a special, local character, reflecting the history that has nurtured its traditions and the expectations those traditions have generated.

It is important, however, not to exaggerate either the division between immanent and critical values or the autonomy of public law from political theory. Immanent values of the sort Cane describes—his list includes such general notions as representation, accountability, and judicial deference—are themselves highly abstract, acquiring their concrete meaning not only from their explicit treatment in case law (or other official sources of law) but also from the way they are understood by critics and commentators as well as ordinary citizens and public officials. We need theory as a means of understanding the relationship between different values, indicating how potential conflicts and inconsistencies should be resolved.[5] Paul Craig, in his response to Cane, even challenges the distinction between immanent and critical values: the real identifying criterion 'is surely that the list captures the values that public lawyers think are or should be important in a regime of public law'.[6] As Craig observes, the relevant values invite recourse to political theory as a way of refining their interpretation. In particular, such central concepts as sovereignty, the separation of powers, and the rule of law are susceptible of competing interpretations; and contrasting conceptions of government or political authority can illuminate their place within the general constitutional scheme. Whether we have in mind abstract legal values or a specific political theory, public lawyers will have to work out the implications for particular legal issues:

There may be issues where the background theory, or abstract legal values, fail to provide concrete guidance, even when one has reasoned through the implications. There may be other issues where guidance is forthcoming.[7]

There remains, however, a certain distance between theory and practice in Craig's account: contrasting theories give competing reasons for different solutions to public law questions. A utilitarian cost-benefit analysis, for example, will generate a different balance of factors relevant to the content of procedural fairness than a rights-based approach.[8] Since the present content of law—the nature and scope of existing rights and duties—can hardly vary according to the chosen political theories of each judge or lawyer, however, Craig's approach is essentially external. The competing visions of law are, in effect, alternative suggestions for change or reform. Alternatively, the law is conceived, in the fashion of legal positivism, as an archipelago—an array of discrete islands, posited by authoritative legal institutions, surrounded by an empty sea, where the lawyer or judge must supplement the law by a form of quasi-legislation (whether by trying to guess what the legislature would do, if seized of the question, or by inserting rules that wise legislators would think appropriate).

---

[4] Cane's essay is, in part, a critique of the distinction between 'red light' and 'green light' approaches to administrative law adopted by Carol Harlow and Rick Rawlings, *Law and Administration*, 2nd edn (London: Butterworths, 1997), 3rd edn (Cambridge: Cambridge University Press, 2009).

[5] Compare Martin Loughlin, 'Theory and Values in Public Law: An Interpretation' [2005] PL 48–66, at 58–60.

[6] Paul Craig, 'Theory and Values in Public Law: A Response', in Craig and Rawlings (eds), *Law and Administration in Europe*, 23–46, at 24.

[7] Ibid, 43.

[8] Ibid, 37.

These conclusions are confirmed by Craig's discussion of the relationship between public law, legal theory, and political theory.[9] He argues that 'the centrality of political theory for public law is compatible with the principal contending legal theories', that is with either legal positivism or anti-positivist interpretivism of the kind associated with Ronald Dworkin.[10] A legal positivist who accepts the 'sources thesis'—that the law is settled when legally recognized sources provide an (empirically identifiable) answer—can have regard to moral or political values when, in the absence of any such answer, a solution to a particular question must be sought outside the law.[11] An adherent of Dworkin's theory of adjudication, by contrast, can invoke such values in the course of interpretation: the judge's personal convictions about justice play a role in distinguishing between competing solutions, when each solution satisfies the initial requirement of 'fit'. While judgements of fit provide a 'rough threshold requirement that an interpretation of some part of the law must meet if it is to be eligible at all', standards of justification will determine the choice between eligible interpretations. A judge must ask himself which view 'shows the community's structure of institutions and decisions—its public standards as a whole—in a better light from the standpoint of political morality'.[12]

Craig observes that political theory is central to an understanding of public law whether one adopts a positivist or Dworkinian (interpretative) account of law: 'Which particular legal theory any public lawyer subscribes to is, of course, an entirely different matter.'[13] It is a different matter, however, only if we treat an exploration of the relationship between political theory and public law as a scholarly enterprise quite distinct from the deliberations of legal interpreter, focused on the specific content of English law. From an internal perspective, characteristic of lawyer or judge, legal and political theory are closely intertwined. Not only is the judicial role in defence of the rule of law ultimately defined by political theory, which must account for the moral value of legality, but our understanding of the concepts of law and legality will in turn suggest the nature and limits of proper recourse to broader dimensions of political theory in the course of adjudication. Legal positivism licenses a freedom of judicial *choice* that an interpretative approach denies. Since a positivist judge may legislate in the gaps between legal rules, she may draw on political theory, in exercise of her quasi-legislative discretion, in a manner that her interpretivist counterpart would think illegitimate. Her recourse to political argument or conceptions of the public interest is not mediated by constraints of legality, which on her positivist understanding do not apply.

---

[9] Ibid, 43–5. See also Paul Craig, 'Public Law, Political Theory and Legal Theory' [2000] PL 211–39, where the pertinence of political theory to the doctrine of parliamentary supremacy is powerfully defended, emphasizing the need for normative justification. The analysis, however, remains external and detached. Craig concludes that it is 'arguable' that the best interpretation, as a basis for 'future constitutional discussion', is that 'Parliament has sovereign power, provided that there is the requisite normative justification for that power'. The way is opened, by way of historical review, 'for legal argument about whether a legally untrammelled Parliament is justified in the present day' (ibid, 230).

[10] See especially Ronald Dworkin, *Law's Empire* (London: Fontana, 1986).

[11] See Joseph Raz, *The Authority of Law: Essays on Law and Morality* (Oxford: Clarendon Press, 1979), ch 3. Raz explains that the 'sources of a law are those facts by virtue of which it is valid and which identify its content'; a law has a source 'if its contents and existence can be determined without using moral arguments' (ibid, 47–8).

[12] Dworkin, *Law's Empire*, 255–6. Dworkin adds, however, that 'even when an interpretation survives the threshold requirement, any infelicities of fit will count against it ... in the general balance of political virtues'. See below for an extended discussion.

[13] Craig, 'Theory and Values in Public Law', 45.

Admittedly, in expounding his interpretative approach Dworkin emphasizes the role of the interpreter's own moral convictions: he can determine the law, reflecting the best construction of legal practice from the perspective of political morality, only by reference to his own moral and political judgement. But making a moral judgement about the best reading of relevant statutes or precedent is quite different from proceeding to legislate in the gaps between plain legal rules. The interpretative approach imposes constraints of consistency and coherence that a legal positivist judge may largely ignore. It sets any doubtful legal issue in the context of a larger corpus of doctrine that a positivist could treat as irrelevant to the gap she has to fill—irrelevant, at least, as a matter of political principle, if not on more limited strategic grounds (such as avoiding obvious inconsistencies that might generate confusion).

Dworkin sometimes invokes the notion of 'choice' in describing the interpreter's deliberations; but that seems infelicitous, blunting the gist of his message. The Dworkinian judge seeks the right answer to any question of law, and even if that answer is controversial, the controversy does not (or should not) betoken a clash of wills or preferences.[14] Legal argument is a specialized form of moral argument, on the interpretative view. Moral argument over the propriety of an action or decision assumes that morality gives an objectively right answer, obtained through careful argument, attentive to all relevant moral considerations as they bear on the facts in question. Political theory may help us to identify such considerations, elucidating features of our practice that otherwise escape our grasp; it is as much a reflection on such practice as an external resource, detached from the experience of government and administration. In interpreting our own tradition we seek to understand what, in any given circumstances, it truly requires—unless, of course, we repudiate the tradition entirely as unworthy of our allegiance. If I am not a sceptic, doubtful about either the sense or the efficacy of the interpretative endeavour, my legal judgement will draw on moral and political theory to illuminate and clarify existing commitments—those entailed by loyal adherence to our legal tradition.[15]

We might, then, treat Cane's plea for an emphasis on immanent values rather than general theory as, in part, a recognition of the distinctive and qualified role of political theory within an interpretation of public law. From an external perspective, at least, legal practice exhibits a marked autonomy, somewhat detached from an interpreter's more abstract accounts of democracy or justice or human flourishing. Cane observes that law and politics 'can be thought of as distinct normative systems that are open to influence from each other'; just as the law may absorb political values, so 'the political realm may be cognitively open to legal values'.[16] When a political theory is specifically addressed to the circumstances of British political history—as, for example, John Locke's *Treatises of Government* were offered as an interpretation and defence of the English Revolution of 1689—it may assist in illuminating features of legal theory and practice.[17] I suggest (in Chapter 3) that Locke should be viewed in the perspective of a larger republican tradition, emphasizing the link between law and liberty. The work of such theorists as Immanuel Kant and Friedrich Hayek may also cast light on the general character of British government as a liberal democracy, underpinned

---

[14] See especially Ronald Dworkin, *A Matter of Principle* (Oxford: Clarendon Press, 1986), chs 5–7.

[15] See Ronald Dworkin, *Justice for Hedgehogs* (Cambridge, Mass: Harvard University Press, 2011), Parts 1 and 2. Dworkin distinguishes helpfully between 'internal scepticism', which denies the truth of certain sorts of moral judgement, from 'external scepticism', which asserts a second-order view *about* morality, denying the objective truth of moral judgements.

[16] Cane, 'Theory and Values in Public Law', 19.

[17] John Locke, *Two Treatises of Government* (originally published 1690; London: Dent, Everyman, 1924).

by the value of respect for the autonomy and dignity of the individual citizen.[18] General political theory must, however, serve more as a source of inspiration than political preference: it must help us clarify a vision of the legal order that consists in a practice dependent on the attitudes and assumptions of lawyers, politicians, and public officials.[19] Theory is helpful chiefly in illuminating ideas and values that we already recognize and honour—if only in inchoate form—as implicit within existing legal doctrine and practice, capable (we trust) of generating wide recognition and assent.

From Paul Craig's external perspective—his treatment of political theory as an external resource on which lawyers may draw, according to their preferences—it is 'open to public lawyers ... to choose between the contending views of the rule of law' that he delineates.[20] Yet the different views embody contrasting conceptions of the nature of law itself, raising philosophical questions directly relevant to an internal viewpoint, focused on constitutional principle and legal doctrine.[21] Because legal positivists treat law largely as a matter of empirical fact—it consists in the rules laid down by authorized lawmakers, whatever their content may be—the rule of law is viewed as an independent political ideal, imposing certain formal or procedural constraints to which the law ought to conform. According to Joseph Raz, the rule of law is a 'negative value': it is intended to minimize the danger of arbitrary power created by the law itself.[22] If we identify the rule of law as the 'rule of good law', the ideal collapses into a general social philosophy and the term is deprived of any useful function.[23] The law should consist of general, clear, and published rules, fairly applied by an independent judiciary; but its *content* is an independent matter of political morality. As Craig emphasizes, echoing Raz, the rule of law is (on this account) only one virtue of a legal system, which may have to be sacrificed to other desirable ends: 'We may feel that the rule of law virtues of having clear, general norms must be sacrificed if the best or only way to achieve a desired goal is to have more discretionary, open-textured legal provisions.'[24]

By contrast, according to Craig, on Ronald Dworkin's interpretive theory of law, in which questions of justice are relevant to the content of law, 'there is no place for a *separate* concept of the rule of law as such at all'.[25] Since Dworkin's theory, as Craig understands it, 'directs us to consider what is the best theory of justice as part of the decision as to what rights people presently have', the need to preserve a distinction between the law and political philosophy is removed. Accordingly, Craig invites us to choose between a largely formal or procedural account of the rule of law, on the one hand, and a specific theory of substantive justice, on the other. A substantive conception of the rule of law of the kind advanced by Sir John Laws, inspired by Kantian liberalism, is questionable because 'that phrase ceases to have a function independent of the rights-based theory of law and adjudication'; such a

---

[18] See Chapter 3, above.

[19] Compare Mark Walters's reflections on Dworkin's legal humanist predecessors, linking liberal and republican conceptions of the state and the individual by way of common law theory: Mark D Walters, 'Legal Humanism and Law-as-Integrity' [2008] CLJ 352–75, at 374–5.

[20] Paul Craig, 'Formal and Substantive Conceptions of the Rule of Law: An Analytical Framework' [1997] PL 467–87, at 487.

[21] Martin Loughlin concludes that the debate between Cane and Craig is conducted within a legal positivist framework: Loughlin, 'Theory and Values in Public Law: An Interpretation'. But see in reply Paul Craig, 'Theory, "Pure Theory" and Values in Public Law' [2005] PL 440–7. For Loughlin's 'pure theory' of public law, based on the idea of an autonomous political sphere, see Loughlin, *The Idea of Public Law* (Oxford: Oxford University Press, 2003); see further below.

[22] Joseph Raz, *The Authority of Law*, 224.

[23] Ibid, 211.

[24] Craig, 'Formal and Substantive Conceptions of the Rule of Law', 469.

[25] Ibid, 478.

conception is a theory of justice earning unwarranted prestige from (an empty) association with the 'rule of law'.[26]

From a non-positivist, interpretative viewpoint, however, the rule of law is a political ideal that informs our grasp of the concept of law itself. The precise nature and dimensions of that ideal may be contested, but it serves to connect our concept of law with such related moral values as liberty and justice. Government according to law is itself a moral ideal: law is not merely an instrument of power in the hands of officials, awaiting the safeguards of an independent doctrine of the 'rule of law'.[27] The various precepts of formal legality, associated mainly with the proper form of legislation, are requirements of a larger political ideal; and that ideal imposes other, more substantive, safeguards that amount to a theory of constitutionalism, underlying and informing the practice of British liberal democracy. Sir John Laws's understanding of the rule of law entails, we may reasonably suppose, adherence to the requirements of English law, interpreted in the light of the governing ideals of freedom, certainty, and fairness that he identifies.[28]

Dworkin defines the 'rights conception' of the rule of law, by contrast with the positivist 'rule book conception', as an 'ideal of rule by an accurate public conception of individual rights'; and he states that it 'does not distinguish, as the rule book conception does, between the rule of law and substantive justice'.[29] But we must understand Dworkin to refer not to any theory of rights or justice that someone might think an ideal candidate for legislation on a fresh slate, but rather to the theory of justice that makes most sense of the legal tradition in which an interpreter works.[30] Dworkin's ideal of *integrity*—his more fully elaborated theory of law—entails the search for coherence within an existing tradition, accommodating the diverse demands of such values as justice, political fairness (as regards the distribution of political power), and due process. Integrity insists that the state should 'act on a single, coherent set of principles even when its citizens are divided about what the right principles of justice and fairness really are'.[31] It is that unity of vision, distinct from universalist notions of justice, that 'explains why judges must conceive the body of law they administer as a whole rather than as a set of discrete decisions that they are free to make or amend one by one, with nothing but a strategic interest in the rest'.[32]

---

[26] Ibid, 479–81; see for example Sir John Laws, 'The Constitution: Morals and Rights' [1996] PL 622–35.

[27] Compare Nigel Simmonds, *Law as a Moral Idea* (Oxford: Oxford University Press, 2007), especially chs 2 & 3.

[28] Craig's critique of my own account of the rule of law is further developed in Paul Craig, 'Constitutional Foundations, the Rule of Law and Supremacy' [2003] PL 92–111, at 97–102. He objects that my inclusion of rights to freedom of speech, conscience, and association within the rule of law aligns the principle with a specific theory of justice, giving pride of place to those rights. But my argument was intended merely to stress the centrality of such rights to any fully interpretative approach, founded on *argument* over principles of liberty and justice. It was not my purpose to denigrate other fundamental rights; nor do I suppose that 'our discussion about free speech, association, would be "about the rule of law", while discourse about the meaning of other rights would not' (ibid, 102).

[29] Dworkin, *A Matter of Principle*, 11–12.

[30] Dworkin's 'principle of integrity in legislation', for example, 'asks those who create law by legislation to keep the law coherent in principle': Dworkin, *Law's Empire*, 167.

[31] Ibid, 166.

[32] Ibid, 167. Compare ibid, 404: 'We accept integrity as a distinct political ideal, and we accept the adjudicative principle of integrity as sovereign over law, because we want to treat ourselves as an association of principle, as a community governed by a single and coherent vision of justice and fairness and procedural due process in the right relation.'

Joseph Raz articulates a similar vision when he observes, in subsequent work, that 'in insisting on the integration of legislation and other current measures with legal tradition enshrined in doctrine, the rule of law respects those civil rights which are part of the backbone of the legal culture, part of its fundamental traditions'.[33] Such an account chimes with a conception of the rule of law as constitutional doctrine, underpinning liberal democracy:

On the one hand it requires legal institutions to be loyal to legislation emerging from a democratic legislature, thus enhancing its power. But the rule of law also sets limits to majoritarian democracy, represented in the legislature. It requires principled, as well as faithful, adjudication.[34]

Legislation conferring public powers should 'be applied in a manner which is both faithful to the legislative purpose and principled in integrating it with traditional doctrines of the liberty of the citizen'.[35] What from Craig's detached descriptive viewpoint is an apparently unstable 'middle way' between formal and substantive conceptions of the rule of law is merely the outline of an interpretative approach—the idea of legality as constitutional justice, as participants would understand it.[36] From an internal, interpretative perspective, the dichotomy of form and substance largely disappears: principles of natural justice and basic presumptions of 'legislative intent', limiting the scope for vague or retrospective statutes, are rooted in a broader philosophy of individual freedom.[37]

Adopting a descriptive, analytic stance, we can distinguish between various techniques or approaches that courts might adopt in seeking to integrate legislation with general common law principle. Craig distinguishes a number of such techniques, the majority falling short of outright invalidation of statutes that contravene fundamental rights.[38] Because the courts have not generally acknowledged any such power of invalidation, we can (it is supposed) affirm the absolute sovereignty of Parliament while recognizing the various practical constraints on its exercise. For example, the Human Rights Act 1998 instructs the courts to read legislation compatibly with European Convention rights whenever possible; but it will not always be possible and validity is unaffected. In the case of European Community law the courts invoke a 'priority rule' that preserves merely 'the formal veneer of legal sovereignty'.[39] Parliament can override Community law only by making its intentions 'unequivocally clear'.

From an internal, interpretative stance, however, these analytic distinctions are less clearly marked.[40] Questions of sound interpretation depend on a broad range of factors that call for judgement that is highly sensitive to the specific context. Compatibility with either common law rights or Convention rights may, for example, depend as much on the importance of the right, as it applies to the case in view, as on the specific language of the legislative provision. What is 'possible' as a matter of interpretation depends, in part, on what aims or intentions it is reasonable to attribute to a 'Parliament', conceived as a body

---

[33] Joseph Raz, *Ethics in the Public Domain: Essays in the Morality of Law and Politics* (Oxford: Clarendon Press, 1994), 360.

[34] Ibid, 358.

[35] Ibid, 359.

[36] Craig, 'Formal and Substantive Conceptions of the Rule of Law', 484.

[37] See also Jeffrey Jowell, 'The Rule of Law and its Underlying Values', in Jeffrey Jowell and Dawn Oliver (eds), *The Changing Constitution*, 7th edn (Oxford: Oxford University Press, 2011), 11–34. As Craig fairly observes, however (in respect of an earlier edition) the principles regulating judicial review, which Jowell makes central to the rule of law, can only be one component of a larger theory of constitutionalism (see Craig, 'Formal and Substantive Conceptions of the Rule of Law', 485–6).

[38] Craig, 'Constitutional Foundations, the Rule of Law and Supremacy' [2003] PL 92, at 107–11.

[39] Ibid, 108.

[40] See Chapter 7, above.

responsible for securing the common good within the constraints of justice. Whether such an approach is consistent with an affirmation of unqualified sovereignty, to which the rule of law must finally bow, is extremely doubtful, as I argue in the chapters above.[41] From an interpretative standpoint, focused on the demands of legality as a fundamental value, it is not even clear that such an affirmation is really intelligible.

II

I have defended an account of legal and constitutional interpretation that unites legal analysis and moral judgement. The law on any matter, however mundane or even trivial the issue, is always determined by recourse to underlying theory: it is the product of deliberative engagement with the moral or political considerations that inform and underpin our over-arching interpretation of English public law. There are no facts of the matter that any viable interpretation or analysis must simply accept, as non-negotiable elements of a legal practice that every competent lawyer understands and endorses. The pertinent facts—whether regularities of institutional practice or lawyers' opinions about what the practice requires—obtain their significance, if any, from the theory that (in the interpreter's view) makes best sense of the practice. We need the theory, placing legal practice in a moral context that supplies criteria of justification, in order to identify which features of that practice are central and important and which marginal and dispensable. Just as an Act of Parliament has the meaning that the best theory of that statute indicates—the meaning that follows most persuasively from our moral commitments both to democracy (and legislative supremacy) and legality (or the rule of law)—so the law as a whole has the content and implications that the best interpretation of our practice or tradition dictates. There is no escape from this deep moral and political engagement, and assertions about the content of constitutional law that seek to avoid it are simply confused and misguided.[42]

I believe my account of constitutional interpretation is broadly consistent with Ronald Dworkin's influential account, on which I have gratefully drawn—though subject to the reservations and qualifications I explore in Chapter 4. Just as my account of statutory interpretation invokes Lon Fuller's insistence on the interaction of fact and value—enacted text and attributed intent or purpose—so my portrayal of legal interpretation in general echoes Dworkin's insistence on a similar interplay of fact and value, uniting historical inheritance and moral judgement about its strengths and weaknesses. While standard summaries of Dworkin's approach typically emphasize his important distinction between interpretative criteria—between requirements of fit and those of justification—they often fail to notice how, in practice, these criteria operate in harness, each highly sensitive to the demands of the other. Matters of fit are as responsive to the interpreter's moral or political judgement (in the case of any social practice) as are more substantive considerations of justice or human well-being. Neither is constrained by any facts of the matter that must be accommodated before they are interpreted.[43]

---

[41] See especially Chapters 3–5. In Chapter 6, I explore the implications of different approaches for recent debate over the constitutional foundations of judicial review, seeking to articulate a fully developed interpretative standpoint.

[42] Some of the implications for doctrinal scholarship are considered by N E Simmonds in 'Protestant Jurisprudence and Modern Doctrinal Scholarship' [2011] CLJ 271–300.

[43] At the 'pre-interpretive' stage there is only a preliminary identification of rules and standards 'taken to provide the tentative content of the practice', and even though there must be a 'very great

In the course of his discussion of literary interpretation, expounding an analogy between legal judgement and the writing, by several authors *seriatim*, of a 'chain novel', Dworkin cautions that the contrast between artistic freedom and textual constraint should not be misunderstood:

It is *not* a contrast between those aspects of interpretation that are dependent on and those that are independent of the interpreter's aesthetic convictions. And it is not a contrast between those aspects that may be and those that cannot be controversial.[44]

In law as in literature there is a complex interplay between the different requirements of fit and justification: the explanatory power of an interpretation, as regards its direct relevance to the subject matter, is part of the case for its overall plausibility and appeal. There is a 'delicate balance among political convictions of different sorts', such convictions being 'sufficiently related yet disjoint to allow an overall judgement that trades off an interpretation's success on one type of standard against its failure on another'.[45] A wider departure from the literal text of a dubious statute would be justified, we may infer, the greater the threat to important principles of (common law) justice: a looser reading of the text, less complimentary to the draftsman's apparent powers of expression or foresight, is redeemed by the urgency or scale of the challenge to constitutional principle.

Admittedly, Dworkin sometimes treats the requirement of fit as a preliminary or threshold test, ruling out immediately a range of interpretations that might otherwise have seemed attractive. There is sometimes the suggestion that the second criterion of justification must adjudicate between several potential interpretations that each satisfy the requirement of fit, as if constraints of fit could operate independently:

Convictions about fit will provide a rough threshold requirement that an interpretation of some part of the law must meet if it is to be eligible at all. Any plausible working theory would disqualify an interpretation of our own law that denied legislative competence or supremacy outright or that claimed a general principle of private law requiring the rich to share their wealth with the poor.[46]

Any such 'rough threshold requirement', however, must be provisional only: it may turn out (even if it is rather unlikely) that further argument would show how quite radical or surprising conclusions do follow from what, when fully explained, is a persuasive interpretation of legal practice taken as a whole. Even acknowledged paradigms—features of legal practice so well established as to be largely taken for granted by all competent lawyers—are vulnerable to challenge by reference to other aspects of a shared tradition, reinterpreted to bring it closer to ideals of justice latent within, or consistent with, significant elements of current practice. Established paradigms, though necessary for interpretative debate to flourish, need not be mere matters of convention; they may instead display 'agreement in conviction', points of convergence within a lively debate over legal and political principle. There need only be a sufficient level of agreement in conviction to 'allow debate over fundamental practices like legislation and precedent' to proceed within the ordinary course of legal argument in particular cases, 'contesting discrete paradigms one by one, like the reconstruction of Neurath's boat one plank at a time at sea'.[47] The precise nature and limits

---

degree of consensus' at this early stage, the true content of the practice will be determined at the 'post-interpretive or reforming' stage in accordance with the justification accepted at the interpretative stage: Ronald Dworkin, *Law's Empire* (London: Fontana, 1986), 65–6.

[44] Dworkin, *Law's Empire*, 234.
[45] Ibid, 239.   [46] Ibid, 255.   [47] Ibid, 139.

of legislative supremacy, however firmly rooted the general doctrine, will be open to interpretative debate.

The distinction between fit and justification, then, is primarily an explanatory device to illuminate the manner in which an interpretation is the product of a tussle between competing considerations—an accommodation that reflects the balance of argument, all things considered:

> So the distinction between the two dimensions is less crucial or profound than it might seem. It is a useful analytical device that helps us give structure to any interpreter's working theory or style.[48]

What is plainly crucial is that certain, more formal criteria should constrain the application of other, more substantive criteria. It is only the existence of interpretative criteria relating to textual form or the general shape of a practice, independent of criteria for determining artistic or literary success or (in the case of law) the requirements of political morality, that enable us to distinguish interpretation from invention.[49] But the precise nature of that interplay of contrasting convictions depends on the interpreter's own intellectual makeup; he is guilty of invention only if there is no such deliberative process at all: 'Whether any interpreter's convictions actually check one another, as they must if he is genuinely interpreting at all, depends on the complexity and structure of his pertinent opinions as a whole.'[50]

It is clear that there is very broad scope for interpretative disagreement. Two lawyers whose conceptions of adequate fit or appropriate justification differ markedly will defend very different accounts of any particular area of law. Their disagreements in what Dworkin calls 'pivotal' cases, testing the power or scope of fundamental principles, will reflect their divergent theoretical standpoints; these disagreements may be profound even if the two lawyers also reach similar conclusions about the law in many other instances, when their different theories point in the same direction. If, then, certain features of constitutional law are 'settled' and agreed, they are so only in virtue of that overlap of theory or conviction: they become unsettled and contentious as soon as a plausible and coherent argument is directed against them, especially if such an argument is deployed in a dissenting judgment in a superior court. The dependence of legal judgement on moral and political conviction is greater than lawyers usually acknowledge, perhaps because their pertinent moral convictions are generally understood and examined as elements of their professional commitment to the rule of law—ways of understanding and practising law that give meaning and force to that shared and fundamental commitment.

I have attempted, in Chapter 4, to give an account of legal interpretation that reveals its close dependence on personal moral conviction, doubting aspects of Dworkin's own account that appear, in certain circumstances, to displace such conviction with capitulation to received opinion or majority sentiment. I have argued that, in the context of legislation that threatens fundamental rights or common law principles, Dworkin's 'protestantism' is somewhat too weak—weaker than his own theory of interpretation requires, when consistently applied. If no competent interpretation of the British constitution could deny legislative supremacy, that must be so because there is agreement in conviction that some version of that doctrine is demanded by democratic principle. Parliamentary sovereignty is the product of moral and political theory; its nature and limits depend on the correct articulation of that theory, a matter likely to provoke debate and controversy in cases where an enactment, while formally valid, threatens the values served by adherence to the rule of law. There is nothing to prevent any conscientious judge or lawyer denying the power

---

[48] Ibid, 231.
[49] For the distinction between interpretation and invention, see ibid, 66–8.
[50] Ibid, 237.

of a statute to wreak serious constitutional damage. His duty is always to defend (so far as possible) a reading that secures a proper balance between legislative purpose and legal principle, preserving both the legitimacy of state coercion and his own integrity and self-respect in maintaining his loyalty to the legal and constitutional order. The limits of the possible, as regards interpretation, define those boundaries of legitimacy and allegiance. Our conscientious lawyer must respect the workings of a legal order that he cannot simply redesign according to his own moral or political preferences; but the mode of constraint matches that applicable to the chain novel:

It is not the constraint of external hard fact or of interpersonal consensus. But rather the structural constraint of different kinds of principle within a system of principle, and it is none the less genuine for that.[51]

From the internal perspective of lawyer or legal reasoner, the constraint is genuine enough: judgements of law are not the same as proposals for fresh legislation or radical constitutional change. But legal argument in hard cases, when acknowledged general principles pull in different directions, must be a species of moral and political debate, albeit a controversy generated by a tradition that claims the loyalty of all participants (or all those acting in good faith, at least). As Lon Fuller argued, in his own confrontation with legal positivism, we cannot determine the law in isolation from our beliefs about what, ideally, it ought to be: every judgement of law is a struggle to bring the whole system of law closer to the ideals of justice to which it implicitly aspires.[52] Present law is always a pale reflection of what Dworkin calls the purer law within:

Present law ... contains another law, which marks out its ambitions for itself; this purer law is defined by pure integrity. It consists in the principles of justice that offer the best justification of the present law seen from the perspective of no institution in particular and thus abstracting from all the constraints of fairness and process that inclusive integrity requires.... It declares how the community's practices must be reformed to serve more coherently and comprehensively a vision of social justice it has partly adopted ...[53]

So legal argument is largely over how to understand and further the vision of justice embedded within existing practice when correctly understood; and no lawyer's views on that matter could, in any context, be divorced from her broader moral opinions about what justice or human well-being, in any political community, truly require. We are constrained by history and precedent only in the sense that interpretation is ultimately a collective endeavour: we are free to read the tradition in the light of our most basic moral and political ideals, but we are shouting into a void if we do not elicit cooperation and support. Our individual protestantism is an equal one: we must appeal to conceptions of justice and well-being that others can recognize, seeking common ground on the basis of fundamental values that are widely endorsed, if only at a relatively abstract level of agreement.

We must nevertheless confront the objection that if practice is interpreted in the light of theory, and theory reflects the divergent moral convictions of interpreters, we may have some doubt about how far competing interpretations actually focus on the same practice. Alan Brudner complains that, while fit and justification must be separated to forestall invention, that very separation is suspect:

Since theory determines what is settled in a practice, the practice that the theory must fit tends to be absorbed into the theory, leaving the latter with nothing to fit; since what reveals the practice in its

---

[51] Ibid, 257.
[52] See especially Lon L Fuller, *The Morality of Law*, revised edn (New Haven: Yale University Press, 1969), 82–91, 224–42.
[53] Dworkin, *Law's Empire*, 406–7.

best light is a matter of controversy between the competing conceptions of justice, that criterion is incapable of arbitrating among these conceptions.[54]

While there is undeniably some force in this objection, we have seen that the distinction between fit and appeal (or justification) is admittedly provisional and tentative. We aim to achieve broad agreement on a 'single and comprehensive vision of justice', which by showing us how best to understand and develop an existing tradition fuses fit and justification.[55] Justification is partly a matter of conformity to a vision of justice capable of eliciting broad assent; fit is partly a matter of broad agreement about the power of such a vision to illuminate a shared tradition.

Brudner's own elaborate interpretation of liberal constitutionalism seeks a comprehensive fit with a practice in which competing ideals of justice vie for primacy: 'certifying fit means exhibiting the theory's ability to integrate what, apart from the theory, appears as a practice riven by competing conceptions of fundamental justice—conceptions such as liberty, equality, community, and the good life'.[56] In Brudner's 'inclusive' conception of liberal justice—one that meets all the conditions essential to individual human dignity—the criteria of fit and justification merge:

The theory that best fits the practice because it integrates the (putative) conceptions of fundamental justice competing for control thereof also exhibits the practice in its best light because it reveals the practice as governed by a conception that is impartial—truly public—vis-a-vis the others.[57]

Brudner seeks an overall or overarching conception of liberal justice appropriate to the idea of human dignity, reflecting what he calls the 'liberal confidence', which is the idea that 'the individual agent possesses final worth ... so that there is no *more* fundamental end to which it may be unilaterally subordinated'.[58] The individual's worth is possessed 'as a separate individual, distinct from (that is, not immersed in or obliterated by or subsumed under) other individuals as well as from the larger groups, society, or political association of which it is a member'; and the individual's worth is inviolable, which means that 'everyone is under a duty to respect it by forbearing from attempts to subdue the individual's agency to his own ends or to some supposed superior end such as tribe, nation, society, or state'.

While there is no *more* fundamental end than the individual, however, in Brudner's conception of 'dialogic community' the polity itself enjoys an equal and independent status: 'the political community is neither an end to which the individual is unilaterally subordinate nor a means to the pre-political ends of the individual'.[59] Instead, 'each is a means to the end-status of the other, and so each is equally a final end'. The structure of 'mutual recognition' between individual and community differs according to the distinctive paradigms—libertarian, egalitarian, and communitarian—that together constitute the inclusive conception of liberal justice. Starting from a libertarian conception of public reason, in which the self is detached from all social relationships deriving from custom and contingency, Brudner traces 'a conceptual path by which the individual person, in order to satisfy its claim to final worth, is driven to richer conceptions of public reason—to the egalitarian conception, the communitarian conception, and finally to the conception of the public that integrates all of these as necessary to a political life that is sufficient for dignity'.[60] The ambition is to

[54] Alan Brudner, *Constitutional Goods* (Oxford: Oxford University Press, 2004), 17.
[55] Dworkin, *Law's Empire*, 134.
[56] Brudner, *Constitutional Goods*, 16.
[57] Ibid, 17.		[58] Ibid, 13.
[59] Ibid, 31.		[60] Ibid, 15.

vindicate the contemporary style of liberal constitution, which superimposes on the classic libertarian safeguards of freedom the further protections of group rights, while qualifying the traditional civil liberties by state powers to secure the conditions of individual autonomy or self-authorship.[61]

Brudner contrasts his own 'complex whole' with Dworkin's 'simple whole', which connects diverse political values with a single egalitarian principle of governmental concern for the lives of citizens; but both writers exhibit the search for a unified scheme of political values. Legal positivism, with its emphasis on authoritative determination of conflicts over justice or the demands of the common good, is a natural bedfellow of pluralist conceptions of value: public reason is powerless to adjudicate between the claims of competing and incommensurable rights or goods. Law is whatever has been explicitly adopted to determine specific rights or duties. An interpretative approach, by contrast—denying authority to any features of practice, treated as given independently of theoretical appraisal and ordering—must be resistant to assertions of moral pluralism and incommensurability. It must appeal to all members of the community, or at least all those who share the liberal confidence, by finding ways of integrating shared basic values in a larger scheme, able to reconcile divergent conceptions of liberty, equality, and justice. Our legal and constitutional practice must be interpreted in the light of the values that inform our wider moral and political discourse; but the practice must extend to argument over the correct understanding and arrangement of these values as they apply in the context of particular cases.

Dworkin's defence of the unity of value, in *Justice for Hedgehogs*, capitalizes on the independence of value—its existence as a separate domain of inquiry and argument.[62] If a moral judgement is objectively true, it is true in virtue of a substantive moral argument, invoking moral values or assumptions capable of being defended in a similar way. We try to interpret our moral concepts in the light of each other so as to form a coherent web of moral conviction: 'We are morally responsible to the degree that our various concrete interpretations achieve an overall integrity so that each supports the others in a network of value that we embrace authentically.'[63] If value judgements are true in virtue of the case we can make on their behalf, they cannot be *barely* true in the way that physical features of the world may be simply true. And if we confront conflicts of value, as we often seem to do, it must be because there is something wrong with our interpretative reconstruction of our moral concepts, or perhaps because certain conflicts of value best serve our moral responsibilities if we conceive them in that way. (Brudner's conflicting constitutional paradigms provide an instructive illustration of this latter mode of thought.) Faced by any practical moral dilemma, we reinterpret our concepts to help resolve it: 'the direction of our thought is toward unity, not fragmentation'.[64]

When legal or constitutional interpretation is placed in its proper context, as a special province of moral and political argument, we can see a promising way to reconcile interpretative protestantism, on the one hand, and the demands of collective, collaborative deliberation, on the other.[65] What may seem at first to be antithetical modes of reasoning—one highly individualistic, the other much less so—can be understood as complementary.

---

[61] For fuller discussion, see my review 'The Rule of Law as Liberal Justice' (2006) 56 UTLJ 283–90.

[62] Ronald Dworkin, *Justice for Hedgehogs* (Cambridge, Mass: Harvard University Press, 2011). There is a summary of what Dworkin calls 'Hume's Principle', at 44–6.

[63] Ibid, 101.

[64] Ibid, 119.

[65] Compare Gerald J Postema, '"Protestant" Interpretation and Social Practices' (1987) 6 Law & Phil 283–319.

An insistence on the truth of one's own conclusions about constitutional rights or public law duties, even when they differ from those of other lawyers or even Supreme Court judges, is only an exercise of moral responsibility: it is what we owe to other lawyers and our fellow citizens. Any legal argument derives its power from an appeal not merely to formal legal sources, but to the moral values that enable us to interpret and apply relevant legal materials to particular cases. And the appeal to moral values is as much an appeal to shared practice as the citing of statutes and precedents; we appeal to the ideas and ideals that best make sense of our mutual commitment to what Brudner calls the liberal confidence.[66]

The web of moral conviction on which any legal interpreter must draw is a fully public one—it is her own present understanding of a scheme of moral value implicit in the social and political context in which she works. On what else could any conscientious lawyer draw in her interpretation of the moral and political values of her community—in this case the political community that claims a monopoly of legitimate force—than her own best understanding of what these are? Her protestantism, if the genuine product of moral conviction, represents her participation in the interpretative legal community. She adheres to the tradition she accepts and supports by holding it to its own standards: in challenging apparent inconsistencies or contradictions, she keeps faith with the legal and constitutional order that claims her allegiance. Her challenge may, of course, go unheeded; she must work for a moral consensus capable of changing the way legal practice is conducted and developed. But it remains an internal, not external, challenge: the moral debate concerns the requirements of the scheme of constitutional justice now in place—what we are already committed to in view of our adherence to the liberal and democratic tradition whose moral authority we grant.

III

Martin Loughlin emphasizes the gulf between analysis conducted within a legal positivist framework and an approach (like the present work) that treats law as an interpretative discipline.[67] Public law is defined as a 'set of practices concerned with the establishment, maintenance and regulation of the activity of governing the state'; and he maintains that 'the nature of these practices can be grasped only once that activity is conceptualized as constituting an autonomous sphere: the political realm'.[68] A somewhat dubious separation of the moral and the political is thus envisaged, Loughlin insisting that public law cannot be equated either with positive law (rules adopted in accordance with officially recognized procedures) or with moral reason. Public law reflects a form of political reason quite distinct from moral argument about the compatibility of state authority with individual

---

[66] Such mutual commitment must not be confused with the much narrower conception of public reason that John Rawls defends, which is artificially insulated from more comprehensive moral or philosophical opinions or doctrines: Rawls, *Political Liberalism* (New York: Columbia University Press, 1993), Lecture VI. For effective criticism, see Brudner, *Constitutional Goods*, 3–11; Dworkin, *Justice in Robes* (Cambridge, Mass: Harvard University Press, 2006), 251–4.

[67] Loughlin suggests that the gulf between positivism and interpretivism is so wide that 'what appears to an author on one side as rational argument is received by the audience on the other as incoherent noise': Loughlin, 'Theory and Values in Public Law: An Interpretation', 64. According to Loughlin, public law within positivist thought 'is that body of positive law concerned with regulating the activities of the governing institutions of a state': 'By analyzing the pattern formed by this body of law, positivists claim that the values underpinning an existing order can be revealed' (ibid, 54).

[68] Loughlin, 'Theory and Values in Public Law: An Interpretation', 58.

human freedom and dignity: 'Politics as a set of practices concerning the art of the state constitutes an autonomous domain operating in accordance with its own rules and principles.'[69] Loughlin substitutes 'prudence' for moral reason as the method of public law: even restraints on governmental action are ultimately designed to enhance and maintain the capacity to rule.[70]

Loughlin is right to maintain that, being expressed through established institutional forms that allow articulation of the general will, sovereign authority 'has nothing in common with the exercise of an arbitrary power'.[71] Understood as an expression of the relationship between the state and the people, or sovereign and subject, the general will takes the form of law: 'sovereignty in reality means the sovereignty of law'. The command-style or rule-based conception of law, characteristic of legal positivism, accompanies a view of political power as 'an empirical rather than a relational phenomenon': positivism overlooks the idea of the 'constituent power'—the people themselves—as the repository of sovereignty (rather than particular institutions such as Parliament or the executive).[72] Loughlin is keen to stress the political as well as legal dimension of sovereignty—it stands 'as a representation of the autonomy of the political'—but notes that it must not be confused with power of the sort conferred by economic wealth, feudal dominion, or despotism. Certain basic constraints are intrinsic to a conception of sovereignty 'as being generated through an institutional framework established for the purpose of maintaining and promoting the peace, security, and welfare of citizens'.[73]

Invoking Michael Oakeshott's distinction between *societas* and *universitas*, Loughlin contrasts competing conceptions of the state as a formal association, constituted by rules, and a form of joint undertaking in pursuit of common objectives: 'Is modern government a formal engagement concerned with maintaining order through the establishment of general rules of conduct? Or is it a purposive engagement in which the rules of conduct are to be interpreted as being incidental to the pursuit of some common good?'[74] It is, however, arguably both; and legal and political theory must help us to secure an appropriate accommodation between them. Public law, Loughlin maintains, is a highly polarized discourse: the polarities elsewhere 'characterized as being between the normativist and functionalist styles of thought, are replications in legal consciousness of unresolved tensions between *societas* and *universitas*'.[75] We cannot make progress, the argument goes, by 'devising some ideal construct of law—whether as a model of rules or a model of rights—and then seeking to reinterpret the world in accordance with its precepts'.[76] In the absence of some guiding ideal, however, it is doubtful whether we can make any progress at all—we are merely stuck with the tensions Loughlin identifies. Whether our conception of the rule of law can cope with the complexities of modern governance depends on the sophistication of the model of rules or rights it invokes.

According to Loughlin, the 'error of constitutional legalism' consists in 'mistaking a part for the whole': it fails to acknowledge the provisional character of constitutional arrangements, or that constitutional frameworks are only the contingent result of irresolvable conflict.[77]

---

[69] Martin Loughlin, *The Idea of Public Law* (Oxford: Oxford University Press, 2003), 156.
[70] Ibid, 148–52.   [71] Ibid, 87.   [72] Ibid, 88–90.
[73] Ibid, 92.   [74] Ibid, 27.
[75] Ibid, 28. For the distinction between normativist and functionalist styles of thought, see Martin Loughlin, *Public Law and Political Theory* (Oxford: Clarendon Press, 1992).
[76] *The Idea of Public Law*, 28 (citing H L A Hart, *The Concept of Law*; Ronald Dworkin, *Taking Rights Seriously* (Cambridge, Mass: Harvard University Press, 1977), and Dworkin, *Law's Empire*).
[77] Ibid, 49.

But lawyers' efforts to find coherence and orderliness are a necessary part of the construction and consistent application of constitutional law; in downgrading or belittling such necessary efforts Loughlin is himself guilty of mistaking a part for the whole—subsuming the legal within a larger, undifferentiated sphere of the political. Modern constitutions are 'prone to this type of orderliness', Loughlin surmises, because 'one of the basic legal myths is that an answer to any issue can be found in the body of the law'.[78] But the answer provided by law will in many instances be that the legislature or executive has power to decide the matter in issue, within what are often broad jurisdictional boundaries. The conflicts and tensions that Loughlin's broad historical and political viewpoint highlights are resolved in practice through a highly nuanced accommodation between the legal and the political, sensitive to the particular governmental context.

The 'primacy of the political' that Loughlin emphasizes is largely a reflection of his chosen subject matter: he fixes his gaze on political practice to the exclusion of legal practice, which is dismissed as little more than a reflection of politics—a 'set of practices embedded within, and acquiring its identity from, a wider body of political practices'.[79] If, however, with Loughlin, we acknowledge that the 'establishment of a legal system that operates in accordance with its own conceptual logic while remaining free from gross manipulation by power-wielders is an achievement of considerable importance', it must be worthy of our attention.[80] That conceptual logic is a fit subject of theoretical study, even if the connections with political practice must be borne constantly in mind. An internal perspective, rooted in the pertinent legal values, will illuminate questions in the kind of detail that Loughlin's overarching and detached perspective cannot. He is right to observe that we cannot simply identify the rule of law, in the present context, with adjudication between citizens or the provision of rigorous procedures in criminal trials; constitutional law is indeed 'much more complicated'.[81] But that means only that our theory of the rule of law must be more sophisticated, not that we should abandon it for a sweeping account of political practice.[82]

Loughlin is right to remind us of the special functions of public law: we cannot simply equate our conception of the rule of law, in this context, with the governing ideal of private law; public law rights (as I emphasize above) are very different creatures from their private law counterparts. The complexities of governance impose great burdens on the judiciary when asked to ensure legality: the rule of law must accommodate the demands of the political system for adaptation to changing circumstances and responsiveness to a fluctuating political will. We cannot (as again I emphasize) expect legal doctrine to do too much: the delicate balance between prudence and law—political realism and legal or constitutional logic—is invariably a function of all the circumstances, more a matter of wise judgement in the light of experience than rigorous adherence to published rules or official guidelines. So we should not deny that the 'rights revolution' of modern governance is a challenging experiment: its displacement of the sovereignty of rulers by the sovereignty of the individual, whose liberty and dignity are treated as ultimate values, has had profound implications for the institutions of government:

> Law, once a form of coercive order, now presents itself as a means of maintaining freedom. Once founded on sovereign authority and authorized by representative democracy, law is now based on rights and legitimated by an appeal to moral autonomy. Law, in short, is no longer fundamentally a matter of will, but an aspect of reason.[83]

[78] Ibid, 50 (citing Ronald Dworkin, *Taking Rights Seriously*).
[79] Ibid, 43.   [80] Ibid, 42.   [81] Ibid, 43.
[82] For comment on Loughlin's 'dismissive attitude to self-understanding in the British context', see the review by J W F Allison at (2005) 68 MLR 344–8, at 347–8.
[83] Loughlin, *The Idea of Public Law*, 128.

Loughlin is entitled to remain sceptical, doubtful of the ability of judges to reach persuasive answers on the relative importance, in specific contexts, of conflicting social and political claims or interests. But we cannot escape the internal debate over constitutional interpretation that Loughlin would prefer to avoid. Nor is the political domain wholly autonomous, divorced from our ordinary moral judgements about what sorts of treatment of other persons are acceptable and which are not.[84] If it is 'an error to reduce our understanding of politics to that of a struggle for domination', as Loughlin concedes, it is an error to treat the political sphere as wholly detached from ordinary moral debate and appraisal.[85] Public law reason cannot be reduced to a species of political reason focused wholly on the 'survival and well-being of the state', unless the well-being of the state means the welfare of its inhabitants.[86] And the latter is a question of moral reason in which the rights and interests of persons, whether as citizens or individual human beings, take centre-stage. Loughlin's attachment to the notion of public law as pure reason of state—denying the connections between political prudence and objective moral truth or value—reflects a view of governance that, by his own admission, has been overtaken by attitudes and convictions that broadly affirm the vision he decries.[87]

The pure theory of public law is plainly an abstraction somewhat removed from the reasoning and experience of public lawyers, compelled to search for legal answers to questions of constitutional authority and legitimacy. Loughlin's method entails an important distinction between the roles of scholar and actor—the former limited to identifying patterns of thought in the manner of external critic, detached from the moral and political argument relevant to the content of constitutional law.[88] This book defends a different kind of interpretative inquiry: it looks at public law from the inside, trying to make sense of lawyers' reasons and arguments as they are actually presented and defended. It supposes that we can best understand public law by participating in the interpretative endeavour its practice entails. And if our arguments are sufficiently persuasive we may even change it—if only by holding others to the implications of basic ideas and values they purport already to acknowledge and endorse.

---

[84] Compare the critique in N W Barber, 'Professor Loughlin's Idea of Public Law' (2005) 25 OJLS 157–67, at 158–65. Barber's discussion underlines the difficulty in making moral sense of a rigid division between the moral and the prudential, as if the survival of the state could be an ultimate end, wholly detached from the interests of its citizens.

[85] Loughlin, *The Idea of Public Law*, 156.

[86] Ibid, 150.

[87] Compare Tom R Hickman, 'In Defence of the Legal Constitution' (2005) 55 UTLJ 981–1022, especially 992–1004. Hickman rightly observes that Loughlin fails to challenge 'liberal legalism' on its own normative ground, attacking what is mainly a caricature of that approach. In Hickman's view, moreover, 'the central problem for Loughlin is that in any state that holds itself out as a modern liberal democracy, the practices of public law will inevitably require a large dose of liberal legalism, and the dosage will increase according to the extent of its support and observance' (ibid, 1004).

[88] Loughlin, 'Theory and Values in Public Law: An Interpretation', 65–6.

Index

A v Secretary of State for the Home Dept [2004]
UKHL 56: 22, 93, 114–19, 185, 273
abode, right of 117, 235, 287–95, 300
access to the courts, right of 86, 145, 229, 231,
257, 290, 305
Ackner, Lord (formerly LJ) 237, 271
act of attainder, *see* bill of attainder
administrative discretion:
danger of arbitrariness 12, 35, 89, 106
see also Dicey; Hayek; legitimate
expectations; quasi-judicial discretion;
reasonableness
Afonso de Silva, Virgilio 294–5
Alexy, Robert 45, 248, 294
Allison, John:
critique and characterization of Dicey 51–4
critique of Loughlin 348
Dicey and Hayek compared 106
*Anisminic Ltd v Foreign Compensation
Commission* [1969] 2 AC 147: 35,
214–15, 219–20, 223, 230–1, 236, 304
Anti-terrorism, Crime and Security Act 2001:
23, 114–17
arbitrary power, *see* rule of law
assisted suicide 69, 180–4
*Associated Provincial Picture Houses Ltd v
Wednesbury Corporation* [1948] 1 KB 223:
113, 208, 250
association, freedom of 129, 324
Atkin, Lord 21, 23
Attorney-General, independence of 67–8
Attorney-General v Jonathan Cape [1976]
QB 752: 65–7, 81
*Attorney General for New South Wales
v Trethowan* (1931) 44 CLR 394 (HCA),
[1932] AC 526 (PC): 152
Austin, John:
law as the sovereign's commands 52, 120,
137–8, 172
legal positivism 11, 52
validity of unjust laws 143
*Australian Building Construction Employees'
and Builders' Labourers Federation v The
Common wealth* (1986) 60 ALJR 584: 297
autonomy, *see* dignity; liberty as independence
AXA General Insurance Ltd v Lord Advocate
[2011] UKSC 46: 145, 301

Bamforth, Nicholas 239
Barber, Nick:
analysis of constitutional conventions 61–3,
66, 72–5

critique of Finnis and Fuller 46–8
critique of Loughlin 349
Barendt, Eric:
analysis of *Fire Brigades Union* 77, 84
critique of *ProLife Alliance* 28, 30
separation of powers 130
Barton v R (1980) 32 ALR 449: 67–8
Bastarache, Justice (Canadian Supreme
Court) 280, 283
Belfast City Council v Miss Behavin' Ltd [2007]
UKHL 19: 263–4
Bellamy, Richard:
critique of legal constitutionalism 14, 286–7,
309–18
statutory interpretation under Human Rights
Act, s 3 200, 317–18
Bellinger v Bellinger [2003] UKHL 21: 286–7,
318–22
bill of attainder 19, 34, 93–4, 116, 124, 140–1,
185
Bingham, Lord (of Cornhill; Sir Thomas
Bingham):
common law and Convention principles
(*Daly*) 255–6
Dicey and administrative law 104
dissent in Chagos Islanders' case
(*Bancoult*) 289, 294, 300
effect of Parliament Act 1911
(*Jackson*) 151–3
equality (*A v Secretary of State for the Home
Dept*) 115
judicial deference to democratic judgement
(*Lichniak*) 179, 273
judicial deference to administrative
judgement (*Begum*) 262
limits of interpretation under Human Rights
Act (*Anderson*) 188–90
literal interpretation (*Gillan*) 306–7
political questions and legitimacy of judicial
review (*A v Secretary of State for the Home
Dept*) 117–18
procedure and substance (Convention
rights) 265
purposive interpretation and constitutional
practice (*Robinson*) 75, 206
resistance to doctrine of deference
(*Huang*) 272–3, 276
right to commit suicide denied
(*Pretty*) 181–3
rule of law 90, 92, 118
unreasonableness in human rights context
(*Smith*) 245, 288

Black-Clawson International Ltd v Papierwerke Waldhof-Aschaffenburg AG [1975] AC 591: 192, 258
Blackstone, William 97, 295
Bonham's case (1609) 8 Co Rep 107: 155
Bribery Commissioner v Ranasinghe [1965] AC 172: 152
Bridge, Lord:
  natural justice 228
  parliamentary sovereignty and EC law (*Factortame* cases) 148–50
British North America Act 1867: 70
Brooke, Lord Justice 260
Brown, Lord (of Eaton-under-Heywood; formerly Simon Brown LJ) 27, 153, 184, 272
Browne-Wilkinson, Lord (formerly LJ):
  common law protection of fundamental rights 266
  defence of common law liberties (*Wheeler*) 250–3
  dissent in *Pierson* (and *Venables*) 191, 253–4
  judicial review of prerogative powers (*Fire Brigades Union*) 78, 84
Brudner, Alan:
  democracy and judicial review 324–5
  interpretation of liberal constitutionalism 343–5
Builders' Labourers Federation (Special Provisions) Act 1986 (New South Wales) 295–6
Building Construction Employees and Builders' Labourers Federation of New South Wales v Minister for Industrial Relations (1986) 7 NSWLR 372: 292–3, 295–301

Campbell v Hall (1774) 1 Cowp 204: 290, 299
Canadian Charter of Rights and Freedoms 175–6, 280, 283–4, 324
Cane, Peter
  public law and political theory 333–7
Carswell, Lord 153, 288, 290, 294, 300
Chahal v United Kingdom (1996) 23 EHRR 413: 87
civil disobedience 40–1, 126–7, 142–3, 157–61
Clyde, Lord 175, 187
Coke, Chief Justice 53, 155
common law:
  common law constitution 3, 8, 15, 32, 35–6, 74, 85–6, 121, 132, 135, 144, 159, 168, 189, 216–17, 221, 239–40, 251, 287, 323–6
  fundamental common law rights 21–3, 26–8, 35, 43, 91, 114, 132, 142, 148, 169, 178–9, 187–8, 216–17, 229, 242–3, 250–1, 255–9, 287–301, 324
  judicial review of administrative action, basis of 208–40

nature of common law rules 49, 53–4, 55, 64, 71, 100, 109–10, 121–2, 125, 143, 178, 230, 284
ordinary or private law 32, 92, 94, 101–4, 232
presumptions of legislative intent 41, 74, 91, 112, 169, 173, 197, 202, 207, 214, 217, 252
see also interpretation of statutes
concordats (between UK Governent and devolved administrations) 77
conscience, freedom of 126, 129, 136, 160–1, 251–3, 260–2, 265, 307, 324
Constitution Act 1902 (New South Wales) 292–3, 296
constitutional conventions:
  Barber's account 61–3, 66, 72–5
  comparison with statute and common law 49, 57, 58, 64, 71, 81
  Dicey's distinction between law and conventions 11, 49–50, 56, 59
  dissolution of Parliament 61, 75–6
  Elliott's account 72–7
  interpretation of 58–61, 63–5
  Jaconelli's account 63–5, 67, 76–7
  Munro's account 70–1
  positive and critical morality 60–4
  royal assent 58–9, 63, 71
  Sewel Convention 72
  see also Attorney-General; Director of Public Prosecutions; federalism; ministerial responsibility
constitutional rights, *see* common law; European Convention rights; public law rights; liberty as independence
constitutional statutes (*Thoburn*) 148–9
constitutionalism, legal and political 1–4, 14, 17, 50, 57–8, 74, 77, 82–7, 200, 286–7, 302–17, 347–8
  see also common law
Council of Civil Service Unions v Minister for the Civil Service (GCHQ case*)* [1985] AC 374: 8, 57, 68, 72, 78–9, 85, 232, 252, 274, 288, 301
Craig, Paul:
  common law constitutional rights, conception of 256, 339
  common law theory of judicial review (and critique of ultra vires) 211, 214, 226, 232–40
  normative dimension of constitutional theory 19
  parliamentary sovereignty, approach to 210, 339
  public law and political theory (response to Peter Cane) 334–40
  rule of law, analysis of 104, 125, 337–40
Criminal Law (Special Provisions) Act 1962 (Ceylon) 298

Cross, Sir Rupert
  Act of Parliament as a norm of present
    law 205
  presumptions of intent as fundamental
    principle 197

de Freitas v Benny [1976] AC 239: 79
democracy:
  constitutional versus majoritarian
    democracy 207, 218, 300, 303, 324–5,
    329–31
  liberal-democratic body politic 292–3, 300
  see also constitutionalism; liberty as
    independence; rule of law
Dicey, A V:
  administrative law, rejection of 104–5, 112
  Allison's characterization 51–4
  bills or declarations of rights 24, 103–4
  common law, fundamental place of 24, 32,
    101–4
  constitutional conventions, account of 11,
    49–50, 56, 59
  contrasting interpretations of (positivist and
    interpretivist) 10–11, 50–4, 105
  equality, formal and substantive 94–5,
    100–1, 107
  habeas corpus 101, 103
  legal and political sovereignty 24, 52–3, 172
  legal positivism, orientation to 10–11
  methodological approach 24, 50–4, 105
  parliamentary sovereignty, account of 18, 24,
    33, 36, 120, 133, 137, 140–1, 171–2, 203,
    206–7, 258, 296
  press freedom 103–4
  rule of law, conception of 24–5, 31–6, 53–4,
    89, 94–5, 100–8, 111–12, 119, 206–7
  statutory interpretation, approach to 206–7,
    258
Dickson, Chief Justice (Canada) 176, 283
dignity, human 19, 38, 43, 47–8, 89, 91–2,
    96, 100, 110–11, 120, 123–4, 131,
    160, 177, 181, 184, 194, 207, 215,
    243, 248–9, 267–8, 323–4, 326, 328,
    330, 344, 347–8
  see also liberty as independence; rule of law
Diplock, Lord 252, 301
Director of Public Prosecutions 68–9, 180–3
disagreement over rights, *see* Waldron
Doctrine of Right, *see* Kant
due process 79–80, 86, 92, 107–10, 112–13,
    142, 186, 223, 235, 242–4, 252–4, 261–8,
    296–300, 304
Dworkin, Ronald:
  Bellamy's critique 310–15
  civil disobedience 161–7
  concurrent and conventional morality 63
  democracy, constitutional versus
    majoritarian 329–31
  equality, formal and substantive 124–6
  Fugitive Slave Act 162–4

grounds and force of law, distinction
    between 127, 162–4
  human dignity 91
  integrity, theory of law as 46, 92, 125–8,
    136, 162–7, 197–8, 335, 338
  interpretation, account of 12, 61, 162–7,
    170, 340–6
  law as legal philosophy 9
  legislative history and legal practice 204–5
  objectivity of law and morality 170, 284–5
  parliamentary sovereignty and
    integrity 166–7
  political obligation (obligation to obey the
    law) 165–6
  principle and policy, distinction between 281
  protestant interpretation 126–7, 136, 163–7,
    342–6
  rights as trumps 281
  rules and principles 177
  scepticism, internal and external 163–5,
    284–5, 336
  Siegfried (sceptical judge in Nazi
    Germany) 164
  sociological and doctrinal concepts of
    law 140
  speaker's meaning (in statutory
    interpretation) 195–6, 198, 204–5
  strong and weak discretion 279
  unity of value, theory of 295, 345
  unjust laws, as challenge to integrity 161–7
Dyzenhaus, David:
  Dicey's blue-eyed babies statute as bill of
    attainder 121, 142
  Dworkin's theory of integrity and wicked
    regimes 167
  incoherence of constitutional positivism 329
  justice and the rule of law 124
  public emergency, judicial acquiescence 118
  suspension of habeas corpus during both
    World Wars 23
  ultra vires debate and implicit challenge to
    legal positivism 213, 224

Ekins, Richard
  legislative intention as a group intention 196
Eleftheriadis, Pavlos 146
Elliott, Mark:
  constitutional conventions and parliamentary
    sovereignty 72–7
  constitutional foundations of judicial review
    (modified ultra vires theory) 225–31
  critique of *Bancoult* 290
  intensity and standards of review 246–7
  parliamentary sovereignty and political
    reality 72–4, 172–3
  proportionality and judicial deference 271
Elmer's case, *see Riggs v Palmer*
Entick v Carrington (1765) 19 St Tr 1029: 90
equality:
  Canadian Charter of Rights, s 15: 283–4

equality (*Cont.*)
  equality and rationality 33–4, 79, 107–10,
    112–19, 141, 185, 244–9, 254, 281, 301
  formal and substantive equality 12, 32–3,
    43, 54, 90, 93–4, 99–100, 107, 113–14,
    121–6, 141, 163–5, 178, 183–5, 243–4,
    283, 301, 330–1
  Fourteenth Amendment to United States
    Constitution 126
  see also Dicey; Dworkin
error of law, doctrine of 235–6
European Communities Act 1972: 147–8
European Convention rights:
  human rights adjudication compared with
    ordinary judicial review 264–6
  overlap and comparison with common law
    rights 4, 13, 22, 26–7, 38, 42–3, 181,
    187–8, 242, 255, 264–5, 282, 320
  public policy, and 319–21
  procedure and substance 242, 259–68
  see also Human Rights Act 1998
Ewing, K D 119, 310

fair trial, right of 34, 41–3, 68, 93–4, 186–8,
    324, 328
federalism (Canadian) 59, 69–70, 82
Feldman, David:
  authority and justification 8
  constitutional convention and judicial
    creativity 12
  judicial review and national security 118, 270
Fenwick, Helen 322
Finnis, John:
  central case of idea of law 45
  judicial review under a bill of rights 282
  statutory interpretation (under Human
    Rights Act, s 3) 117
Forsyth, Christopher
  defence of ultra vires doctrine 217–18,
    221–2, 228–31
Fraser, Lord (of Tullybelton) 237
freedom, *see* association; conscience; habeas
    corpus; liberty as independence; speech and
    expression
Fugitive Slave Act, *see* Dworkin, Ronald
Fuller, Lon L:
  common law precedent, account of 49, 121,
    315
  critique of legal positivism 159, 203–4, 343
  internal morality of law 46–7, 110–11, 119,
    122–3, 220
  interpretative perspective on law 19–20,
    46–7, 343
  racial distinctions in apartheid South
    Africa 124
  statutory interpretation, approach to 47–8,
    170, 203–4, 340
fundamental rights, *see* democracy; common
    law; European Convention rights; rule
    of law

Gardbaum, Stephen:
  contrasting constitutional models 37
  Human Rights Act, s 4 as mark of hybrid
    British model 321
Gearty, Conor
  statutory interpretation and Human Rights
    Act 43, 177, 317
Gee, Graham 83
Ghaidan v Godin-Mendoza [2004] UKHL 30:
    29, 169, 201–2, 317–18
Goldsworthy, Jeffrey:
  contrasting constitutional models 36–7
  legal positivism and rule of law 38–9
  objections to Schauer's account of *Elmer's*
    case 199–200
  parliamentary sovereignty as rule of
    recognition 12, 73, 154–8, 172,
    197–200
  statutory interpretation and meaning 40–2,
    193–4, 197–200
  unjust statutes 38–42, 157–9
Goodwin v United Kingdom (2002) 35
    EHRR 447: 318, 320
Green, Leslie 165
Greene, Lord 113
Griffith, J A G:
  political constitutionalism and legal
    positivism 57–8, 82–3, 308
  proposed limits to judicial review 303–4
  separation of powers 3

habeas corpus 23, 101, 103
Hale, Lady (of Richmond) 116–17, 144, 150,
    188, 264
Halsbury, Lord 292
Harrington, James 98
Harris, B V
  theory of secondary justiciability 79, 278
Hart, H L A:
  concept of law; rule of recognition 70, 82,
    133, 137–40, 145, 147, 154–6
  critical and positive morality 63
  internal aspect of rules 19–20, 44, 138
  legal obligation 141
  legal positivism 10, 44–5, 134
  open texture of rules 204
  parliamentary sovereignty 134–5, 138,
    154–6
Hayek, F A:
  adjudication, account of 98–9, 107–8
  administrative discretion, treatment
    of 105–8, 111–12, 316
  Bellamy's critique 310–11, 315–16
  law as rules of just conduct 98, 105–6, 124,
    315–16
  liberty as independence 89, 97–9
  legal positivism, rejection of 229
  private law, central place of 97
  rule of law, conception of 98–9, 105–8
Hershovitz, Scott 165

Heuston, R F V
  'new view' of parliamentary sovereignty 135,
   147, 153
Heydon's case (1584) 3 Co Rep 7a 193, 203
Hickman, Tom R:
  common law and Convention rights
   265–6
  contrast between public law before and after
   Human Rights Act 13–14, 249–55
  critique of *Bellinger v Bellinger* 319–21
  critique of Loughlin 349
  Fire Brigades Union case, defence of 84
  judicial deference, non-doctrinal
   approach 276
  procedure and substance (Convention
   rights) 264–5
  public emergency, judicial acquiescence
   118
  Simms case, defence of 85
  standards of review and standards of legality,
   distinction between 241–2, 250–5
Hirst v United Kingdom (No 2) (2004) 38
  EHRR 40: 259
Hobbes, Thomas 139
Hobhouse, Lord (of Woodborough) 205
Hoffmann, Lord:
  absolute parliamentary sovereignty 23, 258
  freedom from arbitrary arrest and detention
   (*A v Secretary of State for
   Home Dept*) 22–3, 101
  interpretation of Northern Ireland Act on
   basis of British constitutional practice
   (*Robinson*) 75–6
  principle of legality (*Simms*) 38, 169,
   251, 256–9
  procedure and substance (Convention
   rights) 260–1
  right of abode denied (*Bancoult*) 288–94
  separation of powers (*ProLife Alliance*;
   Rehman) 29–30, 269–70
  statutory interpretation and freedom of
   speech (*ProLife Alliance*) 26
  statutory interpretation and ultra vires
   defence (*Wicks*) 236
  statutory meaning and legislative history 205
Hood Phillips, O 60
Hope, Lord (of Craighead) 144–5, 152, 181,
  183, 186–8, 254, 273–4, 320
Huang v Secretary of State for the Home Dept
  [2007] UKHL 11: 272–3, 276
Human Rights Act 1998, sections 3 & 4: 4,
  13, 28, 35, 38, 42–3, 72, 117, 135, 149,
  168–9, 175, 185, 187, 189, 201–2, 287,
  317–23, 327
  see also European Convention rights;
   interpretation of statutes
Hunt, Murray
  doctrine of due deference 268, 274–5
Hurtado v California 110 US 516 (1884): 34
Hutton, Lord 187, 189, 190, 206

Iacobucci, Justice (Canadian Supreme
  Court) 280
Ibralebbe v R [1964] AC 900: 291–2
incommensurability 278–85, 294–5
integrity, *see* Dworkin
intensity of judicial review, *see* standards of
  review
internal morality of law, *see* Fuller
*International Transport Roth GmbH v Secretary
  of State for the Home Dept* [2002] EWCA
  Civ 158: 272, 280
interpretation:
  conventions or political practice 58–61, 63–5
  interpretative approach to law 5–15, 17–25,
   31, 36–40, 45–9, 52, 125–8, 137, 155,
   157, 210–11, 227, 340
  protestant interpretation 36, 40, 126–8, 136,
   163–7, 342–6
  scepticism (internal and external) 163–5,
   284–5, 336
  see also; Dicey; Dworkin; interpretation of
   statutes
interpretation of statutes:
  common law compared with bill or charter of
   rights 169, 174–7, 187–8, 323–9
  legislative intention 37, 41–3, 84, 151, 169,
   172, 191–202, 219, 225, 229, 233–4, 239,
   300, 303, 329
  open texture of language 204
  see also common law presumptions of intent;
   Dworkin, Fuller, Human Rights
   Act 1998, ultra vires doctrine; unjust
   statutes

Jackson, Justice (United States Supreme
  Court) 115
Jaconelli, Joseph
  nature of constitutional conventions 63–5,
   67, 76–7
Jennings, Sir Ivor:
  constitutional conventions 60
  critique of Dicey 105
  entrenchment of legislation (manner and
   form requirements) 147
Joseph, Philip A 240
Jowell, Jeffrey:
  common law as source of fundamental
   principle 242
  constitutional foundations of judicial
   review 225
  Human Rights Act and democracy 4, 273
  judicial deference and separation of powers 3,
   269–70
  judicial review and constitutional
   review 238–9
  standards of administrative legality and the
   rule of law 339
judicial deference (to Parliament or
  Government):
  deference and non-justiciability 274–5, 290

judicial deference (to Parliament or
    Government) (*Cont.*)
  doctrine of deference 14, 117–18, 241,
    268–78
  first and second-order considerations 277–8
  Hoffmann's analysis 29
  institutional approach 278–81
  see also proportionality principle
judicial independence, *see* separation of powers
judicial restraint, *see* judicial deference
judicial review:
  compared with human rights
    adjudication 264–6
  procedure and substance 112–13, 242,
    250–2, 259–68
  strong versus weak review (of legislation for
    conformity to fundamental rights) 14–15,
    287, 325–31
  see also administrative discretion; due process;
    judicial deference; justiciability;
    legitimate expectations; natural justice; ouster
    clauses; proportionality
  principle; public law doctrine; quasi-judicial
    discretion; reasonableness; royal
    prerogative; standards of review; ultra vires
    doctrine
justiciability:
  Canadian *Amendment* reference (Canadian
    Supreme Court) 70, 80
  see also constitutional conventions; judicial
    deference; political questions; royal
    prerogative

Kant, Immanuel
  Doctrine of Right 92–3, 128–32, 159
Kavanagh, Aileen:
  analysis of Human Rights Act 1998,
    ss 3 & 4: 42, 202, 287, 318, 320–3
  creative dimension of statutory
    interpretation 170
  doctrine of judicial deference 276–8, 320–3
  judicial review and national security 119, 310
Keith, Lord (of Kinkel) 78
*Khawaja v Secretary of State for the Home
    Dept* [1984] AC 74: 23, 235
King, Jeff
  institutional approach to judicial
    restraint 278–81
Kirby, President (New South Wales Court
    of Appeal) 298–300
Kyritsis, Dimitrios
  second-order considerations of judicial
    deference 277–8

Lakin, Stuart 145, 149
Laws, Lord Justice (Sir John):
  common law theory of judicial
    review 216–25
  constitutional and political
    sovereignty 216–17

constitutional statutes (*Thoburn* case) 148–9
freedom of political speech (*ProLife Alliance*
    case) 26–30
grounds of review (*Wednesbury* and
    illegality) 266
judicial deference, approach to 272, 280
legal positivist assumptions 217
legitimate expectations, analysis of 238, 263
negative liberty, priority accorded to 129
parliamentary sovereignty and judicial
    construction 35, 222–3, 229
right of abode (*Bancoult*) 288, 292
rule of law, conception of 216–17, 219,
    222–3, 337–8
Strasbourg jurisprudence, treatment of 266
Thoburn case (effect of EU law on
    parliamentary sovereignty) 148–9, 230
Le Sueur, Andrew 222
legal constitutionalism, *see* constitutionalism,
    legal and political
legal positivism:
  adjudication and political theory 334–40
  constitutional positivism (Dyzenhaus) 329
  detached, external perspective on law 38–9,
    80–3
  Dicey as legal positivist 10–11, 51–4
  division of legal from political practice 57,
    81–3
  Goldsworthy's defence 38–9, 157–9
  Griffith's theoretical stance 57–8, 82–3, 308
  Hart's defence 10, 44–5, 57
  Hayek's repudiation 229
  law limited to authoritative sources 300–1
  legal and moral or political
    obligation 157–67
  Simmonds's critique 39, 213
  value pluralism, and 345
  see also Austin; Dworkin; Fuller; Laws;
    Loughlin; Tomkins
legality, *see* rule of law
legislative intention, *see* interpretation of
    statutes; ultra vires doctrine
legislative supremacy, *see* parliamentary
    sovereignty
legitimate expectations 68–9, 72, 77, 100,
    108–9, 233–4, 238, 263, 304
Lester, Anthony 242
Lewis v Attorney-General of Jamaica [2000] 2 AC
    50: 57–8, 79
liberty as independence 12, 32, 54, 89–92,
    95–101, 111–13, 119, 122–4, 128–32,
    207, 293, 316, 324, 331
Liversidge v Anderson [1942] AC 206: 21–3,
    101
Liyanage v R [1967] 1 AC 259: 290, 297–301
Lloyd, Lord (of Berwick) 84, 191
Lloyd v McMahon [1987] AC 625: 228
Locke, John
  conception of law and liberty 89, 96–8,
    336

Loughlin, Martin
  conception of public law 217, 334, 337,
    346–9
  legal positivism versus interpretivism 346–9

M v H [1999] 2 SCR 3: 280
MacCormick, Neil:
  European Communities Act 148
  orientation of law to the public good 45, 222
  political change and constitutional
    integrity 146
Mahoney, Associate Justice
    (New South Wales) 299–300
Mance, Lord:
  fundamental right of abode (*Bancoult*) 289,
    294, 300
  equality as a principle of the rule of law
    (*AXA General Insurance*) 301
Mansfield, Lord 290, 299–300
Marshall, Geoffrey:
  Attorney-General's discretion to prosecute 67
  positive and critical morality (constitutional
    conventions) 60–1
  rule of law as convention limiting
    parliamentary sovereignty 74
  scepticism about novel interpretative
    obligation (under Human Rights
    Act) 175
Matadeen v Pointu [1999] 1 AC 98: 115
Maugham, Viscount 21
Mead, David 201, 265
mercy, *see* royal prerogative
Miller, Bradley W
  critique of two-stage reasoning under
    Canadian Charter 283–4
Millett, Lord 75, 201–2
Ministerial Code 75
ministerial responsibility 55, 58, 65–6, 75
Munro, Colin
  nature of constitutional conventions 70–1
Mustill, Lord 78, 83

natural justice 79, 112, 220–1, 223, 228, 238,
    250, 263, 295–6, 328
Nazi law 46–7, 164
Neuberger, Lord (of Abbotsbury) 184
New Zealand Bill of Rights Act 1990: 327
Nicholls, Lord (of Birkenhead) 26, 151, 201–2,
    319, 321
Norris v United States (No 2) [2010] UKSC 9:
    282
Northern Ireland Act 1998: 75, 205
Northern Ireland Assembly 75, 205
nulla poena sine lege 90, 122, 194, 328

Oakeshott, Michael 347
obligation to obey the law 39–40, 45, 126–7,
    135, 157–67
office, Kant's distinction between person
    and, 131

Oliver, Dawn 231
ouster clauses (precluding judicial review) 35,
    214–15, 219–23, 230–1

Padfield v Minister of Agriculture [1968]
    AC 997: 220, 228, 304
Paley, William 98
Parliament Acts 1911 and 1949: 143–4, 150–3
parliamentary sovereignty:
  continuing and self-embracing
    conceptions 135–6, 147
  democratic justification of 9–10, 12, 18–19,
    32–4, 120, 139–42, 157, 172, 177, 342
  Dicey's conception of legal fact 18, 24, 33,
    36, 120, 137, 140–1
  Elliott's account 72–7, 172–3
  entrenchment of special legislation 147–8
  European Community (Union) law 145–50
  Goldsworthy's defence of absolute
    sovereignty 12, 73, 154–8, 172,
    197–200
  rule of recognition or fundamental rule 12,
    13, 133–40, 144–61
  Wade's conception of political fact 73,
    145–50
  Woolf's view 215
  see also bill of attainder; common law; ouster
    clauses; ultra vires doctrine; unjust
    statutes
peace, order and good government
    (of a territory) 288–301
Pearce, Lord 152
Pepper v Hart [1993] AC 593: 193
Perreau-Saussine, Amanda 290
Perry, Stephen 165
personhood, *see* privacy
Pettit, Philip:
  liberty as independence 96
  separation of powers 130
Phillips, Lord 223–4, 282
Phillipson, Gavin:
  analysis of Human Rights Act,
    ss 3 & 4: 321–2
  Convention rights and private law 38
political constitutionalism, *see* constitutionalism,
    legal and political
political obligation, *see* obligation to obey the law
political questions 77–80, 82–7, 118, 274–5,
    303–5
  see also constitutional conventions; peace,
    order and good government
political reality, notion of 72–4, 136, 144–7,
    152–3, 230
Poole, Thomas:
  danger of judicialization (*Begum*) 260
  judicial protection of rights and
    administrative context 266–8
Postema, Gerald J
  collaborative dimension of legal practice and
    interpretation 127

prerogative, *see* royal prerogative
press, freedom of, *see* Dicey
presumption of innocence 129, 174–6
Pretty v United Kingdom (2002) 35 EHRR 1:
    181–3
Prevention of Terrorism Act 2005: 119, 188,
    322, 328
Priestly, Associate Justice (New South
    Wales) 296, 299
privacy, right of 181–2, 244–5, 247–9, 282,
    307, 318
private law rights, *see* common law; public law
    rights
procedural fairness, *see* due process; fair trial;
    natural justice
proportionality principle:
    doctrine of European Court of Human
    Rights, Canadian Supreme Court, and
    Bundesverfassungsgericht 174–6, 247–9,
    251–2, 271
    see also interpretation of statutes; legitimate
    expectations; standards of review
public law doctrine, nature and function 2–3,
    13–15, 30, 76–7, 112–13, 235–40, 243,
    278–80, 284, 304–5, 311–13
    see also judicial deference; ultra vires doctrine
public law rights:
    contrast with private law rights 92, 232–4,
    237–8
    nature of 232–3, 244, 257–8, 261–2
public reason, *see* Rawls
punishment:
    ad hominem punitive statute 298–9
    assisted suicide 182–3
    automatic life sentence 43
    mandatory life sentence for murder 179,
    190, 273–4
    tariff sentence of imprisonment 179,
    188–91, 253–4
    see also bill of attainder
pure theory of public law, *see* Loughlin

quasi-judicial discretion 67–8, 79–80, 108–9,
    188–91, 253–4

R v A (No 2) [2001] UKHL 25: 41, 155,
    186–8, 318
R v Director of Public Prosecutions, ex p Kebilene
    [2000] 2 AC 326: 69, 273–4
R v Halliday, ex parte Zadig [1917]
    AC 260: 21–3, 101
*R v Horseferry Road Magistrates' Court, ex p
    Bennett* [1994] 1 AC 42: 68
R v Lambert [2001] UKHL 37: 91, 174–5
R v Lichniak [2002] UKHL 47: 179, 190,
    273
R v Lord Chancellor, ex p Witham [1998]
    QB 575: 229
*R v Lord President of the Privy Council, ex p
    Page* {1993} 2 AC 682: 235

R v Lord Saville of Newdigate, ex p A [1999] 4
    All ER 860: 246
R v Ministry of Defence, ex p Smith [1996]
    QB 517: 77, 244–9, 255, 288
*R v North & East Devon Health Authority,
    ex p Coughlan* [2001] QB 213: 233, 238
R v Oakes [1986] 1 SCR 103: 175–6, 283
R v Offen [2001] 1 WLR 253: 5, 43, 317
*R v Panel on Take-overs and Mergers, ex p Datafin
    plc* [1987] QB 815: 231
R v R [1992] 1 AC 599: 122, 315
R v Registrar General, ex p Smith [1991]
    2 QB 393: 207
*R v Secretary of State for Education and
    Employment, ex p Begbie* [2000]
    1 WLR 1115: 109, 233–4, 238, 263
*R v Secretary of State for the Home Dept,
    ex p Bentley* [1994] QB 349: 79
*R v Secretary of State for the Home Dept,
    ex p Brind* [1991] 1 AC 696: 271
*R v Secretary of State for the Home Dept,
    ex p Fire Brigades Union* [1995] 2
    AC 513: 77–8, 83–4
*R v Secretary of State for the Home Dept,
    ex p Leech* [1994] QB 198: 86, 256–7, 304
*R v Secretary of State for the Home Dept,
    ex p Pierson* [1998] AC 539: 139, 190–1,
    253–4
*R v Secretary of State for the Home Dept,
    ex p Simms* [2000] 2 AC 115: 38, 85, 169,
    243, 251, 256–9, 305–7
*R v Secretary of State for the Home Dept,
    ex p Tarrant* [1985] QB 251: 238
*R v Secretary of State for the Home Dept,
    ex p Venables* [1998] AC 407: 109,
    189–91, 254
*R v Secretary of State for Transport,
    ex p Factortame* [1990] 2 AC 85: 148
*R v Secretary of State for Transport, ex p
    Factortame (No 2)* [1991]
    1 AC 603: 73, 146, 148–50
R v Wicks [1998] AC 92: 236
*R (Anderson) v Secretary of State for the Home
    Dept* [2002] UKHL 46: 188–91, 206
*R (Bancoult) v Secretary of State for Foreign
    and Commonwealth Affairs* [2001]
    QB 1067: 288, 292
*R (Bancoult) v Secretary of State for Foreign
    and Commonwealth Affairs (No 2)*
    [2007] EWCACiv 498; [2008]
    UKHL 61: 8, 77, 85, 287–95, 299–301
*R (Begum) v Head Teacher and Governors of
    Denbigh High School* [2006] UKHL 15:
    160, 242, 260–6
R (Cart & Ors) v The Upper Tribunal [2009]
    EWHC 3052 (Admin); [2010] EWCA
    Civ 859; [2011] UKSC 28: 35, 222–3,
    229, 236
R (Daly) v Secretary of State for the Home Dept
    [2001] UKHL 26: 247–8, 255–6

R (Gillan) v Metropolitan Police
 Commissioner [2006] UKHL 12: 306–8
R (Jackson) v Attorney General [2005] UKHL
 56: 143–5, 150–3, 157, 301
R (Pretty) v Director of Public Prosecutions
 [2001] UKHL 61: 180–3
*R (ProLife Alliance) v British Broadcasting
 Corporation* [2002] EWCA Civ 297,
 [2003] UKHL 23: 5, 7, 25–31, 35,
 85–6, 269, 308–10
R (Purdy) v Director of Public Prosecutions
 [2009] UKHL 45: 69, 183–4
*R (Quila) v Secretary of State for the Home
 Dept* [2011] UKSC 45: 272
Railway Express Agency Inc v New York
 (1949) 336 US 106: 115
Rawlings, Richard
 constitutional concordats and judicial
  review 77
Rawls, John:
 civil disobedience 159
 conception of public reason 313–4, 346
Raz, Joseph:
 law and the rule of law 92, 110–11, 123, 337
 rule of law as constitutional doctrine 339
 sources thesis 335
reasonableness
 see equality and rationality; proportionality
  principle; standards of review
Reed, Lord 145, 301
*Reference re Amendment of the Constitution of
 Canada (Nos 1, 2 & 3)* (1982) 125 DLR
 (3d) 1: 58–9, 69–72, 80, 82
Reid, Lord 220–1
religion, freedom of, *see* conscience
republican government, *see* liberty as
 independence
Ridge v Baldwin [1960] AC 40: 220–1
Riel v R (1885) 10 App Cas 675: 292
Riggs v. Palmer (Elmer's case) 22 NE 188
 (1889): 198–200
Ripstein, Arthur
 interpretation of Kant's theory of law
  128–31
Rivers, Julian:
 judicial restraint and judicial deference 241,
  271
 proportionality doctrine 248
Robinson v Secretary of State for Northern Ireland
 [2002] UKHL 32: 75, 193, 205–6
Rodger, Lord (of Earlsferry) 153, 169, 201–2,
 264, 289–91, 294, 300
Rodriguez v Attorney General of Canada [1994] 2
 LRC 136: 182
Roskill, Lord 85
royal prerogative:
 and convention 56, 68, 72, 75–7, 79–80
 colonial governance, *see R (Bancoult)
  v Secretary of State for Foreign and
  Commonwealth Affairs (No 2)*

justiciability 8, 57–8, 76–80, 83–4, 232,
 290, 294
prerogative of mercy 77, 80
rule of law:
 arbitrary will of officials, antithesis of 35, 79,
  86, 89–90, 95–7, 101–7, 119, 206, 212,
  231, 305
 Bellamy's conception 310–17
 Bingham's account 90, 92, 118
 common law, and 34, 121
 Craig's analysis 104, 125, 337–40
 Dicey's conception 24–5, 36, 53–4, 89,
  94–5, 100–8, 111–12, 119, 206–7
 Dworkin's 'rights conception' 124–8, 338
 Fuller's conception 46–7, 110–11, 119,
  122–3, 203–4
 Hayek's conception 89, 98–9, 105–8, 124,
  315–16
 Laws's conception 216–17, 219, 222–3
 legality and justice 91, 99–100, 118–19,
  124–8
 legality and legitimacy 23, 87, 119–20,
  151–3, 165–6, 210, 230
 principle of legality (in administrative
  law) 38, 243, 251–9, 306–7
 procedure and substance 113, 242–4, 254,
  259–68, 304, 339
 Raz's conception 92, 110–11, 123, 337, 339
 separation of powers, and 34, 78–9, 97,
  117–18, 130–1, 253–4, 269, 305
 standards of administrative legality, and 86,
  112–13, 220–1, 224, 339
 see also dignity; due process; equality; liberty
  as independence; natural justice; ultra vires
  doctrine
rule of recognition, *see* parliamentary
 sovereignty

Salmond, John 145
Schauer, Frederick:
 analysis of *Riggs v Palmer* (*Elmer's* case)
  199–200
 open texture of language 204
 semantic autonomy 195, 199
Scotland Act 1998: 72, 301
Scott, Lord (of Foscote) 28, 188
Scott Baker, Mr Justice 26
Secretary of State for the Home Dept v AF (No 3)
 [2009] UKHL 28: 142, 188, 322, 328
Secretary of State for the Home Dept v MB [2007]
 UKHL 46: 142, 188
Secretary of State for the Home Dept v Rehman
 [2001] UKHL 47: 29, 270
Sedley, Lord Justice:
 judicial review of Orders in Council 290,
  300
 peace, order and good government of a
  colony (*Bancoult*) 292–3, 300
 scope of judicial review of prerogative
  powers 8, 77, 85

separation of powers:
    contrasting attitudes to (legal versus political
        constitutionalism) 3–4, 50, 83–7
    Hayek's account of 106–7
    Hoffmann's analysis 29–30
    Jowell's analysis 3, 269–70
    Kant's account of 130
    separation of judicial power 28–9, 34, 53,
        93–5, 97–8, 101, 118, 188–91, 222–3,
        236, 254, 295–9
    see also bill of attainder; judicial deference;
        ouster clauses; rule of law
Shaw, Lord 21
Simmonds, Nigel:
    critique of legal positivism 39, 134, 213
    critique of Raz's account of the rule of
        law 110–11
    Fuller's connection between law and
        morality 110–11
    interpretation and doctrinal scholarship 340
Simpson, A W B 7, 10
Skinner, Quentin 96
Smith and Grady v United Kingdom (1999) 29
    EHRR 493: 248–9
Sopinka J (Canadian Supreme Court) 182
sovereignty of Parliament, *see* parliamentary
    sovereignty
speech and expression, freedom of 25–31, 35,
    65–6, 85–6, 103–4, 129, 132, 140, 216,
    218, 251–3, 256, 263–5, 307–10, 324, 328
Staatspresident v United Democratic Front 1988
    (4) SA 830(A): 221
Stafford v United Kingdom (2002) 35 EHRR
    1121: 190
standards of review (and standards of
    legality) 3–4, 30–1, 113–14, 184–5, 238,
    241, 244–9, 250–7, 266, 271, 287
statutory interpretation, *see* interpretation of
    statutes
Steyn, Lord:
    assisted suicide (*Pretty*) 182
    entrenchment and parliamentary
        sovereignty 150
    Human Rights Act, section 3 as 'remedial'
        (*Ghaidan*) 202
    legislative intention versus Government
        intentions 193
    literal construction of statute (*Lambert*) 175
    presumption in favour of preserving fair trial
        (*A(No 2)*) 186–7
    proportionality versus reasonableness standard
        of review (*Daly*) 247–8
    reference to *Hansard* when interpreting
        statutes (critique of *Pepper v Hart*) 193,
        205
    rule of law (*Pierson*) 139
    separation of judicial power (*Venables*; *Pierson*;
        Anderson) 188–91, 253–4
    'strict legalism' versus 'constitutional legal
        principle' (*Jackson*) 143–4, 301

Street, Chief Justice (New South Wales)
    rule of law and democracy (*Builders' Labourers
        Federation*) 292–3, 295–300
Sunstein, Cass
    incompletely theorized agreements and case-
        by-case reasoning 14, 275, 286, 311–15
*Supreme Court Advocates-on-Record Association v
    Union of India* (1993) 2 SCC 441: 71
SW v United Kingdom [1995] 21 EHRR
    363: 122

Taggart, Michael
    deference doctrine and intensity of judicial
        review 269
Templeman, Lord 253
Terrorism Act 2000: 306, 308
Tham, Joo-Cheong 119, 310
Thoburn v Sunderland City Council [2002]
    EWHC 195 (Admin) 73, 148–9, 230
Thorpe, Lord Justice 319
Tomkins, Adam:
    absolute versus qualified (European
        Convention) rights 307–8
    constitutional versus administrative law
        (*Fire Brigades Union*; *ProLife Alliance*;
        Simms) 84–7
    critique of legal constitutionalism 1–2, 14,
        31, 83–7, 286, 302–10
    judicial protection of liberty 84, 305–10
    legal positivism, informing critique of legal
        constitutionalism 57–8, 86, 302
    parliamentary sovereignty, nature of 135
Turpin, Colin 136

ultra vires doctrine 3, 13, 112, 152, 208–40
*Union Steamship Company of Australia Pty Ltd v
    King* (1988) 166 CLR 1: 291
unjust statutes 34, 37–43, 47, 127, 141–3,
    155, 157–67, 329

Wade, Sir William:
    parliamentary sovereignty and ouster
        clauses 214–15, 220
    parliamentary sovereignty as political fact 73,
        133, 145–50
    ultra vires doctrine of administrative
        law 212–15, 226
Waldron, Jeremy:
    justice and integrity 126, 166
    law as coherent scheme of justice 45
    legislative intentions, doubtful status of
        192
    opposition to strong judicial review 14, 287,
        325–31
Walker, Lord (of Gestingthorpe) 30, 116
Walters, Mark D:
    characterization of Dicey as
        interpretivist 52–3, 108, 207
    common law ancestry of Dworkin's theory of
        law 128, 337

Wandsworth London Borough Council v Winder
[1985] AC 461: 237
Webber, Gregoire C N 83
*West Virginia Board of Education v
Barnette* (1943) 319 US 624: 161
Wheeler v Leicester City Council [1985]
AC 1054: 242, 250–3, 265
wicked laws, *see* unjust statutes
Widgery, Lord 66, 81
Wilberforce, Lord:
ouster clause (*Anisminic*) 223

statutory construction and the rule of law
258
Williams, Alexander 38
Woolf, Lord (of Barnes) 115–6, 173, 215,
233, 237, 246

Young, Alison L:
analysis of *Jackson* 153
constitutional statutes (*Thoburn*) 149
doctrine of deference 272